ELIZABETHAN
NON-CONFORMIST TEXTS

ELIZABETHAN NON-CONFORMIST TEXTS

VOLUME I
Cartwrightiana
Edited by Albert Peel and Leland H. Carlson

VOLUME II
The writings of Robert Harrison and Robert Browne
Edited by Leland H. Carlson and Albert Peel

VOLUME III
The writings of Henry Barrow
1587–1590
Edited by Leland H. Carlson

VOLUME IV
The writings of John Greenwood
1587–1590
Edited by Leland H. Carlson

VOLUME V
The writings of Henry Barrow
1590–1591
Edited by Leland H. Carlson

VOLUME VI
The writings of John Greenwood and Henry Barrow
1591–1593
Edited by Leland H. Carlson

ELIZABETHAN NON-CONFORMIST TEXTS

VOLUME II

The writings of Robert Harrison and Robert Browne

Edited by Leland H. Carlson and Albert Peel

LONDON AND NEW YORK

First published 1953
by George Allen & Unwin Ltd

This edition reprinted 2003
by Routledge
2 Park Square, Milton Park, Abingdon, Oxfordshire OX14 4RN

Simultaneously published in the USA and Canada
by Routledge
711 Third Avenue, New York, NY 10017

Transferred to digital print 2013

Routledge is an imprint of the Taylor & Francis Group, an informa business

First issued in paperback 2013

© 1953 Leland H. Carlson and Albert Peel

Typeset in Times by Keystroke, Jacaranda Lodge, Wolverhampton

All rights reserved. No part of this book may be reprinted or reproduced or utilised in any form or by any electronic, mechanical, or other means, now known or hereafter invented, including photocopying and recording, or in any information storage or retrieval system, without permission in writing from the publishers.

British Library Cataloguing in Publication Data
A catalogue record for this book is available from the British Library

Library of Congress Cataloging in Publication Data
A catalog record for this book has been requested.

ISBN 978-0-415-31990-4 (hbk)
ISBN 978-0-415-86451-0 (pbk)

Publisher's note
The Publisher has gone to great lengths to ensure the quality of this reprint but points out that some imperfections in the original book may be apparent.

THE WRITINGS OF
ROBERT HARRISON
AND
ROBERT BROWNE

Edited by
ALBERT PEEL
LITT. D.
and
LELAND H. CARLSON
PH. D.

Published for
THE SIR HALLEY STEWART TRUST

GEORGE ALLEN AND UNWIN LTD
RUSKIN HOUSE
MUSEUM STREET LONDON

THIS VOLUME IS DEDICATED TO
CHARLES E. SURMAN
RESEARCH SECRETARY OF THE
CONGREGATIONAL HISTORICAL SOCIETY
WITH GRATITUDE AND RESPECT

PREFACE

THIS is the second volume in the series on Elizabethan Nonconformist Texts. Volume I was issued as *Cartwrightiana* in 1951. Although Thomas Cartwright was not a Brownist, a Barrowist, an Independent, or a Congregationalist, the unpublished writings of this Presbyterian leader were so interlocked with those of the Independents that they were issued as the first in the series.

Volume II presents for the first time the collected works of Robert Harrison and Robert Browne. There are five separate works of Harrison and ten separate works of Browne. Although this volume is as complete as we have been able to make it, there is always the possibility that some lost work may be discovered. This is especially true of Browne, whose writings, known to have been written but undiscovered, are listed in the present volume (p. 5). Inasmuch as Harrison was slightly older than Browne, and since his writings as a group antedate those of Browne, they have been placed first.

It is the hope of the present editor that these writings of the early nonconformists will further the work of students of Tudor history. After the completion of a corpus of nonconformist writings, Dr. Peel had planned to write a volume on Elizabethan Puritanism, but his untimely death precluded that hope. He took great satisfaction, however, in the knowledge that he was making available source materials that would facilitate the work of other scholars in the field of Elizabethan Nonconformity.

The task of assuming the editorship upon the death of Dr. Peel has not always been easy. I have sought to continue his work in the same way that he would have planned, and I can only hope that the present volume would meet with his approval. Where our judgments differ, I have preferred his to mine. For example, in the matter of putting the writings of Harrison before those of Browne, I should have preferred to have those of Browne come first, since they are more important, but I deferred to the judgment of Dr. Peel, whose knowledge is greater than mine. I have tried to make the text as accurate as possible, but the variants in the sources, the difficulties in the reading of manuscripts, and the peculiarities of Elizabethan writing, spelling, and abbreviations have made me painfully conscious of the possibility of errors.

At the present time I am engaged in the work of editing the third and fourth volumes on the writings of Henry Barrow and John Greenwood. Volume V is to be devoted to the writings of John Penry, and Volumes VI - VII to *A Parte of a Register*.

There remains the pleasant task of making acknowledgments. To Mrs. Albert Peel and Miss Margaret Peel I feel deeply grateful. For their interest in this series, and their suggestion that I undertake it, I express my thanks to Professor Herbert Heaton of the University of Minnesota, Professor Marshall Knappen of the University of Michigan, and Professor J. E. Neale of the University of London. I owe a debt of gratitude to the attendants at the British Museum, the Public Record Office, the Lambeth Palace Library, Dr. Williams's Library, Union Theological Seminary Library, New York Public Library, Library of Congress, Northwestern University Library, Newberry Library, and the Huntington Library. Likewise, to the officials and staff of the Bodleian Library, the University Library, Cambridge, Trinity College Library, the Houghton Library at Harvard, and the Sterling Memorial Library at Yale, I wish to acknowledge my great indebtedness.

My obligations to Northwestern University are heavy. To Dr. Gray C. Boyce, chairman of the department of history, I express my sincere thanks for assistance, encouragement, and unfailing kindness. I feel deeply grateful to Dean Simeon

Preface

E. Leland, who made possible my trip to England, and to Dean Arthur R. Tebbutt, who has given generous financial assistance to my research. To the Committee on Research of the Graduate School of Northwestern University, and to Dr. Moody E. Prior, Dean of the Graduate School, and to my colleagues in the department of history, I wish to record my appreciation.

I have drawn inspiration from the friendship and books and ideas of Professor Pieter Geyl, of the University of Utrecht, and to him I express my gratitude for his reading and correcting the introduction.

To the American Philosophical Society, and to its executive officer, Luther P. Eisenhart, I am deeply indebted for a generous grant which made possible my return to England, and which enabled me to complete this volume and see it through the press.

It is a pleasure to acknowledge the many hours of unselfish toil which Charles E. Surman gave to the reading of this work. The dedication of this book to him is a joy to me personally, and a tribute to him for his work as research secretary of the Congregational Historical Society and for his close association and friendly co-operation with Dr. Peel.

My obligations to my wife and family exceed the Miltonic sentiment that they also serve who not only stand and wait, but help in so many other ways. To Miss Dallas Fincham I tender my thanks for her expert typing of very difficult material.

Lastly, I wish to thank Mr. W. Gunns and the sorely tried printers for their patience and courteous co-operation. To the publishers, George Allen and Unwin Ltd., and to the trustees of the Sir Halley Stewart Trust I express my sincere and heartfelt thanks for making this series possible.

LELAND H. CARLSON

Northwestern University
Evanston, Illinois
August 22, 1952

CONTENTS

PREFACE   PAGE vii

INTRODUCTION

    Robert Harrison   1

    Robert Browne   4

HARRISON'S WORKS:

    I. Preface to Lavater's *Of ghostes and spirites walking by nyght.* 1572   26

    II. A Treatise of the Church and the Kingdome of Christ. [1580?]   29

    III. *A Little Treatise vppon the firste Verse of the 122 Psalm. Stirring vp vnto carefull desiring & dutifull labouring for true church Gouernement.* 1583   70

    IV. *Three Formes of Catechismes.* 1583   124

    V. Letter on Robert Browne. [1584]   149

BROWNE'S WORKS:

    I. *A Treatise of reformation without tarying for anie.* 1582   150

    II. *A Treatise vpon the 23. of Matthewe.* 1582   171

CONTENTS

III.	A Booke which sheweth the life and manners of all true Christians. 1582	221
IV.	A True and Short Declaration. 1584	396
V.	An Answere to Master Cartwright His Letter [1585 ?]	430
VI.	Submission and Commentary. 1585	507
VII.	Fragments collected from Stephen Bredwell's Writings :	
	(a) From a "Conference with M.F. and M. E[dmondes]." [1586 ?]	509
	(b) From a "Replie for the doubts." [1586-7 ?]	510
	(c) From a "Raging Libell." [1586-7 ?]	512
VIII.	Fragment of "a treatise against one Barowe." [1588]	515
IX.	An aunswere to Mr. Flowers letter. 1588/9	516
X.	Letter to Lord Burghley. 1590	530

APPENDICES :

(a)	Notes owt of Harrysons booke	532
(b)	Royal Proclamation of 1583	538
(c)	The Will of Robert Browne	540

SELECT BIBLIOGRAPHY 545

INDEX 557

INTRODUCTION

ROBERT BROWNE AND ROBERT HARRISON

During the present century much has been written about Robert Browne and Robert Harrison, but he would be a bold man who claimed that the definitive word had been spoken about them — about their characters and personalities, or even their careers. For a few years their lives were interwoven, but Browne lived on half-a-life-time, indeed nearly fifty years, after Harrison had died as an exile (1585 ?) in Middelburg in Walcheren in Holland, where already some of his children had died.

ROBERT HARRISON

If Browne is one of the most enigmatic figures in the history of the Christian Church, Harrison never emerges into the full light of day, so much so that his Christian name is often given as Richard, and the dates of his birth and death are uncertain.

He matriculated as a pensioner in St. John's College, Cambridge, in 1564, transferred to Corpus Christi, and proceeded B.A., 1567, and M.A., 1572. He was probably a native of Norfolk, and it is with that county and with Middelburg that he was almost entirely connected after his departure from the University. Apart from references to his Cambridge life, all that we know of him is through his own writings, from Browne's *True and Short Declaration*, and from Stephen Bredwell's *The Rasing of the Foundations of Brownisme*[1] (1588). Accounts of his life and work are to be found in Dexter's *Congregationalism*

---

[1] Generally quoted below as *Rasing*.

of the Last Three Hundred Years and the present writer's *The Brownists in Norwich and Norfolk about* 1580. Here is a summary :

1572.	Translates Lavater's *Of ghostes and spirites walking by nyght.* For Preface, see below, p. 26.
1573.	Married at Aylsham.
1573-4.	Master of Aylsham Grammar School. Deprived for Nonconformity.
?	Revisits Cambridge.
1580.	Emerges as Master of the Old Men's Hospital, Norwich, where Browne joins him. A Congregational Church formed in Norwich.
1580-1.	Persecution and probable imprisonment. Writes, but does not publish, " A treatise of the Church and the Kingdome of Christ." (below, p. 29).
1581.	Emigrates with the congregation to Middelburg.
1582.	Helps to finance publication of Browne's books in Middelburg.
1583.	Publishes *A Little Treatise vppon the firste Verse of the* 122 *Psalm* (below, p. 70) and *Three Formes of Catechismes* (below, p. 124).
1581-3.	Death of children in Middelburg.
1583.	Royal Proclamation against the books of Browne and Harrison published abroad. Coppin and Thacker hanged at Bury St. Edmunds for dispersing the books, 40 copies of which were burned.
	Dissension in the congregation, and quarrel between Harrison and Browne.

Introduction

1583-4. Harrison becomes leader of the congregation on Browne's departure to Scotland, and attempts to unite it with the congregation of English merchants of which Thomas Cartwright was minister.

1584. Writes a letter to Cartwright which has not survived. Cartwright's reply to it was printed by Browne (below, p. 432 and in *Cartwrightiana*, p. 49),

1585. together with an *Answere* (below, p. 430), Browne probably undertaking the *Answere* because of Harrison's death.

The writer of the article on Harrison in the *D.N.B.* attributes to him *A Booke of the Forme of Common prayers, administration of the Sacraments*: &c. *agreeable to Gods Worde, and the use of the reformed Churches*, but no evidence is forthcoming, and Harrison is unlikely to have had anything to do with a work of this kind. The book was first printed in London by Waldegrave in 1584 or 1585, and other editions[1] were printed by Schilders in Middelburg in 1586 and 1587. The attribution to Harrison may have been due to the mention of Middelburg, but the author is much more likely to be Dudley Fenner, Cartwright's successor there. Hall, *Reliquiæ Liturgicæ*, suggests Cartwright, Travers, Fenner, and Snape, but does not mention Harrison.[2]

A perusal of the works here printed suggests that Harrison was a considerable figure who might have played a prominent part in the history of Nonconformity but for his untimely death. The Catechisms, like many of those published by his contemporaries, are wooden, but there is liveliness about much of his controversial writing, and here and there a striking phrase catches the attention — " wishers and woulders ", " sleep on both ears ", etc.

---

[1] A careful comparison of any changes made might be suggestive.
[2] See Peter Hall, *Reliquiae Liturgicae* (5 volumes ; Bath, 1847), I, p.p. xiii, xiv.

Robert Browne

If Harrison's brief career is shrouded in mist, what figure of speech must be used to describe Browne's long life, about which blunders continue to be made despite the researches in the present century of Ives Cater, T. G. Crippen, and F. J. Powicke, and especially of Mr. Champlin Burrage? All these correct their predecessors, and sometimes correct themselves, and it is always necessary to make sure that one is reading the latest version. The best sketch of Browne's life to date, incorporating the researches of the scholars just mentioned, is Dr. Dwight C. Smith's doctoral thesis, "Robert Browne, Independent," available in summary in the American *Church History*, (VI. 289-349), and even here there are slips — Robert Harrison was not the " R. H." who wrote " A pythie letter to the Bish. of Nor [wich] " in Nov. 1576 (in *A parte of a register*, 365-70) and Coppin and Thacker were not ministers.

There are few terms, of laudation or of abuse, that have not at some time or other been applied to Robert Browne. It has been maintained, on the one hand, that he had one of the keenest minds of his day, and, on the other, that his vagaries and vacillations can be accounted for only on the supposition that he was mentally unstable — an hypothesis which appears in both contemporary and modern estimates. He is held to have been a pioneer in the field of religious liberty, but even those who have accepted his views have hastened to repudiate his name, his first disciples, Barrow and Greenwood, leading the way. Dexter's careful appraisal and the more recent biographies of Dr. Powicke, Mr. Burrage, and Dr. Dwight Smith should be read by those who think it justifiable to regard him as hypocrite, deceiver, and timeserver. And dogmatism must at all costs be eschewed, for if it is impossible to pierce the gloom and discover what his outward practice was in the second half of his life, what must be the darkness which surrounds his inward convictions?

Now that his writings are for the first time collected together and made easy of access, his character and his outlook

Introduction

may begin to take more definite shape, though it should not be forgotten that all the writings extant belong to a single decade in the life of one who became an octogenarian. It has to be remembered, too, that many of them, even in that decade, are known to us only in part and through quotation by opponents : most of these never reached the medium of print ; others may reveal themselves to some fortunate scholar who will carry on Mr. Champlin Burrage's work in this field.

In one place we have parted company with Mr. Burrage. The reasons for assigning to Thomas Cartwright *A Reproofe of Certeine Schismatical Persons*, printed by Mr. Burrage in 1907 under the title *The 'Retractation' of Robert Browne,*— are stated in *Cartwrightiana*, where the work is printed.

The writings to which reference is made which are not, so far as is presently known, extant in their entirety, are :

(1) A paper of Separation. (See *A True and Short Declaration*, below, p. 423).

(2) Letter from prison to the Norwich congregation (*True and Short Declaration*, below, p. 423).

(3) "Our table of Nature" (*Booke which Sheweth*, below, p. 383 N 4 *recto*) : this *may* refer to a previous section of the *Booke which Sheweth*).

(4) A Treatise on *Revelation* (see *Booke which Sheweth*, p. 225); this seems to be partly incorporated in " A Letter to Mr. Flower " (see below, pp. 516 f. 69 *recto-verso*).

(5) Latin treatise on herrings. (Letter to Mr. Flower).

(6) Letter to "Far. and Har., Londoners ", (*Rasing*, 135), 1585.

(7) " Dispersed writings, as of chalenge against the lecturer [Edmondes] at Dertford for discouering to his auditorie the danger of that schisme " (*Rasing*, 139). The writings seems to be a challenge, a paper on " Reasoning by Sillogismes ", and subsequently, the Report of a Conference. [1586 ?].

(8) Two writings in controversy with Stephen Bredwell :
   (a) " A replie for the doubts and obiections of his Disciple ".
   (b) " A Raging Libell ". [1586-7].

(9) A letter to " a seelie woman of Olaues in Siluerstreete ", so large that, thinking six sheets must confute one, she is confirmed in her separation, contemns the church's excommunication, and boasts that Browne spreads his writings against Bredwell to a hundred miles distance from London (*Rasing*, 138). [1586-7].

(10) Latin tables and definitions (see letter to Burghley, below, p. 530). 1590.

(11) On the arts and the rules and termes of Art (see letter to Burghley, below, p. 530). 1590.

Here are the main events and dates in Browne's life :

1550 ? Born of good family, place unknown ; distantly connected with Lord Burghley, to whose protection he was to owe much.

1572. B.A. Corpus Christi, Cambridge.

? — ? Taught school for some years (? Oundle, Stamford, Bury St. Edmunds).

1578/9. With Richard Greenham at Dry Drayton. Preaches there and in Bene't Church, Cambridge.

1579. Refuses Bishop's licence to preach, and dissuades Harrison from accepting same.
Possible visit to Middelburg.

1580. Follows Harrison to Norwich, where a Congregational Church is formed.

1580 ? Marries Alice Allen, by whom has a large family.

1581. In Bury St. Edmunds. Complained of by the Bishop of Norwich, protected by Burghley, and continues activity in Bury.
Imprisonments (the first of 32 in all) in Norfolk, Bury, and London.

Introduction

    Writes from London opposing emigration of congregation, but later goes with them, to Middelburg.
1582. *A Treatise of reformation without tarying for anie.* (below, p. 150).
    A Treatise vpon the 23. of Matthewe (below, p. 171).
    A Booke which sheweth (below, p. 221).
1583. Coppin and Thacker hanged at Bury for dispersing these and Harrison's works, which were the subject of a Royal Proclamation.
1583-4. Dissension in the congregation, described in *A True and Short Declaration* (below, p. 424).
1584. In Scotland, where controversy with Presbyterians. Returns to England.
1585. *An Answere to Master Cartwright His Letter* (below, p. 430).
    Imprisoned. Signs form of submission, 7 Oct.
1586. April. Presented to the Bishop of Peterborough for not coming to church.
    Nov. Appointed, on terms, master of St. Olave's School, Southwark.
1586-8. In many controversies, notably with (*a*) Stephen Bredwell, (*b*) Barrow and Greenwood.
1588 ? Discharged from St. Olave's.
1589. A Letter to Mr. Flower (below, p. 516).
1590. Letter to Burghley about various writings (below p. 530).
1591. Instituted Rector of Little Casterton, later of Achurch.
1610. Death of Alice Browne.
1612. Marriage to Elizabeth Warrener, which turns out unhappily.
1616-26. Gap in Achurch parish registers.
    Various suits against Browne, now living in Thorpe Waterville, where he is said to have had a gathered church in his house.
1629. Presented for nonconformity.

1631. Pronounced contumacious; excommunicated and deprived.

1633. Last imprisonment and death. Buried in St. Giles', Northampton.

Harrison's works are first printed, and then Browne's, but the reader is advised to read first *A True and Short Declaration*, which provides the historical framework for the writings prior to 1584. The following analysis of the writings may help the reader to secure a general introduction to the entire volume.

* * * * * *

Harrison's writings are neither extensive nor profound. They are, however, clear reflections of those dauntless individuals who lived in the latter half of the sixteenth century, of those nonconformists who challenged the spirit of authoritarianism in ecclesiastical affairs. These men, strongly opposed to the absolutism of the Roman Catholic Church, had witnessed the persecutions in the reign of Bloody Mary; they had learned of the excommunication of Elizabeth in 1570; they had followed anxiously the struggles of William the Silent and the Dutch against the Duke of Alva and his Council of Troubles; they had watched the civil wars in France, and they had recoiled from the reports of St. Bartholomew's Massacre. The Elizabethan nonconformists had been especially alarmed by the growing power of Spain and the fixed determination of Philip II to extirpate the " heresy " of the Reformation.

In the reaction against spiritual authoritarianism, men sought to erect a counter-authority which could deal effectively with dissent. That authority was the State. The prevalence of Erastianism, therefore, was understandable, but to the nonconformist it was illogical. To go from one extreme to another, to exchange a spiritual taskmaster for a civil magistrate, did not make sense. What safety was there if religious pilots avoided the shoals of a papal Scylla only to run aground on a secular Charybdis?

Introduction

In analyzing the writings of Harrison and Browne, we must keep in mind the former dominance of the medieval church, the ideology of the Reformation, the reaction to it, and the national efforts to achieve a solution. These factors helped to produce the *Zeitgeist* from which the nonconformist writings emerge.

The earliest known writing of Harrison is his preface to Ludwig Lavater's treatise, *Of ghostes and spirites walking by nyght*. In his preface, Harrison sets forth his reasons for undertaking the translation of the Swiss writer's work. One of these reasons is to expose the teachings of the Roman Catholic Church on the subject of spirits and ghosts. Since Catholics believed in the doctrine of Purgatory, they held that ghosts were the returned spirits of those who had left Purgatory for some specific reason, and who should be aided if possible. Lavater and other Protestant writers, however, denying the doctrine of Purgatory, believed that souls went immediately to heaven or hell. Therefore, ghosts were usually regarded as demons, who sought the spiritual downfall of their victims, and who should be resisted.

Lavater's work, *De Spectris*, was first published at Geneva in 1570 ; two years later it was translated into English by Robert Harrison. It was answered vigorously by two Catholic apologists : Pierre Le Loyer, *Discours et Histoire des Spectres* (Angers and Paris, 1586) ; Father Noel Taillepied, *Psichologie ou traité de l'apparition des Esprits* . . . (Paris, 1588). The latter work is available in an English translation, *A Treatise of Ghosts* (London : Fortune Press, n.d.), with an introduction and commentary by Montague Summers.

Harrison's most significant work is *A Treatise of the Church and the Kingdome of Christ*. In this treatise he discusses five main subjects. One pertains to the characteristics of the true church and the aspects of the false church. A second relates to the qualities of true preachers of the Word. A third subject treats of the proper form of church government. A fourth topic is concerned with the kind of communicants who participate in the sacraments. The final portion of his treatise relates to objections which have been made by a minister, Mr. Fentome [Edward or John Fenton], and the answers to the objections.

The Church of England cannot be the true church, Harrison contends, because it persecutes the church of Christ. It cannot be the true church because it is filled with manifest pollutions. It is all too clear that persons deserving excommunication are not removed, but are allowed to remain in the fold. Thus, the few corrupt the many. Furthermore, the Church of England cannot be the true church because its ministers are not sent by the Lord but derive their authority from the bishops.

What then is the true church? It is the kingdom of Christ, prevailing wherever Christ reigns supreme. Unfortunately, this is not the case in the Church of England, where archbishops, bishops, deans, and chancellors hold the scepter. These officials are labelled the "pope's bastards," whose authority is derived from Antichrist.

Harrison denounces the ministers of the Established Church as blind guides, "dumbe dogges, destroiers and murtherers of soules." He accuses them of submitting without resistance to ceremonies, mumbled prayers, popish traditions, fees, and seals. By an easy and fallacious logic, Harrison convinces himself that the clergy of the Church of England are not apostles — men sent from God. Quoting St. Paul, he asserts that no one can preach except he be sent. Since the Lord does not send wicked preachers, and since the clergymen of the Church of England are wicked, such preachers are not sent of the Lord. Harrison's argument really rests upon his easy assumption that the preachers of the Established Church are wicked. Therefore, he slides easily into the conclusion that they are not sent by God. Thus, he is able to explain why they are dumb dogs — that is, that they do not preach but merely recite set prayers. The reason is that men cannot preach unless they be sent. Not having been sent (previously proved), the clergy do not and cannot preach.

Introduction

Thus, it is also clear why wolves instead of shepherds are thrust upon the parish churches.

The true government of the church of Christ is a *sine qua non* in the thought of Harrison. Reduced to its simplest elements, his system is that in the apostolic times each congregation was a separate independent unit. The minister must be sent from God, appointed to preach the gospel, and called by the congregation. The locus of authority for the church resides in the congregation and the ministerial power derived therefrom. The trouble with the ecclesiastical government of the Church of England is that the ministers have submitted to the usurped authority of the bishops. The keys of the kingdom were delivered into the hands of ministers and churches, but bishops and deans have arrogated to themselves the power of binding and loosing. It is imperative that "reformation without tarying for anie" be achieved, but the parish clergy refuse to effect the reformation themselves. What is more, they dislike being reminded of their duty, and excuse themselves by saying that they must tarry for the warrant of the civil magistrate. Harrison scornfully observes that in older times kings and princes hearkened to the voice of God as spoken by prophets and priests, but that in Elizabethan England prophets and priests meekly submit to the voice of man as expressed by the magistrates. Harrison's conclusion is that the church must be separated from the power of the magistrates. Until true government of the church is established, the gospel of Christ will continue to be blasphemed.

Harrison believes that if true church government and reformation can be achieved, then it will be possible to correct one of the crying abuses of the time — the participation in the sacrament by the morally unqualified and the spiritually unfit communicant. Harrison bluntly denies the validity of the sacrament in the Church of England. He contends that sacraments are seals of the promises made by God to the church. Since the Church of England is a false church, it has received no promises. Hence, there are no true seals, and their alleged sacraments are but dead signs. The Church of England, he asserts, does not discriminate between the true believers and the mere hangers-on. Occasionally, he admits, a parish clergyman prohibits some egregious sinner, some well-known whoremonger, from participation in the Lord's Supper. But other persons, far worse, whose sins are more of the spirit than the flesh, more sly, secretive, and diabolical, are readily admitted to participation in the sacrament.

The concluding portion of Harrison's treatise is a reply to the accusations of a parish clergyman. The Rev. Mr. Fentome [Fenton] had charged Harrison with drawing people away from the true preaching of the Word, with schism, with impudence and blasphemy, with keeping communicants away from the sacrament, and with dishonoring preaching by the term "prattling." Harrison's efforts to defend himself, and his counter-charges, though interesting and vigorous, are neither convincing nor conclusive. There is much talk about logic but neglect of its principles. Casuistry and quibbling lessen the force of the argument. One example will suffice. Mr. Fentome had depreciated an argument by saying that the speaker's tongue was tipped with a marvellous heat. Although the meaning was obvious that the speaker's words were characterized by indignation and passion, Harrison protested that he had never heard of a tongue tipped with heat. He had heard, however, of a preacher whose tongue was tipped with gold and his lips with silver.

Harrison's reply is that Mr. Fentome is guilty of negligence, disobedience, and wilfulness. He has wrongly divided the Word of truth and mangled the Scriptures. He had justified all his arguments by an appeal to his own conscience. This is tantamount to an appeal to blind prejudice. Thus, Fentome is nothing more than "an unskillful cooke that maketh but one sauce for eu[er]ie meate, & yt an unsau[or]ie sauce to[o], wch tasteth but onelie in his owne mouth."

A Little Treatise uppon the firste Verse of the 122 *Psalm* affords a few details of biographical interest. From this

Introduction

writing we learn that Harrison wrote *A Treatise of the Church and the Kingdome of Christ* first, but that it was not published because of the expense involved. There is a brief reference to Robert Browne, and there is a manifest concern to heal the wounds caused by the differences between Browne and Harrison.

Harrison asserts that he is writing for edification. This he seeks to do by an exegesis of the first verse, to which he devotes approximately fifty-three pages. Actually, *A Little Treatise* is less an exegetical work and more a program of action. He seeks to strengthen the faith of his followers and readers. By faith, he assures them, the walls of Jericho came tumbling down. The canon law, which constitutes the wall of a modern Jericho, likewise will come tumbling down if the people have sufficient faith, blow the blasts of their trumpets, and compass the city.

He urges zeal and love for God's house. In the primitive church, the tabernacle of God was a beautiful sight. To-day the church has neither beauty nor glory, for it is fashioned according to the counsels of men. The pride of man constitutes the greatest obstacle to the completing of the Lord's house. The house will not be built by the clergy of the Church of England, for they are spiritually blind and unable to preach the Word. They dare not face persecution because their calling is not from God but from Antichrist. Therefore, Harrison contends, there is no necessity of ordination by the prelates. By analogy and by reference to first-century history, he seeks to strengthen this unorthodox teaching. He asks : " Is it not a dishonour to Christ Jesus the head of every congregation, which is his body, to say that his body together with the heade, is not able to be sustained and preserued in it selfe ? " Then Harrison observed that the dispersed disciples of the Church of Jerusalem were not ordained men, but were true shepherds for the Lord as they fed their sheep. In sixteenth-century England, however, the law requires that men must return to their own parish, there to feed upon barren rocks. No man would leave his cattle to graze in an area where not a blade of grass grew, but ecclesiastical officials are causing people to starve spiritually for want of food.

The concluding portion of the treatise is a discussion of the respective jurisdiction of church and state. Harrison does not advocate a rigid separation of the two institutions, as may be seen in his own words :

> And woe unto him, saye I, whiche shall holde this, and teache men so, that there is no use of the Magistrates sword among Christians. For that is to remoue ye doole [boundary] of the great and large fielde which the Lorde haue measured out vnto them.

Harrison goes further. Just as the kings of Judah utilized the civil power to reform religious practices, even so should the English magistrates utilize their power to extirpate idolatry and destroy the abominations. Specifically, they should eliminate deans and deaneries, prebends and prebendships, bishops' chancellors, archdeacons, commissaries, proctors' officials, ecclesiastical courts, canon laws, blind and dumb (non-preaching) ministers, and the service according to the Book of Common Prayer. This is the task of the civil magistrates, who should complete the reformation begun under Henry VIII, Edward VI, Somerset, Northumberland, and Elizabeth. It is not the function of the church to interfere, but to keep the sword in Caesar's hand. God's people should pray for the hastening of this process, keep themselves separate from abominations, choose spiritual leaders, rebuke sinners, admonish the weak, and excommunicate the obdurate. Let the true church develop spiritually, but insist that the state wield the secular sword and cut off the remnants of Antichrist.

There is one work of which mention should be made. This is *Two right profitable and fruitfull Concordances, or large and ample Tables Alphabeticall*. This concordance first appeared as an integral part of the Geneva version of the Bible, 1580 edition. The name, Robart F. Herrey, is printed

Introducton

in the preface, together with the date, 22 December, 1578. By some persons Robert F. Herrey is regarded as a pseudonym for Robert Harrison. This identification is given in T. H. Darlow and H. F. Moule, *Historical Catalogue of the Printed Editions of Holy Scripture in the Library of the British and Foreign Bible Society*. 2 vols. (London, 1903 - 1911), I, 91. No evidence is given for this identification, and in recent correspondence I have been unable to secure data which would substantiate the ascription to Harrison. I have found no hint in Harrison's writings that he compiled such a work. There is evidence to the contrary, if Harrison's words may be accepted as the full truth, in *A Little Treatise vppon the firste Verse of the* 122 *Psalm*. In the opening paragraphs Harrison tells us that he " hadde thought neuer to haue set foorth any thinge publikely," that he did write a work on church government which remained in manuscript, and that then he began work on *A Little Treatise vppon the firste Verse of the* 122 *Psalm*. Since these two works were written in the period 1580 - 1583, his own statements seems to rule out any concordance written in the 1570's.

* * * * * *

The best known work of Robert Browne is *A Treatise of reformation without tarying for anie*. Its purpose is fourfold : to refute accusations against the Brownists ; to clarify the role of church and state ; to urge the immediate reformation of the church ; and to condemn those preachers who evade their responsibility for reform by pleading dependence on the secular authority.

The Brownists were criticized because they had left England to go to the Netherlands, because they had forsaken the true church, and because they had manifested ill-will toward their sovereign, Queen Elizabeth. On these charges, the position of the Brownists was that persecution and imprisonments had necessitated the migration to the Netherlands, and that the persecutors, not the persecuted, had forsaken the true church. So far as the Queen was concerned, Browne admitted that on this point the adversaries had wrought great trouble. He asserted the sovereignty of Elizabeth, declared that neither pope nor popeling had any authority over her, and that in all things civil she was the chief magistrate under God for all persons and causes.

Browne's emphasis on Elizabeth's civil power, and his denunciation of the pope as antichrist, were calculated to elicit general approval, but they were irrelevant to the real question — the role of the civil power in ecclesiatical affairs. Browne's position was that neither Queen Elizabeth nor Parliament had jurisdiction over the church. The spiritual kingdom is not subservient to earthly rules. Jesus Christ is superior to civil rulers, and the pastor is superior to the magistrate. The sheep do not lead the shepherd.

Browne certainly wishes the magistrates to wield the civil sword, but he denounces their use of religious powers, which the clergy have surrendered so cravenly. This usurpation hinders the reformation of the church. The kingdom of Christ is not dependent on civil power. In fact, the church in centuries past has flourished most in the face of opposition. Therefore, the clergy should realize their obligation of reforming the church without tarrying for the commands of the magistrate. St. Paul tarried for no such command. If the clergy plead that times are troublous, let them remember that Jerusalem was rebuilt in troublous times. If magistrates are in sympathy with the true pastors, there can be no tarrying. If they are out of sympathy with the true builders or oppose them, they are not Christians. Therefore, whatever excuse is offered, there can be no tarrying.

Although Browne pleads for a separation of the civil and ecclesiastical power, he makes one statement that qualifies that separation. He wrote : " And therefore also because the church is in a commonwealth, it is of their [magistrates'] charge ; that is concerning the outward provision and outward justice, they are to look to it." Such an argument imposes upon the magistrates an obligation which could easily be used as a justification for greater interference in the

Introduction

affairs of the church. It comes close to the argument of the adversaries that in outward policy the church must await the sanction of the civil power.

A Treatise vpon the 23. of Matthewe is one of Browne's most interesting works. Ostensibly, it is a discussion of how to handle the Scriptures in preaching. Actually, it is more a denunciation of current preaching, which is akin to that of the Scribes and Pharisees, and a plea for the kind of speaking exemplified by Jesus, who spoke as one having authority. Written in a vigorous style, this work is scarcely less trenchant than the Martin Marprelate tracts.

One fault of preaching, said Browne, was that it was wrongly motivated. Too many sermons reflected an ostentatious vaunting of the preacher's knowledge of Hebrew, Greek, and Latin. When the Cambridge graduates stand in the pulpits, resplendent in their scarlet gowns and hood, pride shines forth.

They preach for the sake of preferment.
They seek to display their own learning.

Another fault of preaching is the undue interjection of logic into the sermon. Browne confesses that logic *per se* is good, but the light of Scripture is better. Graduates of Cambridge are so enamoured with logic that they consider it a heavenly art. But their abuse and misuse of logic make it a mingling of filth with sweet water, a mixing of dross with gold. Browne is particularly scornful of the use of the syllogism in preaching. Job was an expert at disputation, but his proofs did not "walke vppon a *Maior* and a *Minor*." Paul and Timothy were logical forthright preachers, but they warned men against vain philosophy and profane babblings. True preaching produces goodness and wisdom, prevents ungodliness and folly, but modern sixteenth-century preaching displays disparates, kinds, sorts, species, genus, *consentanie*, *dissentanie*, differences, divisions, definitions, agreements, predicables, and predicaments.

Essentially, Browne's indictment of logic is that preachers have made it an end in itself. His criticism is reminiscent of Bacon's scornful denunciation of the scholastics, of Galileo's criticism of the philosophers who tried to spirit away the rings of Saturn by their logic-chopping incantations, and of Huxley's reminder that the end of life was not knowledge but action. Browne's own statement summarizes the danger to which the teaching of logic is prone : " But nowe their Logike hath helde them so long in learning what they shuld do, that they have done little or nothing at all."

Browne displays the same scorn for rhetoric as for logic, and is contemptuous of the kind of learning acquired at Cambridge during seven years of study. There is too much emphasis upon pseudo-terminology and mere vocabulary. Among the terms which Browne singles out for special derision are the following : anadiplosis, anaphora, aporia, aposiopesis, apostrophe, catachresis, *correctio dicti*, epanados, epanalepsis, epanorthosis, epiphonema, epistrophe, epizeuxis, metaphor, metonomy, paranomasia [paronomasia] polyptoton, prolepsis, prosopopeia [prosopopoeia], *reticentia*, symploce, synechdoche [synecdoche], and trope. This is the kind of vocabulary a student acquires, instead of a knowledge of the Scripture, of theology, literature, science, and true philosophy. Form is stressed more than content, analysis more than creativity, shadow more than substance. In mocking denunciation Browne cries out :

> O Rhetorik farre fetched, even from the dunghils of *Greece*, those rottē deuisings of vaine Philosophers .... O mysteries, O Rhetoricke so faire and so glorious a Ladie, thou art, worthie to be the Queene and the Mother of Universities, such is thy grace, and so gracelesse are they that loue thee not.

To support his thesis, Browne adduces history. The apostolic period, he believed, was a century of common sense and wisdom, but the Ante-Nicene period witnessed a falling away from the pristine purity. The early fathers spun out attenu-

Introduction

ated webs of logic, rhetoric, and nonsense. From the Post-Nicene fathers, such as Jerome, Ambrose, and Augustine, there proceeded vile errors, philosophical delusions, and prophane fables. But the worst of all was that monstrous heretic of the third century, that "logicall and rhetoricall mocker" — Origen.

Browne's longest work is *A Booke which sheweth the life and manners of all true Christians*. This book has a unique format, consisting of material on the left-hand page for the general reader, on the right-hand page for the learned student, and is separated into four columns. Column I, entitled "The state of Christians," has 169 questions and answers, which constitute a kind of catechism for the spiritually uninstructed and a guide to the Christian in his daily religious life. Among the topics included are doctrine, instruction, church policy, ceremonies, the priesthood and prophetic calling of all Christians, the Lord's Supper, calling church leaders, and knowing God's will.

Column II, entitled "The state of Heathen," gives the contrariety of the first column. By contrasting the ideas, institutions, and behaviour of the heathen with those of the Christian, Browne seeks to present clearly what is evil and what is good.

On the right-hand page Column III, which is an amplification of Column I, and Column IV are given over to definitions and divisions. Here Browne seeks to bait the lion in his den — the scholars who like deepness, the logicians who are sticklers for syllogistical reasoning and formal demonstrations. Browne confesses that he has taken great pains to anticipate the objections of the forward and sophistical divines, those peevish troublers who insist on definitions, divisions, axioms, and proofs. By fighting them with their own weapons, Browne is convinced that he can shut their mouths and leave them without excuse — all those perverse individuals who resist the truth.

The most interesting, the most valuable, and the worst printed of Browne's writings is *A True and Short Declaration*,

Harrison & Browne

Both of the Gathering and Ioyning together of Certaine Persons: and also of the Lamentable Breach and Division which fell amongst them. The interest and the value of this treatise derive from the autobiographical details, the strong anti-episcopal bias, and the account given of the early history of the first significant experiments in separatism. From this work the reader obtains details about Browne's student life at Cambridge, his early teaching and preaching career, his meeting with Robert Harrison, Richard Greenham, Robert Barker, Philip Browne, William Harrison, and Richard Bancroft, and his leadership among the pioneer Congregationalists.

Browne's anti-episcopal bias is evident at the beginning of his career as a preacher, when he refuses to procure the bishop's license. The burden of his argument is that bishops are antichrists possessing usurped power. They practise popish government, force their own laws upon the people, compel devotion, and pollute the Lord's sanctuary by a too lenient granting of the sacrament to the spiritually unfit. Browne's denunciation of the bishops, which ante-dates the Martin Marprelate tracts by at least a decade, is historically significant, since the anti-episcopal attitude of the 1570's and 1580's becomes a national factor, which in the 1630's and 1640's is reflected in the policies of Laud, the writings and barbarous treatment of Bastwick, Burton, and Prynne, and the debates in the Long Parliament to extirpate episcopacy root and branch.

For the student of early Congregationalism, this writing is important, since it reveals the early stages of nonconformity. One learns of the discussions of Browne and Harrison on doctrines and polity, of differences of opinion, and of the growth of dissent. As the heavy hand of persecution makes itself felt, the dissenters consider exile to Scotland or the Channel Islands, but finally decide to migrate to the Netherlands. After settling at Middelburg, the exiles encounter difficulties, become home-sick, disagree, and fall apart. Browne tells the story of these lamentable divisions with remarkable fairness and objectivity.

Introduction

In this treatise Browne touches upon the question of church polity. He argues that the authority of every whole church is superior to that of apostle, prophet, evangelist, pastor, teacher, or bishop. He also argues that the " joining and partaking of manie churches together, and of the authority which manie haue, must needes be greater & more waightie, then the authoritie of anie single person." This statement involves a question about the unit of authority. Shall that unit be the separate church, the classis, the provincial synod, or the national assembly ? Historically, the Congregationalists have answered that the separate church is the authority, whereas the Presbyterians have placed power in the classis, the synod, and the assembly. Browne's statement quoted above seems compatible with both systems.

An Answere to Master Cartwright His Letter for Ioyning with the English Churches is Browne's second longest work. It approximates 100 pages in print, is filled with Scriptural arguments, proofs, and allusions, and seems somewhat prolix. This writing had its origin in a controversial letter sent by Robert Harrison to Thomas Cartwright regarding the status of the English churches. This letter, which Browne never saw, unfortunately has disappeared, but Cartwright's reply became available to Browne, who sought to refute it.

The major issue of Browne's answer, as well as of the original controversy, is the question : what is the true church of Christ ? Cartwright had maintained that if an assembly contained only one true believer among many unfaithful members, such an assembly should be regarded as the church of God for the sake of the one true believer. Such a position was anathema to Browne, who believed that the faith of one or even of a few was insufficient to constitute numerous wretches and scandalous persons the true church of God. For Browne a rightly constituted church was a gathering of regenerate persons whose oral confession and sincere beliefs attested to their salvation. The marks of such a church, in the order of importance, were reformation of life, ministering the sacraments, and preaching the word.

A related issue in this controversy was the question of what constituted a true minister. Some idea of Browne's intolerance of Cartwright's tolerant attitude toward non-preaching ministers, and some awareness of the depth of his feeling, as well as the height of his folly, may be obtained from his statement that

> there were [would be] holiness in the dumb ministery, if all the dumbe ministers were hanged vp in the Churches and publike assemblies, for a warning & terror to the rest, that are readie to enter such a function. Then indeede they were [would be] a holy signe and remēbrance of iudgemēt against such wretches, but other holines haue they none in th .

A third point of dispute was that of discipline. Cartwright's attitude was that discipline constituted merely an adjunct of the Church. He believed that assemblies might still be the true churches of God, even though discipline were lacking, so long as faith in Christ remained. The latter was essential, the former accidental. Even as Jerusalem was a city before Nehemiah had re-built the walls, he contended, so a church was the church of God, though it lacked discipline. For Browne such a distinction and such an analogy were not only irrelevant but also blasphemous. They revealed that Cartwright desired a dead Christ to be the life of the church.

Two observations may be noted about Browne's technique of controversy. One is his use and misuse of Scripture. There are frequent marginal references to specific verses in the Bible. These indicate an intimate and detailed knowledge of the Old and New Testament. They also reveal that occasionally his Scriptural proofs do not prove, and that texts wrested from their contexts appear as pretexts to an impartial reader. Sometimes Browne uses a text as a springboard, and where he will come up is anyone's guess.

A second observation is that of Browne's method of reasoning. He assumes that what is relevant to Jeremiah's time is relevant to the sixteenth century, and that what is

Introduction

applicable to Benjamin and Judah is equally applicable to England. Sometimes he is guilty of such fallacies as illicit process, undistributed middle, ambiguity, false analogy, *petitio principii, ignoratio elenchi.* Some of his specious arguments could be interpreted as sophisms. An example of Browne's reasoning may be seen in the following syllogism :

> Every plant which the heavenly Father hath not planted shall be rooted up.
> The English parish churches have not been planted by our heavenly Father.
> Therefore they shall be rooted up.

It would be easy, of course, for any disputant to alter the minor premise by substituting " Presbyterian," " Catholic," Anabaptist," or " Congregational " in place of " English " and arrive at the same conclusion. Convinced that the English parish churches shall be rooted up, Browne seeks to hasten the process. The way to further the extirpation of the churches, he suggested, was to abolish their governing and guiding, because they are blind leaders of the blind.

In contrast to the militant spirit reflected in the aforementioned works, Browne's submission to Archbishop Whitgift reveals a chastened spirit and also some changed opinions on what is the true Church of God. The " Submission and Commentary " does not make pleasant reading for one who has admired the uncompromising position of Browne in his previous utterances. By his submission Browne not only yields to Archbishop Whitgift as the representative of Queen Elizabeth, but also acknowledges the civil authority of the episcopacy. Browne repudiates his own arguments on the nature and discipline of the true church by confessing that the Church of England is the church of God. By promising not to preach unless lawfully called to the ministry, Browne is reversing his former stand as seen in his advice to Harrison and in his refusal to seek episcopal sanction for his ministry. And by promising to behave himself and to keep the peace of the Church of England, Browne certainly retreated from the extreme position signalized by his words : " To deny Christes discipline and gouernment, is to denie Christ."

From the fragments extracted from Stephen Bredwell's works we learn of two works of Browne, the " Replie to the First Answere for Communicating," and the " Raging Libell," neither of which is extant. In " A Treatise against One Barowe," Browne denies two charges made against him by Henry Barrow.

The same spirit which Browne reveals in his submission is manifest in *An Aunswere to Mr. Flowers letter*, written in December, 1588 (o.s.), three years after his submission. Browne tactfully reminds Mr. Flower that this letter has been written in response to his inquiries. Therefore, he urges Mr. Flower to be circumspect, and cautions him about using the letter to the danger and prejudice of the writer.

The work is of interest because of Browne's judgment on the matter of church officers, such as pastor, doctor, presbyter, elder, and deacon, whom he deems to be scriptural and lawful. Even more interesting is his discussion of Presbyterianism in Scotland and his denunciations of the clergy. Browne asserts that the preachers of discipline, both in England and Scotland, had wronged him more than the bishops. It seems that Browne is revealed as a kind of Erastian Congregationalist when he writes :

> If it be asked who be of cheifest guifts or ought to haue cheifest authoritie, I answere that the ciuil Magistrates haue their right in al causes to iudge & sett order, & it is intolerable praesumption for particular persons to skan of euerie Magistrates guifts or authoritie or to denie them the power of iudging ecclesiastical causes. For murthers, felonies, Adulteries, rebellions, blasphemies, vsurpings / Idolatries, oppressi[ons] & all other causes should be & are ecclesiastical, from which if we debar the magistrat, we vtterlie make voied his office, & leaue him nothinge of a Magistrate but the bare name.

Introduction

The final work of Browne is a letter addressed to Lord Burghley. To some the letter may seem presumptuous, a kind of anticlimax to a career that is unsuccessfully completed. But it testifies to Browne's belief in the all-sufficiency of Scripture as a compendium of knowledge. It also evidences what Browne had written of himself : " For I am pore enough & broken to to [*sic*] much with former troubles, & therefore had no need of further affliction." At the age of forty or thereabouts, probably with gray hair and bodily infirmities, Browne indeed had lived a full life, full of experience, trouble, frustration, physical and spiritual imprisonments, and defeat. But he had fought the good fight, had challenged the mighty power of the Elizabethan state and hierarchy, and had dared to remain a nonconformist in a conforming world. From him came ideas and principles that have enriched the world.

LELAND H. CARLSON.

THE WORKS OF ROBERT HARRISON

I. Preface to Lavater, *Of ghostes* . . .

VI. The Preface to Lavater's *Of ghostes and spirites walking by nyght*, though only bearing the initials " R. H ", has always been attributed to Harrison. The title-page reads :
Of ghostes and spirites walking by nyght, and of strange noyses, crackes, and sondry forewarnynges, whiche commonly happen before the death of menne, great slaughters, & alterations of kyngdomes One Booke, Written by Lewes Lauaterus of Tigurine And translated into Englyshe by R. H.
Printed at London by Henry Benneyman for Richard Watkyns. 1572.

Another edition (London, for Thomas Creede, 1596) is practically identical, though towards the end the page endings often vary, one or two lines being transferred overleaf.

J. Dover Wilson, with May Yardley, did a line by line reprint in 1929. Professor Dover Wilson's Introduction deals with the relationship of the book to Shakespeare's Ghosts, and especially to *Hamlet*, Miss Yardley's Epilogue with a Roman Catholic reply to Lavater. There seems to be no mention of the identity of the translator. The treatise is strongly anti-Roman, the kind of work which would appeal to Harrison, and whose translation he would effect with zest. Perhaps it would be his first task after taking his M.A. in 1572.

The Preface is copied from the British Museum copy (718. d. 52) : the Museum has a second copy (718. c. 47).

TO THE READER
[B]Eyng desirous (gentle Reader) to exercise my selfe with some translation, at vacant tymes, and seeyng, that since the Gospel hath benne preached, this one question, touchyng the appearyng of spirites and soules departed, hath not ben much handled amongst vs, and therefore many, otherwise wel affected in religion, vtterly ignoraunt herein, I thought it not amisse to take in hande some good and learned treatise concerning this matter. Wherein as many haue both learnedly, paynfully, & religiously traueyled : so

Preface to Lavater, Of ghostes

amongst others, none in my iudgement hath more handsomely and eloquently with more iudgement and better methode discoursed the same, then *Lewes Lauaterus*, minister of Tigurine. Others haue handled it in dede wel, but yet *nihil ad nostrum hunc*, beyng eyther to[o] short, or to[o] long, or to[o] dark, or to[o] doubtful, or otherwyse so confused, that they leaue the reader more in suspēce in the end, then they founde hym in the begynnyng. As for maister *Lauaterus* his discretion herein, I wyll no otherwise commend it, then to desire the reader to view, & iudge hym selfe. For thus much at the first syght he shal see: A cleare method, with a familier and easie style, the matter thoroughly handled *pro* and *con*, on both sides, so that nothyng seemeth to be wantyng, nor any thyng redoundyng. And if it be true that Horace saith, *omne tulit punctum, qui miscuit vtile dulci*, that is, He wynneth the price, that ioyneth pleasure with profite: I thinke this author may also in this respect be pronounced *victor*, & adiudged to the best game. For he so intreateth this serious and terrible matter of spitites [*sic*], that he now and then insertyng some strange story of Monkes, Priestes | Fryers, & such like counterfeyts, doth both very lyuely display their falsehood, and also not a litle recreate his reader: and yet in the ende he so aptly concludeth to the purpose, that his hystories seeme not idle tales, or impertinent vagaries, but very truethes, naturally falling vnder the compasse of his matter. And howe profitable this his work is, those may best iudge, which are most ignorant in this question, some thinking euery small motion and noyse to be spirites, and some so fondely perswaded that there are no spirites, who being better enfourmed herein by this author, I suppose wyl confesse his worke to haue done them some profite: if knowledge be profitable, and ignorance discommodious. And agayne, those which beyng hytherto borne in hande that mens soules returne agayne on earth, crauyng helpe of the lyuyng, and haue spent much of their substance on idle Monkes & Fryers, to relieue them, wyll confesse the lyke. For when they shall see they haue ben falsly taught, & that they were not the soules of men whiche appeared, bvt eyther falsehood of Monkes, or illusions of deuyles, franticke imaginations, or some other friuolous & vaine perswasions, they wil thinke it profitable to haue knowen the trueth, aswel to auoyde error hereafter, as to saue their money from such greedy caterpillers. Some also whiche be otherwise well trayned vp in religion, and yet not knowyng what to thynke of these matters, wil not iudge their labour euyl imployed, nor the worke vnprofitable, wherby thei may be brought out of doubt, and knowe certainly what to beleue. There be many also, euen nowe a dayes, which are haunted and troubled with spirites, and knowe not howe to vse them selues, who when they shall learne howe a Christian | man ought to gouerne hym selfe, beyng vexed with euyl spirites, wyl thynke it a very profitable poynt of doctrine, that shal teache them to direct them selues. Profitable therefore it is, and shalbe, no doubt, vnto many, and disprofitable vnto none, except perchaunce vnto popishe Monkes and Priestes, who are like hereby to lose a great part of their gaynes, which somtimes they gathered together in great abundance, by their deceiptfull doctrine of the appearyng of dead mens soules. But this their wicked and deuyllishe doctrine, together with all the patches and appendices therto belongyng, he so notably teareth and cutteth in peeces, that I am well assured they shal neuer be hable to cobble and cloute them vp agayne. And this doth he with suche a moderation of breuitie and tediousnes, that I may rightly say: He hath sayde well, and not to[o] much, and written truely, and not to[o] litle.

Nowe as touchyng my translation, although I haue not made hym speake with like grace in Englishe, as he doth in Latin: yet haue I not changed his meanyng, nor altered his matter, endeuouring my selfe rather to make thee vnderstande what thou readest, then to smoothe and pollishe it with fine and picked wordes, which I graunt others myght haue done more exquisitely, and perchaunce I my selfe also somewhat better, yf I would haue made therof a study and labour, and not a recreatiō & exercise. But howsoeuer I haue done herein, verily good reader, I trust thou wylt take it in good part, which is all that I esteeme: yf any man shal mislike therof, let hym amende it. I trust it be sufficient to testifie my good wil to do thee good, and to let thee vnderstande the authors meanyng. Fare well.

II. A Treatise of the Church and the Kingdome of Christ

From the manuscript in *The Seconde Parte of a Register* (I. 441-65) in the Dr. Williams's Library, London, (pp. 533-554 in the " Transcript " volume). See the present writer's Calendar, II. 64-6, where the treatise is summarized, and also his *The Brownists in Norwich and Norfolk about* 1580/ (1920), where it is printed. In the latter work reasons are given for the attribution to Harrison. In the Epistle prefixed to *A Little Treatise vppon the firste Verse of the* 122. *Psalm*, Harrison says (below, p. 71):

And I went about a piece of work touching Church gouernement. But partlie by sicknes, & partly by weying the cost of the print, and finding it to be aboue my reache of abilitie: I was hindered, and haue let staye that worke, vntill the Lorde further inable mee.

It seems clear that the work here mentioned occupies the first six pages of the manuscript in *The Seconde Parte of a Register*. The reference to the cost of printing is of interest because Harrison is supposed to have helped to finance the publication of Robert Browne's books in 1582 (below, p. 71, 396). Possibly it was lack of funds as well as dissention which brought the printing of Browne's *Treatise vpon the* 23. *of Matthewe* to an abrupt stop at the end of Sheet H, the words " by reason of trouble the print was staid " being written by hand in the B.M. copy (see below, p. 220).

The personal controversy which occupies the second portion of the manuscript is of great importance : if only it had given names instead of initials, and one or two dates and places, it would have made clear many obscure points in the history of the Brownists in Norfolk. Almost certainly it can be dated before the migration to Middelburg, probably in 1580 or 1581. The Puritan minister against whom the treatise is directed was either Edward Fenton, Rector of Booton (five miles from Aylsham) from 1564 to 1610, or John Fenton, Rector of Swainsthorp (presented 1571), about five miles from

Norwich. No one with the initials " T. W." is mentioned in Browne's *A True and Short Declaration* as belonging to the Norwich company.

It would be interesting could we discover whether the treatise was written before or after the publication of Browne's *Treatise of reformation without tarying for anie*. Had it been *published* first, perhaps Harrison's name rather than Browne's might have been attached to these early Independent groups.

Another version of the first part of the treatise is to be found in manuscript in the Congregational Library, Memorial Hall, London (MSS. I. e. 14, referred to below as " C. L.") in a volume which contains items by Giles Wiggenton, Henry Barrow, and John Greenwood.

Headed " Proffes of aparant churche ", it occupies 12 pages, and is numbered in paragraphs 1-20 (two being numbered 3 and two 4) the last four pages being unnumbered. It lacks the " Argument " at the beginning, and the word " Aparant " is its key-word; it is not verbally the same, and oftener is a little fuller; the main divergences are indicated below. Towards the end, the versions differ. After the paragraph " Wheras they say ", numbered 19 in " C. L." (below, p. 37), comes 20 ("David speaketh thus " and " The Tabernacle "). Then " C. L." picks up again at " Allso David speaketh thus ", the " Allso " suggesting this is the correct order. The paragraph " In ye 2^d of the Reuelat " is missing in " C. L.", which jumps to " Thus (for this) being manifestlye pved " and the new ending below. " C. L." is reprinted with some slight inaccuracies, in *Trans. Cong. Hist. Soc.*, III. 257-65, without any attribution of authorship.

The need for an accessible edition of the works of these writers is emphasized by the fact that these versions have both been in print for thirty years without anyone noticing that they are substantially the same document !

[441] A Treatise of the Church and the Kingdome of Christ. By R.H.

Quaestio: *Ecclesia Anglicana non est Chri Ecclesia.*
Arg: *Ecclesia Chri est regnū Christi.*
  Ecclesia Anglicana non est regnū.
  Ergo nō est ecc̄lia Chri.
Conf: *Min. Ubi Christus non regnat ibi non est regnum eius*:
  At in Eccles: *Ang*: *non regnat.*
  Ergo non est ibi Ecclesia.
Confirm: *Min. Ubi non est vera Disciplina ibi non regnat Christus.*
  At in Eccles. Ang. non est.
  g⁰ ibi non regnat Chrus.

The Church of Christ is his Kingdome, therfore where as this Kingdome of Christ is not, his Church is not.

Where Christ doth rule & raigne there he is King, but where rule and regim* is taken out of his handes, he is dispossessed of the right of his inheritance, wch is his Kingdome; but o^r mynisters[1] confes that we haue not the true Church goūnm^t, that is as much as to say, Christ his regim^t & scepter, therfore thei haue not his Kingdome, & therfore not his Church.

If thei awnswer that the whole world is the Kingdome of Christ, & y^t he ruleth eu̇ie where, the question is not of y^t ruling wherby he being god equall w^t the Father ruleth & goūneth all thinges, but as to him being man his heauenly father hath giuen the inheritance of *Mount Sion*, wch is his Church, as it is writen: *I haue set my King vpon Sion, my holy mountaine. Allso*:   Psal : 2 : 6.
The Lord hath chosen Sion and loueth to dwell in it saying, Psal : 132
this is my rest for eu̇, there will I make ye horne of Dauid to [13, 14, 17]
bud, for I haue ordained a light for myne annointed. This Sion is the Church, this horne of *Dauid* is the strength of the scepter of the Kingdome of Christ.

If thei awnswer y^t in some pt thei haue this goūnm^t, because as thei say thei p̄ch the word wch is the scepter of the Kingdome of Christ, first thei are faine to call backe y^t wch thei before haue p̄ched, y^t is, y^t Church goūment is wanting. Allso, I demaund of them, if there be any patcher or haulter[2] w^t the lord, or if thei may yoke an oxe or [*sic*] an asse together in the L.

---

[1] *I.e.*, the Puritan ministers, supporters of Thomas Cartwright; C.L. version says "your ministers or rather tymeservers".
[2] One of the meanings of halter or haulter is one who wavers or limps, a waverer or a cripple.

tillage. allso what agreem^t is betwixt God & Beliall, and what felowship hath the scepter of Christ w^t Antichrist, y^t thei should ioyne together in goūnm^t. The lord is a Jelous god, & will not suffer his hono^r to be giuen to another. Lastlie, I awnswer them, y^t the worde, wch is ye scepter of the Kingdome of Christ, is his word of message, p)ched with power & authoritie by them wch are sent wch p)ch with goūing and gouerne wth preaching how thei do this shall appeare afterward.

1. Cor : 2: 4.

[442]

Where the chiefest and highest Eccliall authoritie, is in the handes of Antichrist, there is not the Church of Christ, for Christ hath giuen authoritie to his owne seruantes, bvt in the Churches of o^{rl} mynisters, the L.Bb[2], Deanes, Chauncelo^{r}s, Comissaries, & such like, being ye popes bastardes, haue greater & chiefer authority then thei, & exercise authority[3] oū them & thei suffer y^t yoke: therfore thei haue[4] [not] ye Church of Christ among them.

In the Church of Christ eūie man may execute y^t wch o^r Savio^r hath comaunded in ye 18 of *Matt.* conꝺning ye bringing of due complaintes to the Church in these wordes : *Tell ye Church*; but in ye Churches of these mynisters this can not be executed, no not when a wolf is thrust vpon ye people instead of a shepheard, or any otꝸ most grosse & horrible iniquities are done, thei can not complaine to the Church except thei will call the Bb. the Church, and he is allwaies ye workmast^r of that mischief, of sending wolues & dumbe dogs vnto them: therfore thei haue not the Church of Christ. Let them awnswear where eū this comaundem^t of Christ could be put in practise among them, as in ye Church of Xpst may be daylie

Allso *Matt.* 18 in the Church of Christ there be the keies of ye Kingdome of heauen, to binde & to lose in outward goūm^t, but in ye Churches of these mynisters thei haue not this authority, but thei must fetch it from otherwhere, namely from their chappitall Courtes:[5] therfore they haue not the Churche of Christe.

Thei wch being put in office by a king, & haue giuen oū their authoritie into the handes of a straunge king

---

[1] " these " in C.L., which adds " archdeacons "
[2] Lord Bishops.
[3] C.L. has " these straunge prelassye execut dominion ".
[4] " not " clearly omitted.
[5] C.L. has " the comisaryes cortes or other chapell cortes which ar contrary to christ & therefor antychristian, & againste christ."

A Treatise of the Church

are traito^rs to their kinge, and haue not his kingdome among them: but these mynisters haue betraied the keies of the Kingdome of heauen, wch are com̃itted to them & ye Churches, into ye handes of L.Bb[1] : Chauncelo^rs & Com̃miss: wch are straunge magistrates: therfore thei are traito^rs to Christ haue spoiled his Kingdome: therfore thei haue not ye Kingdome of Christe or Church.

The Churche of Christe is sanctifyed and made glorious without spotte or wrinckle: but in their Church thei confes there bee great pollutions[2]: therfore thei haue not the Churche of Christe. Eph: 5 : 27.

We acknowledge there may be manie pollutions in ye mañs of men, but being secreat, & not openly indaungering ye state of ye Church[3] : but many grosse pollutions openly appearing in ye outward state of ye Church goũnm^t, are such spottes & wrinckles, as declare ye Church not to be glorious nor sanctified to Christ: & therfore to be none of his. *Know yee not y^t a litle leauen leauenth a whole lumpe*, saieth Paule speakinge to haue one euill member cut of[f]. If then one wicked man worthie excom̃unication, not being reproued[4], tendeth to the sowring of the whole lumpe, wch is the Church, how much more, shall so many wicked offi∂s & so many wicked men, wch vse them, & so many wicked guides wch submit themselues to them, & so many people, some ignorant, & some willfull, wch are holden captiue by these guides, & those offi∂s continuinge so long in this sorte, not onelie make sower, bvt make to stinke ye whole lumpe of the Church[5]: therfore such Churches be not ye Churches of Christ, seeing thei are all corrupt, and haue done that wch is abhominable, there is none that doth good, no not one. [1 Cor. 5. 6.] Psal. 14.

But this is ye com̃endation of ye Church, by the mouth of ye pphet: *The people shall be all righteous, ye graft of my planting shall be ye worke of my handes, y^t I may be glorifyed*: meaning that outward iniquitie must be farre from ye children of the Church, & those children wch be planted there be ye Lordes plantes : & the pphet sayeth: *A litle one shall become a thousand, and a small one* [443] Esay : 60 : 25 [sic., 21.]

---

[1] No apostrophe or commas in MS. It is uncertain whether the writer means Lord Bishops, Chancellors, and Commissaries, or Lord Bishops' Chancellors and Commissaries ; probably the latter.
[2] C.L. adds: "and ar bothe mayntained & Retained."
[3] C.L. adds: " goũment " here but omits it later in the sentence.
[4] C.L. has " reconsiled " : *Brownists in N. & N.*, has " removed ".
[5] C.L. adds : " in the nose of god ".

a strong nation: as we may see this day, y^t the whole[1] bandes of ye Lordes enemies can not stand against the power wch the L. hath giuen to a simple[2] one, speaking in his name to the confounding of them all.

Esay : 60 : 18   Allso the pphet speaketh of ye Church of Christ : *Violence shall be no more heard of in ye land, neyther desolation nor destruction in these borders, but thou shalt call saluation thy walls, and praise thy gates*: but in these Churches whosoeu̅ desireth to liue godlie in Christ Jesus, & to keepe a good conscience[3], worshipping god wi^tout the bondage of read prayers, in popish wise, & beggerly Ceremonies, thei suffer violence, both of the wicked guides, & of their lordes[4], & these abhominations of desolation are set vp[5] instead of Christes worship, & of all these mynisters ye moste doe vse them, & the rest consent vnto them by holding their peace, increasing[6] the bandes of them wch suffer for witnessing against them[7], yea thei cry for the Ciuill Magistrates sword, & still craue more violence against them, as though thei had not suffered violence enough, at ye handes of vnlawfull p̄lacy: therfore their Church is not the Church of Christe.

The harlot wch hath not taken her fornications out of her sight, & her adulteries from betweene her brestes, is not ye spouse of Christ, noe though shee haue bene

Osee : 2 : 2.   the mother Church, as it is writen: *Plead w^t thy mother y^t she is not my wife*: but to chaunge ye true Church offices wth false & Antichristian offices, are spūall fornic̄ons and adulteries wch in the Churches of these mynisters, are not yet taken away therfore they be harlotes & not the Church of Christe.

Psal : 132. 17   In the Church of Christe the horne of *Dauid* doth budde, & his Crowne flourish vpon him, bvt in their Churches the horne of Antichrist doth not onelie budde but allso flourish, & ye Crownes flourish vpon ye heades of Bs Chauncelo^rs, Archd: & Commiss : plantes wch god the father hath not planted, must be plucked vp by the rootes before the horne of *Dauid* can budde and spring: therfore thei haue not the Church of Christe.

---

[1] C.L. has " wicked ".   [2] C.L. has " small ".
[3] C.L. has " in the true worship & service of ".
[4] C.L. has " ther byshops with others ".
[5] C.L. has " thrust into the people ".
[6] C.L. has : " and all the mynisters must vse them & the Reste of the people must Joyne with them / & so confyrme them / & so altogether with the lawe add to the bonds."
[7] C.L. has : " the children of god vnconuinced or vncondemned ".

A Treatise of the Church

In *Sion*, wch is the lordes Church *The priests are clothed* Psal: 132: 16
w^t *saluation*, but in these Churches the mynisters are
clothed w^t destruction, for most of them are blinde
guides, & dumbe dogges, destroiers & murthers of
soules, the rest wch seeme to haue knowledge, are
malitious, & obstinate against the lordes house building,
& will not build themselues, nor suffer those that would,
so destruction not saluation cometh by them, to themselues
& other: therfore thei haue not *Sion* wch is the
Church of Christ among them.

In the Church of Christ thei may easely be disċned
from those wch are w^tout, as it is writen: *For what haue* 1. Cor: 5: 12.
I to do to iudge them y^t are w^tout? do not yee iudge those y^t
are w^tin? but in these pishes all be one felowship, we
see not who are w^tin or who are w^tout, or whome
we should count for brethren, & publicans[1] by the
determination of the Churches censures: therfore these
parishes are not the Church of Christe. [444]

The psalme saith thus, *Out of Sion, wch is ye pfection* Psal: 50. 2.
of bewty, hath ye Lorde shined: but thei that speake most
fauourablie of these Churches confesse that in the outward
goūm^t the[re] be many impfections & deformities
wch darke the face therof, yea such deformities thei be
as make it ouglie as is pued: therfore thei haue not *Sion*
wch is ye Church of god.

Allso of the people of the Church it is written: *Let y^e*
high acts of god be in their mouthes, and a two edged sword,
in their handes, to execute vengeance vpō ye heathen, and correc-
tions among ye people, such honor haue all his saintes: but in
their Churches there is not authoritie, nor any such
hono^r to ye S^{ts} y^t thei should execute vengeance &
correction vpon the wicked, but thei themselues are
smitten by the sword of ye wicked, & despitefully vsed
for righteousness sake, yea ye guides them selues lay
downe their neckes willingly & shamelessly[2] to Antichristian
officės to be displaced by their suspensions[3],
and such like Censures so farre are thei from binding
them in chaines and fetters of iron: therfore thei haue
not the Church of Christe.

Paule to the *Rom*: speaketh thus: *Wheras we haue many* Rom: 12 4.
members in one body, and all ye members haue not one office,
so we being many and [sic] *one body in Christ, and every one,*

---

[1] C.L. has: "or whom we should count for heathen & publycanes".
[2] C.L. has "slauishly".   [3] C.L. reads: "those courts".

one anothers members: seing then y^t we haue gifts y^t are di{u}s, according to ye grace y^t is giuen vnto vs, whether we haue prophecy according to ye proportion of faith or an office let us waite on ye office or he y^t teacheth on teaching, or he y^t exhorteth on exhortation, he y^t distributeth, let him do it w^t simplicity, he y^t ruleth w^t diligence, he y^t sheweth mercy w^t chearfullnes: thus hath the Apostle set downe ye offices & callinges of ye Church & the mynistrie of them : namely of y^{e1} pasto^{r}s, docto^{r}s, elders, relie{u}s, & widowes, declaring y^t in the house of god, we are made one anothers members, by the di{u}sities of these callinges & guiftes of grace, wherin we serue one another[2]: but in their Churches thei haue not these offices, much lesse the executing of them, neither any guiftes of grace tending therto: for if anie such guiftes spring vp in any, for want of stiring vp such guiftes & practising it is quenched as the talent hidden in the ground, so y^t their pishio{n}s are not by these guiftes & callinges ioyned together as felow members, or knit by these as by ye sinewes & bandes of ye Church: [er]g^o the^{ei} haue no[t] ye Church etc.

If thei say thei haue some of ye offices as pasto^{r}s & docto^{r}s, we deny y^t a pson or Vicar placed by a patrone and a L: B: can be a pasto^r w^{t}out renouncing ye euill calling[3], & further executing of his dutie, not in tithe[4] gathering of good & bad, but in sepating good from ye badde, and as for the Docto^r, in some few places where he is, he cometh in[5] much after the same ma{n}, ioyning w^t some Idoll shepheard, or some time seru{}, & w^{t}draweth not ye people from abhominations mentioned, nor planting the Church among them: so y^t the light of these Churches is nothing but darknes, & the chiefest order is full of confusion, what then is [?] the disorder of them ? these thinges are not so in ye Church of g.

Allso those wch pseсute ye Church of Christe. are not ye Church of Christe: for Christe is not diuided w^{t}in himself, & thei which hate *Sion* [445] are not of *Sion*: but thei pseсute them wch are gathered together in ye name of Christe, holding one law & gou{n}m^t vnder him, whome thei are not able to charge w^t any abhominations vnremoued, either in ye outward worship of god or in manners : g^o thei pseсute ye Church of Christ, & are not his Church.

C.L. here has " profyts ".
C.L. : " on to anothers perfection & going forward vnto godlyness ".
C.L. adds : " & then to be lawfully called both by god & by the consent of godlye christians to be ruled and guided by hime so fare as the word of god does lead them ".
C.L. omits " tithe ", but adds " together " after " bad ".
C.L. : " to smalle effecte for most comonlye he is adioyned ".

A Treatise of the Church

Wheras thei say we rende oʳselues from yᵉ Church it is childish[1]: for allthough thei were the Church, we might haue[2] one Congregation as many occasions may fall out, so yᵗ we ioine wᵗ another wᶜʰ is the Congregation of gods people: If thei can pue yᵗ we haue ioined against Christe in anie Antichristian manner, or keeping any Antichristian order, we will returne to them and reforme our selues.

Allso *Dauid* speaketh thus of Jerusalem: *Jerusalē is* [Psal. 122. 3,5][3] *builded as a city yᵗ is compact together in itself, wherunto yᵉ tribes even yᵉ tribes of yᵉ Lord goe vp according to yᵉ testimony of Israel to praise yᵉ name of yᵉ Lord, for there are thrones erect or set for iudgemᵗ, even yᵉ thrones of yᵉ house of Dauid.* Jerusalem is a figure of the Church, the thrones of *Dauid* a figure of the Consistories of[4] Holy Eldershyp in the Church: but in their Churches thei haue neither courte nor consistory, Counsell nor Synode holden to oʳ *Dauid*, Christ Jesus, nor in his name, but onely those vnlawfull courtes, consistories, & Synodes holden by the strength of the Canon law, euen the sharpest edge of Antichristes sword, & yᵗ by yᵉ confession of them all, therfore they haue not the Churches of Christe Jesus.

[5]In yᵉ 2ᵈ of the Reuelat: the mynister of the Church of *Ephesus* is comēnded for laboʳ & patience, not forbearing [them] wᶜʰ are euill, examyning them, wᶜʰ are false Apostles, laboʳing wᵗout fainting, yet oʳ Sauioʳ Christ threatneth him *to remoue his candlestick shortly* [Rev. 2. 5] *except he repent, and come to his first loue wᶜʰ he hath left.* Our mynisters deserue bare comēndation in any of these thinges, as for laboʳ, thei laboʳ well yᵗ rule well, thei are patient that suffer pseoution patiently for righteousnes sake [while] thei haue taken a safe way for not suffering pseoution & auoiding daungᵉs: how thei haue forborne yᵉ euill euen dumbe mynisters, sauing in a wordes [*sic*] of winde, notwᵗstanding companying wᵗ them, they are witnes, wᶜʰ haue seene it to their grief, how thei examine false teachers & mynisters callinges, the Church hath seen more to her hinderance then to her furtherance: for thei call eūie wandering p̱chʳ yᵗ roueth about, & can spend an hower in a pulpit, howsoeū it be, &

---

[1] C.L. adds: "and slaundering of us".
[2] C.L. rightly has "leue".
[3] For *Ps.* 122.3. In the letter prefixed to *A Little Treatise uppon the firste verse of the* 122 *Psalm*, Harrison says his first intention was "to haue spoken somewhat brieflie upon the whole Psalme" (see below, p. 71). This paragraph should probably come later, before that beginning "This being thus manifestly pued" below, p. 39.
[4] C.L. omits "consistories of". [5] C.L. omits this paragraph.

[sic, a] p)ch^r & a broth): but those wch haue a care to walke faithfullie in all ye lords house, both in their entrance in & folowing their calling, according to the rule of the word, thei terme despitefullie by the name of newe Apostles: but I reason thus, besides all their faultes, thei are fallen not onelie from the first loue, zeale, wordes, pceeding there of wch were in the Primitive Church: but allso from the state of go(i)nm^t wch is a far greater thing, & thei haue not repented nor returned being warned, but refuse vtterly to returne therin, therfore their candlestickes are remoued, though thei e(i) had any, therfore thei haue not the Churches of Christ, wch are ye Candlestickes, as Reu. 1. 20: if thei say thei refuse not. but tary for the aduantage of ye Ciuill magistrates hclpe, [446] it is an euill excuse,[1] wch will not serue before the lorde. who will require at their handes, those wch haue pished for want therof.

Psal. 50; [51. 18. 19]

Dauid speaketh thus: *Be fauorable vnto Sion, for thy good pleasure build ye walls of Jerusalem, then shalt y^u accept ye sacrifice of righteousnes, the burnt offering and oblation, then shall they offer calues vpon thine aultar*: so that the accepting of o^r sacrifices, euen of all o^r prayer, & thãksgeuing in the worship of god, depend vpon Gods fauo^r toward Sion & the building of the walles of Jerusalem. god is fauorable only to the place where his hono^r dwelleth, his hono^r dwelleth where his Arke resteth, & departeth when his Arke depteth: As

1. Sam : 4 : 22 *Phinees* wife speaketh: *The glory is departed from Israel, for ye Arke of god is taken*, but in these Churches thei haue not yet brought home ye Arke of god from ye Philistines, wch is Christ bearing his scepter, therfore ye glory of god is not among them, & thei refuse to bring it home, & y^t wilfullie therfore thei refuse the L. hono^r. The Arke is the face of god & the p)sence of his grace, therfore, thei not hauing it in his resting place, nor going about to fetch it in, can not behold the lord, nor the face of his annointed; then for the walls of the lordes house thei refuse for to build them, not as the *Israelites*

Aggeus: 2 : 15 did in ye daies of *Haggai*, who pphesied vnto them from the lord, that all wch they did was vncleane, becaus the L. house was not built; for thei being admonished

Nehem: 1 : 3. spedelie obeied; neither as the *Israelites* did in ye daies

---

[1] This idea is treated fully by Browne in his *A Treatise of reformation without tarying for anie* (1582). But compare also Browne's altered opinions on the role of the magistrate, in *An Aunswere to Mr. Flowers letter*.

A Treatise of the Church

of *Nehemiah* & *Hanany* wch saide it was a time of tribulation, & rep)ch because the walles of Jerusalem were not builded, for thei then applied themselues carefully to the worke till it was finished. But as the *Israelites* did in *Meribah* and as in the daies of *Massah* in the wildernes *when they tempted and proued God*, though they had seene his workes, and would not enter into his rest, when they were comauuded, to whom *the lord sware in his wrath y^t they should not enter into his rest*: now these wch haue not the walles of Jerusalem, nor of the temple builded, & refuse obstinately to builde being admonished their sacrifices are not acceptable[1], and therfore thei haue not the Church of Christe. Psal: 95 : 8 Numb: 14 : 22

The Tabernacle was a figure of ye Church, & ye L. gaue streight Charge y^t it should be made according to ye paterne shewed *Moses* in the mount: and so o^r Sauio^r Christe, was 40 daies confusant w^t his Apost. after his resurrection, teaching them those thinges wch concerned ye building of his Church & Kingdome, & ye Apost: according as thei receiued instruction from him so thei builded & haue left vs a paterne: now these Churches are not framed according to y^t paterne, yea thei faile not onely in a pin or hooke or curtaine, wch want might be suffered, but thei faile in the chiefe pillars & walls therof: therefore they are not the Churche of Christe. Exod: 25 : 40

This being thus manifestly pued, that thei be not ye Church of Christe, thei y^t be gathered together in them are not gathered together in ye name of Christe neith^r is he among them, neither can thei haue the Sacram^ts [447] wch be seales onelie to y^t promise made to ye Church, neith^r can thei haue the worde p)ched, for *none can preach except he be sent*, & ye lord sendeth none wch by open & grosse wickednes endaung^e ye state of ye Church: the open wickednes in them is this : y^t thei knowing it to be ye mynisters dutie & calling, to gouerne ye flocke Eccliatllie, & seeing ye want of this gou)m^t, stay notw^tstanding for further warrant from Ciuill Magistrates, & so by this negligence & slacknes are guiltie of ye bloud of them, y^t pish for want of it : allso thei hate to be reformed, & are obstinate against them, wch admonish them of their duty therin: allso they hate & psecute those wch admonish them, allso thei submit themselues to be placed & displaced by those, wch vsurpe Antichristian authority ou) ye flocke, & in their

---

[1] C.L. adds : " & ther relygion but a burden to the lord ".

negligence & slacknes mentioned, thei w^t draw not the people from open abhominations of Antichrist, no not from blinde guides & dumbe dogges: not planting ye Church, nor separating ye cleane from ye vncleane: but submit themselues to fees, seales, & popish orders, mumbled prayers, & many other Ceremonies & popish traditions. Those thinges thei doe & admit, vnworthie ye mynisters of ye gospell of Christe, wherby thei leade ye people astray: so y^t thei are not sent of Christe, nor come in his name : therfore thei p̱ch not ye worde of message, as by authority & pow^r, but onelie speake of ye word of god, as a man w^{t}out calling might doe.

Instead of this last paragraph C.L. has a new ending :

Thus being so manifestlye p̱ved y^t they be not the churches of christ / they which be so gathered together in them ar not gathered together[1] in his name as he hath apoynted to hear them // so they haue no p̱myse of time to hear them[2] / neyther cane they haue his sacraments which be seales only to the p̱myses maed to the church //. For there sacraments ar but dead synes / & pretended sacraments becouse they cane proue no church // and the true sacraments aptayne[3] vnto the aparant church / and to be grafted into the church of god // nather haue theye the word of messag from the mouth of the lord preched among them // but Rezytall [recital] or historycall out of other historyes.

For none can preach the word of message but those that ar sent from the mouth of the lord / onlye and alone // but they com not only & alone from the mouth of the lord / but taketh ther warrant by antichristian auto^{r}ytye from the byshope. So they Ronne and ar not sent of god only and alone // and so they speak gracious words & so minister graces to the hearers as anye child may doe or any other man without callyng.

Now lett this Reason teach yow yf a man in a town com to the wicked and disobedient & saye I com in the name of a constable / & say I charg you in the princes name y^t you leue your wickednes & flowe [sic] me[4] / & is no constable nor haue no lawfull autorytye nor callyng / the wicked will not nor hath not to obey hime / but yf the lawfull offesser come that hath his

---

[1] The last five words are omitted in the transcript in T.C.H.S., II. 264.
[2] " So . . . . . them " omitted in transcript.
[3] Transcriber, puzzled by a difficult abbreviated word, reads " aplay ".
[4] that you leave your wickedness and follow me.

A Treatise of the Church

autoritye from the prince // hime they will and must obay and so do wee.

The callyng of these ministers & autorytye that they haue cannot be warranted by the Word of god / therfor no autorytey—

now lett every on xamine hime self by the Word of god / & show his obedience / fo[?] withowt his obedience ther is no promyse and without a promise ther is no true fayth.

Now That preaching and goũning ar Joyned togethere and can not be sepated the Word of god is manifest // Matt. 24. 45. Mat. 24 / acctt. /20 / 28 / 1 tim. 5 / 17 / 1 petter 5 / 2 / Ezra: 3 / 9. Zacha[1].

and wheras they mak ther escuse of doing of ther dutie / for[2] tarieng for the miestrats [sic] begining that is that the maiestrat must warant them by lawe / because they dar not do ther dutye for fear of lawe / yea I say againe for feare of trobell by law in lossing of ther lyuings / as thowgh the maiestrats wear against the truth of god & did lett the buildyng of the church of god / I saye in this they slander the maiestrat for the maiestrate is not against the bylding of the house of god & fodaryng[3] of his glory for the maiestrat being a christian maiestrat. hathe bed them go forthe & build the church of god // or elsse lett them challeng the maiestrate in that poynt yf they dare[4].

Proffes for sepratione vpon Just cause being dulye examyned by the Word of god //

1 *Corenth.* 5/9/10/11/12/13. [ ][5]. *Rom.* 16/17/. 1 *Cor.* 7. 23 / 2 *tessal*: 3/14/2 *Cor*:6/13/14/15/16/17/ 18. *ephess*: 5/6/7/8/9/10/11/. *acts*/19/8/9/.

christ saythe he y^t hearethe lett hime tack head what he hearethe // bewar of the leauen of the pharises.

Yf they aleadg the Kyngs of Juda & Moses & Kings of Isreall / ffor beginning of refformation in[6] the church —we answer that y^t they did in ecclesiasticall or spirituall matters they did it as they wear fygurs of christ / & that y^t they did syvillye in fforsyng they did it bye the sevyll sword for they had autoritye in bothe casses y^t our Kings & Princes want ffor the fyguratyue maner was ended in Christe //.

I haue bene often moued by diũs of my friendes to

---

[1] An abrupt break at the end of a line suggests the paragraph is incomplete, especially as a line is drawn underneath and the next line begins a new subject.
[2] "for" may be crossed out.
[3] Feeding. By extension, improving or furthering.
[4] A line is drawn partly across the page and another topic begins.
[5] An unreadable abbreviation.   [6] "in" may be crossed out.

write to M^r. Fentome, for thei haue made report to me of a weightie matter, y^t he charged me w^t, in their hearing, namelie blasphemie: yet I was allwaies vnwilling to write, because I had small hope of doing him any good, seeing he hath p͡ceeded to such open enmity against vs: For we ought to spend all o^r time, & to vse eūie occasion & opportunitie, in dealing w^t those y^t are most worthie, in whome some good talentes of hope appeare, as o^r Sauiour Christe hath com̄aunded. But seing his stomacke still boiled, & he could not digest y^t morsell, but powred it out in writing, I haue iudged it to be most for ye glorie of God, y^t I should cleare my self, least any dishono^r should be to ye L. cause, or any stumbling blocke laied in the way of them, wch otherwise would more readilie interteine it.

therfore I haue taken in hand to replie vpon a lre, wherin this accusation against me is contained, wch is an awnswer to a lre of one of my felowe brethren: who allthough he hath matched and oūmatched his adūsarie; & therefore needeth not my helpe, yet I haue shewed ye cause why I tooke it in hand. In wch busines I am irke before I begin to deale w^t such beastly stuffe, as I thinke was neū painted on pap by a p͡ch before, yea it were a shame to hono^r it w^t a awnswer, if a man were not notably constrained: and thus the lre beginneth[1]: If thei had bene ye open enemies of god, as papistes, or any wicked, you would not as you say haue complained, &c. but because thei are ye deare children of god & tenderlie beloued of him, you are as it seemeth therfore bold to insult vpon them [448] and so by yor rash boldnes haue rushed forth w^{t}out either guide of yor minde or stay of yor pen. T.W. did verie fitlie allude to y^t place in ye psal: *If it had bene an open enemie wch had done me this harme I could haue borne it, but it was euen my companion etc*: for of open enimyes we neū loke for otħ measure but a suddaine mischief, coming from a companion & a supposed friend goeth to ye harte, & causeth an vnkinde grief. Now you awnswer (but because thei are ye d[e]are children of god, & tenderlie beloued of him) these be tender wordes & would better haue become yor neighbo^{r}s, to haue bene spoken by them

---

Extracts from Fentome's letter are quoted, but sometimes it is difficult to tell where they, or the quotations from T.W., or R.H.'s comments begin. One wonders if T.W. could possibly be Thomas White, an early advocate of separation who later changed his mind. The Brownists regarded Richard Bernard, Henoch Clapham, and Thomas White as " the most fearful Apostates of the whole nation." See John Smyth, *Paralles, Censvres, Observations* (1609), p. 5, and Champlin Burrage, *The Early Dissenters in the Light of Recent Research* (1550-1641), Vol. I, 155, 156, 159, 161, 164, 167, 186, 187, 197.

A Treatise of the Church

of you, then by yo^rselues touching you, but marke ye reason: Because he counted them not open enemies, or such as before time had shewed themselues openlie wicked, therfore he must needes count them the deare children of god, as those [? though] close & secreat enimies were not euill yea more daungerous then open enimies, wch in time when men hope rather to enioy their helpe & comforte, burst forth into open enmitie & hatred, as you & manie of your felowes haue done against vs: yea you know y^t the treacherous dealing of *Absolom* was worse & grieued *Dauid* tentimes more then ye dealinges of *Shemei*: for thus he testified: *behold myne owne sonne wch came out of my bowells seeketh my life, how much more may now this sonne of Jerminy*[1] *Suffer him to curse &c*: now if a man should reason thus *Shemei* was an open enemy to *Dauid* when he cursed *Dauid* therfore he was a wicked man: but *Absolom* was a secreat enemy when he saide to his father, *I pray thee let me goe to Hebron to render my vow &c*: therfore he was a good man, he should make as faire a piece of matter of it, as you haue done, & this is fine handsell for ye beginn*y*ng. 2. Sam : 16. 11.

It foloweth (you say it is the lordes cause not yo^{rs})[2] I would to god he had wiser and better defenders of his cause then you, or els I feare it will fall to the ground, & in the fall get a great & deepe wound, & so in ye end crush you to pouder, except in time ye repent)[2] he saith it is ye L. cause and not his, & you denie it not y^t I see: belike you confesse it franckly, onlie you wish y^t it might haue better & wiser defenders then he is: he hath defended the cause more ualiantly then you haue done when you were defender of it: for he hath defended it twise by sufferinge imprisonm^t in lothsome prison houses, & w^t Iron fetters, but you defended it once by suffering imprisonm^t in a faire chamber & on a softe fetherbed[3]; & as for wise defenders, it tendeth to ye praise of a workman, to make his worke handsome, w^t vnhandsome tooles: euen so ye lord by weake & foolish instrum^{ts} oùturning ye wise & strong thinges of this world, getteth to himself the greater renowne: you know who hathe saide, *God hath chosen ye foolish thinges of this world to confound ye mighty thinges.* Allso, *the Lord hath* 1: Corinth : 5 : 27. [*sic.,* 1 : 27] Psal : 8 : 2.

---

[1] For the Bible's Benjamite.
[2] The sentence between the brackets seems to be T.W.'s, and the next three—to the second closing bracket—Fentome's answer.
[3] *Cf. Stiffkey Papers*, 200, where, of some imprisoned for supporting the Puritan, John More, Sir Francis Wyndham says: "yt ys to be marveled at how many came to them to pryson, & how they were banqueted, wyne brought to them & on Fryday night even feastes made them in pryson both of fleshe and fyshe".

put strength in ye mouthes of babes and sucklings to still ye enemy: and allso o^r Sauio^r Christe worshipped before his

Matth : 11 : 25 heauenly father and gaue thankes y^t *he had hidden these things from ye wise and prudent, and reueiled them to babes* : therfo.e ye wise men tarie & spie out yor fit time to build ye Lordes house, for it is not yet time w^t you, & we foolish rash children, will god willing, step to it nowe according to the good hand of god vpon vs, & will stay no longer for you as we hath hetherto done, the Lord forgiue vs. Therefore as [449] Dauid awn-

2. Sam. 6 : 22. swered *Michol saying of those maydens, wch thou hast spoken of shall I bee had in honour*: See [*sic*, So] say I to you of those verie same foolish defenders, wch you thinke should be a shame to the L. cause, will the L. get glory & renowne to his cause to still & daunt you all. Then you feare ye L. cause will fall to ye ground if it haue no better defenders: this is wholesome doctrine: it becometh you to know, y^t whosoeũ fall ye L : cause cannot fall, but you, if you w^{t}stand it shall fall before it. Paule saieth, *Let god be true and every man a lyar* : y^t *thou mayest*

Rom : 3 [3]. *be iustified in thy words, and ou^{r}come when y^u art iudged, allso our vnrightousnes, comendeth ye righteousnes of god: allso ye verity of god hathe more abounded through my lye to his glory, and our vnbelief can not make the faith of god of none effect.* If the euill handling of gods cause by ye children of Israel wch came out of Egipt could haue

Deut : 1. p̱uailed against ye L. truth (his truth is his cause, & his cause his truth) then should ye rest of Canaan neũ haue been atteined : but ye L. destroyed y^t genertōn [*sic*] wch sought to turne his truth into a ly, & caried vp a new people: so y^t ye L. cause wente forward, but ye euill handlers therof fell in their sinnes before ye L., whoe made his truth in pforming his pmise so much ye more p̱tious, when by such notable murmuring he was not hindered, to pforme m̃cy, truth, & couen^t on his side: So if we faile in o^r defense ye L. will make vs fall, but his cause shall stand: for he will mainteine his right & cause, he keepeth his throne for y^t purpose, he will vphold ye same for eũ:

1 Sam : 5 : 4. Now it foloweth that ye L. cause in falling should get a great & deepe wound)[1] this is great, & deepe diuinitie, for M^r. F : maketh ye L. cause as [*sic*, an] Idoll, & likeneth it to Dagō the Idol of y^e *Philistines*, wch in his fall brake his head & both his handes but M^r. F: must

[1] Bracket apparently marking the end of Fentome's words.

A Treatise of the Church

marke, y^t allthough *Dagon* gatte such woundes before the Arke, yet y^e Arke ne$\bar{u}$ gat wound before *Dagon*, nor yet before Israel, when thei caried it so vntowardly vpon y^e stumbling oxen, when it should haue ben caried vpon y^e priestes shoulders, though *Uzzah* got a deadly wound, for euill handling of it. 2. Sam. 6 : 6 : 7.

Now to go forward T.W: chargeth some of M^r. F: side y^t ye name of god is much dishono^{r}ed & blasphemed by them: M^r. F: answereth y^t speach can not be vttered by ye Spirit of god & whie? becaus it is a ly saith he, & how pueth he y^t? becaus saith he I for my pt take heauen & earth to record y^t it is a ly: now it is dead sure, as if M^r. F. should stand before a iudge accused by witnesses of some matter of life & death & the Iudge should aske him how he could cleare himself, I will swere saith he y^t I am not guilty: but ye Judge & those y^t stand by will say: I am sory for thee if thou hast nothing to say for thy self but y^t. But seing you can no better clear yo^{r}self as guiltles, I will a litle help forward for yor inditem^t & p)ue you guilty thus, you cause ye name of god to be dishono^{r}ed & euill spoken of, that is to say blasphemed, by ye papistes, for thei sticke much vpon ye authoritie of the Church, & cast in yor teeths rep)chfully demaunding, where this saying *tell the Church* can take place, & becaus you can not, as Matt: 18 : 17. indeed you are not able to giue them any reasonable awnswer in y^t point, therfore thei say you haue a goodly Church & a goodly gospell; so y^e gospell of Christ Jesus is blasphemed by you, in neglecting to establish y^e due go$\bar{u}$m^t of the Church, y^t it might appeare where & how such complaintes might be heard, as o^r Sauio^r Christ hath co$\bar{m}$aunded e$\bar{u}$ie one, by occasion mynistered, to bring to y^e Church. I omitte y^e forme of praiers wch you vse, wch y^e papistes haue boasted full oft in despight of the [450] protestantes, y^t for all their goodly reformation, thei are faine to borrow their forme of praiers & a numb) of Ceremonies of them. It is not time to handle y^e hundred pt of these thinges, wch might be spoken in this cause.

Next of all you aske, where you & yor felow deceiũs, as it is set downe, haue spoken against this go$\bar{u}$m^t, then you make a great ptestation of yor praying for it both priuately & publiquelie. Lesse of yor praiers, & more of yor help: y^e scribes & pharisees praied openlie to be sene of men, & you in times past keeping such a stirre Matt: 6 : 5.

for Church goũmᵗ in yʳ pulpit, & quieting yoʳ selue so quickly, when you are out haue declared, yᵗ you ratñ would seeme to be yᵉ fauourers therof, & would lay a burthen vpon yᵉ backes of otñs, wᶜʰ you will not lift at wᵗ yʳ litle finger, but I would see all yᵉ sort of you pray as *Nehemiah* did, who when he had praied, buckled himself to yᵉ busines of the wall building, & went closelie to yᵉ matter, not making many wordes, before he setled to yᵉ deed doing.

Nehem : 2 : 12

Then you take God to witnesse yᵗ you wish it from yᵉ bottome of yoʳ hearte. Faire wordes make fooles faine, but wise men will looke to yᵉ deedes. I can tell you where once were spoken as faire wordes as these, & yet yᵉ deedes spake anotñ thing; namely of *Saul*, when he came from yᵉ *Amalekites*: for he saide to *Samuel blessed be yᵘ of yᵉ lord, I haue fulfilled yᵉ comaundemᵗ of yᵉ lord*: but Samuel was not so awnswered, but sifted him further & sayde *what meane then yᵉ bleating of yᵉ sheepe in myne ears, and yᵉ lowing of yᵉ oxen wᶜʰ I heare*. So I awnswer you, if you wish for this goũmᵗ so intirelye, what meaneth such yelling and roaring, wᶜʰ cause so many pulpits in *England* to ring against a fewe silly soules, whome you are not able to charge, as swerving anything at all from this goũmᵗ, wᶜʰ you woulde beare vs in hande yᵗ you loue: but sure if you loue it, you loue it absent and farr of[f]: as a man may say he loueth a lyon because he hath heard say, it is a Kingly beast, but yet he would be loth to come in the lyons armes: but you neede not to feare this so, except you will be vnfaithfull labouřs, then indeed you may feare, for it will kill all such & breake their bones, before thei come at ground. Well, Church goũmᵗ & you then be loũs & friendes, but as it should seeme of no great acquaintance, for eitñ you know not her, or she knoweth you: but paduenture she hath chaunged her voice & speaketh like a childe, but yᵉ next time she cometh to offʳ her seruice, or to checke you for her seruice refused, she will make a lowder rowse[1] in yʳ eares be ye sure.

1 Sam : 15 : 13 : 14.

Afterward you say, you practise it as farre as your consciences are assured by yᵉ word you may: & so you leaue yᵉ practise therof allso, as far as yoʳ consciences are pswaded you may: & euen so did *Saul* destroy the *Amalekites* & their cattcll, for he thought in very conscience, yᵗ a few of yᵉ fairest of yᵉ cattell, for no worse end then yᵉ Lordes sacrifice were better spared the[n]

---

[1] Variant of rouse, meaning an arousal, violent stir, excitement.

A Treatise of the Church

spoiled: but as *Saul* was rep̃ued for not doing yᵉ whole will of yᵉ lord, so shall you be rep̃ued for not practising yᵉ whole Church goũnmᵗ, in all pointes as the L : hath com̃aunded, the L: will not be awnswered wᵗ (as far) yᵗ same as farre, squoreth for as [*sic*] euil cõscience[1] :

And in yᵗ you say yoʳ consciences are assured by yᵉ word: this is but a dazeling of yoʳ owne eies, & a foule begging of yᵗ wᶜʰ is in controũsie, of wᶜʰ kinde of Logick, yoʳ whole Ire consisteth : we know manifestly there is no word of god, wᶜʰ pmitteth a mynister to slacke his duty in any point: yea if the sinne of *Saul* was so great in sparing some of the *Amalekites*; what is yᵉ sin of oʳ mynisters in *England* wᶜʰ spare to separate [451] the pphane from the holie, seing yᵉ death of yᵉ bodie is so much lesse then the death of the soule: them whome the Lord hath giuen charge, yᵗ thei should be giuen vnto Sathan by sepation, will he lesse seũelie aske account of their slaughter then he did of the slaughtʳ of yᵉ *Amalekites*.

But oʳ mynisters awnswer yᵗ thei sepate some, because phaps once in a few yeeres thei keepe backe some whoremʳ yᵗ is a poore siely rascall, from yᵉ L. table, & wᶜʰ was neũ of yᵉ Church: but yᵉ fat cobs, wᶜʰ be whoremʳˢ, usurʳˢ, opp̃ssors, forestallers, com̃on swearˢ, vndoers of the poore men by the lawe, ignorant of yᵉ most groundes of X̃pian religion, thei will talke wᵗ thes afterwarde: euen such a reckoning made *Saul* to[o], for he killed the euill fauoured ones, but the faire & fat ones he spared : but yᵉ L. as he was ielous then, so is he now, & if he could not suffer those enemies vnslaine, wᶜʰ once many yeeres before had shewed one cruell pt toward his Church, how will he now suffer vnslaine wᵗ the scepter of his sonnes kingdome, those vnholie wretches, wᶜʰ still day by day, do pphane his sanctuary ? he will not do it but cause in his ielousie yᵉ lives of them wᶜʰ haue spared them for their liues, as was saide to *Ahab* conõning *Benhadad* by the mouth of the pphet. [1 King : 20 : 24 [*sic.*, 42].]

Now it foloweth in yoʳ lre, you tell me yoʳ iudgemᵗ is yᵗ oʳ p̃chers crept in at yᵉ window /[2] alas yoʳ iudgemᵗ is verie siely and weake iudgemᵗ, & as it is weake so it is fowlie corrupted, & wo to yᵉ Church yᵗ should stay on so weake a staffe /: there is all you say for yᵗ :

---
[1] The meaning is that the Lord will not accept half-hearted performance as a satisfacto settlement. The last phrase is evidently "squareth for an evil conscience."
[2] From this point in this MS. the close of many of the extracts from Fentome's letter, & of many of the answers to it, are marked with a line, thus : /.

alas this is yet the simplest awnswer yᵗ eũ I heard in my life: those p̃chers whosoeũ thei be are pitiously beholden to you, who hearing such a great matter against them, & taking vpon you their defense, & yᵗ wᵗ a man of so weake iudgemᵗ as you say should be able to help nothing at all in such a pinch: paduenture you sought for yoʳ arrowes & thei were lost, therfore you came & saide, what should you shoote at such a litle white: but go to I will make it a litle broader yᵗ you may see it: you & thei haue confessed, yᵗ the Lordship & supioritie wᶜʰ yᵉ BB. haue oũ yᵉ flocke is vnlawfull, & not standing wᵗ yᵉ simplicitie of yᵉ gospell: *Marke* : 10 : 43. if you be not still of yᵗ minde, signify to me against yᵉ next time, & I will bestow the laboʳ to p̃ue it: if it standeth not wᵗ yᵉ gospell of Christe it is against Christe, & so Antichristian, but yᵉ BB. by yᵉ vertue of yᵗ supiority & lordship haue giuen you yoʳ l̃res of disorder, & by yᵗ calling you come in, & vpon yᵗ calling you hold, & by comãundemᵗ from them you & thei will cease yoʳ mynisterie, as diũs of yᵉ chiefest haue spoken & done, & therfore yoʳ entring in was by antichristian meanes, so not being by Christ wᶜʰ is yᵉ doore, it must needes be by yᵉ window: now if you haue any strength yoʳ self, pluck downe this window, wᶜʰ is set vp in yoʳ way:

then after vpon T. W. concluding yᵗ we can not heare you, you awnswer onely to yᵉ conclusion, & say, we can not becaus we will not, & we will not, becaus oʳ will is not ruled by gods will, how p̃ue you yᵗ? but you leave of[f] & fall to threates saying yᵗ both will & power shall be taken from vs, & yᵉ doore shut /. nay we will not becaus we dare not, & we dare not, becaus yᵉ word of yᵉ lord hath bound vs by many streight comãndemᵗˢ, as this for one, *saue yoʳ selues from this* Acts : 2: 40. *froward generation*: ene¹ yᵗ froward generation of whome he speaketh there, held yᵉ groundes of religion better then you, as we are able to p̃ue : & yᵗ you are froward it appeareth for yᵗ nothing will p̃swade you to do yᵗ wᶜʰ you acknowledge to be yᵉ mynisters duty, therin we charge you of negligence & flat disobedience. *Paul* 1 Tim : 5 : 21. chargeth *Timothy* wᵗ a solemne charge : *to keepe all those things inviolate wherof he gaue commaundemᵗ*, wᶜʰ chiefly in yᵗ Epist. were about Churchgoũnmᵗ : but you haue not kept them, neithʳ will p̃fesse to keepe them: so you vphold this horrible sinne of disobedience wᵗ a high hand, wᶜʰ endaungʲeth yᵉ state of yᵉ Church,

¹ *I.e.*, e'en — even.

A Treatise of the Church

most grieuouslie, & you colo^r all this w^t a cloake of tarying for furth[er] authority, & yet you say you are sent of God, & called of ye Church, & yet you stay for further authority then these .2 offered you, for this cause which containeth in it a great sort of especiall causes [452] yf I had time to speake of them, you continuing vnreformed, & frowardly w^{t}standing admonition are seuen times worthie to be sepate from ye Church yo^{r}selues, y^t is ye cause that we can not ioine w^t you in any felowship, much lesse in ye felowship of worshipping god togeth[er] w^t you /.

then for alledging this saying of o^r Sauio^r Christ [Iohn 10. 10] *my sheepe heare my voice, a straunger will they not heare* : you say it is like o^r oth[er] doinges, so it is, & yor awnswer is like yor oth[er] awnswers: you must not cast it out of yor handes before you haue vnknit the knot. I haue p[ro]ued y^t you are double worthie sepation, all such are Exod : 12 : 45. strang[er]s, & may not eate of ye L. passeou[er], therfore if we should heare you, we should heare the voice of straung[er]s. you say we bow & bend ye scriptures as pleaseth o^r heades; are you not ashamed to awnswer after this man[er]? is it enough for you to awnswer another man y^t he wresteth a place of scripture, & not tell him in one word short or long, how he wresteth, & where ye fault is ? whie haue you set downe no places, wch we haue bent & bowed ? thei bow & bend ye scriptures to their owne measure, wch make ye com[m]aundem^t of gou[er]nm^t of ye Church a litle com[m]aundem^t, & teach ye people y^t it may be tollerated, to be still forborne, & so thei breake y^t wch thei count a litle com[m]aundem^t, & teach men so, therfore ye lord hath spoken of such, Matt: 5 : 19. y^t they shall be litle in ye kingdome of god. But for wrong alledging of ye scripture, you haue vsed a good caueat in this letter for that you haue not cited one place of scripture in this long lasie lre: but only borrowed a couple of *phrases* from thence, as good neu[er] a whit as neu[er] ye better. this is notable barrennes, but the L. will drie you vp more, if you take not heede.

It foloweth (yor tale of a messeng^r you might haue put vp & vsed at another time, & to anoth[er] people: as for vs we haue o^r warrant from the L. who hath sealed o^r calling surely in o^r conscience, & the children whome ye L: hath giuen vs, are allso o^r Epist. writen in o^r heartes /. the tale as you call it of ye messenger may not be put of[f] till anoth[e]^r time, neith[e]^r can it be fitlier applied to any people then you, it sitteth neare yor

skirtes, it is no m̃uaile though you would be ridde of it, but tarie, it will talke w^t you againe : yf a gentleman send his man to borrow mony at his neede, & he go & borow a cloake, & no mony; is there any hurt in ye cloake borowing may ye seruant say, yet it is but a cloake, & no mony, & therfore will not serue his m^{rs} turne, so it was but a pranke of an euill messeng^r: euen so you mynisters are sent on this errand, first to plant Churches, wch is ye speciall building of ye L. house, excepte you had come vnto them not as ruinous heapes, but as Churches visiblie planted: & then you are to do in the L. house such thinges as you are com̃aunded: if you build not ye house, yor oth̃^{r} labo^r is
Aggee : 2 : 15. but lost, as *Aggee* witnessed to the Jewes, y^t their sacrifices & all y^t thei did was vncleane, till ye temple was builded: much more then is yor p̃ching vncleane : for ye true spuall house being vnbuilded, wch should sanctifie all vnto you, & speciallie when you refuse to do it being charged, wch y^e *Israelites* refused not against ye charge of ye pphet *Aggee*, & yet behold a greater then
Matt : 11 : 11. *Aggee*, hath the lord sent to speake vnto you: for you know he wch is leaste in the kingdom of Christ is greater then he: well then you are set to worke in the vinyeard, but because of a litle flash of water, wch was in ye way, you fearing to go ou̅ yor shooes, haue turned aside into ye field, & wrought there all day: will yor M^r accept of it when you come home, though you say you haue wrought ? nay, but he will say becaus you were not in ye vinyeard, nothing is done of y^t, wch I would haue had done, the messeng^r whome ye lord sent to cry
1 King : 13 : 2. against ye aultar in *Bethel* did his whole message, but failed onely in a circumstance, in y^t he did eate bread in ye place being greatly inticed by anoth̃ pphet: but ye L. brought vpon him ye reward of an euill messeng^r ; & what will he then do to those wch faile in ye first & chief point of their message: we say y^t ye beginning is more then ye half of any thing: & indeede if any of you could shew a Church planted, [453] allthough it were but of ten X̃pians, it were more worth, then the half, yea then the whole y^t eu̅ you haue all done yet :

Now to defend you from strokes wch are due vnto an euill messseng^r, you haue yor stale excuse, y^t is ye warrant of yor cōscience, wherby you say ye lord hath sealed yor calling /. how should I know y^t ? you testifie of yor self therfore yor testimonie is not good : euen as I haue heard of a man, wch being taken w^t a

A Treatise of the Church

fault, was threat to be put to death: nay saide he I shall not dy for this: how knowest y^u y^t quoth ye accuser? I thinke so quoth he. thus doth M^r F: seale all his warrantes vnto us, by my conscience is so pswaded, & ye L. hath so sealed my conscience: eith̃ ye word of god hath giuen him oũ, or he hath giuen it oũ in this defense: for we have not from thence one pofe of matter neither[1].

M^r F: pceedeth & saith: *ye children whome ye L. hath giuen vs are our epist: writen in o^r hartes*: adde therto, *wch is vnderstood and read of all men*, or els you are but a mangler: this is one of ye 2 phrases of scripture wch I spake of, & yet it cometh before it is wellcome as we shall see anone. *Paul saieth he wch praiseth himself is not alowed but he whome the lord praiseth*: but no m̃vaile though you make much of a litle, for you measure yor selues w^t yor selues & compare yor selues w^t yor selues: but we will compare you a litle w^t ye Apost: whose glorie you haue clothed yor selues w^t all, & plucking of[f] yor stollen feath̃s, we shall see y^t you are naked, & as far from the glorie of ye Apost: as you are neere his mañ of speach. *Paul* planted many Churches, so y^t the worke of his handes appeared, & gaue testimony y^t ye grace wch god had giuen him was not in vaine: yea ye verie Churches being his building in the lord were a testimonie of his calling: therfore as manie Churches planted by himself, so manie epistles or l̃res of ɔ̃tificate be to be read of all men, y^t he was sent of god, & y^t the good hand of god was vpon him: therfore so manie of you as haue bene so long in the mynisterie, & can not yet shew a Church planted, do wante yor chief testimoniall & epist: wch should com̃end you vnto vs, as ministers sent of god: therfore instead of ministers you must goe for vagabondes, vntill you can shew vs this testimoniall: but then we will receiue you in ye name of ye lord: now we heare yor wordes, but then we should see yor workes, & know yor power.

O^r sauio^r Christe being demaunded whether it was he y^t should come or thei should looke for anoth̃, awnswered not thus: I am he y^t should come: but saide, *goe shew what things you haue seene and heard: ye blinde receiue their sight, ye halt go, ye leapers are clensed, ye deaf heare, ye dead are raised vp, and ye poore receiue ye ghospell*: so our sauio^r Christe did not compell any to receiue him further, then he made ye workes wch by ye testi-

2 : Cor. 13. 2 [*sic*., 3 : 2]

2 Cor : 10 . 18.

Matt : 11 : 4, 5.

---

[1] A blank, perhaps covering two words, in the manuscript.

monie of the pphetes pteined to his calling apparent in the sight of all men: wch workes the pphet *Esay* beareth record vnto in ye 61 ch: thus: *The spirit of ye lord [is] vpon me, therfore hath he annointed me, he hath sent me to preach good tidings to ye poore, to binde vp ye broken harted &c*: as he speaketh of his workes awnswering therto in ye 11. of *Math*. Therfore allso in the 5 of *Iohn* he saieth: *I haue greater witnes then ye witnes of Iohn, for ye workes wch ye father hath giuen me to finish, ye same workes y^t I doe beare witnes of me y^t the father sent me*: but you haue no outward witnes at all, but inward, by ye witnes of conscience as you pswade yor selues. But we ask you, are ye the true ministers sent of god or shall we looke for oth̃? except ye canne awnswer thus, behold what is seene, we haue o^r Churches planted, the vncleane sepate from ye cleane, all open abhominations of Antichrist expelled, & o^r poore flockes redeemed from his iron yoke, & goũned by ye due order of Christes goũnm^t, & we haue ye keies of outward binding & losing, w^tout borowing them from any Antichristian Courte[1]; and so forth: manie thinges more, as ye word of god hath measured out ye lines of yor dutie: we must needes awnswer you [454] y^t it is not you y^t be sent we must needes seek vp oth̃s. But ye will say ye haue after a fashion Churches in yor pishes, for you would els be ashamed to bragge thus. Looke upon the Church of *Corinth* w^{ch} *Paul* calleth his Epistle, though you among you make it a verie deformed Church, as I haue heard w^t myne eares, see if you can know yor owne by it, or it by yo^rs. *Paul* witnesseth thus of them, that thei were *ritch in Christ in all kinde of speach and in all knowledge*, so that thei were not destitute of any guift, wating for ye appeareing of our *lord Jesus Christe*: but now see ye children, wch the lord hath giuen you as you say, of how manie can you say, loe here was he borne? Indeed there were manie in whome some good towardnes did appeare, wch resorted to you M^r F: because when a man can not haue candlelight, he is faine to leane downe his head to see a glim̃ing by ye coales on the hearth. yet if a man should ask a questione, if you were their father, were not ye children forwarder then their fath^r: I know manie of their hartes were grieued at ye patching of yor prayers, & some of them haue not letted to tell you of it, who indeed were the chief begetters of those children, by fruitfull edifying of gratious

---

[1] "yoke" crossed out "Courte" substituted, may be "Courtes".

A Treatise of the Church

speach & godly conference, of whome you chalenge to yo^{r}self ye hono^r of parentage. But be it y^t the L gaue some blessing to yor labo^r, when you laboured somewhat against Antichrist, you now refusing to striue lawfully & to reforme yor self & yor charge, according to ye L his commaundem^t, but bearing yor self an open enemie to them wch are frowarder then you, be sure ye lord will cut you shorte, & giue you *a barren wombe and dry breasts*: & in token therof these children, whome you spake of, the chief of them haue forsaken you, & yo^{r}self haue missed a gratious time, wherin you might haue wrought such a worke by them, as would haue cōmended you, both before god & his people, & for yor default, y^t hono^r is giuen to another, though it grieue you. Thus yor Epist. wherof you boast, is writen w^t ye l̄res so wide asunder, y^t no bodie can reade it but yor self.

It foloweth the marke of the beast, wch you say we haue vpon vs is vtterlie vntrue/. this is the truest thing wch I had yet: for you may say y^t & sweare it to[o] y^t it is a false marke, & witnes of a false calling.

It foloweth we are surely pswaded, y^t we are of the number of those y^t are marked w^t ye marke of god in their foreheades/. M^r F: scripture is nothing but surelie pswaded, & pswaded in conscience: he is an vnskillfull cooke that maketh but one sauce for eūie meate, & y^t an unsaūie sauce to[o], wch tasteth but onelie in his owne mouth: well it is all we can get, we must hold vs content till better come.

But note y^t T.W. obiecteth conc̄ning ye marke of the mynisterie, ye marke of outward pfession, & M^r F: awnswereth of the L: election. But let y^t go it is one of the least faultes[.] that you haue the marke of the beast we p̄ue, for eūie Antichrist is ye beast, & of the beast, but you haue receiued their waxen seales in yor handes, & their handesfull of benesons[1] on yor heades, whome I before proued to be Antichrist, & you do not repent it nor renounce it: therfore you haue receiued ye marke of the beast. If not, teach me what ye marke of the beast is, I would learne: And y^t the marke of god in y^r forheades doth not appeare I p̄ue it thus : thei onelie were marked by ye marke wch mourned & cryed for all the abhominations that were done in *Jerusalem*, but you account notable abhominations of Antichrist but pretty tollerable spots & impfections, therfore yor mourning & crying must needes be

Ezech : 9 : 4.

---
[1] That is, benisons, blessings.

therafter, as it appeareth w^tout care or Jelousie: neither [455] doth the zeale of gods house eate you vp, neith̄ doth it pitie you to see her stones in the dust. *Moses* spake softlie, but the cry of his praier was exceeding loude: but you declare y^t in speaking verie loud, you pray verie softlie: so as surelye pswaded as you are if you looke not to this matter, yor worke will be worne out before you be aware.

 In y^t you charge vs as marked w^t impudencie, it is but a bare taunt, we will beare more then y^t against o^r selues: but wheth̄ we giue you any tauntes in wordes onelie, w^tout matter & notable occasion ministred, and y^t not in o^r owne priuate cause, I submit it to the iudgem^t of all men. you say, if we hold on the course we haue begun, we shall shew o^r selues impudent to the world. Judge you not to be verie skillfull of the right way yor self, wch can tell oth̄s y^t thei are out of the right course, & speake not one word when thei went out, no[r] where, nor how thei should come in againe.

 It foloweth / as for coming in ye name of gods enemie, I haue shewed before my certificate in Conscience /. you thinke you are of good credite w^t us, or els you would at one time or oth̄ bring some surety out of the word of god, more sufficient then yor owne conscience: you will make yor conscience weary & ouercharge it, if you lay all vpon it. but I rase yor conscience thus: you came not in the name of gods friend, therfore in the name of an enemie, for he y^t is not w^t him is against him: if you came in the name of gods frende you would surely doe y^t you are sent for, & discharge yor message at least in ye chief pointes therof: for he tha[t] *loueth god will do his cōmaundem^t* : therfore you not planting ye Church wch is euie ministers dutie, to doe when he seeth it vndone, euen w^t as much speed as *Nehemiah* & those y^t were w^t him builded ye wall, wch put not of[f] their clothes all the while, but for washing till ye worke was finished: you declare y^t you came not in the name of a lou̇ of god for allso thei y^t loue him loue his glory, & ye increase therof, & y^t w^t jelousie, the increase of gods glorie is especiallie in enlarging ye boundes of his Church. how can y^t [*sic*] boundes be enlarged, before thei be set, when thei are set, then it appeareth from day to day who are added to the Congregation, as appeareth in the first planted Church by the Apost:, & the numb̄ of them wch increased is set downe in three places at y^e

A Treatise of the Church

least in the *Acts*, according to ye time of their increasing: Acts : 1 : 15. euen so you, if you could haue planted ye Churches, 2 : 4, 5 : 14. 6 : 7, 4 : 4. should haue seen, what haruest, ye Lord would haue giuen to yor sowing frō moneth to moneth, & from day to day: but wheras now you can not tell wheth̄ you haue more or fewer, at thend of those many yeeres, then you had at the beginning. You yor selues haue latelie complained, some of you y^t you haue none, & some of you y^t you haue but one y^t feareth the lord, in any outward appearing in yor pishes: euen a iust plague for all them, y^t make pishes & Churches all one: & those few wch you haue, if thei waxe more forward then yor selues thei finde heavie friendes of some of you.

You are charged y^t you seeke flesh & bloud for yor arme, you cleare yor selues of y^t, & howe? I see (you say) clearlie w^t ye eies of my soule, y^t I am free from y^t curse wch thei deserue wch make flesh & bloud their arme, & therfore you pray y^t yor adū́sarie may see it to[o], & you count him dimme sighted because he can not see it, & this is all you can say for yor self: if we stand in doubt y^t the eies of yor soule are dimmed in this matter, what shall we be ye hender[1], thus you may tell a wise man, & kepe yor self vnwise still: the lord make vs to get more wisdome by yor punishm^t, then we are able to do by yor instruction: for full well I see y^t the Lord taketh when it pleaseth him wisdome from ye wise, wordes from ye eloquent, & grace from them that haue abused it, by sinning to quenching of it: but to come to the matter. They wch account them selues mynisters sent of god, & allowed by the Church, staying from their dutie for [456] further strength from ye Ciuill Magistrate, to make them strong in their mynisterie, make flesh & bloud their arme: allso to you, M^r F: they wch get them selues in, to be noble mens Chapplaines, as thinking therby to winne credit to the gospell, & some backing to them in their mynisterie, do extoll ye strength of man, & abase ye strength & glorious scepter of Christ Jesus, & so take flesh & bloud for their arme: now as cleare as you see w^t ye eies of yor soule y^t you are cleare from this euill, more clearlie we do heare w^t ye eares of o^r bodies y^t this euill hath oūtaken you.

It foloweth wheras you say, we leaue all obedience till we be comaūnded: indeed we are loth to come before we be comaūnded as you do, but rath̄ waite w^t

---

[1] "hender" repeated in margin. See "Hende, Hender" in *N.E.D.* Probably means "nearer".

patience & praier, what the lord will say by the mouth of godlie & Christian Magistrates./ often haue I heard y^t kings and princes should waite what ye L. should say vnto them by the mouth of pphets & priestes, but neu ye contrarie, y^t the pphets or any mynisters, should waite what god should say to them by the mouth of Magistrates, except you meane by their mouth their sword: This is a browne bred loafe of M^r F : owne moulding, euen so euill moulded, y^t it breaketh asunder as soone as one toucheth it, yea it is such a lumpe of leuen, y^t if it should fall into a whole batche of dough, it would marre all; & no m̃uaile though their bread be very sower wch vse to leuen all w^t this. but let us assay to put away their leuen, by the sweete word of god:

1 Sam : 13 : 13. *Saul taried for Samuel to heare what he should say to him from the lord*, because he taried not for all the great haste till *Samuel* came, who taried longer then appointm^t, ther-
Sam : 15 : 27. fore the lord cast them of[f]. *Dauid* being himself indued w^t the spirit of pphecie yet waited what ye lord should say to him by the mouthes of pphets & seers: for he saith in one place to Zadock, *art y^u not a seer ? I will tary in ye fields of ye wildernes vntill there come some word from you (meaning Ahimaaz & Jonathan the priests) to be told me*: he allso did attend, what ye L. saide vnto him by
Kings : 19 : 2. *Nathan* the prophet & *Gad* the seer. *Ezekiah* sent to *Isaiah* for an awnswer from the L., vpon the despight-full dealing of the *Assirians* : *Josiah* searched for a prophet, to aske Counsaile what ye L. should say to him, & finding
Kings : 22 : 13, 14, 15. none in *Judah* but onelie a woman pphetess *Huldah*, waited carfullie what the lord should say to him by her: but now I heare a whisping y^t ye priests in *Judah* waited for *Josiahs* reformation. Indeed we haue offten hearde such thinges, wofull disputers be they all : those priestes waited for reformation, as ye wicked people of *England* waite for death: for ye longer it tarieth the better leaue shall it haue: yea so waite allmost all o^r mynisters & people to[o] for Church goũnm^t, for thei know it is a heauy friend for their licentious living: but say in good sadnes, did those priestes well in taryinge vnreformed, till *Josiah* constrained them? yea thei did see[1] well, y^t thei kindled the consuming fier of gods wrath, w^{ch}
2 Kings : 23 : 20. for all ye reformation of *Josiah*, would not be quenched in ye land, but his jelousie susteined him, & his arme was stretched out still.

yet behold ye best p̃tence o^r mynisters haue for their

[1] ? "So".

A Treatise of the Church

waiting, also a wofull p̄tence, is this: & haue not oʳ Christian Magistrates, com̄aunded all the mynisters in this land, to guide their flockes by the rule of the gospell of Christ Jesus: yf it be so wherfore do their waite vnreformed against their owne knowledge & conscience: but to pceade. It is writen in yᵉ 9ᵗʰ of the 1 of *Samuel*: ¹ Sam : 9 : 9. *In Israel when a man went to seeke an awnswer of god, thus he spake, come, let vs go to yᵉ seer*: but Mʳ F : will teach vs a better way though not so readie; *the priests lippes were wont to keepe knowledge*, but now belike yᵉ case is altered; so when a man hath a euill matter in hand, it will shame the Mʳ¹: Well then Mʳ F: hath put his hand to yᵉ plough, and now he standeth & looketh backe, wherfore thinke you? for one yᵗ should come & bring yᵉ whip after him, and [457] therfore when it cometh, my sentence is, yᵗ he should haue the first handsell of it, for if he had not bene more lasie then the horses, there had bene ploughed by this time of the day more then an akre of ground: but a loitering seruaunt he is glad to haue such an excuse to stand still, yea hee quarelleth wᵗ vs because we go on saying we be not com̄aunded: but I would haue him awnswer me if this trumpet haue not yet sounded to vs to yᵉ marching, or his standerd haue not yet bene displaied, wᶜʰ hath said, *I am wⁱ you* Psal : 20 : 5, 7. *to yᵉ end of the world, but we reioice in yᵉ saluation of our king, and set vp our banner in yᵉ name of our god, when yᵉ lord performeth our petitions of dwelling in Sion*: thei waite for flesh & bloud, but we waite for yᵉ name of yᵉ L. oʳ god: *they are brought downe and falne*, but we are risen and stand vpright, and hauing turned oʳ backes vpon the Antichristian *Egipt*, we are prest & readie to goe wᵗ oʳ true *Josue* euen Christ Jesus, vnto yᵉ place where yᵉ L. hath pighte his tabernacle: yea the L. hath saide a great while since *how long will it be ere this people will go vp*? yea all this time of quiet peace, wᶜʰ yᵉ L. hath giuen vs in this land, for wᶜʰ you say we are not thankfull, hath bene yᵉ patience of the lord waiting for oʳ going vp into his rest, euen the visible Church: *for in yᵉ middest of Sion his honoʳ dwelleth, and there is his habitation for euer*. Ps : 84 : 6. [Ps. 132. 13] Judge then who are vnthankfull, thei wᶜʰ despise yᵉ louing suffering of the lord, by not returning from *Babilon* to him in *Sion*, or thei wᶜʰ are obedient to the heauenly voice wᶜʰ speaketh thus *Seeke ye my face*, this is oʳ obedience to go through yᵉ vale of wearines

---

¹ *I.e.*, Master.

digging fountaines to quench o^r thirst, till we appeare before ye L. in *Sion*.

But because I haue bene long in this form pt, & the more worke we do, the more we haue to do, to set this disordered geare in order, euen for redeeming the time, wherof we haue small store, wch may be better spent then in going oũ euĩe pt, I will take but a litle of the scumme to cast in the fier, & suffer ye rest to vanish away in the smoke till it be consumed. Thus T.W. confesseth that he can not discerne how this or that thing should be, therfore (saieth he) must he needes confesse himselfe blinde / this is as good a reason: M^r F: could neũ see a white crow nor a blacke swan, therfore M^r F: is starke blinde. Now afterward M^r F: goeth about to p)ue *schismatiques* & how? first (saith he) because we draw the people from the true p)ching of the word of the eternall god/. here is the best side turned out & y^t w^t a goodly glosse set vpon it, of true p)ching of the word of the eternall god: I awnswer you w^t *Job*: *Will you speake wickedly for gods defense, and talke deceitfully for his cause, will you accept his pson, and will ye contend for god? is it well y^t he should seeke of you? Will ye make a lye for him as one lyeth for a man*? though the wordes of yor mouth be as a mightie winde, yet o^r corne will stand vnshaken: for we are free from the thinges wheiof you accuse vs; but the euill lighteth vpon yor owne pates. how p)ue you y^t eũ we did draw any from the true p)ching of the word of god? yea we call them to it w^t all our power, & vse what meanes we can to haue ye exercise of ye word p)ched to flourish among vs.

But I see well enough you haue forsaken the feare of the Allmightie in y^t you throw out yor railings you care not how sclaunderouslie. But I know yor disease: we come [not] to yor [*sic*] nor to yor felowes, therfore not to ye word p)ched. I deny yor trifling argum^t: We haue the word p)ched among us. we haue p)ued y^t you stand excõicate, till you be reformed, therfore we refuse yor felowship, & you for spight to revenge yor quarell, & to make the matter [458] heinous, say we refuse the worde, no I say, not the word but you, & not you so soone as you haue eithei cleared yor selues, or reformed yo^{r}selues in those thinges wheiof we charge you: for you standing in these open abhominations, indaunging the state of the Chuich, p)ch not ye worde of message, as we shall see anone. But you say you p)ch

A Treatise of the Church

Christe: the Diuells confesse Christe, must we go heare them therfore? but of your p̃ing occasion is giuen to speake anone.

You charge vs allso w^t drawing ye people from ye sacram^{ts} we embrace them dulie mynistred, & the true vse of them, thei are seales to the p̃mises & the p̃ises are onelie to ye apparent Church, for it is saied: *the lord from out of Sion b[l]esse thee, and there ye lord appointed the blessing and life for euermore*: but contrary wise it is writen *he that bringeth his sacrifice, and not to ye doore of ye tabernacle of ye Congregation, shall bee cut of[f] from ye lordes people*: so the Sacram^{ts} are not dulie ministred, nor the worde dulie p̃ched, but in the apparent Church, & about ye apparent Church planting. As for publique prayers from wch you say we drawe the people: if you meane read & stinted prayers in popish wise, we had rather you should be at them then we: We pray publiquely when the congregation meeteth, you say prayers, when yor parish meete, grudge not at o^r praying, & we will not envie yor saide prayers: but eũ you goe on, y^t we draw the people: we would be ashamed to hale & pull the people as you do: I thinke you feare y^t all the best will away: we drawe none but whome the lord draweth by touching their consciences: yea *the youth of our wombe be ye willing people*, wch come w^t as small drawing and as litle noise, as the morning dew falleth vpon the grasse.

Ps. 128. 5.
Ps. 133. 3.
Leuit. 17. 1
2
3
4
5

Ps. 110. 3.

Now cometh yor heavy quarell against me: namely blasphemie, for y^t I should call p̃ching pratling as you say. I deny that eũ I called p̃ching pratling, the lord is my iust Judge, p̃ue it, it standeth you in hand for yor honesty: for you haue accused me more then ten times: but this was saide, when you had nothing to say for yor selues, but allwayes obtend this worde p̃ching p̃ching: I saide y^t p̃ching w^{t}out power, or p̃ching by them wch are not sent, is no p̃ching but rather pratling or as the sound of brasse and a tinckling Cimball: that it is no p̃ching I p̃ue it by *Paules* doctrine, for he saith *how can they preach except they be sent?* Now I say none such as by open abhominations, as submitting themselues to Antichristian Church goũnm^t, or such like sinne do openlie endaunger the state of the Church, can be sent of god, or come in his name; for thei can not so much as be of ye Church so long as thei continue. Now M^r F: I haue giuen you a litle *aqua vitae* to help you to digest this morsell of blasphemie, wch hath stucke so

Rom. 10. 15.

long in yor stomacke. Then you recken vp other thinges wherw^t the p̱chers are charged, thinking it verie absurd: & to it you go againe twise before the end of yor Îre, as to be blinde guides, deceiuers & such like: you guide vs not vp to *Canaan* the lordes rest, but leade vs vp into *Egipt*: for you goũne vs but not according to Christes true goũnm^t wch you confesse to be wanting from you: therfore you are blinde guides: allso you are placed & displaced by the BB.: therfore when we haue most neede of you, you are gone: this is deceiuing; if it were nothing but this [459] for I speake of one of the last matters: for so accounted *Job* of his friedes [*sic*], saying, *my brethren haue deceiued me as a brooke, and as the rising of ye riuers they passe away: in time they are dryed vp w^t heate and are consumed, and when it is hotte they faile out of their places, or thei departe from their way & course, they vanish & perish*: now I say that thei that went from about Windham considered them, and they that went from about Aylessam,[1] waited for them, but thei were confounded when thei hoped, they came thith͡ and were ashamed[2]. I could as easelie proue the rest but for wasting of time: but here is enough proued vntill you disproue it, either by writing or wch I had rather if it were the Lordes will, by shewing yor selues other men.

Then you charge vs that we pswade the people to be rather in houses and corners then to be where there is the publique face of the Church: y^t is as much to say that the Congregation can not publiquelie meete in a house, except it be a great house of lime & stone. But M^r F: & manie mo deale w^t vs thus thei set bandogges[3] on vs to baite vs from their doores, & since thei looke out and say there came no bodie there, and thei chide vs when thei meete vs, because we came not to their house. for o^r mynister p̱ched first & we heard him in a Church of lime & stone, from thence we were driuen into the Churchyard, from thence into a house adioyning vpon the Churchyard, from whence we being had to prison after y^t some of vs had got some liɓtie out, we got in that Church againe, from whence we were had to prison againe. yet now we are charged as people wch will not come to the Church, thus reasonablie are we dealt w^t. Now Mr F. clappeth his handes and saith

Job. 6. 15.

---

[1] Wymondham is about ten miles south-west of Norwich, and Aylsham is approximately thirteen miles north-west of Norwich.
[2] What welcome light on the history of the early Separatists would have been thrown had these sentences been fuller and clearer.
[3] Bandogs are watchdogs, bloodhounds, or ferocious dogs.

what is this but a foule schisme? It should seeme he is foulie ignorante what a schisme is, y^t called it a foule schisme, to go from a great house for ye Church exercises to a lesse: he hath heard somewhat of a schisme & he hampereth about it: but M^r F:, a schisme is this to make a wilfull depting from y^t which is ye appant Church of god. Put on yor harnesse againe, & fight till you proue this by vs, & we will cast downe o^r bann̄ & betake o^{r}selues to yor m̄cie.

Then you say we coū this schisme w^t erro^{rs} & heresies: this is scarce either rime or reason, to coū schisme w^t an heresy. Mr F. coūeth one ill fauored speech w^t anoth^r: nay if we should coū we would turne ye best side outward, & coū foule thinges not w^t fouler then thei but w^t fayrer. a man going to market to sell a bushell of brandie wheat, will not lay a litle dracke or darnell on the top of it, for then his market were done: but we are not ashamed of o^r wheat neith̄ do we coū it: it is faire & cleare thankes be to god & good seede, wheras yo^{rs} is full of durcockle & tares of yor owne deuises, wch I will name anone, & for feare least those Chapmen wch looke on o^r wheat should neū buy of yo^{rs} after, you would p̄uent them & hold them by the skirtes, y^t thei should not come to vs[1], saying to them y^t o^r corne is nought before thei see it: but p̄ue any erro^r or heresie, euen the least shew therof in vs, euen the bredth of an heare, we will cleare o^{r}selues or reforme o^r selues: if you can p̄ue none we must call vnto the L. ye righteous Judge of o^r innocencie, to coole the heat of such tongues, *whose wordes are as sharp as raso^{rs} or as ye coles of Junip̄.*

Now conc̄ning yor selues, because you speake what you list, you must heare what you list not. I can not discōmend yor wisdome in coūing, for you coū wiselie in yor kinde, coūing many erro^{rs} & heresies w^t a faire p̄tence of true p̄ching, & you adde ye word of ye eternall god, this is to coū, & to paint oū ye coūinge, [460] but let vs remble or remoue, & see what is vnderneath. You teach y^t a true mynister lawfullie called must stay for authority from the Ciuill Magistrate, if thei be X̄pian for reforming his charge by Eccliall goūnm^t you teach y^t he must waite what the L. saith to him by the mouth of ye magistrate, you teach y^t a man may receiue the Sacram^{ts} of blinde guides and dumbe dogges, and that he ought so to doe, if there be

---

[1] The words from " would " to " vs " omitted in error in *The Brownists in Norwich & Norfolk*, p. 56.

none otħ in y̆ᵉ pish, you teach that thei be Sacraments by what man soever thei be mynistred: you Mʳ F. [Edward or John Fenton], have taught that blinde guides and dumbe dogges are, after a sort, builders of the house of God: you teach yᵗ the cōmaundemᵗ of Church goūnmᵗ is lesse then otħ commaundemᵗˢ; you teach yᵗ Churchgoūnmᵗ (& so Christes goūnmᵗ of yᵉ keies of binding & losing) is not matter of saluation, yᵗ is as much to say yᵗ wᶜʰ is bound on earth by yᵗ meanes is not bounde in heauen, nor contrarywise: you teach yᵗ it is a handmaide to doctrine, making yᵉ kinglie office of Christ, but handmaide to his office of teaching: you teach yᵗ a man may receiue the Sacramᵗˢ, in company of them wᶜʰ are knowne open offendours: you teach yᵗ there can not be due sepation of cleane from vnclean, wᵗout sepating yᵉ soule from yᵉ bodie: you teach yᵗ theı wᶜʰ are starued for want of sptuaĨ foode by Idoll shepheardes yᵗ can not feede, must wᵗ humble suite attend vpon yᵉ BB: & patrones curtesie, till thei bestow better vpon them: you teach yᵗ a shepheard wᶜʰ can feede, ought notwᵗstanding to leaue his flocke, at yᵉ commandemᵗ of yᵉ lordly Elders, wᶜʰ vsurp authority oū them, yea though it be but for a quarell of bringing them into subiection to a tradition of men as a white linen garmᵗ & such like: you teach yᵗ those thinges wᶜʰ are amisse in yoʳ Church are but impfections not hindering yᵉ peace of the Church, & yᵗ no man may disturb yᵉ peace wᶜʰ you haue for them. Alas what peace *so long as y̆ᵉ whoredomes of Jesabel euen yᵉ whore of Babel do remain?* thes thinges you teach & an 100 more I dare take vpon me to name, wᶜʰ bee grosse erroʳˢ, & some of them oūturning yᵉ groundes of religion, being vpholden of you wᵗ high hand, are euen plaine heresies:

Mat. 16. 19.

Eccles. 10. 1.

Thus you digg pittes and fall into them yoʳ selues: *dead flyes cause to stincke and putrefy the ointmᵗ of y̆ᵉ Apothecary: so doth a little folly him y̆ᵗ is in estimation for wisdome and for glory*: so thei being so many dead flies of erroʳˢ amongest yoʳ ointmᵗ of some true doctrine wᶜʰ you speake make all to stinke, & especially this great lumpe of dead carion of yoʳ frowardnes against yᵉ L. building, being not a litle follie but a great mischief do make you & yoʳ felowes, wᶜʰ heretofore were estemed for wisdome & loving¹ euen contemptible, & euen as a rush wᶜʰ was greene sometime, & fadeth for want of mire: for yoʳ estimation must needes fall if you be not faithful in all

Job. 8. 11.

¹ Possibly "liuing".

A Treatise of the Church

the lordes house: for that is the vpholding of your credit, and euen your wisdome, and hon^r before all people.

T.W. did aske you a question or two, & you bid him awnswer them himself. *K[n]owledge should dwell in yor lippes*: but you know, if you should haue awnsered them, you should haue been as well shackled as thei, wch should haue awnswered o^r Sauio^r Christ about *the baptisme of John*.

Next y^t place of *Paul* being cited to sepate o^r selues *from them wch walke inordinatly* : you say if we meane as *Paul* meaneth we must looke to o^r felow disciples for Idlenes, as you charge vs afterward: Thinke you y^t the word is not more generall, because *Paul* vsed it against those y^t walke idlie, therfore he meant none oth͡? you shew yor cunning: if you heare a man sweare, & you say to him he that breaketh gods cō-maundem^ts is accursed, and you say to him you meane to touch him specially for that [461] present time, therfore do you meane to charge nobodie els, therfore a whoremaister standing by, whose¹ you knew not, may say w^t himself, he meant the swearer. But you runne on as though you had the winde at the sterne, and as though T.W. had got a staffe for his owne backe, you plucke it out of his hand & fall a beating of him and vs w^t it: you charge vs for not labouring as before, for letting our wiues and children wepe for want, for going backward wth the world & waxing poorer. The *Israelites* were counted grieuouslie opp)ssed, because straw was taken from them, & thei had not made their whole tale of bricke, yet had thei their handes & legges at will, & the field before them to scratch vp stubble, & such poore fewell as thei could finde: but we are more cruellie vsed, for we were shut up betwene walls most of vs, w^t our legges chained, all of vs put to great expense, & those wch were out of prison not able to stirre out of the doores, when thei were at home, nor able to be at home except it were a litle by stealth, for the bursting open of o^r doores & violent handling, yet now we are beaten by M^r F : tongue & others, because we haue made no more bricke, & coined no more money. You know M^r F : what was o^r lot, except we should haue done as you did in prison, to haue taken mony of them that would haue giuen it vs, for then we could haue saued some part of o^r charges: but we know we shall haue thinges enough cast in o^r teeth, **though what**

2. Thess. 3. 6.

Exod. 5. 12.

---
¹ Either mistakenly for "whome" or a following noun omitted.

you know by any of vs we can not tell: I for my pt do not know of any of o^r companie poorer then thei were at the beginning of o^r trouble I thancke God hartily, but I know some of the companie richer euen in out-

Psal. 23.

ward thinges wch is euen the m̃cifull bountie of god, who is o^r shepheard, therfore we want not, *he prepareth a table for vs in spight of our foes, he annointeth our heads w^t oyle and our cuppes do ou̇flow, and for his kindnes &. truth* we desire to spend our dayes in his house.

Whose wiues you should meane to haue wept for want, I know not, but if *Moses* wife called her husband *bloody husband*, because [of] the Circumcision of the childe, we will not thinke it straunge though some mans wife of o^r companie, call her husband poore husband because of the psecution of the Church allthough her husband be no more in fault, except it were in tarying to[o] long, before he put his hand to the lordes busines, then *Moses* was in fault for the circumcision of the childe, sauing that he draue it of[f] to]o] long. But M^r F: what if we should loose houses, landes, or all the rest of o^r goods, wiues, children, & all, (as we durst make none other reckoning, if any better measure come we shall put it among o^r gaines) what then I say, would you checke vs by our poũtie and miserie: it is our glorie and not our shame, we haue receiued all from the lord, and we hold all in our handes euen wth our liues, to offer to the lord, at his good pleasure, thinking it a happie thing, if the lord will vouchsafe to serue his glorie, of any thing that we haue, and if we maie make vs such a debter of o^r *vnrighteous Mammon*, we are happie, for that whatsoeuer we lay out[1] in silũ, he will pay it in gold & pretious stones, and seuen times the weight, *heaped measure, pressed downe, and running over*:

Hebr. 10. 25.

You charge vs for running from house to house, we are cõmaunded by the Apostle [462] *to exhort one another* and that so much the more *because ye day draweth nigh*: now we can not do much except we meete often, and goe one to anothers house, if we behaue not o^r selues well when we meete blame vs: now I have awnswered for o^r idlenes[2], let vs come a litle to yor sore working: there are a companie of p)chers as thei call them about you, & you vse to go 2 or 3 daies a weeke, on foote or on horsbacke, as the weather maketh most for yor ease,

---

[1] "out" repeated in MS.
[2] Transcript mistakenly has "weaknes".

A Treatise of the Church

half a dosen miles perhaps, as it falleth out more or lesse, & there you spend an hower in a pulpit, to get a litle praise, to cōmend or discōmend one another, and all the day after feast & talke of prophane thinges; all this may you do and say w^t the frier *heu quanta patimur*[1]: but sometimes you feast not but fast, but after a worse maner, then did the *Pharisees* whome our Sauio^r Christ reproued as fasting to be *seene of men*: for you fast in open sight, and cause all the people to do so: & in the meane time there is nothing named as the cause of the fast, nor any thing at all reformed: yea the goūno^{rs} of the exercise most vnreformed of all: we reade in the scriptures of better fastes then these wch the lord reiected. But some of the p)chers I graunt are more carefull & sober, and worke some what better then this cometh to, both in sermons making and studying: but though thei rise earlie thei are neū the nearer, so long as thei poure their water into a conduite wch hath so manie holes, except thei prouide to stop, though thei should toile neū so sore, yet should their worke be neū the more seene: & if yor pasture fence lie outwardly broken, you may driue out the swine eūie houre of the day, sweating and runnyng yor self out of breath, & yet haue them there againe so soone as yor backes are turned. But cease you to draw water in a bottomlesse bucket, or els the lord will close vp yor wages in a bottomlesse bagge.

Afterward you charge vs to ly one on another vsing one anothers liberality, saying you feare y^t the cōmunitie of the *Anabaptistes* and *family of loue*[2] will fall among vs: now I must needes liken you to y^e *children* to whome our savio^r likened y^t *froward generation* w^{ch} *would not daunce when their felowes piped vnto them, nor weepe when thei mourned to them*. for we help one anothers wantes as we are able, & you say behold *Anabaptists* and men of the *family of loue*: some of vs as you beare vs in hand weepe for want, & you say behold *bankroutes & beggers*: if you had but one drop of that Charity wch is not suspitious you would rather hope of that cōmunitie wch is spoken of Acts 2 & 4 would flourish among vs then misdeeme y^t ye cōitie of the *Anabaptistes* should fall in among vs: but we are despised & cast downe, therfore

Matt. 11. 6.

---

[1] Oh, how many things we suffer, or, alas, how much we endure.
[2] The literature on the Family of Love, or Familists, is not extensive or easily accessible. For an introduction to the subject, see Robert Barclay, *The Inner Life of the Religious Societies of the Commonwealth* (3rd ed.; London, 1879), pp. 25-32; Champlin Burrage, *The Early English Dissenters in the Light of Recent Research* (1550-1641), Vol. I (Cambridge, 1912), Ch. viii; F. Nippold, "Heinrich Niclaes und das Haus der Liebe," *Zeitschrift fur die historische Theologie* (Gotha, 1862), pp. 323-394.

you passe litle to spurne vs : well you feare for y^t wch will come after, & you accuse vs, but it is of y^t wch we shall do, or you feare we will do, indeed such thinges you p)ch: there are will witnes to yor face M^r F: y^t you spake thus in a pulpit, *surely this matter will p̄ue an heresy*: so you being not able to charge vs w^t heresy (as we defie you all therein in ye name of the L., do it if you can) you charge y^t we shall be heretiques hereafter. Seldome haue I read in the hystorie of ye Bible of any wch accused other of y^t thei would do afterward, except their surmise were grounded on something going before: as in *Ezra* 4 ϑtain enimies accused the *Jewes*, y^t if the city should be built, thei would w^thold their tribute from ye King. [463]. Indeed they had plaied so w^t *Nebuchadnezzar*, hard before ye captiuity: so though thei were spightfull enimies, yet had thei some p)tence for their cruell suspition: but w^tout any reasonable colo^r of p)tence, or any liklihood of heresie to charge vs y^t we will surelie be heretiques. I can not finde a yard wand in all ye scriptures of so large a scise, as to measure this outstretched crueltie, but of the divells shap[e] as mention is made in ye 1 & 2 of *Job*, for there the deuill beholding *Jobs* singular innocency yet is bold to say to god that if he will handle *Job* thus & thus *he will blaspheme him to his face*, euen thus are we accused y^t if we might haue libertie we would proue *Anabaptistes*. Therfore M^r F: you may see that you being not able to finde any example of any wicked man, to shape yor cruell surmizinges by, haue shaped them by the divells owne paterne. But he tormoiled w^t cruel mischief & brought forth a lye, so shall you. And lastlie for lying on anothers charge, you may euill checke vs by it for we are content when we meete w^t a drie morsell, & we take what heede we maie of y^t inconuenience: but some of yor company haue so vsed the matter, I wot where, that you haue made one kitchin to chaunge her Ma[1]. you make vs betwitched & beside o^r selues, because we haue meate & will not eat it: we dare not eat y^t meat wch hath poison in it, neith^r dare we receiue o^r meat at the carving of those seruaunts, whome our householder hath charged not to meddle w^t ordering the house: so it is not for malice as you charge vs but for feare of o^r M^{rs} displeasure: & that o^r M^r hath forbidden you to order his house, till you be reconciled to him, we haue p)ued.

---

[1] The meaning is not clear, and we are not helped by the fact that " Ma " is at the edge of the sheet : apparently the charge is that the ministers secure refreshment at the Queen's expense.

A Treatise of the Church

Next after T.W. saying, y^t the L. hath opened his eares to heare the charm̅s voice, you say you thinke so, & yet you say he refuseth to heare the p)chers voice: as though he y^t stoppeth his eares at ye voice of ye true p)chers of gods word, may not be saide to be like *the deafe adder y^t stoppeth his ears at ye voice of ye charmer*. Psal : 58 : 4. But if a man take *Davides* meaning thus, y^t one wch singeth sweetlie, can not wth his sweet singing charme an adder from his sting: what can you except against the exposition, wch is more probable in my iudgem^t then the other, all though I leaue it free. But you know com̅on speach speaketh thus: such a tongue would be charmed, wch is not meant by enchantm^t : allso who hath bewitched you, y^t is so greatlie deceiued you, & it is not meant by witchcraft, but by false teaching as *Paul* speaketh to the *Galath*.

But let y^t go, you in the next line of your letter, whilest Charmer is fresh vpon yor tongue, compare vs to sorcerers, because we go into corners, as you say: we haue sought no corners, but were driuen from open places into corners, you plucke vs out of the house by the haire of the head, & since complaine that we will not tarye wthin : we loue not the darke, you haue *loued darknes more then the light*, as the light it self bewraieth & will betwray, to all those to whome god hath giuen & will giue eies to see. I pray you M^r F : were those of whome the Author to y^e *Hebr.* sayeth *they liued in dennes and holes of the earth*, were thei sorcerers or like to sor- Hebr. : 11 : 30 [*sic.*, 38]. cerers: so you see o^r going into corners maketh vs no more like sorcerers, then o^r pseeuted forefathers haue bene; & yor standing in pulpites maketh you no more like publique teachers, then the popish priestes haue bene. But let vs be called sorcerers of yor mouthes we are content, seing o^r Sauiour [464] Christe was saied to haue the Diuell: but as o^r Sauio^r awnswered the[m] *If I by Beelzebub cast out diuells, wherby do your* Matt. 12 : 27. *children cast them out: but if I by ye spirit of God, cast out diuells, then know y^t ye kingdome of God is come vnto you*: euen so we awnswer you, if we be sorcer^{r}s whie do you call his blessed gou̅nm^t as you do in this letter: but if wee by the grace of gods spirit, haue taken in hand this busines of reforming o^r selues, know you that the sinne of blasphemie wch you lay vpon oth^r will rest vpon yor owne skirtes. Afterward T.W. vsing some sharp speach, you tell him his tongue is tipped w^t a m̅uailous heate. I neū heard of a tongue tipped wt heate afore: but I heard yt one of yor neighbour p̄chers was sayde to haue his tongue tipped wt gold & his lipps wt siluer : but he wch spake it might be deceiued, for all is not gold yt glistereth[1].

Afterward againe you reckon vp a greate sorte of sharpe speaches, wch T.W. did vse, and you make a bead roule[2] of them: as felow deceiuers, false brethren, menpleasers, blinde guides, trees wtout fruite, etc : and you say p̄cisely that thei are not wordes proceeding from the Spirit of god: but thei and such like are wordes proceeding from or Sauior Christe, the apostles, and prophets. therfore by yor reason, or Sauior Christe, the apostles, and prophetes had not the spirit of god. I pray you where are these speaches, *generation of vipers, painted sepulchers, hypocrits, foxes, painted walls, adulterous generation, princes of Sodom, people of Gomorrha, trees wt out fruite, cloudes wtout rayne*, and a thowsand moe[3]. I am sure you know them and where to finde them : so yt the most yt you could haue saide, therfore, had bene that the wrong appliing of these speaches proceeded not from the spirit of god: then if you could haue proued them falslie applied, you had saide something, wheras now being so hastie to giue T.W. a blow, haue missed him and striken the childe in his armes, for you haue spoken vntruelie of the Spirite of god, but your proof is because the Spirit of god is gentle; so were these gentle whome I haue named, and *Moses* was an exceeding gentle and meeke man, yet was he angrie in the lordes quarell in so much that he threw the tables out of his handes, and brake them, he was notablie angrie when he did that. I know we are to deale with meeknes at the beginning wt them in whome there is hope, & so were you dealt wth, but thei wch after two or three admonitions remaine willfull and obstinate, and specially to the hurt of others are more roughlie to be handled.

Manie thinges there are more yea more then as many more, which for verie want of time and wearines I am faine to let passe, hauing in this wch I haue writen giuen a taste of the rest. At last you make a praier, but cleanse yor handes of the bloud of them wch pish by yor negligence : for els the p̄phet *Esay* telleth you: *though*

Shakespeare's wording in *The Merchant of Venice*, Act II, Scene VII, is : "All that glisters is not gold."
Breadroll.
Cf. Peel, *Seconde Parte of a Register*, I. 89, for a similar reply by John Field.

A Treatise of the Church

*you make many prayers the lord will not heare you, your hand*ʳ *being full of bloud*: as you haue prayed in the end of yo*s* letter so do I pray wᵗʰ faithfull *Nehemiah*, a glasse for you all [465] if you would looke vpon him. I pray I say wᵗ him not in myne owne iniurie, but in the lord his quarell, not against you if you repent & obey, nor particularlie against any of your companie, whose repentance I wish rather, but generallie against the professed enemies, wᶜʰ will not builde gods house and hold backe those that would. *Heare o our god for we are despised, and turne their shame vpon their owne heades and give them vnto a pray in the land of their captivitie, and couer not their iniquitie neyther let their synne be put out of thy presence, for thei haue prouoked vs before the buylders.*
      Not yours excepte you repent.
               R.H.

Nehem : 4 : 4.

III. A Little Treatise on Ps. 122. 1.

A Little Treatise vppon the firste Verse of the 122. *Psalm. Stirring vp vnto carefull desiring & dutifull labouring for true church Gouernement.* Psalm. 133. 8. Arise O Lorde, to come into thy rest, thou, and the Arke of thy strength. R.H. 1583.

The copy used is B.M. 3090. a. 15.

Blank leaf; t-p., with *verso* blank; "To all our Christian Brethren", 3 *recto* — 4 *recto* (Black letter); An additional note, 4 *verso* (Roman); *A Little Treatise* (A 1 — H 5 *recto*, in 8's, Black Letter); blank, H 5 *verso*; verses from the Psalms (Roman type), H 6 *recto* — H 7 *recto*. Other copies in Bodleian, Lambeth, and Union Theol. Semin. Library, New York. One of the books against which proclamation was made in 1583. There are still extant signs of the examination of this particular book. In the B.M. (Add. MS. 29546, ff. 113 *recto* — 115 *verso*) is an item endorsed on f. 116 *verso*, "Notes out of Harrysons booke"; it contains 44 extracts, with page references, most of them with captions. Among the Domestic State Papers in the Record Office (CXLVI. 20) is what seems to be another copy of these "Notes", which were no doubt prepared before the issue of the Proclamation.

Another edition was published by the Brewster Press in Leyden in 1618. For collation see Harris & Jones, *The Pilgrim Press*, 1922. Copies of this edition are in the Dexter collection (Zd. 992) in the Sterling Library at Yale — this is probably Brewster's own copy — and in the Bodleian (101. g. 320).

The Scripture references have been amplified where necessary (additions in square brackets) and in one or two places corrected.

[3][1] To all our Christian Brethren in Englande, which wayte for the Kingdome of Christ, increase *of the knowledge of the trueth bee multiplied vnto them, with strēgth* and patience, and perseuerance vnto the ende.

---
[1] These page numbers are inserted in ink in the B.M. copy.

A Little Treatise vppon the first Verse

[M]y state is known vnto manie of you (my Brethren) how that of certaine time (though weakely & vntowardly) I haue striuē, and withstood the yoke of spirituall bondage in the worshippe of God, which the man of perdition haue yet left behinde for our sifting and trial. Frō the which that I might bee deliuered (the Lorde God the searcher of heartes I take to recorde) that it haue bene myne onlie quarell, and the cause of stirring me vp to do that, which I did. Concerning the whiche cause, I did not thinke it lawefull for mee (though I coulde haue escaped in time ynough) to withdraw my selfe into any other place, for myne owne liberties sake, vntill I had more openly witnessed the same cause.[1]

Which when it seemed good vnto God, that I with some others should doo, by abyding imprisonment a certayne time: Then ha-[4]uing offered ourselues to suffer whatsoeuer our vexers should lay vpon vs, and espyinge nothing like to be done vnto vs, but to bee holden with lingering imprisonement, and that without libertie of communicating vnto others the instruction of the same cause, which we professed: wee thought good rather to vndergoe some exile (as it were) for redeeming at least some libertie of worshipping God with safetie of conscience. Which when we did, and diuers of our Brethren, which were willing to come vnto vs were restrayned: and we were persuaded, that to returne vnto them thither, whereas by imprisonment we should againe be holden from them, would little auayle: I haue iudged that we haue bene debters to them to bestow vpon them some thing which might helpe to increase their spirituall courage and comforte. In which behalfe, when the expectation of me and diuers others rested vppon some, who in the ende did but slenderlie answere, and satisfie the same[2]: Then I, which for my vnworthines and poore gifte, hadde thought neuer to haue set foorth any thinge publikely, yet was prouoked to indeuour my selfe, in some parte, as farre as the Lorde should make me able, to satisfie that want, which I thought to be great. And I went about a piece of work touching Church gouernement.[3] But partlie by sicknes, & partly by weying the cost of the print, and findinge it to be aboue my reache of abilitie: I was hindered, and haue let staye that worke, vntill the Lorde further inable mee.

[5] In the meane tyme I thought good to write some other little treatise, and I chose this 122. Psalme, thinking thereby to haue occasion ministred to speak of diuers of those pointes, which concerne the cause mētioned. And I was determined to haue spokē somewhat brieflie vpon the whole Psalme. But in the firste entraunce meetinge with those pointes, which I thought good they should be discussed somewhat largelie for edifyinge sake: Agayne,

---
[1] Compare this outline of events with that in Browne's *True and Short Declaration*, below p. 424.
[2] The reference is probably to Browne.
[3] Above p. 29.

sicknes and other causes cutting me short: I was constreined to
ende at this time skarce finishing the firste verse. Neyther was it
my desire to seeme to speake much vppon a little Texte, (yea I
confesse that I haue passed the boundes of Schollerlike handeling
the Text) but the thinges which offered them selues to be spoken
of, seemed to my iudgement to require so much measure. Herein
my desire vnto the lord is, that my poore labour may be accepted
of him, and may be profitable to his people.

[ORNAMENT]

[6] I Would haue the Reader aduertised, that whereas in one
place of this boke, I haue these woords: *The Authour to the Hebrewes
speake* [sic] *of certaine Christians, which were racked &c.* My meaning
was not, but that I iudged him to speake especially of those which
suffered persecution, before the comming of Christ in the fleshe:
which beleuing in Christ to come, may also well be called by the
name of *Christians.* Yet after it was printed, I suspecting that it
might be an occasion of cauilling to some: I thought good to sett
downe a word or two of my meaning therin.

[7][1]   PSAL. C.xxii. ver. 1.
*I reioyced when they saide vnto me, We will goe into the house
of the Lorde.*

Mat. 6. 19.

Iere. 48. 10.

Right Well is it said, that wher ye treasure is, there
will the harte bee also: which thing is seene in this
seruant of the Lorde, who behaued him selfe worthelie
in the Arke bringinge home. And as it was the Lordes
worke, so did he carefullie acquite him selfe that the
curse shoulde not laye holde on him, whiche belongeth
to the working of the Lordes worke negligentlie. But
that he did, hee did with all his power, and when hee
had finished his ioyfull worke, his ioye was not ended,
but rebowned agayne and agayne, with a sweete Echo
in his soule. So as it was meate and drinke [8] to him to
doo the will of God: so was it also his pleasure to thinke
and muse upon the same, and he hath conceyued the
grace of Gods spirite, and hath brought foorth this
Psalme, as the fruite of so godlie a meditation, leauing
vs a glasse and paterne wherein to see the spottes of
our deformed and lothesome negligence, and a lanterne
he hath set bright before vs, that wee may see to take
our waye to goe and laye hande on the Lordes ploughe,
to doo his acceptable worke. Out of whose example
and wordes in this Psalme, wee minde, by the good

[1] A 1 *recto.*

A Little Treatise vppon the firste Verse

furtherance of God, to gather some aduertisementes to stirre our selues vp, yet whyles it is called to day, least we should be hardned through the deceitfulnes of sinne. *Hebr.* 3. 13.

First we haue to speake of his ioye and the cause thereof, the remēbrance of which, he doth now feede vpon, and chewe the cudd vpon this ioye of that happie daye, whiche hee thus remembreth. The Lord chose Dauid from the sheepefolds to feede his people in [9] Iacob and his inheritance in Israel. And as it is spoken of him that he fed them in the simplicitie of his harte, so did it euē appeare in his first entrance of his kingdome. For nothinge helde him carefull in comparison of this, to haue the Lorde to vouchsafe to come home agayne vnto his people, and to be at peace with them, to loue them, & remoue shame and rebuke farre from them, by returninge his holie Arke, the token of his presence, and the liuelie image of his countenance vppon them, as the taking away thereof was the turning his backe vpon them, and turning awaye his face, as hee hadde threatned before for sinne. And it was the reprochefull steyning of the glorie of Israel: as it sayde, The glorie is departed from Israel, for the Arke of God is taken. Therfore was the care of Dauid, & his zeale set on fyre within his brest, which thing he mightely declared, and the flame thereof appeared, when he sware vnto the Lord and vowed a vowe vnto the mightie God of Iacob, saying, I will not enter into [10] the Tabernacle of mine house, nor come vpon my palet or bedde, nor suffer myne eyes to sleepe, nor mine eyeliddes to slumber, vntill I haue found out a place for the Lorde, an habitation for the mightie God of Iacob. *Psal.* 78. 71. *Ver.* 72. *Deut.* 31. 17. 1. *Sā.* 4. 22. *Psal.* 132. 2.

Now although it be my purpose, and order requireth to hasten to the cause of Dauids ioye, which he heare mentioneth, yet it standeth with dewe order in this place, as it doeth with edifying to stande vppon his great care, in wayting for that thing, whiche being obteyned, this his ioye succeeded. For liuelie and sounde is that ioye which the harte feeleth, when it is refreshed frō care & griefe going before.

When the Lorde had deliuered his soule out of all aduersities, which hee susteyned in the dayes of Saul, and had brought him to the glorie of his kinglie Throne: herein he shewed the simplicitie of a true harte, in that hee was not chaunged by the suddain alteratiō, nor his hart beguyled by those pleasures, to cause him to forget God. He was not highe minded, hee had no *Psal.* 131. 1.

[11] proude lookes. But he kept his soule, as a childe that is weyned frō his mothers brest. Yea at this time he throughlie weined him self, frō taking pleasure in anie thing, vntill the Arke of God should be brought home & placed in Israel, which hee calleth by yᵉ name of the Lorde, and the mightie God of Iacob. Therevnto doth he sweare and vow, not to haue regard vnto his own tabernacle nor house, nor to coūt it his home, or settle him selfe therein, neyther to take any sound rest, vntil he had seene this busines of the Lord in dew forwardnes. Thus was hee thankfull vnto the Lorde, whiche had remēbred him, and all his afflictions.

Psal. 132. 5.

Let vs examine our selues & call to minde the yeeres that are past, when the fyrie sworde did hange ouer our heades in the dayes of Queene Marie, & that by so weake a threede, that we looked euerie houre when it should fall vpon vs, whē we being straungers frō our own houses, walked frō house to house, at suche time as the Owles and Backes[1] looke foorth and flye: [12] And thought it well if wee might liue so without house or land, or ought else saue bare breade for the life.

Ester. 3. 13.
Ester. 7. 3.
Exod. 3. 33.

We were as Iewes which by *Hamans* meanes were solde to bee slaine, and destinate to a day of death. And we were as humble *Hester*, whiche would make no request but for life onelie. Nowe when wee sighed and cｒied for the bondage, and the crie for our bondage came vp vnto God, and God hearde our mone, & remembred his couenant: Then hee brought agayne our captiuitie, as hee did of Iacob: then were we like vnto them that dreamed. Euen for sodeine ioye, doubting whither we dremed those happie tydinges, or no. Then was our mouth filled wᵗ laughter, & our tongue wᵗ ioy. Thē the Nations about vs said, that yᵉ lord had don great things for vs. And we sang thervnto, the Lord haue done great things for vs, whereof wee reioyce. Christ Iesus seemed then to vs as a shining and burning Lampe, and we seemed for that time to reioyce in the light thereof. But our giuinge of [13] thankes and singing prayse vnto god, was skarse so good as that of the people of Israel, mentioned in the fourth Chapter of Exodus, who when they hearde that the Lord had visited them, and had looked vpon their tribulatiō, they bowed downe and worshipped. But when tribulation was increased vppon them, they murmured against God and his seruaunt Moyses. So could we bowe downe and worshippe in

Psal. 126. 1.

Exod. 4. 31.

Exod. 16. 2.

---

[1] "Backe" is an obsolete form of "bat". (See *N.E.D.*).

A Little Treatise vppon the firste Verse

the day of our deliuerance, but since that time, not through bitter afflictiō as did they, but through too much pāpering with more fleshe, then yᵉ pottes of Egypt haue, we haue waxen fatte, and haue forgotten the day of our penurie and hunger. Yea wee haue forgotten, and forsaken the Lorde the holie one of Israel, in that wee are gone backewarde. And better *Esa.* 1. 3. hath the Oxe knowne his owner, and the Asse his maisters cribbe, then we haue known him that saued vs. For if wee knewe him, we would also surelie know, that he redeemed vs from that firie fornace that we should burne with more zeale [14] of furthering his kingdome vpō earth to the aduauncing of his glorie. But the people of Englande in that daye whē the Lorde did lift vp their heads, were farre from the zeale and practise of Dauid, who beinge aduaunced to his kingdome, had not yet the thinge he would haue, and gaue him selfe no rest, vntill he had done dewe homage vnto the Lordes kingdome, by furthering, procuring, and labouringe about those things whiche appertayned vnto the true worshippe of God, vntill he did see them at a good staye. But our Cleargie firste, which should with great affliction haue laboured about the Lordes worke, to haue seene that firste finished, before they hadde instauled them selues into their owne rowmes: they contrariewise layde holde on the great liuings, catch who catche might the riche Bishoprikes and fatte Benefices.

And as *Achsaph* the daughter of *Caleb*, when her father *Iosua.* 15. 19. hadde giuen her a portion of highe grounde, desired still more, namelie, places with [15] springes of water: so was their desiring, and desiring agayne. For those whiche were serued with Benefices where corne grounde was most, they must haue an other, wher good store of pasture lie. And whē they were serued wᵗ that, they muste long for one where store of sheepe are kept, and then they thinke they should be well. But would to god, it had bin no worse affection & desire, then yᵗ of *Achsaph*, which desired the increase of her portion of that lande, which the Lorde had giuen and blessed vnto her people: but these men haue bene greedie of the fatte spoyle, and haue not bene aware that it was the spoyle of *Iericho*, *Iosua.* 6. 17. which ought not to haue been medled withall, but to haue bene execrable thinges vnto vs. I meane not as though that wealthful spoile might not haue bin takē vse of, by conuerting it another waye. But those things holding still their nature & strēgth which thei receiued of ye Cananitish Roman, ought to haue bin to vs execrable things. And euen as the Lord gaue vnto ye children of Israel the first [16] conquest in y^t land of Canaan, namely, ouer *Iericho*, without bowe or sword, horse, horseman, or anie battel, or anie hande mouing of theirs, in token that he would alwayes stande on their right hand, and their victories should proceede from him, if they would goe forwarde to fight the Lordes battell: so the Lorde gaue us this victorie, not with noise of battle, or tumblinge of garmentes in bloude, but by his owne hande alone from heauen, the thing to vs vnlooked for, thereby incouraging vs to marche forwarde vnder his banner, and vnder the good lucke of this watcheword: The Lord liueth, which brought the children of Israel out of Egypt and out of Babel, & the Lorde liueth which haue brought agayne the captiuitie of his poore suppliantes, from the yron yoke of Antichrist: and the Lorde also giuing vs the earnest of assured victorie in those battels which were to insue in the behalfe of his sonnes kingdome, against his professed enimie Antichrist, if we would haue bene so gracious, as once to [17] haue taken them in hande. But we refused to goe to the battle anie more, though the Cananite dwelled still in the lande, and bare the sworde to slaye euerie true Israelite therewith. I meane that man of Rome, who by his Cananitishe offices, and Canons of his lawes, standing still in their strengthe, beareth the scepter right vp, euē a rodde for the righteous. Thus haue we behaued our selues, not as faithful Iosua, and his souldiours, whiche frō Iericho ceassed not to goe forward to more battels, and therein sawe ye great saluation of God fightinge for them, when the Sunne and Moone stoode still in heauen, and hasted not to goe downe for a season. But we haue done more like the *Amalekites*, whiche inuaded *Ziclag*, which did eate, drinke, and daunce manie dayes, because of the great spoyle they had taken, vntill suddaine slaughter & vengeance came vpon thē in the middest of their mirth. So let vs take heed, that wee do not so long eate and drinke of the spoyle, and daunce in securitie, vntill that Dauid [18] Christ Iesus come at [us] vnawares, and take awaye all, and our liues therewith also in most iust iudgement.

Wee also haue done as that other generation of the

A Little Treatise vppon the firste Verse

Iewes which arose vp after Ioshua, which regarded their owne ease more then the Lords commaundement, and his glorie, which stoode vpon the rootinge out of those wicked ones, whose sinne was ripe & their daie was come: those Cananites Perezites, and Iebuzits suffered they to dwell still amonge them. Therefore the Lorde saide, that they shoulde be thornes to their *Iudg.* 2. 3. sides, and their Gods should be their destruction, as it came to passe. Euen so, haue we tenne times more made couenant with that cursed broode of Antichrists birdes, not only entring into neare familiaritie with the men, but also borowing manie of their ceremonies, intertaining their forme of seruice for the most part, being turned but from Latin to English: and yet which is worse, holding our neckes vnder their gyrdles, by making our selues willing slaues to their [19] Ecclesiasticall sworde. And because this practise could sonest be atchiued, and this vngracious work could most spedelie be iumbled vp: then was it counted Pollicie, to wipe mens noses with, and to giue them amocke. But be not deceiued, God is non[1] mocked, who redemed you from aduersitie to this ende, that you should deale wisely and faithfullie in all his house. Therefore it did stand you vpon to haue takē better aduisement in the reforming of religion, and matters about Gods worshippe, knowinge that aboue all thinges it is a matter most curious. And you shoulde with feare and much trembling, setting apart your owne affaires for a season, as *Dauid* did here and that with a solemne vow making, that you would first seeke the building of Gods kingdome: you should thus, I say, haue bene conuersant in this busines, knowing that thē all things would haue prospered with you. You shoulde also have known y^t the lord in his worship might not admit ani strang deuise under pretense of pleasing some, nor [20] might[2] admit anie mingling of his wisdome with mennes wisedome, anie tolerations of vanities with a smoothe and fayned promise to take them away in time to come. Why did the Lorde shewe such a terrible and fearefull example vpon the two sonnes of *Aaron, Nadab* & *Abihu*, as to skortche them with *Leui.* 10. 1. fire from heauen? Because they tooke fire for their censeres, from the hearthe, whiche they should haue taken from the Altar. And they were but yong schollers in those ceremonies, & the obseruations were manie, and

---
[1] As text.
[2] The catchword missing.

it was at the firste beginninge of their trayning to practise: yet the Lordes ielousie burned w^t fire. And why? Had the Lord so great regarde, for a coale of fire? was it not to leaue a fearfull monument for all men to beholde, that they might take heed least in matters pertaining to the worshippe of God, they alter and chaunge euen the least thinge? If any man want skill, let him withdrawe himselfe. For it is written: Take heed to thy foote when thou entrest into the house of God, & be more [21] neare to heare, then to giue the sacrifice of fooles, for they knowe not that they doo euill. Beholde, howe manie in the Realme of England haue done and dailie doo presume to set in their feete into Gods house, and haue not learned how to sacrifize aright. Offer not they the sacrifice of fooles? And they will not knowe that they do euill.

Ecclesiastes 4. 17. [5. 1.]

But to returne to those which haue bene chiefe maister workemen in the reformation of religion at the firste: Can they not beholde, howe that for wante of this faythefull zeale, whiche was in this seruaunt of God Dauid: For want of dewe feare & trembling, carefull crying for the spirite of wisedome, and whole attending vppon the Lordes worke, with hartes free from worldlie intanglings: And for want of that intier loue and charitie, which seeketh not her owne thinges, but those which are Christes, and her poore brethrens: I say, for want of these things, and being drunken with that new vessell of wine of worldlie concupiscence then set a broche: Can they not espie [22] howe they haue drawne their liues so farre wrong, that skilfull workemen, yea nowe euery bungler can not but wonder to see suche worke. For they haue framed their timber, some toe longe, and some toe short, in such sort, that the buildinge hangeth all on the one side, tottering and reeling with euerie wind, and waiteth but for a blast from the Lorde to cause it to fall, and to slaie all those, which haue committed thēselues to such a false building. And as for the forme & fashion of the house, where was the paterne which God shewed *Moses* in the mount? It was to be foūd, but it was not sought, the hast was so great to other things. Therefore because the Lords paterne was refused: no maruaile thowgh hee refused to send his spirit of wisedome vnto those, which stood in stead of *Bezaleel*, and *Aholiab*, and the rest of the workmen. For veiwe and trie out this reformation. Looke vnto your

1 *Cor.* 13.

Exo. 26. 30.

Exod. 36. 1.

A Little Treatise vppon the first Verse

brethrē of other nations rounde about which haue reformed, if they haue admitted such thinges as you, who yet notwith-[23][1]standing come shorte enowgh of their duetie. But looke vnto the worde of God, and espie out there, how manie coales of fire you haue takē, not from the altar Christ Iesus, but from the smoking chimneis of the Cananites which dwelt in the land, the Papists I meane. Therefore repent and returne, or else take heede of the Lords fire from heauen, who although he use more patience and longe sufferaunce towardes you, then he did towardes *Nadab* and *Abihu*: yet be you assured that he hath not nowe lesse regard and ielousie for the bodie, then he had then for the shadowe.

And whereas some saye, what! It is a house, though it be a downegate[2] thinge, though it want roufe, though some walles, though it want this and that. Manie such songes the babes in the cradle heare, to rocke thē a sleape. But by their own words I will iudge them. For suppose that some noble man mindeth to builde a house, he hireth workmen and manie seruauntes: part of their wages he paieth, for the [24] rest hee appointeth dewe order, and make [*sic*] with his workemen streight couenaunt in all thinges, hastening the worke. Since he goeth into an other countrie, and returne fiue and twentie yeeres after: if he then finde his house halfe vnbuilded, and the tymber which is layde, rotten for default of couering in dewe time, and likewise the morter crumpled away, & the stones some fallen and some readie to fall: the workemen they take their wages, and spende it euerie daye at the alehouses and tauernes, eating, drinking, and playing, when they shoulde be at worke: will not that Noble man at his comming cast in prison those workemen and seruauntes, and giue his stewarde also a great rebuke, and put out his house to other workemen? And yet these chief builders of whom I haue spoken, manie of them, yea most of them haue confessed and doo confesse vntill this daye, that manie thinges are amisse in the Churche, and yet we must be content and beare the. And in deede are there manie thinges [25] wanting and missing to the finishing of the Lordes house, and can they sitt still and eate and drinke, and not buckle them selues to their busines? Or may the Lordes worke aboue other things suffer delaye,

[1] B 1 *recto*.
[2] Falling, used for going down, descending, setting.

and waite our good leysure? Or are they the Lords remembrauncers, which can giue him [no] rest, and them selues also, before they see Ierusalem, the prayse of ye worlde, redeemed and reedified from the ruin therof? Can they so long time vse the tabernacles of their houses hanged & decked with Arres[1], and Tapestrie, and fare deliciouslie euerie daye? Can they so long goe to their palet[2] & bedd, and suffer their eyes to slumber and sleepe, before they haue founde out a place for the Scepter of Christe, his lawful gouernement, and made readie a Throne for him to sitte and rule, and treade Antichriste vnder foote? This is counted but a small want. O deepe securitie! This wee must beare: and we are content so to doo, as longe as the Lorde hath made anie promise to beare with wickednes. But he is mer-[26]cifull, and long sufferinge: but so, as he will not holde the sinner innocent. And if he spake by his Prophete, saying that the Sabothes and solemne feastes of the Iewes (which notwithstanding were after his lawe) were a burden vnto him, and hee was wearie to beare them: Howe thinke we is he wearie to beare so manie Sabothes, which hee neuer made, and so manie ceremonies & other deuises & strange Church gouuernement, which neuer entred into his minde: whither are these thinges a burden or no vnto him thinke we? Yea such a burden, that as he hath spoken concerninge them, so hath he concerning vs also: Ah, I will ease me of mine aduersaries. Yea hee must needes skoure our drosse. For in deede our siluer is become drosse, and our wine is mixt with water, farre otherwise thē it was among them. But they saye, wee must beare nowe, for the time is past, when the matters of reforminge the Churches were chieflie handled, and we must tarie vntill a fitte time come agayne. [27] Indeede, there was a time careleslie slipped at the beginninge, when the yron was whote, but the workemen were lasie, and neglected to frame and fashion the work, before the yron was colde. What gracious libertie might not haue bin obteyned, if they, of whō I haue spoken, had bin as carefull and sorowfull for these things, as *Nehemiah*, who fasted and prayed certayn dayes, and mourned so much because the Wall of Ierusalem was not yet builded, that the king coulde easelie discerne his sorow by his countenāce, and was moued with compassion, to bidde him

---

[1] Arras, so named from the town in Artois. A rich tapestry fabric.
[2] Pallet. A mattress or straw bed.

A Little Treatise vppon the firste Verse

aske what hee would haue, before *Nehemiah* durst mention his sute vnto him. And there is no doubt, but like sorowe and care shoulde haue founde like compassion to haue bin refreshed with, and no lesse furtherance to euerie godlie enterprise. For the Lorde would surelie haue done it, who haue [sic] the hartes of Kinges and Princes in his hande. And as wee haue hearde, there wanted not some gracious offer concerning these thinges. [28] But the Lorde lay not to our charge, that which is past. If occasion offered by him, be not taken, our care, feare, and griefe in repenting, ought to bee the greater, & our indeuour the more vehement to recouer our losses. Seeke the Lord then, whyle he may be foūd. Labour better then before. Disburden you of al, either offices or liuings, which hange on and presse downe, to hinder you in the worke. Giue glorie to God and his sonne Christ Iesus, by setting vp his royall Throne amonge vs, which is that you call Church gouernement, whiche many thousande tongues haue confessed and complayned to be wanting. Once agayne, remember I saye the Lordes deliuerance, howe he saued us as hee did Israel from Pharao in the redde Sea. Lette vs singe as Moses did at the shoare: He is my God, and I will prepare him a Tabernacle. Therfore are we escaped the drowning, that we should make the Lorde a Tabernacle. Lette vs not onelie promise it in singing or sayinge, but perfourme oure [29] vowes vnto the Lorde, whiche wee made in the daye of our distresse: and let this Tabernacle be so made, that being viewed in the ende by our Moyses Christe Iesus, the worke and the workemen, may receyue a blessinge. This let vs doe, and goe on, and prosper, and liue in the Lorde; if not, lette vs be sure, the consumption & plague determined, shal ouerspread and ouerwhelme vs by gods righteous iudgement, who haue [sic] vengeance readie for all disobedience. *Heb.* 12. 1.[1] *Exod.* 15. 2. *Exo.* 39. 43. 2 *Cor.* 10. 6.

Thus haue I shewed, howe especiallie the Cleargie haue acquite themselues in the day of the Lords visiting of vs, if it had not ben hidden from our eyes.

And now concerning the rest of the people (I meane those which had som knowledge and zeale) they also haue bene well agreed with their guids in their necligēce. For they hauing once obtained a seruice in the English tongue, thought it so great a matter, that they myght lawfullie be holden excused though they sought no further: and [30] hauing gotten a shadow, wherein they

---

[1] This reference seems wrong. Correct reference is Is. 55.6.

might coole thē selues in yᵉ heat of the daie, and rest a litle from their weariness : They haue giuen them selues to eating, drinking, and sleaping vnder that shadowe, and forgett the rest of their iournie, vntil darcke night come wherein no man can walke [*sic*, worke].[1] Neyther haue they knowne, that as the Lorde gaue to the children of Israel a clowde by day to shadow them from the heat, to this ende, that they should iournie forward to their resting place. So also yᵉ Lord gaue them a defence from that present heate, to the intent that they goinge throughe the vallie of teares, should iournie forward, and goe from strength to strengthe, vntil vnto euery one of them, God had appeared shining out of Sion the perfectiō of bewtie. No, but the people haue bene as a strong asse couching downe betwixt diuers burdens of spirituall bondage. And they haue sene that rest is good, and that the lande is pleasaunt, therefore they haue bowed their shoulder to beare, and haue bene subiect vnto that [31] yoke, which is contrarie to yᵉ libertie, wherein Christ haue sett vs free. Euē so it is certainly. For the pleasures of this world haue stolen away the harts of many, and haue caused zeale and religiousnes to be frosen vp: so true is it that one can not serue both God and Mammon, but eyther he must loue the one and hate the other, or at the least in leaning to the one, he must neclect and despise the other. For the people of England, I meane those which eyther at that time, or since, haue felte some motions of Gods spirit vnto godlines: the most part of them, I say, whiles they haue applied them selues to eate and drinke largely, as in the daies of rest, to buie and selle, and to smile merelie vpon gaine coming in, and to welcome it with giuing it the hand, their hartes haue bene stolen before they haue bene aware: so that they being once deliuered from the filthines of the worlde, through the knowledge of the Lord, haue againe intangled them selues therewith, and haue returned as the dogge to his vomit, [32] & as the sow that is washed, to the walowing in the mire. For vpon this taking a smatch[2] and tast of worldly ease & welth, wherof I spake, the stomach haue become gredie, & there haue ben no ende of seeking gaine, laiyng vp in store, makinge the barnes wider, ioyning house to house, & land to land. So that nowe if one come and tell thē of further

Iohn. 9. 4.
Exod. 13. 21.

Psal. 84. 6.

Psal. 50. 2.
Gene. 49. 14.

Galat. 5. 1.

Luk. 16. 13.

2 *Pet.* 2. 20.

Esai. 5. 8.

---

[1] But might equally well be " walke ", in apposition to " iourney ".
[2] Smack, flavour.

A Little Treatise vppon the firste Verse

seeking the face of God, & building his kingdome: hee speaketh to the bellie which hath none eares, & his speach is like vnto his, which speaketh with a straunge language, and he speaketh to them which fare as if they were in a dreame. For the wine of the fornication of this worlde haue cast them into a sleape, and they haue not knowne, neither will knowe till it be to[o] late to recouer it, that they haue solde their birth right for a mease of potage: And haue not followed the counsell of him which saieth: When thou eatest honie, take heede thou eate not too much, lest it hurte thee. Neyther haue they boughte the precious Pearle of Gods Kingdome: but they [33] haue solde it for that which glistereth, and yet is no gould. *Heb.* 12. 16. *Prou.* 25. 16. *Mat.* 13. 45.

But we ought to haue taken heede of all such worldie things, especially vntill we had further finished our worke and labour in the lorde: herein folowing the example of those men, which deferre their euentide meele, vntill they haue ended their worke, thoughe in such time of the yeare, as part of the night do ouertake them. For their experience doo teach them, that whilest their hande is nowe in woorke, it is not greatly greuous, though they abide some wearines and colde: But when they haue with eating and drinking bene satisfied, and haue basted themselues well by a good fire, then it is death to goe to worke againe: but forthwith the fealing of that ease craueth more, vntill the time of sleape.

Therefore ought wee to haue holden ease and rest, and worldlie commodities, euen at the swordes point, as enemies to those which fight the Lordes battels, by denying them selues and all things, and taking vp the [34] crosse, and also as clogges & weightes to them which haue a race to rnune [*sic*], except that they were vsed, as though they were not vsed, and let passe as straungers, not entertayned, and welcomed as beloued friends.

Yet notwithstandinge this people haue in the middest of their carelesnes, an answere readie as good as an aperne[1] of figge leaues. For say they, we must abyde a time, and the time is not yet come, and they are not ashamed to call it, the Lords leysure, whiche is their owne leysure, seeing the Lorde haue compleined a longe while since, as being wearie of their lasines, saying: Howe long will it be yer [variant of ere] this people will goe vp? And concerning not being yet time, the Prophet Agge answer-

[1] Obsol. form of "apron".

Agge. 1. 2.
[*Haggai*]

eth them: The Lorde of hostes speaketh: thus sayeth this people: The time is not yet come, that the Lordes house should be buylded. Is it time for your selues to dwell in your sieled houses, & this house lieth waste? And with what courage can this people buylde, yea and that gorgeouslie [35], siele, hang with clothes, & plant: & see the stones of the Lordes house lyinge stil in the dust? Alas that care is wanting which wee haue mencioned here to be in Dauid, who sware and vowed not to take as it were, the possession of his house, the Arke of God beeing from home.

That care, zeale, and indeuour is wanting, which was

Nehe. 4. 23.

in *Nehemiah*, & those which were with him, which in ye speedie buylding of the Wall, did not put off their clothes but onely for washinge, vntill the worke was finished, which indeuour the Lord blessed with mightie successe.

They moreouer in their answering pretende that we must be thankfull to god for that we haue, and charge them with unthankfulnes, who with griefe and great mourning bewayle that is wāting, and bende vnto it: But what unthankfulnes was in *Hanani*, one of the Israelits which came to *Nehemiah*, and being demaunded concerning the state of the Iewes, he sayde, they were

Nehem. 1. 3.

in affliction and great reproche, [36] because the wall of Ierusalem was not buylded vp. Was he vnthankfull to God which had returned their captiuitie, graunted them his true worshippe in their owne lande, with reedifying ye Temple? And was the materiall Wall suche a

Nehem. 1. 4.

matter, to complayne of? And what vnthankfulnes was in *Nehemiah*, to conceyue great griefe thereuppon, and to faste and mourne certayne dayes? It shoulde seeme that they were streight in their owne bowels, when as the Lorde was liberall and bountifull towards them. But they knew, that the full building of Ierusalem was the Lordes prayse, and the honour of his people, and euerie ruine which was to be beholden theare, was to all nations and people which should see it, a witnes of their shame: In as much as it was a monument of the Lords anger, which had dishonoured them, who by their transgressions had dishonoured him.

And if in those materiall things, & figures, the case standeth so: What reprochfull people are we, and what [37] blind, dissolute, and miserable men, which see not our reproche and miserie, neyther doo we feele anie burthen therof, as striuing to be eased of the same. But rather we bost thereof, and glorie in our shame, and say, thankes be to God, we are well, and haue religion

A Little Treatise vppon the firste Verse

reformed better thē manie other countries: And such like smoth speaches and sweet words, which we haue bene taught of diuers of our teachers to heale our deadlie hurt. For that which we want is more then a thousand citie walls: and all the cities in the worlde are not worthe one liuelie church which is Gods Kingdome, wherein the throne of Christ is onlie exalted, and the throne of Antichrist is laide for his footstoole. *Iere.* 6. 14.

And until you see this thing brought to passe, O yee people, and see your selues also the liuing stones of this liuing buildinge: mourne and lament bitterlie. Fast and praye. Bidde farewell to pleasures, and to the daye of mirth. Let yᵉ Bridegrome come out of his chāber, & the bride out of her closet [38] Weepe upon your faire seeled houses your inlarged pastures and fieldes, your sweet gardens, pleasant arbours and bowling allis. Know your selues to be in more greeuous bondage of soule, by being holden from Christ his trewe gouernment: then the people of Israel were in bondage of their bodies, when they walking forth by the riuers of Babel, could not be refreshed from their woo, but they sate downe and wept, when they remembred Sion. It was not the pleasant walkinge by the riuers of waters, that could entice them to be merie, and forget their griefe, and forget their countrey, from which they had nowe longe time bene absent. Seuentie yeares coulde not instraunge them, nor weane them frō the remembraunce of Iurie, and Ierusalem, and mount Sion: Not so muche because there was their dwelling, as because they dwelt there togither with the Lorde, giuing there outwarde tokens of his presence. Therefore they vowed, and wished harde thinges unto them selues, if they pre-[39]¹ferred not Ierusalem before all ioy: or if they shoulde be ioyfull, before they should see Ierusalē full deliueraunce. *Psal.* 137. 1. *Vers.* 6.

Thus shoulde it fare with us. And euen as a woman which full dearelie haue loued her husbande being nowe deceassed this life, can take no pleasure in beholding his garmentes: but rather renue the remembraunce of her losse, and increase her woo and greefe: So shoulde houses, fieldes, pastures, pleasaunt gardens, orchyards, golde, siluer, yea wife & children, and whatsoeuer else of outwarde thinges: wee should inioie them, & looke vpon them, shaking the head, with wailing and wrinking the hands, crying, alas for our husband Christ Iesus, which haue left us all these good thinges, and he is not

¹ C 1 *recto.*

with us: But our sinnes haue caused him to depart aside, seying he haue bene so despightfullie vsed amongst vs, by exalting the sworde of his enemie, and treading his sworde vnder foot. And lest any shoulde think me to ouerreach, in saing we are in greuouser bondage then were the [40] Iewes in Babilon, though to speake of it wil be thought of some, straying from my matter, yet I must regarde edifying more then anie other order.

Therfore I demaunde of those which haue anie eyes to see, whither they can beholde their soules to be solde for handefulles of Barlie, and morselles of bread, euen for tithe sheaues (wheras if we had bene solde for slaues, appointed to bodilie toyle, wee might haue helde our peace) For doeth not he which haue monie, or the letter of some great man, or favoure by other meanes, doeth he not gette the gift of a Benefice of some Patrone, and being presented to the Bishoppe, hee is forthwith sent to be instauled ? and so the guydes of our soules, ar appointed vnto vs without our aduice and counsell, whose life and death of soule it standeth vpon to trie our guydes, that after they haue bene founde able to cutt and deuide our portion of ye bread of life in dewe season, they might bee approued of vs, & receyued. But that whiche is more greeuous, when a [41] blinde leader is come to take vs by the hande, wee haue no authoritie as the Church of God, to refuse him, or to complayne for redresse, or to remoue him, after we haue tried his inabilitie. Are not then our soules in bondage?

1. Cor. 5. 4.
Furthermore, we haue no authoritie to complaine of that, or anie other mischiefe, in our owne congregation, that by the power of our Lord Iesus, whiche there ought to florishe and beare the swaye, euen in euerie Church

Esai. 26. 13.
of his, that mischiefe might be remedied: but other Lords besides Christ doo rule ouer vs, and ouer the whole Church, yea ouer manie hundred churches: and them we must seek vp through the prouince, thē must wee daunce great attendance, and to them we must complaine: and if our complaint be of anie thinge done against the honour of Christ, or against our libertie which hee haue giuen vs, our mouth shall be stopped, and we shal be cutt shorter. But if it bee a matter against their owne honour, touchinge their iniunctions, as of the garmēt of [42] obedience, and the cappe of maintenance, or for taking downe the imagerie worke about the Fonte, or suche thing, then we are good parishioners, they will visite vs, and redresse these thinges well ynough. Are

A Little Treatise vppon the firste Verse

not nowe our soules in bondage ? Furthermore, we can not serue God, or worshippe him publikelie in spirite, as we ought to doo, for we are tyed to the dead letter, and stinted out our measure, that we must giue God this day, euen as muche, and the selfe same, whiche we gaue him the last daye, that muste we also giue him euerie daye in the yeare, all the time of our lyfe. Whither he be pleased or no, that is his stinte and his see, hee maye no more haue. And though he be wearie of that and lothed with it, because it is all one dishe of meate continuallie, (and that would lothe any mans stomache) yet he must haue it all, and neuer a whit lesse. He is a cruell maister, whiche will urge his bonde slaue to eate vppe three or foure meases of potage, when his stomache will not beare [43] one, without regorginge. But the Lorde is worse serued at our handes. And we are forced to mocke the lorde after this manner, in bringinge him such a worshippe, as hee spueth out of his mouth, & that to the endlesse hurte of our owne soules. Are not then oure soules in bondage ? Moreouer, if half a dozen, or halfe a skore, doo consent and agree togither, and chuse a man fitte to guyde them: can they bringe him in ? or for want of him, or anie other man sufficient, maye they freelie go to another place, to heare the word and receyue the Sacramentes ? No, there is a lawe, and by that law, they must come home to their own Parish, there must they feede vpon the rockes and stones, or else starue. Will anie vnmercifull manne deale so with his beaste, as to tye him where there growe not one spire of grasse ? And release canne the poore soules haue none, vntill there maye come newe lawes, whiche maye bringe redresse and graunt further libertie, although they neuer come, but still streighter [44] & streighter. Euen as the Israelites were more *Exod.* 5 17. hardlie dealt with, after they had motioned their sute of going into the wildernes to sacrifize & worshippe God as he commaunded. Are not then our soules in bondage ?

That I speake nothing of our subiection to the iurisdiction of that court, which our owne conscience, and the voyce almost of all the people in the lande, crye out that it is popishe and Antichristian, and yet not one man among a thousand haue spirit and courage to withdrawe him selfe from it, neyther will they knowe it to bee a sacriledge, and treason against Christe, to goe and bowe before the scepter of Antichriste: and flatter them selues, saying, that Christ rule in their harts inwardlie, & they serue him inwaidlie, and outwardlie they serue that idoll, which the Deuill haue set vpp, worse farre awaye then the idoll which Nebuchadnessar set vpp in the plaine of *Dura*.

Dan. 3 1.

But the people saye, If the Masse and images come againe, they wil ra-[45]-ther dye, then they will receyue those. Will you fight the Lordes battelles, and will you needes chuse your owne standing? Must not the Souldioures fight with that bande and wing of the enemies, wherevnto their Captaine appointe them? But O foolishe and blinde men. For whither is greater wickednes? The Masse and images, or that rule and power, which haue authorised, and established the Masse & images? Whither is greater, the apple, or the tree whiche bringeth forth the apple? For the Masse and images & all other wicked ceremonies, were but apples of this cursed and bitter tree of popishe gouernement. And although we haue cut of[f] a few twigges, which bare some kinde of apples, yet the tree remayne, and the roote hath yet very deepe holde in the grounde, and it bringeth foorth other cursed crabbes, to set our teeth on edge withall. And though the Deuill woulde beare vs in hande, that they were as good apples, and set as great a praise on them, as he did on the apple, which [46] he feofft Eue with: Yet in eating thereof, the Lord shall proue our disobedience.

Gen. 3.

These abominations which I haue spoken of, & many more which I haue not named, declare whither our bondage, or the Babylonian bondage of the Iewes, were more greuous and daungerous. And if they hanged vp their harpes vpon the willow trees: Whither haue we cause to sett apart Lute & Cithern, Uiols, Shalmes, Cornets, Sackbuts and Dulcimers, and all the instruments of Musicke with daunsing and mirthe: and to singe the songs of dolefulnes? Lette vs rende our harts and not our garments. Lett vs no more sitt downe to eate & drink, and rise againe to plaie: but lett vs eat the bread of aduersitie, and drinke the water of affliction: and pray continually so, that in praying, our bitter cōplaints may ascende vp to the Lord, & we may rightly speak with like affection, as did the poore banished Iewes saying: Behold as the eyes of the seruants look vnto their masters, and the [47] eyes of a maidē to the hand of her mistresse: so our eyes wait

Psal. 137. 2.

Psal. 123.

A Little Treatise vppon the firste Verse

vpō the Lord our God, vntil he haue mercie vpō vs. Haue mercy vpon us, O Lord, haue mercie vpon vs, for we haue suffered to[o] much contempt. Yea if we had anie grace to take to hart, the reproches of the papists which mock our patched seruice, and skorne vs, as not able to builde our house of religion, without borowing most of our stones and timber from them: And cast in our tethes: Where doo you tell your church? Or whence haue you any iurisdiction or churche gouernement, but from him whom you skorne in words, namelie the Pope? As in deede it is in euerie mans mouth to cry, fy on the Pope: & yet we bowe the knee before him by submission to his Court. Therefore are we mocked of the papists, as our sinnes haue deserued. Which spiritual euil if our dull harts could feele: we might adde also with those carefull Iewes: Our soule is filled full of the mockings of the welthy & ye despight of ye proud. For it is a time of reproch [48] and our shame lyeth open in the eyes of all nations (if we could discerne it) whyles neyther Temple is buylded, wherein we may worshippe the Lord aright, neyther the citie Wall, whereby the Heathen might bee kept out, that they no more come into the lords heritage, to defile his *Psal.* 79. 1. holy Temple, & to make Ierusalē an heape of stones. Nowe therefore, although we at the beginning, haue not done as faythfull Dauid did, to sweare and vowe vnto the Lorde, concerning his acceptable work finishing with all possible speed: let vs yet at the length heare the *Psal.* 95. 8. lords voyce, without hardening our hartes, and sweare & vowe to seeke his face, and builde his kingdome otherwise, then we haue done, and not to rest as heretofore, tyll we haue performed our vowes, and passed euen thorough the vallie of teares & mourning, digging *Psal.* 84. 6. fountaynes to quenche our thirste (I meane abyding all trouble and persecution) vntill we draw neare the *Psal.* 95. 11. lords rest in Sion: before the time that hee sweare, and seale the decree of our ne-[49]-uer entring in thither, and so wee bee shut also from his eternall rest, in his kingdome, for our too much contempt of his glorie, which should appeare in the aduaunced kingdome of his deare Sonne, and for our luke warme professing his name, without doinge his will, and working his worke.

Thus haue we hearde concerninge the care, which Dauid had for ye bringing home the Arke. It followeth to speake of the ioy, which he conceyued, when the

Lorde vouchsafed to be with him, & to bende also the hartes of the people therevnto, when it was brought home.

I reioyced when they sayde vnto mee, we will goe into the house of the Lorde.

1 Chro. 15.

King *Dauid* according to the vowe and promise which hee made vnto the Lorde, so he continued faythefull and stedfast, and prepared a place for the Arke of God, and pitched for it a tent, and longed for the day, when it should be placed there. Yet for all his fayth-[50]-fulnes

1 Chro. 15.

and exceeding great care, it pleased God to humble him, by that great iudgement, whiche fell vppon *Vzzah*, that hee might bee sifted, and tried to the vttermost, and the Lorde spared not Dauid, in that litle thinge which was committed awrye, in that the Arke was caried on a carte, and drawne by Oxen, which ought to haue

Exo. 25. 14.

bene borne vppon the *Leuites* shoulders. Therefore the Lorde made him to beholde a doleful sight in the death of *Vzzah*, and turned his ioye into heauines, for that present time. Thus ielous is the Lorde alwayes for his

Leui. 10. 3.

true worshippe: For he will be sanctified of those, which come neare him. Where is nowe anie place left for toleration of any disorder in the state of the Church? When as the Lord would not tolerate & beare with thus much, for his seruaunt Dauids sake, whose care was so great, whose harte was so faithfull, whose hand was so forward, and his labour so painefull, to restore true religion, & to promote the Lords glorie. But what haue our reformers [51] of religion done? Onely in one thinge haue they followed the example of thē which were with Dauid to help home the Arke the first time: for they to ease their owne shoulders of the burthen, and to auoide that great labour, which belōgeth to ye building of gods church rightlie and effectuallie, haue bene cōtent to shuffle up the matter, and haue committed

Ephe. 6. 15.

the cariage of the Arke to brutishe Oxen: euen dumme & blinde Ministers. And these Oxens feete are not shodde with the preparation of the Gospell of peace, therfore they stūble at euerie steppe, and haue long ago ouerthrown cart, & Arke, & all: althogh there haue bene *Vzzahs* appointed to put toe their hand & helpe the oxen. I meane teachers haue bin apointed, to learn ye ignorant ministers to preach: how thei prosper, men may wel know, except they had power to work miracles, to make ye dumme to speake, and the blinde to see, and that only by teachinge. But lette those

A Little Treatise vppon the firste Verse

Vzzahs, and the appointers of them vnderstande and knowe a more excellent waye [52] namely, that the *Leuites* take the burthen vpon their shoulders, weighe it neuer so heauie, by trouble, persecution, and paynefull labour, and let them cherefullie bring home that Arke, euē Christ Iesus, vppon whose shoulders the gouerne- *Esai.* 9. 6. ment lieth, and place him in his Tente pitched for him, euen his Sion, his Church and Kingdome, that he may beare that rule and gouernement, which vnto him belōgth, without so muche as the print of the foule footesteppes of Antichrist, remaining in his Tabernacle to his dishonour.

And here it shal not be amisse vpon occasion, to touche the courage of Dauid, who although he was a little daūted at the firste, by that miscarying of the Arke, in so much that he said: How shall the Arke of 2 *Sam.* 6. the Lorde come vnto me? yet notwithstanding hee fainted not, neyther gaue ouer his purpose: but feared the Lord more, and sought out more circumspectlie, wher ye fault was, and howe it might be redressed: And agayne girt upp his loynes, and addressed him self with more chere-[53]-fulnes, yet agayne to bringe it home. Manie there be in the Realme of Englande, whiche haue bene zealous of Church gouernement, and of the remouing the ceremonies, of mens traditions, and stinted seruice: and because they haue made long tarying, & haue had a colde offeringe, and haue hoped longe of redresse by Parliamentes, wherevnto they haue made sute, and haue bene disappointed of their hope: Therefore as though they hadde done their whole dewtie, they haue set them downe, and waxed colde and carelesse, and haue slept on both eares, and thinke that the Lord must needes nowe holde them excused, vntill the Lord cast it vpon them, & put [it] into their mouthes. But they muste knowe, that they are not to *Mat.* 6. 33. ceasse seeking the kingdome of God, and for other thinges they shall be caste vnto them without their carefull thought. The kingdome of God must suffer violence *Mat.* 11. 12. of those, which w^t violent zeale doe drawe it vnto them. Many runne, but few gett the crowne. We must so 1 *Cor.* 9. 24. [54] runne, as we may obteyne. It is not ynough to be wishers and woulders, as manie be at this daye counted religious and fauourers of gouernement, because they can saye: O wee muste praye, we must pray: thereby satisfying them selues and others, being not a little gladd, that they may buye it so cheape, to sitt at their ease, and folowe the worlde. Therefore what cryes and complaintes their prayers bee, maye easelie be discerned. Prayers without practise, are but poore prayers, & the harte whiche setteth not the hande a worke, do not burne with much heate. We must so praye, as continuing and increasing in greater feruēcie, giuing ye Lord no rest, nor suffering any nay: though he seemeth to sende vs awaye with a rough answere, as our Sauior Christe did vnto the *Cananitishe* woman, refusing her sute, and calling her dogge: yet shee left him not, but desired at the least that whiche a Dogge might haue, euen the crummes which fall from the children, and so obteyned her sute with cōmendatiō of her faith.

Mat. 15. 26.

[55][1] And we, if we haue wished & desired, & therwith made sute to the higher powers, & laboured in the behalfe of true Ecclesiasticall gouernement, and yet haue returned emptie, & confounded, because the lord haue not vouchsafed to let vs see ye Arke come home: we are to feare so much ye more before the face of ye lord, as it is said y^t Dauid feared the lord, in y^t vnspedie day: he feared God before, but now his feare was increased. And in this feare ought we to examine the cause, why the Lord haue not made our enterprise prosperous, & to search our waies, whither we haue taken the right pathe or no: whither we haue gone to the place where it is, or we haue sought it in a wronge place: whither we haue put our shoulders to the burthen, or we haue gone about to carte it, that it might come easily vnto vs, and as it were, alone without oure helping hande. Thus ought wee to search vntil we finde out in our selues the cause of Gods displeasure, for the whiche wee are depriued of this benefit. And hauinge founde the cause, let [56] vs repent and redresse that is amisse, and strengthen ye feeble knees of ours, making straight steppes to our feete, least that which is halting, bee turned out of the waye. Lette vs recouer the right pathe, from the which wee haue wandred wide, and gyrde vppe our loines, that wee maye with more courage and swiftnes walke therin, then before we haue done in our wronge & false waye.

Sam. 2. 6.
[*sic.* 2 *Sam.* 6. 9

Heb. 12. 13.

Luk. 17. 20.

And some there be whiche haue atteyned vnto this knoweledge, that the kingdome of God come not by

[1] D. 1 *recto*.

A Little Treatise vppon the firste Verse

obseruation, and wayting and suinge, here and there, but is neare vnto vs, euen within vs: and no more is to be required, but that we remoue our selues frō euill, and worshippe God accordinge to his worde, chusing rather to suffer the crosse, then to denye Christ by slauishe giuing ouer of that authoritie & libertie, which he haue giuen vnto his people. Some I saye, haue attayned vnto this knowledge, yet notwithstanding they haue bene dismayed and offended, beholding the wayward foot-[57]-steppes of diuers whiche haue gone before, euen in the right path, though not with steadie foote, but haue slipped, halted, and falne in the waye by committing some thinge whiche haue displeased the Lorde, as sometime in the chiefe Citie in Englande, there were manie whiche withdrewe them selues from this spirituall bondage mentioned. But some onelie making conscience at the Cappe & Surplesse, and therein stoode all their religion. Some entring that waye, despised all other, but pitied them not in the bowelles of compassion, that they might be brought vnto the trueth, but were proude in their owne conceyte. Moste of them also ignoraunt howe they should come to the ende, or yet to the middest of the waye, which they hadd entred, neyther being humble in seeking out the same, but thinking rather that they knew all things. Therefore whē they wer tried and weighed, manie were found too light, and their miscarying of the Lords Arke, and the iudgement which fell vpō some of [58] thē, as sore as did vpō Vzzah, discouraged manie, & weakned their hands. So by their vntowardnes they caused the sauour of the Lords work to stink in the nostrels of the people.

And of late an other attempt haue bene giuen that waie by one[1], of whom I must needs saie, that the Lord vsed him as a meanes to bringe the trueth to light, in manie points concerning the true gouernement of the Churche: who, I wish for the glorie of God, if it had ben his good pleasure, that he had stoode in integrity, without swaruing and leaninge to Antichristian pride, and bitternes. And for me to make mention thereof, may seme very hard, which am not so able therin to saue my self frō the reproch of manie tongues, as I am to cleare my selfe of the deseruing the same. Yet notwithstanding a wound being made in the brethrens

[1] Robert Browne. See below, p. 149.

minds: I have thought it my duetie rather to labour to heale it, thē to faine my selfe not to see it.

Mat. 24. 12.   True it is at all times, that iniquitie preuailinge, causeth the loue of [59] manie to abate. For euerie iniquitie committed especiallie in those enterprises, which beare the cheefest shewe of holines before the Lord, and draw nearest his work, procure a more greuous and speedie iudgement, to cause a lamentable successe therein. For as I haue alledged: The ieleous God will be sanctified of those which come neare him, and he cause his iudgment to beginne euen at his owne house.

Leuit. 10. 3.

1 *Pe.* 4. 17.

This iudgment being beholden, causeth feare, and daunteth the courage of many which had begonne to steppe in the waie. Euen as if two men riding through a water, the former slipp into some groope[1] and perish, the other had rather turne backe, and loose his iournie, then to goe forward, though there be space enough to go by, and auoyd that daunger. At the least with feare and trembling hee seeketh out his waie. And no maruell it is though the beholding of such iudgement, because of iniquitie preuailinge, cooleth greatlye the heat of loue, and dulleth the edge of courage for a time.

Iosua. 7.   [60] For euen valiant *Iosua* thereby was striken full sore. For he rent his clothes and fell to the earth, at the euill successe in the battle at *Ay*. And he cried: Alas O Lord God, wherefore hast thou broughte this people ouer *Iorden*, to deliuer vs into the hands of the *Amorits*, & to destroie vs? Would God we had bene content to dwell on the other side *Iorden*. Oh Lord, what shall I saie, when Israell turne their backes before their enemies? Thus he seemed to repent his coming ouer *Iorden*, As though that iournie had not bene taken in hande in the Lorde, and by him furthered, and the furtheraunce thereof confirmed & honoured by a great miracle of the Lords mightie hand. But the Lorde raised him vp, and tolde him that iniquitie committed in Israel, had caused the reproche of that vnspedie daie.

Leui. 10. 19.   Also *Aaron*, *Eleazar*, and *Ithamar* were so daseled with the iudgement, which fell on *Nadab* and *Abihu*, that they did not eate the Goat in the holie place, as they shoulde haue done.

Exo. 32. 31.   [61] *Moses* was so greued at the euill successe of the children of Israel, not being able to come to their rest

[1] A drain, gutter, small trench, ditch.

A Little Treatise vppon the firste Verse

because of their iniquitie, that he chose rather to be rased out of the booke of life, then to heare and see that reproche, which should come vnto that people, and to the name of God. *Ieremiah* wished that he had neuer been borne, because Israel in steade of a blessing, had rewarded euill vnto their owne soules. *Rebekah* when the children stroue in her wombe, thought it had bene better not to haue conceyued. And *Dauid* when he sawe the deathe of *Vzzah*, brought not home the Arke at that time, but feared and lamented, saying: Howe shall the Arke of God come vnto mee? Great feare came on the church of Ierusalem, at the terrible iudgement of *Ananias* and *Saphira*. Most of these haue bene partly afraide and discouraged, as though their interprise and work, which was of the Lorde, had in it selfe obtayned that harde happe, and vnprosperous euent, which proceeded of some other [62] euill comming in by the waye. But as *Iosua*, when he had founde out the faulte, and purged it, renewed battell agayne, and sawe the mightie power, and great saluation of the Lorde for them, with comfort and gladnes: and as *Dauid* when he also had espied the faulte and redressed it, renewed his indeuour, and brought home the Arke with more ioye and chearefulnes: and as the disciples of Ierusalem ceased not from giuing almes, but their feare tended to this, that they should do it with more singlenes of hart: So let not vs be offended, and stumble at the sinne of anie man, to giue ouer our zeale and loue vnto the Lordes cause, ye trueth whereof his worde hath cõfirmed vnto vs. But rather let vs search out, where the iniquitie is, and let the offender beare his shame and rebuke, howe excellent a personage soeuer he haue bene, for turninge the trueth of God into a lye: and let the Lord haue his glorie, who is alwayes founde true, when euerie manne is founde a [63] liar. And his trueth abounde the more, through the lie of man vnto his glorie.

Gen. 25. 22.

Act. 5.

Rom. 3. 7.

The children of Israel which came out of Egypt to goe into the lande of Canaan, coulde not atteyne thither, but their carkases fell in the wildernesse: Might one haue saide therefore, that they came not out by the Lords commaundement and his conduct? Yes, and greater was the glorie of GOD, who was not hindered from performinge his promise by the vnbeleefe of that people: but their vnbeleefe made his faithefulnes more appeare. And their vnrighteousnes commended the Lordes righteousnesse, whiche recompensed them their

Rom. 3. 5.

iust deserte, and yet raysed vppe a better generation, to enter into his resting place. So will the Lorde euermore make his cause to stande, though they whiche handle it amisse, shall fall before it in the waye. And as for men of greate credit and estimation, the Lorde often times will make theyr [64] weakenesse and vanitie to appeare, that no glorie might bee transferred from him self to mortall men, and that we should neuer make fleshe and bloud our arme, neyther trust in manne, in whose nostrels is breath: for what is he to be esteemed? *Salomon* the glorie of the Kings of the earth, called also the Lordes beloued, a spectacle for wisedome: whom the Lorde vsed also for a speciall instrument vnto manie thinges: yet did not hee perseuere in wisedome, but became a foole in committing wickednes against the Lord. *Iehu*, whiche valiauntlie wrought the Lordes worke at the first, turned also to idolatrie, and forsooke the Lorde. And *Gedeon*, a worthie instrument, which the Lorde chose for his worke, made the *Ephod*, which was an instrument of euill.

Esa. 2. 22.

2 *Sā.* 12. 25. [24]

1. *King.* 11. 6.
2. *Kin.* 10. 31.

Iud. 8. 27.

These and manie more examples there be, which teach vs, that although we see before our eyes neuer so manie which begin in the spirite, and ende in the fleshe, that we condemne not their beginning, neyther feare to enter into [65] that waye, but rather take heede that we walke so fast, and so steadelie, and so well armed, that sinne doo not ouertake vs, & ouerthrowe vs in the waye. The euill example of life shewed by those Nations which are called Christian this daye, make the sauour of the Gospell to stinke before the Iewes, Turkes, and other Heathen, which refuse therefore once to searche, what Christian religion is. Therefore are they still holden backe from Christe & his kingdome. Like recompence shall we reape, if the vntowarde example of anie man quensh our zeale and care of searching out the Lordes cause, that we shoulde not take it in hande.

But there are not wanting, whiche vnto the slowe rūners about the lords busines, laye more weight of lead vppon their feete, and bringe them into a further securitie, by afraying them, by the example of *Vzzah*, that they attempt not anie thinge about matters pertayninge to the Churche, because they haue no callinge. As though that vengeance shewed vppon *Vzzah*, was [66] for taking vpon him a wrong calling and not rather for dooing that whiche was no mans calling to do. For

A Little Treatise vppon the firste Verse

there was no man in Isreal whiche had anie such calling, but if that hee had driuen the Cart and done as *Vzzah* did, it is like hee shoulde haue bene spared as litle as *Vzzah* was. And *Dauid* in the 13. verse of the 15. of the first Chron. speaking to *Sadock* and *Abiathar*, say not, the Lorde haue made this breache amonge vs, because *Vzzah* did euill: But because we (sayeth he) sought him not in dewe order. And although hee saye also, because you were not heare: his meaning is not that they being present, should haue done that which *Uzzah* did.

But admitte he was punished for ouerreaching his calling: (as in deede whosoeuer passe the boundes of dutie, passethe boundes of their calling also in that respecte) Is it not the callinge of euerie Christian, to remoue himselfe from their communion, whiche worshippe God vaynlie, as by the directinge of the blinde and dumbe mi-[67]-nisterie, that execrable abominatiō in Gods sight: and to ioyne onlie, where the Lordes worshippe is free, and not bound or withholdē wᵗ the *Luk.* 17. 20. bands of any iurisdiction of this worlde. Howe can they make the Kingdome of God near vs & within vs, if we can not by gods assistance, make our selues members of his outward church & Kingdome in this worlde, *Psal.* 133. 3. which onely hath the promise of blessing and life for euermore: without the authoritie of man, & wayting their leysure, for a cōmaundemēt therevnto. And wherevnto are all christians made kings & priestes? *Reue.* 1. 6. Haue they no calling therby to seeke yᵉ meanes of their saluation? If my saluation shoulde depende vpon the curtesie of anie in this worlde, I were in most miserable takinge. But the righteousnes of God dealeth other wise: and our saluation dependeth vppon that King, whose baner is alwayes displaied before vs, and he is with vs to the ende of the worlde. *Mat.* 28. 20.

But now cōcerning those which are able to teache & instructe in the way of [68] the Lord, they must not meddle without calling (saye they) although there be no callinge suffered and allowed of in a Realme or Dominion, but that which they confesse to bee vtterlie vnlawfull. So must the flocke of Christe tarie and be starued, whilest we wayte for that, which they can not direct vs where to haue, or howe it should be.

It must be, saye they, by diuers true Ministers calling and allowing him: and so he must be ordeyned. But howe manie of the Ministers in the Realme of England dare be seene in this dooing? If fayth canne not bee

Rom. 10. 13. [14] begotten without a Preacher, and a Preacher can not be without lawfull sendinge: and this be the onlie way: why suffer they the people to be depriued? Why are they afrayde and ashamed of the Gospell of Christe? Why rather doo they not abide persecution? But the lawfull calling and sending of the Ministers, whiche is the onelie meane to make them haue frutefull wombes to begette faythfull children, and frutefull brestes to nource the same: also dewe [69] gouernement, which is the onelie aduauncing of Christe his kingdome, & the cutting short of sinne and wickednes: Also oure Christian libertie to worshippe God with free conscience, according to his worde: and our comfortable ioyning in the true felowship and communion of Saintes: And to conclude, the meanes of our saluation must be kept from vs, vntill a ciuill law send them vnto vs, although there be neuer so long delay: as though they were not sent from heauen, and offred to all that will receyue them. We can defie the Papistes doctrine, for making part of our saluation, to hange vppon oure owne desertes: but wee canne not taste the bitternes of the roote of this doctrine, that the building of gods kingdome, for the meane and furtherance of our saluation must depend vpon ciuile power, and Christ Iesus with all things pertayning vnto him, are made vnderlings therevnto, and caused to daunce attendaunce vpon it. Those which walke after this doctrine and teache men so, doo break [70] not one of ye least, but one of the greatest commaundements, teaching men so: and therefore shall be counted least in the kingdome of God, if they doo not repent.

And agayne, concerning this calling, whiche must needes bee done by diuers Ministers which will not doo it: But admit they would, frō whence haue they their calling, sendinge, and authoritie, such as pertaineth to a Minister? Hadde they it not from those which sitt in the chayre of Antichrist? Yea, howe manie are in all Christendome, which haue bene so rightlie ordeyned, but that their ordination haue come from the popishe Prelacie, within three or foure generations at the most? Nowe if a man take a griffe of a sowre fruite, and plant it, & then take a griffe of that newe planted, & plant that: and take of that agayne & plant it the thirde time, and so continewe vnto the hundreth time: will it loose the sowrenes, and gather sweetnesse? No more can

A Little Treatise vppon the firste Verse

an vnlawefull callinge bring foorth a lawfull, though it des-[71][1]-cende from one to another an hundred or a thousande times. Therefore except they can approue the lawfulnesse of their calling to the ministerie vnder some other title then y^t which thei now haue by ye Clergie: it will fall out, that there shal hardlie be found a Minister duelie called in all the worlde, and also that there is small hope that euer ther shalbe anie. But whatsoeuer burthen they laye vpon vs, I laie no more vpon them, but that they hauinge the approuing and consent of their flocke, doo the works of a Minister, namely, that they feede their flocke wherof the holy ghost haue made them ouerseers, if they make not them selues vnworthie, and that they keepe backe from them, nothing that is profitable. So then they muste not keepe backe nor suffer to be kept backe (they standing still) their libertie & authoritie, which the Churche should haue, and the true worshippe of God in all pointes safe and sounde, the scepter of the gouernement of Christ borne vpright, and hauing dewe honour, remouing themsel[72]ues and their flockes, at least from all open abomination in life and religion, whereby reproch should redowne to the name of God. These thinges if they doo, and whatsoeuer else apperteineth to a ministers duetie: their worke shall commende them, and testifie their calling, and shall be in stead of an Epistle or rather a licence written in their owne harts: undestood [*sic*] also and redd of all men. Our Sauiour Christ being demaunded whither he were the sent Sauiour, or they should looke for an other: did not answere that he was sent a Sauiour, but saide: Tell Ihon what you haue herde and sene: The blinde see, the lame walke, the lepers are clensed, the deafe heare, the dead are raised vp, and the poore receyue the Gospell. As if he shoulde haue saide: I doo the workes of the Sauiour, which the Prophetes beare witnes of, that he should doo: Therefore I am the sent Sauiour: As namelie, *Isaiah* witnesseth, saiyng: He hath sent me that I shoulde preache the Gospell to the poore, and that I should [73] heale the broken harted &c. And our Sauiour Christ witnessethe in another place, saiynge: I haue greater witnes then the witnes of Ihon: For the workes which the Father hathe giuen me to doo, those testifie of me, that the Father haue sent me. Therefore whosoeuer doo the worke of Ministers, and haue not

Act. 20. 20.

2. *Cor.* 3. 2

Mat. 11. 3.

Esai. 61. 1.

Iohn 5. 36.

[1] E 1 *recto*.

known the deepnes of Satan, neyther haue the cursed learning of Antichrist: I iudge none other burthen to be putt vpon them, but that they holde fast the doctrine of Christ vntill his comming: And their worke shall declare their calling, and seale it before all men. Otherwise the answere of our Sauioure Christe to them which came from Ihon, and the proofe of his calling should not be forceable.

Reuel. 2. 24.

And moreouer, whereas they tie the Ordination of euerie Minister, as it were, vnto the girdle of other Ministers, that of necessitie it must at all times depende and staie vppon them: that is to laie a greater bondage vpon ye churches, thē they are able to beare. [74] For admitt there be onelie one church in a nation, and they want a pastour: must they seeke ouer Sea and lande, to gett a minister ordained by other ministers? But what if there shoulde be but only one apparent to vs in the world: shall that church for euer be depriued, after they haue once wanted a minister, for default of authoritie to call and ordaine an other? By this reason, euery church should not be perfect in it selfe, nor haue in it self meanes and power to continue by that measure of lines which the Lord haue measured out vnto it. And is it not a dishonour to Christ Iesus the head of euery congregation, which is his bodie: to say that his body together with the heade, is not able to be sustained and preserued in it selfe?

Moreouer I demaund what calling the dispersed disciples of the churche at Ierusalem had, y^t they did preache and teach the Gospell as they went? Were they all ordained ministers, by whose meanes it is said that manie did beleue, and that the Lorde was [75] with them? And those whom they did begette, and bring forth as new borne children to God through the Gospell of his sonne: did they want authoritie to feede them and giue them sucke being so brought forth? Which if they might doo, then came they very neere to the work of the pastour, which hath his name of feeding. And was not only charitie a calling to these men, who meeting with such as they found worthie, ouerslipped not that occasion of doing so great good? If the Samaritan be commended for doing the part of a neyghbour vnto him which fell among theeues and was woūded: because he hadd compassion on him, tooke him vpp, and washed his woundes, and in all things prouided for the safetie of his life: Why should they be reproued as passing the bounds of their calling, who meeting with soules

Act. 11. 21.

Luke 10. 36.

A Little Treatise vppon the firste Verse

wounded by the sworde of Antichristian robbers, or anie waie bound by Satan with the chaines of ignoraunce: shall helpe to loose them, and mollifie their woundes with the oile [76] of Gods trueth, and bestow vpon them what spirituall gifte they are able, to refresh them, and saue the life of their soules? Yea if they doo it not, they shalbe founde mercilesse, and like to fayle of mercie in the time of their neede.

In all this I denie not but that ther is vse of other Ministers, when they may be had, for mutuall help in trying and examining, & alowinge those whō they finde meete, that by their iudgement the other churches may so much the more be confirmed.

Thus haue I passed the bounds of the texte somewhat in this discourse, I confesse. But I craue pardon of ye reader. For not without due occasiō haue I bin ledde therevnto. And nowe at length I come to speake of Dauids ioye, whiche I thought to haue done long yere nowe.

And firste of all, therein wee espie the footesteps of that fayth whereby the authour to the Hebrewes wit-[77]-nesseth, so manie excellent practises to haue bene atchieved: which is the grounde of thinges which are hoped for, and the euidence of things whiche are not seene. For hereby Dauid despised all the glorious thinges with visible shewe, whiche belonged to his Royall kingdome, and did bidde them giue place, in comparison of the vnspeakeable treasure of Gods fauour, and all the good whiche flowe from thence, whiche he sawe not but by the eyes of fayth, and possessed onely by the title of that euidence, whiche is concerninge thinges not seene but hoped for, yet herein hee ioyed fullie. *Heb.* 11.

The multitude saye: Who will cause vs to see good? *Psal.* 4. 6.
They knowe what they see here, but they knowe not what they shall haue. But the faythefull saye: Lorde lift vp the light of thy countenaunce vppon vs, and so *Ver.* 7.
thou shalt giue vs more ioye of harte, then the people haue of their aboundant haruest and vinetage. They knowe not, or at ye least wil not acknowledge [78] for their owne ye things of this world. But those thinges which out of Gods countenance turned towardes them, they do conceyue, they knowe for their owne, and they declare that they seeke an induring citie.

So then euen as Dauid by faith had ouerquelled the Lion and the Beare, and by fayth had enterprised to fight with *Goliah*, and had preuayled: so by fayth hee obteyned the bringinge home of the Arke. And though he seemed at the firste to be disappointed, & walked on his waye weeping, sowing deare seede (as did *Abraham* when he so long went without an heyre, and at last was commaunded (as it were) to burie ye hope which he had of the promise in his onlie heyre, by appointing him vnto the death): Yet as *Abraham* did, so hee beleeued in hope against hope. Therefore in the Lords appointed day, hee returneth with mirth and gladnesse, bringing his sheaues with him, when as by fayth hee had gotten accesse vnto ye grace wherin he stoode, and reioiced vnder the hope of glo-[79]-rie of God, wherein hee sawe a liuelie image in his holie Arke, with an vndoubted pledge of loue and fauour towards him. Thus hee fayleth not of that wherewith hee strengtheneth his soule in the time of weaknes & temptation, sayinge: Why art thou cast down, O my soule, and why art thou so disquieted within me [1] wayt on god for I shall yet see the time to giue him thankes for the helpe of his presence. He is my present helpe, and my God. Thus he wayted with patiēce, which taught him experience, which experience brought forth the increase of his hope, and his hope made him not ashamed: seeing hee was not disappointed of that he hoped for, but sawe the greater saluation of the Lorde in the daye of his reioycing, to the further sustayning of his hope, to wayte for greater things also at the Lordes hande. So we see that which I haue spoken, that by faith he entred into the Lords rest, when as the Lorde vouchsafed to haue his resting place and holy habitation with him, and by fayth he reioysed in [80] this, esteeming it aboue all other causes of ioye, because he looked to those inuisibe [*sic*] ioyes, whiche hereby were promised and sealed vnto him.

And nowe to applie this vnto our selues. This also is a glasse which we haue not dressed our selues by: for verie manie can saye, Waite, and tarie. But whither doo we thinke, that they meane, vntill the Lorde helpe and further their paynefull indeuour, whiche is neuer a whit, or vntill they haue filled their insatiable and bottomlesse Coffers with uncontrouled traphiking?

---

[1] Text has exclamation mark.

A Little Treatise vppon the firste Verse

For, where is the disquiet and casting downe of the Soule? Where are the afflictions whiche the Lorde shoulde remember, as he did Dauids? Which shoulde whett the edge of patience, that patience might haue *Iames* 1. 4. her perfect worke, that they might be intire wanting nothing. But above all thinges, where is faith, without the which it is impossible to please God? And without the whiche God will not shewe his glorie before anie people, to their saluation, but to their confusion? [81] for want of which, our Sauior Christ wrought not those miracles in some places, whiche otherwise hee woulde haue done? Where is this faith, I saye, when those which are the chiefe and principall leaders of the people, which should beare the Arke vppon their shoulders: they saye, and haue taught the people to say, It is not possible it should come home: and why? For not only the chiefe of Clergie, but also the chief which haue ye reynes of the ciuile regiment, are against the establishing of church gouernement. I demaund, whither it be from heauē, or from men. If frō heauen: with god all things are possible, & hee will then further his cause in our hand, when we beleeue. And when it shall please the Lorde to further his cause: who can resist *Rom.* 9. 19. his will? For thē euerie Valley shall be exalted, and euerie Hill shall be brought lowe, for the loftines of menne shall be abased, and the Lorde GOD onelie shall bee exalted in that daye. The roughe waye shall *Esai.* 2. bee made playne. This will the ielousie [82] of the Lord of hostes performe, & his owne arme shal susteine him to do the worke if we could beleeue: yet we say it can *Heb.* 11. 34. not bee. Where is that fayth, whereby our Fathers subdued kingdomes, wrought righteousnes, obtayned the promises, stopped ye mouthes of Lions, quenched the violence of the fire, escaped the edge of the sworde, of weake were made strong, waxed valiant in battaill, turned to flighte the armies of the aliauntes? Let us feare for the greeuous iudgement of God, which befell to the children of Israell in the wildernes, whiche were readie to haue entred into the Lordes rest: but sodainlie *Deut.* 1. 28. thorough vnbeleefe conceyued of the euill tidinges which the spies brought, they did shutt the dore against them selues. And what was the matter? The walles were so high, and the people were so stronge. But the height and strength of the Lordes arme was forgotten, whiche had bene stretched out vpon *Pharao* and *Egypt* vnto destruction: But vpon them vnto deliuerance. Euen so wee, for wee [83] woulde fayne enter into the Lordes Sion, a true reformed Churche: but some body is against it. I knowe whereof you meane. A Lyon is in the waye: but *Salamon* saye, that that is but the excuse of a sluggarde. Those spies were euill ynough, whiche went into *Canaan*, and brought home an euill answere. But what shall we saye to those spies whiche tell an euill answere before they will steppe one foot out of the doore ? We haue high walls against vs also, and strong Prelates, whose bodyes if they were growne as farre out of square, as their pompe & authoritie is growne from the lines of their calling, they shuld not be like the Anakims in *Canaan*: but rather like vnto the Giaunt, which the Poets haue fayned, to haue stoode but vpp to the knees in the Sea, where it is at ye deepest. But for a meane to plucke downe this height, and weaken this strength, the hande of the Lorde is forgotten, which was stretched out, euen within this generation, vpon the high walles and swelling Babilonishe buil-[84]-dings of the Abbies and Monasteries. Euen when there was no hope or likelihoode of any such thing by mans reason: Then came a daie from the Lorde, vppon euerie high tower, and vppon euerie stronge wall, to make those places voide dennes. For thistles and nettles growe in their highe halles, and priuie chambers, and the owles shrike there, and the crowes & the rauens gaile[1] there by Gods iust iudgement. There came a daie also vppon all their pleasant pictures, and all their galaunt images, where of they were gladd to cast some into hooles to the moules and the backes, to keepe them from the fire. The daie of the Lorde came also vpon the Cedars of Lebanon, & the O[a]kes of Bashan, euen the great & mightie Cardinals, Abbots, Monkes and Friars, and the rest of the Prelats, whiche bare the sway in the land. These wanted not strengthe. For they were like horses prepared to battle, they were cladd with iron habargions, they had Lions teeth. They had also crownes [85] on their heads, and stinges in their tailes. For there was not one of them in whose presence to speake any thing against their idolatrie: but that it was as muche, as a mans life was worth. These also haue the breathe of the Lords mouthe sent into the bottomlesse smoking Lake, from whence they came. These thinges haue the Lord done for vs, euen in our fresh remembrance, to

Prou. 22. 13.

Esa. 2. 15.

Ver. 20.

Ver. 13.

Reuel. 9. 7.

---

[1] = gale, sing, make an outcry.

A Little Treatise vppon the firste Verse

beat downe the hilles, and make the waie smother to the residue of our iournie. He hath opened a wide dore vnto vs: But we being drücken with the ease of this world, haue reeled against the posts thereof, & fallen backwarde and lie sleaping. Let vs take heede lest we sleape so longe, vntill the Lorde shutte the dore, and naile it vppe also with an othe in his anger, if he haue not done it already.

Seing then ye Lord haue giuen such an onset, doing so great things for vs, bringing vs thus farr on our way out of Egypt: let vs take heed there be not in vs an euill harte and vnfaythefull to departe from the liuinge GOD [86] least we be depriued. But let vs go on our way cherefullie: and feare not the heate of the daye, nor the darkenes of the night. For the Lorde shall create vpon euerie place of mount Sion, and vpon the assemblies thereof, a cloude and smoke by daye, and the shining of a flaming fire by night : for vppon all the glorie shall be a defence, and a couering shall be for a shadowe in the daye for the heate, and a place of refuge and couert for the storme and for the rayne. Neither let vs feare for the highe walles of Iericho, I meane the Antichristian Canon lawe, whiche is the strength of his gouernement. For by fayth ye walles of Iericho fell down at the blastes of the Trumpettes. And what are al the execrable buildings of Antichrist, which still remayne amongest vs, that they should stande before the Lords Trumpetters, if they haue fayth, and doo not onely blowe their blastes, but also compasse the Citie as ofte as they shoulde, and blowe their blastes in due time and place, as the Lorde haue appoynted ? Moreouer, let [87]¹ vs knowe, that as the walles of Iericho fell downe, so also by fayth the walles of Ierusalem were builded vp. For *Nehemiah* misdoubted not eyther the fewnes, eyther the pouertie of the Iewes, eyther the malice of the enemies, but stept vnto the woorke in the middest of those vnlikelihoods, for the whiche their aduersaries did mocke them drylie, saying: What doo these weake Iewes, will they fortifie themselues ? Will they make ye stones whole agayne, out of the heapes of dust, seeing they are burnt ? And another answered: Although they builde, yet if a Foxe goe vppe, hee shall euen breake downe their stonie wall.

Heb. 3. 12.

Esa. 4. 5.

Heb. 11. 30.

Nehe. 4. 2.

So therefore when the harte of gods people shall be

¹ F. 1 *recto.*

to worke, encouraged by fayth, so that their hande also bee strengthened, and put to the busines, though neuer so manie *Ammonites* & *Ashdodims* be wroth and conspire al togither to come against *Ierusalem*, & to hinder the building thereof, yet shal God bringe their counsell to nought. For God is in the middest of it: ther[88]fore shall it not be moued: God shall helpe it very earlie. Thoughe the nations rage against it, & the kingdoms be moued: God shall vtter his voyce, and the earthe shall melt: God shall speake vnto them in his wrath, & vexe them in his sore displeasure. He will persecute them with his tempest, and make them afraide with his storme. So shall the haters of Sion be ashamed and turned backwarde. For the Lord of hostes is with vs, the God of Iacob is our refuge, when we are vnder his Baner, and fighte his battles without vaine feare. For he will teach our handes to warre, and our fingers to fight. He will break the Bowe, and cutte the Speare, and burne the Chariots with fire. But our armes will he strengthen, so that they shall breake euen a bowe of steele. And our feete will he make like Hindes feete, that by the myght of our God we shall leap ouer the highest wall, which Antichrist hath reared: And though our haters vexe us manie times: they shall not preuaile against vs. Thoughe they [89] plowghe vpon our backes: the righteous God shall cutt their cordes in sunder. Thoughe they woulde deuoure vs quicke: yet God will not give vs as a praye vnto their teethe. Waite therefore and knowe that the Lord is God. He will be exalted amonge the heathē, he will be exalted in the earth.

Psal. 4. 7.
Psal. 46. 5. 6.
Psal. 2. [5].
Psal. 83. 15.
Psal. 129. [5]
Psal. 144. 1.
Psal. 129. [2,3]
Psal. 46. [10]

Let vs giue him glorie therefore by trusting in him, that we may take his worke in hande, and further it with all our might, not suffering our eyes to beholde, nor our hartes to consider the impossibilities of finishinge the same. For God is faithefull, who hath promised, saying: To him that disposeth his waie aright, I will shewe the saluation of God.

Psal. 50 [23].

Againe concerning Dauids reioysing, in the day when the people assembled willingly to accompanie him at the bringinge home of the Arke, and the Lord made all thinges to prosper: It seemed to be the fullest & soundest ioye that euer he hadd, bothe for that he then daunced, and leaped, [90] and sprange as one rauished, and fullie possessed with an heauenlie pleasure, and also

A Little Treatise vppon the firste Verse

taketh refreshment, as it appeareth in this psalme, in remēbring, meditating, and singing of the happines of that time, whiche teacheth vs what affection wee shoulde put on in matters pertaining to the Lords glorie, as when his kingdome is builded, and furthered, when he is well known amongest vs, and his Name is great as in Israel, & his Tabernacle with vs as in *Salem*, and his dwellinge as in *Sion*. *Psal.* 76.

We reade of Dauid, that when the Lorde had giuen him to see his sonne *Salomon* placed in the throne of the kingdome, he worshipped vppon the bedde, and saide: Blessed be the Lord God of Israel, who hath made one to sitte on my Throne this daye, euen in my sight. 1. *King.* 1.

This also was a godly reioysing, as it is a godlie and commendable thing in all Kinges & Princes, to haue care to see that matter so well ordered & disposed in the time of their life, as [91] much as in them lie, that the people whose safetie the Lorde haue committed to their care and charge, may enioye continuance of peace and welfare after their deceasse, that there bee no inuasion, nor going out, nor crying in the streetes of their dominions afterward: As also it is godly and commendable to ioie, and blesse God whē he giue them to see with their eyes, the hope of a good staie within their kingdoms: which is so farre from derogating from their honour and renowne, that it tendeth greatlie to the increase & aduancement of the same. For Dauid tooke this for an honorable salutation at his seruaunts hands, when they saide: God make the name of *Salomon* more famous then thy name, and exalt his Throne aboue thy throne. This I say, was one ioye of *Dauids*, yet not comparable to the other: as appeared in that his care to beholde this thinge was not so vehement, and he was neere to haue ouerslipped too longe, the laying of his hande to the furtheraunce thereof, in [92] respect of *Adoniahs* ouer hastie attempt, and he had neede of stirringe vp by the sute of *Bethsaba*, and the aduertisement of *Nathan* the Prophet. Whereas in the other busines of bringing home the Lords Arke, he neded no spurres to pricke him on forward. Flesh & bloode kindled not that zeale in him, but the Lorde hadd inflamed his harte with the Spirit of loue and fire. And this burninge affection of loue bare he from time to time, vnto the Lords holy Tabernacle, for his trew worshipps sake, and his glorie therein appearing. And as it was his life to dwell in the Courts of the Lord by often fre- *Psal.* 144.

1. *Kin.* 1. 47.

quenting them: so was it euen death and great distresse for him to be a straunger from the same, as appeareth by his pitifull complaints in the daies of his banishments, as when he sayeth: As the Hart braieth for the Rivers of water: so panteth my soule after thee O God. My soule thirsteth for God, euen for the liuinge God. When shall I come and appeare before the presence of God? [93] His teares were his meate daye and night, and hee powred out his verie harte when hee remembred the deare times past, when he had gone with the multitude, and led them into the house of God with the voyce of singing and prayse, as a multitude that keepeth a feast. But we alas declare what poore and feeble ioye we would conceyue, if the Lorde would restore the glorie of his sonnes kingdome in open sight before our face, and purge his Court and Sanctuarie, & plant vs therein, when as wee being berefte of this benefite, haue so small thirste, so little panting & braying, and so little sadnes of soule, and shedding of teares, for this maner[1] presence of the Lorde.

Yea wee heare the voyces of manie, and the thoughtes of more lie open before the Lorde, whereof some saye, and some thinke, that they haue no great neede of Christ his Ecclesiasticall gouernement, seeing they can gouerne them selues, and liue in the feare of the Lord wel ynough, as they imagine with them selues. Therefore [94] they sett their harts at rest. But haue they more staye of them selues, and towardnes vnto Godlines thē Dauid had? Or doo they thinke, that he was cleane absent from God, that he could not praie and prayse his name? Yet doo hee saie: When shall I come to appeare before the presence of God? And scarse could he comfort his own soule, whiche was then in heauines, though he hoped for a day of returne. Thus he accounted, that he shoulde stande before the presence of God, when he should be present in the place, which the Lorde did chuse to putt his name theare, and shoulde enioye the sight of those things, which the Lorde appointed for the tokens of his presence amonge them. And therein was his great delight, according as he vttereth, saying: O Lord of hostes, how amiable are thy tabernacles? My soule longeth, yea and fainteth for the courtes of the Lorde. For mine hart and my fleshe reioyse in the liuing God. Blessed are they that dwell in thine house: they will

---

[1] As text.

A Little Treatise vppon the firste Verse

euer prayse thee. [95] And although hee behaued him selfe carefullie before God, when hee was absent from the Lords tabernacle: yet he acknowledged his strength not to be so great, but that there was daūger to be feared by the want of those thinges which the Lord had appointed as meanes to holde them in his true worshippe. For this cause he complaineth vnto *Saul* his persecutor, not so much for persecutinge him, as for chasinge him from the place where the Lorde vouchsafed to dwell. For he saith: If yᵉ Lord haue stirred thee vp against me, let him smel yᵉ savour of a sacrifice : but if the childrē of men haue done it, cursed by [*sic.*, be] they before the Lord: For they haue cast me out this day frō abyding in the inheritance of the Lord, saying, Goe serue other gods. ^{1 *Sā.* 26. 19.}

This loue to Gods house, hadde Kinge *Ezekiah*, who in his sicknes (whereof woorde was brought him that hee shoulde dye) was greeued for nothinge so muche as this, that he shoulde no more goe uppe into the Lordes house. [96] For this cause were his prayers and teares. As appeareth by the worde which came from the Lorde by the mouth of the Prophete. Thus sayeth the Lorde God of Dauid thy Father, I haue hearde thy prayer, and seene thy teares. I haue healed thee, and the thirde day thou shalt goe vp vnto the house of the Lorde. ^{2 *Kin.* 20.}

This zeale also & loue to the Lords house appeared in the ancient fathers which returned from the captiuitie of Babilon, who as they coulde not bee cōforted in their exile, but sate down, & wept by the riuers of Babel, when they remembred Sion. So in the ioyfull time of their returne, yea in yᵉ ioyful day of laying the foundation of the Temple, which they aboue all things had desired, in the middest of the ioiful shouting and singing of the residue of the people, their hartes yet melted within them, & they wept with a loude crying, in so muche that the noyse of the shoutinge could not bee discerned from the noyse of the weeping, and all was for this, because they had seene [97] the former Temple. And the foundatiō of this was not cōparable to that. What shall wee saye, Did these old men dote'? Were they fonde vppon an outward shewe of faire building ? No: but as their chiefe delight was in the house of god, so the increase of the glorie thereof, was their ioye, & the diminishing of the glorie therof, was their sorowe and griefe of minde. ^{*Ezra.* 3. 12.}

Thus ielous were they ouer Gods glorie, that in the outward shewes and shadowes they were impatient of any want. But amongst vs, there is small weepinge, though the buylders in their building haue left out the chiefe corner stone, which should be the garnishing of all the worke. They haue left out the gouernement of Christ, without ye which, that their Churche can bee his house, though they face and brace neuer so much, how should they thinke it possible ? For they muste knowe, that Christe dwelleth not, where he ruleth not. He maye not bee an idle Idoll. His Churche and Kingdome in this worlde, is outwarde and visible, and [98] except he gouerne visiblie, euen by his outwarde ordinances: It is vayne for vs to say, He ruleth in our hartes: and in the church that we are ioyned vnto we submit our selues to the ordinances of Antichrist. Wee shall soone banishe Christ frō our hartes, if we haue no more care of his glorie then so, but can abide to see his Sanctuarie prophaned and polluted by that Heathenishe straunger of Rome, whiche not onelie set his foote in there euery day, but also erecteth there his owne altar of incense. For my prayers and thankes giuing must bee measured out and appointed after his fashion.

If euer we had seene the beautie of the first building, I meane in the time of the primitiue Churche, wee might wel nowe, if we had not stonie hartes, weepe and lament with loude crying, in seeinge this buyldinge before oure eyes. Not so much for that it is inferiour to the other in glorie: but for that it hath neither glorie nor beautie at all, being fashioned not after anie paterne shewed of God, but after the de-[99]-uise and counsel of man. In which miserie if our notable anguishe and greeuous grones were hearde in the eares of the Lorde, and in vs there were no want to call and stirre vp one another, and ioyne handes, for the helpe of the furtherance of the worke in bringing home the Arke of God: there were then greater hope of the daye wherein we might & ought to reioyce, as Dauid here did.

Moreouer, we note in Dauid, that his ioye was so great in the Lorde, that he conteyned not him selfe, but so leaped and daunced, that he seemed in the eyes of the wicked, as a foole, whiche vncouereth his shame, and became vile. For after that maner did *Michal* his wife reprochefullie taunt him, as one whiche had so vily vncouered him self, that he should be a mocking

2 Sam. 6.

A Little Treatise vppon the firste Verse

stocke vnto the Maidens of Israel. But hee answered, that it was before the lord, who had performed vnto him so great mercie: for whose cause he woulde bee yet more vile and lowe in his owne sight. And saide more ouer, that of the [100] same Maidens whereof hee had spoken, he should bee had in honour. Whereby we see, how litle he weighed to become base and lowe in the sight of the worlde, so hee might sett foorth the glorie of the Lorde his God.

At this day amongest vs, one of the greatest lettes & hinderaunces of the Lordes worke finishing, is, for that it can not be done without the abasinge of the loftines of manie men whiche are exalted without the Lorde. As for the titles of Gracious and Honourable Lords, our Sauior Christ taught his Apostles that they might not bee amongest them. Therefore if these men so exalted, would loue and care for the Lords honour more then their owne, and would willinglie giue ouer their monstrous liuings, and all their worldlie pompe, though they thinke it were a great shame for them, and that they shoulde seeme vile before men, (whiche they ought willinglie to vndergoe, for his glories sake, who suffered the crosse and despised the [101] shame) yet if they coulde *Heb.* 12. 2. see it, it would tende to their more true dignitie. For of all the people in Englande whiche wayte for a more full appearaunce of Gods glorie in his house, they shoulde be had in honour. Where as nowe contrariewise they receyue honour onelie of a fewe flattering seruinge men, within their owne houses, whiche liue by bringinge dishes to their Table, and almost to all the residue of the people of the lande, their name is in reproche, and they are become a Byworde and a common talke.

Our Sauiour Christ thought it no shame to abase *Iohn.* 13. 5. him selfe to washe his Disciples feete: by that example, and manie more teaching those which will followe him, that they must not thinke much to be base and vile, and dishonourable in the sight of men, if they will looke for true honour in the sight of GOD. The Angel Gabriel *Luke.* 1. 15. sayde vnto Zacharias, that his Sonne Iohn the Baptist shoulde bee great in the sight of the Lorde.

[102] But what greatnes he had in the sight of the worlde, it appeareth, when as his clothing was of **Camels** heare, & his meate was Locustes and wilde honie. The authour to the Hebrewes speaketh of some **Christians**, *Heb.* 11. 35. whiche were racked, and would not be deliuered, that

they might receyue a better resurrection. They woulde needes abide torment and shame, that in the Lorde they might haue their onelie refreshment, and their onelie glorie. And he became their glorie, and the lifter vp of their heade.

Our Sauior Christ who thought it no robberie, to be equal with God, he yet in his nature of man, became vile, and tooke vpon him the shape of a seruaunt: Hee turned his face to the striker: He humbled him selfe, euen to the death of the crosse. Therefore was giuen him a name and dignitie aboue al names, that at his name euery knee should bowe.

Phil. 2. 9.

But great is the darkenes and vngodlines of these dayes, when those which professe them selues to bee his [103]¹ Ministers, doo so order their goings, and conforme them selues so little vnto the image of his life, that wee may sooner trace out the shewe of all the great glorie of this worlde, then of Christian poorenes in spirit by their footesteppes. And it is too manifest, that thei are ouercome with the temptation of him whiche sayde: All these glorious thinges will I giue thee, if thou wilt fall downe and worship me. For they declare howe hardelie they would abide themselues to be plucked vp by the rootes, that they might bee planted in a better resurrection, when as they will not suffer their superfluous braunches to be cut of[f], which do so ouerhange and annoye the lanes, that the Lordes passengers can not ride on their iourneye towardes Sion.

Mat. 4. 9.

There be also of the Temporalitie diuers, which esteme it to[o] uile a thing, and vnfittinge for their dignitie, to come vnder the censure of the church, that their faultes shoulde bee looked [104] vnto, and they should be subiect to the Admonition, Rebuke, and Excommunication of the Minister and the Congregation. Therefore they say: Let vs breake their bandes in sunder, and cast their cordes from vs. But if they vnderstoode the great mysterie of the Lorde, and the decree, which is sealed vp amongst his Disciples: they should well know, that their renowne & glorie is no more impaired by bowing & giuing due homage to Christs Scepter, then the flower and oyle of the widowe of *Sarepta* was diminished, by giuing away part of that litle which she had, vnto *Elias.* For certainly the great and noble Potentates of this worlde, if they doo not

Psal. 2. [3].

Esa. 8. 16.

¹ G. 1 *recto.*

A Little Treatise vppon the firste Verse

intertaine the kingdome of Christ Iesus, thoughe their name reache the clowdes: yet in trueth their honour and renowne is small, and skarcely to be accounted an handfull, which when it is spent, they die. Then their name perishe, and their pompe will not followe them. Then is a liuing dogge [105] better then they. For doth not their dignitie goe away with them? Doo they not die and that without wisdom? Whereas if they would be content to giue away vnto our *Elias* Christ Iesus, a litle of their honour by abasing themselues before his Throne of gouernement: they shoulde haue neuer the lesse, but a great deale the more: yea the continuance of true honour for euer. For they shoulde stand as the faithfull witnesses in heauen, their names being registred in the booke of life. According as the Prophet *Esaiah* speakethe of the renowne of the Church, and accoūteth it the renowne of Kinges and Princes, to worshipp therein with their faces towardes the earth, and to licke vp the dust at the feete thereof.

Ecclesiastes. 9. 4.

Iob. 4. 21.

Esai. 49. 23.

Lastlie as touching Dauids affection of ioye, and his delight which he hadd to see the glorie of God shine forthe: as it was declared by signes, yea the whole disposing of himselfe, to be great at that present time: so did [106] the continual practise of his life afterward, giue token that it was intiere and vnfeined. For he continued his care and studie to be an instrument to aduance Gods glorie.

Of our sone whote[1] & sone colde zeale: and of our gladnes, which bewraied it selfe to be more for the shining hope of our worldlie welfare, then for the hope of the increase of Gods kingdome, and the speedy coming thereof : And of our loue, whiche haue giuen place to iniquitie soone getting the vpper hande: And of all our forwardnes and goodnes, which appeared in the day, when the Lorde opened one dore for vs to come out of prison, and an other dore to haue entred his Tabernacles, if we would haue but strained our selues a litle to haue remoued a fewe blockes in the waie: Of this our goodnes and forwardnes, howe that it proved but as a morning mist, which vanished before any heat of the Sunne brast forth: I have spoken before. Litle was that we had, therfore [107] was taken from vs euen that litle. Great was the true and sincere ioye, faith, zeale & loue which Dauid hadd: therefore was giuen

[1] Soon hot.

unto him more. For he continued faithefull to him which hadd called him through grace, and for the remembrance of his great goodnes, he still in hart desired to add more labour vnto the Lords worke. For the Arke being brought home, & placed in a tent, he desired to builde an house for the same. And if it hadd seemed good in the eyes of the Lord, to haue used his hande therin, as he did accept of his hart and goodwill: he woulde haue chose rather to haue bene destitute himselfe of a princelie pallace, then y^t the Arke of god should haue bene without a royall house, for the more manifestinge of the glorie thereof. And when he receyued answere from ye Lord, that he should not build an house vnto him, but his sonne shoulde builde it: yet as muche as he might, he did with all his power, and became a cheefe builder one waye, [108] when as an other waye hee could not, namelie, in preparinge those thinges which should furnishe the worke, and set

1. *Chro.* 22. [5]. it forwarde with speede, when it shoulde be begonne. For he said: My sonne *Salomon* is yonge and tender, and we must buylde an house for the Lorde, magnificall, excellent, and of great fame and dignitie thoroughout all Countries. I will therefore nowe prepare for him. And hee prepared an hundred thousande Talentes of golde, and a thousande thousande Talentes of Siluer: And of Brasse and of Iron, passinge weight: And also Tymber and Stones, and he had sett Masons to hewe and polish the stones in readinesse. And yet for all this, his hunger for Gods glorie, was not satisfied, but hee complayned that hee was able to doo no more.

Ver. 14. For hee sayde to his Sonne *Salomon*: according to my pouertie I haue prepared these thinges.

There was then no necessitie of an house: For the Arke was kept in the [109] Tabernacle, whiche figured the churche, and that was after Gods institution. And the necessitie of hauinge the Temple came not vntill the Lords commaundement appointed a time thereunto. Neyther was there any ruine of thinges pertaining to Gods house at that time. Yet you see howe *Dauid* behaued himselfe, not constrained by any necessitie of the time, but inflamed by his true affection, which hungred for the further glorie of those things, which represented Gods glorie.

There be witnesses in England, which know, how that exceding manie mouthes of the teachers, and of those

A Little Treatise vppon the firste Verse

which speake as they are taught, haue confessed concerning their Churche: Some, that it is ruinous: Yet will they make the stones whole againe out of the duste, not with a worke, as *Nehemiah* did with building: but with a word or two, in saying, it is the churche of God yet notwithstanding.

[110]. Some saye, It is naked, and yet a Churche: And thoughe it bee both hungrie and naked, they giue it such a beggars almes, as ye Apostle Iames speake of: *Iames*. 2. 16. Goe warme thee, and fill thy bellie. For they saye, God helpe it, wee shall praye for it. In the meane time nothing is ministred to susteyne it with, touchinge that they complayne to bee wantinge vnto it, therefore what helpeth it?

Some saye, It is as a man that wante a legge, and *Heb.* 12 [13]. yet a church. But the Scripture saye, That that which is halting, is neare to bee turned out of the waye. Some saye, It want but an arme, &c. But all this while they espie not wherein the greatest deformitie lieth, namelie, In that it hath a little pretie bodie, and a great sorte of monstrous great heades. I meane those of whome wee maye well complayne with the Prophete, and say: O Christe, Other Lordes besides thee haue ruled ouer *Esai.* 26. 13. vs.

But because I knowe herein my iudge-[111]-ment will be sifted: I say for my selfe, that I iudge them not, nor condemne them. The worde of the Lorde iudgeth all them and mee.

But concerninge the Churche of Englande, as they intitle it: It is a notable dishonour vnto Christ Iesus, to make all the Parishes in England generallie his Churche, hee will giue no thankes for that liberalitie. Yet I am perswaded (the Lorde I take to witnesse) that in the Realme of Englande there bee diuers Churches. And I hope also that there bee manie more true worshippers, or such at the least as the Lorde doeth accept, whiche abhorre and deteste to bowe the knee to the Antichristian scepter, more I saye, then seeme to appeare, as was in Israel in the dayes of the Prophete *Eliah*. But that the booke whiche is for Gods worshippe and seruice, and yet beareth not the name of God, that euer it caused Tabernacle to bee so framed, as that the Lord shoulde knowe it for his owne, I ut-[112]-terlie denie.

But to returne to my purpose. Seeing the case so

standeth that the ruines and decayes of the Churches be apparant by a generall confession almoste of all: yea seeing it is also confessed, that shee is sicke vnto death, and lie panting for breath: let vs not thinke, that sweete and smoothe wordes will heale her deadlie hurte, as to saye: yet it is a famous Churche, and other nations haue thought well & reuerentlie of the Churche of Englande, &c. But let all with whome is yet the feare of the liuinge GOD, and anie desire of his glorie, laye the hande to the worke, no more but euen thus, by eschewing euill, and dooing good, that although they goe forwarde in fewenesse, according to their pouertie for a tyme, yet by their example, and aduertisementes, they maye winne manie vnto righteousnesse, by callinge, and stirringe vppe after this maner: Come, lette vs goe vp to the mountaine of the Lorde, to the house of the [113] God of Iacob, and he shall teache vs his wayes, and wee will walke in his pathes.

Esai. 2. 3.

Let them also saye eche to other, that because we sought not the Lorde in dewe order, therefore heare we this complainte to our rebuke and shame: There was neuer more wickednes then is nowe.

Thus if we do, labouring not more faintlie, because iniquitie hath gotten the vpper hande, but more valiauntlie to redeeme the times, because the dayes be euill, wee shall be foūde in the sight of the Lorde, accordinge to our abilitie, to haue polished & made readie liuinge stones for the Lordes buyldinge, that although wee can see the worke goe but slowlie forwarde in our dayes, yet in the next generation it may rise more speedily to the glorie of GOD, And let none vtter these wordes of vnfaythfulnes, Alas what can I doo, or what can twoo or three of vs doo, or howe are wee like to goe forwarde ? [114] So I maye saye, what can a graine of Mustarde seede doo ? It is small to beholde. But being caste into the grounde in dewe time, and watered, wee see what it dooeth, and howe it spreadeth. So wee maye saye, what can wee doo, if wee sitte still ? But if wee labour in the Lordes businesse, so as wee giue our selues ouer to bee sowne in the earth for his truethes sake, vndoubtedlie, out of oure dead bones or ashes there will springe vp manie more witnesses, vntill the glorious cause flourishe gloriouslie.

But to proceede
   I reioyced when they sayde vnto me &c.

A Little Treatise vppon the firste Verse

It is written in the Chronicles, that Dauid gathered all Israel togither, to goe vp to Ierusalem. And in that the people were so hartilie willinge, sayinge, That they woulde goe vp to the house of the Lorde, and their feete shoulde stande in the gates of Ierusa-[115]-lem, wee maye note this, that the Lorde nowe being with Dauid, after hee hadde feared before his face, and carefullie sought him in dewe order, hee addeth blessinge vnto blessinge vnto him, to make his ioye full. For hee doeth not onelie make him to see the Arke come home in peace, but also giue him the hartes of all the people, as one man reioysinge with him, and praysing the Lorde, then the whiche nothing coulde refreshe and solace his minde more cherefullie ouer his grief paste. *1 Chro. 15.*

Thus doth the Lord make things to succeed with them (yea oftentimes more then they looke for) which seeke him in feare and tremblinge, and attempte to worke accordinge to his will.

Thus *Nehemiah*, when his harte had conceyued that enterprise of building of the walles of Iersualem, hee not onely obteyned leaue of the King to goe thither, whiche thing he hoped not for without feare: but also the [116] Lorde made him obtayne that which was least looked for, euen helpe and furniture of Timber towardes the worke. Moreouer, the Lorde gaue him the hartes of the people, who notwithstandinge their pouertie and fewnesse, yet were incouraged to worke with vnwonted forwardnesse.

So *Moses*, though hee had a frowarde companie to guyde, yet when hee went about the Tabernacle makinge, with all thinges apperteyning therevnto, accordinge to the Lordes commaundement, hee founde the peoples hartes so willinge and readie to offer, and their handes so full of giftes, that hee cryed, Ho, and commaunded them to ceasse from offringe anie more. *Exod. 36. 6.*

Therefore, let there be no vnchearfull wordes amongest vs, to weaken our handes before we begin to worke. As some saye, Howe is it possible? Where shall wee haue fitte men for Elders? Where shall wee haue sufficient Ministers ynough? And where [117] shall we haue this and that?

It is the propertie of a slouthfull seruaunt, to tell before hee goe out, howe hee is not like to speede. Let vs in the middest of all streightnes and impossibilities, take in hande our enterprise in the Lord with humblenes, wisedome, & single hartednes: and we shal see successe not only in those thinges which we can foresee & hope for: but also manie things vnlooked for of vs, shalbe prospered into our bosome.

Nowe whereas the people speak so willingly, saying: We will go vp into the house of the lord: it declareth their forwardnes vnto a good enterprise. But the King had called them & stirred them vp therevnto. So peraduenture it may seeme that the people are not to go vp into the Lordes house: especiallie to go about such an heauenlie busines, as thei now did, without their Kings & Princes going before them. As for ye Arke, though it bare a spirituall representatiō of holy things, yet it was a material thing, & the bringing [118] of it home required outwarde furniture and preparation accordinglie. But what the Priestes and people might haue done as touching it, if the king should haue bene to[o] slacke: when I shall vnderstande it to be doubted of: aunswere shall be made as GOD shall giue leaue.

In the meane time, it is not amisse to speake some thinge of a question whiche flyeth much abroade, whiche haue bene taken vp rather of desire to intangle, then of anie loue of ye truth, as shoulde seeme by the disorderlie framinge and propoundinge thereof. The question is this:

Whither the Prince or the people ought first to beginne reformation in the Church?

I aunswere with propoundinge other questions. Can they tell whether Prince or people ought firste to turne to the Lorde? Whether Prince or people ought firste to do their duetie? [119][1] Or, whither, ye head, the hand, or ye foot ought first to do that, which seuerallie appertaineth to ye office of ech of those mēbers to do? For Kings & Princes ought to reform without delay or waiting for other, so farr as the bounds of their calling reach: and ye people they ought to reforme without al delaye or tarying for other, so farr as the boūdes of their calling reach also. But howe farre the bounds of eche doo extende, therein lieth the chief point.

In the name of God, let *Cesar* haue whatsoeuer vnto him belongeth, euen all ciuile power and Dominion ordayned of God. And woe vnto him, saye I, whiche shall holde this, and teache men so, that there is no use of the Magistrates sworde among Christians. For that

H. 1 *recto.*

A Little Treatise vppon the firste Verse

is to remoue yͤ doole[1] of the great and large fielde which the Lorde haue measured out vnto them. And that is also to depriue Christians of that benefite of peace whiche the Lord haue ordayned that wee should enioye by their menes.

[120] For it is written: Exhoιt, that Prayers, and Supplications be made for Kinges, and all that be in authoritie, that vnder them we may lead a godlie and peaceable life. 1. *Tim.* 2. 2.

Therefore I am thus perswaded, that as the Kinges of *Iuda* did reforme by their ciuile power, those things which outwardly were sett vp for abominations: namely, as they did break downe the altars, cutt downe the groues, burne the images with fire, slaye the Preistes of Baal, and suche like thinges: So also it apperταineth to the Magistrates now, to break downe the idolatrous altars, plucke downe their buildinges, burne their images with fire, & to slaye those, which haue reuolted frō Christianitie to open idolatrie. And herein wee prayse the Lorde, who strengthned our Princes handes, to worke so farre, as was wrought therin. And if our sinnes had not displeased the Lorde, we shoulde haue sene more. For I would to God the Arrow had not bene shott against [121] the ground only three times, but three hundred times three times, that a full conquest for euer might haue bin gotten ouer those Antichristian *Aramits*. 2 *King.* 13. 18

And now concerning those abominations, which remaine, which partly I haue spoken of: As the offices, rowmes, and liuinges of the Lordlie ouerrulers of many churches, together with Deanes, & Deanaries, Prebēds and Prebenshippes, Cathedralles wᵗ the Chaunters therin, and their Marmaiden musick, Bishops Chaūcelors, Archdeacons, Cōmissaries, Proctors Officials, Sūners & Questmen, whiche all do robbe yͤ church of her authoritie & libertie, and strippe her naked: These I say, wᵗ their Courtes & Canō lawes, as also freehold Parsonages & Vicariges, which hinder the free election & deposing of the Minister: Also blinde & dūme ministers, with yͤ forme of stinted seruice to be read, being the staffe of strength of vpholding thē: All these wormewoode dregges of Antichrists cupp, & what soeuer more, it apperταineth only to the office of yͤ ciuile [122] Magistrate, to powre out and rince euen from the

---

[1] **Stake**, boundary, landmark.

bottom. Which ye Lord graunt that it may soone be done.

And whereas we are charged that we will take vpon vs to remoue these things, & establishe newe lawes for other gouernement: we are most iniuriouslie slaundered. For we contrariewise charge al in ye name of God, that they be not so hardie, as by any authoritie whiche they may imagine they haue, as being of the church of God, to meddle once to moue the hand to take away these thinges: For that were to take ye sword out of Cesars hād. Therfore they ought to wayte for this maner of reformation, with cōtinuing in feruent praier to God for the hastning thereof: But herein lieth the duetie of Gods people, to remoue them selues from these & al *Ephe.* 5. 11. other abominations, & not to haue fellowship w^t ye vnfruitfull workes of darkenes: not to ioyne handes with open wickednes, but to keepe our selues vnspotted therof, *Galat.* 5. 1. not to go vnder any yoke of spirituall bō-[123]-dage, to betraye the libertie & authoritie which Christ haue left with vs to keepe, but to stand faste in the libertie wherein hee hath made vs free. By the vertue of which libertie and authoritie, the Church of God haue to trie and examine the giftes, and conuersation, of those which should leade thē, and finding them meet to chuse them, and perceyuinge them afterwarde to fall to anie euill heresie in doctrine, or to loosenes of life, and will not bee reclaymed by dewe admonition, to depose them. Also by the power of the same libertie and authoritie, *Mat.* 18. 17. the churche of GOD haue to use their dewe admonitions, and rebukinges of offendours. Euerie one maye bringe his complainte in due order: And such offendours as will not heare the churche, and bee reformed, must 1 *Cor.* 5. feele the sworde of excommunication by the woorde of GOD, to bee cutte of[f], and to bee deliuered vnto Satan, to stirr them vpp to bewayle their wickednesse and to repent, if the Lorde so [124] touch their hartes. And this authoritie of punishinge the transgressours by *Mat.* 18. 18. the Ecclesiasticall sworde, maye not be taken out of the Churches handes, neither can the Churche giue it ouer without denyinge Christe, who haue left this his power vnder their charge: Although the ciuile Magistrates maye and ought also to strike with their sworde, euerie one whiche beinge of the Churche, shall openlie transgresse against the Lordes commaundements.

Moreouer, it standeth with the libertie of the Lordes

A Little Treatise vppon the firste Verse

Congregation, to vse prayers and thankes giuing alwayes, as the present occasion requireth.

These and suche like things appertayne to the office of the Lordes Ministers, togyther with their Congregations. And as for the reforminge of these thinges, where soeuer anie wante bee: What vngodlie tongue dare bee so bolde, as to saye, we ought to tarie one howre? No, but if we ta-[125]-rie for a newe graunt from men to doo our dueties in the true worshippe of God, when as we haue alreadie sufficient graunt from heauen: we shall die in our sinnes, and our bloude shall be vpon our owne heades.

Nowe, if the Ministers and peoples duetie and charge extende vnto this which I haue mentioned: it followeth, that nothing is wanting vnto true Churche gouernement, but so much as the people, and especially the Ministers which shoulde guide them, are wanting vnto their duetie enioyned to them by the Lorde.

Wherefore in the Lorde, I doo require some of those Ministers in Englande, whiche thinke hardlie of our doinges, and yet perswade them selues that they hartilie desire the full repayring of the Walles of Ierusalem: That they would set downe by proofe of the worde of God, that whiche is wanting to true & full church gouernement, besides that whiche is their duetie to doo, togither with their Cōgre-[126]-gation, whom they ought to stirre vp to their duetie likewise. If there be anie thinge at all: I will promise and vowe faythfullie to tarie and wayte w^t them also. If there be nothing, why do they make so long suing at the Parliaments, & suffer so manie poore soules at Rome to be depriued of their heauēlie well fare, and to suffer sinne so too ouerspreade by their default, which by their keepinge the Lordes watche, might be cutt shorter? For what sewe they for vnto the Prince and Parliament? Euen for a lawe to cōpell them to doo that which the Lord haue commaunded them to doo. Why doo they it not in haste, by the vertue of Gods cōmaundement, alreadie giuē, so long as they can in peace? And when they no longer can, why suffer thei not persecution for his sake, whom they must obeye before man? and who haue said: Blessed are they, whiche suffer persecutiō for righteousnes sake: for theirs is the kingdome of heauen. *Mat.* 5. 10.

Whose kingdome and glorie wee [127] must seeke

both in wealth and woe, both in peace and persecution. His kingdome come with speede. And to him at length, lett vs giue the hande, singing the songe of hartie entertainement:

Hosanna, Blessed be the kingdome that commeth in the name of the Lord of our Father Dauid: Hosanna, O thou which art in the highest heauens.

Mat. 11. 10. [*sic, Mark* 11. 10].

AMEN.

[Ornament]

[128 blank]

[129] Ornament.

Psalm. 80. *ver.*
4. O Lorde God of Hostes, howe longe wilt thou bee angrie against the prayer of thy people?
8. Thou hast brought a Vine out of Egypt: Thou hast cast out the Heathen, and planted it.
9. Thou madest roume for it, and diddest cause it to take roote, & it filled the lande.
10. The mountaynes were couered with the shadowe of it, and the boughes thereof were like the goodlie Cedars.
11. Shee stretched out her braūches vnto the Sea, and her boughes vnto the Riuer.
[130] 12. Why hast thou then broken downe her hedges, so that all they, whiche passe by the waye haue plucked her?
13. The wilde Bore out of the wood hath destroyed it, and the wilde beastes of the fielde haue eaten it vppe.
14. Returne wee beseeche thee, O God of Hostes: Looke downe from heauen, and beholde and visite this Vine.

Psal. 123 *ver.*
3. Haue mercie vppon vs, O Lorde, haue mercie vppon vs, O Lorde, for wee haue suffered much delaye.

Psal. 126. 4
O Lord, bring againe our captiuitie, as the Riuers in the South.

[131] *Psal.* 84. *ver.*
9. Beholde, O God our shielde, and looke vpon the face of thine anoynted.
10. For a day in thy Courtes is better, thē a thousand otherwhere.

A Little Treatise vppon the firste Verse

Psal. 51 *ver.*

18. Be fauourable vnto Zion, for thy good pleasure: Build the walles of Ierusalem.

19. Then shalt thou accepte the sacrifice of righteousnes.

Psal. 80.9 [80.19]

Turne vs againe, O Lorde God of Hostes: Cause thy face to shine and we shall be saued.

So be it.

IV. *Three Formes of Catechismes, conteyning the most principall pointes of Religion.* Deut. 4. 10. I will cause them to heare my words, that they may learne to feare me all the dayes of their life, And that they may teache their children also. R.H. 1583.

Copied from the only known copy, which is bound up with four more tracts in Lambeth 30. 9. 18 in a binding with Richard Bancroft's initials. On the title-page Bancroft has written: "This booke was geven me by the L. cheefe Justice of ye Cōmon place[1]; at Burie Assises 1583 ye sixt of Julye". Coppin and Thacker had been executed for dispersing the books the previous month, and some forty copies had been burnt at the time of the execution. (See a letter of Sir Christopher Wray, the Lord Chief Justice, to Burghley, 6 July, 1583 (Lansdowne MS. 38, ff. 162, 3). For Bancroft's activity in Bury see *The Opinions and Dealings of the Precisians*, By Richard Bancroft (?), edited from the manuscript in St. John's College, Cambridge, by Albert Peel (to be published by Cambridge University Press, probably in 1953).

Collation : T-p. (A 2 *recto*) ; To the Reader (A 2 *verso* ; Black Letter) ; Texts of the three catechisms (A 3 *recto* — E 2 *verso*, in 8's). The Questions are in Roman, the Answers in Black Letter.

For the frequent use of Catechisms in Elizabethan England, see *Cartwrightiana*, (p. 156) in the present series.

[*A.* 2 *verso*] To the Reader.
Thou hast here (Christian Reader) in this litle booke, three Catechismes. The first setting forth the chiefe pointes of religion somewhat at large. The seconde gathering the same in a shorter sūme, for their memories sake, which are not able to committe to harte the longer. The thirde very short, for the alluring of weake and crased memories, as of aged folke, and such like, which at least may soone learne those foure wordes, and the meaning of them, and be brought to saye some thinge of them by their owne knowledge. There be very many Catechismes, thou knowest (good

---

[1] **May** be "places" and no semi-colon : this is the old form of "Common Pleas."
  Sir Edmund Anderson (1530 - 1605) was appointed Lord Chief Justice of the Common Pleas in 1582. Wray (1524 - 1592) was appointed to the Queen's Bench as justice in 1572, and as chief justice in 1574.

Three Formes of Catechismes

Reader) and in very many of them (in my iudgement) a good & perfect order wanting, for beginning where they shoulde beginne, and endinge where they should ende, and making thinges followe in their due course. I submitte my selfe also to the iudgement of others. Peraduenture manye wyll so thinke of these. Therefore I leaue it free to thee to chuse, vntill thou finde that forme of Catechisme, which thou thinkest to agree most aptlye to thy minde, which thou art best able to followe in instructing thy householde. If thou shalt take anye profite by these, giue God the glorie.

[A. 3 recto] *Question*
Who created you, and all things which are created?
Answere
GOD.

Quest. What is GOD?
An. He is a spirit almightie, eternall, and so incomprehensible, that wee are not able to attaine vnto what he is, but as he hath in his worde expressed his owne name and nature.

Quest. What is that his name expressed in his word?
An. The Lorde the Lorde strong, mercifull and gracious, slowe to anger, and aboundant in goodnes and trueth, reseruing mercie for thousands, forgiuing iniquitie, and transgression and sinne, and not making the wicked innocent, visiting the iniquitie of the fathers vpon the children vnto the thirde and fourth generation.

[A 3 verso] Quest. And what is yonr [sic] duetie, and the duetie of all creatures towardes God our creatour?
An. To sett forth his glory. For the Lord made all thinges for his glories sake.

Quest. And how is Gods glorie set forth by his creatures?
An. In respect of the Lord, it is sett forth, in that the glorie of his wonderfull wisedome and power appeareth, wyll we nyl we, in our creation: In respect of his creatures, his glorie is set forth by their obedience to his will and commaundement.

Quest. How is Gods glorie declared by obeying his commaundement?
An. Because the Lord to all things which he made appoynted a lawe, as a token and marke of his soueraignetie and Lordshippe ouer them. In keeping the which lawe, they witnesse that God is he whom they serue, and of dueie [sic] ought to [A 4 recto] obeye, and so giue him the glorie of a Lord and God: and in breaking which lawe, they doo as much as proclayme that they owe him no seruice nor obedience, and so denie him his due glorie, of beyng Lorde and God, maker and gouernour of all.

Quest. Declare some examples as concerning what lawes the Lorde haue giuen to his creatures in the beginning, wherby they myght testifie their obedience, vnto his glorie.

An. To the Sunne the Lord gaue a lawe, that it should rule the daye: to the Moone and Starres, that they shoulde rule the nyght: To the Waters, that they should be gathered into their boundes, and not couer the drie lande as they did before: to the Earth, that it shoulde bring forth the hearbe that seedeth seede, & the fruitfull tree &c. And to Man God gaue a commaundement, to abstayne from eating of the fruit of the tree in the middest of the gardē of Paradyse, called the tree of Knowledge of good and euill.

[A 4 verso] Quest. Howe doo the dumme creatures obeye Gods commaundement?

An. In that they continue in the state, wherein the Lord placed them, & stand to the order and course, wherevnto he assigned them at the first.

Quest. Haue not man also obeyed Gods commaundemēt from the beginning?

An. No. For our first parents Adam and Eue presentlie after the commaundement giuen, turned quicklie out of the waye. For they hearkning vnto the serpents lying temptation, turned also the trueth of God into a lye. For they beleued not that which the Lord had spoken, but did eate of the forbidden fruit, and therby as it were proclaymed, that they ought vnto the Lord no seruice nor obedience, and so denyed him the glorie of their Lorde and Gouernour, and seperated them selues quite from him.

Quest. What befelle of this fall of Adam?

[A 5 recto] An. Most wofull ruine to him selfe, and to all his posteritie. For the Lorde creating him of this nature, to begett seede, and to increase on the earth, after a maner wee were all created in him, seyng wee haue all spronge out of his loines. Therefore as he receyued most happie blessings and guiftes of the Lord, both for him selfe, and for his seede, and wee all in him receyued them: so by this his denying the Lorde, he lost all both to him selfe and to his seede, and wee all in him haue lost them. He made himself a seruant to sinne, wherevnto he had obeyed, and a slaue vnto Satan whom he had serued. Which miserie is come vpon all his posteritie, as it is written: By the offence of one, sinne came on all men to condemnation. And againe, in Adam wee are all dead. So that he hath left vs none other inheritaunce, but the cursed and bitter root of sinne, which inwardly springeth in the grounde of

Three Formes of Catechismes

our soules, euen from our birth. And this is called Originall sinne, and for the playner vnderstanding, we may call it sinne which we haue by nature or kind.

[A 5 *verso*] Quest. What do this naturall corruption bring forth in vs?

An. It bringeth foorth in vs[1] continuall disobedience against the Lord, in breaking his lawes. And it is a verye stronge infecting plague, which infectethe and poysoneth all our thoughtes wordes and deedes, in such sort, as that they be all transgressions against Gods commaundements.

Quest. What commaundements be they?

An. The Ten Preceptes ingrauen by the Lord in two tables, for the more plaine expressing to vs of his reuealed wyll, which was also his reuealed wyll from the beginning.

Quest. Let vs heare how you giue the vnderstāding of these commandements. And first of these words: I am the Lord thy God, which brought thee out of Egypt, &c.

An. The Lorde vseth meanes hereby to [*A. 6 recto*] drawe them to reuerence in hearkning, in proclaiming his Lordshippe and rule ouer thē in these wordes: *I am the Lord*, and to procure them to free, willing, and louing obedience, in testifying his free Couenaunt of loue and meere Grace, entred with thē, in these words: *Thy God*, And his benefites which for his Couenaunts sake he bestoweth on them, in these wordes: *Which brought thee out of Egypt, &c.*

Quest. The first commaundement, Thou shalt haue none other Gods but me, vnto what duetie doth it appoint vs?

An. Euen to giue to God that whiche to him belongeth: As his due Worshippe or Homage, and honorable Reuerence: Feare and Obedience: Loue and Confidence, Calling vpon his name and Thankfulnes: But if we transferre any of these frō him to any other, eyther God or man, wee committ idolatre.

Quest. Shewe by example. For is it not [A 6 *verso*] lawfull to honour, loue, feare and obey men? Also to make petitions to them, and to thanke them, and so forth?

Ans. Who so prostrateth him selfe to the maiestie of any man, yeelding honour and homage, in respect as he is man only, and not in respect, eyther of some authority or magistracie giuen of the Lord to some, to rule and gouerne as in his steade, or in respect of some grace or gift of God, wherein his glorie appeareth, so that alway the honour may redowne to the Lorde: such an one committeth idolatrie.

And they which receyue that homage & honour, and

[1] " to " blacked out in text after " vs ".

yeelde it not againe into the Lords hands, whose seruaunts they be in their offices & callings, commit idolatrie.

And who so feare and obey man, saue in the Lorde, as to doo that which God haue forbidden, because of the commaundement, & for feare of the strength thereof, committe idolatrie.

And they which loue any thing, as wife [A 7 recto] children, house, lande, mony, foode, rayment and such lyke, otherwise then vnder the Lord, that is, as helpes to their life for a time, and as meanes to sette their minde on the giuer, and not to drawe thē from him, to cause them to desire to liue still on the earth, committe idolatrie.

And they which make any sute or petition vnto man, and do not make sute vnto God first and chefely, and vse that man as a means to serue to gods prouidence, do committe idolatrie.

They whiche trust for helpe in man in tyme of neede, as in multitude of souldiours, skill of the Phisicion, or such like, and truste not only in the Lorde, and vse such meanes as he offer: committe idolatrie, sinning against this commaundement: so likewise of the rest.

Quest. Goe to the seconde commaundement: Thou shalt not make to thy selfe any grauen image, &c.

An. Wee are forbidden herein to worshippe God (though the true God, as we [A 7 verso] wee[1] pretende, vnder any outwarde lykenes, or in any other maner or fashion, then he haue appointed.

Therefor they which will make an outwarde shape to putte them in remembraunce of God, are vaine. For it can not putt them in remembraunce of that it is not lyke, but only it cause thē to remember that fantastical toy, which they haue deuised in their owne brayne, and sett vp for God.

They whiche conceyue or imagine of God, according to the reach of any outwarde sense, as if they thinke him to be like the lyght, or any such thing: sinne against this commaundement.

The inuisible things of God, that is his eternal power and Godheade, are to be seene in his word and workes: but spiritually to be beholden.

They which in the worshippe of God bringe in any representations or ceremonies, to signifie any thing, the Lord in his word not beyng authour of them, as whitnes

---

[1] As text; catchword on previous page is "may".

Three Formes of Catechismes

in a garment to signifie in-[A 8 *recto*]-nocencie, or suche like: sinne against this commandement.

They which in the worshippe of God, whiche is free to all, make them selues bond, and worshippe after the precepts of men, by limitation and course, and not by quicknes of the spirit, whiche stirre vp our minds vnto God according to our present necessitie: sinne against this commandement.

They which submitte them selues in the worshipp of God in his Church, to any such, as to whom he by his worde haue not giuen charge ouer his househoulde to guyde and teache them, and therfore can not guyde nor teach them: sinne against this commaundement.

All these and many more committing other thinges, doo imagine of God otherwyse then he is, & do sett vp a false image and representation of him.

Quest. Proceede to the thirde commaundement: Thou shalt not take the name of the Lord thy God in vayne, &c.

[A 8 *verso*] An. Wee are commaunded here to vse the name of God with reuerence and sobrenes, whither wee haue occasion to meditate or speake of him, or his word wherin he haue declared his name most manifestly, or his workes wherein he haue also ingrauen his name: for as much as the glorie of his wisdome and power, whereby he is and maye be knowne, doth shine in them.

Therefore they which name him when they minde him not, as in any sodaine chaunce of mirth, or at any thing happening somewhat straungely: as if one shoulde saye in such a case (*Lord God is that true*) or such like: they offende against this commandement.

They which vse the name of God in cursings, also in inchauntings: sinne against this commaundement.

They which sweare by any thinge sauing God alone, as thoughe any thing in the world were a searcher of the hart besides God: sinne against this commaundement, & make that thing an idoll.

[B. 1 *recto*] They which sweare by the name of God, without high reuerence and homage yeeldinge, in a solemne and necessarie cause, eyther when the trueth can not otherwise be manifestlie founde out, in respect of the time past: or when wee make a solemne vowe or promise to do anie thing, for the time to come: when the parties to whom wee promise, can not otherwise be assured of our certain care to performe y^t thing. They which sweare otherwise, sinne against this commaundement.

They which turne ouer a trifling matter to lott, calling

God from heauen to determine that, which otherwise most easelie might be determined, sinn against this commaundement. For chaunce there is none, though peraduenture the worde may be vsed not vnlawfully, to note those things whiche come to passe to vs vnlooked for. But in respect of ye Lorde, there is no chaunce, but by his prouidence euerie Sparrowe lighteth on the ground: much more by the same prouidence the issue of euery Lotte is [B 1 *verso*] directed.

They whiche hearing the worde of God, haue their minds otherwise occupied: sinne against this commaundement.

And they also whiche in their readinge do not meditate duely.

They whiche presente them selues at a seruice of God, which they vnderstand not: or if they vnderstand it, it agreth not at all to their state, and they are not edified, and yet they stil frequent the same: sinne against this commaundement.

They whiche singe Psalmes or Himnes of the scripture to passe the time in the middest of their vaine mirth, & eyther vnderstande them not, or applie them not to their owne affections, neither meditate soberly on them: sinne against this commaundement.

They whiche idlelye doo beholde Gods workes, and passe ouer them as things of course, not espying nor meditating Gods glorie which shineth in them: as it is written: The heauens declare the glorie of God, and the firmament shew-[B. 2 *recto*]-eth the workes of his handes, &c: they sinne against this commaundement, and so likewise of the rest.

Quest. Declare the summe of the fourth: Remember that thou keepe holye the Saboth day.

An. The seuenth day is commaunded to be kept holy vnto the Lorde, in spiritual exercises, and meditating of the workes of God, which he made excellent & wonderful, and rested the seuenth day, which hee hath commaunded to be kept apart, to celebrate the remembrāce of his rest, as also to put vs in minde, that we are to rest from our owne workes whiche are euill, that we may do the workes which God will and commaunde. And vnto the Jewes a verie streight obseruing of the day was giuen in charge, because it was to them a shadowing of the heauenlie rest. Vnto vs Christ Jesus hath sett an ende to all shadowes, in whom we beholde our rest and blessednes. Howbeit the seuenth day being sanctifyed and put apart of the Lorde from the beginning, [B 2 *verso*] to other vse then the rest, we are to holde a seuenth day, to cease from our outward labours,

Three Formes of Catechismes

which should hinder vs from hauing both our soules and bodies free vnto the whole attendance vpon the diuine worshippe of God.

Quest. The fifth commandement what doeth it appoint vnto vs?
An. All dueties which we owe vnto anie of those, whome God haue placed vnder him to gouerne vs, whither they be Parentes, Magistrates, Church guydes, or whosoeuer. And the Lorde haue comprehended them vnder one kinde, wherevnto the verie bonde of naturall affection, if anie sparke be in vs, binde vs vnto. Therfore we must giue honour to whom honour belongeth: Feare, to whom feare apperteyneth: Tribute, to whom tribute is due, and all in the Lorde, and for him: As it is written concerning submission to Magistrates: Lette euerie soule bee subiect to the higher powers, &c. Concerning Church guydes it is written: Obeye them that haue the ouersight of [B. 3 recto] you, and submitte your selues: for they watche for your soules. Concerning parentes it is written: Children obey your Parentes in the Lord, for it is right, &c. Concerning Maisters, Seruauntes be subiect to your Maisters with all feare.

Therefore they sinne against this comandement, whiche are stubburne against such, and are aunswerers againe, or goe powting and lowring about their message, doing eye seruice, or constreyned.

Also, they which by anie meannes increase their priuate wealth and gayne with the hinderance of the comon wealth, though they can by some shift stoppe the mouth of a good lawe: yet they sinne against this commaundement in the ciuile Magistrates behalfe, who is appointed for the mayntenaunce of that common wealth.

Also, they whiche being admonished of a sinne, by anie brother in the churche, or anie Church guide, eyther wil not heare him, or if they seeme to heare, yet they nourishe still their sinne within them more secretlie, sinne against this com-[B. 3 verso]-maundement, and so likewise of others. For verie many particulers might be gathered in euerie cammaundenent [sic]. But I mention a fewe of the plainest to auoide tediousnes.

Quest. Declare the meaning of the sixt commaundement: Thou shalt not kill.
An. We are forbidden all violence, and all harme conceyuing or doyng, against the safetie of the life of any man.

Therfore they which hate any man though he be their enemie: sinne against this commaundement.

For it is written: Loue your enemies. Doo good to them that hate you. But wee whom we hate, wee woulde haue made out of the waye. Therfore hatred is the cole whiche kindleth the fire of slaughter. Where it is saide: Do I not hate them with a perfect hatred, which hate thee? &c. In deede we may hate the Lords enemies as sinners, and be angrie against them with ielousy ouer Gods glorie: but as liuing men, we maye not hate them, nor doo any thinge which shoulde tende to the shortning of [B. 4 *recto*] their liues: but committe that to God, & to those to whō he haue cōmitted ye sword.

They which giue checke for check, & taunt for taunte: sinne against this commaundement.

They which are angrie vnaduisedly, much more they which brust out into any reprochful words: sinne against this commaundement.

They which for want of loue, withdrawe their helping hande frō the safetie of the life of an other, when as they may stande in stead to do good therein: sinne against this commaundement.

Quest. Pioceede to declare the seuenth: Thou shalt not committe adulterie.

An. Wee are forbidden whoredom, and all filthines of lust, vnclennes and vnchastnes, which tendeth therevnto.

Therefore they which look on any with the eye of concupiscence, whō they ought not so to looke vpon: sinne against this commaundement, & in hart haue committed adulterie, as Chiist haue spoken.

They which vse vnchaste wordes: also they [B. 4 *verso*] whiche decke them selues delicatelie, or gesture with the body pleasantlie, thereby stirring vp the lust of others, declaring their vnchast, & vnmortified minds: sinne against this commaundement.

Also they which pamper their bodies deliciously, which thing increaseth lust: sinne against this commaundement.

Also they, whiche though they vse no straunge fleshe, but conteyne themselues within the boundes of matrimonie, and yet bridle not their insaciable lust, but vse that thing for a prouocation to sinne, and a meane of inflaming thereof, which was giuen of God for a remedie against sinne, and a meane of quenshing thereof: sinne against this commaundement. And so likewise of others.

Quest. Proceede vnto the eyght commaundement: Thou shalt not steale.

An. Herein we be forbidden to hinder the goods of our neyghbour, but are commaunded to be carefull, that euerie man haue his owne iustlie and truelie, as farr as in vs lie.

[B. 5 *recto*] Therefore besides the common theeues & robbers, they also whiche byte with the sharpe teeth of Usurie & extorsion, sinne more grieuouslie against this commandement.

They which seeke altogither to gather to them selues, and are loth that other poorer and yonger then they, should haue anie dealings to thriue by them: sinne against this commaundment.

They whiche keepe backe the hyrelinges wages, yeares, monethes or dayes, yea but one night, when he needeth it: sinne against this commaundement.

They which take a mans cause in hande, & delaye the same one day longer then by necessitie: sinne against this commaundement.

They which haue inough to liue vpon, and great ouerplus, and playe not the good stewards to dispose where need is: sinne against this commaundement.

They which abuse the necessitie of the Buyer, to inhaunce the price of any thing: sinne against this commaundement.

[B. 5 *verso*] Also, they which abuse the necessitie of the seller, to bring the price vnder foote, and cause the poore to sell their goods, especiallie those which they sell before hand, euen halfe for nought: sinne grieuouslie against this commaundement. And this is a gulfe which swaloweth vp manie a man in a yeare, with his poore wife and children.

They which are idle & labor in no calling, eating the bread which is due to thē only that labor: sin against this cōmandement.

They which do eye seruice, & behinde the backes of thē whom they serue, diminish of their work through slouthfulnes, & yet receiue their wages: sinne against this cōmaundement, & so likewise of the rest.

Que. Go forwarde to expresse the meaning of the ninth cōmandement: Thou shalt not bee a false witnes against thy neighbour.

An. Wee be forbidden by any meanes to hinder our neighbours good name, as by lying, slaundering, backebyting, surmising, or anie such way. But we are com-[B 6 *recto*] maunded to defende, mainteyne, and further the same, as farre as we are able in trueth and right.

Therefore they which haue pleasure to sitt descanting of other mens faultes, when they ought to be otherwise occupied, without care to moue them selues or any they talke with, to auoyde the like:

Also they which disclose those faultes whiche are to bee couered, or to be touched first by due priuate admonition.

Also they which make yᵉ fault seeme greater then it is, eyther for euill will, or because they thinke that another mans disprayse is partlie their prayse, or else doo carpe at other mens gifts to lesson their estimation, thinking that so much is added to their owne: these & such like sinne against this commaundement.

Question. The tenth commaundement what doeth it enioyne to vs?

Aun. To absteyne from all wandring desires, wherby we long after, & fansie those [B. 6 *verso*] things which God haue allotted vnto others, and not to us, though we haue no purpose nor consent of minde, vnlawfully to come by the same, as in the other commaundementes. And wee are commanded louinglie to couet and desire our neyghbours profite and welfare euen as our owne.

Therefore they which seeyng an house or peece of grounde, or such like thinge, of their neyghbours next adioyninge to theirs, and their mouthe water thereat, and they think it were excellentlie commodious, if they hadde it, although they would not haue it without payinge the price, yet offende they against this commandement. For the Lord haue appointed it to their neighbour, to whom often-times it serueth for necessitie in his calling, when it shoulde not serue the other but vnto superfluitie. And so likewise of others coueting anything after this maner.

And this is the Lawe of God, the perfect rule of his righteousnes, teaching vs to leade an vpright lyfe, and requireth that [B. 7 *recto*] we be spirituallie endued with entiere loue towardes God, & our neighbour, which is the accomplishment of the law.

Que. Is it possible that this Law should of vs be fulfilled?

An. No. For the Lawe is spirituall, but we are carnal, solde vnder sinne, & therefore too weake to attayne to this perfection.

Que. Why then haue the Lord giuen vs a Law, and taketh punishment for the breache therof, which we are not able to fulfill?

An. Because the Lorde being perfectlie righteous, could not giue a lawe of anie other nature or kinde. Which lawe in it selfe is possible to be fulfilled, for Christ in the nature of man, haue fulfilled it. But we are so infected with sinne, that as sicke stomaches cann not sauour the moste sauourie meate, and the bleared eyes can not beholde the Sunne: so

Three Formes of Catechismes

can not wee brooke the Lawe of GOD, [B. 7 *verso*] the stomaches of our Soules being alwayes sore sicke of this disease of sinne, and the eyes of our soules being dazeled therewith.

Quest. Is there not then life to bee had by the Lawe?

An. Yes, lyfe is promised to the performers thereof, as it is written: Do this, and thou shalt liue. But because of this mine infirmitie: that commaundement which was ordeyned vnto lyfe, is founde to be vnto me vnto death.

Quest. What profite then chieflie doo we reape by the Lawe?

Auns. This, that we being too blinde in seeing our owne sinnes, and too fauourable in iudging them, shoulde haue this lawe, as a glasse therein to espye the multitude, grossenesse, and owghlines of them: And as a right squire whiche shoulde sette more plainely before oure [B. 8 *recto*] eyes, the crookednes of our pathes, to the ende wee should bee driuen to shame and confusion in our owne selues: and also that we shoulde haue this law (beside a streight examiner and searcher of our wayes) a sharpe condemner also for our so manifolde and euident transgressions therof, therby to driue vs to shame and feare of woe: that thus wee beinge bounde with the chaynes of miserie, might of force be driuen more carefullie to seeke to the fountayne & welspring of mercie.

Quest. If there be nothing to bee looked for of vs at the handes of the Law but death and condemnatione, howe is it that such things are spoken of the Lawe: as that it is perfect, conuertinge the soule, and reioysing the heart, giuing light to the eyes, &c. Also, Thy Lawe is my delight, Giue mee vnderstandinge, and I will keepe it with my whole hearte. Also, Blessed is the man, that hath not walked in the counsayl of the wicked, nor stand, &c.

[B. 8 *verso*] But his delight is in the Lawe of the Lorde, and in that Lawe hee doeth meditate day and night.

An. In those places of Scripture, these wordes, Law, Testimonie, Word, Statute, and such like, are takē for the whole reuealed will of God, cōcerning his couenaunt with his Saintes: And so not onelie for the commaundement, whiche bindeth and bringeth wrath: but therewith for the attonement also by grace & mercie in the Lords annoynted, whiche was a Lambe slaine frō the beginning. Of which welspring of grace & life, our Fathers haue drunck, thogh by shadowing sacrifices ledde therevnto. But wee here speake onely of the lawe of the bare cōmaundements, which setteth our misdeedes in order before vs.

Quest. Are we then all tiansgressours of the Lawe of God?
An. Yea all: As it is writtē, ALL haue sinned, & are depriued of the glorie of god. Also, There is none righteous, no not one, There is none that vnderstandeth: there is none y^t seeketh God. Also, all the imaginations and thoughts of mans heart are only euill cōtinuallie. Yea and this our transgression is more increased bv the giuing of the Lawe, as it is written: The Lawe entred therevppon, that sinne might abound. For although there haue bin all one and the same Law from Adam to Moses, which haue ben since: yet nowe the preceptes being engrauen befoie our eyes, euen as lines drawne out for a writer to direct his writing by, we are the more in sinne, and the more manifestlie conuict therof, for not drawing as it were, the writing of our life & conuersation by those streight lines of Gods lawe.
Quest. Who accuse vs of this sinne and transgression before the tribunal seate of God?
An. Euen this lawe, which draweth out the handwriting of our enditement against vs.
[C 1 *verso*] Quest. Who is the witnes for the confirming the same?
An. Euen oui owne conscience is a thousande witnesses, when the Lorde call it to accompts.
Quest. Who is iudge?
An. The Lorde God a ieleous God, into whose hands it is fearefull to fall. Whose Justice as his Shreife fettreth vs with deadly chaines, and is readie to hale vs vnto execution.
Quest. Vnto the execution of what iudgement?
An. Euen of death euerlasting, which is ye reward of sinne, and the effect of Gods curse, which is vttred against the breakers of the law, as it is written: Cursed is euery one whiche abideth not in all these commaundements.
Quest. This is great woo and miserie. Shall he thus die without remedie?
[C 2 *recto*] An. This is the state of the worlde, and thus are ye innumerable multitude slaine by Gods auenging iustice.
Que. Is no pardon offred them by Gods good grace and mercie?
An. Yes: If they would fall downe, humbling their hartes, and turninge to the Lord, abhorring those sinnes which haue procured his wiath.
Quest. Why doo they not so, especiallie in this distresse?
An. They adde sinne to sinne, treasuring vp wrath so long that by gods iust iudgement, their hartes are still harde and can not repent. Also they are absent from the Lords barre, and are sleping in the middest of their pleasures, when their iudgement sleepeth not, but proceedeth thus against

Three Formes of Catechismes

them. And they may be sayde to be absent, because hauing no touche nor remorse of conscience, they can not bee sayde to heare eyther accusation of the Lawe, or sentence of the iudge. And whē the shrieffe Gods iustice calleth to ven-[C 2 *verso*]geance, they thinke he dallie, and are brought in minde as Adam & Eue were by the Tempter, that they shoulde not die. Such vaine hope haue they, vntyl the sworde of death giue them an euerlasting wounde.

Quest. Who are they then, which escape this deadlie dinte of dreadful iudgement?

An. A remnant saued by the Election of grace, of them selues no more worthie then the rest: but by the Lorde called of purpose, and redemed from out of the worlde, and the abominations of other sinners.

Quest. And how doo they escape?

An. They being present before Gods iudgement barre, heare and see the proceeding of all thinges, by the inwarde feeling of conscience, which is giuen thē by Gods Spirit, as the first steppe and entraunce vnto good. Nowe they beholding nothing, but euen the vndeɪgoing of this terrible iudgement: they fall [C 3 *recto*] downe flatt before the maiestie of the iudge. They confesse their sinnes, & hide thē not. They are ashamed of thē, wherein they hadd pleasure before, & are ashamed of them selues. They hate & abhorre them, for that they haue brought thē vnto this woo. They are angrie with them selues for angring their God, whose frowning countenance they can not now beholde. They thinke themselues most vile & detestable, yea the miserablest of all creatures vnder heauen. Death is before their eyes, & they are holden with ye bands therof. They are plunged in the pitt, & gaspe for breath. They burne in ye fire of Gods indignation, hauing hell in their conscience, and darcknes on euerie side. Thus they sorowe with intire purpose, if they may escape, to leade a newe life. This is the paterne of trew repentance, and this is dying vnto sinne.

Quest. What release then vpon this?

An. Christ Jesus sendeth to thē his Spirit ye comforter, to cheare their soules with [C 3 *verso*] these glad tydings: Come to mee ye that labour and are loden, and I will refreshe you. I haue appeased my Fathers wrath. I haue borne the burthen of your sinnes. I haue nayled your inditement to my crosse. Beholde I haue sent your pardon. Then dreadfull iustice giueth place, and tender mercie take them by the hande, to plucke them out of the pitt. Thus the dayspring from an [*sic*] highe doo visite them, giuing light to them sitting in darkenesse, & in the shadowe of death. Then are the poore penitent sinners raised from death to life, from hell to heauen, hearing the spirite soūding in their [sic] eares of their soules, and readinge their pardon thus: Blessed are they whose vnrightuousnes is forgiuē, and whose sinne is couered. Blessed is the man to whom the Lord imputeth no sinne. This rising from death and quickening by fayth in Christ vnto a newe lyfe, after wee were dead through sinnes, is the second birth.

Quest. By what meanes hath Christe appeased his Fathers wrath, and raunsomed vs?

[C 4 recto] An. By suffering death, euen the death of the crosse, & the torment of hell in soule and conscience. So he bare the burthen for vs, which should haue rested vpon vs, and woulde haue pressed vs downe for euer. His blood was a purging sacrifice of a sweet smelling sauour to God, wherin he smelled the sauour of peace.

Quest. We being thus ransomed and redemed from the power of hell and Satans bands: in what name or title can wee looke for the ioyes of the heauenlie life, seing we can yet bring no desert vnto God?

An. Christ hath also fulfilled the Law, and wrought perfect righteousnes, which he imputeth to vs, wherewith he clothing vs being naked in our selues, he presenteth vs to his father, and maketh vs partakers & felloheires of glorie with himselfe in heauenly places. He also hauing receyued abundaunce of the spirit without measure, powreth vpon vs also of ye same spirit, as it is written: Of his fulnes wee haue all receyued, and grace for [C 4 verso] grace, whereby he Sanctifieth vs to the leading of a nue and holie life, whiche may be cōformed to ye image of his life.

Quest. What natures be in Christ?
An. The perfect nature of God, and the perfect nature of Man.
Quest. Why was it necessarie that our Redemer shoulde be God?
An. That he myght haue full power to sustaine his Manhoode to the ouercoming of death, that he myght not be holden with the bands thereof: which thing passeth mans strength.
Qu. Why was it necessarie that he shoulde be perfect man?
An. Because Man had trespassed, Man also was to answere the trespasse, as the iustice of God required.
Qu. How coulde it stand with the Iustice of God to pardon our sinnes, whereof he spake: The day that thou doest so, thou shalt die the death?
[C 5 recto] An. The Justice of God remaineth vndiminished, in that our sinnes were punished by death and bloodshedding

Three Formes of Catechismes

in him, which bare our iniquitie. His mercie also taketh place, and reioyseth againste iudgement, in y^t they are pardoned to vs, and the debt paied by a faithful suertie.

Quest. How do we receyue Christ Iesus, & applie him vnto vs with his merites, and in him all promises and Amen?
An. By faith.
Quest. What is Faith?
An. It is an especial gift of God giuen by inspiratiō, but not without other means. And may well be called the hande of our soule, which we reache foorth to lay hold of all good thinges, which the Lorde doe offer to vs in his woide.
Quest. Howe then and by what meanes is it wrought in vs, or inspired into vs?
An. God giueth it, or worketh it in oure hartes by his spirit, at the outward hea-[C 5 *verso*]ring of the worde taught by any to whō he haue giuen anie lawfull charge or calling to teache vs ye same: though in some case it be done but by a priuate brother, onelie by the charge of charitie, instructing them whom hee finde to haue neede and to be worthie, as did the scattered Disciples of the Churche in Jerusalem, and prospered in begetting faith.
Quest. By what meanes doeth the Lord assure our faith of his gracious promises?
An. By the same meanes, euen his word, wherein they are conteyned, and from whence they flowe vnto vs, and his spirit quickening vs by the same, & sealing it vnto vs by giuing liuely feeling of the power thereof.
Quest. Hath not the Lorde of bountie yet added further assurāce by outward meanes,[1] for the help of our weak faith?
Ans. Yes: He hath also left vs two Sacramentes, as seales vnto his promises.
[C 6 *recto*] Quest. Which be they?
An. The Sacrament of Baptisme, and of the Lords supper.
Quest. What is a Sacrament?
An. It is an outwarde visible signe by the confirmation of the worde, applied therto, representinge spirituall graces vnto vs, for the tesifying of Gods goodnes towardes vs, and confirming our faith.
Quest. What is Baptisme?
An. The Sacrament of regeneration or newe birth, and seale of our receyuinge into Gods house, the kingdom of Christ, to be one of the number of his, and to be brought vp among them.

---

[1] " meane,s " in text.

Quest. What inwarde grace do the washing with water represent vnto vs?

An. It represents two things especiallie: One is, the washing away of our filthines by the bloud of Christ, as it is written: That he might sanctifie his church, and cleanse it by the washinge of water, [C 6 *verso*] through the worde. Otherwise also it representeth a drowning & ouerwhelming: for euē as one that is ouerwhelmed with water, seemeth to be dead and drowned: but if he peere vp againe, he seemeth to haue escaped death: Euen so all that are baptised, doo vndergoe a certaine representation of death, not therby to die, but by escaping that death, to liue in farre better state, and a more excellent lyfe: so it is said, that our Fathers were baptised in the sea, because that going thorough it as through the valley of death, by that passage they escaped death. So was Christe saide to bee baptised by his death, and we are said to be baptised into the image of his death, whē we being wounded in conscience for sinne, doe dye vnto the same, and forsake it, that wee may liue a better life, euen to rightuousnes, and escape the second death. Thus Baptisme representeth dying, and liuing againe as a newe creature. So is it called the Sacramēt of regeneration.

Quest. What doo the Sacrament of the Lords Supper signifie vnto vs?

[C 7 *recto*] An. Euen as by Baptisme wee are receyued into Gods house, to be nourished as his deare children: so the Lords Supper which we are often to receyue, represent[s] vnto vs the foode wherewith our soules are nourished. Namelie the bread signie [*sic*] the bodie of Christ the liuing Manna, which giueth neuer to hunger more: And the wine doo signifie the bloude of Christ the water of life, whiche giueth neuer to thirst more. And as in our bodies we doo taste these elementes, so in our soules by faith wee doo feede on our Sauiour Christ.

Qu. What certaine marke & tokē haue we to examine our selues, whither wee haue the true faith or no, and whither we be in Christ, & he in vs: or that wee haue but a bare opiniō of these things, and deceiue our selues as the most part of them do, which notwithstanding cal them selues Christians?

Auns. Our certaine marke and seale is the Spirite of adoption, whiche testifieth vnto our spirites, that we be his [C 7 *verso*] children: and by the which we crie bouldly, Abba Father. But if any man haue not the spirit of Christ, the same is not his.

Three Formes of Catechismes

Quest. Howe may wee examine whither wee haue this spirit or no ?
An. By the forcible working of the same in vs. Not onely as feeling some motions of goodnes, which are by the spirite illuminating, and afterwarde by returning to our olde nature, wee quenshe the spirit, and drowne those motions, so that our goodnes proue but as the morninge mist, and our light be but as a flashe of lightning to leade vs for a stepp or two. But the grace of the adopting spirit, giueth light to see, and strength to runne on the race with courage: yea with violence to drawe the kingdome of God vnto vs. It is called fire, because it ministreth heate, and taketh away coldnes of zeale and loue, and it will brust foorth in manifest appearance. And being the anoynting oyle wherwith we are anointed, the smell therof will be sauoured of those [C 8 *recto*] whō we drawe neere. The fruites thereof be loue, ioye, peace, long sufferinge, gentlenes, goodnes, fayth, meeknes, temperancie.

Finallie, if our nature be so withered, and grace so flourishing, that wee hate sinne which wee loued before, and delight in the testimonies of the Lord which were ircksome to vs before: this is a token of the quickning spirit. Also if we obey the Lorde, not in the deadnes of the letter, but in the freenes of the spirit: not by compulsion or constreint of the lawe, or feare of hell: but for thankfulnes to the Lorde for his mercie, and deliuerance, for verie loue of righteousnes, thoughe there were no Deuil nor hell at al. These and such like graces, witnes vnto vs the the [*sic*] possession of the incorruptible seede of Gods spirit. And if we examine our selues duely, wee can not deceiue our selues.

Quest. Are then these workes of him that is regenerate righteous & good ?
[C 8 *verso*] An. Their workes can not weigh in the balance of the Lordes examination, but shall be founde to[o] light. If he shall mark what is done amisse, the most righteous can not stande. For the remnant of sinne whiche is not vtterlie slaine in vs tyll death, staineth our best workes with one euill affection or other. But whome the Lorde receyueth to grace, he accepteth their obedience, & couereth their sinnes with the robe of righteousnes of his deare sonne.
Quest. Are not the graces, and euerie good gift proceeding from God, freelie bestowed vpon his people ?
An. Yes, euen of free grace, without any thing of our part mouing thereto.
Quest. Whereunto then tendeth Prayer which is a chiefe exercise

	of a Christian fayth ? And it is saide: Knocke, and it shall be opened vnto you: aske, and ye shall receyue.
An.	It is our bounde[n] duetie to call vppon the Lorde instantlie, for it is a chiefe [D 1 recto] part of his worshippe, howbeit he knoweth before we aske what wee haue neede of. He both giueth the thinge, and frameth the harte to call for the same, yea & ministreth gracious words and zeale to our prayers. For his spirit helpeth our infirmities, and prayeth for vs with inward sighthings. He semeth some time to delay vs: but it is to stirre vp our feruency. For he is purposed before to giue in due time. So our praier of it selfe procure nothing at Gods hande; but he giueth vs the grace to praye, thereby making vs more fitt to receyue at his hande those things, which he do freely giue.
Quest.	Reherse the praier, which our Sauiour Christ taught his disciples.
An.	Our Father which art in heauen &c.
Qu.	What learne you by these words ?
An.	That wee in confidence of the spirit call God Father, hauing faith to be his children in Christ Jesus by adoption, whereas wee were straungers from him before.
[D 1 verso] Qu.	Why is God saide to be in heauen, whom the heauen of heauens can not conteine ?
An.	Because wee thinke of no place so honorablie as of heauen. And there most glorie appeareth, that our dulle minde might the highlier conceiue of him, whõ no place doeth holde, but the seat of his power is in all places.
Qu.	What aske wee of God in this first petition: Sanctified be thy name ?
An.	Wee desire that the name of God, which is his power, and goodnes, wisedom, mercie and trueth, and whatsoeuer he is known by, should haue dew honour and reuerẽce by vs & others, and that all profaning of his name by vngodlines, may be farre away.
Quest.	What aske wee in the second: Let thy Kingdome come ?
An.	We craue that the Lord would speedelie increase the number of true beleeuers, & faithful worshippers, which may [D 2 recto] be receiued into the fellowship of Gods House, which is his Church and Kingdom, so beyng graft into the bodie of his Sonne: & that he would minister plenty of giftes and graces, and giue his worde plenteously for the welfare of his church, and spreading out the curtaines, and inlarging the bounds thereof.
Quest.	What craue wee of God in the third: Lett thy will be done in earthe, as it is in heauen ?

Three Formes of Catechismes

An. That as he is Lord and King to rule ouer all: so we and others may submitte our selues vnto his will, with renowncing our owne, being readie also to execute his will and pleasure, with like readines, as his Angels in heauen doo accorde and are prest to fulfil the same.

Qu. In the fourth petition what require we : Giue vs this day our dailie bread ?

An. We require at the hands of the Lord whatsoeuer is needful to the vse of our bodies. And so we require it, as acknowledging that we are fedde and sustained day-[D 2 *verso*]lie by his gift, howsoeuer wee come by our sustenaunce. And wee are taught to to[1] [*sic*] require it, as they which knowe they are to liue from hande to mouthe, of the Lords prouision, blessing them in their calling, without greedie coueting of superfluitie, or taking care what wee shall eate, or what wee shall drincke, or what clothes wee shall put on hereafter.

Quest. What aske wee of God in the fift petition: And forgiue vs our trespasses as wee forgiue them that trespasse against vs ?

An. In this and the next wee aske all grace needefull for our soules, namelie, Forgiuenes of sinne in this: and in the next, Grace and strength to perseuere, and to stande immoueable of temptatiō. For in the forgiuenes of our sinnes, consist our blessednes, which is made manifest when we perseuere vnto the ende. When we adde As we forgiue thē that trespasse against vs, it is a note to trie vs, whither wee be fitt to craue forgiue-[D 3 *recto*]nes at gods hande, & if we be single harted without hatred or desire of reuenge, but are mercifull, as our heauenlie Father is mercifull and good, causing the raine to fall and the sunne to shine on the iust and vniust.

Quest. What require we of God in that which foloweth: And leade vs not into temptation: but deliuer vs frō euill: For thine is the kingdom, &c ?

An. We desire that yᵉ Lord would not punish our sinne with giuing vs ouer to sin more & more, but would deliuer us frō sinne and Satan, which are contened vnder the name of Euil here spoken of. And wee require these things vnder the name of asscribing vnto him all rule, power and glorie, whereby wee confirme our selues that he is able to do all things and will graunt all that is for his glorie.

Question. Where do the Lorde nourishe and bring vp his people, vntill they be made a perfect people to be receyued to further glorie ?

[D 3 *verso*] An. In the place which the Lorde doeth chuse to

---

[1] ? "so to", or "to so"

putt his name there: euen his Churche, his Sion where he voutsafeth to dwell, the Kingdome of his Sonne, whiche he do gouerne by the Scepter of his Worde a scepter of righteousnes.

Which Churche houldeth one Law and order vnder her Kinge, and therefore is called Catholike. And the members of the same, holde a happie fellowshippe as the members of one bodie, seruinge one to another by their giftes & graces, & sustaininge one an others neede in mutuall charitie. And this is called the Communion of Sainctes. Vppon this Sion the Lorde makethe to fall the first raine and the later, euen the blessings of his good will. For there the Lorde appointed blessing, and Life for euermore, which, those members of the Bodie of Christ instantly seruing God daie and night, waite to come vnto: hopinge also for the Resurrection of the Bodie, which is sowne in corruption, that both the Soules and bodies of the Lords Elect may partake glorie with Christ Je-[D 4 recto]sus for euermore, after that he hath subdued all thinges, and deliuered vp the Kingdome into his Fathers hande, vnto whome God almightie, withe the Sonne and the holie Ghost, be all Glorie & Praise for euermore.

AMEN.

[ORNAMENT]

[D 4 verso] An other briefer forme of Catechisme, and as it were, the summe of that which went before.

Question. Who created you, and all creatures?
Answere. GOD.
Quest. What is the duetie of you, and all creatures vnto God?
An. To set forth his glorie.
Quest. Howe is that done?
An. By keeping his worde & commaundement, whereby we declare that hee is our Soueraigne Lorde, and haue authoritie ouer vs to commaunde vs obedience.
Quest. Howe doo the dumme creatures keepe Gods commaundement?
[D 5 recto] An. By continuing in that order & state whereto the Lorde by his worde firste assigned them.
Quest. Hath man done so from the beginning?
An. No: For oure firste Parentes brake Gods commaundement, in eatinge the forbidden fruite.

Three Formes of Catechismes

Quest. What befell of that?
An. They became sinful, and haue left vnto vs being braunches of the same roote, the inheritance of sinne, which wee call Originall sinne, or sinne which wee haue by nature and kinde.
Quest. What euill come thereof?
An. This originall sinn is a verie plague infecting all our wayes, so that they bee all transgressions of Gods lawe.
Quest. What doeth the Lawe of God require of vs?
[D 5 *verso*] An. That wee should loue the Lorde with all our soule and strength: and our neighbour as our selfe.
Quest. Are wee not able to performe this?
An. No, in no wise.
Quest. Why was it then commaunded of God?
An. Because it is the rule of perfect righteousnes, agreeing vnto ye nature of god, able in it selfe to be obserued and to giue life: but of vs vnable, because of our sinfull inabilitie.
Quest. What profite receyue wee then by it?
An. This, that we being conuicte of oure sinne more manifestlie by ye Law, wherin as in a glasse we beholde the same, we might be ashamed of our selues, & feare Gods wrath, and so bee constreined to seeke for remedie of our miserie otherwhere, namelie in Christ.
[D 6 *recto*] Quest. You saye that in all our dooinges we transgresse Gods lawe, what cal you that transgression?
An. Sinne.
Quest. What is the desert of sinne?
An. Gods curse, and fierce wrath to the vtter spoyling of soule & bodie by euerlasting death, whose iustice thereyppon calleth for the execution of this punishement.
Quest. What followeth thereon?
An. Then they whose eyes God doo open to see their miserie, beholde themselues lost and confounded, yea euen plunged with waues of woe vnto death. Thē they repent and lothe their former sinne, whiche haue brought vpon them this cōdemnation, and hūblie craue pardon, appealing from iustice to mercie. Then doo Christe Jesus take them by the hande, giue them ease of their burthen, & quicken them by his comforting Spirite, restoring them from death to lyfe, so are [D 6 *verso*] they then made newe borne children.
Quest. By what meanes can Christe reskue vs from his Fathers iustice?
An. Because he offered a sacrifice of his owne bodie and

	bloud to his Father, to make the attonement for vs. And he being perfect man, suffered death: and being perfect God, susteyned him selfe to breake the bands of death.
Quest.	And howe do we attaine to euerlasting lyfe, hauing escaped death?
An.	Christ also hath fulfilled perfect righteousnes, which he doeth impute to vs: and of the fulnes of the spirit, whiche he haue receyued, he sanctifieth vs, and so present vs to his Father, crauinge that we may be partakers of his glorie with him.
Quest.	Howe do we receyue, and applie to vs, Christ Iesus, and all this which he haue done for vs?
An.	By Faith.
[D 7 recto]	Quest. What is faith?
An.	A spirituall gift giuen of God, euen the hande of our soule, which wee reache out, to drawe vnto vs all good thinges which are offered and promised.
Quest.	How is this fayth wrought in vs?
An.	By the inward meanes of the spirit, and the outward meanes of hearing the worde taught.
Quest.	What outward meanes hath the Lorde giuen, for the strengthening of our faith, that we may with more full assurance receyue his promises?
An.	The two Sacramentes, of Baptisme, and the Lords Supper, whiche wee call seales vnto the handewriting of the Lords promise of our saluation.
Quest.	What is a Sacrament?
An.	It is an outward visible signe, by the confirmation of the word applied thereto, representing spirituall graces vnto vs for the testifying of Gods goodnesse [D 7 verso] towardes vs, & the confirming of our faith.
Quest.	What is Baptisme?
An.	The seale of our receyuing into Gods house, being before ye heires of hell. And this is done by a great alteration in vs, namelie, dying to sinne, & liuing againe vnto righteousnes, whiche is our newe birth. Which grace this Sacrament do represent, both in that it signifie a spirituall washing from our sinne by Christe his bloud: And also a drowning & passing through death, that wee might escape a more grieuous death, & liue for euer.
Quest.	What doeth the Lordes Supper represente vnto vs?
An.	Our continuall nourishing after wee be receyued into Gods familie with the liuing breade, & the liuing water, the bodie & bloud of Christ, whereon we feede by faith,

Three Formes of Catechismes

        & grow togither into one w^t him.

Qu.   What seale and marke can we finde in our selues, that we haue this faith, & be in Christ? for al can say they beleue.

[D 8 *recto*] An. The spirit which Christ Jesus do giue as a pledge of our adoption, is a certaine seale. Which spirite if it dwell in vs, the fruit thereof as the heat of a fornace will come foorth. Loue to the Lorde and his worde will appeare, and charitie to our neighbour. Generallie a full alteration we must espie in our selues, that wee are dead to sinne wherein we liued in times past, and now we haue pleasure to exercise our selues in meditating the lawe of God, in Praier, Thankesgiuing, and all the exercises of Christianitie, wholy leading a newe life, and houlding the agreement of godlie felloshippe with the rest of the members, whereof Christ is the heade. And alwaies hauing our conuersation in heauenlie things, that our light may shine, & our life may expresse the praise and glorie of him, & our thankfulnes towards him, who haue redemed vs to the hope of the Resurrection to Eternall Life.

[D 8 *verso*]

An other shorter forme
for weake memories.

Question. What chiefe pointes and groundes do you knowe, concerning your Religion?
Answere. Foure pointes especiallie.
Quest. Which be those?
An. First, my sinne.
      Secondlie, my miserie whiche my sinne bringeth.
      Thirdlie, my redemption & deliuerance.
      Fourthlie, the seale and token of my deliuerance.
Quest. What say you concerninge your sinne?
An. I acknowledge, that I was borne & conceyued in sinne, and therein haue continued all my life, transgressinge Gods commaundementes in all my thoughtes, [E 1 *recto*] words and deedes, being onely euill continuallie, thereby highlie dishonouringe God.
Quest. What say you cōcerning your miserie?
An. I acknowledge that for my sinnes sake, I haue deserued gods curse & fierce wrath, to cast mee soule & bodie into hell fire. And his iustice roareth vpon me as a Lion, readie to plucke me awaye, as a pray to death, hell, & Satan, to whom I am inthralled. And this is y^t woefull

	lake of miserie, wherein I am plunged, in respect of myne owne selfe.
Quest.	What saye you concerninge your redemption?
An.	I do beleue, that by the death & bloudshedding of Christ Jesus, my sinnes are ransomed, and so pardoned, & I redemed from my wofull miserie. I beleeue also that Christ hath purchased life for me by his righteousnes. This is my faith, and herein is my comfort.
[E 1 *verso*] Quest.	What say you cōcerning the seale and pledge of your redemption and saluation [?]
An.	The seale and pledge whereby I examine my selfe, whither I be in Christ or no, is his spirit. For if any man haue not his spirit, the same is not his.
Quest.	Howe knowe you whither you haue his spirit or no?
An.	If the fruit appeare: For the spirite worketh faith, loue, obedience, repētance from dead workes: altering my nature to hate sinne which I haue loued, and to loue righteousnes whiche I haue abhorred. And generallie, it conformeth my life to the image of the life of Christe, that as I professe his name, so I may set forth his glorie by Christian conuersation.

FINIS

V. LETTER ON ROBERT BROWNE, written to " one of London " known only from this quotation in Bredwell, *Rasing of the Foundations of Brownisme* (A 2 verso):

In deede the Lorde hath made a breache amongest vs, for our sinnes haue made vs vnwoorthie to beare his great and woorthie cause. M. B. hath cast vs off, and that with the open manifesting of so many and so notable treacheries, as I abhorre to tell, and if I should declare them, you could not beleeue me. Which because this sheete and many more woulde not suffice to rehearse, I will meddle with no particular thing, to declare it. Onely this I testifie vnto you, I am well able to proue, that Caine dealt not so ill with his brother Abel, as he hath dealt with me.

[Againe towards the ende of that letter, hee writeth thus:] Also I would admonish you to take heede howe you aduenture your selfe to be a meane, to spread abroad any of that parties bookes, except it were more tending to the glorie of God then it is. For in the first booke there is manifolde heresie: and the other vpon the 23. of Matthewe, is a patterne of all lewde frantike disorder, whoso haue eyes to see it.[1] And I do not doubt but that the Lord will yet driue him on to worse and worse, seeing he hath so notably fallen [A 3 *recto*] from him. Giue not your selfe ouer to be abused: the Lorde open your eyes, and giue you grace to take profite by my writing, euen as I do giue it with a well meaning minde to doe you good.

---

[1] The " firste booke " alluded to is probably *A Treatise of reformation without tarying for anie*. The other is *A Treatise upon the* 23. *of Matthewe*.

THE WORKS OF ROBERT BROWNE

I. *A Treatise of reformation without tarying for anie.*

II. *A Treatise vpon the 23. of Matthewe.*

III. *A Booke which sheweth the life and manners of all true Christians.*

These three works are placed together because they appeared at Middelburg in 1582, and are often found within the same volume, as in the one copied below (B.M., C. 37. e. 19).

This contains:

1. A title-page which refers to items I. and III. above.
2. *A treatise of reformation without tarying*, in italic (A 2 recto — C 2 verso).
3. "A Preface of the vse of this Booke which followeth, of the life of Christians", in black letter (D 1 recto — D 2 recto).
4. *A Treatise vpon the 23. of Matthewe* (D 2 verso — H 4 verso), ending abruptly at the foot of the sheet, the words "by reason of trouble the print was staid" being written in.
5. A 1 recto. A new title-page for *A Booke which sheweth* proper.
6. A 1 verso — O 4 recto, *A Booke which sheweth*.

The volume presents many problems to the bibliographer[1]: there are not many known copies, and most of them lack the *Treatise vpon the 23. of Matthewe.* The two copies at Lambeth differ from the British Museum copy and from each other. 31. 6. 18. follows the B.M. copy as far as No. 4 above, though

---

[1] For these see J. Dover Wilson, "*Richard Schilders and the English Puritans,*" *Transactions of the Bibliographical Society*, XI (October, 1909, to March, 1911), pp. 65—134.

A Treatise of reformation without tarying

lacking the words written in. The following two leaves (Sigs. 1 and 2) repeat in Roman type the preceding Black Letter Preface, substituting for the final paragraph the words: "If anie will followe our order, we giue them these rules by the Scripture. Not as though they should seuerallie stande alwayes on eche of them, or keepe this course, but as the matter and their iudgement and discretion shall leade them, so are they freelie to deale". That is to say, the reference to the work on *Revelation* is omitted. The six-line heading (top D 2 *verso*) to *A Treatise vpon the* 23. *of Matthewe* is also omitted, the *Treatise* here beginning with the first paragraph, "Hauing first the knowledge", continuing to the paragraph, "So that in handling . . . lesse labour", and ending with the word "FINIS." Then follows the title-page of *A Booke which sheweth* proper; and the text.

L. 3. 47. has the general title-page, *A treatise of reformation*, the Roman Preface as in the copy above, the specific title-page, and *A Booke which sheweth*; it thus lacks the Black Letter Preface and the *Treatise vpon the* 23. *of Matthewe*.

I. A Treatise of reformation without
tarying for anie, and of the wickednesse of those Preachers
which will not reforme till the Magistrate commaunde or compell them.

The original has the text in Italic and the quotations in Roman. This is reversed in the present reprint.

Twice reprinted, once in America, and once in Britain. The "Old South Leaflet 100" (Boston, n.d., but c. 1882) is accurately printed, though the Scripture references are drawn into the text, and three lines are inadvertently omitted, no doubt owing to the fact that consecutive sentences begin with the word "So". The London reprint (1903) was edited for the Congregational Historical Society by T. G. Crippen: it is admittedly from the American reprint and follows its errors, though it is said to have been collated with the B.M. copy!

[A 2 recto] SEEING in this Booke wee shewe the state of Christians, and haue laboured also in good conscience to liue as Christians, It is maruailed & often talked of among manie, why we should be so reuiled and troubled of manie, & also leaue our countrie. Forsooth (say the enimies) *there is some hiddē thing in them more thē plainly appeareth: for they beare euill will to their Princes[s] Queene* ELIZABETH *and to their coūtrie, yea they forsake the church of God, & cōdemne the same, and are cōdemned of all, and they also discredit & bring into cōtēpt the Preachers of the Ghospel.* To aunswere them, we say, That they are the men which trouble Israel, and seeke euill to the Prince, and not we. And that they forsake and condemne the Church and not we.

First concerning our faithfulnesse to our Prince and Countrie, and what our iudgement is of the ciuil authoritie, we aunswere as appeareth in this Treatise. For their other accusations and slaunders of forsaking and condemning the Church, &c. if our doings will not stoppe their mouthes, nor this booke which followeth of the state of Christians, we purpose by the grace of God, to shewe in an other booke, which shall hereafter come foorth, whether we or they be the rebellious children and a false seede. But for the Magistrate, howe farre by their authoritie or without it, the Church must be builded and reformation made, and whether anie open wickednesse must be tollerated in the Church because of them, let this be our aunswere. For chieflie in this point they haue wrought vs great trouble, and dismayed manie weakelings from imbracing the trueth. We say therefore, and often haue taught, concerning our Soueraigne Queene Elizabeth, that neither the Pope, nor other Popeling, is to haue anie authoritie either ouer her, or ouer the Church of God, and that the Pope of Rome is Antichrist, whose kingdome ought vtterlie to be taken away. Agayne we say, that her Authoritie is ciuil, and that power she hath as highest under God within her Dominions, and that ouer all persons and causes. By [A 2 verso] that she may put to death all that deserue it by Lawe, either of the Church or common Wealth, and none may resiste Her or the Magistrates vnder her by force or wicked speaches, when they execute the lawes. Seeing we graunt, and holde thus much, howe doe they charge vs as euill willers to the Queene ? Surelie, for that wee holde

A Treatise of reformation without taryin

all those Preachers and teachers accursed, which will not doe the duties of Pastors and teachers till the Magistrates doe force them thereto. They saye, the time is not yet come to builde the Lordes House, they must *Hag.* 1. tarie for the Magistrates and for Parliamentes to do it. They want the ciuill sworde forsooth, and the Magistrates doe hinder the Lordes building and kingdome, and keepe awaye his gouernement. Are they not ashamed thus to slaunder the Magistrate? They haue runne their owne swordes vppon the Wall and broken them, and nowe woulde they snatche vnto them the Magistrates sworde. In deede can the Lordes spirituall gouernement be no waye executed but by the ciuill sworde, or is this the iudgement that is written, Such *Psal.* 149. honour shall be to all his Saintes? Is this to binde the Kinges in chaines, and the Nobles with Fetters of Iron, by the highe actes of GOD in their mouthes, and a two edged sworde in their handes? Those bandes and chaines, which is the spirituall power of the Church, they haue broken from them selues, and yet woulde they haue Magistrates bounde with them, to beginne Discipline. They would make the Magistrates more then Goddes, and yet also worse then beastes. For they teache that a lawefull Pastour must giue ouer his charge at their discharging, and when they withholde the Church gouernement, it ought for to ceasse, though the Church goe to ruine thereby. Beholde nowe, doeth not the Lordes kingdome giue place vnto theirs? And doe they not pull downe the heade Christe Jesus, to sett *Col.* 1. 18. vppe the hande of the Magistrate? yea and more then this, for they firste proclaime the names and tytles of wicked Bishoppes and popishe officers, and the Lordes name after: Seeing also the Bishoppes must discharge the lawfull Preachers, and stoppe their mouthes, though the Lorde God haue giuen them a charge for to speake, and not to keepe silence. The Lorde hath exalted Christe Iesus, and giuen him a name aboue euerie name, *Phil.* 2. that all thinges should bowe and serue vnto him, and yet haue they exalted the power of wicked Bishoppes aboue him. Beholde a great and moste wholesome riuer, and yet their pudle wa-[A 3 *recto*]ter is preferred before it. Except the Magistrates will goe into the tempest and raine, and bee weather beaten with the haile of Gods wrath, they muste keepe vnder the roafe of Christes gouernement. They must bee vnder a Pastorall charge:

They must obeye to the Scepter of Christe, if they bee Christians. Howe then shoulde the Pastor, which hath the ouersight of the Magistrate, if hee bee of his flocke, bee so ouerseene of the Magistrate, as to leaue his flocke, when the Magistrate shall uniustlie and wrongfullie discharge him. Yet these Preachers and teachers will not onelie doo so, but euen holding their charge and keeping with it, will not guide and reforme it aright, because the Magistrates doo forbidde them forsooth. But they slaunder the Magistrate, and because they dare not charge them as forbidding them their dueties, they haue gotten this shift, that they doo but tarie for the Magistrates authoritie, and then they will guide and reforme as they ought. Beholde, is not all this one thing, seeing they lift vppe the throne of the Magistrates, to thrust out the kingdome of Christe ? For his gouernement or Discipline is wanting (saye they) but wee keepe it not awaye. And who then ? For most of them dare not charge the Magistrates, but onelie closelie, and with manie flatterings, that they might still be exalted by the Magistrates. They leaue their owne burthen, and crie out that it is not caried by faulte of the Magistrate. So they speake against them, and laye all the burthen on them: but they them selues will not mooue it with one of their fingers. Yea they are bolde also some of them, in open places, so to charge the Magistrate. So they make them enimies, because they saye they withholde the Church gouernement: euen enimies doo they make them to the Lordes kingdome and righteousnesse: and why then do they not wage that spirituall battell against them, whiche is to cut them of[f] from the Church ? For the Scepter and kingdome of Christ is not of this worlde, to fight with dint of sworde, but it is a right Scepter, which subdueth the people vnder vs, and the Nations vnder our feete Hee iudgeth the wicked, and by the rebuke of his worde, he filleth all places with the slaine, and smiteth the Heades ouer great countries.

Psal. 47.
Psal. 45.

Psal. 110.

Now then if the Magistrates be enimies vnto the Lords kingdome, why are not these men better warriars to vpholde the same ? For they giue vp the weapons of their warfare into the enimies handes, and then say, they can not doo withall. By their weapons I meane those whereof Paule [A 3 *verso*] doeth speake, that they are not carnall, but mightie through God, to cast downe holdes, and so foorth: These weapons haue they giuen

2 *Cor.* 10.

A Treatise of reformation without tarying

from thē, for they haue not the Keyes of the Kingdome of heauen to binde and lose, and to retaine or pronounce remitted the sinnes of men, seeing they graunt much open wickednesse incurable among them, and also auouche that it must needes be suffered. Yea they haue given vp these keyes to the Magistrates or to the Spirituall Courtes, and therefore haue no right to call them selues the Church of God, or lawfull Pastors thereof. Christ is at the right hande of God, gone vp into heauen saieth Peter, to whom the Angels and powers and might are subiecte, howe then shoulde his kingdome tarie for the Magistrate, except they thinke that they are better able to vpholde it then he. Yea we must presse vnto his kingdome not tarying for anie, as it is written in Luke, & againe in Matthew, The kingdome of God suffereth violence, and the violent take it vnto them by force. In the throng which is made to escape a burning, would they tarie for the Magistrate to make them a waye, and should not they rather if they could, make a way for the Magistrate? They see that the kingdome of God is with strift and great labor, and yet they will haue it with ease and the ciuill sworde must get it them. Ierusalem (saieth the Prophete) and the streetes and Wall thereof, shall be built euen in a troublous time, and to tarie till it be built without troubles, is to looke for a conquest without going to battell, and for an ende and rewarde of our laboures which would neuer take paines. My kingdome, saith Christe, is not of this world, and they would shift in both Bishoppes and Magistrates into his spirituall throne to make it of this worlde; yea to stay the Church gouernement on them, is not onely to shift but to thrust them before Christ. Yet vnder him in his spirituall kingdome are first Apostles, secondlie Prophetes, thirdlie, teachers &c. Also helpers and spirituall guides: But they put the Magistrates first, which in a common wealth in deede are first, and aboue the Preachers, yet haue they no ecclesiasticall authoritie at all, but onely as anie other Christians, if so be they be Christians. Therefore hath God made these teachers fooles, and these spirituall professours as madde men. For woe vnto you, ye Priestlie preachers and Doctours hypocrites, which are a snare to the people, and fill vp their measure of iniquitie, while ye pretende the Magistrates authoritie. For will anie man else giue ouer his calling, or abridge the full execution thereof, when the

Mat. 18.
Iohn 20.

1. *Pet.* 3.

Luke 16.
Mat. 11.

Dan. 9.

1. *Cor.* 12.

Magistrates forbid them, will they cease the [A 4 recto] teaching or due guiding of their housholdes and charge for their dischargings, and should the labourers in Gods spirituall husbandrie giue ouer and ceasse. For it is Gods husbandrie and not theirs, the Church is his building and not theirs. They are but members thereof if they be Christians, and are not anie way to stay the building, neither is it to tarie or waite vpon them. But these wicked preachers eate vp and spoyle the Lords haruest them selues, and then set open the gapp, as though the Magistrates brake in like wild bores, and spoiled the haruest. They say, beholde we haue a Christian Prince, and a mother in Israel: but can they be Christians, when they make them to refuse, or withstand the gouernement of Christ in his Church, or will not be subject vnto it. If they therefore refuse and withstande, howe should they be taried for? If they be with them, there is no tarying: and if they be against them, they are no christians, and therefore also there can be no tarying. For the worthie may not tarie for the vnworthie, but rather forsake them, as it is writtē, Saue your selues from this frowarde generation: and cast not pearles before Swine, nor holy things vnto dogges: and rebuke not a skorner sayeth the wise man, least he hate thee: and inquire who is worthie, sayeth Christ. He that will be saued, must not tarie for this man or that: and he that putteth his hande to the plowe, and then looketh backe, is not fitte for the kingdome of God. Therefore woe vnto you ye blinde guides, which cast away all by tarying for the Magistrates. The Lorde will remember this iniquitie, and visite this sinne vpon you. Ye will not haue the kingdome of God, to go forward by his spirit, but by an armie & strength forsooth: ye will not haue it as Leauen hidde in three peckes of meale, till it leauen all, but at once ye will haue all aloft, by ciuill power and authoritie: you are offended at the baseness and small beginnings, and because of the troubles in beginning reformation, you will doe nothing. Therefore shall Christ be that rocke of offence vnto you, and ye shall stumble and fall, and shall be broken, and shall be snared, and shal be taken. You will be deliuered from the yoke of Antichrist, to the which you doo willinglie giue your neckes, by bowe, and by sworde, and by battell, by horses and by horssemen, that is, by ciuill power and pompe of Magistrates: by their Pro-

1. Cor. 3.

Actes 2.

Matth. 8.
[Sic.] 7.
Prouerb 9.
Mat. 10.

Luke 9.

Zach. 4.

Matt. 13.

Hosea 2.

A Treatise of reformation without tarying

clamations and Parliamentes: and the kingdome of God must come with obseruation, that men may say, Loe the Parliament, or loe the Bishoppes decrees: but the kingdome of God shoulde be within you. The inwarde obedience to the outwarde preaching and go-[A 4 *verso*] uernement of the Church, with newnes of life, that is the Lordes kingdome. This ye despise. Therefore shall ye desire to see the kingdome of God, and shall not see it, and to enioye one day of the Sonne of man, and ye shall not enioye it. For ye set aloft mans authoritie aboue Gods, and the Preacher must hang on his sleeue for the discharge of his calling. In the 32. of Iob, doth not Elihu holde his authoritie, and durst not account of mannes authorising, though learned, wise and aged, yea the Elders or Fathers of the Church, neither would he spare either Iob or them, or submitte him selfe to them in respecte of his calling. I will receiue no mans person, saieth he, and I will vse no title (or preface) before man, for I knowe not to vse tytles, If I vse them a little, he would take me awaye that made me. But these men name them selues, some the Bishoppes Chaplaines, some my Lordes Chaplaines, and some the Queenes Chaplaines, and call them their Maisters, to whom their calling and ministerie must serue at commaundement. Thus the Lordes spirituall message must be beautified with these tytles of men, (*The right Honorable my Lorde. &c. who is my very good Lorde and Maister,*) Yet Christe him selfe saieth, that the Preachers nowe in his kingdome, have greater authoritie than Iohn Baptist, and Iohn Baptist greater then the Prophetes before him. Therefore if Ieremie was set ouer the Nations & ouer the Kingdomes, to plucke vp and to roote out, and to destroye and throwe downe, to builde and to plante, Then haue we also an authoritie against which if the Kings and Nations doo sett themselues, we maye not be afraide of their faces, nor leaue our calling for them. Howe long therefore will these men take the inheritance from the right heire, and giue it vnto the seruaunt? For the spirituall power of Christe and his Church, and the Keyes of binding and losing, they take from Christe, and giue to the Magistrate. The Magistrates haue the ciuill sworde, and least they should strike them therewith, they giue them the Ecclesiastical also. Hoe say they, If we were Prophetes, or if we were Apostles, then shoulde we preache though the Magistrate forbidde

Luke 17.

Iob 32.

Mat. 11.

Ierem. 1.

us, but wee are but bare Pastors or Preachers, and therefore we must feare their frowning and threates, and keepe silence thereat. But let them speake, Had not the Magistrates, as full and the same power ouer Apostles, as ouer other Pastoures, or were Apostles more exempted from their obedience to Magistrates, then other Preachers? For let euerie soule be sub-

Rom. 13.

[B 1 *recto*]ject to the higher powers, saieth the scriptures. Therefore as they coulde not displace, nor discharge Apostles from their office & calling, no more can they doo lawfull Pastours and Preachers: for whether it be right in the sight of God, to obeye men rather then God, let all men iudge. But to this they aunswere, that

Actes 4.

Peter saied this, being an Apostle: But in deede muste Apostles onelie followe their calling, though menne doo discharge them, and may not other doe it likewise? For as God hath distributed to euerie man the gifte

1. *Cor.* 7.

(saieth the Scripture) as the Lorde hath called euerie one, so let him walke, and so ordained Paule in all the Churches. If then the Magistrate will commaunde the Souldiour to be a Minister, or the Preacher to giue ouer his calling, and chaunge it for an other, they ought not to obeye him, for they haue not the gifte, and God hath called them this way rather then that. Yet if the Magistrate call one of a lower calling to an higher, to the which he is fitt and prepared, he ought to obeye, for God hath calleth [*sic*] him thereto. And in all thinges wee must firste looke, what is the Lordes will and charge, and then what is the will of man. For we

1. *Cor.* 7.

are bought for a price, saieth Paule, and we may not be seruauntes to the vnlawfull cōmaundings of men. And this freedome haue all Christians, that they consider what is lawfull and what is profitable, what they

1. *Cor.* 6.

may doo and what is expedient, and in no case bee brought vnder the power of anie thing, as Paule teacheth

1. *Cor.* 10.

vs. What soeuer doth most edifie, that must we chuse, and auoide the contrarie: and what soeuer is most expedient, that must be done, and so we must applie our selues all vnto all, that notwithstanding we holde our libertie. For if either Magistrate or other would take that from vs, wee must not giue place by yeelding

Galat. 2.

vnto them, no, not for an houre, and this libertie is the free vse of our callings and guiftes, as we see most agreeing to the worde of God, and expedient for his glorie. Therefore the Magistrates commaundement, must not

A Treatise of reformation without tarying

be a rule vnto me of this and that duetie, but as I see it agree with the worde of God. So thē it is an abuse of my guifte and calling, if I cease preaching for the Magistrate, when it is my calling to preach, yea & woe vnto me, if I preach not, for necessitie is laied vpon me, and if I doe it unwillinglie, yet the dispensation is committed vnto me. And this dispensation did not the Magistrate giue me, but God by consent and ratifying of the Church, and therefore as the Magistrate gaue it not, so can he not take it away. Indeede if God take it away for my wickednesse and euill deserte, he may remoue me from the Church, [B 1 *verso*] and withholde me from preaching: but if God doo it not, and his worde doeth approue me, as most meete for that calling, I am to preach still, except I be shut vp in prison, or otherwise with violence withhelde from my charge. For the Magistrate so vsing me can not be a Christian, but forsaketh the Church; and howe then should my office in the Church depende on him which is none of the Church? And the welfare of the Church must be more regarded and sought, then the welfare of whole Kingdomes and Countries, as it is written: Because thou wast precious in my sight, and thou wast honourable and I loued thee, therefore will I giue man for thee, and people for thy sake. And againe he saieth, I gaue Egypt for thy raunsome, Ethiopia and Seba for thee. The Lorde shall therefore iudge these men, and cut them of[f] both heade & tayle, braunch and rushe in one day. The auncient and the honorable men, which take on them to put downe the Lordes authoritie, and to stoppe the mouthes of his messengers, they be the heade, and the wicked teachers which exalte men aboue God, they are the tayle. They are afrayde of the face of the Magistrate, & do flatter and currie fauour with them, and they would haue vs also to doo the like. But ye the Lords faithfull seruauntes trusse vppe your loines as Ieremie, which in your charges haue greater authoritie than Ieremie, as we proued before. Arise and speake vnto them, all that I commaunde you, sayeth the Lorde: Be not afrayde of their faces least I destroye you before them, sayeth the Lorde. For I, beholde I haue made you as defenced cities, and yron pillers, & walles of brasse, against the whole lande, against the Kinges and against the Princes, against the Priestes and against the people. For they shall fight

Cor. 9

Isa. 43.

Iere. 1.

against you, but they shall not preuayle, for I am with you to deliuer you euen to the ende of the worlde. Therefore yee vanishe in vanitie yee wicked Preachers: for knowe ye not, that they which haue their full and sufficient authoritie and calling, are not to tarie for a further authorising. And hath not euerie lawfull Pastor or Preacher his full authoritie? Are they not to teache the whole will of God, and guide accordinglie, and haue they not then their whole authoritie? For herein was Paule free frem [*sic*] the bloode of all menne, because he had kept nothing backe, but hadde shewed them all the counsell of GOD. But (say they) Paule taught them in deede the whole counsell of God, and so maye wee, but we may not gouerne: we may tell the Magistrates, that gouernement is wanting, but we may not take vppon us, to be refor[B 2 *recto*]mers. In deede, did not Paule both in worde and deede testifie his faithfulnesse, did he not in practise as well as in wordes, fulfill his calling? For (sayeth he) you knowe my manner of life: and addeth further, that in seruing the Lorde, he kept backe nothing that was profitable. Howe then shoulde hee keepe backe the gouernement of the Church, whiche is all in all. And in the 35. verse, he setteth himselfe for example, for I haue sheweth [*sic*] you all thinges, saieth hee, howe that so labouring, ye ought to supporte the weake. Noting that hee sheweth in worde and example, not that onelie, but all thinges else, for due guiding of the Church. And therefore let them not flee to their odde disti[n]ction of ordinarie ond [*sic*] extraordinarie, as though Paule might guide the Churche without tarying for the Magistrate and wee may not. For Paule set downe him selfe for an example: and in the 28. verse, and in the 31. he applieth all vnto them, that they shoulde followe him, that they shoulde watche night and daye in teaching and guiding the flocke as he did. Yea they must not onelie preache, but teache them the practise. They muste obserue and doo all thinges which Christ hath commaunded. And the Lorde did not onelie shewe them the Tabernacle, but badde them make it. But these menne will not make it at all, because they will tarie for the Magistrate. Christe is before vs and his Apostles: as Moses a figure of Christe was before them, and yet we must tarie for the Magistrates. And for what Magistrates? For

A Treatise of reformation without tarying

those of our charge, trowe ye, or for those which are none of our charge ? Muste wee not in all thinges looke duelie to our charge, and let them goe which are none of our charge ? For wee shall not giue accounptes vnto God for them which are out of our charge. For we must take heede to our selues, sayeth the Scripture, *Act.* 20. and to all the flocke whereof the holie Ghoste hath made vs ouerseers. But these men teach, that we must let our charge alone, and lay from vs the gouernement thereof, for their sakes which are none of our charge. Shal not these men be hurled out of their place and charge, whiche thus doe mocke with the Lord, and dallie with their charges ? Yea the Lord shall take them awaye with a swifte destruction, and menne shall clappe their handes at them and hisse them out of their places. Euerie Preacher must runne to the Queene and to the Counsaill forsooth, as though they were of their charge, and the Magistrates must plant & reforme al Churches at once. If they be of their flockes, why should they tarie for thē ? [B 2 *verso*] vnlesse they will have the sheepe to force the sheepehearde vnto his duetie. Indeede the Magistrate may force him, but it is his shame to tarie till he be forced. Be ashamed therefore ye foolish shepheardes, and laye not a burthen on the Magistrates, as though they should do that in building the Lordes kingdome, which the Apostles and Prophetes coulde not doo. They could not force Religion, as ye woulde haue the Magistrate to do, and *Song* 8. it was forbidden the Apostles to preache to the vnworthie, or to force a planting or gouernement of the Church. The Lordes kingdome is not by force, neither *Mat.* 10. by an armie or strēgth, as be the kingdomes of this *Hosea* 2. *Zach.* 4. worlde. Neither durst Moses, nor anie of the good Kings of Iuda force the people by lawe or by power to receiue the church gouernement, but after they receuied it, if then they fell awaye, and sought not the Lorde, they might put them to death. For the couenaunte was firste made, as it is written, they made a couenant to 2. *Chro.* 15. seeke the Lord God of their fathers, with all their harte, and with all their soule. And then followe the next wordes which are to be vnderstoode of thē which made the couenaunt, for of them which so sware vnto the Lorde, whosoeuer did not seeke the Lorde God of Israel, should be slaine, whether he were small or great man or woman. And therefore did the whole Congregation of Israel gather them together, to warre against the children of Reuben and Gad, because they seemed to forsake the couenant. Yet woulde not Hezekiah fight against Israel, though they laughed him to skorne and mocked at his doings, for they had not receiued the couenaunt, but their forefathers, and they were nowe called to the couenaunt againe, which the Lorde had disannulled with their forefathers: as it is written, that for a long season Israel had bin without the true God, and without Prieste to teache, and without lawe. Nowe therefore let the wise vnderstande these things, and the Lorde be mercifull, and deliuer vs from these vnreasonable and euill men. For there is no ende of their pride and crueltie which ascende vp and sit in the Magistrates chaire and smite the people with a continuall plague, and such of them as haue not yet gotten the roume, do crie for Discipline, Discipline, that is for a ciuill forcing, to imprison the people, or otherwise by violence to handle and beate them, if they will not obeye them. But the Lorde shall bring them downe to the dust, and to the pitt, as abhominable carkasses, which would be aboue the cloudes, yea which dare presume into the throne of Christe Iesus, and vsurpe that authoritie and calling in his Church, which is opposed and [B 3 *recto*] contrarie to his kingdom and gouernement. This shall appeare afterwarde: In the meane time let them knowe that the Lords people is of the willing sorte. They shall come vnto Zion and inquire the way to Ierusalem, not by force nor compulsion, but with their faces thitherward: yea as the hee goates shall they be before the flocke, for the haste they haue vnto Zion, and they them selues shall call for the couenaunt, saying, Come and let vs cleaue faste vnto the Lorde in a perpetuall couenaunt that shall neuer be forgotten. For it is the conscience and not the power of man that will driue vs to seeke the Lordes kingdome: as it is written againe, Remember the Lorde a farre of[f] and let Ierusalem come into your mindes, for they see the fierce wrath of the Lorde, where the Lordes kingdome is not, and they flee from the same going and weeping as they goe, as the Prophete saieth, because he hath bin angrie so long. But nowe they haue escaped his displeasure, they goe on and stande not still till they appeare before the Lorde in Zion. Yea and the Lords people shall come willinglie in the day of his assemblies, euen his armies in holie

Ioshu. 22.

2. *Cro.* 30.

2. *Cro.* 15.

Ierem. 50.

Ierem. 51.

Ierem. 51.

Psal. 84.

A Treatise of reformation without tarying

beautie. Yet the frowarde wilbe frowarde still, for (say *Psal.* 110. they) Moses and the kinges of Iuda did reforme the Church, and they were taried for, therefore we also must tarie for our Magistrates. Beholde nowe howe the shame of their faces doeth testifie against them, which dare against their consciences, make our Magistrates prophetes with Moses, yea high Priestes as he was and figures of Christ, as both he was and the Kings of Iuda also. Howe boldelie also dare they peruert the trueth, affirming that some which ought to reforme, did it not, because they would tarie for Moses or for the Kinges of Iuda. For did Zacharie (say they) or the Prophet Haggaie, builde of them selues, and not rather call on the ciuill Magistrates and tarie for them? But they knowe not (as men that are willinglie ignoraunt) that their building of the Temple stoode in outwarde furniture of timber, stone, cariage, and therefore had neede of the helpe of Zerubabel the Prince: but our spirituall prouision, as the guiftes, callings, & graces of the Church neede not anie worldlie preparation in such outwarde cerimonies. Therefore we aunswere, that Zerubabel being a figure of Christ, as appeareth in Zacharie the 4. he was to be chiefe in the worke. Neither were they in that worke as ciuill Magistrates nowe a dayes, but as Spirituall guides, representing Christe and his spirituall kingdome. Neither did Haggaie or Zacharie tarie for the Magistrates, but went before them, for in the name of God they com-[B 3 *verso*]maunded them to builde, and the test sayeth further, that they ioyned with them and helped them. So *Ezra.* 5. that neither by worde nor deede they taried and were behinde: yea when the King (whose subiectes they were) commaunded them to cease, they refused to giue ouer the building. This appeareth in Ezra 4. 23. and in *Ezra.* 4. 23. Ezra 5. 1. And before also, because they ceased and *Ezra.* 5. 1. lingered the building, for that the Magistrates were *Hag.* 1. 2., *Hag.* 2. 15. against them, they were sharpelie reproued of Haggai, and it was a most grieuous curse vnto them. Yet dare these menne laye sinne vpon the Prophetes, as tarying & lingering for the Magistrates. And wherefore? Forsooth they did not hewe timber, and carie stones first of all to further the worke. But in deede, were not they firste when they commaunded and the other obeyed, and when they ioyned with them & helped them? For otherwise might Salomon also not to be saied to builde the Temple, but to tarie for others, because he him selfe brought not the stones, neither hewed them, but commaunded others (as the text sayeth) and they obeyed and brought great stones, and costlie stones to make the foundation of the house. But if Zacharie or Haggai had taried, it proueth not that we must tarie for our Magistrates. For both Iehoshua the high Prieste, and Zerubbabel the Prince, were figures of the high priesthoode and princedome of Christe, and also had an ecclesiastical gouernement ouer the Church, which our Magistrates haue not. And further also, euerie lawfull Preacher at this time hath that authoritie of building Gods Church equall with Zerubbabel and Iehoshuah, or rather superior, for they are compared with them, as the 11. of the Reuelation, and the 4. of Zacharie will testifie, and in the 11. of Matthewe, and the 3. to the Corinthes the seconde Epistle, they are preferred afore them. We knowe that Moses might reforme, and the Iudges and Kings which followed him, and so may our Magistrates: yea they may reforme the Church and commaunde things expedient for the same. Yet may they doo nothing concerning the Church, but onelie ciuillie, and as ciuile Magistrates, that is, they haue not that authoritie ouer the Church, as to be Prophetes or Priestes, or spiritual Kings, as they are Magistrates ouer the same: but onelie to rule the common wealth in all outwarde Iustice, to maintaine the right, welfare, and honor thereof, with outward power, bodily punishment, & ciuil forcing of mē. And therfore also because the church is in a commonwealth, it is of their charge: that is concerning the outward prouision & outward iustice, they are to look to it, but to cōpell religion, to plant churches by power, and to force a [B 4 *recto*] submission to Ecclesiastical gouernement by lawes & penalties belongeth not to them, as is proued before, neither yet to the Church. Let vs not therfore tarie for the Magistrates: For if they be christiās thei giue leaue & gladly suffer & submit thē selues to the church gouernemēt. For he is a christian which is redeemed by Christ vnto holines & happines for euer & professeth the same by submitting him self to his lawes & gouernmēt. And if they be not christians, should the welfare of the church or the saluatiō of mens soules, hang on their courtesie? But they aske how we proue that

1. Kin. 5. 17.

Reuel. 11.
Zacha. 4.
Mat. 11.
2. Cor. 3.

A Treatise of reformation without tarying

Moses & the kings of Iudah & the Iudges before thē, were figures of Christ. They know it true, & dare not denie it, & yet to quarel & trifle with the trueth, they must haue it proued. Yea they charge vs as Anabaptistes & denying Magistrates, because we set not vp them, nor the Magistrates aboue Christ Iesus and his glorious kingdome. How often haue we proued by word & writing these matters. For the Scepter shal not depart frō Iuda, saieth the Scripture, nor a law giuer *Gene*. 49. frō betwene his feete, vntil Shiloe come. By these wordes Iacob did prophesie, that one should take the spiritual kingdom & be Lord thereof, namelie Christ Iesus, and euer more one of the tribe of Iuda & house of Dauid, should foreshew the same as in figure, & sit also in the throne of iudgemēt, to declare it more liuelie, and that the throne of Dauid and the raigne of his children did so signifie, the Scriptures declareth, as it is written, In mercie shall the throne be established, *Isa*. 16. & he shal sit vpon it in stedfastnes in the Tabernacle of Dauid, iudging and seeking iudgement and hasting iustice. And again it is written, In steade of thy fathers *Psal*. 45. shal thy children be, whom thou shalt make Princes throughout all the earth. And this is spoken of the posteritie of Salomon, which as figures of Christ, were Lords of the world, though their dominiō in wordly wise was not so large. For all that Psalm is to magnifie the kingdome of Christ which is his church, which was prefigured by Salomon & his posteritie, and by the mariage of Salomon, which shadowed the church & the childrē thereof. And againe it is writtē, that Christ *Isa*. 9. shall sit vpō the throne of his father Dauid, & vpon his kingdom, to order it & to stablish it with iudgement and with iustice for euer. Wherefore was it called the throne of Dauid & his kingdom, but because in a cōtinual course it shadowed out the kingdom of Christ till his cōming. Therefore also are Dauid, Salomon, Iehoshaphat, Hezekiah, Iosiah, and others, set downe in the Scripture as figures. Yea and the euill Kings of Iuda, though not in their wickednesse, yet in that authoritie and calling whiche they should haue rightlie vsed, were figures.

[B 4 *verso*] For they all had their entrance at the East gate of the Temple, at the which the people might worshippe, but not goe in: they might pray for the people, *Ezek*. 46. and by their sacrifices attonement might be made: as

Psal. 20.   it is writtē, Let him remember all thine offerings, and turne thy burnt offerings into Ashes. And againe, Saue Lord, let the King heare vs in the daye that we call. Yea all those Kings were to looke to the Temple, to the building and restoring thereof when it was decayed, as did Iehoash, Iosiah, Hezekiah, and others.

Let them looke the 4. of Zacharie, the thirde of Hosea, and 5. verse, the 33 of Ieremie, and manie other places, especiallie in the Psalmes, and they shall finde Dauid and his children after him, in the throne of iudgement to foreshewe the comming of Christ. And if the high Priestes and Kings of Iudah in their spiritual ministration *Zacha.* 4.   were glorious, because they figured Christ Iesus, & for the glorie of their office were cōpared to two Oliue trees, and two golden Candlestickes, Then also must their ministration be glorious, to whom God shall giue *Reuela.* 11.   power in these latter dayes to be his witnesses. For they also stande before the God of the earth, as it is written Reuel. 11. And if anie man, whether Magistrate or other, would hurt them, the fire of their message proceedeth out of their mouthes, and deuoureth their enimies. Therefore is their authoritie of God and not of man, and much lesse doeth it depende on man, or on the Magistrate. For vpon what man did the authoritie 2. *Cor.* 3.   of Moses depende? yet Paule affirmeth, that the ministration of the spirite committed to all faithfull teachers at this time, exceedeth in glorie the ministration by Moses and the Prophetes before time. Yea the Church hath more authoritie concerning Church *Isa.* 45.   gouernement then Magistrates, as it is written, They shall followe thee, and shal goe in Chaines: they shall fall downe before thee, and make supplication vnto thee. For who knoweth not, that though Magistrates are to keepe their ciuill power aboue all persones, yet they come vnder the censure of the Church, if they be Christians, and are openlie to humble them selues in vnfained repentaunce, when they haue openlie and grieuouslie trespassed. They are in deede to keepe their Royal dignitie, yet keeping that they are to abase them selues vnto God before the face of the Church. *Isa.* 60.   For all powers shall serue and obeye Christ, saieth the Prophete: and that kingdome and nation which will not also serue his Church (for so is the text) shall perishe, and the Nation shall be vtterlie destroyed. And the *Psal.* 47. [*Sic.* 45] daughters of Tyrus, saieth [C 1 *recto*] the Psalmist, with

A Treatise of reformation without tarying

the riche of the people, shall do homage before thy face with presentes. And further it is writtē in Isai: Euerie tounge that shal rise against thee in iudgement, shalt thou condemne, this is the heritage of the Lords seruauntes, and their righteousnes is of me, saieth the Lorde. But *Isa.* 54. all this would the aduersaries shift of, with this aunswere, that concerning outwarde policie we must tarie for the Magistrate: See howe they grope for the wall, as menne without eyes. For when wee speake of spirituall power and authoritie in the Church, doo we speake of ciuile policie, trowe ye? So then they condemne them selues least wee should doo it, that the spirituall power and Ecclesiasticall reformation, must proceede without tarying, but to redress things ciuille, the ciuile Magistrate must meddle, and none is to take his authoritie from him. For we knowe that when Magistrates haue bin most of all against the Church and the authoritie thereof, the Church hath most florished. Woe to you therefore ye blinde Preachers and hypocrites: for ye spread a vaile of darkenes vpon the people, and bring vpon them a cursed couering, because by your policie you hide them vnder the power of Antichrist, and keepe from their eyes the kingdome of Christe. The Lordes kingdome must waite on your policie forsooth, and his Church muste bee framed to your ciuill state, to supplie the wantes thereof: and so will ye chaunge the Lordes gouernement, and put your deuises in stead thereof: but his shalbe alwayes the same, when yours shall chaunge with your wittes, his lawes shall alwayes abyde whē yours shal turne in your hoodes, his hath the same offices, but yours haue newe and renewed offices. Goe to therefore, and the outwarde power and ciuil forcings, let vs leaue to the Magistrates: to rule the common wealth in all outwarde iustice, belongeth to them: but let the Church rule in spirituall wise, and not in worldlie maner: by a liuelie lawe preached, and not by a ciuill lawe written: by holinesse in inwarde and outwarde obedience, and not in straightnesse of the outwarde onelie. But these handsome Prelates, would haue the Mase and the Scepter in their handes, and then hauing safetie and assuiance by a lawe on their sides, they would make a goodlie reformation.

Ex. 25. 29, 40.
Mat. 28. 20.
1 *Tim.* 6. 13.

Beholde the Lorde hath seene this their villanie, and he hath made them despised and vile in the sight of the people. They haue refused knowledge, and the Lorde hath refused them, they shall beare no more the name of his message.

[C 1 *verso*] *Of their wicked aunswere, that they can not remedie things, and therefore they will tollerate.*

Mala. 2.

Mala. 1.

Beholde, the Lorde hath cast dunge on their faces, euen the dunge of their solemne feastes, as of their Christmasse, and Easter, and Whitsuntide, and of all their traditions, receyued from Baal. For in their solemne meetings, then doeth their iniquitie most woefullie appeare. And they haue saide plainlie (as in the dayes of Malachie) the table of the Lorde is not to be regarded. For though hogges and Dogges come thereto, yet who can redresse it: or why should the Communion be counted polluted vnto vs? Thus they pollute my name saieth the Lorde, and yet they say Wherein haue we polluted thy name? In that ye suffer such wickednesse amongest you, saieth the Lorde, and say also that it is sufferable, and can no way be remedied. O goodlie teachers, which eate vp the sinne of the people, and deuoure seelie soules whyle they wil tollerate forsooth: For by tolleration, they make vnlawfull things lawfull: and by a protestation they iustifie all iniquitie. Indeede they be euill say they, but yee must beare with them, for there is no remedie. So not onlie they practise and vse them them selues, and drawe on others by their wicked example, but also commaunde and teache all men the like, yea hate and persecute all those which stande not with them. O notable Protestantes, whiche both witnesse euil & do the same. Darkenes hath certainlie couered vs, and grosse darkenesse hath filled vs, that we could not hitherto espie this great follie. For no wickednesse is tollerable, except for the hardnes of mennes hartes, we yeelde them vppe to their

Isa. 35.

Isa. 60.

1. Tim. 3.

wickednesse. For the Lordes way sayeth the Scripture, is holy, and no polluted shall passe by it. And againe it is written, That the Lordes people (he speaketh of the Church) shal be all righteous, that is, no open wickednesse shal so shew it selfe in the Church, that it shoulde be incurable. For either the parties which offende, shalbe separate, or else they shalbe reclaymed by due admonition. And therefore the Church is called the house of the liuing God, the piller and grounde of trueth. For by the due order therein, Religion and

A Treatise of reformation without 'arying

holinesse is vphelde, and all heresies, euill maners, and wicked examples put awaye. If then anie open wickednesse must needes be suffered, it is suffered in those which are none of the church : as it is written, 1. *Cor.* 5. What haue I to doo to iudge them which are without, doe yee not iudge them which are within? for God iudgeth them which are without. [C 2 *recto*] Knowe ye not (saieth the Scripture) that a little leauen leaueneth the whole lumpe. Howe then shall we suffer but a little wickednesse, whiche indeede is not little if it can not be remedied. Yea Paule would not bee brought 1. *Cor.* 7. into bondage of the least thing that is, and it is horrible iniquitie to be seruauntes to men, that is, when we are bought for so great a price to glorifie God as his free men, that we should be made seruaunts to menne to suffer their wickednesse. Goe to therefore yee tolerating Preachers, this you get by your tolerating, to haue no name amonge the righteous, nor to be of the bodie of the Church. For Ierusalem is called a citie of trueth, and the mountaine of the Lorde, the holie mountaine. *Zacha.* 8. But ye are vnholie, in that ye saye, some pollutions can not bee clensed awaye, but muste needes be suffered among you. And this is a certaine trueth, that where anie open disorder is incurable, there is not the Lords Zion, to the which he is turned to dwell therein: that is, they are not the Lordes Church, ouer whom he doeth raigne to shewe his kingdome and gouernement. For the Lordes kingdome is not as mannes, and his rule in his church is not the rule of man. Man is not able to reforme al things, and in the commonwealthes manie thinges are suffered. But in the Church, though hypocrites which are called the tares, can not bee rooted out, yet no open disorder shall so spreade it selfe, that it can not be remedied. Else should not the Church be called the pillar and ground of trueth, the Lordes resting place, his holie habitation, his kingdome and glorious renowne. Therefore doth Paule call that 1. *Cor.* 5. parte of church gouernement, which is to separate the vngodlie, the power of our Lorde Iesus Christ. For thereby are the Kings bounde with chaines, and the Nobles with fetters of yron, that they may execute *Psal.* 149. vppon them, the iudgement that is written, Such honor bee to all his Saintes. And in deede this is a great honour we haue, as Paule sayeth, that though we walke 2. *Cor.* 10. in the fleshe, yet we warre not after the fleshe. For the weapons of our warfare are not carnall, but mightie through God, to caste downe houldes, casting downe the imaginations, and euerie high thing, that is exalted against the knowledge of God, & bringing into captiuitie euerie thought to the obedience of Christ. So then there is nothing which the Lorde will not breake, if it be against his glorie, neither anie wickednes which the gouernement of his Churche is not able to put downe.

Psal. 45. For the Scepter of Christ is a right Scepter, hee will keepe in awe his [C 2 *verso*] people in this life, and put aparte from them the vnrulie: he shall be Iudge among the Heathen, and fill all with dead bodies, and smite *Psal.* 110. the heades ouer great Countries, and after this life he hath made readie the last vengeance against all disobedience, when the obedience of his people is fulfilled. Howe then dare these menne teache vs, that anie euill thing is tolerable in the Church, as though the church gouernement could not remedie it: yea and so tolerable,
that all men should be brought into bondage
thereby: yea into so foolishe bondage, that
they should protest a thing to be euill,
and so thinke they are excused
to practise the same.

II.

[D 2 verso] *A Treatise vpon the* 23. *of Matthewe,* both for an order of studying and handling the Scriptures, and also for auoyding ¶ the Popishe disorders, and vngodly comunion *of all false christians, and especiallie of wicked Preachers and hirelings.*

Hauing first the knowledge of that tongue and speach, wherein we reade the Scriptures, and being assured eyther by our owne iudgement and skill in the languages, or by the faithfulnes of the Church in receyuing true translations, that the text is not corrupted: we must then looke out the true meaning and doctrine of the wordes.

Proofes of Scripture for the knowledge of tongues, 1. *Cor.* 14. 5, 18. *Act.* 2. 4. *Act.* 19. 6. *Daniel.* 1. 4, 19. &c.

For the credite of the Church in the letter and translation, 1 *Tim.* 3. 15. *Eze.* 43. 11. *Dani.* 7. 1. *Haba.* 2. 2. *Iere.* 30. 2. *Iere.* 29. 1. *Isa.* 30. 8. 1 *Pe.* 1. 19.

For the doctrine and meaning of the wordes, Nehe. 8. 8. 1. *Cor.* 14. 28. *Marke* 4. 34. *Isa.* 28. 11. 1. *Cor.* 14. 19. *Tit.* 3. 13. *Luke* 4. 16.

Then must we searche out wherefore such doctrine is shewed by such wordes, if the wordes be doubtfull, or harde to vnderstande.

For doubtfull and harde wordes, Prouerb. 1. 4, 6. *Ioh.* 6. 60, 63. *Rom.* 6. 19. *Nehem.* 8. 8. 2. *Pet.* 3. 16.

Also we must finde out the agreement and difference of the doctrine from other pointes of diuinitie, and what is the order & following of the matter.

For agreement and difference of doctrines, and for the order, Phil. 1. 10. *Phi.* 4. 8. 1. *Cor.* 2. 13. 2. *Cor.* 6. 6. 1. *Tim.* 1. 7. 2. *Cor.* 8. 7. 1. *Cor.* 1. 5. 2. *Ti.* 3. 15, 16. 1. *Cor.* 14. 29. 1. *Cor.* 12. 8. *Heb.* 5. 11, 12. *Heb.* 6. 1. *Eccles.* 7. 29.

Further we must take heede to all doubtes and questions, that may well be gathered and followe vpon it.

For doubtes and questions, Mat. 22. 43. *Luke* 2. 46, 47. 1. *Cor.* 7. 1. *Tit.* 1. 9, 10. *Ioh.* 3. 10, 11, 12. *Mat.* 15. 16. 1. *Kin.* 10. 1, 3.

Then may we further declare the contrarie thereof, and make both of them plaine, by some parable, similitude, or ceremonie of the olde lawe.
For contraries, parables, similitudes, ceremonies, Tit. 1. 9, 10.   1. *Tim.* 1. 10.   *Phil.* 1. 10.   1. *Tim.* 6. 11. *Gala.* 5. 19, **22.**   *Pro.* 1. 4, 6.   *Hose.* 12. 10. *Ezeck.* 17. 2, 12.   *Marke.* 4. 42, 43.
[D 3 *recto*] But chieflie the **applying** must not be forgotten. For defaultes and erroures, must be improued by the Scriptures, with rebuke, and iudgementes, denounced as there is cause, and the truth must be proued.
For improuing and rebuking, and prouing the trueth, Tit. 1. 9.   2. *Tim.* 4. 2.   *Isa.* 58. 1.   *Ezek.* 20. 4.   *Luke* 24. 27.   *Mat.* 20. 34, 46.   *Act.* 9. 22.   *Act* 18. 28. *Mat.* 3. 7.
Exhortation also must be vsed with confirming and strengthninge of the weaker.
For exhortation, 2.*Tim.* 3. 16.   2.*Tim.* 4. 2.   1.*Thes.* 2. 11.   1. *Tim.* 5. 1.   2. *Cor.* 10. 1.   *Ezek.* 34. 4.
So that in handling of the Scriptures we looke to these thinges, yet not as straitlie to them all, but that by occasion we omitt and let passe some of them. And though we be more carefull in them at the firste, tyll we be skilfull, yet afterwarde it wil be easie to meditate, write, or speake of the Scriptures, with more readines and lesse labour.

Against the abuse of Tongues in preaching.

But somewhat it is meete to shewe the disorders of some in that firste point for knowledge in the Tongues. For their hoctpotch at Paules crosse, or at Saint Maries in Cambridge, must needes be sauced by vaunt of the tongues. Paule doeth wishe, *That they all could speake languages,* therefore these will speake Latin, when no man doeth neede it. *They spake the languages* (saieth the scripture) *as the spirite gaue them vtteraunce.* And you may smell out their spirites by the sent of their Greek or Ebrewe sentences. They cast them foorth, as he that giueth flowers to feede the hungrie, or would make a feaste with the smell of a posie. They spake the languages, in the 19. of the Actes, and also prophesied: and so these speake Greeke and Latin, and I warrant you, doe edifie withall. They gather such stuffe from

1. Cor. 14. 5.

Actes. 2. 4.

Actes. 19. 6.

A Treatise vpon the 23. of Matthewe

Ambrose or Chrysostome, or from some common place booke of Doctorlie sentences.

These Maidens of the Bishoppes, are called to the Pulpit, and their euerie Maiden must hurle to them her dressing out of a hoode. If Iohn London do not sauce it with a Methode of preachinge, if they haue not his Rhetoricke to make the hearers heedfull, welwillers, and teacheable (o pure diuinitie) or if their cookerie be not welcomed with the Beadle & the typstaffe, to bring it to the pulpit, then may it go for no seruis. Their Latin is phisik to make hole the sicke, and their greeke and hebrewe will blesse you frō euill spirites. By these & by their booke of the order of preaching, they may stand before the Queene, as did Daniel before the king. For so soone as they haue stood vp in famouse places, & shewed their vniuersitie degrees, and how wel they become their hoodes, or their skarlett [D 3 *verso*] gownes, and what standing in Cambridg, and reading they are of in the tongues and Doctors: There may then be none like them: then must you needes call thē Rabbie, Maister Doctor, My Lords Chaplen, Maister Preacher, and our Diuinitie lecturer. This Phisicke will heale all at Paules Crosse in one day. For so soone as they haue shewed it and receyued a Dinner, and their honour and the hope of some preferrement; all is made whole, and they goe away as if no bodie were sicke. There be some also which count it a fault in Pulpites, to recite Doctors sentences, or to speake straunge language, and yet will descant vpon the translation, and shewe what varietie there is, least their learning should be hidd. So because they will seeme to fetche nothing from the Doctours or other authours, they will picke out some matter from their owne fingers endes.

Dā. 1. 4, 19

Agaynst vayne Logicke, being their helpe in the seconde point.

Nowe for the other point of searching out the doctrine, they picke it out by Logike. Beware ye Preachers, that ye haue your Logik: that will be good foode for the sheepe. Coulde Ezra giue the meaninge of the Scriptures, as in Nehem. 8. or coulde the people vnderstande his meaninge without your Syllogismes, without Predicables and Predicamentes, and your argumentes of Inuention ? Did he digge out such stuffe from Cam-

Neh. 8. 8.

bridge horned capps? Or because the light of the Scriptures was not great enough, did he fetche the rest from vnder the earthe? Logike is an heauenlie art, saith one, it came from heauen, saith an other, he that handleth the Scriptures saith an other, and hath not gott his Logike, doth defile them with his vnwashed handes. Did euer anie godlie professe their Logike before that Christ came in the flesh, or since his coming tyll the coming vp of Antichrist, was it studied and learned? Was it then nothing needefull, and is it

Col. 2. 8.

nowe so needfull? Doth not Paul speake of Logike, in that place where he writeth of spoilinge by Philosophie, & vaine deceat? For suche vaine Philosophie, or wisdom of men did the false Apostles vse, which the godly did refuse. And by that haue all heretikes, and all the broode of Antichrist both troubled and spoiled vs: for by it is the exercise of prophecie or mutuall edifyinge, also the righte vse of Synodes or generall meetinges, of determining controuersies, of discussing matters, of communinge, disputing, and searchinge out the truth, cleane taken awaye. By that also the people whiche haue not learned Logike, are shutt out and discouraged from talking, pleading, and mutuall edifying in the churche meetinges. I knowe they saye contrarie to this, and affirme that Logike dothe teache vs the way

Pro. 38. 13 [sic, 18. 13].

of disputing and discussinge matters. It is written, *He that answereth matter before he heareth it, it is a follie and a shame vnto him.*

Nowe to reason bye Syllogismes is the cheefe deepenes of their Logike, and they stande altogether in chopping and cuttinge of one an other, in vaine bablinges, braw-

Actes. 9. 22.
Ioh. 6.
Ioh. 8.
Luk. 2. 46.

[D 4 *recto*]linges, and strife of wordes. Paul disputed, but did he vse Syllogismes? Christ also disputed, and had he suche Logike, and when he harde and posed the Doctours, did he shewe anie suche skill? But they answere that the Apostles had no neede in deede of suche helpes as we haue. So belike they wil make them, thoughe they learned not Logike, yet to haue it bye reuelation: and to shewe the vse of it in their preachings and writinges. Nowe suerlie they that picke Logike out of their doctrine or writinges, doe mingle their filthe with sweete water and putt in drosse to beautifie pure

2. Ti. 1. 13.

goulde. When Paul saide to Timothie: *Keepe the true Paterne of wholesome wordes, which thou hast hard of me:* did he bidde him keepe Logike, or learne it out of his

A Treatise vpon the 23. of Matthewe

doctrine? yea rather he sayth: *Proteste before the Lord,* 2. Ti. 2. 14. *that they striue not about wordes, which is to no profit, but to the peruerting of the hearers.* And in an other place he 1. Ti. 6. 20. saith: *O Timotheus keepe that whiche is committed vnto the[e], and auoide prophane and vaine bablinges, and oppositions of science falselie so called.* But they say we can not proue that Paul doth meane Logike in those places, and bring Caluin and Beza and the auncient fathers against vs. We answere, that both here and in the seconde to the Coloss. he condemneth all vaine Philosophie, and especiallie that whereby cheefelie they did striue to vphold their false doctrine, that is vaine Logike. For that only hath those vaine words of art which Paul calleth here κενοφωνίας βεβήλους[1] & it hath onlie those oppositions or contrarie reasonings of one against an other, which he saith are oppositions of science falselie soe named. Soe then he speaketh here of false doctrine, and of a false knowledge and science in vpholding the same, which is Logike: so dothe he in that place to the Coloss. not as Beza woulde interpret it of the three sortes of corruptions: The first of specu- Col. 2. 8. lations, the second of, he himselfe can not tell what, saue that he saith, it standeth vpon custome and fained inspirations: the thirde was of ioyning the Lawe worshippe with the Gospel.

Thus he woulde pointe at Paules meaninge, and doth driue an other waye. For Paul nameth the vanitie & deceatfulnes of Philosophie, & sheweth that that is after mens traditions, after the rules and principles of this worlde, and not after Christ: and so he doeth strike at that strong tree of vanitie, whiche is Philosophie, and the roote thereof which is mannes traditions, or the rules and principles of their worldlie artes. But Beza for one tree hath gott himself three: namelie, Speculations, Customes and Inspirations, and the Ceremoniall worshippe. In steade of Philosophie, which Paule calleth, vaine deceite, he nameth curious speculations: As if one shoulde aske a Hatchet, and he should giue him the Helue[2]. Paule woulde roote out all their philosophie, and Beza but some parte, namelie some curious speculations. For the roote of Philosophie, which is mannes deuisinges and rules, hee maketh two other plantinges of his owne: the one is Custome and Inspirations, and the other the Cere-

[1] That is, vain babblings. See I Tim. 6. 20 and II Tim. 2. 16.
[2] Handle.

moniall worshippe. I graunte that Paule afterwarde forbiddeth and reasoneth against such vayne vsages, and ceremonies of the lawe, and should therefore Philosophie be after them, or according to them (for the worde is *kata*)[1] and not rather they stande and be grounded on Philosophie? If he digge for the roote in the toppe of the [D 4 *verso*] tree, he can not cutt it vp, and while he maketh the ceremonies of the lawe, and false inspirations or worshippinges, to be the roote of vaine Philosophie, he doth no better. Be not all their Syllogismes in striuinges? yet Paul saieth, *The seruaunte of God muste not striue, but muste bee gentle towardes all men, and apte to teache.* But when the Syllogisme cometh, then cometh babbling and contention: for the leafe will shake with the winde, & churlishe wordes are sone moued, by suche boisterous reasoninges. Thoughe you warne such disputers to beware of heat in disputinge, yet they are sooner in the fire, then you can tell howe it kindled. *If the serpent bite when it is not charmed, no better are such babblers.*

2. Ti. 2. 24.

Eccle. 10.

Job disputed with his friendes, but did he vrge them with Syllogismes? Did his proofes walke vppon a *Maior* and a *Minor*, or did two such stumpes beare vp his *Conclusions*? Did the faces of three Moodes out of *Aristotle*, fraye them with their frowninges? Or did he make it blasphemie to denie a Syllogisme? Did he bringe as in a roule the places of Inuention, or was it euil tydings to his aduersaries, that Logick was against them? were both parties filled with Axioms, or did they poure them out in forme of demōstration? Did they make ado for anie simple or compounde proposition, or make anie outcries for want of fine Methodes & handlings of the matter?

But what, saye they, is there no vse of Logike? what saye you then to a thinge, and the Cause thereof? For the Effect is knowne by the Cause, and the Cause by the Effect. So they giue vs foure sortes of Causes, but wee returne them vpon them, as the spillinges of their drunckennes. For the matter of a thing they make the cause of a thing, which is but a part or some vse thereof: and the forme they call the Formall cause, which is eyther the nature or the fashion in the making: and the Ende they call the finall cause, whiche is eyther the vse, or the working thereof.[2] Yet I graunt there

---

[1] This Greek preposition ordinarily means "down," "about," "according to," and less frequently, "after." The more common preposition for "after" is "meta."
[2] See Aristotle, *Physics*, Book II, ch. III.

A Treatise vpon the 23. of Matthewe

be Causes. But when a cause is giuen, must it be written vp for Logike ? If a man shewe an Effecte, could he no where fetche it, but from their Logike Tables ? Is Logike the Trumpet of Gods workes, for they are all effectes: Or doth it shewe his power and holines, as the causes thereof. Who is ignoraunt but that there are Causes ? And will Logike cause vs to knowe the Causes, or can we sett the face thereof, or the eyes to looke them out for vs ?

If one be wicked (say they) it will shewe you the causes of goodnes, or if you lacke wisedome it telleth you also the causes of follie. This is a great commendation, these be sweete wordes for a sicke bodie, but they will giue him no health. For if you want wisedome, Logike doeth onely tell you that there be causes thereof, but this is mocke foole, when I am out of the way, to saye, there is a right way, and not to shewe me the same.

Beholde all their Logike is in names and wordes, without anie vse. These wordes *Consentanie* and *Dissentanie*, *Genus* and *Species*, and other such like be mysteries, because they be Latin. But translate thē into Englishe, and you neede not goe to Cambridge to learne them. Some things agree, say they, and partake togither: If you call not this a secrete, they will byte you or prepare themselues to battle. Some things also differ and [E 1 *recto*] can not well be ioyned, as to saye, a good man is naught. To learne so harde a lesson is worth a Cambridge degree. When things doo differ, as being of an other kinde, you must call them *Disparates*, that is in English, the sortes of thinges which are sundrie, but you marre the game, if you name not their owne worde *Disparates*. You take away their wisedome, if you speake so playne English. O ye Merchauntes, strengthen you[r] hands vnto marchaundise, by this Logike. Can you tell what sortes ther are ? and what sundrie kindes of traffike, and yet were neuer made Graduates ? This is deepe kookerie, not to knowe howe to dresse and make readie all meates, but to knowe what is a Sorte, or what is meant by thinges sundrie, What is a *Species* and what is *Genus*. O the light of Logike, it dothe rippe vp such secretes. It will teache the Carpenter to hewe chippes for trees, and the Souldiour to kill strawes in steade of men. Will any man knowe what is meant by things contrarie, reache vs this meaning, O gentle Logike, lift vs vp this Parable.

What is an exception, and what is diuers, what is a relate, or priuation, or similitude?

But they aske what we say to definitions. Haue you not had, say they, much vse by thē? Likewise haue you not hadd much profit by Diuisions? I answere with Ecclesiastes that I *finde the count sekinge one by one*. But seekinge out bye twoes and by threes their curious Diuisions, I finde out their follie and madnes. Lett a man compasse about, as did Salomon, and turne him selfe and that from his hart, to knowe and to inquire, and to searche wisedome and reason, and he shall see that in light, which Logike doth shutt vp in darcknes. A Definition, they make the right hande of Logike, and a Diuision is the twoe eyes thereof. It is an euill right hande whiche doth allwaies reach forth, and doth neuer laye holde, and they be euill eyes, which looke towards manie thinges, and see nothinge at all. A Definition must haue his *Genus* and *Difference*, and it must shewe you what a thing is. So they saye it must shewe: But who doeth finde it for all their saying? Giue an hungrie man meate, and saye not here is a table whereon meate may be sette. You must shewe a thing by his *Genus* saye they. O deepe wisedome, for by the *Genus* they meane the name of that kinde, which being diuided, hath that thing whiche is defined, to be one sorte vnder it, that is to bee a *Species* as they call it. Marke this and learne nurture, O ye Logike professours. Will you define a hounde, why, call him a dogge, for that is the *Genus*: and lette an horse be named a beast. Can you doo this without Logike? No, no more then the childe can saye Father to him, whome he knoweth for his father, and call him a man, whom he knoweth to stande as a straunger at the doore.

So then when we knowe the kindes and sortes of things, we shall easilie giue them names, but to teache vs onelie, as Logike doeth, that there are names, and there are sortes, and that wee must seeke them out, is to counsell vs not to walke, because we muste bee long time in learning whether our feete will beare vs. Likewise we say of the Difference, which they call an agreemēt or predicable, or the forme of a thing, that we neede not stande on the name, nor care for the helpe of [E. 1 *verso*] Logike therein which doeth onely call for differences, and biddeth vs goe seeke them as if a man shoulde seeke his eyes, or forget his armes whether they hang on his

A Treatise vpon the 23. of Matthewe

shoulders. For what man which would know a thing, would not seeke out the nature thereof whereby it worketh, and keepeth itselfe, which they call the defining Difference: we should seeke out the workes of God, so should we be readie in the kindes and sortes of things, in the Names and Natures which belong vnto them. But nowe their Logike hath helde them so long in learning what they shuld do, that they haue done litle or nothing at all. They demaunde here whether Definitions be vnlawfull. We answere that to name the kindes and sortes of thinges, and to name their natures is not vnlawfull. But their idle arte of Defining is vnlawfull, and to thrust their Definitions as mysteries into our bosomes, or to terme the naminge of thinges, or their natures whereby they are called, by the wordes of their vaine arte, is wholie vnlawfull.

If they aske why we then vse the names, and haue laboured also so much in Defining, we tell them, that wee returne their owne weapons vpon them: not that wee care for such weapons, but because they feare them so much, we haue tryed if they may dismaye them in their follie, and turne them to the truethe. *Salomon* was so wise, yet had hee no wisedome in their definitions, nor vnderstanding of such Diuisions[.] I knowe they saye, yea, because it is written, *That God gaue Salomon wisedome, and vnderstanding exceeding much, and a large harte, euen as the sande that is on the sea shoare. For it excelled the wisedome of all the children of the East, and all the wisedome of Egypt.* But did he (as they saye) excell them in Logike? Their chief Logicians were long after *Salomon,* and til these latter times, as it is euidentlie proued, they haue neither founde out good Methode nor Diuisions the chiefe thing in Logicke, neither true Definitions, neither yet the true forme of Syllogismes. The doctrine of *Salomon* in Prouerbes, Parables, and wyse sayings, with searching out and speaking of the workes of God, as of trees, beastes, foule, fishe, and creeping thinges, and with due and peaceable gouernement, this was his wisedome. *The Countries marueled at him* (saieth *Ecclesiasticus*) nor for his Logike and Rhetoricke, but for his *Songes, Prouerbes, Similitudes and Interpretations.* And *Salomon* him selfe sayeth, That his way of studying and searchinge out of things, was by minding and pondering

1. Kin. 4. 29.

Ecclus. 47.17.[1]

---

[1] This reference is to the Wisdom of Jesus the Son of Sirach, or Ecclesiasticus, in the Apocrypha. The following three references are to Ecclesiastus, in the Old Testament.

them *one by one*, by turning him self to beholde wisedome
and madnes and follie, yea by experience especially:
For he sayeth, *I haue giuen myne hearte to searche and finde
out wisedome, by all things that are done vnder the heauen.*
And to this labour he sendeth them, but not to Rhetoricke and Logike. For this sore labour (saieth hee) hath
God giuen to the sonnes of men, to humble them thereby.
As for Moses learning, which they say was in Rhetorik
and Logike, because he knewe the wisdom of the
Aegyptians, they wolde teach vs that he allowed vaine
Artes: In deede such thinges as were lawfull to be
studied, those thinges he liked: as were the workes of
God, and that knowledge whiche Salomon knewe
better then did the Egyptians. For they [E. 2 *recto*]
had knowledge, but *he hath giuen me* (sayth Salomon) *the
true knowledge of the thinges that are, so that I knowe howe
the worlde was made, and the powers of the elementes, the
beginninge and the middes[t] of tymes: howe the times alter,
and the change of seasons, the course of the yeare, the situation
of the starres, the nature of liuinge things, and the furiousnes
of beastes, the power of the windes, and the imaginations of
men, the diuersities of plantes, and the vertues of rootes: and
all things both secret and knowne doo I knowe: For Wisdome
the worker of all things hath taught mee it.* Soe then the
Egyptians, the Chaldeans, and the children of the East,
the Grecians, and the Romanes knewe such thinges,
but they hadd not the true knowledge. For *when they
professed them selues to be wise* (saieth Paul) *they became
fooles*, and though they wer wise after their kinde, yet
because they wolde not knowe God aright, God gaue
them vp to a reprobate mind. Therfore Salomon had
the true knowledge, & he nameth also what it was, yea
he reckoneth vp all knowledge in this and the next
chapter (I meane the generall sortes, and kinds of all
knowledge, for so must that 21. verse be taken) and yet
Logike and Rhetorike are left out.[2] If they say that by
subtilties of wordes, and the solutions of darke sentences
(as it is in the 8 chapter) is ment Retorik and Logike,
that is interpreted by the firste of the Prouerbes and the
47 of Ecclesiasticus. For by a parable and the interpretation, by the woides of the wise, & their darke
saiynges, he ment as much Rhetorike and Logik, as he
ment that Parables sholde come onlie from *Aristotle*,

Eccl. 7.
Eccl. 2.
Eccl. 1.

Act. 7. 22.

1. King. 4.

Wisdō. 7. 17.[1]

Rom. 1.

Wisdō. 8. 8.
Pro. 1. 4. 6.
Ecclus. 47. 17.

---

[1] The Wisdom of Solomon, in the Apocrypha.
[2] The Wisdom of Solomon 8. 21.

A Treatise vpon the 23. of Matthewe

and wisdome sholde liue and die with him. Yea I saye of those triflinge bookes of *Aristotle* and of all that vaine Philosophie, that God hathe smittn vs withe madnes and with blindnes, and with astonishment of hart, that we sholde not see the follie of them, but dote so much vpon them.

O ye foolishe Disciples of suche heathenishe wiserdes, yee meete with darknes in the daye time and grope at noone daye as in the night. What doth take awaie your hartes, and what doo your eyes aume [*sic* aime] at ? For ye say ye may not looke on holye Scriptures, nor search out wisdome and knowledge, tyll you haue throughlye learned *Aristotle*, or spent your seauen yeares at Cambrige, in studying of the sciences. Then shal you handle the Scriptures with your cleane washed handes. Daniel was so broughte vp you saye, and he learned first the Chaldean speach and wisdome. But reade the text better, and you shall finde, that first he was instruct in all knowledge (that is in all the generall sortes of knowledge) and was well seene in knowledge, and able also to vtter knowledge, and then it is saide, that he was to be taught the tongue and learninge of the Chaldeans. So then he was instruct in all knowledge, and yet knew not their Rhetorike nor Logike. And if they say that the Chaldean learning was in Logike and Rhetorike, their owne prophane authors doe proue them lyars, as also the 20 verse of the first of Daniel. For the Inchaunters and Astrologians were the best learned of those countrie men. And their knowledge was in the starres, and tymes, and natures of thinges, and in the gouernement of common welthes. And of the wise men of Greece and Athens, neither those seauen, wherof chiefelie they boaste[1], neither the rest, had anie art of Rhetorike or Logike from [E. 2 *verso*] Aegypt, or from the Chaldeans: and yet notwithstandinge hadd muche other knowledge from them. Ye haue too long therfore doted about wordes, O ye vaine men, and wearied your selues with your Logik fopperies, and fedd your selues with the winde. Therefor shall the Wynde take you awaye, and vanitie shall pull you awaye. You clense your handes with Logike, you say, to handle the Scriptures purelie: nay rather you haue swallowed vp such filthye stuffe, and haue cast the vomite thereof vpon the Scriptures. You haue

---

[1] The " Seven Sages " (Bias, Chilon, Cleobulus, Periander, Pittacus, Solon, Thales) 620—550 B.C.

fedd also others with those your berayinges,[1] therfore shall the Lord feede you with wormewoode, and giue you the water of gall to drinke.

For their Methode and Diuisions, looke the fourth point. Against their Rhetorike in that point, of doubtfull and harde wordes.

Seinge we say that doubtfull and harde wordes are to be vnderstoode, why shoulde not Rhetorike be needful to this ende? When the disciples sayed, *This is an hard saying, who can heare it*, was it not trowe ye because they knewe not Rhetorike? Let vs heare the trumpe of Rhetorike, it will sounde her owne prayses. If they had knowne an Allegorie or an Hyperbole, they should haue knowne these wordes: *The breade which I will giue, is my flesh.* Speak for thy selfe, O Rhetorike, we wil heare thy sweete voice. Thou wilt tell vs thy Tropes and thy Figures. A Trope is a maner of speaking. Knowe you not the maner or the way to speake? your mother hath not taught you well, the growne wiserdes must become babes againe, for yet they knowe not colours. There is a *Metonomie*, an *Ironie*, a *Metaphor* and *Synechdoche*. These be secrets beneath, who can fetche them vp? An *Hyperbole*, an *Allegorie*, and the harde *Catachresis*. These be deepe waters, who will drawe them out? when I say, this is a riatous citie a carelesse citie, you can not knowe my meaninge, except you knowe a *Metonomie*, A *Metonomie* is a by name, or a nickname. For the citie is put for the people in the citie. So to say *Virgile* for the booke of *Virgile*, syluer for monie, hastie anger, because it makethe vs hastie, he is lost, for his goods are lost: these be *Metonomies*, that is by names or nicknames. And doo we vnderstande such speaches anie whit better, because we call them bynames or nicknames. He that looketh on a wall, can he tell by that where the winde is? What if I shoulde call them chaunged speaches, haue I founde a newe Trope? Or if I call them Parlour wordes, and not Kitchin wordes, doo I make by this two other kindes of Tropes? Will the Parlour or the Kitchin make me vnderstande them the better? Euen so when they say, this speach is a *Metonomie*, and this is a *Metaphor*, they may as well say, that the one came from your elbowe, and the other from your knoockles.

Ioh. 6. 60.

6. 51.

---

[1] To beray is to defile, disfigure, befoul, or abuse.

A Treatise vpon the 23. of Matthewe

[E. 3 *recto*]   To saye, O well done, or, O honest man, to him that is vnhonest, or is vntowarde in his busines, is made a *Trope* called *Eironie*, that is, the way or manner of mocking or iesting, or contrarie speaking. So skorning of wickednes is a Trope of Rhetorike, and wherefore ? Because one skorneth it. So he that rebuketh hath a Trope of rebuking, and he that laugheth of laughing. For there may be a pretie laughter, and why then should it not be a Trope ? If one say to mee, O honest man, and I aunswere, you mocke me, doth he vnderstande my aunswere. For I shoulde haue sayed, you doe Trope me, or you are *Eironicall* towardes me. But to say, you ieste at me, is to[o] plaine. Because iesting speache must needes be made a Trope of Rhetorike. So this speach, *The Elephant would drinke vppe Iordan*, is their Trope called *Hyperbole*, that is ouermuch or ouerloftie. So the name they giue to it, is more harde then it is. For by this, *He is swifter then an Eagle*. And *stronger then a Lion*, is meant, he is verie swift & verie stronge, and if I call it an *Hyperbole*, I do as if I cast away my cappe, that it might seeke me out such mysteries. So this speache, He hath a deepe heade, for he is a wyse man, they make a *Synecdoche*, for the parte is put for the whole, the heade for the whole man. And *Synechdoche* doeth signifie a contayning or houlding within a thinge. For belike the whole man is contayned in the heade. And if they put contayning for meaning, then must it be called the Trope of meaninge. And when I saye, This hande shall doo it, for I will doo it, you must goe seeke the meaning Trope, or the containing Trope, for there is muche meaninge or contayninge in myne hande: yea also in my finger. For if I saye, This finger shall doo it, for this, I will do it, then all my bodie (saye they) is contayned in my finger. And this speache, Giue us this daye our dailie breade, they call a *Synecdoche*, the speciall say they, for the generall. For breade is putte for all outwarde prouision. This is also the Trope of contayning: for breade contayneth all meate, they saye. But if not, and they all will expresse it more handesomely, that all meate is meant by it, then why should it be Rhetorike: For will they call this worde *Meaninge, or to meane* a Trope of Rhetorike. Yea the snuffe of a candle, and the scraping of their Trenchers shal be Rhetoricke.

A *Metaphor* is a goodlie Trope, as to saye, A minde

lightned with vnderstanding, a man set on fire with anger, and boyling in displeasure. This is called the Trope of translation or of carying ouer or cleane beyonde. O witte to stoppe shoes. O Rhetorik farre fetched, euen from the dunghils of *Greece*, those rottē deuisings of vaine Philosophers. To draw iniquitie with the cordes of vanitie and sinne as it were with cartropes, This is translating: for the rope is caried from the Carte, or is taken of the wicked to plucke to them their wickednes. If God say to his people, He will breake the yoake from off their necke, and take the burden from their shoulders, they must goe learne Rhetorike to vnderstande him. It is a Metaphor, a carying ouer, for the yoake is translated from the Oxenecke, and the burden from the Asses backe, to be vpon the people. [E. 3 *verso*]. But if one say, that by the yoke is meant distresse and affliction, or suche grieuous euilles are likened to a burden, then their Rhetorike dooth lose her vauntage. For they hedge vppe the right way that they may take toll of them that goe their wrong way.

And if (I say) a thing is likened or a thing is compared, or it hath an other meaning, must I needes make Tropes of such speaches, as to saye, the lickning Trope, the comparing or the meaning Tropes. For let the meaning be shewed, and wee neede not stande vpon such words. And if they say, we can not know the meaning without such wordes of Arte, I aunswere, that a man needeth not spectakles to see the Sunne shine, and yet their Rhetorike is so farre from being spectacles to see the trueth, that it is rather a couering vnder which they playe Bo peepe, and mocke holydaye with the trueth. Yea alas, many notable witts haue bin euil occupied by it, & trifled away their days both in learning and writing thereof, and in framinge their speache and practise to an Apishe Rhetoricall imitation. If *Tullie* say (*A Citie besieged, distressed, weakened, and spoyled*) this is *Epizeuxis* saye they, wee must imitate this: So to bring in such a figure, they will eyther go cleane from the matter, or else frame the matter tootoo childishlie to it. For *Epizeuxis* is a ioyning togither, or vpon, and whereof? Of a vaine sounde in the ende of a worde. For these foure wordes, *Besieged, distressed, weakened*, and *spoyled*, doo ende all in *Ed*. So a quicke witte, of what soeuer he writeth, or speaketh, must needes imitate this, if it come into his heade: as for

A Treatise vpon the 23. of Matthewe

example, He speaking of Justice will saye, That a Juste man, doeth esteeme, examine, determine, resigne right vnto euerie man. Thus hath he gotte an hobling *Epizeuxis*, And because these wordes, *Esteeme* and *Resigne*, doe not ende in *Ine*, as the other two, he will make them *similiter desinentia*,[1] an other way. For he will saye, that Justice is in esteeming, examining, determining, resigning right and due. Nowe they ende all in *Inge*, and this whisling sounde of *Ing* is made deepe Rhetoricke: yea, an Oracle of so great a power, that if an Orator doe liuelie pronounce it, thē they which heare it, must leape out of their cloathes for delight thereof, and must be as men rauished with such eloquence. Who may not see by this howe vayne their Rhetorik is ? Or who doth not know, that Pith and wisedome must drawe after it wordes and speache, and not the words drawe and rule wisedome, except they meane that the cloathes shoulde putte on a manne, and not a mann his clothes, and that the sadle shoulde beare the horse, and not the horsse the sadle. If wordes do fall out well in speaking, it is because the matter doeth give them[2] But we may not vse preatie speache, as if therefore the matter should be pretie.

If a woman saye of her Sonne which is drowned, My childe, my childe: O my child, he is drowned, this also is made Rhetorike. For the same worde is repeated together as before the same sounde, and that is a Rhetoricall repetition. So the note of the Cuckowe shall be made Rhetoricke, if you repeate it after her. But a dubling againe which they call *Anadiplosis*, they make an other figure from repeating agayne, as also *Anaphora*, *Epistro*-[E 4 recto]-*phe*, *Symploce*, and *Climax*. For *Climax* is the Ladder, or the staire figure, and *Symploce* the infoulding figure, *Anaphora* the Figure of returning and giuing agayne. *Epistrophe* a turning too, or togither. Likewise also *Epanalepsis*, a taking vp agayne, and *Epanados*, a going back againe. In this speache, *This was done by me, by me I say*, a man vnworthie of a deede so worthie, there is a dubling againe of these wordes *By mee*, and this dubling you may not call a repeating againe, but a dubling agayne, for then you make two Figures one. Also, if I say, that I sawe a thing and seeing it, I desired it, and desiring it, I bought it, & buying it I vsed it, then this is *Climax*, this is a ladder

---
[1] From *med. lat.*, meaning a desinence or termination — an ending in like manner.
[2] Clearly a word missing.

to clyme vp into the towers of Rethoricke, and there men shall see you aloft, and say you are in heauen. Also to repeate *What if* in the beginning of sentences, as What if reason will shewe it you, What if your conscience will tell it you, What if your friends will so counsell you? This is *Anaphora*, that is, neyther a repeatinge agayne, nor a dubling againe, but a returning or giuing agayne. O mysteries, O Rhetoricke so faire and so glorious a Ladie, thou art, worthie to be the Queene and the Mother of Universities, such is thy grace, and so gracelesse are they that loue thee not. A man can not say, *What if* thrise togither, but he hath wonne the Garlande, he shal be crowned and beare the ensign of *Anaphora*. It were to[o] long to lay out all their follie: For as they began to wander, so because they returned not, or stoode not still at firste, they haue wandered the further, and the more greeuouslie. If a man crye out againste wickednes, they call it the figure of *Exclamation*, if hee wonder, or make *Lamentation*, or *Intreate*, or *Denounce*, all these are made figures. What should I write of their *Epiphonema*, of their *Aposiopesis*, and *Epanorthosis*, For by those, if a graue or greater matter bee vttered, they followe it with an after crie, and a weaker speache they followe with a call backe, or make amendes: and a high speache, with a keepe silence, or say nothing. When a man sayeth, O cruell murtherer, when a tale is tolde of his murthering, this is that worthie figure *Epiphonema*, and when Christe did weepe ouer Jerusalem, and for grief could not make an end of his words, this was great Rhetoricke, this was the figure *Reticentia*. And to saye, such a one did rebuke, yea rather, he did rayle and brawle, this is *Epanorthosis*, or *Correctio dicti*.

But for all these Figures, and for the rest, I demaunde, Are they wordes onelie, or are they wit and wisedome? They are but wordes of Arte, they saye, yet they teache vs wisedome. Nowe surelie, wordes without witte can shewe little wisedome: and seeing that, as our iudgement is, and we conceaue the matter so the wordes muste followe. It is but follie to learne and shewe wordes in steade of matter. The right vse of these Figures is but to knowe them when wee finde them, but a better vse is, that when we finde them, we leaue them as we founde them, and haue no medling with them. But to seeke them vp, is euen to hawke for flies, or to hunt after mise, because you haue litle else to do. For if one would

A Treatise vpon the 23. of Matthewe

rebuke his brother, must hee seeke to *Paranomasia*, and dis-[E 4 *verso*]-cante on his name, as to chaunge the last letter *R* into *L* and so make him a brothel, or should he devise a *Polyptoton* and saye a brother, of all brethren the worst, which was a good brother, whome nowe the brethren hate, whose doinges are vngracious. Doo you marke this Rhetorike ? For these wordes, *Brother, Brethren, Which, Whom, Whose*: And agayne, *Brother, Brethren* doo make a *Polyptoton*. So also you may make an *Apostrophe*, to the other Brethren, and saye, O ye brethren, be yee witnesses against this our brother. Likewise also to his attire vpon him, as to speak to them, that they doo not clothe him, nor warme him. So may you fetch in an *Aporia*, a *Prolepsis*, a *Permission*, or a *Prosopopeia*. All this is gallant stuffe, and without this can neither Diuinitie stande, nor any point of wisedome or of knowledge be in vs. O woefull delusion. The Lorde hath suerlie bin sore displeased, which hath so long giuen vs uppe to such vayne imaginations.

If the Lorde made the wisedome of those men to perishe, and hid their vnderstanding which were the Scribes and expounders of the Lawe, no maruell if he shewe the thoughts of these men, to be vaine, and the euill imaginations of these heathen Philosophers. Yea howe doe they flie as birdes without eyes, which will followe such wilde Geese for wisedome, and gather after them, as in the ayre, such their wholesome droppinges. They will teache them an *Exordium*, as if one coulde not beginne to tell a tale, except the *Grecian* taletellers had tolde him howe to tell it. You must haue your *Exordium*, saye they, also your *Narration, Proposition, Confirmation*, and then shutte vp all with a seemelie conclusion. If a man must goe a iourney, will he staye it till their Rhetorike bidde him beginne ? Or if one goe to Dinner, must he beginne it with Rhetorik, must Rhetoricke teache one to goe into the Citie, or reach out her hande to helpe to blowe your nose ? For a man can neither write a letter, nor tell a tale, nor discourse of anie matter, but Rhetoricke must shewe him the *Exordium*. It doeth firste teache him to beginne, and then doeth shewe him howe: As if reason, duetie, and experience, should be thrust out, that Rhetorike might come in. For duetie will teache vs to make them *Beneuolos*, whose good will wee ought to seeke, and surelie they haue small good manners, which

Isa. 29. 14.

1. Cor. 3. 20.
Gen. 8. 21.

for Rhetorike sake, and not for conscience sake, doo seeke a mannes good will, or would appease his displeasure. Likewise if we would haue one to knowe a thing, doeth not reason leade vs to tell and shewe that thinge ? Will not the matter make them *Dociles*, or our duetie in vttering it rather then their Rhetorike ? And why should the rule of *Narration* be cleane another from the rule of making *Dociles*, seeing they both doo shewe and tell a matter ? Should one forget to tell his tale or the goodnes of his cause, except Rhetorike did put him in remembrance ? And why rather should hee not forgette his Rhetorike, then to tell his matter, or to make best of his cause. Likewise to proue his cause, or to make a Refutation, and an humble *Peroration*, for these, is Rhetorike so needefull, as to spitte in ones face, is needefull to giue beautie ?

For if Rhetorike proue and confirme, what [F 1 *recto*] should Logike do ? And if Rhetorike disproue and refute, to what vse is Logike ? And wherefore doth Logike shewe the Methode and order of handling matters, as to begin, to proceede, and to conclude, if Rhetorike do the same ? Well, they helpe one another like two good sisters, whiche else should be idle, or haue litle to do. If a man do pleade for his life, will he say nothing for him selfe, will he neither proue his innocencie, nor answere his accusers, nor crie out of their wronges, because he hath no Rhetorike ? Or should the Judges heare him for his Rhetorik, or blame him for not learning it ? Behold they which are wise vnto that which is good, and simple concerning euill, haue no neede of such deepenes. The righteous in times past haue knowen no such wisedome, and in the length of their dayes they sought out no such mysteries. But in these latter dayes, and since the Apostles age, they haue wouen such Spiders webbes for goodlie garments, and wrapped vp such dunghill stuffe for good and precious marchaudise. Yet forthsooth for warranting of such stuffe, *Augustine and Origen, and Ierom*, with such auncient fathers must be brought in.

And was there not a declining euen presentlie after the Apostles times ? Did not great abuses and errours spread verie largelie, both in preaching & guiding the church, and in iudgement, opinions, and manners: in so much that *Anno Do.* 120. there were great and uniuersall disorders almost in all the West Churches, a

A Treatise vpon the 23. of Matthewe

by fastings, mariages, Images, Jurisdictiō, and orders of the church. Also by contention, either in some or in all these, besides other matters. And if they did stagger in these things like the drunken, How shoulde we knowe their vprightnes in Rhetorike and Logike? In the yeere 310. Bishops did clyme aboue Pastours, and Archbishops aboue Bishopps, which though they did many yeres before, yet then it was established vniuersallie, so that the chusing of Ministers, the controuuersie of church matters, the excommunication of men, the reformation of abuses, the determination of Church decrees, were either forced by Antichristian power in some Bishop or Archbishop, or Metropolitan, or by some of their officers vnder them, or else, did wholie hang vpon them alone. Now seeing that all those ancient Doctors or Writers, haue liued in those corrupted daies, and most of them in times more declining then before, and haue lefte also their corruptions to other ages after them, who can folow such halters, to learn to walke vprightlie. Or who can take their iudgement to be sounde about Rhetorike and Logike, which by such vaine Philosophie haue left behinde them so much rotten Diuinitie. How manie foolish toyes, prophane fables, and vile errours be in *Augustin*, *Ambrose*, *Chrysostom*, and others, and what monstrous heresies, and Philosophicall delusions, are forged & maintayned by others, and especially by *Origen*, that Rhetoricall and Logicall mocker. Howe therefore should they leade vs in the light, whiche themselues do grope in darknes? The Lord hath taken such wise men in their craftines and hath also cast away our Counsell, and layed our follie on vs, which would thus be mocked by them.

[F 1 *verso*] *Against their curious Methodes and Diuisions, which is their onelie helpe in the fourth point, for the agreement and difference, and following of matters.*

We see Paules forme of doctrine, & maner of handling thinges. Also the order, which in teaching and writinge, both Moses did keepe and all the Prophetes after him, yea Christ also and all his Apostles. For they did reckon things and laye them togither, and handle them one after one, and so did shewe their difference. Nowe these by their Methodes will set them farre a sunder, to

Phil. 1. 10.	make the better order, and will scatter them by Diuisions, to haue the counte more readie. Paule teacheth vs, *to discerne the thinges that differ*, and he sheweth vs the manner, that is, that we take them before vs, and counte the waye as it were, pase after pase. As firste to seeke and handle one thing, and after that an other, and so the reste, as occasion serueth, and as good discretion leadeth vs, and also to haue eche thing in readines, *that
Phil. 1. 9.	we may abounde in knowledge and in all iudgement*. And therefore the *Philippians* hadde both learned, and receyued, and hearde, and seene in Paule, what things soeuer were true, or honest, or iuste, or pure, or par-
Phil. 4. 8.	tayned to loue, or had good reporte, or vertue, or prayse in them, and were commaunded to thinke on those things as they had learned and seene them in Paule. But did Paule teache them by Diuisions, to leape be-
Ephe. 3. 3.	yonde the middes before they had the right beginning? *I wrote* (sayeth he to the *Ephesians*) *this mysterie aboue in few wordes, whereby whē ye reade, ye may knowe myne vnderstanding in the mysterie of Christ.* So by this writing they might knowe that which did differ from this mysterie, and yet not by Logicall Diuisions. Paule doeth often set downe things, but neuer by Diuisions, though it
Eccle. 2. Eccle. 7.	please them otherwise to charge him. *Salomon* also did seeke out thinges one by one, and by experience, as that whole Booke of *Ecclesiastes* doeth testifie, and the seconde and seuenth chapter especiallie. Howe often doeth
1. Cor. 1. 17. 1. Cor. 1. 22. 1. Cor. 2. 13.	Paule fall into this question of the Rhetoricke and eloquence of the *Corinthes*, and of vaine wisedome, such as the *Grecians* delighted in. In so much that often times, he sheweth the proude face of Rhetoricke, and the poyson and filthines of Logike, and teacheth to handle spirituall thinges in spirituall wise, that is to compare and laye them together, and to iudge them one by an other. They define Methode to be *Dianoian*, that is a deriuing or finding out of one matter by an other. Also they call it a iudging of one matter by an other.

But what wise man woulde call an order or waye, eyther a findinge out, or a iudginge? For an order is the manner of setting or handling anie matter, and the maner of handling is the ryght vse of our counsaile, in applying it to practise. But Judgement or Inuention be cleene an other thinge. For Judgement is an aduising or minding of a thinge, whereby we agree thereto for the reason thereof. And Inuention is a mindynge

A Treatise vpon the 23. of Matthewe

and a ponderinge of thinges, that wee maye knowe the reason and maner of them. [F 2 *recto*]. Now therefore order or Methode is not Inuention, neyther is it Judgement, no more then the worcke of a man, is the man himselfe, or the thinge founde out and iudged, is the findinge or iudging thereof. For Inuention dooth finde out order, and iudgemente dooth iudge order, and they call order the Judgement or Inuention it selfe. Behoulde therefore the Art of Methode is without Methode, and woulde teach others that, which it hath not yet learned. It setteth vp a signe of good order, & calleth others to it, but can not come there it selfe, it is so vnorderlie. Paul did approue the thinges whiche he taught by puritie, by knowledge, and by the worde of truth: let vs see if the Art of Methode can approue her selfe by the truth of her Methode.   2. Cor. 6. 6. 7.

The Definition, say they, must first be giuen, and then must follow the Division, But disordereth [? *sic*, disordered] *Aristotle* made Diuisions and parts of Logike, and yet no Definition was giuen tyll manye hundreth yeares after. Well you must pardon *Aristotle* the master of order, thoughe he kept none order. For he that may teach what he liste, and speaketh all Oracles, maye doo what he liste, but none can finde fault. Logike is called reason, or reasoninge, nowe it is defined to be the Art of reasoning or vsinge reason: But wisdome onlye doth teach the right vse of reason, or of the mynde and vnderstandinge, therefore Logike is made wisdome, and so is made a vertue, and so also is made a part of the word of God, and so also we must haue one Art of one vertue and an other of an other, and for seuen liberall Artes we shall haue seuen hundreth. Againe if Logike be reasoning or disputing, howe can they define it to be the Art of reasoning, or disputing ? For then reasoning is called the art of reasoning, and disputing the art of disputing. For what is *Dialectike* but *Dissertio* or *Ratiocinatio*, & what is *Dialogizesthai*, but *Disserere* & *Ratiocinari*. Also if Logike be wisdome, what *Genus* hath it ? For it must be called a vertue, & not an art. Thus behold the Art of defininge can not define it self. It would giue a *Genus* to eche thing, and appoint all things their Difference, but it hath none at all for it selfe. O poore Logike, thou hast great bagges, and doest promisse much by them, if there were anie thinge in them. Pull out thine hande we praye the[e], and reache a Diuision of Logike, for Definition thou hast none.

Forsoth Logike is diuided into Inuention and Judgement. I shewed before howe both these they doo put for one, and so they make two partes one, and leaue the whole still vndiuided. But I saye that both Inuention & Judgement are partes of counsail, or of mindinge and pondering thinges, and how then will they make them partes of Logike ? except they say that the mindinge, counsaile, and ponderinge of thinges be all one with Logike. For Deuiuising [sic] is a counsail, mynding or pondering of any thinge, so also is Judgment, so also is Remembraunce, Counting, Foresight, Purpose: So also is Conscience, and all agreeyng and consentinge to matters. If, therefore all these be Logike, whye is onlye Inuention and Judgement made the partes of Logicke, and if they put Logicke for reason, and so make it containe the mynding and pondering of things, why is not minding, or pondering set downe for a part of Logicke ? And why is knowinge forgotten ? [F 2 verso]. For knowinge also is a parte of our vnderstanding and reason. For the minde and soule worketh, which is by minding and considering thinges, or hauing founde out anie thinge, it knoweth it, and so hath rest from that labour in searching it.

But looke further into the Methode of Logike, & you shall finde it so patched, as is the cloake of a beggar, and so filled with good order, as is a tubb of kitchin sincke draffe. For inuention, they saye, is that parte of Logike, whiche is in findinge out Argumentes. Soe the difference of finding is finding, as before the Definition of reasoning was the Art of reasoning. Now the Argumentes they make artificiall or without art. So a part of their Art they make to be without Art, and yet will handle it also as belonging to their Art. This is to playe handie dandie, & to turne both sides of the hoode, and to finde witt in neyther. Inuention, they say, is onlye of Argumentes, as if Axioms and Syllogismes had noe Inuention, or as if argumentes were not to be iudged. The partes of an Axiome be founde out, but the ioyning of them together, is Judgement, say they, and not Inuention, as though if the partes be founde, the whole is not found, or as if, when the whole is iudged, the partes wer not iudged. O miserable dotage, how should men thus trifle with learning, except they willingly woulde make it an Idol or ba[u]ble to play with ?

A Treatise vpon the 23. of Matthewe

But see what leaping, skipping, turning and returning there is in their methode?[1] for frō artificial they goe to inartificial, and then turne back to artificial, from that they goe to the first argumentes, as if that were first that hath an other before it: for artificial was first named: or as if first & second, or former & after, did make a diuision, and not rather an enumeration. Then frō the after argumentes, they returne to the former, & from thē they goe to the simple & compared: and setting by comparinges, they come againe to simples: and so they goe dauncing to & fro, through their whole Logik. This method wil not weary thē, for it is a daunce, and they know their turnings so well, that they can neuer turne frō them to goe right on their way. It were toe much to shew all their mockeries, and would require many volumes. Let thē answere to those which ar shewed, or rather let thē be ashamed of them, & trouble vs no further about thē. I thought good to write these things, that in hādling of the scriptures, we might take heed of such vanitye, know that our wisdom to saluation, is by the holy scriptures, & not by vaine Logike, as 2. Tim. 3. 15. Paul doth teach vs. They are able, sayth he, to make vs wise enough, and are *profitable ether for teaching, or improuing, or correcting, or instructing.* And in the Corinth. 1. Cor. 12. 8. he reckoning vp all the graces or guiftes of edifiyng, doth put Logik, and the vaine methodes and diuisions thereof, for none of thē. If then they haue no edifying, let vs leaue thē to their forgers, which would lift vp heathenish fopperies, to ouerlook and trouble vs. If any yet thinke that we are deceaued & out of the way, Prouer. 16. let thē beware of the issue of their owne way, which though it seeme cleane in their eyes, yet death will be the ende, except they returne.

We make hast to shew by exāple, how to meditate & hādle the Scriptures, and could not but breifly touch these former thinges before hande.

Now letting other thinges passe, we come to **the Scripture.**

[F 3 *recto*] Matthewe. 23.

The Text. Then spake Iesus to the multitude and to his Disciples. I said before, That hauing the words of the Text, & knowledge of the tongue wherein we reade the Scriptures,

[1] Interrogation mark as text.

we must looke out the true meaning, and doctrine of the wordes, and for this cause we must be readie and skilfull in the Scriptures, and in the pointes of Diuinitie, which are grounded thereon.

The doctrine therefore out of these wordes, agreeing with other scriptures, and with our 34[1] question, is this.

	That all are called, and may be led to saluation if they will obeye: but especially the Disciples and they of the church. For	How needles *Logike* & *Philosophie* is, to gather the doctrine of these words. They stand first *vpō* the proposition, as whether it be simple or
Ro. 10.	haue thei not heard saith Paule ? No doubt their soūd went out through al the earth, and their wordes vnto the ends of the	copulat, general or special. Now *Iesus spake* say they, this is a copulate and speciall proposition. Yea they will not call it a particular but a proper
Tit. 2.	worlde. · For the grace of God, that bringeth saluation vnto al mē (if they	*Axiom*. For *Iesus* is a proper name, and when the Antecedent is proper, the whole *Axiom*
Psa. 50.	will receiue it) hath appeared. Yea the Lord God hath spokē and called the earth frō the rising vp of the sun vnto the going down thereof. But of Israel he saieth, Out of Zion, which is the perfection of beautie hath God shined. And heare O Israel, and I will testifie vnto thee. Yet again of Israel he saith, All the day long haue I	must needes be so. O foolish *Logicians*, ye conceyue *chaffe*, and bring forth *winde*: ye sowe *follie*, and reape the *fruite of madnes*. For what wit is in this, whether there be an Et, or a neq, or other cōiunction to making a coupling: or whether a thing be affirmed or denied, or be necessarie or happining, or name an other thing, or be named it self, or be general, or haue cōtradictiō. Also they
Ro. 10. Isa. 65. Matt. 22.	stretched forth mine hande vnto a disobedient and gainsaying people. Therfore did Christ sende his seruaunts out into the high waies to cal all that they founde vnto his mariage. And this Gospell of the	teach, that the Antecedent *Iesus* is a cause, and the consequent (*spake*) is an effect. For he is the instrumentall cause of his speach. This is their first part of *Logike* called *Inuention*. O *Wisedome* blowen out of a bladder. Nowe their doc-
Mat. 24.	Kingdome saieth Christe, shall be preached through	trine by morall *philosophie*, doeth teach vs *Magnanimitie*,

[1] *I.e.*, third and fourth instructions in the " order " set out (above, p. 171).

A Treatise vpon the 23. of Matthewe

the whole world for a witnes vnto all nations.

and saieth, It was foolishnes for Christe, to bee so much among the people. The wise Philosophers or famous schooles were more meet for his doctrine, if we count it so worthie.

For doubttfull and harde wordes. Because it is saide, that Christe spake to the multitude or companie, and not to the people, this they say is Rhetorike: It is a *metanomie* the *Adiunct* for the *Subiect*. The multitude or number is put for the People which are numbred and are manie. [F 3 *verso*]. But I saye, Is this a *Metonomie*, that is a byname, or nickname: If one call the people the multitude, or name an Assemblie to be a companie. If names be giuen which doo plainely shewe the meaning, and what a thing is, why should they be called nicknames? Or why shoulde multitude or companie be put for people? As though the people were not a multitude or companie when they are assembled? If ten friendes be mett, and they are all called by this name *Iohn*, thē a man may speak ten pointes of Rhetorike at once, if he say the ten men are together, meaning the ten friends. For to saye men for so manie *Iohns* is their *Synecdoche*, the generall for the speciall. And then they make euerie generall an efficient, or materiall cause of euerie speciall: and therefore to say, men for *Iohns*, is a *Metanomie*, the cause for the effect. Yea and they canne picke out both these two sortes of *Metanomies* in this worde *Men*, and also their *Katachresis*, for howe should men be put for friendes, but by the Trope so called.

Thus they make mountaines of Moulhilles, and turne the droppes into riuers, and out of motes, will fetche the whole worlde, as also some of their Philosophers taught them. Yea and what will they not finde out by such foolishe descanting.

For the difference of the doctrine from other poinres [sic] of diuinitie, and for the agreement of the same. We see that Christ speak-

The Methode by Logike, howe this doctrine is to be handled. when they haue their Thesis, as such a sentence, that GOD *calleth all menne to*

eth to all, but chieflie to his Disciples : All are called to the trueth, but chieflie the Church. For the seede of the worde is sowne in the world but where it taketh, it is made the Lordes vineyarde, they are planted in his vineyarde that is, they are ioyned to his Church and people, whosoeuer receyue this seede as good grounde, and bring forth fruite worthie of the same.

Mat. 13. 38.
Mat. 21. 33.

Nowe, howe must wee followe on this doctrine, not for applyinge firste (for that doeth come after) but for better knowledge. He that will thorowlie speake of this, how men are called and shold be fedde vnto happines, is to speake of the meanes of saluatiō and happines, and so is to shewe howe it cōmeth to passe that we are called [F 4 recto] or taught by the worde, and what doth follow after, or vpon that calling and teaching. For the Lord did thinke on vs in our miserie, & tooke coūsail: he did still remēber vs, and his bowels were troubled for vs. Yea he is gracious & merciful, slowe to anger, and of great kindnes: therfore he remēbred his couenaunt and promise made to a thousand generations. So hath he giuen

Mica 4.

Iere. 31.

Joel. 2.

Psa. 105.

Isa. 49.

laye holde of their saluation, they runne to their Topicke places, to fetche their Diuinitie. For their foure sortes of causes, will finde you out all mysteries: as it is written in their Prophete, so well renowned for his honestie and chastitie: Foelix qui potuit rerum cognoscere causas.[1] *If they giue the efficient cause of our calling as the mercie of God, what shall we saye of his loue, of his purpose and counsaile, of our predestination & free election, and to finde out these, what neede we seeke to Logike ? For the groundes of Religion will teache vs these things. Not because that Logike doeth helpe vs to finde them out, but because the readie way is by reckoning and following things one by one. As for example, it commeth thus to passe, that God doeth call vs to happines. Firste, God did knowe that we woulde sinne and become vnhappie, before he made vs. Yea, he knewe and doeth knowe our miserie and sinne.* So hee did pitie our state, and is still mooued with mercie and loue towardes men, the worke of his handes: not for mans sake, but for his Sonnes sake. Hee hath foreseene and purposed by him to remedie our miserie. So hee hath chosen and predestinate vs to saluation. He gaue his Sonne for vs, who being God, became

---

[1] It is interesting to note that both Browne and Francis Bacon cite this passage. See Virgil, *Georgics*, II, 490.

A Treatise vpon the 23. of Matthewe

Rom. 8. his Sonne for a light of the Gentiles, that hee might be the saluation vnto the end of the earth. And those whō he knew before he hath also predestinate to be made like to the image of his son.

Rom. 8. Moreouer, whom he predestinate, them also he called, and whō he called, thē also he iustified, and whom he iustified, them also he glorified. If thē the Lord haue appointed vs to glorie, he will suerelie call vs, we shall heare

Luk. 16. Moses & the Prophets, and if we regarde not them we will not beleeue, though one should rise from the dead againe.

also man. He suffered our miseries for vs: He ouercame and tooke them awaye. Hee restored vs to happines with him selfe. And nowe hee calleth all menne, and would leade them to this happines, if they would obeye. Thus it appeareth both plainelie and in order, howe our callinge and leading to happines, doth agree with that doctrine, whiche is to goe before it.

But if wee seeke to Logike for the foure sortes of causes, or for order and following, wee shall finde manie wordes, but little matter, and manie Diuisions, but nothing ioyned, or duely framed togither.

Thus by the Scriptures we lay downe that doctrine, which is to go before. For we speaking of calling or teaching, do speake of the meanes of our happines. And then hauing all such meanes, and euery point verie readilie in our mindes, we shall knowe the order, agrement, and following of euerie thing the better. For the Lorde did knowe our miserie, and the remedie of it, and was mindfull of the same. Therfore we begin with his *Knowledge, and mindefulnes of vs.* Then followeth, *His mercie, and loue in Christ, his Will and Counsell, his Foresight and Purpose to helpe vs, his Chusing and Predestinating of vs to be saued, his Sending and giuing of his Sonne, Christ Iesus, who became man. who suffered our miseries, who ouercame and tooke them away, who restored happines.* And then commeth this point, *Howe he calleth and leadeth vs to happines.* Nowe that whiche followeth this point, is to be stoode on also. Not that wee must binde our selues to doo thus alwayes, for we may shewe, or leaue vnshewen, both that which is before a thing, and that which followeth: except wee will searche out the order, and gather further knowledge, for meditation or edifying.

Therefore our calling and leading to happines is thus: Firste, *God doeth Plante and gather his Church vnder one kinde of gouernement,* [F 4 verso] *he maketh a couenaũt with it, and doeth promisse to be God and Sauiour vnto it, he giueth his promisses to the seede of the church, he giueth it his spirit, he receaueth it to suffer and dye vnto sinne by repentaunce, he giueth Baptisme as a seale of this suffering and repentaunce, he receaueth it to one communion of graces in the church, as first to attonemẽt by the Priesthoode of Christ*: *By this his Priesthoode he is our Mediatour, and prayeth for vs, our sinnes are forgiuẽ vs, wee are Iustified and Sanctified. Also by his Prophecie he receaueth vs to Instruction and knowledge, hee teacheth and appointeth vs our duties. Also by his Kingdome and rule, he ouerseeth and trieth out our faultinges, he rebuketh vs, and separateth from vs all those, which are wilfull and greuous offenders. Also we are called and led vnto happines, by all those graces and offices, which are from Christ, and Vnder Christ.* All these thinges we handle in our booke of diuinitie, from the 23 question to the 82 question[1]. Some will say, that if we handle all these thinges, we shall goe from the matter. In deed we shal do so if we stand not on them, ether for the order only, that it maye leade vs to the matter, or for knowledge thereof howe it shoulde bee and what vse there is of it. Therefore both the order and the vse of this doctrine we speake of, will be plaine, if we search out as before, how it cometh to passe that we are called, and taught the will of God, and what be the partes and pointes of this calling, firste in planting and gathering of the Church, and then in a further building thereof. But afore we can either meditate or speake of this thing roundlie, we must knowe the thinges before, and also their contraries, and be readie to count and giue thẽ without anie staye. Thus shall wee finde out those deepe pointes of Logike without the arte of Logike, euen the right order without their curious Methodes, and howe to frame proofes without their Sylogismes, also eche true saying and doctrine without their goodlie Axioms, and lastlie, all things belonging to the matter, and eche point agreeing thereto, or disagreeing from it, without their places of Inuentiõ. For the order should be, to count things one after one, and not by Diuisions, and the profes are, when the things which are knowen in order, are applyed to proue or disproue, as any doubt

[1] Below, pp. 240—296.

A Treatise vpon the 23. of Matthewe

leadeth vs, and the sayinges, doctrine, or other points belonging, are the particular things which are knowen and follow in their order. If anie doo yet agayne alledge, that for one point, all these thinges neede not be sought for, I aunswere, that if we know Religion and godlines, we neede not seeke for them: for they will be readie without seeking. But why then should we seeke to Logike for them, which not onely doeth shewe vs none of them, but also trifles for them. Yet I say, that for that one pointe *of teaching and calling all men*, the other pointes are needeful which are withall mencioned. For the doubtes and questions which may followe thereof, can not be determined without them, neither can the trueth be proued, nor errour be disproued nor rebuke, counsaill, or exhortation bee vsed, but by them and with them. The like we say of al other pointes and doctrine, which is shewed in this 23. of Matthewe, and we wishe all that will write, speake, or meditate, of anie doctrine of Diuinitie, that they bee [G 1 *recto*] first readie in the order agreement and vse thereof. Howe needfull this is, that which followeth will shewe vs.

The Doubtes and Questions about the doctrine.

Seyng Christ spake to all the multitude, it maye be asked, whether they which haue his message, may preach where they list, and to whomsoeuer they will. As whether they maye goe to Rome, and preache to the Pope and his Cardinals. and if anie Bishoppe should sende for them, or the King or Queene should commaunde them, whether they should come and preach before them, and if they place them in a benefice, or anie parishe doo call them, whether they be tyed to that benefice, or the whole Parishe be their charge. Likewise also if anie blaspheme, or be frowarde and persecute the truthe, whether still we must offer it to them, and preache amonge them.

The applying with proofe, rebuke, and exhortation.

Against disordered preachinge at Paules crosse in London, Also before the Queene, before Bishoppes, and Noble men,

and against Sermons by turne and course, in famouse places, Against preaching Lecturers hired thereto, and against Popish Parishes.
And lastlie, against all preaching to those which by resisting and frowardnes, doe shewe them selues vnworthie.

As the doctrine was proued by the Scriptures, that all are called, soe the doubt must be answered, first by the Scriptures, and then by other proofes, namelie such as are grounded on those pointes which eyther did followe the doctrine, or went before it. and so we see how needfull it is to set downe and know the agreement of euerie doctrine with other pointes of diuinitie. It is written that God will remoue the Candlesticke out of his place, that is, they which nowe appeare to be his people, shall no more be so. For the abomination of desolation shall be sett vp, and stande in the holie place, as we knowe it is at Rome, which some tyme had more grace, and then must we flee and stande not still. For the Lord hath taken mercie and compassion from that place. And if in all England, or in some more famous places of Englande, whether great cities, or uniuersities, or the Court it selfe, we see not the kingdom of God maintained but persecuted, and the true worshippe of God refused a false worshippe and idol seruice wilfullie suffered, and many popishe abominations vphelde and established, from thence the Lorde doth take awaye his kingdome, as it is written: *The Kingdome of God shall be taken from you, and shall be giuen to a nation which shall bringe forth the fruites thereof.* Yea none maye continue [G 1 *verso*] to preach the truth vnto those, when once they haue boldly testified it, and they put it from them, and make theselues vnworthie therof, but they must turne awaye from such: and if a companie in anye citie be such, then muste they forsake that companie. For Paul departed from those which were hardned and disobeyed, speaking euil of the waye of God before the multitude. Yea he separated the disciples and taught no more amonge them. And if a citie or a countrie do likewise refuse, they must forsake that citie or countrie, it shall be easier for the land of Sodom and Gomorrha in the daye of iudgement, then for that citie or countrie. But if it be said, what if some desire the trueth, must they also be forsaken? I answere that if they desire the kingedome and sell

Reuel. 2. 5.

Mat. 24.

Mat. 21.

Act. 13. 46.

Act. 19. 9.

Mar. 6.
Mat. 10.

Mat. 13. 44.

A Treatise vpon the 23. of Matthewe

not all that they haue to buye it, and the place where it is, and will not come and dwell there, they are vnworthy therof. It is come to passe vpon those, as it is written, that they desire to see one daye of the sonne of man, and can not see it. If the whole church be persecuted, it ought wholye to flee, and if lawes be made against all, thoughe as yet they be not executed on some, yet the persecution is generall, and they are called awaye. Iere. 50. 5. Deut. 12. 11. Luke 17.

In Egipt the whole church was in bondage, and it wholy departed. yet did Pharaoh giue leaue there to worshippe God rightlie. But answere was made, it is not meete so to do in this place. For lo, can we sacrifise the abomination of the Egiptians before their eyes, and they not stone vs? Soe also in Englande, thoughe the magistrates shoulde giue vs leaue to worshippe God rightlie, yet the true worshippe and reformation of the church, is an abomination to the Bishoppes, and other wicked Preachers and people, & what stirringes and hurlie burlies would they make? But they saye we must abide such troubles. In deede we must beare thē, when we can not auoide them, and in auoiding thē, we must take heede, to houlde still a good cōscience: but we tempte God, as did manie of the Jewes, if when we maye goe out of Egipt, and auoide such troubles, we will not, or murmur against it. Yea and their coming out of Egipt, as also their fleeing from Babel, did figure our remouing from persecuters, and enimies of reformation. For it is written: *Goe out of her my people, that ye be not partakers of her sinnes, and that ye receaue not of her plagues.* Yet they saye wee must not flee, because there is hope to wynne others. Nay there is danger sayeth the Scriptures, lest those which are wonne, shoulde be partakers of their sinnes, amonge whom they tarye, or lest they shoulde receaue of their plagues. For eyther the subtiltie of the enemyes shall beguile them, because their teachers are shutt vp from them, and they are in the handes of their enemies, or else the persecution shall discourage them being but weake of themselues without the church meetynges. When the Priestes and the Leuites left their Cities and suburbes, and all their possessions, and came to Juda and to Jerusalem, did they euill in this? For they also might haue taryed for hope of winning others. But they are commended for departing. For there fell manye straungers vnto Juda out of Israel, [G 2 recto] sayeth the text, and were ioyned Exod. 8. 25. Reuel. 18. 2. Chr. 11. 2. Chro. 15.

with them as one people, and the Lorde was with them. For let others followe them, as it is written in that 11. chapter: *And after them, there came men of all the tribes of Israel in like maner.* Yea let *tenne men take houlde of the skirt of* him that fleeth from that spirituall Babel, and saye, *wee will goe with you, for wee haue hearde that God is with you.*

<small>Zach. 8. 23.
Zach. 8. 20.</small>

But nowe for Preachynge at Paules Crosse *in London* and before the Queene in that maner, and for Parishe Preachers and hired Lecturers, we neede not here stande vpon them, because they are afterwarde answered in the text.

Yet as I gaue warninge before, if wee knowe those pointes, which both followed the doctrine and went before it, and haue proofe of them by Scriptures, wee maye shewe the Trueth and take awaye suche doubtes, by sufficient proofe and exhortation.

For example to proue such their preaching and Parishes vnlawful, and that neither they preache the worde of message, nor are his church & people, we alledge the firste point which followeth the doctrine. For wee *saied that God calleth and leadethe to happines, but yet by planting and gathering his church vnder one kinde of gouernement.* So then the proofe is this:

Whosoeuer are not gathered from all false churches, and from their false gouernement, can neither be the Church of God, nor Preachers in the same, Ierem. 3. 17. *Act.* 8. 12. *Ezek.* 43. 11. 7. *Psal.* 94. 20. *Mic.* 4. 2. *Exod.* 19. 6. 1 *Pet.* 2. 9. *Reuel.* 1. 6. *Reuel.* 6. 2. *Psal.* 45. 3. *Psal.* 110. 2. *Isa.* 2. 3. *Nowe whether their Parishes, and such Preachers in them be thus gathered, and whether they be rather grounded on the Popish church and stande thereby, It will afterwarde appeare,* onelie we write this to shewe the waye of following or prouing matters, yet without Logicke.

Of the seconde point we giue this proof, *That whosoeuer are not receyued to the Couenaunt of Christ, which is made with all his people, before they can he his people, they are not the Church of Christe, neither canne be Preachers therein. Ierem.* 31. 33. *Gene.* 17. 1. 2. *Deut.* 5. 2. *Exod.* 19. 5. *Iere.* 50. 5. *Ezra.* 6. 21. *Exod.* 12. 43. *Nehe.* 9. 38. 2. *Chro.* 15. 12. *But whether their Parishes haue made this couenaunt, or rather doo make a mocke of the same, and are still vnder the yoake and bondage of Antichriste, let it afterwarde be iudged.*

A Treatise vpon the 23. of Matthewe

Of the thirde point may be this proofe, *If to their Parishes God haue not giuen his Promises, nor made them partakers of them, howe are they his people?*
For his people are alwayes made partakers of his promises, Ephes. 2. 12. *Psal.* 133. 3. *Rom.* 9. 4. 1. *Pet.* 2. 9. *Psal.* 147. 20.

The like proofes may be gathered, and not onely Proofes, but Rebuke, Exhortation, and Counsell, vpon other pointes following.
As of the gifte of the Spirite, of Suffering and dying vnto sinne by repentance, of the due vse of Baptisme, of the Kingdome, Priesthoode, and Prophecie of Christ, &c. And of the contrarie of all these.

[G 2 verso] For if in their Parishes, or in the Prelates whiche ouerrule them, a spirite of delusion and errour, a desperate hardening, a Popish Baptisme or the Priesthoode, Kingdome, and Prophecie of Antichrist be in steade of these thinges aboue named, howe should they be the church of God, or what should we account of their preaching therein?

Nowe to handle these thinges more largely by the scriptures, we haue no neede of Logike. For except we seeke smoke to geue vs light in stead of the sunn, wee must iudge, that so great a light as the scriptures geue, hath no neede of such rush light. As for example, Iere. 3. 17. Jerusalem is called the Throne of the Lorde, and in that citie is the name of the Lorde, and to it must the people be gathered. So by warraunt of such Scriptures the Bishopes will call the Preachers to Pauls Crosse, or to preach before the Queene. For a Logike Subiect is their warrant. Paules Crosse or the Courte, they make Jerusalem, that is the subiect, to which they make the Preachers an Adiunct, and therefore there must they Preache. See how this Logike doth pull a sacke vpon the truth, to make it seeme the fairer. For a Subiect doth signifie vndercaste, and Adiunct a cast to, or hangbye. Therefore because Preachers depende on the Church which is their subiecte, the Bishoppes maye call them to Paules Crosse, for that is the Church or *Ierusalem*. Agayne they picke more Logike out of this scripture, as bones out of Marow. For *Ierusalem*, or the Church is the whole, and the Preachers are the part. Nowe the parte must come to the whole, and therefore by their argumēt of the whole, the Preachers as the partes, must ioyne and seeke to it. O Logicke full of fine deuises, it doth flie aloft in the cloudes to cast vs down these mysteries. But let wise men vse their wisedome, and not picke it out of milstones[1]: let them speake the worde of God as it shoulde be spoken, and not put chaffe for wheat, nor dregges for wholesome licour. We saye therefore, O ye prelates, not by your Logike Oracles, but by the worde and doctrine, Is Paules Crosse Jerusalem, or is the Lordes name there? Is not your name sounded there, as by the blast of a Trumpet? My Lorde Bishoppe there controlleth, in his name the Preacher standeth vp, as the wolfe doeth in a visarde, he hath the Bishoppes name in parchement, for that is his licence, it is a Theeues quittance though he came in by the windowe, it is the Scourecoastes Passeport, though he roaue out for his praye. My Lordes face is in the waxe, a print and marke of holines. Who can preache without it? It is the seale of ghostlie message. Three such seales, haue threefolde grace, but the money which buyeth them, hath that grace seuenhundreth foulde.

 Is this nowe the Lordes name, when his Ghospell must hange on parchement, or on the name and markes of those Romish beastes? Is this his name, when his glad tydinges ceasse, except the parchement holde, and his message misseth, except a waxe marke giueth it? Is this *Ierusalem* where such Bishoppes raigne, or should we call it the throne of the Lord? Is it not rather the seate of iniquitie, to which (as the Prophete sayeth) the wicked doo approche? The Lorde hath sayd, Buylde vp myne house, and in it will I be fauourable. But they preach at Paules Crosse, and call this [G 3 *recto*] a building. They are fedde with their Bishoprickes, and herein call the Lorde fauourable. Do they meane to plante his church at Paules crosse? Or if they meant it, could they there gather his people to him, and subdue them to his gouernement? Doo not there those Bishops make the word of the Preacher to serue, and his message to be slauishe? I haue not sent you saieth the Lord, to those places, where my Scepter must come vnder. Can you preache my worde there, where I take my kingdome from you? And doo you hold my kingdome, when you cast downe my crowne at the feete of those Bishoppes? The Lordes worde can not serue: but your worde both there and in your parishes is made to serue.

Marginal references: 1. Pet. 4. 11. Ierem. 23. Reue. 13. 16. Amos. 6. 3. Agge. 1. 8.

---

[1] See *N.E.D.* for this use. The reference is to a kind of learning characterized by a pretended extraordinary acuteness.

A Treatise vpon the 23. of Matthewe

The Lorde doeth ride on, prospering in his glorie, because of Psal. 45. 3.
the worde of trueth and of meekenes and of righteousnes, and he Reuel. 6. 2.
*hath guirte his sworde vpon his thigh. Hee sitteth on his white
horse, and hath his bowe and a crowne is giuen vnto him, and
he goeth forth conquering that he might ouercome.* This his
conquering and this his Prospering is his gouernement
which he winneth by the power of his worde. This is
the Crowne, his Bowe, and his Sworde. *For the Lawe* Isa. 2. 3.
shall goe foorth of Zion, and the worde of the Lord for Ierusa- Mich. 4. 2.
lem: He shall iudge among the nations, and rebuke manie Psal. 110. 2.
people. And this worde he calleth *the Rodde of his power,
by which he will rule.*

Nowe therefore ye Preachers, because ye subscribe
that the Lordes gouernement is wanting, and yet set vp Lamen. 5. 8.
other Lords, or suffer them in his place, and because
you can not, neither will you preache, but by their good
leaue and license, therefore you can not preache my
worde. What doo you at Paules Crosse, or what shoulde
my messengers doo there? Doo not there the Bishoppes, Isa. 63. 18.
as also in your Parishes, *treade downe* the Lords Santuarie?
And are not the people as they ouer whom the Lorde did
neuer beare rule. Yet you saye, the Bishoppes gouernement is tolerable, and take the teeth of those Wolues,
for a discipline to the sheepe. Some tymes you call
their rule a false Popishe gouernment. And againe,
when they call you to Paules Crosse to preache for your
honour, or place you in a benefice, then their warrantes,
and their Purseuauntes muste bee made the worde of
trueth and meekenes. To smite the people with crueltie
and pride, is the Discipline of Christ. Such sharpenes
doth much good, as he that breaketh the Bones helpeth
the Ague. *Hath the throne of iniquitie* (saieth the Scrip- Psal. 94. 20.
ture) *anie fellowshippe with God, which forgeth wrong for a
lawe?* This is nowe the Throne of the Bishoppes, which
in their Dioces, Parishes, and Cathedrall Churches is
lift vp against Christ. From it doeth come foorth their
lawes and Iniunctions, by which all menne euen small
and great, riche and poore, free and bounde, are made Reue. 13. 16.
to receyue a marke in their hande or in their forehead.
For all are made thraules and slaues to their policie, to
builde the church, and to worshippe God after their
deuisinges. They are all turned backe after bablinge
Prayers and toying worshippe, after priestlie Preachers,
blinde Ministers, and Canon offices, after Popishe attire
and foolishe disguising, after fastings, tythings, holydayes,

and a thousande moe abominations: and their feete doo sticke [G 3 *verso*] faste in the myre and dirt of all Poperie, that they can not gett out.

Mala. 1. 10   Beholde nowe, whyle these things are, *will I haue pleasure in you, saith the Lorde? will I accept an offering at your handes?* Will I smell the smoke of suche incense as is your Letanie, and Collectes, and all that pretie

Leui. 10.   Beadrow? Is it not the incense of *Nadab* and *Abihu*? And came it not frō *Baal*? It was to[o] spiritual to keepe still within the Popes Massebooke, the stomack therof could not brooke it, and therefore did vomitte it out. Why rest you in those Parishes, O ye stubburne

Iere. 7.   children? Are they the Lordes housholde, or is his gouernement in them? Doe you trust in lying words, [s]aying our Parishes, and our churches, and surelie

Hose. 2.   we are Gods people. Pleade against their Popishe Parishes saith the Lord, euen against their mother church. For shall the Harlot be honest because her bastardes so call her? Shall her fornications remayne in my sight, and her adulteries bee kept betweene her brestes, and shall I take her for my wyfe, or will I be her husbande? O ye my messengers, take ye no charge

Isa. 59.   of such Parishes, for they be not *Zion*, and the Redeemer shall onelie come to Sion, and they are not Jacob, yet he shall onelie come to *Iacob*, and to them that turne from iniquitie in Israel. They are not *Ierusalem*, and his name

Iere. 3. 17.   of sauing vs is onelie in Jerusalem. For beholde, can they be Jerusalem, which is called the Throne of the Lorde, when there the Bishops sitt as in the Throne of Antichriste? What Throne hath Christe, but by his gouernement, which they say is wanting, and what is the Throne of Antichriste, but that Lordshippe in their Dioces, with such swaye of Popishe officers, and with such Romishe traditions. If there be no calling nor leading to happines without the Lordes kingdome and gouernement, what shall we make of that preaching, or of those Parishes and Churches, whiche are without this gouernement? If they say, they haue his gouernement, their owne mouthes, their subscribing and preaching to the contrarie, will condemne them.

What shall we answere? They say, They call no Preachers to preach, but God and the church, because their authoritie is of God and of the Church and the Queene and the people agree to receyue them. So their Parishes are Churches, and those great Assemblies

A Treatise vpon the 23. of Matthewe

are the flocke of Christe. For they are faire Cages, though the birdes be vncleane. Know you not an honest woman, for shee doeth loue fornicators? So may you knowe the true Church, for shee loueth such Prelates. O Churche of price, O the famouse church of Englande. Tell ye the Church, that is, tell ye the Bishoppe of the Dioces. The church can geue him Mat. 18. 17. authoritie, to authorise both the church it selfe, and the Ghospell, as if God should intreate such a Prelate to be good vnto him: and as if the church should pul him by the sleaue, that he put not out her eyes. O church without eyes. For thy light is shutt vp at the Bishops *Beneplacitū*. Art thou the church of Christe, when thy Reue. 1. 10. starres be not in his hande, but the fystes of thy Bishoppes 1. Ti. 3. 15. doo pull them downe from thee? Yet is this church of Englande the pillar and ground of trueth. For the Bishops ouerryde it. They are [G 4 *recto*] the trueth and it is the ground. It is the Beast and they are the Ryders. It stoupeth as an Asse for them to get vp. The whippe of their spirituall Courtes, and the Spurres of their lawes, and the Bridle of their power, do make it to carie them. We giue say the Bishops, then wee take saye the Preachers. Holde take you Authoritie, but on this condition, that you preach no longer then we list. Mark you this say the Preachers: for wee haue no authoritie but by the Bishops, & if they giue it vs, why may they not take it away? So the theefe taker doeh [*sic*] please the theefe giuer, and the yong wolfe wanteth, when the olde wolfe is angrie. O yee wolues, and worse then hirelings, which not only leaue the flock when ye see the wolfe come, but also rauen and deuoure the Iohn. 10. 12. flocke, as the Bishoppes giue you leaue. For ye feede on the sinne of the people, whyle ye suffer their wickednes, and say, who can mende it, for discipline is wanting. Therefore O ye Prelates and priestlie Preachers, you confesse the Lordes gouernement & the discipline of his house to be wanting, and howe can you say, yee haue planted his Church? Yes, say they, wee haue planted it, for we haue the worde and the Sacramentes. They proclayme in Pulpittes and subscribe with their handes, That a Popishe discipline and gouernement is among them: yet say they, we haue the worde and the Sacramentes, and so also haue the true gouernement in Part. What Parte hath Christ with Belial, or howe can they be subiect to that Antichristian gouernement, & chal-

Matt. 6. enge also a parte of Christes gouernement? Can two contrarie lords rule ouer one householde? Or can they serue twoo contrarie Maisters? Haue they not open abominations and wicked men amongst them, which they say must be tolerated, because they are incurable? Can they then haue anie Parte of Church gouernement, when neither by rebuke, nor by separation, they can cleanse the church of such greeuous wickednes, but as it pleaseth the Popishe officers?

Psal. 149. Is this to binde the Kinges in chaynes, and the Nobles with fetters of Iron, or to execute the iudgement that is written, *Such honour bee to all his Saintes*? Is this to fight with the spirituall weapons, whiche are not carnall, but
2. Cor. 10 mightie through God, to caste down houldes: yea all
1. Cor. 7. proude imaginations, and euerie high thing? Is not
Actes 4. this to bee seruauntes to menne, yea to obey men rather then God? Beholde they shewe their sinnes as Sodome, and hyde them not, and say, that the Lordes gouernement is not able to redresse them, and therefore they muste bee tolerated. Thus they houlde still the priesthoode of Antichriste, which is the tolerating and dispensinge with wickednes, by such wicked Preachers, to make Christe and Belial agree. Therefore thus sayeth the Lorde, I
Song. 1. feede not my flocke at Paules Crosse in London, or *Saint Maries in Cambridge*, or in your Englishe Parishes. O ye my sheepe, goe ye not thyther, as though there were my foulde, and there I rested & fedd my flocke: for there be
Mat. 24. shepheards and flockes also that followe thē, which are
Luke 17. not of Christ, for they hold of Antichrist. *Beleeue not*
Iohn 10. 5. *euerie one whiche saieth, Loe here is Christ, or there is Christ, but let the Lords sheepe heare his voyce, and forsake a straunger* [G 4 verso] They knewe those sheepefoldes before time that the wolfe ruled in them, and there they sawe playnelie the face of Antichrist looking ouer them. But nowe they hide the wolfe in the folde, and saye, here is Christe: they put a visarde on his face, and say that Antichriste is gone, he shall deuoure them no more. Thou are deceyued O Englande, thou art gone from one destruction vnto another: Thou hast escaped the snare, but art fallen into the pitte. Woe to thee, for thy fall is great, and who shall rayse thee vp?

But we haste to that which is chiefe in this Chapter, and though wee would gladlie handle thinges more fullie, yet that whiche followeth, wee must shut vp brieflie, because of other matters.

A Treatise vpon the 23. of Matthewe

Verse 2. and 3. The Scribes and the Pharises sit in Moses seate.

3 *All therefore whatsoeuer they bid you obserue, that obserue and doo: but after their workes doo not: for they saye and doo not.*
Against Parishe Preachers and hired Lecturers, and all that Popishe rabble, and against the hearing and receyuing of them as lawfull Pastours, and messengers from God.

THE Lorde doeth shewe thee O Englande, if thou wilt searche the Scripture, and knowe his voyce therein, the crooked pathes which thou hast made thy selfe, & thy great rebellions. But thou art obstinate, thy necke is an Iron synewe, and thy browe brasse. Behoulde thou seest not because thou wilt not see: a visarde hath deceaued the[e], and the sheepes clothing hath mocked the[e]: and thou saiest, I will follow my shepherdes which haue put away Antichrist, and yet behoulde such raueining & mischeefe as was neuer the like, and wickednes is gone forth from thy shepherdes into all the land. But let them heare his voice which sheweth them what their church and state is, and what is that reformatiō whereof they boast. *The Scribes & Pharises sit in Moses seat*, saieth he.

The doctrine of these wordes agreeing with other Scriptures and with our 114. *question.*[1]

The doctrine is, That the Scribes and Pharises, being eyther *Leuites*, or trained vp in the Schooles of the Prophetes, were lawfullie called to teache the people. And this Christ alloweth and commaundeth to be, so that he is a straunger, a hireling, and a false prophete, which is not sente nor lawfullie called, & yet will preach and take charge of the people. *For he that entreth not in* Ioh. 10. 1, 5. *by the doore into the sheepefoulde, (sayeth Christe) but climeth vp an other way, he is a theefe and a Robber. And my sheepe heare my voyce.* [H 1 recto] *They will not followe a straunger, but they flee from him, for they knowe not the voyce of straungers. And the straunger which cometh neare the Tabernacle, shall be* Num. 1. 51. *slaine. And if anie shall come in their owne name, we may* Iohn 3. 42. *not receaue them. If they be blinde guides,* The Lorde Mat. 15. 14. chargeth vs to *let them alone. It is not for such to builde*

---

[1] See *A Booke which sheweth the life and manners of all true Christians*, p. 221.

<small>Ezra. 4. 3.</small>
<small>Matt. 7. 15.</small>
<small>2. Thes. 3. 6.</small>

the Lordes house: as it is written in Ezra 4. Neyther must we be carelesse *of the false Prophetes, which come to vs in sheepes clothinge, but inwardlye are raueninge woulues.* And Paule commaundeth vs, *in the name of our Lorde Iesus Christ, to withdrawe our selues from euerie brother, which walcketh inordinatlye, and not after the instruction receaued.*

We shoulde in those wordes againe shewe the abuse of Logike and Rhetorike, but because we woulde dispatch in fewe wordes the things which followe, we cut of[f] that labour. We haue partlie declared their vanitie in this point, and therefore will stande on more needfull matters. They interprete Moses seate, to signifie Moses Pulpit, or else Moses doctrine. Howe happe here they forget their Rhetorike, and make not seate to signifie Gouernement, authoritie, and calling, and so put the signe, for that which is signified. In deede some of them thus interprete it, though they neede not searche out Tropes for this purpose. For in manie places of Scripture, Throne, Seate, Place, Chaire, are taken for gouernmēt, Authoritie, callings. As in Jere. 3. Isa. 16, Isa. 9. Pro. 16. Prouer. 20. Eccl. 3. and other such like. Nowe let them shewe by the worde, or their best writers for them, that by Seate in this place should be ment Moses pulpitt, or teaching true doctrine, and we agree to them.

But wherefore would they, that *Moses* seate should so bee taken? Belike, to iustifie the Pope, and *Peters* chaire at *Rome*. For if the Pulpit or the Seate be so forceable, or the preachinge of some true doctrine, with much other false, why should not the Papistes reasons be good, which say they preache Christ, and they haue Peters seate, & succede the Apostles? But these men forsooth, will defie the Pope, euen as the Marchaunts of that harlot (as it is written) which stande a farre off from her, for feare of her torment, and yet weepe and wayle for her marchaundise: namelie, for those Tythings, and Benefices, for their Palaces, Bishoprickes, Fees, and poulinges, and canon exactions, and for all their popish traditions. But no maruell, though they stande so much on Moses seate. For they teache most earnestlie, and with persecution of those, which receyue not this doctrine, that if anie Minister haue the seate, though they be vtterlie vnmeete for that calling, either for want of giftes in knowledge and teaching, or for lyfe and behauiour, yet we may lawfullie receyue the Sacramentes

<small>Reu. 18. 15.</small>

A Treatise vpon the 23. of Matthewe

of them: yea they sitt in Moses seate say they, and that is sufficient to vs, though not for themselues. And so somme of them do teach and counsell, and some doo tolerate, and some doo force others to come to blinde guides, or wretched preachers, and to present their publike prayers to God by their mouthes, to giue thankes, and receyue the Sacraments by their guiding.

Beholde, is not this to giue vs gall and wormewoode mingled in our [H 1 *verso*] drinke? Is it not to set vp a Beetle[1] for our guide, and a stocke to teache vs knowledge? It is not to call a foole to be our maister, and to welcome a messenger as bringing good tydinges, from the Deuill and Satan? Is it not to take a straunger to feede the flocke, whose teeth are of yron, & his tongue and voyce as the sent of a pitt, which breatheth forth death and destruction? Is it not to put the sheepes clothing on the rauening wolfe, and then make sport that the sheepe are beguiled? Is it not to call him to builde the Lords house, which hath sword and fire in his hands to destroy it? Is it not to bidde the polluted make an other man cleane, and to putt dunge in the bosome to make a sweet smell!? Is it not to beate the souldiour from the battle, and the workman from the building, because we will get the victorie by a blinde and lame people, or by him that hath no weapon nor strength to vse it, or because we will haue an house made without hands? Is it not to make the dunghill beautifull, and to boast of the beggar, as borne of great bloud? Is it not to proclame that whosoeuer will, shall be more then a Saint, and who so can reade and will take the orders of Priesthoode, though he be a foole him selfe, yet shall he rule seuen hundreth wise men. Is it not to make him an ouerseer for good order, which hath hornes to pushe the flocke, and lifteth vp by the feete and the shoulder to thrust and treade downe the sheepe if they call for their meate? Is it not to make the meate sauorie with salte that stinketh, and hath lost his sauour? Behold, dare they preache such thinges, or that by Moses Seate the Lorde Jesus did suffer vs, to receyue the Sacramentes of such kinde of Ministers? yea they are more boulde and shameles then thus, and haue made their faces more harder then stones. For

Mat. 15. 14.
Iohn 5. 43.
Iohn 10. 5.

Ezra. 4. 3.
Ezra. 6. 21.
Num. 1. 51.

1. King. 12.
1. King. 13.
2. Thes. 3. 6.
Ezek. 34. 4.
Luk. 14.

---

[1] May be Betle. A beetle is a heavy wooden instrument for ramming, crushing, or pounding paving- stones or wedges. It is also used as a type of heavy dullness or stupidity (" dumb as a beetle "). A stock is a block of wood ; also, it is a type of that which is senseless, lifeless ; a stupid person.

though they haue such waight of Scripture to beate downe this follie, yet one poore delusion alledged falslie out of *Caluin*, must shift it of all. For it maketh no matter say they, who bring vs a letter or a gift, so that the gift and the letter be good. So they will take goulde of a theefe to Justifie his theeuerie, and he that doeth steale a message, and counterfet an handwriting, is welcome vnto them. But indeede, is the Lordes message a blinde reading of seruice, and though they preache, yet is that the Lordes goulde whiche they bring, when they take and leaue the flocke as the wicked Bishops appoint them, and neither can nor will plant, or reforme the Churche? Haue I sente them saieth the Lorde, or commaunded them, when they cause my people to erre, by their lyes and by their flatteries, saying, ye are his people and church, though ye be polluted and abominable? Haue these dumme Dogges or tolerating preachers, my letters and seales? I neuer gaue them sayeth the Lorde, they are stolen and counterfet. Yea they haue the seales and licenses of their wicked Bishoppes, and if they haue my message, why holde they their peace at the wicked Bishoppes discharging, as if they had his message onelie. Be it therefore O ye Prelates, that yee put Moses seate for Moses doctrine. Can you preache the Lordes worde and doctrine, or minister his Sacramentes? To preache some trueth as wicked menne may doo, and to preache the Lords word of message is not all one. For his message can not be without his gouern[H 2 recto]ment, & his gouernment is the Lordship he hath in the cōmunion of his offices. But you haue the Popishe lordeship & cōmunion of his offices. You haue not yet planted my Church sayth the Lord, by gathering it from the wicked and ynworthie, and yet this is the first dutie of all my messengers. Act. 2. 40. Ezra. 4. 3. 2. Chron. 15. 3. 12. Act. 19. 9. Act. 13. 46. Ezra. 6. 21. Mat. 10. 11. Nehe. 9. 38. Ye haue not yet cast of[f] the yoke of Antichriste, & receiued al things concerning my kingdome and gouernment, as Mat. 28. 20. Act. 8. 12. Exod. 25. 40. 1.Tim. 6. 13. Therefore because ye haue not planted and builded my Church, sayeth the Lorde, that it may be visible, nor purged and cleansed it from open abominations, both yee and all the workes of your handes, with your Prayers and Sacramentes are vncleane and accursed vnto you.

Ierem. 23.

Isa. 56.
Mala. 1.

1. Cor. 9.

A Treatise vpon the 23. of Matthewe

For so it is written, Hag. 1. 4. Hag. 2. 15. And if this iudgement came on the Jewes, which hadd the true worshippe and ordinaunces accordinge to Moses lawe, what is their iudgement, which haue their worshippe, traditions and gouernement, grounded on Antichriste, and taken from him? Yet forsooth it is made great wickednesse, not to heare these Preachers, for they sitte in Moses Seate, and are not blinde guides. Nay they sitte in the seate of Antichriste, and if they were blinde, they should not haue had this sinne: But nowe they saye that they see, therefore their sinne remayneth. For they confesse, as dyd the Pharisees, That Christe ought to raigne ouer them, yet they raigne without Christ, and haue sente an ambasage after him, saying, Wee will not haue this man to raigne ouer vs, except our Magistrates will suffer him, or make him to raigne. Yea wee will none of his Disciples, except our Parliamentes decree, that wee shall haue it. Is not this to make the kingdome of God to come with obseruation? To be by an arme and strength, and not by his Spirite: To be by Bowe and by Battle, by Horses, and by Horssemen, and not by the Lorde? Is not this to skorne the Lordes Kingdome, because it groweth as the Musterdseede, and is hidden as the leauen, and commeth vp as the corne sowen in the fielde. But yet these wicked Preachers rise vp against this, and crie out that they haue the cheefe. They haue the worde and the sacramentes, and as for the Gouernement or Discipline, it is but an accessarie and hangbye, needefull in deede, but yet they maye be without it, & be the church of God notwithstanding. But for this mater looke the 16 verse & the meaning thereof. In this place we saye that their preaching is not the worde of message frō God, neither may wee partake with thē in the Sacramentes. For the Lorde is come in iudgment against thē, that though they see yet they might be made blind, and therefore we must leaue them, as it is written, Mat. 15. 14. They stagger through their spirituall giddines, & at noone daye doo grope for the wall. For what blockishnes is this to saye they are Christians and we must partake with thē in the Sacramentes, though they haue but the popish Baptisme, & popish kinde of churches. For thus they reason, Circumcision say they, was the couenant in times past, and now is

Iohn 9. 41.

Luk. 19.

Luk. 17. 20.
Zecha. 4. 6.
Hos. 1. 7.
Math. 13.

¹Marke 4. 16.

Gene. 17.

---

¹ This reference seems incorrect; possibly Mk. 16. 16.

Baptisme, and therefore we haue the couenaunt, and are Christians, seyng we are baptised.

[H 2 *verso*] So they teach also, that Papistes haue the couenaunt, and the promise, because they are Baptised. But the Baptisme of them both, saieth the Lorde, is no more my couenaunt: Then the Popish communion and sacrifice of the Heathen was the offeringes which I accepted. Can an Assemblie of Idolaters bee my Church, saith the Lorde? And howe then should the Papistes haue my promises and couenaunt, for I haue onelie giuen them to my people and to none other. But they saye, their children and the children of Papistes are baptised into my name. Yea doo they not blasphemouslie abuse my name, and doo they not baptise them into their Popishe parishes filled with all iniquitie? Is their blinde reading, or popishe inchaunting a baptising in my name? Is not this rather baptisinge in my name, when the signe of washing or sprinckling of the parties baptised, is applied to my worde duelie preached, and that by him whom they knowe to haue his Message from me. The Sacramentes are markes of the outwarde church, as the Scripture doth testifie, Actes. 2. 42. Mat. 28. 20. Actes. 8. 12. Deut. 33. 10. Exod. 12. 43. Marke 16. 16. Gene. 17. 14. 1 Corint. 10. 16. Nowe therefore if they be not that outwarde church as we haue proued they are not, what shall wee account of their Sacramentes? Can they be Sacramentes without the spirituall communion? But they are without this communion, whiche can haue no gatheringe, planting, separation or reforming of their church, but by their spirituall Courtes, Popishe officers, and their excommunication, absolution, lawes and penalties, which are altogether Antichristiā. Are we not baptised into the bodie of Christ, to die vnto sinne, are we not also baptised into the gouernement of Christ in his Church? For by it we are receyued vnto grace and felloshippe, by partaking with the church in one Christian communion. And this also doeth the Lords supper signifie. What is then the Baptisme of those, which can not be of the bodie of Christ, whom also his gouernment doth separate from the church? Now whereas they aunswere that the Ministers sinne which baptise thus disorderlie, or thus vse the Lords Supper, & say it is their sinne & not ours, we aske them, doth not the Church partake with the Minister, and is not euerie Christian a King

A Treatise vpon the 23. of Matthewe

and a Priest, to rule with Christe by open rebuke, if no other doo in season rebuke, and by withholding of those from their communion and fellowshippe, which are without the couenaunt? _{Exod. 19. 6.} _{Hose. 2. 2.} _{Col. 4. 17.} _{Ro. 16. 17.}

And let them answere, whither are the baptised presented to the minister, or to God and the church, or whither doth the minister receaue anie to felloshippe, or rather the church? For though the minister be guide in receauing them, yet it is the church which doth partake vnto them that felloshippe. *For wee Preach not our selues*, sayeth Paul, *but Iesus Christ, and our selues your seruauntes*. And againe he saieth: *We are yours, and ye are Christs*. Soe then the church is cheefe, though Paul be greater in the church vnder Christ, then anie one single person in the church. And therefore is the Church called the Pillar and grounde of Trueth: And though the Minister should fail, yet the Church must stande sure. And though all men should do wic-[H 3 *recto*]-kedlie, yet may not we followe a multitude to doo euill. Yea we must saye to *Archippus*, Take heede to thy Ministerie: and if *Archippus*, or an Angell from heauen, or a whole congregation will not be reformed, we must pleade against them, yea forsake them, and houlde them accursed. _{2. Cor. 4.} _{1. Cor. 3.} _{1. Tim. 3.} _{Exod. 23.} _{Col. 4.} _{Hose. 2.} _{Galat. 1.}

Yet againe for this matter they bring in *Caluin* against vs, and accuse vs for Anabaptistes and *Donatistes*. For we say of that fifte to the Corinthes, That Paule doeth speake of that spirituall communion, which is onlie in the Church, and this they call heresie. For Paule him selfe sayeth, that if we leaue the other communion, which is in a common wealth, we must goe out of the worlde. And therefore he teacheth the woman whiche beleeueth, to abyde with the vnbeleeuing man, and the seruaunt whiche beleeueth, to keepe with his Maister, except they bee frowarde and persecute, or the whole Church be helde there in bondage, or they can not holde the true worshippe and all christian dueties, with the sufferance of other, & the safetie of their liues. For then they may flee, as we proued before. For the Seruaunt that fledde from his Maister to the Church of God, might not be deliuered vnto his maister, but hee might dwell where hee would among the Lordes people. Did not *Iaacob* abide with *Laban*, till he founde quarelles against him, & he was in daunger? For neither Brother, nor Sister, no not Husbande and _{Ioshua 24.} _{1. Cor. 5.} _{1. Cor. 7.} _{Deut. 23.}

	Wife, are in bondage saith Paule in such things. Yea
1. Cor. 7. 15.	whether did the Lorde speake these wordes to all,
Iere. 5. 1.	*Remember the Lorde a farre off, and let Ierusalem come into your minde.* If the Husbande would not goe, should the wyfe tarie, for all are commaunded to goe, and not one to stande still. And if they say, that they had this speciall commaundement, and we not the like, are not all thinges that are written, written for our learning and example? And is not the same commaundement, in
Reuel. 18. 4.	the newe Testament belonging to vs, as Reuela. 18. for
Deut. 12.	that Captiuitie was a foreshewing of our captiuitie at this time. And nothing happened in Ceremonie or in miracle then, but the same is nowe verified in trueth, and in a maruelous working of the Spirite of God. The Church was neuer vnlike it selfe, saue that it put away ceremonies when the substance came, and shadowes when the true light was come. Yea the same commaundements remayne vnto vs, which were giuen
Psa. 27.	vnto them. For to vs it is commaunded, That wee seeke the place whiche the Lorde hath chosen to put his name there. And seeke ye my face sayeth the
Psa. 42.	Lorde in that Psalme. And shewe me O thou whom my soule loueth, sayeth the Church in that Songe,
Song. 1.	where thou feedest thy flocke, and causest it to rest in the heate of the daye. And aunswere is made, That it must holde the true flocke, and seeke the right shepheardes and depart from the others. This is commaunded to all, and therefore, though the husbande will not, yet the wife must doo it, or the husbande, though the wife bee against it. But this we haue added by occasion, yet also needful to the matter. For we shewe that so farre we must be from hearing or receyuing of such Pastours and Ministers, and from dwelling in their Parishes, and vnder their charges, that the wyfe may not tarie for the husbande to flee [H 3 *verso*] frō thē, if he be vntoward.

Now for their calling, because they stande vpō that, let vs see what it is. It is inwarde and outwarde, they saye: And they haue them both. For they alledge that they haue the spirite of God, a good conscience, and a good minde to doo good to the Churche, and they haue also knowledge sufficient. Thus they speake faire, & will shewe a good countenaunce. But is this a good minde, or a good conscience, to strewe greene rushes vpon the mouth of the pitte, and then bidd vs

A Treatise vpon the 23. of Matthewe

walke ouer it, for they minde vs no hurt? So doo they in that they will fullye tolerate, or with outrage vpholde such greate abominations: which also are blinde to see the woes of the Churche, and those which they see, they woulde hide from our eyes, with their dispensinges and mitigations, and will wincke at grosser corruptions, and saye they see them not. If they walcke thus after the fleshe, howe can they saye, that they haue the spirite or be inwardlie called? Hath not the Lorde turned their harte to hate his people, and to deale craftelie with his inheritaunce? For they are our enemies, and hate not only vs, but the gouernement and kingedom of Christ, and the trueth which wee bringe, that they maye come out of Egypt, and the yoake of Babel, they are hardned, accordinge as it is written: *God hath giuen them the spirite of slumber, eyes that they should not see, and eares that they shoulde not heare.* And what is this their inwarde calling? For this was the slumber of the Scribes and Pharises. They helde the groundes of Religion as wee doo, but they could not applye them to Christ, when he came in an other gouernement then ceremoniall. Euen so these while they would holde the groundes, they cleane ouerthrowe them, because the spirit of slumber doeth so harden them, that they can not applye them to Christ, when he cometh without their popishe gouernement, and Antichristian bondage. If it be verified vpon them, *I will destroye the wisdome of the wise, & will caste awaye the vnderstandinge of the prudent*, howe are they inwardlye called? And where is their wisedome, when they refuse Christ Jesus to raygne ouer them, except he come by ciuile lawes and decrees of Parliamentes, and had rather be vnder the raigne of Antichrist, then in simplicitie and basenes, together with persecutions to receyue Christes kingdome? If darcknes, and grosse darcknes doo couer them, what inwarde callinge haue they? If their eyes be not turned awaye from regardinge popishe vanities, and they be not quickned in the right way, what inward calling haue they? If the good spirit doo not leade them as it were by the playne waye which the church gouernement sheweth them, what spirit or inwarde callinge haue they? For they goe the crooked wayes of Antichrist.

Nowe whereas they alledge for their inwarde calling, that they pray and preach for Discipline, and are sorow-

Rom. 8.
Psal. 105.

Rom. 11.

1. Cor. 1.

Isa. 60.
Psal. 119.
Psal. 143.

full also for thinges amisse, and carefull to redresse them, we answere, that their backwardnes and frowardnes doeth shew the contrarie, as is proued before. For though some of them refuse to weare a surplesse, or be precise in some other pointes, yet it is with horrible tolerations of the same things in others, and with doubling[1] also, [H 4 *recto*] & mitigatings, relentings & protestings, in most shamefull maner. Therefore this fayre shewe of deuotion is but greater hypocrisie: and seeing they would hyd suche horrible wickednes, by the shewe of straightnes in some pointes, why should thei not be those spirits of Diuils working miracles, and as the Frogges which go out of the mouth of the beast, to gather the Magistrates and people against vs. For their subtilties, colourings, faunings, and fayned deuotions, are maruelous, and their persecutions and raylings toto[2] grieuous. As for the Bishops and their officers, and fellow partakers, they succeede the Martyrs, they saye, and are carefull for the vnitie and prosperitie of the Church, and therefore they are inwardly called.

Reu. 16.

O most reuerende Lordes and Fathers which are carefull and mindfull of our spirituall woes: they count them so often, as men walke vppon hedges, and forget their traditions, as he that goeth forgetteth his feete. Their thoughtes and deuises are onlie for good, this you may knowe, by their foure deuisinge corners of their horned cappes. They are readie to the Gospell, as the yuie bushe is readie to drawe you the wine. Neyther *Cranmer* nor *Latimer*, nor *Hooper*, nor *Ridley*, were so meete for the prison houses, as these are for their Bishoprikes. They loue the fleece and thinke on the fatte, and this is their inwarde calling. Doo not all menne tell you whom they like best, they suffer the forwarde among them, as did Bishop *Boner*[3]. For eyther they prouide them such houses, where no light nor ayre can come to them, belike least it choake them, or else they dryue them away and set them farre of[f], because they loue not to hurt them. They feede on the fatter, as on the riche Papistes, and on others also by suspensions, and penalties, whyle they can beare out the charges. But the forwarde, they fetter, because they will runne to[o] fast without boultes. As for the sleeping sheepe whiche are neuters, they charme them

---

[1] May be " doubting ".
[2] A common use, familiar to readers of Shakespeare.
[3] Edmund Bonner, bishop of London (1500 ? — 1569).

A Treatise vpon the 23. of Matthewe

with their Mattins, and mumbling seruice, for they are formall protestantes. Beholde, haue they not nowe an inwarde calling? They professe & vowe in their hartes to helpe Christes little flocke. But doo they paye their vowes in their palaces and parishes, as *Philpot*[1] did his vowes in Smithfielde? Their state in the church is their statelines, and their calling is their cutting with the sword, for ther pryde is a right inward calling, & their crueltie is the good mouing of their spirite and conscience. They threaten, pursue, imprison, and smite the sheepe because they loue them, and are inwardlie called therto. The Popes olde house was destroyed in Englande, and they are called to builde him a newe. In the time of King *Edward* the 6. they began such a building. They had gotte the Popishe tooles, but they coulde not holde them. God was mercifull by the rodde of Queene Marie, and dyd beate such euill weapons out of their handes, yet these haue gotte againe that false popish gouernment, and by it they will blesse vs frō all euill sicknes and plagues. Haue they not knowledge and skil sufficient, as another inward calling? Haue they not the whole worlde in their heades to be sure of the church? Let vs welcome wise Gentlemē: they toke in hand to build the Lords house, and now moe then xx. yeeres are past in studying for the groūdwork. O perfect work, whē shal it end, which is so lōg in beginning.

[H 4 *verso*] Thus we see their inwarde calling. Nowe let vs come to their outwarde. How got they their roumes, Benefices and liuings? Did we send for such guesse to *Rome*, or to *Louane*, for they get into the sheepfolde thoughe the dores be shut aganst them. Came they not in at the windowes, trowe ye. Doethe not the Torche of Ambition shewe them a windowe? Be not Cambridge degrees an high ladder to go vp? Be not their bribes or flatteries, or vaunt of their learning, a ladder to goe either vp or downe, And is not the fauour of some Patrone or Bishoppe, or worldly man, the strength of these ladders? Did they not finde out a liuing before they foūd out meete people for their calling? And did they not gather their stipendes and tythinges before they had gathered the scattered of the flocke? Doo not the lawes place them in their liuings, and is not this a good outwarde calling? They hunte the praye

[1] John Philpot, Archdeacon of Winchester, burnt at Smithfield, 18 Dec., 1555.

by the sente of the Lawe. It calleth them and they answere with the bragge of their pulpitbarking, and with the tune of sweete pleasing, or with the charme of high fauour, and commandinges. This, this is a due outwarde calling. They haue looked vs in the face, and haue stolen away our libertie. They tooke vs by the hande, as though they would leade vs, but they haue bounde our handes behind vs. For when we looked to chuse them for Pastours, they came vpon vs by force, and yoked vs to their parishes, and snared vs with inioynings, and did beate vs with penalties. O worthie outwarde calling. Doo not the Bishoppes pray when they make Ministers, and shal we condemne their prayers? For the Foxe is a Father in the Church, when he prayeth for grace. Are not our Ministers duelie examined? They are Posed by master Examiner. Beware ye Priestes that ye can speake Latin. And in anie case forget not your Catechisme. By these two shall you spitte out your grace vpon others, and men shall feede on your graceles spuinges. Breath[e] vpon them, ye Bishoppes, and giue them your gracious spirites, which ye call the holy Ghost. So shall they bee those good spirites, like Frogges which come forth of your mouthes to make battell against vs. Kneele downe ye Preachers, that the Bishoppe may ordayne you sitting in his chayre. His holie handes shall blesse you. They are washed from blood as was Pilates, and as the nose of a Wolfe whiche will rauen no more. Then must you take your Licenses in parchement, and paye well for them. Prepare a Boxe for your waxe, printe your message therein, and keepe touche with the Bishoppe, least he open your Boxe, and your calling flye awaye.

Beholde, this is their outwarde callinge, and if a man haue this, they are called (they say) and sitte in Moses seate. For may not a reading minister serue for a better, if he be thus called? And may not an Idoll serue well ynough, when God doeth forsake them? Should a blinde guide bee displaced, if he be thus called, for he may become learned. So Satan doth call Theeues to steale, and should they not freelie doo it? For they haue a calling, and by stealing they may learne to become true menne. Should not one murther seuen thousande to learne not to kyll? Or should not these[1].

[1] This is the end of H. 4 *verso*. There is the catch-word " Bussards ", and then these words are written in: " by reason of trouble the print was staid ".

[A 1 recto]   A BOOKE
WHICH SHEWETH THE
life and manners of all true Christians,
and howe vnlike they are vnto Turkes and Papists,
and Heathen folke.
Also the pointes and partes of all diuinitie, that is of the reuealed will and worde of God, are declared by their suerall Definitions, and Divisions in order as
followeth.

ROBERT BROVVNE
MIDDELBVRGH,
Imprinted by Richarde Painter.
1582.

Parts of the *Booke which sheweth* have been printed in (i) Williston Walker, *Creeds and Platforms of Congregationalism* (1893); see pp. 1 - 27, where there is a valuable Introduction and Sections 1, 35 - 63, 110 - 127; (ii) *Transactions of the Congregational Historical Society*, XII, 11 - 18, the same sections as in Walker.

The book is printed across two pages in four columns, headed, " The state of Christians ", " The state of Heathen ", " Definitions ", and " Diuisions ". The " Definitions " in the third column expound the terms in Column I, while the " Diuisions " split up the " Definitions " according to the methods of logic. As Browne explains in his Preface, the unlearned need read only Column I, or at most Columns I and II; Columns III and IV are for " the learned, which seeke deepnes, and stande on their methodes and curious diuisions ". The answers in the first column are generally in Black Letter, the questions in the second column in Italic, and Column IV in Italic : the rest in Roman. In addition to the general headings, each column has another caption at the head of each page.

III.　　　　　　　A Booke
WHICH SHEWETH THE
life and manners of all true Christians,
and howe vnlike they are vnto Turkes and Papistes
and Heathen folke.
Also the pointes and partes of all diui-
nitie, that is of the reuealed will and worde of God are
declared by their seuerall Definitions
and Diuisions in order as fol-
loweth.

¶ *Also there goeth a Treatise before of*
Reformation without tarying for anie, and of the wickednesse of those Preachers, which will not reforme them
selues and their charge, because they will
tarie till the Magistrate commaunde
and compell them.
By me, ROBERT BROWNE.
MIDDELBVRGH.

¶ *Imprinted by Richarde Painter.*
1582.

[D. 1.] A Preface of the vse of this Booke which followeth, of the life of Christians; and how to studie and reade the Scriptures with profite and edifying.

For the vse of this Booke which followeth, I thought good to write somewhat. I sett it foorth for all sortes of menne, and applyed my selfe both to the learned and to the vnlearned. If any require plaines[1], let them reade onely the first questions and aunsweres, which are vnder this title, *The state of Christians*, & so let them reade the first halfe page, throughout the Booke. If any would knowe the sinne, ignorance, and errours of these dayes, and so finde out trueth, and duetie by their contraries, as by falsehoode and faultings, let them read the contrarie questions and aunsweres, which are in the other halfe page. We haue diuided them by line from the firste questions, and haue set them also in another letter, one against an other, for their better viewe, and vnder this title, *The state of Heathen*. For

[1] *I.e.*, plain-ness.

A Booke which sheweth the life and manners

we woulde not, that the weaker sorte should charge them selues, but onelie with the chiefe and former things firste, as be the groundes of Religion. And therfore we leaue it free vnto them, eyther by the former questions and aunsweres, to learne these groundes, or by the other to search out the contrarie, or to iudge by them both, whether we and our companie, haue learned and holde the true Religion: we leaue it free (I saye) to them, to followe or not to followe, our wayes and doctrine, except they see it good and meete for them. As for the learned, which seeke deepnes, and stande on their methodes and curious diuisions, we haue for their cause, takē some paines. Not that we tye Religion or Diuinitie vnto such Diuisions, or Definitions, or Logicall demōstrations, or cōdemne all which bring not such learning: But we leaue thē without excuse, which refuse the trueth, except it be hidden with curious art, and handled after the maner of their Schooles. With such frowarde & Sophisticall diuines, I was before time driuen to deale, as I might best shut their mouthes, that is in writing to set downe the question, and doubt, then euerie worde of the question, because of their quarrellinges, the definitions of euerie thing, the proofes gathered on them, and all things applied to the Scriptures, and the Scriptures to warrant them. This haue I done, because they stand so much [D 1 *verso*] on Demonstrations, and Sylogisticall reasoninges, for that is their deepnesse: and call our proofes weake, and confused. But I saye, are they professours of Logicall demonstration, & will they call proofes by definitions, by their Axioms, and belaboured Diuisions, to be weake proofes? Doe not Definitions containe the natures, the causes, the differences, the kindes and sortes of thinges, & will they make conclusions vpon Principles to be weake matters? Suerlie either let thē disproue, & take away such proofes or els they are weake aduersaries, which thus would weaken the trueth. And the Lord be Judge of such weake & euill consciences, which do cast forth so strong a sauour of malice & enuie. For such peuish truoblers [*sic*] haue I troubled myselfe if it might be to beate them with their owne weapons, & haue geuen thē in the other page, which doeth answere to the questions, the Definitions which they call for.

Now the vse of this book in studiing of the scriptures

is this. As we did gather it out of the scriptures, so do we againe apply it vnto them, and that in this sort. First we take heede to the wordes of the text that we vnderstand the meaning. If some wordes bee doubtfull, or the manner of speakeing, we search out that. For the simple as Salamon teacheth vs, should haue sharpenes of witt, & the childe knowledge and discretion: also the wise should heare and increase in learning: he shuld vnderstand a parable and the interpretation, the wordes of the wise, and their darke sayings. And this is it that is writtē in Nehemiah: *They redd in the booke of the lawe of God distinctlie, and gaue the meaning, and caused the people to vnderstande the reading.* So that first the wordes, and then the matter and doctrine must be looked vnto. That this may be rightlie done, we must be skilfull and readie in the pointes of Diuinitie, that is in the knowledge and doctrine of Religion and godlines, and in Questions, doubtes, & controuersies, which belonge therto. Nowe this our booke of Diuinitie containeth such knowledge, and doth also make plaine such doubtes & questions, that soe sone as we haue the wordes of the Scripture, so sone may we know what is the doctrine therof, or what doubtes and questions do followe thereon. For wee must consider what point of Diuinitie it is, and how it agreeth and keepeth order with other pointes wherof it is grounded, and what followeth thereon, also what is against it, or like vnto it. And then that beinge founde out, we shall easilie see the reason, wherof it is spoken and sett downe in such wordes. Thus both the hardnes in the wordes and maner of speakinge being taken awaye, and also the doctrine made plaine and manifest, first by an agreement, and difference from other pointes of diuinitie, then by the order, thirdlie by some question or doubt, if there be anie; and lastlie, by that which is against it, or like vnto it, as bee contraries, similitudes and Parables: Then must we come to applying, that is we must skanne and examine what defaultes and erroures bee in anie, to improue and rebuke the same, as Paule teacheth vs, and to dehorte, denounce, and counsell otherwise: Also wee must exhorte and confirme them in their right iudgement, and in all dueties of godlines to goe forwarde therein. This will not be easie vnto vs, except God doo giue [D 2 *recto*] them grace, and a

Prouerb. 1.

Nehem. 8.

Hos. 12. 10.
Ezec. 17. 2.

1. Ti. 4. 16.
1. Tim. 5. 2.

spirit of discretion, and except we take paines, both to labour with others in vsing their helpe, and also with our selues, to get experience in these thinges.

This paynes I tooke, to searche out of the Scriptures, all the pointes of Diuinitie, and to sett them in order as is shewed in the booke. And then also to applie the whole Scriptures vnto them, not onelie in meditation and writing, but also in speache and mutuall edifying. If anie will follow our order[1], we giue them a proofe or example thereof, by a Treatise which we hope shall come foorth of the *Reuelation of Saint Iohn*[2]. We haue chosen to this purpose that parte of Scripture, because in these dayes it is so needefull, and yet so smallie regarded, and because men counte it so harde, which is so easie and playne. Also because we haue brieflie gone ouer the ceremonies of the olde lawe, and shewed their meaning, and nowe onelie remayneth this difficultie, as they make it, for the *Reuelation of S. Iohn*. The abhominations of Antichriste we shall brieflie there touche, and some chiefer thinges we shall handel more largelie, Because they are the cause of such troubles vnto vs, and for which we haue left our Countrie. In the meane time, for some order of studying and profyting in the Scriptures, wee doo here shewe by that *xxiii of Matthewe*, what is our manner of handling them, that as others see cause, they may iudge what is meete, & do accoidingly.

---

[1] See above, pp. 221, 523, f or a form of the Preface which differs from this point on.
[2] Part of this seems to be incorporated in *A New Years Guift* (below, p. 516) in an intrusive section (beginning " Then followeth the sixt degree " and ending " the seuenth plague ") which follows a missing passage.

The state of Christians.	The state of Heathen.

[A 1 verso — A 2 recto]

Christians. Their Knowledge The Godhead.	Heathen. Their ignorance. Fals Gods.
1. Wherefore are we called the people of God and Christians? Because that by a willing Couenaunt made with our God, we are vnder the gouernement of God and Christe, and thereby do leade a godly and christian life.	1. *Wherefore are the Heathen forsaken of God, and be the cursed people of the worlde?* Because they forsake or refuse the Lords couenaunt and gouernement: and therefore they leade an vngodly and worldly life.
2. Howe should we leade a godlie and Christian life? By knowing God & the dueties of godlines: and by keeping those dueties.	2. *Howe do the Heathen leade an vngodlie and worldlie life?* By ignorance of God, and deceyuing them selues: and by sinning and faulting to their owne destruction.
3. What beleefe and knowledge of God must we haue? We must knowe the Godhead: and the all sufficiencie or moste blessed state thereof.	3. *Howe are the Heathen deceyued & ignorant of God?* They take those for gods whiche are no gods, and they put blessednesse in them which vanishe in them selues, & haue their wantes and harmes.
4. What knowledge of the Godhead muste we haue? We must know our God to be one God. To be three persons. To be of an vnsearcheable nature.	4. *Howe doe the Heathen mistake the Godhead?* They beleue that there ar many gods. They make them as dreames and imaginations. They will needes searche out their natures and dispute thereof.

A Booke which sheweth the life and manners

Definitions. Diuisions.

Christians. Their Knowledge[1] The Godhead.		
1. Christians are a companie or number of beleeuers, which by a willing couenaunt made with their God, are vnder the gouernement of God and Christ, and keepe his Lawes in one holie communion: Because they are redeemed by Christe vnto holines & happines for euer, from whiche they were fallen by by the sinne of Adam.	Christians whiche should leade a godlie life.	By knowing God and the dueties of godlinesse. By keeping those dueties.
2. The knowledge of God and godlines is a right and stedfast iudgement of his Godheade, and moste blessed state: & of his whole will in his worde: which doeth gouerne vs wholy to do all things wisely, as his worde doeth binde vs.	Knowledge of Christians, as first	Of God: as of { The Godhead. The all sufficiencie Of the dueties of godlines.
3. By the Godhead we meane the right Iudgemēt which we should haue, concerning his Name, both in vnitie and Trinitie, which in nature and essence, is past finding out, and vnsearcheable.	Of the Godhead.	In the vnitie of the Trinitie. In his vnchaungeable nature.
4. The vnitie of the Godhead is one and the same nature of the three persones, which hath neither separation, nor vnlikenes of partes.	The vnitie of the Trinitie is	One God a liuing Spirit. Three persones.

---

[1] These are page-headings.

5. Howe is GOD knowne to be one?
The three persones are but one liuing spirite.
They haue one and the same nature.
They haue no partes nor vnlikenes of partes.

5. Howe doe the Heathen make them selues manie Goddes?
They made such thinges to be gods, which they haue handled or tasted, or seene with their eyes.
They haue chaunged their gods, and taken newe vnto them being wearie of the olde.
They make them contrarie and vnlike to themselues, and of sundrie natures.

[A 2 *verso* — A 3 *recto*]

The all sufficiencie of God. His Maiestie. Infinitnes.

The Wantes. Vilenes. Limiting of false gods.

6. Whiche be the three persons?
God the Father.
God the Sonne begotten of the Father from euerlasting, and after an vnspeakeable manner, whiche also is called IESVS CHRIST.
God the holy Ghoste, proceeding of the Father, and of the Sonne.

6. What dreames and imaginations haue the Heathen of sundrie persons in the Godhead?
They haue their Baals, Popes, & fatherhoode in mischiefe: They haue their sonnes also & children of their Gods, as mightie Gyaunts & subtile wretches, which drawe frō their fatherhoode a course and force which is mischeeuous.
They haue also their seducing and wicked spirites, which they say are of God.

7. How is God all sufficient and most blessed?
His all sufficiencie and moste blessed state appeareth by his incomparable Maiestie, & by the shewe of his wonderfull glorie.

7. How do the Heathen Gods vanish, and haue their wantes and harmes?
They are vile and nothing worth.
They are vnprofitable and can doo nothing, except they be helped of others.

5. The Trinitie is the difference or distinction of the three persones, in perfect order and mutuall working without diuision of nature, or vnlikenesse of partes. } Three persons. { Father — Of the Father, as { His onely begotten Sonne: as the holy Ghost proceding of the Father and of the Sonne.

The persons of the Godhead.   The all sufficiencie.   Maiestie.   Infinitnes.

6. A person is a difference of the Godhead in the names and working in one mutual agreement. } *The persons.*

The Father is a person of the Godhead, which is, and worketh by his Sonne begotten of him from euerlasting, in a mysterie vnsearcheable. } *The Father.*

The Sonne is a person of the Godhead, which is, and worketh with his Father, who begate him from euerlasting. } *The Sonne.*

The holy Ghost is a person of the Godhead, which is, and worketh from the Father, and from the Sonne. } *The holy Ghost.*

7. The all sufficiencie and blessednesse of God, is his perfect state, whereby he wanteth nothing, nor hath neede of anie thing, to better the same, but all things haue neede of him, and haue their beeing by him. } *All sufficiencie of God.* { *In his Maiestie & excellēcie aboue al.*

In the shew of his wonderful glorie.

8. How is his Maiestie incomparable? Because he was neuer made nor created, nor seene of mortall man. Because he staineth and confoundeth all things being compared with him. And because he is onely infinite.	8. *Howe doo they shewe them selues vile and nothing worth?* They are made, handled, and led by others. They are worse then their makers, & more vile, then they whiche handle and vse them. They are limited by others whiche rule them.
9. Howe is he infinite? He is and cōtinueth from euerlasting to euerlasting. He is vnchaūgable & w^tout corruptiō. He is incomprehensible, and contained of nothing.	9. *How are they Limited?* Their beginning is vile, & their ende is worse. They chaunge and fade away. They are caughte and taken in their corruption.

[A 3 verso — A 4 recto]

The glorie, power, holines, wisdome of God.	*The vilenes and vnprofitablenes of false Gods.*
10. Howe hath God shewed vnto vs his wonderfull glorie? First, by his power & almightines. Secondlie, by the name of Chieftie, which he hath by his power. Thirdlie, by his holines in vsing his power.	10. *Why are they vnprofitable, & can do nothing, except they be helped.* Because of their weaknes and deadnes in them selues. Because they are maistered, & haue their basenes. Because they are misled and do fault by their weaknes.
11. How is God knowen by his power and almightines? By his creating of all things. By his vsuall guiding of all. By his meruailes & wonders which he sheweth besides vse.	11. *How are they weake, and dead in them selues?* They haue their making & marring. They are driuen & drawne by their course & destinie. Their best woorke is trifling to no profit.

A Booke which sheweth the life and manners

8. The Maiestie of God is his incomparable excellencie or greatnes, whereby he differeth frō all thinges, in a wonderfull mysterie and stayneth and confoundeth them, being compared with him.	Maiestie of God.	Being vncreat and inuisible. Being incomparable.	Stayning & confounding all things. Only infinit.
9. His infinitnes is a perfection of his Maiestie, whereby he limiteth all thinges, and is limited of nothing: and therefore he limiteth time and place vnto all things, and their working & chaunges.	His infinitnes.	In his eternitie. In his incōprehensiblenes	Without time. Without chaunge.

The glorie of God, his power, holines, wisedome.

10. His glorie is the shew of his excellencie in all his workes.	His glorie	In power In the use thereof.	In chieftie In holines.
His power and almightines, is a perfection of his excellencie, whereby nothing is to[o] hard for him, and he bringeth to passe whatsoeuer he will.	His power	In creating all things. In guiding all things.	Vsuallie. More strāgelie.
11. His creating is a worke of his allmightines whereby he made all things of nothing.	Creating.		
His guiding is a woorke of his power, in vsing all things to serue his purpose, that nothing chaunceth but by his will and commaundement.	His guiding.		
His maruailes and wonders, are his extraordinarie workes, teaching man that he hath power ouer all his workes, to vse them against their nature, to doo him seruice, and set foorth his glorie.	Maruailes.		

12. Howe is hee knowen by the chieftie whiche he hath by his power?
He is Lord and Ruler of all.
He is God and Possessor of all.
He hath the honour and and prayse of all.

12. *Howe are they maistered, and haue their basenes?*
They are seruile and slauish.
They are the curse, and the euill of those that seeke to them.
They are the shame, and skorne of the wiser.

13. Howe is hee knowen by his holines in vsing his power?
He sheweth his holines in perfect wisdome.
Allso in his iustice & righteousnes.
Allso in his goodnes and grace.

13. *How are they misledde, & faultie by their weaknes?*
Those men or euill spirits which haue bene made Gods, haue their fondnes or foolishnes.
Also their vnrighteousnes.
Also their hurtfulnes and harming.

14. What say you of his wisdom?
By his wisedome hee knoweth all thinges.
He is perfect in counsaile.
He worketh all things in theyr due manner.

14. *What say you of their fondnesse and foolishnes?*
Thei haue their ignorāce & blindnes.
Also their rashnes and lightnes.
Also their euill handling & marring of matters.

[A 4 *verso* — B 1 *recto*]

The counsaill of God. His due working. His Iustice.   The rashnes. Disorder. Iniustice of false gods.

A Booke which sheweth the life and manners

12. His Chieftie is the power which he hath to vse all things as he will. } Chieftie in { Lordship & Authoritie Honour. { Rule. Possession

His Lordship is his chieftye wherby he hath all things subdued and obedient vnto him. } Lordship.

His Rule and Gouernement, is his Lordship, in vsing the obedience of all things, to do his will. } Rule and Gouernement.

His possessing of all, is his Lordshippe in vsing their seruice, for his purpose and will. } Possession.

His honour is the chieftie which he hath by the homage and seruice of all. } Honour.

13. His holines is, the right and perfect vse of his power, to do all things most vprightly, and innocently. } Holines. { In his wisdom. In using his authoritie. { In Iustice. In goodnes

His wisdome is his holines, by the perfect vse of all vnderstanding. } Wisdome of God is { In knowing all things. In vsing the same. { By counsail. By the manner of working.

14. His knowledge is that point of his wisdome, wherby nothing is hydd and secret from him, but he hath thorowly found out the same. } His knowledge.

His counsaile is his minding and pondering of all things from euerlasting, according to knowledge. } His counsail. { Deuising. Aduising.

The counsaile of God. His due working. His Iustice.

15. What saye you of his counsaill?
He mindeth and searcheth oute all thinges from euerlasting.
He remembreth and counteth them.
He foreseeth & purposeth all things.

15. *How doo they shew them selues no godds, by their lightnesse and rashnesse?*
Their [sic] may carelesnes and dulnes be spied in them.
Also forgetfulnes.
Also vnwarines, and headdines.

16. How doth he worke things in their due manner?
He doth al things in perfect readines and order.
Also with speed & forcible indeauour.
Also in stedfastnes and finishing his enterprises.

16. *What say you of their euill handling and marring of matters?*
They are disordered and vntoward.
They haue their slacknesse and fainting.
They haue their backwardnes, and disuauntage.

A Booke which sheweth the life and manners

15. His deuising, and serching out of things, is his counsaile from euerlasting, how all things shall be and fall out. } *Deuising* { For *Aduising*, look after in the wisedome of man.

His iudginge and markinge, is his counsaile of all things present how they are. } *Marking.*

His remembrance, as we vnderstand it, is his aduising or counsaile of things which are past, as it were, by occasion of things present, though nothing is occasioned to God. } *Remembrance.*

His counting, or reckoning, is a whole and full aduising of things passed: because he will take accounts of them. } *Counting.*

His foresight is his counsaile, wherby he is aduised of all things comming. } *Foresight.*

His Purpose and Praedestination, is his counsaile, whereby he is setled how all things shall be. } *Purpose and Predestination.*

16. His manner of worcking, is the right vse of his knowledge, in applyinge the same vnto practise.

His readiness is his perfect maner of preparing al things, which may further his workes.

His order is his perfect manner of setting and compassing the worke it selfe.

His speed is his hastning to dispatch the worke.

His force is the endeuour, whereby the woorke wanteth no strength to bring it to passe.

His Stedfastnes and finishing, is the continuance of his enterprise without fayling or letting tyll it be done.

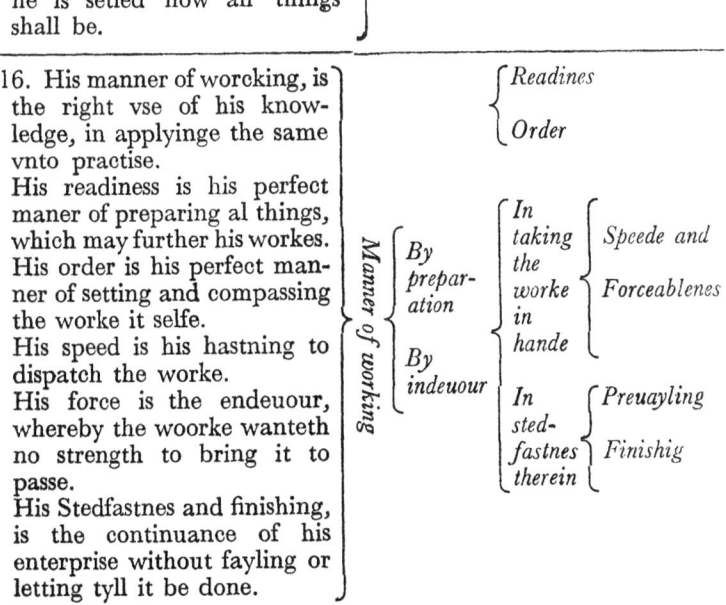

{ *Readines*

{ *Order*

Manner of working { *By preparation* { *In taking the worke in hande* { *Speede and Forceablenes*

{ *By indeuour* { *In stedfastnes therein* { *Preuayling* *Finishig*

17. Howe is hee iust and righteous?
His righteousnesse standeth in esteeming right and due. Also in vpholding the same: by appointinge to all thinges their worke and dutie. Also in takinge accountes of their workes and duties.

17. *How are they vnrighteous?*
They mislike the right, and fauour the wrong.
They leade others vnto wickednes.
They suffer and lette them alone therein.

[B 1 *verso* — 2 *recto*]

The estimation, appointing, and taking accounts of dueties. Misliking right. Misleding & suffering sinne

---

18. Howe doeth he esteeme of right and due.
He is zealous and iealous for equitie and innocencie. Hee loueth those and reioyceth ouer them which do right and dutie.
He hateth al vanitie and wickednes, and is angrie therewith.

18. *Howe doo they mislike right and due?*
They make light therof.
They loath it and take greefe therat.
They rest and please them selues in euill and wrong.

A Booke which sheweth the life and manners

17. His Iustice and righteousnes, is his holines, in the right ruling and governing of all things.

His Esteeming of right is that point of Iustice, wherbey he is pleased therewith, and displeased with the contrarie.

- Iustice
  - In esteeming right.
  - In doing right.
    - Appointing duties.
    - Taking accoūts.
- Esteming right.
  - Pleased with right.
    - Loue & ioye.
    - Zeale and ielousie.
  - Displeased with contrarie as
    - Hatred
    - Anger and wrath.

The estimation, appointing, and taking accountes of dueties.

---

18. His zeale and iealousie, is his estimation of right and duetie, for the worthines thereof: whereby he is saide, as it were, prouoked to hasten the same, and maketh it sure with all straightnesse and watchfulnesse. } *Zeale.*

His Loue and Ioy is his high estimation of any in their goodnes, whereby he yeeldeth him self to them in one mutuall happines, and taketh them as precious and deare, which haue so sought his name and his glorie. } *Loue.*

His wrath & hatred is his troubled disliking of wickednes in anie, for the contrarietie thereof to his holines, prouoking him to pursue them as accursed, and to set him self wholie against thē as hateful vnto him. } *Wrath and hatred.*

19. Howe doeth he appoint vnto all their worke and duetie? He hath geuen vnto all things power and meanes to obey and serue him, if they had kept it. He teacheth vs his will and worde. He directeth vs by his example and guiding.	19. *How do they mislead?* They leaue them in their weaknes, or peruert their gifts. They geue them vp to their ignorance, or deceaue and beguile them. They forsake the vntoward, or make them more auke[1].
20. How doeth he take accounts? He watcheth vs himselfe, and by his Angels and messengers: He examineth, and trieth vs by his word and our consciences, and by outward affliction. He recompenceth euerie one according to his workes.	20. *How do they suffer, and let alone in their wickednes?* They hyde wickednes, and shift it away, and seeke occasions of euill. They ouerslip wickednes, and passe by the same. Thei flatter and excuse them in their sinne.

[B 2 *verso* — 3 *recto*]

The goodnes of God, and our redemption.	The Curse by false goddes and Antichrist.

[1] Auk, awk, now obs. Survives in "awkward". See *N.E.D.*

A Booke which sheweth the life and manners

19. His appointing of dueties is that part of his gouernement, or that worke of his Iustice, whereby all haue their office and charge at his handes. } *Appointing dueties.* { *Giuing power.* | *Directing the same* { *By teaching.* | *By exāple & moderating.*

His teaching is, whereby hee reuealeth and maketh knowne his will. } *Teaching.*

His Moderating is a work of his gouernement, vsing the obedience of his creatures in following him, to put in practise, a duetie or office appointed vnto thē. } *Moderating.*

20. His taking of accountes, is a woorke of his gouernement, whereby he reckoneth with all things, howe they execute his will. } *Taking accoũts.* { *In knowing right and due.* | *In recompensing.* } { *By watching.* | *By examining.*

His watching is his continuall mindinge of all his creatures, whereby he marketh their obedience and seruice. } *Watching.*

His examining and trying in his forceable taking of accountes, whereby he maketh knowne that whiche anie would hyde. } *Examining.*

His recompensing is a worke of his Iustice, whereby euerie thing, as it sheweth foorth his glorie, so it hath the name and the vse thereof, in good or euil. } *Recompensing.*

The goodnes of God and our redemption.

Hitherto of the Iustice of God.	Hitherto of the vnrighteousnes of Heathen gods.
21. What say you of his grace & goodnes [?] His goodnes is in preseruing & blessing his creatures, & especially man: both in his firste estate, wherein he was made after the image & likenes of God: And in restoring him againe being fallen away from his state.	21. *What say you of their cursednes and harming*? They are a present mischeefe. They faile most, when they should cheeflie helpe.
22. How doth he maintaine and blesse things in their state? He giueth to al their natures. Also their glorie and excellencie. Also all outward furniture needfull vnto them.	22. *How are they a present mischiefe*? The course of nature is corrupted & chaunged by them. All things are defased and stained. All come to marring and spoile.
23. What say you of the restoring of man being fallen away from his state by the sinne of Adam? God hath prouided the meanes of saluation. First, in his secrete counsaile. Secondly, in his redines to helpe vs. Thirdly, in the shew of his helpe.	That we may apply this vnto Antichrist: 23. *How hath he most failed vs, when he seemed to helpe vs*? Antichrist hath euer an euill minde to the church of God. He is alwaies vntoward and vnfit to helpe it. He is a plague and destroyer thereof.

A Booke which sheweth the life and manners

21. His goodnes is his holines in doing good, and increasing his blessings towardes his creatures, more then the goodnes which is in them deserueth. } *his goodnes* { In maintayning things in their state. / In restoring them being fallen. }

His preseruation or sauing of things is, a worcke of his goodnes, whereby he keepeth all his creatures, in their state of excellencie and difference of kinde, by continuance of his blessing vppon them. } *Preseruation.* { In themselues by their natures, and glorie. / By outwarde furniture. }

22. The natures of things, is the proper ablenesse which euerie thing hath, to kepe it selfe in his perfect kinde. } *Natures of thinges.* { In the working and powers { By life & quickning, / Without life. } / In the outwarde making. }

Their glorie and excellencie, is the gifte which they haue to shew forth the glorie of their Creator. } *Glorie and excellencie.*

Their outward furniture, is the prouision and stoare of outward helps and furtherances of their welfare. } *Outwarde furniture.*

23. The image of God in man, was the greatest shew of his excellencie in man: whereby he resembled his God most liuely in a wonderfull happines. } *The image of God in man.*

His restoring and sauing of man being fallen away, was the work of his wonderful goodnes, wherby he did remedie our miserable estate, and brought vs againe vnto happines. } *Our redēption by* { The causes & preparation of helpe. { The coūsel of God. / His readines thereon } / The shewe of his help. { In his promises. / In keeping the same. { Sending his Sonne. / Sauing us by him. } }

241

16

24. What is his secret counsell?
Hee knoweth oure miseries and wantes.
He mindeth and counteth them.
He foreseeth & purposeth what helpe we shall haue.

24. *Who is an Antichrist by his his euill mind to the church of God?*
The wilfull hyders of the woes of the church, & blind to see the grosse corruptions thereof.
They that forget & ouerslip the same but watch to vphold their traditiōs.
They which haue wicked deuises against it.

[B 3 *verso* — 4 *recto*]

The meanes of our redemption. The Manhood of Christ.

Damnation by Antichrist.

25. Howe is the Lorde readie to helpe vs?
He is full of mercie and compassion.
He loueth his people & desireth their welfare.
He is zealous & iealous for them.

25. *Who be Antichristes by ther towardnes and fitnes to destroye?*
They which are fierce, and cruel in a false church gouernement.
They which loath the righteous, and are at reste in their absence.
They which pursue & put frō them the righteous as being their plague.

26. Howe doeth hee shewe his helpe?
He hath giuen his promises to helpe.
He is faithefull of his promise in sending his Sonne into the worlde for our redemption.
He hath redeemed and saued vs, by his Sonne, Christ Jesus.

26. *Who be Antichrists by the plague and destruction which they bring vnto soules?*
They which haue professed and vowed it by their calling and state.
They which hold the same course of profession, and begin the mischiefe.
They whiche make the destruction and hauocke.

24. His counsaile.
　　His knowledge.
　　His mindfulnes.   } *were before defined, but here we*
　　His foresight and purpose,   *haue them applied vnto our re-*
　　　&c.   *demption.*
　　His readines

The goodnes of God and our redemption.

---

25. His mercie and cōpassion,
　　is as it were, a troubled dis- } *His mercie.*
　　liking of our miseries, as if
　　they were his owne.
　　His loue was defined before.
　　Likewise his zeale and ielousie

---

26. The promises are the Ioy-
　　full shewe and teaching by   *Promises.*
　　message, speache, and writing }
　　of his purpose to remedie our
　　miseries.

　　　　　　　　　　　　　　　　　　　　　　　By his office & message
　　　　　　　　　　　　　　　　　　　　　　　　as before.
　　　　　　　　　　　　　　The　　　　*By*　　*Of the*
　　The sending of his Sonne into *sending* *generation* *spirit be-*
　　the worlde, was the office and   *of*   *which*   *getting.*
　　charge whiche hee gaue him,   } *his*   *was*   *Of the*
　　to worke our saluation, by   *Sōne*   *seede of*
　　taking our Manhoode vnto his   *the Virgin*
　　Godhead.   *made a*
　　　　　　　　　　　　　　　　　　　　　　　　quickning
　　　　　　　　　　　　　　　　　　　　　　　　spirit, &
　　　　　　　　　　　　　　　　　　　　　　　　yet a
　　　　　　　　　　　　　　　　　　　　　　　　liuīg soule
　　　　　　　　　　　　　　　　　　　　　　　　& bodie.

27. Howe did he sende his Sonne into the worlde?
He being God became also man, and tooke our nature vppon him, sinne onely excepted.

Hee was conceyued of the holye Ghoste.

Hee was borne of the Virgine Marie.

27. *How doo all Antichristes holde their course and profession to begin the mischeefe?*
They take on them the name and callings of shepheards in the church, but haue no message.

They are bred from beneath in the bottomles pitte, Reuel. 9.

They breake foorth as Locustes, out of the smoke of the pit.

[B 4 *verso* — C 1 *recto*]

Our redemption. The sufferings of Christ. His victorie.	Damnation by Antichrist.

28. How hath Christ redeemed vs?
He suffered our miseries for vs.
He ouercame and tooke away our miseries.
He restored happines vnto vs.

28. *How do Antichristes destroy, and vndoo the people?*
They first will be sure of their outward welfare, and maintenance by the people.
They then vpholde or bring in one spiritual plague or other, which peruerteth all.
They weare, & spend away the whole spiritual welfare of the church.

27. The Manhoode of Christ, was the making of him a reasonable, liuing man, so that in fashion, nature & qualitie, he was like one of vs, sinne onely excepted. } *The Manhoode.*

His conceauing by the holy Ghost in the wombe of the Virgine, was the working of the holy ghost in the wombe of the Virgine, without carnall copulation with manne, wherby the seede of her bodie, became a liuing man, hauing both soule and bodie.

His conception was without sinne, because the cursed seede was sanctified by the spirit, so that it could no more sinne, yet must it nedes abyde the curse and punishment of sinne. For the bodie sinneth not but by the soule. Nowe his soule was holie, and therefore also his bodie was holy, though it was of the seede of the Virgin. } *The conception.*

His birth was the bringing foorth of the liuing seede into the worlde, being perfect man, and yet without sinne. } *The birth.*

Our redemption. The sufferings of Christ. His victorie.

28. The sufferinges of Christe, is the seruice and yeelding vp of his bodie and soule, to feele and indure in them both the extremitie of all miseries for our cause. } *His sufferings.* { *Of the cause of miserie.* { *The burden of our sinne. The wrath of God.* *Of the miserie it selfe.*

29. How did he suffer our miseries?
Because he was man, he did also abide the wrath and dreadfull curse of God, which was due vnto man.
He suffered death, and the tormentes of hell for vs.
He suffered also in his mēbers, which are his people and church.

29. *How are they sure of their welfare first?*
They get the fauour of some patrone or Byshop, or worldly man.
They get the graunt of some benefice or stipend, without planting the church.
They liue in iolietie, hauing ease and fauour of men.

30. Howe hath he overcome our miseries, and taken them away?
By his righteousnesse, hee ouercame sinne, the cause of our miserie, & tooke it away.
Also by his death and tormentes, hee ouercame and tooke away the wrath of God, and the debte of the Lawe.
Also by his rysing againe, hee ouercame the miserie and curse it selfe.

30. *Howe doo they vpholde, or bringe in one or other spiritual plague?*
By some open wickednes, or false doctrine, they ouerthrow the groūds of religion, and the gouernment of the church.
They make thē selues, and their followers guiltie of the breache of the whole lawe, by peruerting the cheefe lawes: and so procure the wrath of God against them.
The curse of God doth light vpon their labours: so that their shame & plague appeareth.

[C 1 *verso* — C 2 *recto*]

The causes and meanes of happines.   The causes leading to damnation.

31. Howe hath he restored happines?
He hath him selfe obteined the loue of God by his iustification.

31. *How doo they weare and spende awaye the whole spirituall welfare of their flockes?*
The people are vnder them whom God hateth.

A Booke which sheweth the life and manners

29. His suffering of the wrath of God, and the burthen of our sinnes, was his forsaking for a time, as vnworthie of the fauour and blessing of God, being accursed and a castaway. } *His suffering of the wrath of God and burden of sinne.*

30. His ouercomming was the worke of his patience, whereby he gotte his whole purpose in discharging al things wherewith man might be charged, and in taking away all thinges, which hindred our happines. } *His victorie.* { Of the cause of miserie. { Sinne by his righteousnes. Wrath of God. his tormentes.

Of the miserie it selfe by rysing againe from death.

His ouercomming of sinne, was his taking away of the guiltines thereof. } *Ouercomming sinne.*

His ouercomming of the wrath of God was the appeasing of his anger, and satisfying of his Iustice, by induring the curse thereof. } *Ouercomming of the wrath of God.*

The causes and meanes of happines.

31. His restoring of happines was his work of redemptiō, wherby the meanes is offered to all men for to be saued. } *His restoring of good was* { By getting it himself as the { Loue of God by his Iustification. The happiness it self by his ascension.

By getting it for vs.

247

He hath obteined his owne happines by ascending vp into heauen.

He hath also obteined the like for vs, by his mediation.

Also vnder them whome God curseth.

Also they are made like vnto them by obeying and following them.

32. How hath he gotten happines for vs ?

He hath gotten the causes of our happines which are in god. Also the meanes of our happines as proceeding from God. Also he hath gotten the inioying of the happines it selfe.

32. *Howe doo they make the people cursed like to them selues* ?

They ar altogither brought into the displeasure and disliking of God.

They are left helples & without the meanes of saluation.

All woe and miserie waiteth vpon them.

His Iustification was the perfect fulfilling of the will of GOD, accepted of him by pronouncinge his innocencie. } *Iustification.*

The Happines which he got, is the perfect sufficiencie or most blessed state which he hath in God, or it is the blessing of God vppon him, whereby he wanteth nothing, nor hath neede of anie thing else to better his state. } *Happines.*

---

32. The causes of our happines in God, is the secrete sufficiencie which he hath in himself to saue mankinde. } *Christ hath gotten* { *The causes of happines for us* { *In God* { His Counsaile { *In electing* / *In predestinating* / His readines thereon, as before / The meanes from God / *The happines it selfe*

33. What be the causes of our happines in God?
His chusing, and predestinating of vs vnto this happines.
His mercie.
His loue towardes vs.

33. *How are they brought into this displeasure of God?*
They shewe them selues appointed and iudged vnto damnation.
Also that presētly they are vnder the fierce wrath of god & his bitter curse.
And that God hateth & loatheth thē.

34. What be the meanes of our happines from God?
Our calling & leading vnto this happines.
Our obedience thereto in mortifying our selues.
Our raysing and quickning againe.

34. *How are they left helples, & without the meanes of salvation?*
They are called away, and misled to destructiō without any hope of help.
They are desperatly hardened.
They are most fearfully discouraged and troubled, when their euill state appeareth.

A Booke which sheweth the life and manners

33. His Electing or chusing is his free consent or will in his eternall counsell, to saue vs for his names sake, without anie desert of oures, to make knowne his exceeding great mercies. } *Election.*

His Predistinating of vs, is his full consent or counsaile, whereby he is setled to saue those whom he hath chosen, and after that manner which pleaseth and liketh him. } *Predestination.*

34. The meanes of our Happines from God, is the helpe which hee giueth vs in our selues, and among our selues. } *Meanes of happines from God.* { *Calling*

Obedience thereto.

His calling of vs, is his using of all meanes and occasions, to moue vs to the seking of saluatiō in Christ.

His calling of vs in trueth, is when the meanes which moue vs to seeke vnto Christ, are cleare to the conscience, without[1] the outwarde signes thereof. } *Calling.*

---

[1] " Wihthout " in text.

C 2 *verso* — C 3 *recto*.

The calling, Planting, and Couenaunt of the Church.	Misleading. Supplanting. A false couenaunt.
35. What is our calling and leading vnto this happiness ? In the new Testament our calling is in plainer maner: as by the first planting and gathering of the church vnder one kinde of gouernement.	35. *How doo Antichristes call awaye and misleade the people* ? Some are Antichristes, which professing the newe Testament, peruert the same: as they which supplant & ouerthrowe the good state and gouernement of the church.
Also by a further plāting of the church according to that gouernement.	Whiche also establishe their false churche and gouernement in steade therof.
But in the olde Testament, our calling was by shadowes and ceremonies, as among the Jewes.	And some are Antichristes, by peruerting the olde Testament: as the Iewes, which holde stil the shadowes and ceremonies of the olde lawe, & denie Christ to be come in the fleshe.

A Booke which sheweth the life and manners

The calling, Planting, and Couenaunt of the Church.				
35. The new Testament which is called the Gospell or glad tidings, is a ioyfull and plaine declaring and teaching by a due message of the remedie of our miseries thorowe Christe our Redeemer, who is come in the fleshe, a Sauior vnto those which worthelie receyue this message, and hath fulfilled the ould ceremonies.	The newe Testament.	*Our calling and leading to happines*	In the newe Testament more plainly	By the firste planting & gathering of the church under one gouernement.
Our calling in plainer manner, is when the meanes, which moue vs to seeke Christ, are cleare to the conscience, without the outward shadowes and ceremonies thereof.	Our calling in plainer maner.			By a further building according to the gouernmēt.
The Church planted or gathered, is a companie or number of Christians or beleeuers, which by a willing couenant made with their God, are vnder the gouernment of god and Christ, and kepe his lawes in one holie communion: because Christ hath redeemed them vnto holines & happines for euer, from which they were fallen by the sinne of Adam.	The church planted or gathered		In the olde Testament more darkelie	
The Church gouernment, is the Lordshipp of Christ in the communion of his offices: wherby his people obey to his will, and haue mutual vse of their graces and callings, to further their godlines and welfare.	The church gouernement.			

36. Howe must the churche be first planted and gathered vnder one kinde of gouernement?

First by a couenant and condicion, made on Gods behalfe.

Secondlie by a couenant and condicion made on our behalfe.

Thirdlie by vsing the sacrament of Baptisme to seale those condicions, and couenants.

36. *Howe doo they supplant, and ouerthrowe the good state and gouernement of the church?*

They wrest and mocke the Lords couenant, as if he offered thē grace.

The people doo yoake and binde away them selues by their couenant, from the Lord and his grace.

They make their Baptisme a pledge, and seale of gracelesnes & mischeefe.

---

37. What is the couenant, or condicion on Gods behalfe?

His promise to be our God and and Sauiour, if we forsake not his gouernement by disobedience.

Also his promise to be the God of our seede, while we are his people.

Also, the gifte of his spirit to his children as an inwarde calling and furtheraunce of godlines.

37. *How doo they wrest and mocke the Lords couenaunt?*

By a blasphemous abusing of the name and promises of God, they make thē selues their Gods, by holding thē bondslaues to ther government. Also they holde their children and seede in like bondage. Also they intāgle thē with a spirit of error & cōtinual misgeuīg frō good.

A Booke which sheweth the life and manners

The first planting & gathering of the Church.
- By the couenant,
  - On Gods behalfe.
  - On our behalfe.
- By the Sacrament thereof.

36. The couenant on Gods behalf is his agreement or partaking of condicions with vs that if we keepe his lawes, not forsaking his gouernment, hee will take vs for his people, & blesse vs accordingly.

The couenant on Gods behalfe.
- His promise.
- His Spirit.

37. His promisse to his church, is his sure couenant, remembred, taught, and held by the church, and the seede thereof: whereby it onely hath assurance of saluation in Christ.

His promise
- To the Church.
- To the seede thereof.

The spirit of God in vs, is an inwarde working of the holy Ghost in our hartes, stirring and d r a w i n g vs to take Christe for our Sauiour, and preparing and strēgthning vs vnto all goodnes.

The Spirit of God in vs.

C 3 verso — 4 recto.

Our covenant with God. Our baptising.	A false couenant, and false baptisme.
38. What is the covenant or condicion on our behalfe? We must offer and geue vp our selues to be of the church and people of God. We must likewise offer and geue vp our children and others being vnder age, if they be of our householde and we haue full power ouer them. We must make profession, that we are his people, by submitting our selues to his lawes and gouernement.	38. *Howe doo the people yoake and binde awaye them selues from the Lorde and his grace?* They cutt of[f] and keepe awaye them selues from the true church, to be amonge the wicked. They geue vp them selues & others to be of their popishe parishes, and felloshippe. They beare the image and markes of Antichristian people, by obeying and keeping the lawes of Antichrist.
39. How must Baptisme be vsed, as a seale of this covenaunt? They must be duelie presented, and offered to God, and the church, which are to be Baptised. They must be duelie receiued vnto grace and fellowship.	39. *How do they make Baptisme a pledge and seale of gracelesnes & mischiefe?* They are brought to bee baptised vnto Antichrist, and his popish parishes. Then also in stead of due receauing, there is a gracelesse forceing, and rauening of them vnto damnation.

A Booke which sheweth the life and manners

Our couenant with God. Our baptising.

38. The couenaunt on our behalfe, is our agreement and partaking of conditions with God, that he shalbe our God so long, as wee keepe vnder his gouernement, and obey his lawes, and no longer.
The giuing vp of our selues and our seede to be of the church, is a duetifulnes in seeking holines and happines by Christe, in his Church, which onely we haue, by a couenaunt to be vnder his gouernement in the Church, and by obeying thereto.
Our profession and submission to his lawes & gouernement, is the keeping of our couenant, by leading a godly and Christian life.

The couenaunt on our behalf

In offering & giuig up to be of the church. In professing & leading a Christian life.

Our selues. Our children. and seede.

Offering and giuing vp to be of the Church.

Professing and submitting to the Church gouernement.

39. Baptisme is a Sacrament or marke of the outwarde church, sealing vnto vs by the washing of our bodies in water, and the word accordingly preached, our suffering with Christ to die vnto sinne by repentance, and our rising with him to liue vnto righteousnes, and also sealing our calling, profession, and happines gotten by our faith in the victorie of the same Iesus Christ..

The vse of Baptisme is,

By due presenting and offering of the parties to be baptised.

By due receyuing of them to grace and fellowshippe.

| 40. How must they be presented and offered? | 40. *How are they geuen vp vnto popish parishes?* |

40. How must they be presented and offered?

The children of the faithful, though they be infantes are to be offered to God and the church, that they may be Baptised.

Also those infantes or children which are of the householde of the faithfull, and vnder their full power.

Also all of discretion which are not baptised, if they holde the Christian profession, and shewe forth the same.

40. *How are they geuen vp vnto popish parishes?*

The children of the wicked and vnfaithfull, are offered by godfathers and godmothers, and brought to their parishes.

The parentes and gouernours haue no authoritie to present them.

They hould not the christian profession, nor shew forth the same.

C 4 *verso* — D 1 *recto*.

| *Due receyuing and baptising into the Church.* | Popishe baptisme. |

41. How must they be receaued vnto grace and felloshippe?

The worde must be duely preached in an holie assemblie. The signe or Sacrament must be applied thereto.

41. *What is their gracelesse forceing and rauening of them?*

A lawe doth binde the priest and people to a popish reading, or to a dead & frutelesse forme of wordes. The signe is made a superstititious trifling & colouring of abominations.

A Booke which sheweth the life and manners

40. Presenting and offering of persons to be baptised, is a duetifulnes in the parentes and gouernours which offer, or in the parties which offer themselues, whereby they seeke t h e i r saluation by ioyning with the church in one christian communion. } *Presenting and offering* { *By the gouernours,* { As parents and Rulers which offer their children, or them of their houseMolde.

By the parties them selues, hauing discretion.

The due receyuing vnto grace and fellowship is a duetifulnes of the Church in partaking with those in one Christian communiō, which are meete for the same. } *Due receyuing.* { By due preaching of the Worde.

By right applying of the signe thereto.

Due receyuing and baptising into the Church.

---

41. By preaching the worde of Baptisme, we vnderstande not the blinde reading, or fruitles prating thereof at randome, but a due teaching by lawfull messengers, of our redemption, mortifying, and raysing with Christ. } *The word of Baptisme preached, as* { Of our whole redemption, and the promises to the Church.

Of taking vse therof { By mortifying.

By raysing.

42. How must the word be preached?

The preacher being called and meete thereto, must shewe the redemption of christians by Christ, and the promises receaued by faith as before.

Also they must shewe the right vse of that redemption, in suffering with Christ to dye vnto sinne by repētance. Also the raising and quickning again vpon repentance.

42. *What is their dead reading or frutelesse forme of teaching?*

A blind guide or priestlie Preacher, by a shewe of reading or telling a redemption by Christ, doth snare thē with the abominations of Antichrist[.]

They lead them to desperate hardning, by the wicked guiding of their parishes or charges.

They are vtterlye withdrawne from goodnes to sett them selues on mischeefe and wickednes.

---

43. Howe must the signe be applied thereto?

The bodies of the parties baptised must be washed w^t water, or sprinckled or dipped, in the name of the Father, and of ye Sonne, and of the holy Ghost, vnto the forgeuenes of sinnes, and dying thereto in one death and burial with Christ.

The preacher must pronounce thē to be baptised into ye bodie and gouernement of Christ, to be taught & to professe his lawes, that by his mediatiō & victorie, they might rise againe with him vnto holines & happines for euer.

The church must geue thankes for the partie baptised, and praye for his further instruction, and traininge vnto saluation.

43. *How is the signe made a superstititious trifle?*

They blasphemously abuse the name of god in baptising thē, wherby they further come vnder the fierce wrath of god & his bitter curse, to be more desperatlie hardened in their sinnes.

Thei are pronounced to be baptised into their wicked fellowship and gouernment, to be taught & to professe with some lawes of Christ, the lawes of antichrist especially, & to be set on mischiefe, and left helplesse therein. The parishe with a false worship and idoll seruice geue thankes, and pray vnto God as to an idoll: wherby there is a further increase of wickednes & miserie to the partie baptised.

A Booke which sheweth the life and manners

42. Our redemption is defined before.

Our sufferings and raysing do followe after to be handled.

---

43. Baptising in the name of God, is a due applying of the signe of washing or sprinckling to the worde duelie preached, by him which is knowne to be sent of God.

    Baptising in the name of God.

Baptising into the bodie and gouernement of Christ, is when the parties Baptised are receyued vnto grace and fellowshippe, by partaking with the church in one Christian communion.

    Baptising into the bodie and gouernement of Christ.

Thankes giuing and Prayer doo followe after to be spoken of: here they be mencioned by occasion.

Harrison & Browne

[D 1 verso — D 2 recto]

The graces and offices in Christ: and first his priesthood.	The offices of Antichrist: & first his priesthood.
Hitherto of the first gathering and planting of the Church. 44. How must it be further builded, accordinge vnto churche gouernement? First by communion of the graces & offices in the head of ye church, which is Christ. Secondly, by communion of the graces and offices in the bodie, which is the church of Christ. Thirdly, by vsing the Sacrament of the Lords Supper, as a seale of this communion.	Hitherto of supplanting of the true Church. 44. *How do they establish their false church & gouernmēt in stead therof?* They are first vnder one chiefe Antichrist the Pope, or vnder other Antichrists, which resēble him: or sprang vp of him, and receaue their image and markes. They draw corruptions, and partake wickednes one with an other, in one common plague. They make their supper of communion, a pledge & seale of their wretched confusion.
45. Howe hath the churche the communion of those graces & offices, which are in Christ? It hath the vse of his priesthoode: because he is the high Priest thereof. Also of his prophecie: because he is the Prophet thereof. Also of his kingdome and gouernement: because he is the kynge and Lord thereof.	45. *How are they vnder some one chiefe Antichrist, and receaue his image and markes?* They put religion, & holines in their fellowship vnder his abominations, and so he is their priest. They follow his lawes and ordinances: and so he is their prophet. They hould his gouernment, and so he is their kinge.

A Booke which sheweth the life and manners

The graces and offices in Christ: and first his priesthood.

44. The communion of graces, is a mutuall vsing of friendshippe and callings, to pleasure and be pleasured in all christian charitie.
Christ is the Sonne of God, made by his Father the Heade and Lorde of the Churche, because he hath anoynted and filled him with his Spirit, and hath giuen him an office and charge, and the fulnes of all graces to worke our saluation.
Antichrist is the childe of the Deuill, filled with the spirit of delusion and hypocrisie, who hath an vsurped office ouer false christians, named the church of God, and by the strength of his lawes, gouernement, and superstitious ceremonies, doeth ouerthrowe their redemption by Christ.

{ *Communion of graces* { *In the Head & highest as in Christe, by* { *His Priesthood. His rule.*

Christ. *In the body which is the Church.*

Antichrist.

45. The Priesthoode of Christ is his office of mediation and seruice in the church, for attonement and sanctification, whereby all sinne and vncleannes is taken away.
The Priesthoode of Antichrist is his office of tolerating and dispensing with wickednes, that it may remaine, and agreement might be made betweene Christ and Belial.

Priesthood of Christ.

Priesthoode of Antichrist.

{ *In making attonement* { *By forgiuenes of sinnes. By iustification.*
In sanctifying vs.

46. What vse hath the churche of his priesthoode? Thereby he is our mediatour, and we present and offer vppe our praiers in his name, because by his intreatie, our sinnes are forgeuen.
Also he is our iustification, because by his attonement we are iustified.
Also he is our Sanctification, because he partaketh vnto vs his holines and spirituall graces.

46. *How is Antichrist their priest?*
A vile person presenteth their prayers to God, as a spokesman for them, and pronounceth absolutiō of their sinnes: and that by stinting and limiting in popish wise.
Also hee tolerateth, and dispenseth with wickednes, to iustifie iniquitie.
Also by a vaine hallowing and blessing them selues vnder him, they draw and increase their corruption and filthines by him.

[D 2 *verso* — 3 *recto*]

| *The Prophecie, & Kingly office of Christ.* | The Prophecie, & Kingdom of Antichrist. |
---

47. What vse hath the church of his prophecie?
He him selfe hath taught vs, and geuen vs his lawes.
He preacheth vnto vs by his worde & message in the mouthes of his messengers.
He appoynteth to euerie one their callinges and dueties.

47. *How is Antichrist their prophet?*
He geueth them lawes and iniunctions, which they receaue.
He sendeth his hirelings to preach and vphoulde, with some lawes of Christ, his owne lawes especially.
He misleadeth euerie one to his mischeuous busines.

A Booke which sheweth the life and manners

46. His Mediation is a duetie of his Priestlie office, in seeking and getting the helpe & blessing of God towardes vs, by the fauor of God towardes him: and therfore he complaineth & intreateth for vs, as belonging vnto him. } *Mediation of Christ.*

The forgiuenes of sinnes is the mercifull graūt of God to the prayer of Christ, that the sinnes of his, for whom he answered in righteousnes, might be taken away. } *Forgiuenes of sinnes.*

Our Iustification, is the ful discharge of al dueties wherewith the lawe charged vs, which deliuereth vs from the guiltines of sinne, by the righteousnes of Christ. } *Iustification.*

Our Sanctification is the partaking of the holines & spiritual graces of Christ Iesus, whereby we serue God in newnesse of spirite. } *Sanctification.*

The Prophecie, & Kingly office of Christ.

47. The Prophecie of Christ is his office of teaching and giuing lawes to his people, wherby he vseth their obedience to learne and know the same. } *Prophecie of Christ.* { In teaching. { By him selfe. By his messengers. By example. By charging. } In directing.

His preaching by his seruauntes, is the message he giueth to those whom he sendeth, to vse the obedience of his people in learning, that they might knowe his lawes and his will. } *His message.*

265

48. What vse hath the churche of his Kinglie office? By that he executeth his laws: First, by ouerseeing and trying out wickednes.
Also by priuate or open rebuke, of priuate or open offenders.
Also by separation of the wilfull, or more greeuous offenders.

48. *How is Antichrist their King?* He forceth his religiō by civil power, or by binding their consciences: whereby he hideth & shifteth away their guiltines, which the word doth bewray.
His officers chide and braule to increase their power & riches by those which offend them.
They excōmunicate some frō their churches, to communicate damnation more surely to those, which are in their churches.

His appointing and moderating, is whereby all haue their office and charge at his handes. } *His appointing of dueties.*

The prophecie of Antichrist, is his office of teaching and giuing lawes to his people, whereby he abuseth their obedience to holde and learne with some lawes of Christ his owne lawes especiallie. } *Prophecie of Antichrist.*

48. The kingdome of Christ, is his office of gouernement, whereby he vseth the obedience of his people to keepe his lawes & commaundements, to their saluation and welfare.

Kingdom of Christ by { *Ouerseeing and trying out wickednes.* { *Rebuke.* *Recompence.* *Separation.*

The kingdome of Antichrist, is his gouernmēt, confirmed by the civill Magistrate, whereby he abuseth the obedience of the people, to keepe his euill lawes and customes to their own damnation. } *Kingdome of Antichrist.*

The ouerseeing and trying out of wickednes, is his forceable taking of accountes, by the watch in his church, and the skāning of things by his worde, whereby he maketh known that which anie would hyde. } *Ouerseeing and trying out of wickednes by Christ.*

[D 3 verso — 4 recto]

Graces and offices vnder Christ.	Antichristian officers with their corruptions.
49. What vse hath the churche of the graces and offices vnder Christ? It hath those which haue office of teaching and guiding. Also those which haue office of cherishing and releeuing the afflicted & poore. Also it hath the graces of all the brethren and people to doe good withall.	49. *What is the common plagne* [sic], *in drawing corruptions, and partaking wickednes together vnder Antichrist?* Some haue office of deceauing, and misleading the people. Some of prouiding for the belly and kitchin. All the company do partake, & further wickednes, in a false worship & vngodly behauiour.

A Booke which sheweth the life and manners

Rebuke, is a pronouncing of the knowne wickednes of anie with condemning the same in the hearing of the offēder only if his fault be priuate, or of witnesses, if he be wilfull therein & openlie iustifie it, or of the church if he yet bee more wilfull, or else if his faulte be open in the presence and hearing of those whiche see his fault, or if he be wilful, before the churche, whereby he may be ashamed and others feare. } *Church rebuke.*

Separatiō of the open wilfull, or greeuous offēders, is a dutifulnes of the church in withholding from them the christian communion and fellowship, by pronouncing and shewing the couenaunt of christian cōmunion to be broken by their greeuous wickednes, and that with mourning, fasting, and prayer for them, & denouncing Gods iudgements against them. } *Separation from the Church.*

Graces and offices vnder Christ: and the sortes of them.

---

49. The office of teaching and guiding, is a charge or message committed by God vnto those which haue grace and giftes for the same, and therето are tried and duelie receyued of the people, to vse their obedience in learning and keeping the lawes of God. } *Offices of teaching and guiding.* { *Participate.* *Seuerall.* }

50. Who haue the grace & office of teaching and guiding?
Some haue this charge and office together, which can not be sundred.
Some haue their seueral charge ouer manie churches.
Some haue charge but in one church onelie.

50. *Who haue the office of deceauing and misleading the people?*
Some haue their authoritie, & power of rauening, ioined together and participate.
Likewise some haue their seueral power, to rauene manie churches.
Also some are tied toe particular churches.

51. How haue some their charge and office together?
There be Synodes or the meetings of sundrie churches: which are when the weaker churches seeke helpe of the stronger, for deciding or redressing of matters: or else the stronger looke to them for redresse.
There is also prophecie, or meetings for the vse of euerie mans gift, in talk or reasoning, or exhortacion and doctrine.
There is the Eldershippe, or meetings of the most forwarde and wise, for lookinge to matters.

51. *Howe haue they their Antichristian authoritie ioyned & partaking?*
They haue their popishe Synodes, & counselles, and conuocations. &c.
They haue their prophecies, commō places, colleges, &c: for the abuse of mens guiftes, by trifllinges and stintings, by inioyninges and charginges in popishe wise.
They haue their spirituall courts, c h u r c h w a r d e n s sydemen, &c.

A Booke which sheweth the life and manners

50. The offices or charges participate and ioyned, are, whiche haue their execution and gouernement, with consent and counsell of diuers in the same office and charge. } *Offices participat.* { With manie, as } *Synodes.* / *Prophecie.* ; With fewer, as } *Eldershippe.*

51. A Synode is a Ioyning or partaking of the authoritie of manie Churches mette togither in peace, for redresse and deciding of matters, which can not wel be otherwise taken vp. } *Synodes.*

Prophecie is a ioyning or partaking of the office of manie Teachers in peaceable manner, both for iudgement and tryall, and also for the vse of euerie mannes gifte, in talke, reasoning, exhortation, or doctrine. } *Prophecie.*

Eldership is Ioyning or partaking of the authoritie of Elders, or forwardest and wysest in a peaceable meeting, for redressing and deciding of matters in particular Churches, and for counsaile therein. } *Eldership.*

[D 4 *verso* — E 1 *recto*]

Apostles. Prophets. Euang. *Pastors. Teach. &c.*	*Popish Commiss. Legates.* *Byshopes &c.*
52. Who haue their seueral charge ouer many churches? Apostles had charge ouer many churches. Likewise, Prophetes, which had their reuelations or visions. Likewise helpers vnto these as Euāgelistes, and companions of their iourneis.	52. *Who haue their false charge ouer manie churches?* High popishe Commissioners, and Legates, &c. Archbishoppes, and Bishoppes. &c. Also helpers vnto these, as Chaūcelours, Commissareis, Sumners, &c : rouing and wandring Ministers.

Apostles, Prophets, Euang, Pastors. Teachers. Elders. &c.

52. An Apostle is a person hauing office and message from God, for the which he is meete, vnto all persons and churches, to shewe them their state of damnatiō for some notable want or wickednes, and to vse the obedience of all persons and churches whiche receyue him, to plante, reforme, and set order for auoyding that damnation.

A Prophet is a person hauing office and message from God, for the which hee is meete, to foretell of plagues or of blessings which GOD hath shewed to the Prophet, & to vse the obedience of all which receiue him, to plante, reforme, and set order for the auoyding of the plagues, and the obtayning of the blessings.

Euangelistes are persons hauing office & message of God, for the which they are tried to be meete and thereto are chosen where the church is planted, or receiued by obedience, whē they plant the church, to helpe the Apostles or Prophetes, either by preparing a way for them to do the more good, or by holding that waye & course which the Apostles and Prophetes appointe vnto them.

{ *Apostles.* / *Prophetes* / *Euangelistes* }

{ Teaching and guiding many churches, }

{ Chief laborers / Helpers vnto thē. }

{ *Apostles.* / *Prophetes.* / *Euangelistes.* / Cōpanions of their iourneys. }

53. Who haue their seuerall charge in one Churche onely, to teache and guide the same?

The Pastour, or he which hath the guift of exhorting, and applying especiallie.

The Teacher, or he whiche hath the guift of teaching especially: and lesse guift of exhorting and applying.

They whiche helpe vnto them both in ouerseeing and counsailinge, as the most forward or Elders.

53. *Who haue their false charge ouer one churche onlie, to deceaue and misleade it?*

Priestes, Parsons, Vicars, Curats, and the rest of that rable, which ar thrust vppon the flocke.

And helpers vnto these, as euerie Questman, and the Clarks, and Readers, and Singers, &c.

54. Who haue office of cherishing and releeuing the afflicted and poore?

The Releeuers or Deacons, which are to gather and bestowe the church liberalitie.

The Widowes, which are to praye for the church, with attendaunce to the sicke and afflicted thereof.

54. *Whoe be for the kitchin, and for feeding the bellie?*

They haue their civil collections popishlie established.

A l s o, Amners, Almsemen, Beade-houses, M o u r n e r s, Stewards, Cookes with all that rable.

A Booke which sheweth the life and manners

53. A Pastor is a person hauing office and message of God, for exhorting & mouing especially and guiding accordinglie: for the which he is tried to be meete, & thereto is duelie chosen by the church which calleth him, or receyued by obedience where he planteth the Church.

A Teacher of doctrine is a person hauing office and message of God, for teaching especiallie and guiding accordinglie, with lesse gifte to exhorte and applie, for the which he is tried to be meete, and thereto is duelie chosen by the church which calleth him, or receyued by obedience, where he planteth the church.

An Elder or more forward in gifte, is a person hauing office and message of God, for ouersight and counsaile, and redressing thinges amisse, for the which he is tried. &c.

54. The Releeuer is a person hauing office of God to prouide, gather & bestowe the giftes and liberalitie of the church, as there is neede: to the which office he is tried and receyued as meete.

The Widowe is a person hauing office of god to pray for the church & to visit and minister to those which are afflicted & distressed in the church, for the which she is tried and receyued as meete.

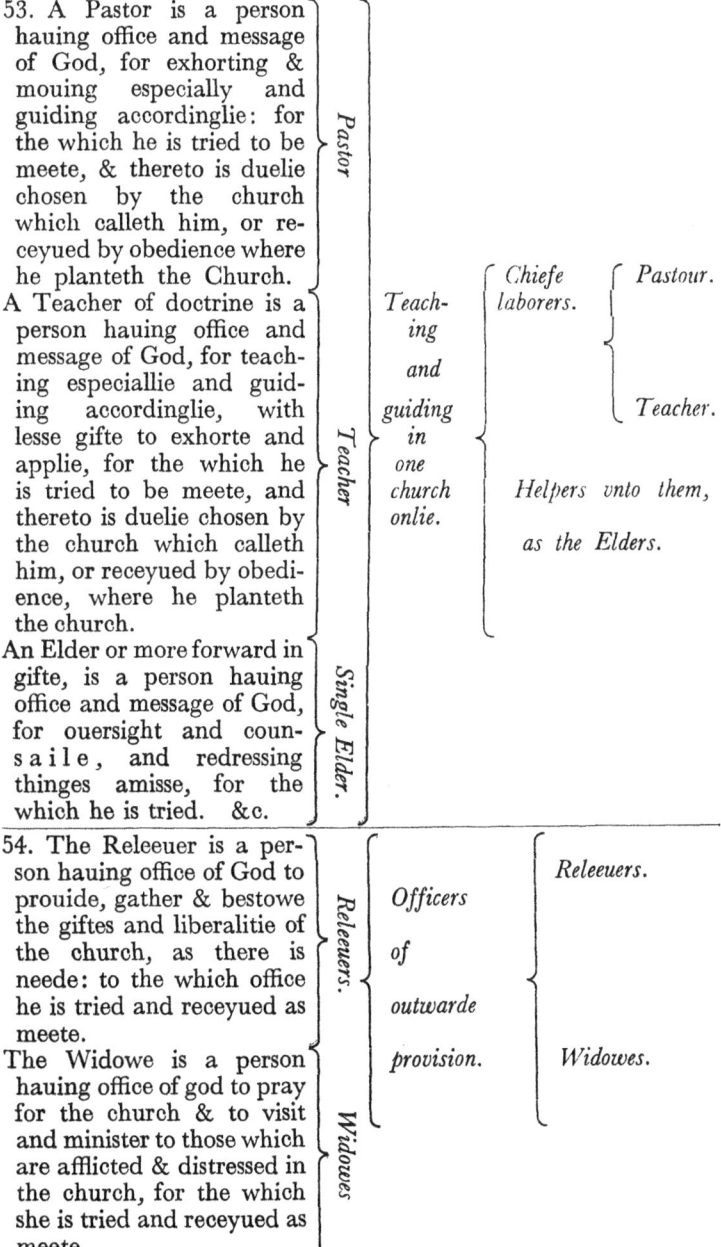

Pastor · Teacher · Single Elder. } Teaching and guiding in one church onlie. { Chiefe laborers. { Pastour. Teacher. } Helpers vnto them, as the Elders.

Releeuers · Widowes. } Officers of outwarde provision. { Releeuers. Widowes.

[E 1 verso — 2 recto]

All Christians made Kinges, Priests, & Prophets.	All the wicked a common Plague.
55. How hath the church the vse of those graces, which al y̆ᵉ brethrē & people haue to do good withal ? Because euerie one of the church is made a Kinge, a Priest, and a Prophet vnder Christ, to vpholde and further the Kingdom of God, & to breake and destroie the kingdome of Antichrist, and Satan.	55. *Howe are the people of the euill churches a plague to them selues, by partaking wickednes one with an other ?* Euery one is a captaine and ringleader to mischeefe. Also a spirituall infection, and abomination. Also a false & wretched deceauour.
56. Howe are we made Kinges ? We must all watch one an other, and trie out all wickednes. We must priuatlie and openlie rebuke, the priuat and open offendours. We must also separate the wilful and more greeuous offenders, and withdraw our selues frō them, and gather the righteous togither.	56. *Howe is euerie one a captaine and ringleader to mischeefe ?* Thei all seek occasions of euill, and hunt for the bloud of the righteous. They chide & brawle without shame both priuatlie and openlie. They drive and chase from them the righteous, and loath their companie.
57. How are all Christians made Priestes vnder Christ ? They present and offer vp praiers vnto God, for them selues & for others. They turne others from iniquitie, so that attonement is made in Christ vnto iustification. In them also and for them others are sanctified, by partaking the graces of Christ vnto them.	57. *Howe are they a spirituall infection and abomination ?* By a shewe of deuotion in their false worshippe & idol seruice, they make others like them in their wickednes. They tollerate & cherish wickednes, to iustifie the same. In them also and by them others be accursed, by drawinge their corruptions.

A Booke which sheweth the life and manners

All Christians made Kings, Priestes & Prophetes.

55. The kingdome of all Christians is their office of guiding and ruling with Christ, to subdue the wicked, and make one another obedient to Christ.	*The kinglie office of al Christians.*
Their Priesthoode is their office of cleansing and redressing wickednes, whereby sinne and vncleanes is taken away from amongst them.	*The Priesthoode of euerie Christian.*
Their Prophecie is their office of iudging all thinges by the worde of God, whereby they increase in knowledge and wisedome among them selues.	*Euery Christian a Prophete.*

56. *Looke question 48.*
- Kinglie office of all Christians.
  - For watching & trying out wickednes. → In watching and trying out wickednes.
  - For private and open rebuke. → In recompensing. → Rebuke.
  - For separation. → Separation.

57. *Looke question 46.*
- Priesthood of all christians.
  - For praying for others. → In attonement and appeasing → By prayer vnto forgiuenes.
  - For Iustification. → By Iustification.
  - For Sanctification. → In Sanctification.

58. How are all Christians made prophetes vnder Christ?
They teach the lawes of Christ, and talke and reason for the maintenaūce of them.
They exhorte, moue, and stirre vp to the keeping of his lawes.
They appoint, counsel, and tell one an other their dueties.

58. *How are they false and wretched deceauers?*
They stand & reason for their lawes and traditions.
They incourage & strēgthen one another, with flatterings & pleasinges.
They misleade by their counsell and example, to their mischeeuous busines.

[E 2 *verso* — 3 *recto*]

The Lordes Supper. Preparation to receaue it. Ministration thereof.   Popish Communion.

Hitherto of the communion of offices and graces in the church. Nowe followeth the right vsing of the Lordes Supper, as a seale of this communion.
Howe men should enter and take on them Church callings, and offices, and execute the same: Looke question 114.

59. How must we vse the Sacrament of the Lords supper, as a seale of this communion?
There must be a due preparation to receaue the Lords Supper. And a due ministration thereof.

59. *How do they make their supper of communion, a pledge & seale of their wretched confusion?*
They are most toward and fit to receaue their owne supper, but not the Lordes.
They handle their supper in a vile, & abominable maner.

A Booke which sheweth the life and manners

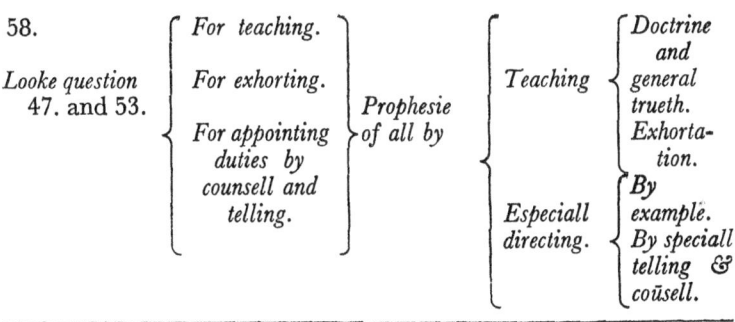

58.

Looke question 47. and 53.

The Lordes Supper. Preparation to receaue it. Ministration thereof.

59. The Lords supper is a Sacrament or marke of the apparent Church, sealing vnto vs by the breaking and eating of breade and drinking the Cuppe in one holie communion, and by the worde accordinglie preached, that we are happilie redeemed by the breaking of the bodie and shedding of the bloud of Christ Iesus, and we thereby growe into one bodie, and church, in one communion of graces, whereof Christ is the heade, to keepe and seake agreement vnder one lawe and gouernement in all thankefulnes & holy obedience.

A shorter definition.
Or brieflie, It is a seale of our partaking and growing togither in one bodie, whereof Christe is the heade in one Christian communion.

The Lordes Supper.

In due preparation to receyue it.

In the due ministration thereof.

60. What preparation must[1] there be to receaue the Lords supper?
There must be a separation frō those which are none of the church, or be vnmeete to receaue, that the worthie may be onely receaued.
All open offences and faultings must be redressed.
All must proue and examine them selues, that their conscience be cleare by faith and repentance, before they receaue.

60. *How are they most toward and fyt to receaue their owne supper?*
They partake open wickednes in one wicked fellowship.
Open offences & sinnes, are amongst them incurable.
All do flatter them selues with a superstitious likeing off an outwarde shew of some holines.

61. How is the supper rightlie ministred?
The worde must be duelie preached.
And the signe or sacrament must be rightlie applied thereto.

61. *What is their vile and abominable handling thereof?*
The law doth bynd the priest & people to a popish reading: or to a dead and fruitlesse teaching.
And the signe is made a superstitious trifling, & colouring of abominatiōs.

---

[1] "nust" in text.

A Booke which sheweth the life and manners

60. Preparation to receiue, is a duetifulnes in vsing meanes, that it maye be in right and due manner.
Separatiō of the vnworthie, is a withholding of them from that communion and fellowship in the supper, beeing not prepared nor meete thereto.
Redressing open offences and faultings, is a duetifulnes in vsing meanes, that the parties which doo offende, may be openly knowne to be amended, or separation made.
Examining our Cōscience, is a due applying of the worde of God vnto the same, to know our good and euill life, least the guiltines of our secret sinnes and priuate offences doo make vs vnworthie receyuers.

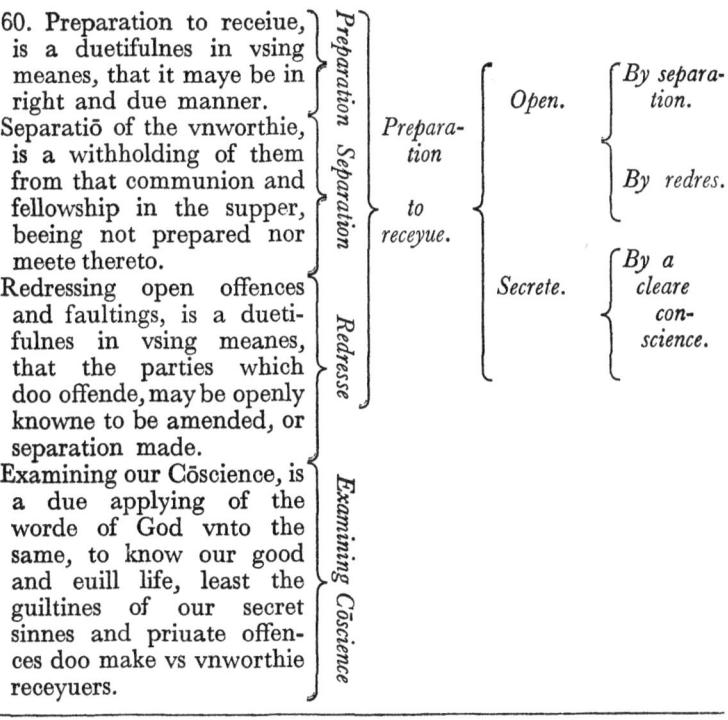

Preparation Separation Redresse } Preparation to receyue. { Open. { By separation. / By redres. }
Secrete. { By a cleare conscience. }

Examining Cōscience

---

61. Ministration of the Supper, is a due manner of vsing the same by applying it to a right communion.
By preaching the worde of communion we vnderstande not the blinde reading, or fruitlesse pratlinge thereof at randome, but a teaching by lawful messengers, of the right vsing of the bodie and blood of Christ in one holie communion, and that with power.

Ministration of the supper. } { By preaching the word. / By applying the signe. }

Preaching the word of Communion.

281

[E 3 verso — 4 recto]

The Word and the Sacrament together.	A vaine worde applied to a vaine trifling.
62. How must the worde be duelie preached ? The death and tormentes of Christ, by breaking his bodie and sheading his bloud for our sinnes, must be shewed by the lawfull preacher. Also he must shewe the spirituall vse of the bodie & bloud of Christ Iesus, by a spirituall feeding thereon, and growing into it, by one holie communion. Also our thankefulnes, and further profiting in godlines vnto life everlasting.	62. *What is their popish reading, or dead and fruitlesse teaching* ? By a shew of reading, or telling of the body & bloud of Christ, which were geuen for them, they mocke them with a shadow of his body, or rather a counterfet. They make them guiltie of the bodie and bloud of Christ Jesus. They are imbouldned, & made carelesse in their wickednes.

The Worde and the Sacrament together.

62. *The death and torments of Christe, were defined before.*

The spirituall vse and feeding of the bodie & blood of Christ, is an applying of his whole worke of our redemption by that outwarde signe, to feele effectuallie the remedie of our miseries by that partaking & growing togither in one bodie of Christ and spirituall Communion.

Feeding by faith of the bodie and bloud of Christ.

Thankesgiuing and profiting in godlines are afterwarde defined.

[E 4 verso — F 1 recto]

The appliing of the signe to the Worde.	*The Signe made mockerie and trifle.*
63. How must the signe be applied thereto? The preacher must take breade and blesse and geue thankes, and thē must he breake it and pronounce it to be the body of Christ, which was broken for thē, that by fayth they might feede thereon spirituallie & growe into one spiritual bodie of Christ, and so he eating thereof himselfe, must bidd them take and eate it among them, & feede on Christ in their consciences. Likewise also must he take the cuppe and blesse and geue thankes, and so pronounce it to be the bloud of Christ in the newe Testament, which was shedd for remission of sinnes, that by fayth we might drinke it spirituallie, and so be nourished in one spirituall bodie of Christ, all sinne being clensed away, and then he drinking thereof himselfe must bydd them drinke thereof likewise and diuide it amōg them, and feede on Christe in their consciences. Then must they all giue thankes praying for their further profiting in godlines & vowing their obedience.	63. How is the sign made a superstitious triflinge and colouringe of abominations? They take breade or a wafer cake, and inchaunte it by reading a grace ouer it, and a number of other prayers: they reade it to be the bodye of Christ, which is but an Idole in stead thereof, and they feede on it by their superstition, and growe into one wicked communion: so the priest doth eate of it himselfe, and carieth it rounde about vnto them, with a vayne babling ouer euery one, which receyue and eate it kneeling downe before him. Likewise also they take the cuppe, and inchaunte it, by reading a grace, or other prayers ouer it: then they reade it or by the booke pronounce it to be the bloud of Christ, which is but an Idole in steade thereof. And so he and they drinking it, doe euen drinke their iniquitie, and feede thereon. So are they imbouldned and further strengthned in ther sinne.

Hitherto of our calling in the newe Testament.

The applying of the Signe to the worde.

63. Applying of the signe, is a due manner of giuing, taking, and vsing it in an holy communion vppon the worde preached. } *Applying the signe.*

Pronouncing the breade to be the bodie of Christe, is a warranting and sanctifying thereof, by the authoritie of God in the message of the Preacher, to bee an outwarde religious signe, seale. or pledge of his bodie broken for vs, and of the spirituall grace receyued thereby. } *The breade the bodie of Christ.*

Pronouncing the drinke to be the blood of Christe, is a warranting or sanctifying thereof, by the authoritie of God in the message of the Preacher, to bee an outwarde religious signe and seale or pledge of his bloudsheading for remission of our sinnes, and of the spirituall grace receyued thereby. } *The drinke the bloude of Christ.*

The Jewish State before time, and at this day.

[F 1 verso — 2 recto]

Calling by Ceremonies.	Misleading by Ceremonies.

Now followeth what calling the Iewes had in the olde Testament, as by shadowes and ceremonies, which nowe are abolished.

It were to[o] long to write of all the Iewishe Ceremonies, seeing wee would haue this Booke so small as we could. For the order of handling them, there is no difficultie, for looke as the pointes and matter of our redemption be, so must the ceremonies be applied thereto.

64. What calling is there by ceremonies and shadowes?	To apply this to the Iewes at this tyme.
By outwarde sensible signes, they teach vs spirituall graces: as the ceremonies of the oulde law, which are abolished.	64. *How are the Iewes called away, & misled by the ceremonies?* Their outward sensible signes, are a mockerie of the spirituall graces: yea Idols be they and superstititious trifles in stead of grace and truth, which is by Christ Iesus.
And in the new Testament, the two Sacraments before mencioned.	

A Booke which sheweth the life and manners

Definitions.	Divisions.

Calling by Ceremonies.

64. The olde Testament was a declaring & teaching by a due message from God, of the redemption by Christ, who was yet for to come: but yet in darker manner, by the shadowes a n d ceremonies applied to the doctrine, to represent Christe Iesus.	The olde Testament.
Ceremonies be outwarde sensible signes, sanctified and applied by the worde duelie preached, to be religious shewes of some spirituall graces, which are meant thereby.	Ceremonies { *Remayning as the two Sacramentes.* / *Abolished.*
Ceremonies remaining (which rather are to be called Sacramentes) are Religious Signes and seales, confirming and sealing vnto vs by the worde duly preached, a spiritual Grace receaued alredy.	Sacramentes.
For they be rather seales of graces receyued, then shewes and shadowes of graces comming.	
Ceremonies abolished a r e, which being fulfilled in Christ, whom and whose dooinges they did signifie, doo cease to be helde anie longer: because Christe Iesus hath made our saluation so cleare, that to vse the olde ceremonies, were to darken the light with shadowes, and to chaunge Christ Iesus him selfe, for the signes and shewes of him.	Ceremonies abolished.

[F 2 verso][1]

²Calling by Ceremonies.

65. Which be the ceremonies of the ould law?
Some were ceremonies of the whole church, and of our whole redemption. As the Garden of Eden after the fall of man. For the Tree of lyfe which before the fall of Adam was but a token of his obedience, of his welfare and happie life thereby, was nowe made a signe of life in Christ Iesus. Also his driuing from the tree & garden, was a signe that he should seeke life and redemption, by Christ in his Church. For the Garden also did shadowe out the Church, as the Tree did shadowe Christ Iesus.

Also the Altar, and place togither where it stoode before the Tabernacle was commaunded. For the Church of God is as holie grounde, for the Altare Christ Iesus: and we, are yᵉ place which he hath chosen to put his name there. Christ is the Altar, because that as by the Altare, the place and all that was done in it, was sanctified, so by Christ both we and all that we doo in our regeneration is cleansed and sanctified. And therefore is Christ the Altare, because that as it was for burnt and sinne offerings, and for meate offeringes, and peace offerings, &c. So Christ was slaine to be our burnt and sinne offeringe, and he ouercame and tooke awaye sinne and miserie, and restored our happines, to be our meate offering and peace offering.

[F 3 recto][3]

Calling by Ceremonies.

The Arke of Noah, and the doare thereof, and the safetie of his familie therin, did signifie the spiritual house, and Church of God, whereof Christ is the doore: and also the spiritual safetie and happines therein, which shal be perfected after this life.

---

[1] Running title now: F 2 verso: "The Jewish state before time, and at this day"; F 3 recto — G 2 recto: "The Jewish state".
[2] From some pages the fourfold columns disappear; in F 2 verso — F 3 recto they are replaced by two columns, the "Definitions" and "Diuisions" disappearing: then from F 3 verso — G 2 verso (SS. 66-81) the columns disappear altogether.
[3] Running title: "The Iewish state".

Misleading by Ceremonies.

65. *How doe they make the ceremonies Idols, & mockeries of the truth* ?

They haue some Ceremonies in place of the Church, and of the redemption by the Messiah, whiche are Idoles in steade of the Church and of the redemption.

As the Garden of Eden, and the Tree of life therein, they make an idol in stead of Christ & his church if stil thei holde thē as ceremonies, that the Messiah our tree of life, is not come, & that he daily doth not gather his church, which is our garden of Eden. For therein we haue our spirituall beautie, & looke for an end of this outwarde basenes & miserie.

Likewise, their Altares at this day, and the places where they stande, they doo make Idolles in steade of Christ and his church, because thei hold them as ceremonies, that the Messiah our altare, is not come, & that the true Christians are not the place of the Altare and churche of God, which the Lord hath chosen to put his Name there, and there to dwell.

But they looke to come againe to their Ierusalem and Mount Zion, and that their Messiah shall bring them thither, who as yet they say, is not come into the worlde.

Misleading by Ceremonies.

But of this the Iewes haue their Idoles and mockes, because they looke for safetie otherwise then by Christ in his Church.

The land of Canaan, and the increase, and blessinges therof, were figures of the Lords Church and people, and of the spirituall graces which the Lorde bestoweth thereon. For as the landes of the kingdome is the Kinges inheritaunce, so we are the Lordes spirituall inheritaunce, and his Canaan, ouer which he raigneth. The same also is to be saied of some places in the lande of Canaan.

The Passeouer and comminge out of Egypte did foreshew our redemption from Satan and Antichrist, and from all wickednes and miserie. For we eate the Paschall Lambe Christe Iesus when we feede spirituallie on his death and tormentes, and so die with him by repentaunce vnto sinne, and when we receyue the graces of his resurrection, and happines with God, and so partake and growe togither in one bodie and church, in one Christian communion of graces, whereby wee goe out of Egypt, as did the Israelites.

[F 3 *verso*]¹   *Ceremonies abolished: but the Truth retained.*

The like may be saied of other such ceremonies and shadowes of the whole Church, and of our whole redemption. As the Rocke from whom doth flow the spirituall drincke. The Tabernacle framed and made for a dwelling to the Lord wherein he delighteth. The Citie Ierusalem. Mount Zion. The Temple. The Sanctuarie. The Slaughter of the Midianites: and such great Deliuerances. The Returne from the Captiuitie &c. Also certaine Families houlding the ceremonies, and true Religion: As the familie of Noah: and those before him, which were raised vp in Abels roume. Abraham and his seed. Moses and the Kingdome of Israel in the handes of good Kinges and Iudges: Aaron & his seed the Priestes and Leuites. Dauid & his seed in the seat of Iudgment, tyll the coming of Christ. And other such like.

66. Some were Ceremonies of some pointes of our Redemption: as of the Lordes secret Counsel and readines to helpe vs, which are handled in the 24. and 25. and 33. question. For his loue and mercie towardes his people, and his electing and predestinating of them vnto saluation, with care and mindefulnesse ouer them were shewed, and figured by the Tythe, the first borne, the firste fruites. The numbring of families, The choosing of the Leuites, The perfect numbring and measuring of thinges about the Tabernacle and Temple. The Paschall Lambe kept tyll the daye of the Passouer, figured that Christ was appointed for the slaine Lambe before the worlde was. Lottes, and diui-

¹ Now one column only.

A Booke which sheweth the life and manners

Of this the Iewes haue their Idoles and mockes, because they dreame of a wordlie [sic] Canaan, to the which they shall come, not knowing that it ceased to be a figure, when it was polluted with Idolatrie, and when Christ came, and raigned in his Church, as a King in his spirituall Canaan.

Of this the Iewes haue their Passeouer as an Idole and mockerie: because they denie Christ Iesus the Paschall lambe to be offered alreadie, and because they do not feede on his death and tormentes, nor receiue the grace of his resurrection and glorifying.

sions of the lande by lotte. The summes which Salomon raysed for the building of the Tabernacle. The casting of lottes mencioned in Nehemiah for to dwell in Ierusalem. The writings in Ezra made to shewe their kindred. And other such like.

67. Some were ceremonies of the sufferinges of Christe in his Manhoode: which are handled in the 26. 27. 28. and 29. question. For hee bare the burthen of our sinnes vppon him. Which was shadowed by the sinne offeringes, with confession of sinnes vppon the heade of the sacrifice. Also by the fatte and the kalle[1] and the kidneis: by the woode whereon the fier did kindle. Also by the false accusations & slaunders of those which were figures of Christ. And diuerse such like.

[F 4 recto] 68. Also some were ceremonies of the wrath of God vppon him for our cause. And of his death, tormentes, and bitter curse. As the fier of the Altare euer burning. The fier which came frō heauen sundrie times to consume the sacrifices. The grate of brasse like networke vppon the Altare. The Rodde in the Angels hande that touched the sacrifice. The rosting with fier of the Paschall lambe, and the burning of that which remained till the morning. The tables & stones of slaughter. The fleshhookes, the knives for slaughter, the herthstones, the beasomes, the panes, the slaying of the sacrifices, the pouring & sprinkling of the bloud, the burnt sacrifice. Also the fleaing, cutting in peeces, and cleeuing of the sacrifices, the seasoning them with salte, the afflictions, tormentes, and troubles in conscience of those men which were figures of Christ, as of Dauid, Ionas, &c.

[1] *I.e.*, caul. See *Lev.* ix. 10.

69. Some were ceremonies of his ouercomming and taking awaye of our miseries. Looke the 30. question. As of the taking awaye of our sinnes. As washings and cleansings with water. The cleansing of the Altare, the washing of the Sacrifices, the sending away of the scape goate, and of the liue Sparow, the offering of Sacrifice with vnleauened breade, the taking away of the excommunicate thing: the high Priest bearing the iniquitie of the people, the taking away of the Ashes and excrementes. And such like.

70. Some were ceremonies of his victorie ouer death and hell, and the power of the wicked, and of our victorie with him. As ye going out of Egypt by strong hande, the going thorowe the red Sea, the passing ouer Iorden. Great cōquestes by them which were figures of Christ: the swimming of the Arke of Noah vpon the waters: the escaping frō the daungers of the captiuitie: Iaacobs preuayling when he wrestled with the Angell: the taking downe from the tree, the cursed that was hanged: the eating of the Passeouer, with their loynes girded, and shoes on their feete and staues in their handes, and eating it in haste: the remoouing of Iosephs bones from Egypt. And such like.

[F 4 *verso*] 72[1]. Some were ceremonies of the happines, which he also obteined for vs. As of the causes of our happines which are in God: mentioned before: And of the meanes of our happines proceeding from God, as first of the communion of the graces and offices in the heade of the Church, which is Christ.

The ceremonies therefore of his mediation and Priesthoode were, Euerie lawefull high Priest and Sacrificer, till his comming. As Abel, Noah, Abraham, Melchizedecke, Iob, Moses, Aaron, &c. Also ye Mercie-seate vppon the Arke, the Altare of burnte offeringes, the altare of incense and sweete perfume, the clensinges and perfumings of the high Priest. The high priest going into the holie place for attonemente once a yeare, the Bels on the skirts of his garmentes, when he wente in for attonemente. The familiar appearing of Moses and others in the presence of God, and their pleading and praying for the people. Incense of hallowed fier, and not of straunge fier, the fierie and brasen Serpente, the dore of Noahs Arke and the Tabernacle, the Porch of the Temple, certaine Pillars and stones, and such like.

---

[1] As text. For 71 see between 74 & 75, where a note refers it to its rightful place.

A Booke which sheweth the life and manners

73. Some were ceremonies of our Iustification by his mediation and Priesthoode. As the grauing of the names of the Tribes of Israel vppon stones, and imbossing and setting them in golde, to be presented and borne on the breast of the high Priest, the table of the Shewbreade with the thinges therof: the stones of the Temple perfected before they were brought to be laied on: the purenes and perfection of all the stuffe of the tabernacle, and such like.

74. Some were ceremonies of our Sanctificatiō by his priesthoode. As the holy garmentes of the Priestes: the seeling, gilding, and hanging of the temple and tabernacle: the anoynting of all thinges with holy ointement: the sanctifying of the Priestes: the Sabbath a signe of holines, and such like.

[G 1 *recto*]
71[1]. Some were ceremonies of his restoring of happines, looke question 31. And first of his owne Iustification and happines. As the Sacrifices without spotte and blemishe: the stones of the Altar whole and vnheawen: the writing of holines to the Lorde, to make the high Priest acceptable: the making of the Arke and Altar of Shittim wood.

The ceremonies of his happines were, The precious ointment, wherwith mans flesh might not be anoynted: the taking vp into heauen of holy men, which were figures of him: the budding and fruite of Aarons Rodde: the riches and glorie of Salomon, and such like.

75. Some were ceremonies of the prophecie of Christe, and of his worde and promises, and our calling to happines. As the testimonie & Oracles from the Arke: the Urim & the Thummim vppon the breastplate of Aaron: the ringes and barres to carie the Tabernacle and the thinges thereof, that the people might follow it to the lande of Canaan: the pillar of a cloude, and the pillar of fire, to leade them both day and night, that is the Lordes Name of power and Maiestie: Manna from heauen: the giuing of the Lawe in glorious manner: the raysing vp and sending of the Prophetes: the trumpettes and Lampes, and Lightes, and Candlestickes: the windowes of the temple: the place where God did putte his name by the Arke and Altare therein: the chiefe workemen about the tabernable [*sic*] and temple to make and builde them.

---

[1] As text. Should follow 70.

76. Some were ceremonies of Christe our King, and of his Kinglie office. As the lawfull Kings and Iudges of Israel: as Moses, Ioshua, Gideon, Sampson, Dauid, Salomon, &c. The Crownes of golde: the Rodde of Moses; the Thrones for iudgement, and such like.

77. Some were ceremonies of the communion of those graces and offices, which eyther the guides and teachers, or all the brethren and people haue to doo good withall. As the wisedome and towardnesse of those which made the tabernacle and temple: the summe that Salomon raised to bring and prepare for the building of the temple: the foure score thousande Masons, and the seuentie thousande that bare burthens. Also the Priestes and Leuites, were figures of euerie Christian, a priest and Leuite, and such like.

[G 1 verso]

78. Some were ceremonies to vs of the vsing of our redemption. And therefore our mortifying and miseries were shadowed by circumcision, by fastinges and sackecloth and rentinge of garmentes. The eating of the Passeouer with sower hearbes, the going through the wildernes, and through the sea, dwelling in boothes, the crie for the bondage of Egipte, buying & selling of bondmen, the bloude of the couenaunte sprinckled on the people, the bloude sprinckled vppon the dore postes, the goings and iourneyings of Abraham, abstaining from wine & strong drinke, the law of the captiue maide. The clothes rent, and the heade bare, and a couering on the lippes of the Leper, the humbling of the people on certaine dayes. Sundrie trialles of the Iewes in the wildernes, the Vaile of separation in the Tabernacle and Temple. The markes and threates that none should touch the mount, the fleeing of the people from the presence of God, the oxen stoned and not eaten, which goared and killed anie man, taking vsurie on straungers, the courte of the Tabernacle and Temple, the going out of all, while the high Priest made attonemente by incense, separation from all vncleannes. The redeeming of the vncleane, by that which was cleane, the vaile on Moses face, because the people could not looke on him. The bloud of the sacrifice of consecration put vppon the right eares, and thumbes and toes of the Priest, the sacrifice for sinnes of ignoraunce and such like.

79. Some were ceremonies of the iudging and condemning of our selues. As the geuing of a redemption, when the people was numbred: the cursinges vppon mounte Ebal, the touching of vncleane things, the crie of the leper, I am vncleane, I am

vncleane, The Lawe of purifying weomen, and of clensing garmentes and other thinges polluted, and of receyuing a leper, or other polluted, being healed and cleane: the bitter and cursed water, and the curse therewithall. And such like.

[G 2 *recto*]

80. Some were ceremonies of our regeneration and newnes of life. As the Nazarites, the refraining from fatte and from bloud, the abstaining frō vncleane meates, the eating of vnleauened bread: the shewbread, the offeringes to the building of the Temple, or Tabernacle: the making and paying of vowes. And such like.

81. Some were ceremonies of the happines wherevnto we are called, and which in Christ we enioye. As the comming into the lande of Canaan, which shadowed the Church, and our happines in the heauens with Christ. The meate offeringes and peace offeringes with ioye and gladnes. The feast of Tabernacles and of especiall deliueraunces. The Sabbaths & Iubiles. The blessing pronounced of the high Priest, as of Melchizedeck, Aaron, &c. The beautifying and adorning of the Temple and tabernacle. The outwarde blessinges of the lande of Canaan, a figure of the spirituall blessings. Long lyfe in that lande, of the euerlasting lyfe in the heauens: Also certaine Welles and Springes in that lande. The best remnaunt of the meate offeringes belonging to the Priestes. The redeeming of the freedome of bondmen. The redemption of the saile of landes and houses, and their returne to the owner. The lawe that the Priestes should not mourne for the dead, and such like.

Hitherto of our calling both in the olde and newe Testament.

[G 2 verso — 3 recto][1]

Mortifying, Iudging, and afflicting of our selues.	Hardning, flattering, and cherishing in sinne.

Now followeth our obedience thereto, by mortifying, and *the contrarie of these things in the wicked.*

82. How must we obey to our calling by mortifying? We must iudge and condemne our selues. We must suffer affliction. We must repente, and chaunge our mindes and disposition.	82. *Howe are the wicked hardened in their sinnes, and desperately refuse their calling?* They flatter and please them selues. They pamper and cherishe themselues. They are froward and stiffe.
83. Howe must we iudge and condemne our selues? We must counte & reckon the multitude of our sinnes. We muste knowe the greeuousnes of them. We must applye the deserte receyued or comming.	83. *Howe doe they flatter and please themselues in their sinnes?* They forgette and passe ouer their sinnes. They trifle and sporte them away. They boast of their worthines.

---

[1] The four columns, " The state of Christians," " The State of Heathen," " Definitions " and " Diuisions " are resumed.

A Booke which sheweth the life and manners

Mortifying, Iudging, and afflicting of our selues.

82. Mortifying of our selues, is a daily decaye and wearing away of our wicked nature, and readines to sinne, by an effectuall feeling of the curse and miserie we are in, whereby the loue and liking of our selues is taken away.
Iudging and condemning our selues, is a sure and certaine consent in our selues, by due examination of our state, that we are most wicked and wretched.

{ *Mortifying*

{ *Iudging our selues by*

{ *By iudging and condemning our selues.*

{ *Afflicting & killing the fleshe.* { *By suffering.* / *By repenting.*

{ *Reckoning* { *The multitude of sinnes.* / *The greatnes.*

{ *By applying desert.*

83. Reckoning and counting our sinnes, is a duetie of right aduising of our selues, wherein and howe often we sinne, by a due calling of our selues to accountes.
Knowledge of the greeuousnes of sinne, is the vnderstanding or wisedome whereby we haue founde out howe farre we haue disobeyed and broken the lawes of God.
Applying desert, is a iudging of our selues worthie of such punishment, as the sinne and trespasse hath offended and abused the lawe giuer which is God.

{ *Reckoning sinne.*

{ *Knowing the greeuousnes.*

{ *Applying deserte.*

84. Howe must wee suffer affliction?
Wee must bee inwardly troubled in dread and horrour.
Wee must bee greeued and heauie vnto death.
Wee must suffer outward affliction, and at last death it selfe.

84. *Howe doe they pamper and cherish themselues in their sinnes?*
They are stoute and sturdie against euils.[1]
They are merie and pleasaunte.
They haue their nicenes and tendernes.

[G 3 verso — 4 recto]

Repentance. Renewing. Happines.	Hardning. Discouraging. All Wo & Miserie.

85. How must wee repente?
We must be ashamed of our disposition and state.
We must be angrie and displeased therewith.
We must hate & abhorre the desires and thoughts of our hartes.

85. *How are they froward and stiffe in iustifying them selues?*
They are bould and maliperte.
They are still and at rest in their sinnes.
They loue their fansies and pleasures and delight in the same.

---

[1] As text.

A Booke which sheweth the life and manners

84. Suffering miseries is a yeelding ouer of our bodies & soules to feele in them both such measure of the miseries, that Christe indured for vs, that the liking of our selues being taken away, we may onelie like and take Christe for our happines. } *Suffering* { *Inwarde* { *Feare and dread.* / *Greefe.* } / *Outwarde.* }

Greefe is a troubled disliking of our wickednes, whereby we feele the hurt and daunger we are in, by the displeasure of God for our sinnes. } *Greefe.*

Feare and dreade is a troubled disliking of our curse and miserie which shall come vpon vs by the wrath of God, whereby we fayne woulde escape and get from it. } *Feare and dread.*

Suffering outwardlie, is in withholding or wanting things needefull for the bodie. And this is defined before. } *Sufferings outwardlie.*

Repentance. Renewing. Happines.

---

85. Repentance is an vtter disliking of our selues by the feeling of our miserie and contrarie nature to God, whereby we wishe for the estimation of him, that we had neuer offended him } *Repentance.* { *Shame.* / *Anger and hatred.* }

Shame is a troubled disliking of our owne vilenes, by the feeling not onely of the excellencie of God aboue vs, but contrarie to vs: whereby wee are stricken as dead at the shewe of the same. } *Shame.*

86. How must wee be raised and quickned againe vppon our repentaunce?
Wee must haue faith to apply our redemption by Christ vnto vs particularly.
Wee must haue cleare consciences that our sinnes and miseries are taken away.
Wee must be sanctified vnto newnes of life.

86. *How ar they vtterlie discouraged vpon their frowardenes, and fall away more and more?*
They are vnfaithfull and withdrawe themselues from God.
They haue their guiltines as neuer to be better.
They are sette on mischeefe and wickednes.

A Booke which sheweth the life and manners

Anger against our selues, is a troubled disliking of our shamefull iniurie done to the glorie of GOD, whereby we are prouoked to afflict, yea to destroye our selues, wishing that we had neuer bin borne, but that some hope of mercie doeth staye vs. } *Anger.*

Hatred of our selues, is an vtter dislking of our selues, as being contrarie to the nature of God and his enemies: and therefore by his hatred against vs, doo feele our selues a curse to our selues, and would that we were not, in respect of our selues. } *Hatred.*

86. Raysing and quickening, is a daily renuing and strengthening of the godly nature and spirit of Christ within vs, by an effectuall feeling of the remedie of our curse and miserie through C h r i s t. whereby we profit in grace & godlines vnto life euerlasting. } *Raysing and quickning.*

Faith is a full consent by heauenlie inspiration, to our redemption in Christ, prouoking vs to take him for our happines, and wholie to yeelde vp our selues vnto him. } *Faith.*

A cleare conscience is a ioyfull consent, that by repentance and faith in Christ, we haue peace with God, and are made his children and heires of happines. } *Cleare consciences.*

{ *By faith.*
By working of faith. } { *Cleare cōscience.*
Newnes of life. }

87. What is the happines which wee shall enioy?	87. *What woes and miseries dooe they abide?*
A blessed and holie life, which for euermore wee shall haue with our God in the heauens. The fellowshippe and communion of Saintes. The rising againe of our soules after this life, and of our bodies at the last Iudgemente day to be blessed for euer.	A woefull and wicked life in hell for euer. They haue their portion with deuilles and abominable men. They are condemned both bodie and soule vnto eternall torment.

[G 4 *verso* — H 1 *recto*]

Newnes of life. Religion. Esteeming God.	Wickednes. prophanes. Despising God.
Now followe the dueties of godlines, whiche in newnes of life we ought to keepe.	
88. Which be the dueties of godlines in newnes of life[?]	88. *What be the sinnes and faultes of the wicked?*
All godlines is in the generall dueties of religion and holines towards God. Also in the speciall dueties for his name and Sabbath. Also in the dueties of righteousnes concerning man.	All wickednes or sinfulnes sheweth it selfe in prophanes and worldlines. Also in that speciall sinne of hindering Gods name, and breaking his Sabbathes. Also in vnrighteousnes concerning man.

A Booke which sheweth the life and manners

Newnes of life is, a straight obedience to the will of God, shewing the chaunge of our wicked nature for a heauenlie and godlie nature, which is by partaking the spirit of Christ Iesus. } *Newnes of lyfe.*

87. Our happines is the perfect sufficiencie, or most blessed state which we haue and shall haue in Christ: or it is the blessing of God vpon vs, whereby we want nothing, nor haue neede of anie thing else, to better our state. } *Happines.*

The fellowship and communion of Saintes is the enioying of that happines which we haue & looke for, by mutuall vse of the companie, graces and dueties one of another. } *Fellowship & communion.*

The raysing againe of our soules and bodies, is a restoring of vs in both, by putting away the olde nature decayed, and making vs new creatures in Christ, hauing a pure and perfect nature, in steade of our former corruptions. } *Resurrection.*

Godlines. Esteeming God. Reuerence. Bashefulnes.

88. Godlines is the right vsing, or continuall occupying of our giftes and powers, both in soule and bodie, in such perfect duetifulnes, as is taught and commaunded vs by the Lorde our God. } *Godlines*

Religion and holines is that part of godlines whereby we continually doo glorifie God as we ought. } *Religion*

{ In Religion and holines towards God.
  In righteousnes with man. }

{ In generall dueties of holines.
  In speciall dueties. }

89. What be the generall dueties of religion and holines towardes God?
They consist in esteeming him.
In honouring and worshipping him.
And in seruing him faithfullie with all our endeauour.

89. *How doeth wickednes shewe it selfe in prophanes and worldlines?*
Prophanes is in dispising God.
In making him a shame and a skorne so much as lieth in them.
In vnrulines.

90. How must wee esteeme and accounte of God?
Wee must esteeme him in his Maiestie and excellencie.
Also in his iustice.
Also in his goodnes.

90. *Howe do prophane and worldlie men despise God?*
They make lighte of his worthines.
Also of his lawes and commaundementes.
Also of his grace and blessinges.

91. What estimation must wee haue of his maiestie?
Wee must reuerence him highlie.
Wee must be ashamed and abashed in comparison of him.

91. *Howe doe they make lighte of his worthines?*
They sette vile thinges before him.
They are bould and maleperte before him.

A Booke which sheweth the life and manners

89. Esteeming God is a duetie of Religion and holines whereby we take him for our only happines and consent, that he onely hath all worthines in him. } *Esteeming God.* { In his Maiestie. / In his authoritie { In Iustice. / In goodnes. }

90. Esteeming God in his Maiestie, is a duetie of Religion, whereby wee are striken with a feeling of the great excellencie of God aboue all, and of our vnworthines in repect of the same. } *Esteeming in his Maiestie* { Reuerence. / Bashefulnes. }

91. Reuerence of God, is an estimation of God for his worthines in him selfe, and for his owne cause though he had made none of his creatures. } *Reuerence of God.*

Bashefulnes and shame of our selues before God, is a troubled dislking of our owne vnworthines, by the feeling of the excellencie of GOD, whiche striketh vs with the great estimation thereof. } *Bashefulnes before God.*

[H 1 verso — 2 recto]

Esteeming and honouring God.	A light account and skorne of God.
92. How must we esteeme him in his iustice?	92. *How doe they make lighte of his lawes?*
Wee must feare and tremble thereat, least wee displease him.	They haue their hardnes and stoutenes of hart.
Wee must be zealous for his righte and glorie.	Also their doubling and halting.
Wee must hate all vanitie and wickednes, and be displeased therewith.	Also they rest and flatter themselues in their wickednes.

Esteeming God in his iustice and goodnes. And honouring him.

92. Esteeming God in his Iustice is a duetie of Religion, whereby we take him for our Lorde and gouernour, for his holines in ruling vs most worthelie.	*Esteeming God in his iustice.*	*Feare, Zeale.* *Hatred of wickednes.*
The feare of God, is an estimation of his Iustice, whereby we take heede to please him in all thinges, and abhorre to prouoke him against vs, because we are sure, that as we set foorth his excellencie, so wee shall haue the name and the vse thereof.	*Feare of God.*	
Zeale to the glorie of God, is an high estimation thereof, for his worthines, prouoking vs most earnestlie to hasten and further the same as being our happines.	*Zeale to the glorie of God.*	
Hatred and anger against wickednes, is a troubled disliking thereof, for the cursednes and contrarietie thereof, both to God and our godlie nature, prouoking vs to set ourselues wholie against it.	*Hatred of vanitie and wickednes.*	

93. How must wee esteeme him in his goodnes?
Wee must loue the lord our God with all our hartes.
We must continually reioyce in his presence.
We must alwayes hope and trust in his helpe.

93. *How doo they make light of his grace and blessinges?*
They haue their misgeuing from goodnes.
They take greefe thereat.
They shrinke awaye & doubt to goe forward.

94. What honour and worshipp is due vnto God?
We must humble our selues before him.
We must seeke to him, for his fauour and helpe.
We must be thankefull, for his goodnes towards vs.

94. *How would they make God a shame and a skorne?*
They haue their loftines and pride or els their superstition and Idolatrie.
They forsake the Lords goodnes & withdraw themselues like straung children to seeke to false Gods.
They esteeme their owne worthines and are vnthankfull to God.

93. The loue of God is an high estimation of God for his most perfect goodnes, whereby we take him for our happines in feeling his presence and good will towardes vs, and therefore yeelde vp our selues wholie vnto him. } *Our loue of God.*

Our Ioye in God, is an high estimation of the vse of his goodnes, whereby wee feele him to bee our happines therein. } *Ioye in God.*

Hope and Trust in God, is an high estimatiō of the helpe of God towardes vs, prouoking vs to doe all thinges in his name, with assurance of his promises and graunte to preuayle. } *Hope and Trust in God.*

We Hope when we haue but the promise: wee Trust, when we feele a further helpe vpon his promise. } *The difference of Hope and Trust.*

94. The Honouring and worshipping of God is our holines in shewing by our lowlines before him, howe much wee esteeme him aboue vs.

Humbling of our selues to God, is an honouring or worshipping of him, by abasing our selues, according to our vnworthines and his excellencie aboue vs.

The honor & worship of God. In using his goodnes.

Humbling our selues.

In hūbling our selues to his gretnes. In seeking to him. In thankefulnes.

Inwardlie { *In meeknes. In patience.*
Outwardlie in homage.

[H 2 verso — H 3 recto]

Humbling & seeking to God. Thankefulnes.	Loftines. Forsaking God. Vnthankfulnes.
95. How must we humble our selues vnto God? We must be meeke, as despising our right and welfare. We must be patient in abiding miseries. We must be lowlie in our hartes, and in our speach and behaviour.	95. *What is their loftines and pride or their superstition and Idolatrie?* They are stoute and stubburne: and yet slauish to false gods. They storme and grudg in aduersitie and yet superstitiously torment thēselues. They will be gallaunte and lordlie, and yet bowe and abase themseules to vile Idoles.
96. How must we seeke to him, for his fauour and helpe? We must confesse our faultes and offences. We must aske pardon & forgiuenes. We must complaine of our wantes & craue his helpe.	96. *How doe they forsake the Lords goodnes, and withdrawe themselues like straung children to seeke to vaine gods?* They excuse and iustifie themselues in their sinnes, or make confession vnto Idoles. They are frowarde and wilfull in their sinnes, or seek their false pardons. They chaleng desertes or complaine and seeke helpe by false gods.

A Booke which sheweth the life and manners

Humbling and seeking to God.   *Thankefulnes.*

95. Meekenes is an humbling or abasing of our selues in despising our right or welfare as vnworthie to haue or to seeke it. } *Meekenes.*

Patience is an humbling or abasing of our selues, gladlie to suffer miseries and temptations as being meete for vs. } *Patience.*

Lowlines and homage is an humbling or abasing of our selues as beseemeth his worthines, whereby we wholie yeeld vp our selues to giue him his honour. } *Lowlines and homage.*

96. Seeking to God is a worshipping of him by a willing desire to vse his goodnes towardes vs. } *Seeking to God.* { *For remedie of sinne.* *For the remedie of euil for sinne.* } { *Confessing faultes.* *Asking pardon.* *Complayning of wantes.* *Crauing helpe.* }

Confessing faultes is a seeking to God for his mercie, by shewing wherein and howe greatlie we haue offended. } *Confessing faultes.*

Asking pardon is a seeking to God to haue our sinnes forgiuen vs, with an humble intreating of him for his Christes sake. } *Asking pardon.*

Complayning and Crauing, is a seekinge to God by shewing wherein and howe much we haue need of his helpe, with an humble intreating him for the same. } *Complaining and Crauing helpe.*

97. How must we be thankfull ?
We must acknowledg his goodnes towardes vs ?
We must giue him thankes for the same.
We must praise him in his marueilous workes.

97. *How doe they esteeme their owne worthines, and are vnthankefull to God ?*
They sette light and thinke skorne of his graces.
They talke of their deseruinges.
The vaunte and boaste in their workes.

[H 3 *verso* — 4 *recto*]

| *Seruing God. Learning his will. Obedience thereto.* | Vnrulines. Foolishnes. Disobedience. |

Hitherto of Esteeming and Worshipping God. Now followeth, Howe to serue him.

98. How must we serue God ?   98. *How are the wicked vnrulie ?*

We must learne his will.
We must obey thereto in our calling.
We must giue good accountes of our calling.

They are foolish & full of ignoraunce and errour.
They disobey the Lords will.
They are altogether sette on their willes, and flee from the Lord.

A Booke which sheweth the life and manners

97. **Thankefulnes** is an honouring or worshipping of God by abasinge our selues for his blessinges receyued, whereby we take our selues wholie indebted vnto him, and to be altogether vnprofitable vnto him, and neuer able to make him amendes.

Acknowledging his goodnes is a ful cōsent & conscience thereof, by continuall mindefulnes and examining of his particular blessings.

Giuing thankes is a witnessing or shewing of the Lords deseruings both in our hartes, or by voyce & speach, whereby we cōfesse the greatnes of his blessings and our vnworthines.

Praysing God, is a confessing or reckoning vp in our selues or to others, of his great workes and blessings to set forth his glorie.

Thankefulnes to God.
— In acknowledging his goodnes.
— In dutifulnes for the same,
  — Giuing thankes.
  — Giuing prayse.

Acknowledging his goodnes.

Giuing thankes.

Praysing God.

Seruing God. Learning his will. Obedience thereto.

98. Seruing God is a duetifulnes in folowing our calling and vsing our giftes with earnest indeuour, whereby the Lorde hath his whole honour by all things we doo.

Learning of his will is the seruice of our mindes and vnderstanding, in vsing his goodnes in teaching vs, that we may knowe his will & leade our liues thereafter.

Seruing GOD
— By learning his will.
— By obedience thereto
  — In our calling.
  — In accoūtes therof.

Learning the will of God
— By getting knowledge.
— By vsing the same to followe.
  — The example of God.
  — His guiding.

99. How must we learne the will of God?
We must gette the knowledge of his word and workes.
We must follow him guiding vs.
We must follow his example, so farre as we are made according to his Image.

99. *How are they foolish and full of ignoraunce?*
They seeke deepe to deceiue themselues, and increase their follies.
They follow lyes and the lustes of their hartes.
They become cleane contrarie to God, and are wholy peruerted.

---

100. How must we obey the will of God in our calling?
We must take counsaile in all things we doe.
We must be forwarde thereon.
We must doo all things in their due maner.

100. *How doe the wicked disobeye the Lords will?*
They do all thinges in ligthnes [*sic*] and rashnes, or with subtletie and crafte.
They are backward and vntoward.
They haue their euill handling and marring of matters.

A Booke which sheweth the life and manners

99. *The knowledge of the worde and workes of God, is defined before in the 2. question.*

Following the Lorde guiding vs, is an vsing of his gouernement, to put in practise a duetie or office by his particular appointing. — *Following God guiding vs.*

Following his example, is a fashioning of our lyues to his image and likenes, in such thinges as he would we should be like him, to shewe forth his holines. — *Following his example.*

100. Obedience to the will of God, is the seruice of God by our giftes and graces in vsing them rightlie as his worde doeth binde vs. — *Obedience*
- *In taking counsaile.*
- *In dutifulnes thereby, as*
  - *Our forwardnes vpō coūsaile.*
  - *Our maner of working.*

Counsaile, is a minding and pondering of all dueties, whereby wee examine and trie howe the Scriptures or worde of God doeth warrant them. — *Counsaile*
- *Deuising.*
- *Aduising.*

A more full diuision of the pointes of wisdom & counsaile, looke for in our table of Diuinitie, & Nature, & of Ordering Common wealthes. — *Aduising.*
- *Of present things.*
- *Of absent*
  - *Past*
  - *Comming*

Marking and examing.
- *Consenting.*
  - *Iudgement, &c.*
  - *Conscience. &c.*
- *Remembraunce.*
- *Counting.*
- *Foresight.*
- *Purpose and decree.*

[H 4 verso — I 1 recto]

Counsaile. Forwardnes. Skill. Labor.	Rashnes. Vntowardnes. Idlenes.
101. How must wee take counsaile? We must attend and watch to our dueties. We must remember and count the same. We must foresee and purpose what to doo.	101. *How are they light and rash in their doings?* They haue their carelessnes and dulnes. Also their forgetfulnes. Also their vnwarines and headines.
102. How must we be forward? We must desire to doe our dueties, with hope and trust of obtaining our desires. We must haue zeale & courage therto. We must be ioyfull and comfortable therein.	102. *How are they backward and vntoward?* They haue euill will to their dueties, with shrinking and doubting to goe forward. They are could[1] & doe better things by halues. Their dueties are wearisome and irksome vnto them.

[1] *I.e.*, cold.

A Booke which sheweth the life and manners

Counsaile. Forwardnes. Skill. Labour.

101. Our attendance and watching, is a continuall minding of euerie duetie, whereby we take heede that we faile in no duetie. } *Attendance and watching.*

Our reckoning and counting is due aduising or cousaile of things done, wherby we cal our selues to accounts what things are amisse. } *Reckoning.*

Foresight is our counsaile whereby we are aduised of things which may fall. } *Foresight.*

Purpose is our cousaile, wherby we are setled, how any thing shal be by the good help of god. } *Purpose.*

102. Forwardnes is a due preparation and stirring vp of our mindes, whereby nothing can withholde vs from beginning the worke. } *Forwardnes.*

Desire to our dueties is a liking thereof, wherby we willinglie consent for to do them. } *Desire.*

Forwardnes. { *Inclining* { *Desire.* / *Ioye.* } *Prouoking* { *Zeale.* / *Ielousie.* } }

Ioye, Hope, Trust, Zeale, were defined before.

103. In what manner must wee doe our dueties?
Wee must be actiue and skilfull.
Wee must labour and worke.
We must be steadfast and constant.

103. *What euill handling and marring of matters haue they?*
They are vnfitt and vnskilfull.
They are idle and slothfull.
They are wauering and geue ouer.

104. What skill or actiuenes is required?
Wee must order thinges by their times and course.
Also by their measure of worke.
We must be semely & handsome therin.

104. *How are they vnfitt and vnskilfull?*
They are disordered and doe things by hazard.
They haue their disuantage.
They are vntydie and boisterous.

105. What labour is required?
We must vse our force and might.
Wee must be speedie and quicke.
We must be painefull and strait that nothing faile.

105. *How are they idle and slouthfull?*
They haue their weaknes and fainting.
Also their slacknes and slownes.
Also their loathing and letting.

A Booke which sheweth the life and manners

103. The maner of working is the right vse of our counsaile and forwardnes, in applying the same vnto practise. } *Maner of working.*

Actiuenes and skil, is a due readines in doing things in such due maner, as best may further the busines. } *Skilfulnes.*

104. Ordering by time and course, is a due maner of setting and cōpassing our works, to bring thē to passe in their due season. } *Ordering by time.*

Measuring our worke, is an ordering thereof, by dispatching so much as wee did wiselie purpose. } *Measure.*

Seemelines and handsomnes, is a due maner of doing things in discretion and warines, that nothing be hurt or hindered by hastines. } *Handsomnes.*

105. Labor is a maner of working whereby we ouercome the hardnes or hinderances of anie worke or busines. } *Labor.*

Force and might, is a labor or indeauour whereby the worke wanteth no strēghth to bring it to passe. } *Force.*

Maner of working. {
  Gaines or actiuenes { Order. { By time and course. / By measure of worke. } / Handsomnes. }
  Labor and diligence { Painefulnes, { Speede. / Forceablenes. } / Stedfastnes, { Patient bearing. / Preuayling. } }
}

[I 1 verso — 2 recto]

Constancie. Accountes to God. Special Dueties.	Vnconstancie. Fleeing God. Special Sinnes.
106. What steadfastnes or constancie is required? We must be patient whatsoeuer successe we haue. We must preuaile & gather strength. Wee must dispatch and finish our worke.	106. *How are they wauering and vnconstant?* They are discouraged if anie thing miscarie. They shrinke and faile by their backwardnes. They loose their labour and misse of their purpose.

A Booke which sheweth the life and manners

Speede is our indeavour in hastening to dispatch the worke.	*Speede.*
Painefulnes is a labor or indeavour vnto wearines, to bring any thing to passe.	*Painefulnes.*

Constancie.   Accountes to God.   Special dueties.

106. Stedfastnes and cōstancie, is a continuance of labor & busines, without chaunging and letting, tyll our counsell and purpose take place.	*Stedfastnes*	*In patience.* *In preuayling.*
Patience in labour is a stedfastnes in sufferinge the euilles that come to vs by anie worke, so that they can not discourage vs.	*Patience in labor.*	
Preuayling and gathering strength, is a stedfastnes whereby we gette vauntage and further ablenes to bring anie thing to passe.	*Preuayling*	*Gathering strength.* *Finishing.*
Dispatching and finishing is a stedfastnes to the end of a worke, bringing our coūsaill & purpose to passe.	*Dispatching and finishing.*	

107. What accountes must wee make vnto God of our seruice?
We should alwaies feele our selues cleare from the guiltines of sinne.
We should be free from the troubles and punishmentes of sinne by peace in God.
We should vse all thinges as a blessing and token of our iustification.

107. *How are they sette on their willes and flee from God?*
They haue alwaies a guiltie conscience for their sinnes.
They are alwaies troubled and afflicted by some thing amisse.
In all thinges they feel the Lordes curse, and their condemnation, when God doth withdraw his peace from them.

Hitherto of the generall dueties of religion and holines.
Nowe followe the speciall duties for the name and kingdome of God, and for keeping his Sabbathes.

108. What be the speciall duties for the name and kingdome of God?
They are for the worshippe of God, on some speciall occasions. Or for some speciall furtheraunce of his kingdome.

108. *Which be the speciall sinnes of hindering Gods name and kingdome?*
They be when we giue speciall occasions for men to skorne & be ashamed of our profession.
And when we hinder the building of his kingdome.

107. Our giuing of accountes, is our obedience in the seruice of God, whereby wee make a good reckoning of all dueties towardes God. } *Accountes* { *Of dueties by a cleare conscience.* / *Of blessings by vsing them.*

A good conscience was defined before, quest. 86. But here we define it as it should haue bene, if man had not fallen. A good conscience, is a ioyfull consent vpon the examination of our liues, whereby we feele our selues happie in ioy and peace with our God. } *A good cōscience* { *Without guiltines of sinne.* / *Without trouble.*

Peace & Quietnes in God, and the blessed vse of all thinges, is an inioying of the goodnes of God in all thinges, whereby wee feele him to be our happines therein. } *Peace and blessings.*

108. Special dueties for the Name of GOD are whereby God is chieflie glorified on greater, or some times more rare occasions. } *Special dueties for* { *The name of God.* / *His Sabbath.*

The Name of God is the knowledge of his excellencie and worthines, whereby he is glorified accordinglie.
To vse his name rightlie, is to glorifie him according to the knowledge we should haue of his excellencie. } *The name of God.* { *By his special worship.* / *By the furtherance of his kingdome.*

For the difference of the name and glorie of God, looke the 10. *question and this* 108. *question.*

The speciall worship of God is our holines in giuing him honour on greater or more rare occasions } *The special worship of God.* { *Our special humbling by special iudgements.* / *Our speciall thankfulnes in straunger blessings.* } { *By praysing God.* / *By vowing vowes, and performing them.*

[I 2 verso — 3 recto]

Special dueties for the Worship, Kingdom, & Sabbath of God.	Speciall sinnes against the same.
109. What speciall worshippe of God is there? Our speciall humbling with praier in straunger iudgments. Our speciall thankfulnes, and praising of God in straunger blessinges. Our speciall vowes which we are for to keepe and performe.	109. *What speciall occasions giue the wicked of shaming and skorning the worshippe of God?* They shewe their hardning and willfulnes in straunger iudgementes. Also their sottishnes, in straunger blessinges. Also they hould their wicked course still, and are soulde[1] to do euill.
110. What speciall furtheraunce of the kingdome of God is ther? In talke to edifie one an other by praising God, and declaring his will by rebuke or exhortation. In doubt and controuersie to sweare by his name on iust occasions, and to vse the lottes. Also to keepe the meetinges of the church, and with our especiall friends for spirituall exercises.	110. *What hinderances be there of building Gods kingdome?* In talke to encourage to vanitie and wickednes, and discourage from goodnes. To speake blasphemies, or to vse idle othes, or gaming & tryfling by Lottes. To forsake the church meetinges or be negligent therin, and to be neare & friendlie to the wicked to the increase of wickednes.

---

[1] Was "boulde" intended?

Speciall dueties for the Worship, Kingdom, & Sabbath of God.

109. *The definitions of humbling, prayer and thankefulnes are giuen before: but here the speciall occasions are to be considered.* } *Humb. Pray. Thank.*

A Vowe is a faithfull promise made by an othe, vnto God in our hartes, or by voyce & speache, whereby we bynde our selues to him, for some speciall blessing which we haue or looke for, to shewe our thankefulnes in some speciall duetifulnes, which before we knewe not, or did neglecte. } *Vowes.*

110. The kingdome of God which is called his church is defined before.

Edifying is a cōmunion or bestowing of our graces in knowledge, coūsel, & due behauiour, to further all godlines in our selues & others. } *Edifying*

Rebuke is a pronouncing of the knowne wickednes of anie, with condemning of the same by the word of God, wherby they haue shame that others might feare. } *Rebuke.*

A Booke which sheweth the life and manners

Exhortation is an edifying by all comfortable wordes & promises in the Scripture, to worke in our hartes the estimatiō of our dueties with loue and zeale therevnto.	Exhortation.	Our speciall furthering of the Kingdom of God.	In spirituall edifying.	In talke by praysing God, exhorting & rebuke.
An Othe or Swearing by God is an honoring of God in his Iustice, when wee call him to be a Iudge and witnesse of that truth, which can not otherwise be founde out, and an auenger of our lies, if we speake any thing faslie [sic].	An Othe or Swearing			In doubt and controuersies, as by swearing & lottes.
Lotting is an applying of some thing which is chaunce vnto vs, to be a token of Gods will in such doubts and controuersies as he only is to determine. We honor him by Lottes when we call & take him for our Iudge & Guide in thē.	Lotting.		In meetinges for the same	With the Church.
The Church meetings are the due resorting & comming togither of Christians, for mutuall comfort by their presence, and communion of graces to further all godlines.	Church meetings.			With speciall friendes.

111. What special duties be ther for the Sabbathe?
All the generall duties of religion & holines towards God, and all the speciall dueties of worshipping God, & furthering his kingdome, must on the Sabbath be performed, with ceasing from our callinges & labour in worldlye thinges.
Yet such busines as can not be putt of tyll the daie after, nor done the daie before, may then be done.

111. *What is the speciall sinne of breaking the Lords Sabbathe?*
It is notable prophanes and worldlines, and a cheefe hinderaunce of the name of God, when wee followe our worldlie busines, and callinges on the Sabbathe, or giue our selues to other vanitie and wickednes.

[I 3 verso — 4 recto]

Righteousnes with men.
Gouernours. Theyr calling & giftes.

Gouernment Abused.
Ambition.

Hitherto of the dueties of religion & holines. Now followe the dueties of righteousnes concerning man.

112. Whiche bee the dueties of righteousnes concerning man?
They be eyther more bounden, as the generall duties in gouernement betwene gouernours and inferiours:
Or they be more free, as the generall dueties of freedome.
Or else they be more speciall duties for eche others name, and for auoyding couetousnes.

112. *Which be the sinnes of vnrighteousnes concerning man?*
They be either in the abuse of gouernement.
Or in the abuse of freedome and libertie:
Or in speciall faulting by our owne and others euill name, and by couetousnes.

A Booke which sheweth the life and manners

111. The Sabbath or rest, or keeping of the Sabbath is an holy vsing of euerie seuenth day in all dueties of Religion and holines & worshipping God and furthering his kingdome, and that with resting and ceasing from our calling and labour in worldly things. Our Sabbath is on the Lordes day which is the day of his rysing from the dead, and is held by the church for a Sabbath or rest vnto God, the next day after the Iewish Sabbath. So that we counte euerie Sabbath from one Lords day to another. } *The Sabbath.*

Righteousnes with men. Gouernours. Their calling & guiftes.

112. Our gouernement is our Lordshipp, authoritie, or chieftie, ouer anie, whereby wee vse their obedience and seruice, to partake vnto them the vse & graces of our authoritie and guiding. } *Gouernement*

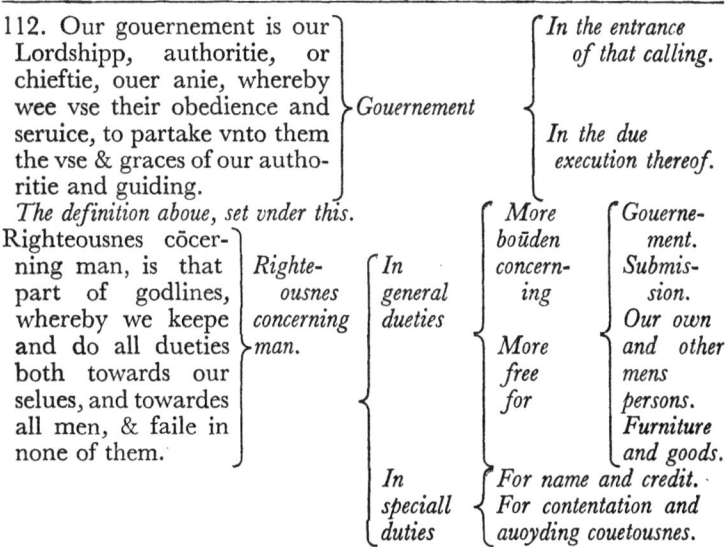

The definition aboue, set vnder this. Righteousnes cōcerning man, is that part of godlines, whereby we keepe and do all dueties both towards our selues, and towardes all men, & faile in none of them. } *Righteousnes concerning man.*

{ In general dueties { More boūden concerning { Gouernement. Submission. Our own and other mens persons. Furniture and goods. More free for

In speciall duties { For name and credit. For contentation and auoyding couetousnes.

113. What be the dueties of Gouernours?
They consist in the entraunce of that calling.
And in the due execution thereof by ruling well.

113. *How is gouernemente abused?*
By an ambitious seeking and vsurping of that calling which belōgeth not to them.
And by an euill handling thereof for their pleasure and lustes.

114. How must Superiours enter and take their calling?
By assurance of their guift.
By speciall charge and commaundemente from God to put it in practise.
By agreement of men.

114. *How do the wicked ambitiously seeke and vsurpe their gouernment?*
They are vnfitt and vnskilfull to gouerne.
They are forbidden by God, and vnsent to that calling.
They steale into that calling, or get it by force and rauening.

115. What gift must they have?
All Gouernours must haue forwardnes before others, in knowledge and godlines, as able to guide.
And some must haue age and eldershippe.
Also some must haue parentage and birth.

115. *How are they vnfitt and vnskilful to gouerne?*
They are vntoward through their ignoraunce, and are worldlie minded men.
They are children or of childish condicions.
They haue no right nor succession by parentage or birth.

113. Entrance or taking on vs the calling of gouernement, is a due maner of beginning the same, being prepared and meete thereto. } *Entrance of that calling.* { *By assurance of our giftes.* *By our calling to vse them.* { *By Gods commaundement.* *By agreement of men.*

114. Assurance of our gifte, is a conscience of our ablenes to followe that calling, because we knowe our owne readines, to doo all the dueties thereof, with preuayling and prospering by the helpe of God. } *Assurance of our gift* { *In our selues* { *Knowledge, age, godlines, &c.* *Outward furniture, &c.* *By others, as parētage & birth, &c.*

115. Knowledge is the right iudgement or wisedome which they should haue, whereby they shoulde haue all thinges sought and founde out belonging to that calling. } *Knowledge.*

Godlines is defined before.

Age and Eldershippe is a gifte whereby they haue greater authoritie as by naturall deserte of their wisdome, if so be by cōtinuāce of time they haue gotten that wisedome. } *Age and Eldership.*

Birth and Parentage, is a gifte whereby they haue greater authoritie as by naturall deserte of kindred and bloude, or of begetting and bringing vp, if so bee they aunswere in worthines otherwise. } *Birth and Parentage.*

[I 4 verso — K 1 recto]

God giuing Charge. Agrement. of men.	Men taking charge, when God dischargeth.
116. What charge or commaundement of God must they haue to vse their guift?	116. *How are they forbidden by God and vnsente to that calling?*

They haue first the speciall commaundement of furthering his kingdome, by edifyinge and helping of others, where there is occasion and the persones be worthie.

Also some speciall prophecie and foretelling of their calling, or some generall commaundement for the same.

Also particular warninges from God vnknowne to the world, as in oulde time by vision, dreame and reuelation, and now by a speciall working of Gods spirite in our consciences.

They are chiefly forbidden to hinder the building of the Lords kingdome.

Also their is some generall commaundement, or some speciall warning and example to stay them from that calling.

Also their owne fancie, ambition or lust doth thurst them on to that calling.

God giuing charge. Agreement of men.

116. A commaundement to vse our giftes is a pronounced or written lawe or forme of wordes, appointing vnto vs that duetie, by the authoritie of God in the pronoūcer or writer. } *Comaundement to vse their gift.* } *Generall lawe.* { *Prophecie.* *Special* *Warning.*

The speciall commaundement for this is defined before.

Prophecie or foretelling of their calling, is the pronounced or written decree or will of God for their calling shewed before hande, whiche appointeth vnto them that calling, by the authoritie of God in the pronouncer or writer. } *Prophecie of their calling.*

Particular warnings is the stirring vp and prouoking of them, by the worde, their consciences, and the spirit of grace in them, and by the occasions of doing good by their giftes, wherby they are compelled to vse their giftes in that calling. } *Particular warnings.*

117. What agreement must there be of men?

For Church gouernours there must be an agreement of the church.

For ciuil Magistrates, there must be an agreement of the people or Common welth.

117. *How do they steale into that calling, or gett it by force & rauening?*

They will shift & thrust themselues into the Church gouernment as Antichristes.

They will shift or thrust themselues into the ciuil gouernment, as Tyrantes.

For Houshoulders, there must be an agreement of the houshouldes. As Husbandes, Parents, Maisters, Teachers, or Scholemaisters. &c.

They wil shift and thrust thē selues into home gouernment, like Lord-danes,[1] or maisterly troublers.

---

[1] Obsolete; see *N.E.D.* under "lurdan".

A Booke which sheweth the life and manners

117. Church gouernors are persons receyuing their authoritie & office of God, for the guiding of his people the Church, receyued and called thereto, by due consent and agreement of the Church. } *Church Gouernours.*

The Church gouernement and gouernours are defined before.

Ciuill Magistrates, are persons receyuing their authoritie & office of God, for the due guiding of the common wealth, where to they are duely receyued and called, by consent and agreement of the people and subiectes. } *Ciuill Magistrates.*

A larger definition may be this:

Ciuill Magistrates are persons authorised of God, and receyued by the consent or choyse of the people, whether officers, or subiectes, or by birth and succession also, to make & execute lawes by publike agreement, to rule the common wealth in all outwarde iustice, & to maintaine the right, welfare, & honour thereof, with outwarde power, bodily punishemens [*sic*], and ciuill forcing of men. } *Ciuill Magistrates.*

Housholders or house keepers are persons authorised ouer their housholdes and charges. } *Householders.*

} *Agrement of men.* { *Ecclesiasticall.*

Ciuill { For Magistrates { In peace. / In war. } / For housholders.

[K 1 verso — 2 recto]

Agreement and choise by the Church.	Intruding & shifting into Church callings.
118. What agreement must there be of the church, for the calling of church gouernours ? They must trie their guiftes and godlines. They must receyue them by obedience as their guides and teachers, where they plante or establish the church. They must receyue them by choyse where the church is planted. *The agreement also for the calling of ciuill magistrates should be like vnto this, excepting their Pompe and outward power, and orders established meete for the people.*	118. *How doe they shift or thrust themselues into the church gouernment, as Antichristes?* They hide away their vntowardnes and wickednes, and colour the same by an outward bragge, or countenance of authoritie, or by flatterings and pleasings. They vndermine, and take away by craft the libertie of the church, and bring them into bondage. They come vppon them by power and force, and yoake them by cruel lawes and penalties. *The like may be saide of Tyrauntes which vsurpe ciuile authoritie.*

A Booke which sheweth the life and manners

Agreement and choise by the Church.

118. Agreement of men is the willingnes or glad consent both of the Gouernors to rule, & the people or inferiors to obey, for the assurance they have in God, of welfare by eche other.

Trying of their giftes and godlines, is a taking of accountes of the same, by a right iudgemēt of them, by that which we haue knowne and seene in them, whiche doeth sufficientlie warrant their meetenes.

Receyuing of them by obedience, is a duetifulnes in partaking to them the vse of our submission or seruice, because they partake vnto us the vse of their authoritie and guiding

Receyuing by choyse, is an agreement or partaking of condicions betweene Gouernours and inferiours, That so long as the Gouernours haue right vse of the submission and seruice of inferiours, and the inferiours also haue the right vse and welfare of their authoritie & guiding, they shall hold that com-

Agremēt of men.

Trying giftes & godlines.

Receyuing by obedience.

Receyuing by choyce.

Agreement of the Church.

By trying their giftes and godlines.

Receiuing thereon

By prophecie.

By life & manners.

By obedience.

By choise.

337

munion, or else make a breache thereof, when once it shall tende to confusion and destruction.
We giue these definitions so generall, that they may be applied also to the ciuill state.

119. What choyse should there be?
The praiers and humbling of all, with fasting and exhortation, that God may be chiefe in the choise.
The consent of the people must be gathered by the Elders or guides, and testifyed by voyce, presenting, or naming of some, or other tokens, that they approue them as meete for that calling.
The Elders or forwardest must ordeine, and pronounce them, with prayer and imposition of handes, as called and authorised of God, and receyued their charg to that calling.
Yet imposition of handes is no essentiall pointe of their calling, but it ought to be left, when it is turned into pompe or superstition.

119. *How doe they come vppon them with power and force, and yoake them with crueltie?*
With pride, threates, or wicked lawes, they are thrust vppon the people, by their owne might or by the strength of others: As of Bishops Patrones. &c.
The most wicked haue gotten from all, the libertie of vsing their voice and sentence: and doe at their pleasure present, name and approue whom they will. As the Examiner, the Patrone, the Bishoppe. &c.
They commaunde and giue Licences with seales and fees and kneelings, and blasphemously also will giue the holie Ghost and the authoritie of preaching, though they haue not the guift: both which the lord onely can giue.

A Booke which sheweth the life and manners

119. Prayer at the chosing is vpō the word preached, a pronouncing of their earnest desire to haue God their gracious Gouernor, in so waightie a matter, with an hūble cōfessing wherin and how much they haue need of his help, & an intreating for the same in the name of Christ Iesus.

The gathering of voyces & consent of the people, is a general inquirie who is meete to be chosen, when firste it is appointed to thē all, being dulie assembled to looke out such persons among thē, & then the nūber of the most which agree, is taken by some of the wisest, with presenting and naming of the parties to be chosen, if none can alledge anie cause or default against them.

The ordayning by some of the forwardest & wisest, is a pronoūcing thē with prayer & thanksgiuing, & laying on of hands (if such imposition of handes bee not turned into pompe or superstition) that they are called and authorised of God, & receyued of their charge to that calling.

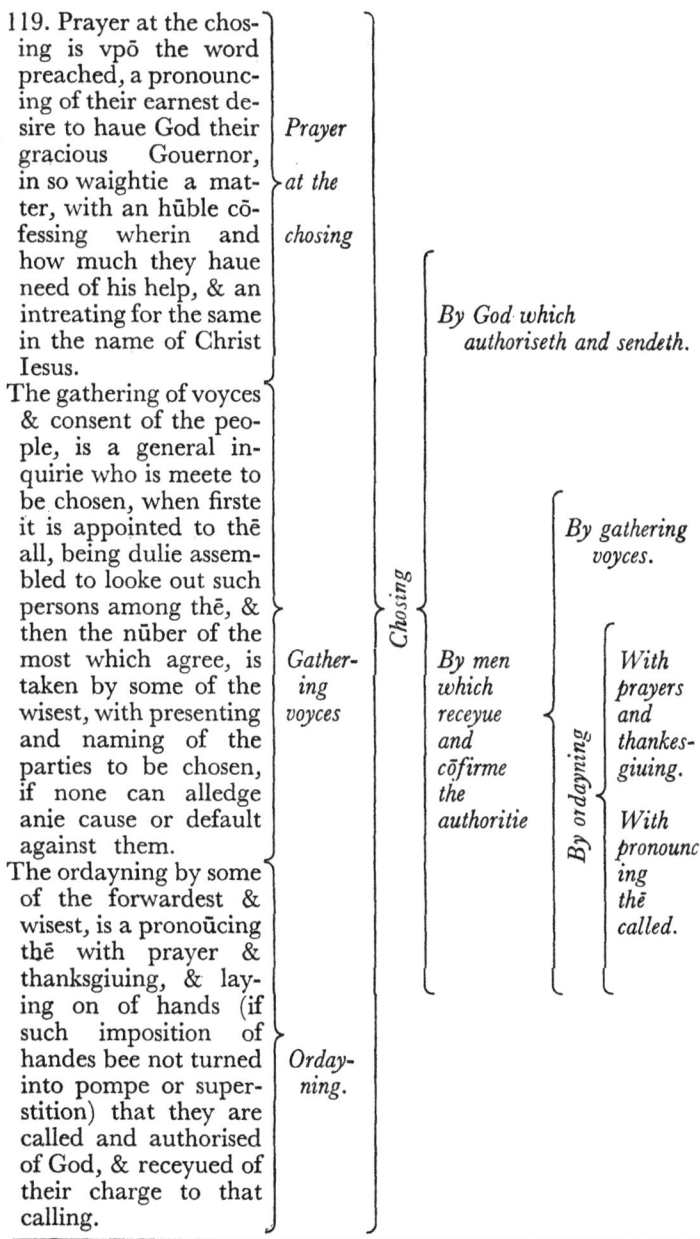

Prayer at the chosing — By God which authoriseth and sendeth.

Gathering voyces — By men which receyue and cōfirme the authoritie { By gathering voyces. With prayers and thankesgiuing.

Ordayning. — By ordayning { With pronouncing thē called.

[K 2 verso — 3 recto]

Agreement and choise by househouldes.	Intruding & shifting into home gouernment.
120. What agreement must ther be in the househouldes, for the gouernement of them?	120. *How doe they shift and thrust themselues into home gouernment?*
There must be an agrement of Husband and Wife, of Parentes & Children: Also of Maister and Seruant, and likewise of Teachers & Schollers. &c.	There is some disorder, wilines, or wrong in their agreement.
This agreement betweene parentes and children is of naturall desert and duetie betweene them:	There is vnnaturall hardnes in the parentes towards the children, or the children doe refuse and cast of[f] their parents.
But in the other there must be triall & iudgment of ech others meetnes for their likinge and callinge, as is shewed before.	They hide away their vntowardnes by some outward bragge and countenaunce.
Also there must be a due couenaunt betweene them.	By craft, feare, or power, they vndermine them and bring them into bondage.

Agreement and choise by househouldes.

120. The gouernement of the Husbande is, his authoritie, lordshippe and chieftie ouer the wife, whereby he useth her obedience and seruice, to partake vnto her the vse and graces of his authoritie and guiding.	*The gouernmēt of Husbandes.*	By natural agreement, as betwene	Parents.
Parentes are persons authorised ouer their children to rule them, by naturall desert of begetting and bringing them vp.	*Parents*		Children.
Maisters are persons authorised ouer their seruantes to rule them, by couenant of some maintenance, wages, or benefite, for their bodily seruice.	*Maisters,*		Betweene husbande & wife.
Teachers are persons authorised ouer schollers to rule them, by couenant to have maintenance or benefitte by them, for the learning which they gette vnder their guiding.	*Teachers.*	By couenant and choyse made as,	Maisters and Seruantes. &c.
Triall of eche others giftes & meetnes is defined before, quest. 118.			
The couenant of Gouernement, is an agreement or partaking of condicions to hold the communion thereof, so long as it tendeth not to the confusion or destruction of eyther partie.	*Couenant of gouernment.*		

Home Government

As for the couenaunt here betweene husband and wife, we vnderstand not the couenaunt which is in the communion of mariage, but that which is in the communion of gouernement. And this couenaunt is broken if eyther do seeke the destruction of other, or doe persecute religion or goodnes: likewise also it is broken, if by keeping togethr [sic] the one can not hould the true religion through the vntowardnes of the other in a wicked and false religion. And therefore in such cases a brother or a sister is not in bondage but that the husband may depart from the wife or the wife from the Husband 1 Cor. 7. Yet this departing is not a breach of the couenaunt of mariage, but of that communion in gouernment, through leauing one another for a good conscience.

[K 3 verso — 4 recto]

Gouernment by Superiours.   Guiding amisse.

Hitherto of the entraunce and taking on vs the callinges of gouernment: now followeth the due execution of those callings.

121. How must Superiours execute their calling by ruling their inferiours?
They must esteeme right and due.
They must vphould the same.
By appointing to others their dueties.
They must take accountes.

121. *How doe the wicked handle their gouernment amisse, and abuse the same for their pleasure and lustes?*
They mislike the right, and fauour the wronge.
They leade others vnto wickednes.
They suffer and let them alone therein.

122. How must they esteeme right and due?
They must be zealouse for equitie and innocencie.
They must loue those and reioyse ouer them, which doe their dueties.
They must hate all vanitie and wickednes and be angrie and greeued thereat.

122. *How doe they mislike right and due?*
They make light thereof.
They loath it and take greefe therat.
They rest and please themselues in euill and wrong.

A Booke which sheweth the life and manners

Let this Definition be equallie weighed, and it will appeare whether wiues may departe from their Husbandes, when the vntowardnes of the Husbandes in a false religion, and persecution withall, doeth driue them to seeke their saftie with true Religion and a good conscience.

Gouernment by Superiours.

121. *For the definition of rule & gouernement looke question 112.*

Execution of their calling is a duetifulnes in them, in partaking vnto them which obeye and serue them, the whole vse, and al the graces of their authoritie and guiding.	Execution of calling	By esteeming right and due.	
		By vpholdīg the same,	By appointing duties. By taking accountes.
Esteeming right and due in inferiours, is a duetie of their calling, whereby they are pleased with the worthines thereof, and feele or knowe the vse of the same.	Esteeming right.	Pleased with it.	Loue and Ioye. Zeale. Ielousie.
		Displeased with cōtrary	Hatred. Anger and Wrath.

122. Their zeale and Ielousie, is the estimation of right and dutie, for the worthines thereof: whiche prouoketh them to hasten the same, & to make it sure with all straightnes and watchfulnes. } *Zeale*

Their Loue and Ioye is their high estimation of inferiours in their goodnes, whereby they yeelde themselues to them in one mutuall happines, and take them as precious and deare, which are so obedient and rulie. } *Loue.*

Their anger and hatred is their troubled disliking of the wickednes of inferiours, for the contrarietie thereof, to their iust guiding and authoritie, prouoking them speedily to redresse such wickednes, or if that can not be, to cast them off and forsake them. } *Hatred and anger.*

[K 4 verso — 4 recto]

Appointing and teaching dueties.	Misleading and deceauing.
123. How must they appoint vnto others their worke and duetie? They must teach them. They must direct them by their guiding and helpe. They must giue them good example.	123. *How doe they misleade?* They giue them vp to their ignoraunce, or deceiue and beguile them. They forsake the vntoward or make them more auke. They goe before thē in wickednes.

*Teaching
- *Deliuering the groundes of Religion and the meaning of the Scriptures.*
  - By interpreting and opening
  - By gathering vppon it
- *Confirming the same.*
  - By requiring agayne, and priuate applying.
  - By trying in practise.

A Booke which sheweth the life and manners

Appointing and teaching dueties.

123. Appointing of dueties is that point of gouernement, or duetifulnes in Gouernors, whereby their inferiours haue their office and charge at their handes.
Their Teaching is their duetifulnes in using the obedience of inferiours, to learne and knowe their dueties.

{ *Appointing dueties* { *By teaching.* / *By speciall directing.*

Teaching *

{ The wordes.
  The matter, as { The whole meaning. / The partes. }

{ The summe & whole matter breiflie laied out.
  The methode and order.
  Proofes.
  Sentences. }

{ Generall knowledge { Of Religion and holines. / Of righteousnes with men. }

  Applying to reforme { Skanning duties by / Mouing affections }

  { Cōmending, discōmending.
    Exhorting, dehorting. }

124. How must they teach them? They must teach them the groundes of religion, and the meaning of the Scriptures.
They must exhort and dehort particularly for reformation of their liues.
They must require thinges againe which are taught, by particular applying and trying their guift.

124. *How doe they giue them vp to their ignoraunce, or deceaue and beguile them?*
They teache them heresies, or lette them alone therein, and withholde them from searching and learning the truth.
They incourage & strēgthen thē in wickednes by flatteringes and pleasinges: but discourage from goodnes by taunts and threats.
They skoffe and mocke at their graces and knowledge, if they haue anye, or litle regarde their ignoraunce.

[L 1 verso — 2 recto]

Directing and taking accountes.	Forsaking and suffering wickednes.
125. How must they direct them by their guiding and helpe? They must guide thē in the worshipp of God, as in the Worde, Praier, Thanksgiuing, &c. They must gather their Voices, Doubtes and Questions, and determine Controuersies. They must particularlie commaunde and tell them their dueties.	125. *How doe they forsake the vntowarde, or make them more auke?* They are a spirituall infection, and misleade others in a false worshippe and idol seruice. They make them slauish to their decrees and traditions. They force, controule and turne all dueties which waye they will.

A Booke which sheweth the life and manners

124. The groundes of religion are the pronounced, written, or knowen lawes & doctrine of God, teaching vs the first necessarie and chiefe rules of our christian profession, whereof if one of them be denied or refused, it is the ouerthrowe of al religion, & of our whole redēption. } *Groundes of Religion.*

Applying is an examining or trying out of the liues of men by the trueth of Gods word, to make known the secretes of their hartes vnto them, and their iust desertes for the good or euill that is in them, or proceedeth frō them. } *Applying*

For the definition of Exhortation, looke quest. 110

Dehorting is an edifying by sharpe & blaming words with threatnings of iudgement, to worke in their hartes a misliking of some vice and errour, with a hatred and griefe against it. } *Dehorting.*

Requiring agayne is a seconde or after teaching to confirme things which are taught. } *Requiring againe.*

Directing and taking accountes.

125. Their directing and guiding is a duetie of their gouernement, vsing the obedience of others in following them, to do anie thing with them or after thē. } *Direcing* { To doo things with vs { In religion & worshipping God. { In doubtes & controuersies to decide matters. In busines to commaūde & tell them their dueties.

In al other affaires {

To do things after vs by our exāple.

Guiding in the worship of God, is when they worship God with vs, and after our maner. } *In the worship of God.*

Gathering voyces, doubtes, &c, is diligent inquirie of them: and determining controuersies, is an vsing of their obedience to followe our iudgement in them, set downe by the worde of God. } *Deciding matters.*

126. How must they take accountes?

They must continually watch them by visiting and looking to them them selues, and by others helping vnto them.

They must trie out and search their state and behauiour by accusations and chardgings with witnesses.

They must reforme or recompense by rebuke or separation the wicked and vnruly.

126. *How doe they suffer and let alone in their wickednes?*

They hide wickednes and shift it away, and seeke occasions of euill.

They ouerslippe wickednes and passe by the same.

They flatter and excuse them in their sinne.

Hitherto of the dueties of Gouernours, now follow the dueties of submission vnto them.

A Booke which sheweth the life and manners

Particular commaunding and telling of dueties, is a pronoūcing with authoritie what we appoint them to do: whereby we vse their obedience to followe our will. } *Particular commaunding.*

Good example is a duetie of their gouernement in forwardnes before them, to shew vnto others, howe they should followe them, & doe anie thing after them. } *Good example.*

126. Our taking of accountes is a duetie of our gouernement, whereby we reckon with them, howe they do their dueties. } *Taking accounts* { In knowing right and due { *By Watching.* / *By examining.*   /   In recompensing.

Watching, is our continuall minding of them, whereby wee marke their obedience and seruice. } *Watching.*

Examining and trying, is a forceable taking of accountes, whereby we make known that which anie would hyde. } *Examining.*

Recompensing is a duetie of gouernement, whereby as they doo their dueties, so we giue them the name and the vse thereof in good or euill. } *Recompensing.*

For rebuke and Separation, looke questoon [sic] *48.*

[L 2 verso — 3 recto]

Submission. Esteeming Superiours.	Vndutiefulnes. Despising Superiours.
127. What say you of the dueties of submission to Superiours? They consist in esteeming them. In honouring them. In seruing them.	127. *How are inferiours vndutiefull and faultie?* They despise their Gouernours. They make them a shame and a skorne. They are vnruly.
128. How must we esteeme them? We must esteeme them in their Persones. Also in their Iustice. Also in their Goodnes.	128. *How doe they despise them?* They make light of their worthines. Also of their will and pleasure. Also of their goodnes, and the graces, and blessinges which they may haue by them.
129. How must we esteeme them in their persone? By reuerence. By shamfastnes and bashfulnes.	129. *How doe they make light of their worthines?* They are too homelie with them. They are boulde and malepert.

Submission.   Esteeming Superiours.

127. Inferiours or persons gouerned are, which giue vse to their Gouernours of their submission and seruice, and receyue the vse of their authoritie and guiding and houlde this communion so longe, as it tendeth not to the confusion or destruction of either of them.
Esteeming Superiours, is a duetie of submission, whereby we consent, that they are worthie and meete for to guide vs.

— *Inferiours and submission.*
  - *In esteeming them.*
  - *In dutifulnes thereon by*
    - *Honouring them.*
    - *By seruing them.*

— *Esteeming*
  - *In their persons*
    - *Reuerence.*
    - *Bashefulnes.*
  - *In their authority*
    - *In iustice.*
    - *In goodnes.*

128. Esteeming them in their person, is whereby we are moued at their presence, and are stricken with their worthines, for their cōtinuall good example and due behauiour. — *Esteeming their persons.*

129. Reuerence is an estimation of them for their owne worthines, though we had not to deale with them. — *Reuerence.*
Bashefulnes or shamefastnes, is a troubled disliking of our owne vnworthines, because of their presence, whom wee better accounte of then of our selues. — *Shamefastnes.*

130. How must we esteeme thē in their iustice?
By feare.
By zeale for their right.
By greefe for their displeasure.

130. *How doe they make light of their will and pleasure?*
They haue their hardnes and stoutnes of hart.
Also their dubbling and halting.
Also they rest and flatter them selues in their wickednes.

[L 3 verso — 4 recto]

Esteeming. Honouring. Humbling.	Despising. Shaming. Pride. Forsaking.

131. How must we esteeme thē in their goodnes?
We must loue them.
We must reioyse in their presense and welfare.
We must hope and trust of their help in God.

131. *How do they make light of their goodnes, and of their graces & blessinges which they may haue by them?*
They haue their misgiuing frō them.
They are greeued and heauie before them.
They shrinke awaye, and doubt of their helpe.

A Booke which sheweth the life and manners

130. Esteeming them in their iustice, is a duetie of submission, whereby wee take them to be meete and righteous Gouernors. } *Esteeming thē in their Iustice.* { In well doing { *Feare.* / *Zeale.* } In euill doing as greefe.

Feare is an Estimatiō of their Iustice, wherby wee take heede to please them in all things, and abhorre to prouoke them against vs, because we are sure, that they will recompence vs according to our deseruings. } *Feare.*

Zeale for their right is an highe estimation therof, for their worthines, prouoking vs earnestlie to hasten and further the same, as feeling it our curse if they lose their right. } *Zeale.*

Griefe for their displeasure, is a troubled disliking of our wickednes, and iniurie done to them, wherby we feele the hurt and daunger we are in, by their displeasure against vs. } *Greefe.*

Esteeming. Honoring. Humbling.

131. Loue and Ioye is an estimation of thē in their goodnes, whereby we yeelde our selues to them in one mutuall happines, & seeke their welfare before our owne. } *Loue & Ioye.* { *Esteeming in goodnes* { Present { *Loue.* / *Ioye.* } Cōming { *Hope.* / *Trust.* }

Hope and Truste is an highe estimation of their helpe and fauour, prouoking vs to doo anye thing, wherin we haue assurance of their good will or promise. } *Hope and Trust.*

Looke question 93.

132. How must wee honour them?
Wee must humble our selues before them.
Wee must seeke to them for their fauour and helpe.
We must be thankfull for their goodnes towardes vs.

132. *How doe they make them a shame and a skorne?*
They haue their loftines and pride or els toe much slauishnes.
They forsake their goodnes and cast them of[f].
They esteeme their owne worthines and are vnthankfull.

133. How must we humble our selues?
Wee must shewe the lowlines of our hartes by our speach and behauiour.
We must be meeke in despising our right and welfare.
We must be patient in abiding their chastising.

133. *How haue they their loftines and pride, or their toe much slauishnes?*
They will be gallant and lordlie, or ouerwretched in flattering.
They are stoute and stubborne.
They murmure or rage when they are corrected.

134. How must wee seeke to them for their fauour and helpe?
We must confesse our faultes and offences.
Wee must aske pardon and forgiuenes.
Wee must complaine of our wantes and craue their helpe.

134. *How doe they forsake their goodnes and cast them of?*
They excuse and iustifie them selues in their faultes.
They are frowarde and wilfull in the same.
They chalenge their deseruinges.

132. Honouring them is a duetie of submission, whereby wee set foorth their worthines. } *Honouring them.* { In humbling our selues to them.
In vsing their goodnes. } *Humbling.* { Inwardly { In meekenes.
In patience.
Outwardlie in homage.

Humbling ourselues, in an honouringe of them, by abasing our selues; according to our vnworthines and their excellencie aboue vs. }

133. Homage is an Humbling or Abasing of our selues in our behauiour towards them, as beseemeth their worthines, whereby they haue honour therein. } *Homage.*

Meekenes is an humbling or abasing of our selues, in despising our right and welfare, as vnworthie to haue or to seeke it at their hands, when they wittinglie withhold it. } *Meekenes.*

Patience is an humbling or abasing of our selues, gladlie to suffer their correction as being meete for vs. } *Patience.*

134. Seeking to them, is an honouring of thē by shewing our willing desire to vse their goodnes. } *Seeking to them.* { In faultes.
In other miserie or need. } { Confessing faultes.
Asking pardon.
Complayning of wantes.
Crauing helpe.

Cōfessing faultes is a seeking to them for their fauour and good liking, by shewing wherein and howe greatlie we haue offended. } *Confessing faultes.*

Asking pardon is a seeking to thē to haue our faultes forgiuen vs, with an humble intreating them for the same. } *Asking pardon.*

Complayning and Crauing, is a seekinge to them by shewing wherein and how much we haue need of their helpe, with an hūble intreating them for the same. } *Complaining and Crauing helpe.*

[L 4 verso — M 1 recto]

Thankefulnes. Seruing. Learning.	Vnthankefulnes. Vnrulines. Foolishnes.
135. Howe must wee be thankefull ? We must acknowledge their goodnes towards vs We must confesse the same in our words. We must shewe kindnes and duetie againe.	135. *How doe they esteeme their owne worthines and are vnthankefull* ? They sette light and thinke skorne of good turnes and benefites. They talke and vaunte of their deseruings. They vpbraide them and are vnduetifull.

Hitherto of esteeming and honouring of Superiours:
Now foloweth seruing of them.

136. How must we serue them ? We must learne of them. We must obey them in our calling. We must giue good accountes of our calling.	136. *How are they vnrulie* ? They are foolish and ignoraunt. They are disobedient. They are maisterly and set on their willes.

Thankefulnes. Seruing. Learning and following.

155 [sic] Thankefulnes is an honoring of them by abasing our selues for the good we haue by them, whereby wee take our selues indebted vnto them and vnable to make them amendes. } *Thankefulnes to thē* {

In acknowledging goodnes. { Giuing thanks
In dutifulnes for the same, { Kindnes and duetie againe.

Acknowledging goodnes is a ful consent and conscience thereof, by mindefulnes and examining of their particular good turnes towardes vs. } *Acknowledging their goodnes.*

Giuing thankes is a witnessing or shewing of their deseruinges, whereby wee confesse their goodnes towardes vs, and our vnworthines. } *Giuing thankes.*

Kindnes or duetie againe, is a thankefulnes in pleasuring them for all the goodnes whiche they haue shewed towardes vs. } *Kindnes and duetie againe.*

136. Seruing them is a duetifulnes in giuing to Superiours the vse of our calling and giftes, with earnest endeauour to pleasure and profite them. } *Seruing them* {
By learning of them.
By obedience thereto. { In our calling.
In accountes thereof.

Learning of them, is the seruice of our minde and vnderstāding, whereby we vse their goodnes in teaching vs, that wee may knowe our dueties, and do thereafter. } *Learning of them.* {
By getting knowledge.
By vsing the same to follow { Their guiding.
Their example.

137. How must we learne?
We must gett the knowledge of such things as they teach vs, and reforme our selues by them.
We must followe them guiding vs.
We must followe their example.

137. *How are they foolishe and ignorant?*
They are dull and deceaued.
They become more vntoward and auke.
They are contrarie and against them in vnlike behauiour.

138. *How must we followe them guiding vs?*
Wee must worshippe God by their guiding, and daylie keepe the meetings thereto appointed.
Wee must yeeld and stand to their iudgements, and debatings of matters by the word of God.
Wee must take and fulfill our taske and dueties at their appointing.

138. *How are they vntoward and auke?*
They houlde a superstitious or false worshippe with them.
They are froward and contentious.
They are vnprofitable, and bring losse or disuantage.

[M 1 *verso* —][1]

Obedience. Counsaile. Forwardnes. Due Working.

139. How must we obey them in our calling?
We must take counsaile.
We must be forward theron.
We must doe all things in their due manner.

140. How must wee take counsaile?
Wee must attend and watch to our dueties.
Wee must remember and count the same.
We must foresee & purpose what to doe.

[1] From this point to 145 two columns only, then the four columns re-appear.

A Booke which sheweth the life and manners

137. Knowledge of our dueties, is the right iudgement and wisedome wee should haue, whereby we should haue al things sought and founde out belonging to our calling. } *Getting knowledge by them.*

Following them guiding vs is a duetie of submission in vsing of their gouernement, to put in practise anie duetie by their particular appointing, or as wee see them to go before vs. } *Following them guiding.*

Following their example, is an vsing of their godlie life, to frame our owne liues accordingly. } *Following their example.*

138. *The worship of God, and the meetings for the same, are defined before.*

Yeelding and standing to their iudgements, is a duetie of submission in vsing of their iudgementes, and aunsweres to learne what is truth and meete in anie matter, to followe the same. } *Yeelding to their Iudgementes.*

For *Taking and fulfilling our taske & dueties*, looke number 146.

Disob. Rashnes. Backwardnes. &c.

139. *How doo they disobey them in theyr calling?*
They doo thinges in lightnes and rashnes, or with subteltie and craft.
They are backward and vntoward.
They haue their euill handling and marring of matters.

140. *How are they light and rash in their doings?*
They haue their carelessnes and dulnes.
Also their forgetfulnes.
Also their vnwarines and headines.

141. How must we be readie and forward vpon counsaile?
   We must desire to doe our dueties, with hope and trust of obteining our desires.
   We must haue zeale & courage thereto.
   We must be ioyfull and comfortable therin.

142. In what manner must wee doe our dueties[?].
   We must be actiue and skilfull.
   We must labour and worke.
   We must be steadfast and constant.

143. What skill or actiuenes is required?
   Wee must order thinges by their times and course.
   Also by their measure of worke.
   And we must be handsome and tydie in our worke.

[M 2 *recto*]

Labour. Stedfastnes.

144. What labor is required?
   We must vse our force and might.
   We must be speedie and quicke.
   We must be painfull and straite that nothing fayle.

145. What stedfastnes and constancie is required?
   We must be patient whatsoeuer successe we haue.
   We must preuaile & gather strength.
   We must finish & dispatch our work.

¶. *For the Definitions and Diuisions of vntill number* 146. *Looke the number*

A Booke which sheweth the life and manners

141. *How are they backward and vntoward?*
They haue euill will to their dueties, with shrinking and doubling to goe forward.
They are coulde and doe better things by halues.
Their duties are wearisome and irksome vnto them.

142. *What euill handling and marring of matters haue they?*
They are vnfit and vnskilfull.
They are idle and slothfull.
They are wauering and giue ouer.

43 [sic]. *Howe are they vnfitte and vnskilfull?*
They are disordered and do thinges by hazard.
They haue their disuantage.
They are vntydie and boysterous.

Idlenes.   Vnconstancie.

144. *Howe are they idle and slothfull?*
They haue their weaknes and fainting.
Also their slacknes and slownes.
Also their loathing and letting.

145. *How are they wauering and vnconstant?*
They are discouraged if anie thinge miscarie.
They shrinke and faile by their backwardnes.
They loose their labour and mysse of thier purpose.

all these before from number 138.
100. *to the number* 107.

[M 2 verso — 3 recto]

Accountes of calling. Dueties of goodnes.	The wicked maisterlie, cursed and vngracious.
146. What accountes must we make of our calling? We must cleare our selues from all accusation and suspicion of euil. We must shewe and approue our faithfulnes. We must fullfill our taske.	146. *How are they masterlie, and obstinate in their wickednes?* They excuse anb [sic] iustifie their faults. They hide their vnfaithfulnes, and shifte it awaye. They faile of their worke & dueties, and do them by halues.
Hitherto of bounden duties.	Hitherto of abuse in gouerenment.
147. What be the more free duties? They are concerninge other mens persons, in goodnes towards them. Or concerning our owne. Or concerning outward furniture.	147. *What abuse is there of freedome and libertie?* The wicked are cursed and vngracious to others. Also to them selues. Also they marre & spoile all thinges.
148. What be the dueties of goodnes towards others? They be eyther in esteeming them. Or in honouring them. Or in pleasuring them.	148. *How are they cursed and vngracious to others?* They despise them. They shame them or make them a skorne, so much as lieth in them. They are hurtfull and mischeeuous.

Accountes of calling.   Dueties of goodnes.

146. Giuing accountes is our obedience in seruing them, whereby we make a good reckoning, of all dueties towardes them. } *Accountes.* { *In worde* { *In clearing our selues.* / *By shewing our faithfulnes.* } / *In deede by fulfilling taske.*

Clearing of our selues is a giuing of accountes, whereby we discharge our selues of all things wherewith wee are, or might seeme to be charged. } *Clearing.*

Shewing faithfulnes, is a giuing of accountes whereby they marke and perceiue, that we keepe trust and credite with them. } *Faithfulnes.*

Fulfilling taske is an accounts in our deedes, discharging vs of that worke and seruice which they appointed vnto vs, because we haue duelie dispatched the same. } *Fulfilling taske.*

147. Goodnes towardes others is our righteousnes in yeelding and applying ourselues vnto them to their behoofe rather then to our owne. } *Goodnes* { *By esteeming and accounting.* / *By dutifulnes thereon* { *In honouring them.* / *In pleasuring them.* }

148. Esteeming them is a duetie of our goodnes, whereby we iudge and take thē, as worthie thereof, and yeelde our selues to them. } *Esteeming them* { *In prosperitie* { *In their persons.* / *In their goodnes.* } / *In miserie* { *Greefe, mercie and compassion.* }

149. How must we esteeme thē ?
Wee must esteeme them in their person.
In their goodnes.
And in their miserie.

149. *How doo they despise them* ?
They haue respect of persons.
They cast them of[f] and make light of their worthines.
They forsake them in miserie.

150. How must we esteeme thē in their person ?
By reuerence.
By shamefastnes.

150. *How doo they respect persons* ?
By slauish abasing, by wondring, or by disdaine.
By bouldnes and malepertnes.

[M 3 *verso* — 4 *recto*]

Esteeming. Honouring. *Humbling.*	Despising. Forsakeing. Shaming. &c.
151. How must we esteeme them in their goodnes ? By loue towards them. By ioy in their presence & felloship. By hope and truste of their fauour towards vs.	151. *How do they cast them of* [*f*] *and make light of them* ? They haue their misgiuing & anger. Also their enuie and greefe. Also their shrinking & withdrawing.

A Booke which sheweth the life and manners

149. Esteeming them in their person is a duetie of goodnes whereby we yeelde our selues to them, for their owne cause and worthines though wee had no good by the m } *Esteeming person* { *Reuerence.* *Shamefastnes.*

150. Reuerence is an estimation of them for the image of God in them, or for some shewe of his excellencie. } *Reuerence.*
Shamefastnes is a troubled disliking of our vnworthines, which we feele the more by the shewe of their excellencie. } *Shamefastnes.*

Esteeming. Honouring. Humbling.

151. Esteeming them in their goodnes, is our duetifulnes in yelding our selues to them, for some communion of graces or dueties which we haue with them. } *Esteeming thē in goodnes* { *Loue* *Ioye.*
Loue is an Estimation of them, in their goodnes, whereby we yeeld our selues to them in one mutuall happines. } *Loue.*
There is also a loue of our enimies, which is but an estimation of the shewe of some excellencie of God in them, whiche driueth vs for the Lordes cause to seeke their welfare. These we can not loue in their goodnes, being wicked, nor yeelde our selues to them in one mutuall happines. } *Loue of our enemies.*
Ioye is an estimation of them, whereby wee feele the blessings and graces wee haue by thē, how much they further our happines. } *Ioye.*

The definitions of Hope and Trust looke before.

152. How must we esteem them in their miseries?
By mercie and compassion.
By partaking their greefe.
By partaking their shame.

152. *How do they forsake them in miserie?*
They are sauage and vnmercifull.
They are gladd and merie in their euils.
They disdaine them and thinke skorne of them.

153. Howe must we honour thē?
We must humble our selues to them.
We must seeke to them, and request them for their fauour and helpe.
We must be thankfull.

153. *How do they shame them, or make them a skorne?*
They haue their loftines and pride, or their slauish pleasing.
They forsake their goodnes and cast them of[f].
They esteeme their owne worthines, and are vnthankefull.

154. How must we humble our selues to them?
By lowlines in speach & behauiour.
By meekenes in pleasing them.
By gentlenes in sparing them.

154. *How are they proude, or slauish in pleasing?*
They are gallant and lordly, or wretched flatterers.
They are stoute and wilfull.
They are disdainefull and spightfull.

155. How must we be lowlie in speach and behauiour?
By vsing reuerent names and speach towards them.
By courtesie and homage.
By wayting and ministring.

155. *How are they gallaunte and lordly?*
They raile, mocke and iest, or otherwise abuse them by speach.
They are to[o] homelie, vncourteous, or barbarous.
They are nice and straunge.

152. Mercie is a troubled disliking of their miseries as if they were our owne. } *Mercie.*

Partaking griefe is a feeling with them, of the hurtes and daungers they are in, as if they were our owne. } *Greefe.*

Partaking shame, is a troubled disliking of that vilenes they are in, as if it were our owne. } *Partaking shame.*

---

153. Honouring is a duetie of goodnes t o w a r d e s them, whereby we set forth their worthines. } *Honouring* {
- By hūbling our selues to them.
- By vsing their goodnes. {
  - For their worthines { Reuerent speache. Courtesie and Ministring.
  - For agreement { Meekenes in pleasing. Gentlenes in sparing. }

Humbling our selues in an honouring of them by abasing our selues, according to our vnworthines which we feele in comparison of them. } *Humbling.*

---

154. Lowlines is an humbling or abasing of our selues, whereby wee preferre them before vs. } *Lowlines.*

---

155. Courtesie or ciuilitie is an hūbling or abasing of our selues in our behauior towards them, as beseemeth their persons, or desertes at our handes. } *Courtesie.*

Ministring is a duetie of humbling or abasing, whereby we applie our selues to helpe & serue them as their neede is. } *Ministring.*

[N 4 verso — N 1 recto]

Meekenes. Gentlenes. Vsing goodnes.	Stoutnes. Spitefulnes. Forsaking.
156. How must we please them in meekenes towards them? By yeelding to their request, or opinion. By pardoning them anie thinge. By appeasing them being angrie.	156. *How are they stout and wilfull*? They are contentious and churlish. They are fearce and furious. They make trouble and prouoke others.
157. How nust [sic] we spare them in gentlenes? We must be milde in talke or rebuke. We must forbeare their infirmities. We must be patient in their iniuries.	157. *How are they spitefull*? They are waywarde and bitter in talke and rebuke. They stomacke infirmities and seeke vantage against others. They are malicious & seeke reuenge.

A Booke which sheweth the life and manners

Meekenes. Gentlenes. Vsing goodnes.

156. Meekenes is an humbling or abasing of our selues in despising our right or welfare, as vnworthie to holde or seeke it with their displeasure. } *Meekenes in pleasing* { *By yeelding.* *By appeasing anger.*

Yeelding to them is a duetie of meekenes, fulfilling their desire and suite, though it bee against our selues. } *Yeelding* { *To request* { *Of suite. Of pardon.* *To him that striueth for his opiniō.*

Pardoning is a duetie of meekenes in receyuing them to fauour, and shewing our loue, as if they had not offended vs. } *Pardoning.*

Appeasing their anger, is a duetie of meekenes in vsing softe wordes and kinde behauiour to get their fauour in their wrongfull disliking of vs. } *Appeasing.*

157. Gentlenes in sparing is a duetie of humbling or abasing our selues gladlie to suffer their vntowardnes and weaknes, though it be against our selues. } *Gentlenes in sparing* { *By mildnes.* *By patience in forbearing* { *Infirmities.* *Iniuries.*

Mildnes in speache is a duetie of gentlenes in applying of our wordes to their liking, though it be against our selues. } *Mildnes in speache* { *In talke.* *In rebuke and admonishment.*

Patience is a duetie of gentlenes in sparing and forbearing them, dealing wrongfullie against vs. } *Patience.*

Forbearing infirmities is a duetie of gentlenes in sparing of them in their vnaduised or vnwilling dealing against vs. } *Forbearing infirmities.*

Forbearing iniuries, is a duetie of gentlenes in sparing of them in their wilfull dealing against our knowen right. } *Forbearing iniuries.*

158. How must we seeke to thē for their fauour and helpe?
We must complaine of our wantes, and craue their helpe.
We must confesse our faultes and offending of them.
We must aske pardon & forgiuenes.

158. How doo they forsake their goodnes, and cast them of?
They match and compare themselues with them, and skorne their helpe.
They excuse & iustifie their faultes.
They are froward therein.

[N 1 verso — 2 recto]

Thankfulnes. Pleasuring. Teaching.	Vnthankfulnes. Harming. Corrupting.
159. How must we be thankfull? We must acknowledge their goodnes. We must confesse the same. We must shewe kindnes and goodnes againe.	*159. How are they vnthankfull and esteeme their owne worthines?* They sette light by and thinke skorn of their good turnes and benefits. They talke and vaunt of their deseruings. They vpbrayde them and are vndutifull.

A Booke which sheweth the life and manners

158. Seeking to them is an honouring of thē by shewing of our willing desire to vse their goodnes. } Seeking to them. { In faultes. { Confessing faults. Asking pardon.

Cōfessing faultes is a seeking to them for their fauour and good liking, by shewing wherein and howe greatlie we haue offended. } Confessing faultes. { In other miserie or need. { Complayning of wantes. Crauing helpe.

Asking pardon is a seeking to thē to haue our faultes forgiuen vs, with an humble intreating them for the same. } Asking pardon.

Complayning and Crauing, is a seekinge to them by shewing wherein and how much we haue need of their helpe, with an hūble intreating them for the same. } Complaining and Crauing helpe.

Thankefulnes. Pleasuring. Teaching.

159. *For the Definitions and Diuisions in this number* 159. *looke number* 135.

160. How must wee pleasure them?
By prayer for them.
By directing and furthering them.
By maintayning them.

160. *How are they hurtfull and mischievous?*
They curse and wish euill vnto them.
They misleade and hinder them.
They forsake them and faile them, when they should helpe them.

161. How must wee direct and further them?
By teaching and counsayling.
By ayding and moderating.
By our example.

161. *How do they mislead and hinder them?*
They corrupt them and hould them in their errour and ignoraunce.
They trouble or withdrawe them from their dueties.
They are captaines and ringleaders to mischeefe.

162. How must wee teach and counsayle them?
We must vse mutuall conference and edifying in the Scriptures.
We must exhort and comfort.
We must dehort and rebuke.

162. *How do they corrupt them, & holde them in error and ignorance?*
They stand and reason to withdrawe and peruert one an other.
They incourage & strēgthen in wickednes by flatterings and pleasings.
They discourage from goodnes by tauntes and threates.

A Booke which sheweth the life and manners

160. Pleasuring them is a duetie of goodnes and charitie towardes them, whereby wee doo them good. } *Pleasuring them*

Prayer for them, is a seeking to God for his helpe and blessing vppon them, by shewinge wherein and howe much they haue neede of his helpe, with an humble intreating him for the same. } *Prayer for them.*

{ Secrete by prayer for them.
  Shewed } { By directing and furthering them.
  By mayntayning thē. }

For *Directing*, looke number 125.

Furthering is a duetie of goodnes, whereby they gette vauntage, and are profited by vs. } *Directing & furthering*

{ In word { Teaching. Counsell.
  In deede { By ayding, moderatig. By example. }

161. For *Teaching and Counsaill*, looke number 125. and number 53. And also 47.

Ayding and helping is a duetie of goodnes, whereby we vse meanes or indeuour our selues to remedie their wantes and necessities. } *Ayding and helping.*

For *Moderating and example*, looke number 125. and number 19.

162. For *Conference and Edifying*, Also for *exhorting and dehorting*, looke number 110. and 124.

Cōforting is a duetie of goodnes towardes them, whereby we vse kinde wordes and full of godlie hope, either to remedie greefe or impatience, or to make them more gladde and comfortable. } *Comforting.*

[N 2 verso — 3 recto]

Maintayning others: Also our selues.	Fayling others: Also themselves.
163. How should we maintayne them? By iudging and defending their person and cause, and reconciling parties. By giuing and lending and suertishippe, as they haue neede. By visiting and ministring to them in their distresse, though it cost vs our liues.	163. *How doo they faile and forsake them?* They reproch, condemne, and betraye them. They are vnkinde, harde, and pinchinge, and lende vpon vsurie. They haue their straungenes, nicenes, and loathinge.
Hitherto of dueties concerning goodnes towards others.	Hitherto how they are a curse and vngracious to others.

A Booke which sheweth the life and manners

Maintayning others: Also our selues.

163. Maintayning is a duetie of goodnes & pleasuring them, whereby thei want no helpes nor furtherance of their welfare, so much as lyeth in vs.

Maintayning

- *In strift & controuersie, by iudging and defending their cause and person, and reconciling parties.*
- *In peace & quietnes*
  - *In prouiding good things for them.*
  - *In doing good.*

Iudgeing their cause is an assurance or conscience of their right and innocencie, wherebye we determine accordingly. } *Iudging.*

Defending is a maintaining of them in strift by vsing of lawe, power or strength, to vphoulde their right. } *Defending.*

Recōciling is a duetie of goodnes in iudging and determining their cause, whereby the parties offended, do willingly agree and striue no further. } *Reconciling.*

Prouiding things, is a duetifulnes in vsinge meanes to haue them readie, that we may bestowe them. } *Prouiding.*

Giuing or liberalitie, is a duetie of goodnes, whereby we bestowe good things vpon them without their cost. } *Giuing*

Lending is a duetie of goodnes in laying out and bestowing of our goods to their vse, vpon trust or assurance of payment agayne. } *Lēding*

In bestowing our goods
- *Lending.*
- *Giuing.*

164. What dueties are for our owne persons? We must defend and maintayne our state and welfare. We must vse it comfortablie, and remedie our greefes. We must vse it seemelie & honorably, as beseemeth Christians.	164. *How are they a curse and vngracious to them selues?* They faile and are wanting to them selues. They are their owne greefe, and increase their miserie. They shamfullie abuse their welfare, and make them selues vile.
165. How must we defende our state and welfare? By withstandinge the violence of the enemie, when it is for Gods glorie. By bouldnes in answeringe and pleading our cause. By assailing the enemie with force, when the cause requireth.	165. *How doo they faile, and are wanting to them selues?* They miscarie or perishe throughe shrinkinge, or through wilfull indaungering them selues. They are fearfull or ouermatched in holding their cause, & betraie ye same[.] By flight or other vnwarines, they betraye their safetie or welfare.

A Booke which sheweth the life and manners

Suertiship is a warrāting of their faithfulnes towardes others by standing bounde in their behalf, vpō trust of their faithfulnes towards vs. } *Suertiship*	} *Doing good*		{ *Suertiship.*
For ministring, looke num. 155.		In bestowing our selues & our seruice	
Visiting is a duetie of goodnes in partaking vnto them the vse and comfort of our presence and companie. } *Visiting*			*Visiting and ministring &c.*

164. Defending and mayntayning our state & welfare is a dutie of pleasuring & helping our selues by all lawfull meanes } *Defending*	} *Duties for our selues*	In mayntayning our welfare	{ In defending and keeping it. In remedying it.
		In vsing it	{ Comfortablie. Honourablie.

165. Withstāding is a strift against enimies, whereby we defende our selues, vpon trust of some ablenes in God to resist them. } *Withstāding*	} *Defending*	By withstāding	{ In deeds. &c. In word &c.
Pleading our cause is a defending of our right, making it known by proofe & examination. } *Pleading*		By assayling.	
Assayling is a strift against enimies, firste prouoking them to defende themselues. } *Assayling.*			

[N 3 verso — 4 recto]

Dueties of Comfort, Seemlines, Chastitie.	Wretchednes. Vilenes. Vnchastitie.
166. How must we vse our state comfortablie? We must vse the blessinges of God both mutuall and suerall, as a remedie against dulnes and greefe. Also against weaknes and wearines. Also against hurt, or vncomlines.	166. *How are they a greefe and miserie to them selues?* They cast them selues into further heauines and care. They pine away or breake them selues, with fasting and toiling. They increase their disease & beastlines.
167. How must we vse our state seemelie and honorablie? We must refraine from lawfull pleasures, as there is neede, and bridle our lustes. We must be pure and chast. We must be sober.	167. *How are they shamefull and vile?* They pamper & cherish them selues. They are vnchast and filthie. They are giuen to wantonnes and pleasures.
168. What chastitie and purenes must we vse? We must vse mariage duelie. We must have no filthie thoughtes nor lustes. Neither wordes nor behauiour, nor outwarde helpes to further the same, as, euil companie, excesse in eating, & drinking, brauerie, nicenes, &c.	168. *How are they vnchast and filthie?* They abuse mariage. They haue filthy thoughtes & lustes. Also wordes and behauiour, & outward helpes to further the same.

A Booke which sheweth the life and manners

Dueties of Comfort, Seemlines, Chastitie.

166. Vsing our state comfortablie is a bestowing or applying of the giftes and graces of God to haue the full ioye and glorie of the same. } *Vsing state comfortablie.*
Remedying of dulnes, greefe, weakenes, wearines, hurt, and vncomelines, is an vsing of such blessings and graces of God, as may take them away. } *Remedying want of comfort.*

167. Vsing our state seemelie and honorablie, is a bestowing and applying of the giftes and graces of God, to haue our full reuerence and honour thereby. } *Vsing state honourablie* } *In abstinence* { *In nature, as lust, appetite, delightes, ease, &c.*
{ *In other pleasures.*
In moderation { *By purenes & chastitie.*
By sobernes.
Refrayning and abstinence is a duetifulnes in disliking and refusing such pleasures as beeing lawefull in them selues, yet by some occasion are vnmeete for vs. } *Abstinence.*
Moderation is a dutifulnes in gouerning pleasures, that we exceede not measure and honestie. } *Moderation.*

168. Purenes and chastitie is a moderation of naturall lust, that no filthines be in vs. } *Purenes & chastitie* { *In mariage* { *By preparing thereto.*
By due ioyning.
In single life.

169. What is the right vse of mariage?
There must be a due triall and iudgment of eche others meetenes.
Also a due couenaunt made on all parties.
Also a due ioyning in mariage.

169. *How doo they abuse mariage?*
They are deceaued by some foolish fancie, & drawne together for some worldie cause.
By shifting and wilines, or some wicked bondage, they make the matche sure.
They come together by some wrong and disorder.

[N 4 *verso* — O 1 *recto*]

Meetnes. Couenant. Ioyning in mariage.	Shifting. Wrong. Disorder in mariage.
170. What triall of their meetnes must there be? They must be twoo onely, the man and woman, which for age, sexe and kinred are meete eche for other. They must be meete for eche others liking in behauiour and personage. They must be meete for eche others state and calling.	170. *How are they deceaued, and drawne away by their fancie, &c.?* They fall to all filthines, as incest, buggerie, filthines with beasts, & vntimelie matching &c. or else forbid mariage altogither to some persons. They take them meete for their luste, as for beautie, riches, or for some outward countenaunce or benefite. They trouble and hinder their state and calling.

A Booke which sheweth the life and manners

169. Mariage is a lawfull ioyning and fellowship of the husband and wife, as of two in one fleshe, by partaking the vse o f eche others loue, bodie, and giftes, in one communion of dueties, and especiallie in generation and bringing vp children.
Trying their meetnes is a takinge of accountes with our selues and others to haue warraunte of the same, by a right iudgement of thē, in those things which we haue knowne and seene by them.

	Mariage	By preparatiō thereto	By triall of meetnes in the parties to be maried.
		By a due ioyning.	By a due couenant.
	Trying their meetnes	By nature	Sexe, age, kindred.
			Personage to our liking.
		By nurture & bringing vp.	Godlines.
			Meetnes by trade.

The Definitions of Sexe, age, kindred, persons, looke for in our table of Nature.[1]

Meetnes. Couenant. Ioyning in mariage.

170. Their meetnes ech for other is their state or blessing of God vpō them, whereby they are both most redie and prepared for the vse eche of other, both for liking and calling. } Meetenes.

Meetnes for liking, is the blessing & grace which they haue of behauiour, personage, and comlines, not to be disliked as vnmeete for eche others degree. } Meetenes for liking.

Meetnes for calling is the blessing and grace which they haue, whereby eche others calling and skill may serue sufficientlie to their mutuall maintenance and profite. } Meetenes for calling.

For meetnes by godlines, looke num. 118.

---

[1] ? Another unknown work of Browne's or a reference to some of the previous sections ?

171. What couenant must ther be? There must be a betrothing of eche to other. Also an espousing of the parties by witnesses.	171. *How do they make the match by shifting, wilines, or some wicked bōdage?* They gett a promiss eche of other by forcing, or by some craft & flatterie, Likewise in espousing there is some such craft, wrong and disorder.
Also an agreemente of parentes, or friendes, if the parties to be maried by [sic] vnder their ful power & gouernmēt. *But if not, & the parentes or friendes be froward and none of the churche, the mariage of the godlie is not in bon[d]age to their agreement.*	Also the parentes by craft, feare, or power doo bring them together: or they are stolen or withdrawe them selues from the authoritie of their parentes in that matter.
172. How must they be duelie ioyned in mariage? Their betrothing & espousing must be further made known vnto witnesses. Their friendes must be glad and reioyce together, in some ioyefull and seemelie maner. They must giue the vse of their bodies for generation of children eche to other, and must not giue that vse of their bodies nor anie token therof to anie other, while they liue together, and lawfull diuorcement with deathe doth not followe.	172. *How do they come together by some wrong and disorder?* They haue graunt of secret licenses to marie, or their popish banes are asked in churches, and without a ringe and bablinge praiers, and the minister to marie them they can not be maried. And so they make it a sacrament. They haue their feastes, daūcings & vaine pleasures in heathenish wise. By rape, force, fornication or adulterie, or by vnlawfull diuorcementes, &c. they defile mariage.

A Booke which sheweth the life and manners

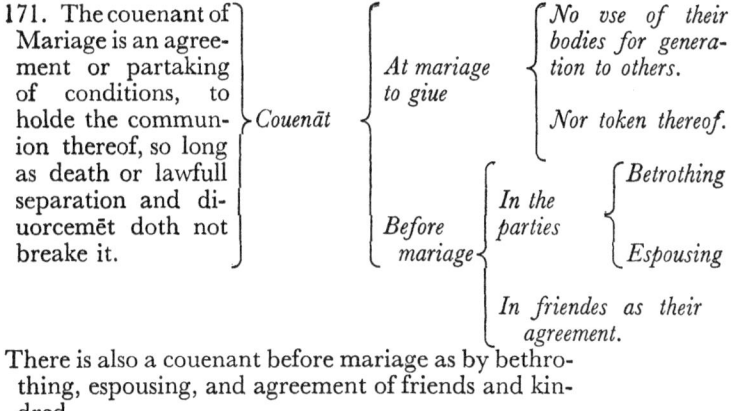

171. The couenant of Mariage is an agreement or partaking of conditions, to holde the communion thereof, so long as death or lawfull separation and diuorcemēt doth not breake it.

 — Couenāt
  - At mariage to giue
    - No vse of their bodies for generation to others.
    - Nor token thereof.
  - Before mariage
    - In the parties
      - Betrothing
      - Espousing
    - In friendes as their agreement.

There is also a couenant before mariage as by bethrothing, espousing, and agreement of friends and kindred.

Bethrothing is a couenant betweene the parties to be married, wherby they giue their troth that they will and shall marrie together, except some lawefull vnmeetnes and disliking eche of other do hinder it in the meane time. — Bethrothing.

Espousing is a couenant betweene them, whereby they are pronounced before witnesses, to giue them selues, and to be giuen eche to other to become husband and wife. — Espousing.

172. Making it further knowne is the professing and shewing thereof, whereby it is further founde out and manifest. — Making it further knowne.

Gladnes and Ioye of friends, is a blessed partaking of the vse and comfort of eche others presence & companie, with mirth & feasting, for the blessing of God towardes them in that mariage. — Gladnes in meeting of friends.

The Mariage and Ioyning it selfe, is defined before, num. 169.

[O 1 *verso* — 2 *recto*]

Sobernes. Profitablenes. Sauing.	Wantonnes. Vnthriftines.
173. What sobernes must we vse? We must haue no wanton thoughtes nor delightes. Neither wordes nor behauiour. neither outward helpes to further the same.	173. *How are they giuen to wantonnes and pleasures?* They haue their wanton thoughtes, delightes, wordes & behauiour, also the outward helpes to further the same; as euill cōpanie, excesse in eating & drīking, brauerie, nicenes, &c.
Hitherto of free duties concerning persons.	Hitherto of the abuse of freedom in vndutifulnes to persons.
174. What be the dueties concerning goods and furniture? They consist in getting, and increasing furniture and goods. In sauing them being gotten. In doing right vnto others about them.	174. *How are they vnduetifull in goods and furniture?* They are vnprofitable, and liue vpon others. They are vnthriftie, and their goods goe to decaye. They do iniurie and wrong.
175. How are we to gett and increase thinges? By our callinges in studies of learning. By worke of bodie in sciences and craftes. By the maner of laboring in these, as appeareth before.	175. *How are they vnprofitable, and liue vpon others?* They are vntaught and without learning. They haue no trade nor occupation. They haue their euil handling and marring of matters.

A Booke which sheweth the life and manners

Sobernes. Profitablenes. Sauing.

173. Sobernes is a moderation of Ioye and delight, that no wantonnes be in vs, neither in thought, worde, nor behauiour.	*Sobernes.*	Inwarde.	In speache.
		Outwarde	In behauiour and furniture.
Duetifulnes concerning goods and furniture is our righteousnes in vsing them, and occupying our selues about them for profite and benefite.	*Duetifulnes in goods*	By getting them.	
		By sauing them being gotten.	

174. Getting and increasing goodes, is a duetie of vsing the blessings of God, vnto further vauntage and gaine.	*Getting*	By labor in our calling	In studies of mind as in the artes.
			In work of bodie as sciences and trades.
		By the maner of labouring, as before.	
Our calling is our appointed charge and maner of life in some honest worke wherein we are dailie to labour as we may best profite therein.	*Callings.*		

175. Studies of learning are callinges wherein the minde laboureth to inable vs with knowledge and wisedome, the better to gouerne and reforme vs in all dueties.	*Studies of learning.*
Trades & sciences in bodily worke, are callings wherein the bodie also laboureth by skillfull and diligent stirring, to make or do somewhat for liuing and maintenance.	*Trades and Sciences.*
For the maner of labouring, looke num. 100	

176. How are we to saue things? By placing and counting them, that they be not lost. By mending and dressing thē before they be marred. By spending and bestowing them without anie wast.

176. *How are they vnthriftie, and lett their goods goe to decaye?* They cast and laye thinges disorderedlie, and are carelesse of them. They spoile and marre them. They wast and lauish them awaye.

[O 2 *verso* — 3 *recto*]

Righteousnes. *Faithfulnes.* *Innocencie.*	Vnrighteousnes. Falsehoode and wronge.
177. How must we do right vnto others in goods and furniture? We must deale faithfullie with them. Also innocentlie in agreement and couenaunt. Also vprightlie in generall equitie.	177. *How do they iniurie and wrong vnto others?* They are vnfaithfull and deceitfull. They are hurtfull and oppressours of others. Thei ar vniust & cōmō doers of wrōg.

A Booke which sheweth the life and manners

176. Sauing goods, is a duetie of profitablenes, whereby wee vse meanes that goods gotten, may be wel kept. } *Sauing by* {
 Keeping frō the losse { *By reckoning and Counting.* / *By placing.*
 Bestowing and vsing wel { *By spending without waste.* / *By mending hurt and vncomelines.*

Keeping from losse is a sauing of them by a diligent watchfulnes, to make them sure, and to haue them readie when neede requireth. } *Keeping from losse.*
Counting them is a sauing of them by the helpe of their number. Likewise placing by helpe of their place. } *Counting and placing.*
Bestowing them is a sauing of them by heedines to haue the full vse and benefite by them. } *Bestowing.*
Spending is a warie bestowing of them, as they may reache furthest and last longest in profitinge our selues and others. } *Spending.*
Mending them is a sauing of thē by remedying their hurt as there is neede. Likewise dressing is in remedying the foulenes or vncomelines. } *Mending and dressing.*

Righteousnes. Faithfulnes. Innocencie.

177. Doing right to others in goods & furniture, is a duetifulnes whereby we yeelde vnto them their due therein. } *Doing right* { *By faithfulnes.* / *By innocencie.*
Faithfulnes is a duetie of righteousnes and Iustice in keeping our trust and credite with anie. } *Faithfulnes* { *Keeping trust.* { *In debtes & borowing.* / *In vsing their goods truelie.* / *In generall equitie,*

178. How must we deale faithfullie?
We must paye our debtes, and keepe our promisse.
We must restore that which is borowed.
We must deale truelie with other mens goods, being in our handes or keeping.

178. *How are they vnfaithfull & deceitfull?*
They are bankerupt and breake promisse.
They borow, and restore not againe.
They defraude, cousin, or beguile men of their goods.

---

179. How must we deale innocentlie in agreement and couenaunt?
We must bargaine, buye or sell, with equall vauntage in price and stuffe, by weight, number, greatnes, measure, time.
We must do our work for our wages.
We must giue the wages for worke.

179. *How are they hurtfull, and grypers of others?*
They bargaine, buye and sell to the losse of others, as by euil ware, false weight, euil measure, tale & count.
They are deceitful laborers, & work by halues for their wages.
They giue wages by halues, or keepe it wholie backe.

---

180. How muste wee deale vprightlie in generall equitie?
We must permitte vnto euerie one their libertie and goods without robberie and oppression.
We must not steale nor beguile with craft.
We must make amends, when we haue hindred or defrauded anie.

180. *How are they vniust and common dooers of wronge?*
They are exactors, robbers, and oppressours.
They are theeues and pilferers.
They holde what they haue euil gotten, and count it their owne.

Hitherto of the generall dueties of righteousnes with men.

Hitherto of generall vndutifulnes towards men.

A Booke which sheweth the life and manners

178. Paying debt is a duetie of faithfulnes in restoring that again which we tooke vpon trust & credite to bestowe to our vse. } *Paying debt.*

Restoring anie thing borowed, is a duetie of faithfulnes whereby wee giue againe that is lente vs to occupie. } *Restoring things borrowed.*

Dealing truely with their goods is a duetie of sauing or keeping thē to their whole benefite. } *Dealing truely in their goodes.*

---

179. Innocencie in agreement and couenaunt, is our righteousnes therein, whereby they haue right at our hands, & no mischief & wrōg is foūd in vs. } *Innocencie in agreement and couenaunt* { *In buying and selling* / *In wages and worke.*

Innocencie in bargaining is in paying duely for that we buye, and deliuering duely that whiche is bought, to the equall gaine of the buyer and seller. } *Innocencie in bargaining.*

Doing work for wages, is a duetie of innocencie, by a diligent dispatching of so much busines, as for which we receyue our wages. And payinge wages is, when the workman hath his whole due for his worke. } *Innocencie in wages and worke.*

---

180. Uprightnes in general equitie is our righteousnes, whereby we suffer all to enioy their libertie & goods in peace & safetie. } *Vprightnes in generall equitie* { *In permitting due* / *In satisfying for wrong.* } { *Without robberie and oppression.* / *Without stealth and craft.*

Robberie is an vnrighteousnes in taking awaye the goods of anie by vsing violence against their person. } *Robberie.*

Oppression is an vnrighteousnes in getting frō anie their right, by vsing our power against their cause. } *Oppression.*

Stealth is an vnrighteousnes in taking secretlie other mens goods away from them, by spying out the time of their vnwarines. } *Stealth.*

Making amendes is a duetie of righteousnes, whereby the person which hath suffered iniurie, is requited againe, as the cause deserueth. And this requiting must be secret in secret iniuries, & shewed in a knowen iniurie. } *Making amendes.*

[O 3 verso — 4 recto]

Dueties for Name, Trueth, Secretnes, &c.	Falsehoode. Slaunders. Couetousnes.
181. What be the special duties for name and creditt? They consist in trueth. In secrettes. In innocent reportinge.	181. *What speciall faulting is there by their owne, and others euil name?* They fault by falsehoode & vntruth. Also by tatling and pratling. Also they do wronge by euill reportinge.
182. What be the duties of trueth? Simplicitie. Steadfastnes in testifying ye trueth. Taking all thinges in the right meaninge.	182. *How are they false and vntrue?* They dissemble and dubble. They chaunge and faine in their wordes. They take their vantage, and peruert the plaine trueth.
183. What be the dueties of secretnes? We must keepe priuat things secret, without tales, whisperings, backbytings, &c.	183. *What tatling and pratling do they vse?* They make rumors of priuate matters, not able to proue them. They whisper, backbite, & cary tales.

A Booke which sheweth the life and manners

Dueties for Name, Trueth, Secretnes. &c.

181. Speciall dueties for name and credit are wherein chieflie we may pleasure or displeasure our selues and others.	*Speciall dueties for name and credite*	*In faithfulnes*	*In Trueth.*	*In secretnes.*
		In innocencie		*Without slaũdering and false witnessing.*
				Without speaking or receiuing euil words.
Speaking truth, is a faithfulnes in our words, to make knowne vnto anie a thing as we know it is.			*Speaking trueth.*	

182. Simplicitie is a speaking of the trueth without shifting or dubling.	*Simplicitie*			
Stedfastnes is a speaking of the same wordes, in the same manner and meaning, so much as we possiblie can remember.	*Steadfastnes*	*Trueth*	*In simplicitie, and taking the right meaning.*	
			In stedfastnes.	
Taking things in the right meaning, is a speaking and vttering of the wordes of an other, as we may charitablie vnderstande them.	*Taking the right meaning*			

183. Secretnes is a faithfulnes in telling to no man such things as are vnmeete to be toulde them, because they are priuate or smaller offences, and the parties tractable.	*Secretnes.*

184. How must we be harmeless in reporting of others ?
We must not slaunder.
Nor beare false witnes.
Nor speake, or receaue euil wordes.

184. *How do they wrong by false reportes ?*
They slaunder.
They beare false witnes.
They speake, or receaue euil wordes.

---

185. What be the speciall duties against couetousnes ?
That we be content with our owne, without a grudging desire to match or excel others, or to haue anie thinge that is theirs.

185. *What speciall faulting is there by couetousnes ?*
They are couetous, and haue a grudging desire to match or excel others, or to haue that which is their neighbours.

---

184. Keeping our selues from slaunder, is an innocencie in wordes, by raysing no false reporte of wickednes in anie to hinder their good name. } *Without slaundering.*

Keeping our selues from false witnessing, is an innocencie, by speaking nothing vntruelie or otherwise then we knowe. } *Without false witnesing.*

Refrayning from speaking or receyuing evil wordes, is an innocēcie wherby we neither suffer nor giue foorth suche wordes nor occasion thereof. } *Without euill wordes.*

---

185. Cōtentation is a conscience of our welfare by the blessing of GOD, whereby we like the same, and condemne our vnworthines aboue others. } *Contentation.*

FINIS

IV. A TRUE AND SHORT DECLARATION.

This work, of which the only known copy is at Lambeth (xl. 2. 23), has as its full title *A True and Short Declaration, Both of the Gathering and Ioyning together of Certaine Persons : and also of the Lamentable Breach and Division which fell amongst them*. It has no name, place, or date, but was probably written by Browne before he left Middelburg at the end of 1583. It contains three sheets, and breaks off abruptly at the end of the third, p. 24. It was not printed by Schilders, as were Browne's previous books, and it seems to have been set up by an amateur, perhaps by Browne himself. It is reproduced here as printed — with apologies to the sorely tried compositor. From Bredwell's *Rasing of the Foundations of Brownism* (1588) it seems as if Harrison had financed, at any rate in part, the printing of Browne's previous books, but ceased to do so when the breach came. Compare the words written in on the sudden ending of *A Treatise vpon the 23. of Matthewe*, " by reason of trouble the print was staid ", and also Harrison's reference to the cost of printing a book on church government as " above my reach of abilitie " (above, p. 71).

The meaning of the penultimate sentence in *A True and Short Declaration* is not clear : perhaps it means that Harrison and his friends insisted on Browne's paying for stocks on hand, and then strove to prevent their sale.

As the third sheet nears its end the spelling, punctuation, capitalization, and abbreviation become wilder than ever, though throughout the choice of capitals is such as to suggest a shortage of type. For the letter " w " we have W, w, vv, vu, vV, Vv, Vu, VV, uu, uv, uV, Uu, Uv ; indeed, every possible combination except UU.

Another mystery is what is supposed to be a facsimile reprint in *The Congregationalist*, London, 1882. The pages are not the same length, and there are hundreds of deviations from the Lambeth copy. Most of this issue was destroyed by fire.

A True and Short Declaration

IV. [A. 1. *recto*] A TRVE AND SHORT DECLARATION, BOTH OF THE GATHERING AND IOYNING TOGETHER OF CERTAINE PERSONS: AND ALSO OF THE LAMENTABLE BREACH AND DIVISION WHICH FELL AMONGST THEM.

THERE Were certaine persons in England, of vvhich, some vvere brought vp in schooles, & in the Vniuersitie of Cambridge, & some in families & houshouldes, as is the manner of that countrie. Some of these vvhich had liued & studied in Cambrige, vvere there knovvne & counted forvvard in religion, & others also both there & in the contrie vvere more carefull & zelous, then their frovvard enimies could suffer. They in Cambrige vvere scattered from thense, some to one trade of life, & some to an other: as Robert Broune, Robert Harrison, William Harrison, Philip Broune, Robert Barker. Some of these applied thē selues to teach schollers: to the vvhich labour, R. Broune also gaue him selfe, for the space of three yeares. He hauing a special care to teach religion vvith other learning, did thereby keepe his schollers in such avve & good order, as all the Tounsemē vvhere he taught gaue him vvitnes. Yet the vvorld being so corrupt as it is, & the times so perilous he greatly misliked the vvantes & defaultes, vvhich he sawe euerie vvhere, & marcked plaīly that vvithout redresse, nether the parentes could long reioise in their children, nor the children profit so much in religion, as that their other studies & learning might be blessed thereby[.] Hereuppon he fell into great care, & vvas soare greeued vvhile he long considered manie thinges amisse, & the cause of all, to be the vvofull and lamētable state off the church. VVherefore he laboured much to knovve his duetie in such thīges, & because the church of God is his kingdom, & his name especially is thereby magnified; he vvholy bent him selfe to searh [*sic*, search] & find out the matters of the church: as hovv it vvas to be guided & ordered, & vvhat abuses there were in the ecclesiastical gouernment then vsed. These thinges, he had long before debated in him selfe, & vvith others, & suffered also some trouble about thē at Cābridge. yet novve on fresh he set his mind on these thinges, & night & day did consult vvith himselfe & others about thē, least he should be ignorant, or mistake anie off those matters. What so euer thinges he ffound belonging to the church, & to his calling as a mēber off the church, he did put it in practis. For euen litle children are off the church & kingdom off God yea off such saith Christ, doth his kingdom consist: & therefore both in his schole he laboured that the kingdom off God might appeare, & also in those of the tovvne vvith vvhom he [A 1 verso] kept companie. So by vvord & practisse he tried out all thīgs, that he might be staied both in iudgmēt & coūsell, & also in enterprising matters, as his duetie should lead him. But this his dealīg got hī much enuie of the preacher & sōe others vvhere he taught, & much trouble also vvhē he broke his mīd more plainlie vnto thē. Presētlie after this he vvas discharged of his schole by the grudge of his enimies. Yet he taught still, vvith great good Vvill & favour of the Tounsemē, till such time as the plague increased in the Tovvne, & he was sēt for avvai by his frēdes. Therfore because his schollers, though neuer so Vvel plied & profited by him, vvere notvvithstanding, ether flitting avvaie Vpon such occasions, or to[o] hastelie sent to the Vniuersitie, or because of their misguiding there, to some occupations, he thought that the fruict of his labour Vvas toe much vncertaine, & tooke counsell if by sōe better vvaie he might profit the church. Then he gaue vvarning to the Toune, & departed to come home, as his father vvilled him. So might he haue liued vvith his father, being a man of some countenaunce, & haue vvanted noethinge, if he hadd beene soe disposed but his care as alvvayes before, so then especially being set on the church of God, he asked leaue of his father, & tooke his Iournie to Cābridge, frō whēse a fevv yeares before he had departed. He ther had dealīg vvith M. Greēhā of dreitō,[1] vvhōe of all others he hard sai vvas moste forvvarde, and thought that Vvith him & by him he should haue some stai of his care & hope of his purpose. Wherefore, as those vvhich in ould tyme vvere called the prophetes & children of the prophetes & liued to gether, because of corruptiōs among others, so came he vnto him. He vvas suffered, as others also in his his [sic] house, to speake of that part of scripture, Vvhich vvas vsed to be red after meales. And although he said, that vvithout leaue & special vvord from the bishop, he vvas to suffer none to teach openlie in his parish, yet Vvithout anie such leaue he suffered R. B. Notvvithstanding, vvhen R. B. savve, that the dishops [sic] feet vvere to much sett in euerie place, & that spiritual infectiō to much spread euē to the best reformed places, he tooke that occasiō vvhich the Lord did first geue him for redresse, & vvhen certaine in Cambrige had boath moued him, & also vvith consent of the Maior & Vicechancelar, called him to preach among them, he delt in this manner.

[1] Richard Greenham, minister of Dry Drayton, 1570-91. See *D.N.B.* His *Works* appeared in five editions between 1599 and 1612.

A True and Short Declaration

He first considered the state of Cambrige, hovve the church of God vvas planted therein. For he iudged that the church vvas to call and receaue him, if he should be there chosen and appointed to preach. Then did he thinck on this, vvhoe should be chiefest, or haue charge before others, to looke to such matters. For the bishops take vppon them the chieftie, but to be called and authorised by them, he thought it vnlavvefull. And vvhy he vvas of this minde, he had these & such like vvarrantes: namelie thei shoulde be chiefest, vvhich partake vnto vs the chiefest graces, and vse of their callinges. And that doeth Christ, as it is vvritten, of his fullnes haue all vve receaued, and grace for grace. Ioh. 1. 16. And to him hath God made all thinges subiect saieth Paul, Ephes. 1. 22. euē vnder his feet, and hath appointed him ouer all thinges, to be head of the church, vvhich is his bodie, euen the fullnes of him, vvhich filleth all in all thinges. Novve next vnder Christ, is not the bishop of the dioces, by vvhōe so manie mischiefes are vvrought, nether anie one vvhich hath but single authoritie, but first thei that haue their authoritie together: as first the church, vvhich Christ also teacheth, vvhere he saieth, If he vvill not vouchsafe [A 2[1] *recto*] to heare them tell it vnto the church, & if he refuse to heare the church also, let him be vnto the[e], as an heathen mā & a publican, Mat. 18. 17. Therefore is the church called the pillar & ground of trueth. 1. Tim. 3. 15. & the voice of the Vvhole people, guided bie the elders and forwardest, is saied to be the voice of God. And that 149. psalme doth shevue this great honour, Vvhich is to all the saincts. Therefore the meetinges together of manie churches, also of euerie Vvhole church, & of the elders therein, is aboue the Apostle, aboue the Prophet, the Euangelist, the Pastor, the Teacher, & euerie particular Elder. For the ioining & partaking of manie churches together, & of the authoritie Vvhich manie haue, must needes be greater & more Vvaightie, then the authoritie of anie single person. And this alsoe ment Paul Vvhere he saith. 1. Cor. 2. 22. Wee are yours, & you are Christes, & Christ is Godes. Soe that the Apostle is inferior to the church, & the church is inferior to Christ, & Christ cōcerning his manhood & office in the church, is inferior to God. This he iudged, not onelie toe be against the Vvickednes of the bishopes, but also against their Vvhole povver & authoritie. For if the authoritie of the church, & of the forvvardest breethren or elders therein, be aboue the bishopes, hovve should it not follovue, but that the bishopes maie be commaūded, accused & charged bie the church, yea also discharged & separated as is their desert? But novve because of their popish povver & canon lavves, thei haue

[1] Mistakenly "A 4" in text.

lift vpp their authoritie more high, thē the church can take accountes of them: & not onelie by force do thrust out & trouble Vvhome thei list, but also raigne as Lordes & Dukes in their dioces, their authoritie must nedes be vsurped. For the Apostles did geue accoūtes to the church of all their doinges, as Vve read in the Act. 11. 4. Act. 15. 2, 3. & Rom. 15. 31. But these being got aboue the Apostles, Vvill sit in the throne of Christ, & as Christ is not inferior to the church, no more Will thei be. For Christ hath chosē us, saith the scripture, & not Vve him, Ioh. 15. 16.; & therfore he is the greater thē vs all. And seīg the church can not chose the bishopes, nor those hirelinges, Vvhome the bishopes thurst vppon them, therefore thei also Vvill be greater then the church, & Vvith Vvhom then do thei compare them selues in degree, but Vvith Christ? & so make them selues antichristes. Nai thei presume further then Christ Vvhich woulde not thrust his Apostles vpō anie congregatiō, nor suffer them to take charge of anie Vvhich did not Vvillinglie receaue thē. Luc. 10. 10. But these do force vpō the people euerie Vvhere, & in sundrie places against their vvilles, not onelie ministers vnknovūe [sic], but also such as are knovuē to be blind busserdes, Vvicked fellouves & idol shepherdes. Likevvise Christ hath al rule in his hande; as it is Vvritten that vve are compleat in him, Vvhich is the head of all prīcipalitie & povver Col. 2. & he can not sinne, nor offend the lavve of God, nor be accused by the same; For so the scripture testifieth, that none could reproue him of sinne, though he offered him selfe to them to accuse him if thei could. Ioh. 8. And he is that high priest, as againe it is Vvritten. Heb. 7 vvhich is holie, harmlesse, Vndefiled, separated from sinners, and made higher then the heauens. Hovve high then do thei lift them selues Vvhich Will rule alone as lordes ouer the flock, though the vvord hath saied it shall not be so? Luc. 22. 26. 1. Pet. 5. 3. Which vvill be Rabbies, Doctors & reuerend fathers, though Vv[e] haue but one doctor & Father, as saith that high doctor Christ, Mat. 23, vvhich also take vpō thē, not as seruāuts in the house as vvas Moses, Heb. 3. but haue sent after him that is soone & heire in his ovvne house saing thei vvill not haue him to raigne ouer thē Luc. 19. 14. For thei haue refused his gouernment, & chosen their ovvne popish discipline in stead thereof.

[A 2 *verso*] This appeareth, because they enter & take on them their offices in popish vvise, & as that lavve præscribeth thē, & also do misguid the people by that popish tyrannie. For vvho knovveth not, but that they vvatch for the liuing or byshoprike, vvhen it shall fall, & then sevve[1] & paye vvell for the same, if they obtaine it. So are they rauenous & vvicked persōs, as saith the scripture, Zac.3.

---

[1] *I.e.*, sue.

A True and Short Declaration

They are makeshiftes & troublers, seing they rule rather because they seeke their ovvne aduantage, or glorie, or mischeuous purpose, then the vvelfare & benefit of the church. Yea they all looke to their ovvne vvaye as saieth the Prophet, Esa. 56. 11. euerie one for his aduātage & for his ovvne purpose. Who knouveth not also, but that they vvhich are not duelie receaued & called to guide, & that by due consent & agremēt, they are ether Antichristes in the church, or Tyrantes in the common vvelth, because they vsurp in the church or commōvvelth. Such are they of vvhom Paul speaketh. 2. Cor. 11. 20. that the corīthians did suffer them to much. For they did suffer if a man brought them into bondage, if a man deuoured, if a mān tooke, if a man exalted him selfe, if a man smote them on the face. For in deed the people do suffer the byshops, though they take from them their libertie of chosing good pastors & refusing euill, yea they suffer them selues to be robbed & beaten by those spiritual courtes, they suffer the great vntovvardnes & vvickednes of the byshops to be coloured & hidden by their outvvard bragge & countenance, as by their pomp, authoritie, tytls, & povver, & some times by their fair flattering sermons & pleasings. For they rule by three sortes of lavves, as by the ciuil, the canō, the commō lavve, vvhich are three kingdomes vnto them, or as the Popes triple crovvne, & by pretending the fourth lavve, vvhich is the vvorde of God, they ouerrule totoe much: they spare not to come vppon the people vvith force & povver, & they care not to bridle them vvith nevv & yearly iniunctions, & also vvith the oulde lavves & penalties of the court of Rome. While R. B. thought these thinges in him selfe he moued the matter diuers times vnto others. Some did gainsay & those of the forvvardest, affirming that the byshops authoritie is tolerable, & he might take license & authoritie of them. Others of them saide they vvoulde not coūsel nor medle for an other mās cōscience in that matter, but they them selues iudged, that the byshops preached the vvord of God, & therefore ought not lightlie to be reiected. Also they said, that seing they had the vvord & the sacraments, they must needes haue vvithall the church & people of God: & seing this vvas vnder the gouernmēt of the byshops & by means of thē, they could not vvholy condem the byshops, but rather iudge them faultie in some parte. Then did R. B. againe & againe discusse these matters, as he had often before, as vvhether the byshopes coulde be saied to preach the vvord of God & minister the sacraments or no. For if that vvere trevve, then also might they call & place ministers: & seing they them selues did minister so great a thing as is the vvorde & the sacraments, they might also minister their help in other things not so great. Therfore to knovve vvhether they preached the vvord of God, he searched & foūd by the scriptures, vvhat it is to preach the vvord: namely to do the Lordes message, as it is vvritten in Jeremie 23. 22. in teaching the people those thinges, vvhereby they might turn them from their euill vvaies & from the vvickednes of their inuentions. Therefore except they haue a due message, they can not preach the vvord off message. For I sēt them not saieth the Lord in that place, nor commaunded them, therefore they bring no profit vnto this people. Againe except they preach those things first, ffor vvhich first & chiefly they vvere sent [A 3 *recto*] namelie vvhat soeuer is to reclame the people, first from some especial vvickednes, vvherein they sinne, & so ffrom all other deffaultes, they can not be said to preach the vvorde. Therefore seing the byshopes calling & authoritie vuas shevved before for to be vnlavvefull, & seing also they call not the people from the cheifest abominations, Vvhich are the cause of the rest, but rather vvilfully & vvith crueltie do leade them in the same, as vvill aftervvarde appeare, they can not preach the worde of God. For to make a sermon is not to preach the vvord of God, no, nor yet to make a true sermon. For the seruaunt that telleth a true tale hath not done his maisters message, nor the arraunt[1] for the vvhich he vvas sent, except he tell & speake that for the vvhich his maister sēt him. Therefore though the byshops teach the people, and geue them lavves, & make manie iniunctions, yea, though they be lavves of Christ, yet if they abuse the obedience of the people, to houlde and follovve vvith some lavves of Christ their ovvne lavves especiallie, vvhat are they but antichristes? And hovv can they then but onelie in name & in shevve, preach the lavves of Christ? For example vvhile they peruert the lavve of God in this, they can not be saied to preach his lavve: namelie vvhereas God commaundeth to plant & to build his church, by gathering the vvorthie and refusing the vnvvorthie. Mat. 10. 11. Act. 19. 9. Ezr. 6. 21. they hooke by their contrarie lavves both papists & careles vvorldlings, as crooked trees, to build the Lordes sanctuarie, & force the vvretched to their vvorshippings & seruice, as if dogges might be thurst vpon God for svveet sacrifice. Proud forceing is meeke building vvith them & deuotiō compelled is their right religiō. Thus herein they pollute the Lordes sanctuarie & vvrest his lavve, hovv much more by a thousand moe abominatiōs vvhereof aftervvard vve brieflie touch some. For by thē do they feed them selues & the people vvith the bread of vncleannes, in stead of the puer vvord of God. They make it readie vvith the dongue that cometh of man, euen vvith their traditions, tolerations & falsifiinges. And if the Pharises made the vvorde of God of none effect or authoritie by their traditiōs, as it is vvrittē. Mark 7. 13. much more these. They by their corbans or

---

[1] = errand.

offering of guiftes, gaue occasion to children to dishonour their parēts & these by their spirituall courtes, by their fond excommunications, dispensations, absolutiōs, &c. yea by their taking of bribes & fees, do let so manie lose to all misrule & filthines. They taught the gould of the Temple to be greater then the temple, vvhich sanctifieth the gould: Mat. 23. 17. & these teach that to sinne is damnable: but to pollute the Lordes spiritual temple by mingling the cleane & vvretched together vvhich is the cause of all sinne, is noe matter of damnatiō: forsooth it is a thing tollerable because they can not remedie it. They taught that the offering on the altar vvas greater then the altar, though it sanctifie the offering; and these teach that to vvant the sacraments, that is lamentable, but to vvant the kingdō of God, & the visible shevve of his rule in his church, vvhereby the sacramēt is sāctified that they make no matter. If then for such doctrine they vvere called blind guides & fooles by Christ himselfe, Mat. 23. 16, 17. yea & though they sate in Moses seat, that is at first vvere lavvefullie called to teach the people, yet the people vvere charged by Christ toe lett alone such blind guides, & not to be guided by them. Matt. 15, 14. hovve much more should vve let these blind guides alone, vvhich neuer vvere lavvfully called, and also sit in the seat of Antichrist: for vvhat is the seat of Antichrist but that Popish Gouernment and lordship in the communiō of such Romish offices, & horrible abuses by them. And vvhile they syt in the tē-[A 3 verso]-ple off God 2. Thess. 2. 4, & exalt their traditions aboue Gods, vvhat are theie but antichrists? Doe theie then preach the Lordes vvord of message? or is not his vvord a fier, and like an hāmer that breaketh the stone? Iere. 23. 29. But all their preaching can not breake & bring men from anie smaller or greater disorders, vvhich vuicked church lavves or church Prelates cōmaund them. Thus vvas he setled not to seeke anie approueing or authorising off the bishopes. But because he knevue the trouble that vvould follovue, iff he so proceeded, he sought meanes off quietnes so much as vvas lavueffull; & for dealing vvith the bishopes, he was off this iudgement, that men maie novve deale vvith them, as before thei might vvith the pharises: that is, so far as vve nether sinne against God, nor geue offence vnto men: Thereffore iff Christ did his Fathers vvill, when he sate in the middes of the doctors, heareing them, & asking them quæstions. Luc. 2. 46. & iff Paul did his duetie, vvhen he sate doune in the synagogue, as it vvere offering him selfe, & seeking leaue to speake to the people. Act. 13. 14. iff he also did lavueffully applie him selfe to their ceremonies, Act. 21. 26. then thus far also is there medling vvith the bishopes, to trie & proue them, or to be tried off them, as vve see the like did fall out in Christ, also to yeeld to their povver, so that, vvherein vve yeeld, it be not against the trueth, & vve do

not establish it: as vve knovue Paul did to the povver off the
priests, off the pharises, & off the chiefe of the synagogue. Therefore he thought it lavuefull first to be tried off the bishops, then
also to suffer their pouver, though it vvere vnlauveffull, iff in aniẹ
thing it did not hinder the trueth. But to be authorised of them,
to be svvorne, toe subscribe, to be ordained & to receaue their
licensing, he vtterlie misliked & kept hī selfe cleare in those matters.
Hovve be it the bishopes seales vvere gotten him by his brother,
Which he both refused beffore the officers, & being vvritten for
him vvuold not paie for them, & also being aftervvard paied for
by his brother, he lost one, & burnt an other in the fier & an other
being sent him to Cambridge, he kept it by him, till in his trouble
it vvas deliuered to a Iustisse off peace, & so from him, as is supposed, to the bishop off Norvvich. Yet least his dealīg on this
manner, should encourage others to deale in vvorse manner, he
openlie preached against the calling & authorising of preachers
by bishops, & spake it offten also openlie in Cambrige, that he
taught among them, not as caring for, or leaning vpon the bishopes
authoritie, but onelie to satisfie his duetie & conscience. And this
his duetie he saied vvas, first to discharge his message before God, &
deserue no reproofe of them, & then also, ether toe finde them
vvorthie, or else, iff thei refused such reformation, as the Lord did
novve call for, to leaue them, as his duetie did bind him. For he
did not take charge off them, as he oftē gaue them vvarning, & also
did often shevve the cause, namelie for that he savve the parishes
in such spirituall bondage, that Whosoeuer Would take charge off
them, must also come into that bondage With them. Therefore
he finding the parishes toe much addicted, & pliable to that lamentable state, he iudged that the kingdom off God Was not to be
begun by vvhole parishes, but rather off the vvorthiest, Were thei
neuer so feuve. For it is as a graine off musterd seed, saieth Christ,
at the first, Mat. 13. and as a litle leauen hidd in three peckes of
meale. So he hauing tried about halfe a yeare, both by open
preaching, & by daielie exhortation in sundrie houses, that ether
bie bondage off the bishop in that dioces, or of the Colleges, or of
vvicked ministers & readers of seruice, or bie the prones[1] off the
parishes to like of that bondage, no redress could be Waited for,
he knevve that the Lord had appointed [A 4 *recto*] him theree to be
occupied, onelie to trie & prepare him to a further, & more effectual
message, & to be a vvitness of that vvofull state of Cambrige, vvhere-
into those vvicked prelats and doctors of diuinitie haue brought it.
This he foresavve before he preached among thē, & therefore vvhen
they gathered him a stipend, & vvoulde haue had hime take charge,

---

[1] *I.e.*, proneness.

A True and Short Declaration

he refused, and did both send backe the monie thei vvould haue giuen him, and also gaue them vvarning of his departure. So he continued preaching a vvhile, till he fell soare sick: and in his sicknes vvhile he ceased his labour, he vvas forbidden to preach bie a letter shevved him from the counsell. For indeed he had delt bouldlie in his duetie, and prouoked the enimies. The bishops officer named Bancraft,[1] did read the letter before him, but he nothing moued therevvith did ansvvere, that if he had taken charge in that place, he woulde no vvhitt lesse cease preaching for that, but as he Vvas he tooke not on hī he said, though the letter Vvere not, to preach there anie longer.

OF R.B. COMING TO NORWICH
& hovve the companie there ioined together.

After these thinges, Vvhen he Vvas recouered of his sicknes, & had gotten his strength he took counsell still & had no rest, Vvhat he might do for the name & kingdom of God. He often complained of these euill dayes & Vvith manie teares sought Vvhere to find the righteous, Vvhich glorified God, Vvith vvhome he might liue & reioise together, that thei putt avvaie abominations.

While he thus Vvas carefull, & besoughte the Lord to shevue him more comfort of his kingdom & church, then he savue in Cambrige, he remembred some in Norfolke, Vvhome he harde saie vvere verie forvvard. Therefore he examined the matter, & thought it his duetie to take his voiage to them. First because he considered, that if there vvere not onelie faultes but also open & abominable vvickednes, in any parish or companie, & thei vvould not or could not redresse them, but vvere held in bondage, bie antichristian povver, as vvere those parishes in Cambrige by the bishops, then euerie true christian vvas to leaue such parishes, & to seek the church of God vvheresoeuer. For vvhere open vvickednes is incurable, & popish prelates do raigne vphouldīg the same, there is not the church & Kingdom of God: as it is vvritten, 2. Chro. 15. 4. for a long season, Israel hath bene vvithout the true God, & vvithout priest to teach, & vvithout lavve. So that though there be a name of priests, & of preaching, and of God amongst anie, yet if there be sett ouer them idol shepherdes, popish prelates, & hireling preachers vvorse then thei, that vphoulde antichristian abominatiōs, there God doeth not raigne in his kingdom, nether are thei

---

[1] Richard Bancroft, afterwards Bishop of London and Archbishop of Canterbury. See "The Opinions and Dealings of the Precisians," edited Peel, to be published about 1953 by the Cambridge University Press.

his church, nether is there his vvorde of message. For no man can serue tvvoe contrarie maisters, saieth Christ. Mat. 6. nether can thei be the Lordes people vvithout his staffe of beautie & bandes. Zach. 11. 7. that is, vvithout the Lordes gouermēt. For his couenant is disanulled as it follovveth in the 10 verse. Novve his gouernmēt & sceptre cā not be ther, vvhere much opē vvickednes is īcurable. For if opē vvickednes must needes be suffered, it is suffered in those vvhich are vvithout, as Paul saieth, vvhat haue I to do to iudge those vvhich are vvithout? 1. Cor. 5. 12.

[A 4 verso]. And againe he saieth euen of these latter times, that men shall be louers of them selues, couetous, boasters, proud, cursed speakers, disobediēt to parents, vnthāckfull, vnholie, vvithout naturall affection, truce breakers, false accusers, intemperate, feirce, dispisers of them vvhich are good, traiters, headie, high mīded, louers of pleasures, more then louers of God, haueing a shevve of godlines, but hauing denied the povver thereof. From such vve must turn avvaie as Paul vvarneth. 2. Tim. 3. 5. that is, vve must count them none of the church & leaue them, vvhether in all these, or in some of them, theie be openlie soe faultie, as that thei be incurable.

Also if anie be forced by lavves, penalties & persecution, as in those parishes, to ioine vvith anie such persons, ether in the sacramentes, or in the seruice & vvorship of God, thei ought vtterlie to forsake thē, & auoid such vvickednes. For the abomination is set vp, antichrist is got into his throne, & vvho ought to abide it. Yea vvho ought not to seeke from sea to sea, & from land to land as it is vvritten, Amos. 8. 12. to haue the vvorde and the sacramentes better ministred, & his seruice and vvorship in better manner. So vvhile he thought on these thinges, and vvas purposed to trie also in Norfolke the forvuardnes of the people, it fell out that R. H. one vuhom he partlie vuas acquainted vuith before, came to Cambridge.[1] What vuas his purpose in coming, and hovue he thought to haue entred the ministerie, & did vse some meanes to that end, it is needles to rehearse, onelie this I shevue, that he seemed to be verie carefull in that matter, & though he leaned to much vpon men for that matter, as vpon M. Grenham, M. Robardes,[2] & others, & vuas carefull amisse for the bishops authorising, yet his mind and purpose might be iudged to be good, & no othervuise but vuell did R. B. iudge of him. When he had talcked vuith R. B. and shevued him the matter vuhereaboute he vuent, he receaued this ansvuere at his handes, that it vuas vnlauufull to vse ether maister Greenhams help, or anie mans else for the bishops authorising. Soe

---

[1] Robert Harrison came to Cambridge in 1580, and returned to Norwich the same year.
[2] Thomas Roberts, Archdeacon of Norwich, a leader of the Puritan ministers there (see *Seconde Parte of a Register*, I. 143 ff.)

A True and Short Declaration

he shevued him hovue before he had delt concerning the bishop, & vvas novue so far frō seeking license, ordainīg or authorising at his handes, that though he neuer had thē, yet for that he knevue of them, he abhorred such trash & pollutions, as the marckes and poison of Antichrist. Notvuithstanding he saied that if his conscience led him, to deale as before he had delt, he vuould do for him vuhat he might. for he had before requested his help. But R. H. ether chaūging his mind, or disappointed of his purpose, returned to Norvvich Vuhether also a short time after R. B. tooke his iournie. He came to R. H. house, Vuhoe then Vuas Maister in the Hospitall at Norvvich. He there finding roume enough, and R. H. VVillinge enough that he should abide Vuith him, agreed for his board, & kept in his house. They often had talcke together, of the lamentable abuses, disorders, & sinnes Vuich NoVVe raigne euerie Vuhere. At the first they agreed Vuell together, but yet so as that in some things R. H. doubted: notVVithstanding he came on more and more, and at last VVholie yeelded to the trueth, Vuhen he sauue it began to preuaile and prosper.

THE TALKE AND COVNSEL VVHICH
R. B. and R. H. had together, about matters of the church & Kingdom of God.

Their commo[u]ning about such matters Vuas much and often, as of the state of the [B 1 *recto*] church vvherein it was then: & VVhat vvas both their dueties to do in such matters. Their talck did fall out much after this manner. For Vvhen thei were vvalcking alone R. B. said I vvas glad M. H. that God did keep you at Cambrige, at your last being there, and disposed your vvaie not to haue anie medling With those bishops, but to geve them ouer. Whereto R. H. ansvvered, that he asked it off God, and God hard his praier, that if it vvas not meet for him so to enter the ministerie, he vvould let and disappoint him off his purpose. Then after this at sundrie times, there grevve other talck: as of the Lordship, offices and discipline off Antichrist in stead of the Lordship and gouernment of Christ. Then fell out these questions betvveene them, Whether those preachers that submit them selues vnto such popish povver, or anie Vuay so iustefie or tolerate it, as lavvefull in some part, or partlie to be liked & ysed, can thēselues be liked off, or do their duetie as lavuefull pastors & preachers. Hereat

R. H. did stick, because off M. Robardes, M. More[1], M. Deering[2], & others, vvhome he thē did greatlie like off. But more he doubted & as it vvere drevve back, vvhē he should geve ouer such preachers, or else forsake & shrincke from our ovvne good purpose. For he vvould haue the consent of such preachers in the matters that vvere determined, & also vuould haue them to ioine, though it vvas made plaine vnto him, that thei nether Vvoulde, nether could ioine, takeing that course Vvhich thei did. And as for chaūging of their course there Vvas no hope or likelihood, that thei Would do it. For their liuing, their glorie, & credit With the people, stood on it: & thei had sought out manie fetches, & got an euē vvaie on both sides. Thei haue their tolerations, mitigations, & other trim distinctiōs, as of things partlie lavvefull & partlie vnlavvefull, necessarie & lesse needful, matters of faith & matters besides faith, ordinarie & extraordinarie, vvith a number such like. Thus thei both please the people, & the bishops also: & so are praised & mantained bie the people, & also suffered off the bishops, because forsooth thei are somevvhat conformable. Then from this talck thei fell into other, namelie of the parishes, guided ether bie such preachers, or by the bishopes & their officers. Off this it did follovve, that if the guides & their guiding Vuas vnlavvefull then also the parishes so guided vvere vnlavuefull, & so could not be the churches of God. For thei that shut vp the kingdom of heauen before men, Mat. 23. 13. can not belong to the Lord, no more can thei, to vvhome it is manifestlie shut vp because their follovue and praise such guides. This being thus it Vvas debated; What profit thei had bie the preachers, and vvhat good thei had reaped bie the parishes: as vvhether faith might be vvrought bie their preaching, & men called to goodness, & vvhat vse there vvas off the blind reading off service & the chapters bie the ministers ? Then bie both tould hovv faieth Vvas first Wvrough[t] & bred in thē. But herein thei agreed not, because R. H. said that faith might be bred & first vvrought in some. onelie bie reading the scriptures: & R. B. saied, no. For though it might be nourished & increased bie such reading, yet the first Vvorcking thereof, is by hearing the vvord preached: as Paul saith, Rom. 10. 14. hovve shall Vve beleue on him on Vvhom VVe haue not hard, & hovve shall VVe heare Vvithout a preacher. And least reading shoulde be taken for preaching, it is said, hovve shall thei preach except thei be sent. So also least hearing the Vvord, should be taken for hearing it read, Paul saith aftervvard, that faith cometh by hearing

---

[1] John More, an outspoken Puritan minister called " The Apostle of Norwich," minister of St. Andrew's church from leaving Cambridge until his death. See *D.N.B.* and *Seconde Parte of a Register*, I. 143 ff.
[2] See *D.N.B.*, *A parte of a register*, 73-85.

A True and Short Declaration

& hearing by the vvord of God; meaning by the Word of God the Vvorde off message in his mouth vvhome God sendeth. So then faith is not Vvrought by reading, ne-[B 1 *verso*]-ther bie preachers, nor bie preaching: but by the preaching of those vvhich are sent bie the Lord, if his grace in our harts do worck therevvithall for else all preaching & our hearing also is fruictles, as it is vvritten againe. Ioh. 6. 45. that thei shall be all taught of God. Wherebie Christ concludeth thus, that euerie one vvhich hath hard the trueth, & hath also learned of his father, he shall come vnto him, but othervvise none can come. But R. H. said, that he for his part did iudg, his first calling & effectuall stirring to goodnes vvas on a certaine time vvhen he red in the Bible. It vvas ansvvered him, that vve maie be deceaued in iudging our selues in such thinges. For vve may haue the spirit of God & good motions before vve haue faith, & so maie vve mistake faith, thincking that such motions & good vvorcking of the spirit is faith. For Christ teacheth, as it appeareth in Ioh. 3. 8. that the vvorking off the spirit & faith is hard to be discerned. For as vve knovve not saith he the reason of the vvind, how, from vvhense, & vvhether it blovveth, no more can vve easilie knovve, hovve a man is born off the spirit of God: that is, hovve he is first renevved & called to goodnes by faith, and the spirit of God. For this is the difference of faith & the spirit, because the spirit is an invvarde Working off the holie ghost in our harts, Which stirreth & prepareth vs unto all goodnes, & vvhen faith cometh, it strengthneth vs much more in goodnes. But faith is a conscience of our redemption & happines in Christ, vvherebie vve Wholie yeeld vp ourselues vnto hī, in all nevvnes of life. So then faith can not be except Vve be so renevved, that no open grosse VVickednes be in vs: as Iames teacheth vs, that faith VVithout VVorcks is dead. Iam. 2. 17. 20. & that Vve are but vaine men iff Vve saie Vve haue faith Vvhen Vve haue no Worckes. And faith may be vvholie Wanting for a time, till the Lord do call vs, & dravve vs vnto him: but the spirit is geuen to the elect euen Vvhile thei are infantes. And this spirit, though for a time it maie be hidden & couered, yet can it not cleane be put out & quenshed. Therfore by it Vve are said to be sealed off God, & it is called in the scripture, the earnest off the spirit, the earnest off our inheritaunce. 2. Cor. 1. 25. Ephes. 1. 13. 14. Wherebie is ment that that spirit shall neuer Vvholi cease io [*sic*] Vvorck litle or much tovvard our saluation. Noe more can it be that faith being once thorovvelie Vvrought, should Vvholie faile, as Christ saith, he that cometh to me shall not hunger, & he thatt beleeueth in me shall neuer thirst. Ioh. 6. 35. For though thei sinne neuer so greuouslie, yet iff thei be elect, thei haue alvvaise some conscience of their Vvelfare in Christ, or forevvarning of some grace vvhich is tovvardes them.

Thei had further this talck, hovve men are called novve a daies: hovve some are troubled in conscience: What hardning of the hart there is: & Vvhat tokens & assurance there is of our saluation. All vvhich matters ech partie did applie to him selfe. Therefore for our calling & hovve faith is vvrought novve a daies, it Vvas said before to be bie the preaching of the vvord, but bie vvhat & vvhose preaching, that remaneth to shevve: for that also vvas skanned betvvene them. R. B. vvas of this iudgment, that euerie Christian hauing faith & knovvledg & speaking the vvord of God vnto others, might vvinn others. This R. H. confirmedd saiing that he found it true, because bie his meanes certaine sisters off his, vvhen he taught & exhorted them, vvere called & vvonne. But hovve far thei & others vvere Vvonne, it is aftervvard declared. Novve iff anie maie be thus vvonne, hovve is faith said to be Vvrought by preachīg of the vvord ? B. saied that preaching is not oneli the publick teaching in the pulpit, but it is rather that duetie of speaking & teaching the trueth, as it ought to be taught [B 2 *recto*] & that in vvhat place so euer. For so it is Vvritten in Deut. 6. 7. vvhere parentes are commaunded to teach the vvord, yea to beat it into their children & to vvhet them on therein, both tariing in the house, & as thei vvalck bie the vvay, and Vvhen thei ly dovvne, and vvhen thei rise vp. Therefore preaching is not tyed to the pulpit, nor to degrees, to persons, to the tippet, or surplisse, or cornerd capp, to the priest sleued cloake, or to the skarlet houne, the attire of bishops, the beadle & tipstaffe and other disguisings. Therefore did Aquila & Priscilla preach euen to a preacher, vvhen thei tooke Apollos vnto them and expounded Vntoe him the doctrine of the ghospel more plainlie. Act. 18. 26. Yet is there a difference of preaching, because some are called and receaued to that office and charge, in publique manner, but others are bound onelie as all other christians, to edifie and instruct one an other: and this also is preaching, but not vvith publique charge. And by this teaching is faith also vvrought as vve knovve by example of that vvoman of Samaria, Ioh. 4. 41. For vvhose vvordes manie beleued, but manie moe beleeued saith the text, vvhen they hard the Vvordes of Christ him self. For thei confessed plainly that he vvas the Christ the sauiour of the vvorld. And if the Vvordes of all christians ought to be such, as may minister grace to the hearers, saith Paul Ephes. 4. then if some heare vvhich yet haue not faith, thei may also haue that grace of faith Vvrought in them by their hearing. Thus vvas it agreed on that faith cometh bie hearing and hearing bie the vvord preached, and the vvord is preached bie those vvhich are sent, & this sending is both of those vvhich haue publique message and authoritie ouer others, and also of euerie christian, vvhich is called & commaunded bie all occasions to edifie others. For vvhere tvvoe or three are gathered in mie name saith Christ, there am I in the middest of them: & if tvvoe shall agree in earth vpon anie thing, Vvhat so euer thei shall desire of the Father, it shall be giuen them. Mat. 18. 19. Who therefore can doubt, but that one or tvvoe maie vvinne others to the Lord, and praiing also for the faith of those, vvhom thei teach, then faith maie be giuen them of the Lord?

WHAT GOOD THE PVBLICK PREACHING DOTH
novve a daies in England.

But this matter vvas not vvholie agreed on Vvhat good vvas doone by the preachers and vvhat fruict follovved their doctrine. For R. H. made great accountes of some preachers, and said that much good vvas done by them. Whereto it vvas ansvvered, that some preachers vvhile thei vvere forvvard, and did striue for reformation, soe long thei did good: but Vvhen thei relented, and fell to mitigations and tolerating, thei did not so much good before, but then thei did tvvise soe much hurt. Euen as the Scribes and Pharises vvhich compassed sea and land, to make one of their profession, and uvhen he was made, thei made him tvvoefould more the child of hell, then thei them selues Mat. 23.
[B 2 verso] So these vvhen thei vvere gone a litle forvvard, & had brought others after them, thei then turned aside, & made their follovvers more careles of goodnes then euer thei Vvere, yea & not onelie careles, but also dispightfull & most bitter persecuters, if anie vvent beyond thē, or vvere more tovveard then thei. Therefore vvell maie that vvo in Mat. 23. 13. be pronounced against such euill preachers, because thei shut up the kingdom of heauen before men, for thei them selues go not in, nether suffer thei those that vvould enter, to come in. Woe to them hypocrites, vvhich saie thei desire reformation & yet thei them selues are most vnreformed. Thei sai thei mourne & praie for amendment, & behould thei are fed of the rich & Vpheld bie great men, they liue in pleasure & haue courtlie honour, & no man is the better but all are vvorse & vvorse. Yea others also do rightlie learne their hypocrisie: for as thei vvill streine & make much a do at some thinges, as at the capp & the surplisse & crossing in baptisme &c. and so vvill shevue their zeale & deuotion in smaller thinges, & let greater ouerpasse: so also their follovvers Vvill seeme godlie, yea touched in hart & humbled, yet are thei openlie defiled vvith greuous offences & vvickednes. So haue thei a shevve of godlines, as Paul saith, but haue denied the povver thereof. 2 Tim. 3. 5.

HOWE AND VVHEREFORE THE COMPANIE
left the preachers & their follovvers: and of the ignorance
& sinne in the preachers & people.

But because R.H. named such & such often times, vvhich he said, feared God, & vvere sorouefull for their sinnes, it Was made plaine vnto him both bie vvord and vvriting, that he had small cause to saie so. First for the preachers, though R.B. did iudge the best of some, as of M. Robardes, M. Moare & some others, vvhose dealing at the first he did not throughlie knovve, yet aftervvard he found them to be like their fellovves, & frō them he said plainlie that vvickednes vvent forth into all the land. Iere. 23. Their ignorance and vvretched dealing vvas often declared: as hovve thei being teachers of others are theselues vntaught, euen in some groundes of religion, & in the chiefe partes of their callings. This vvill aftervvard appeare, as likevvise their foolish distinctiōs & shiftinges, vvhich thei haue partlie inuented them selues, & partlie taken frō others, that as it vvere an other Antichrist is begotten, borne & made strong off them, & a nevve persecution practissed. Thei Vvilfully tolerate the things Vvhich are against Christ, yea & vvith persecution & outrage vphoulde them, & hovve then are their not against Christ, that is hovve are thei not antichrists? And these things against Christ, are not onelie lamentable vvantes among them, but alsoe most greeuous vvickednes & horrible abominations. Therefore both to R.H. & to the companie that aftervvard ioined, vvere such things spoken as follovve, & also set dovvne in Vvriting: namelie that vve are to forsake & denie all vngodlines & vvicked fellovveship, & to refuse all vngodlie communion vvith Vvicked persons. For this is it that is most & first of all needfull: because God vvil receaue none to communion & couenant Vvith him, Vvhich as yet are at one vvith the Vvicked, or do openlie them selues transgresse his commaunde-[B 3 *recto*] mentes.

Novue it vvas shevued thē, that the foundacion of that state, is the popes canon lavve: the headstones in· the building, is the povver & authoritie of canon officers, & that therefore thei could not ioine vvith them, as in one spiritual building. For so it is vvritten. Ezr. 4. 2. 3. like vvise other scriptures vvere alleged to this end, as Ezr. 6. 21. Act. 2. 40. Ephe. 4. 3. Rom. 16. 17. Ioh. 10. 5. 2. Thess. 3. 14. 2. Cor. 6. 17. But because the enimies sought it out deeplie, hovue to iustifie all such antichristiā offices: he taught them herein also to take heed of their leauen. For thei bring for their vvarrant the Queenes commaundement. Shee appointed

A True and Short Declaration

them saie thei, & thei are not novue antichristian but ciuill orders, & iff you Vvill not haue them to be callinges in the church, yet let them be offices in the common Vvelth. For ansvuere hereof it Vvas said, that in deed in the parlaments, the bishopes had set doune their traditions & orders, & the Queene Vvith the Counsell did agree & graunt vnto them. But such traditions, except thei vvere Warranted bie the Word off God, are but the precepts & doctrine off men. And the scripture saith plainlie, Hos. 5. 11. that Israel is oppressed & broken in iudgment, because he Willingli vvalcked affter the commaundement: that is, because mens commaundements Vvere so much made off, & the Will off the Lord not regarded. Therefore saith the Lord in Esa. 29. 13. because this people come neare vnto me vvith their mouthes, & honour me vvith their lippes, but haue remoued their hart ffrom me, and their feare tovvard me is taught by the precept off men, therefore the vvisedom off the vvise men shall perish, & the vnderstanding off the prudent shall be hid. Therefore though thei be nobles or bishops, or vuho so euer, yet iff thei reiect the lavve off the Lord, for their ovvne traditions, vvhat vvisdom is in them? Novve vvhereas thei mingle ciuil & church offices, it vvas ansvvered bi the vvord off God that such mingling vvas flatt antichristianitie. For Christ him self refused to be a ciuil iudge & diuider of landes. Luc. 12, 14. & forbad his apostles to medle in such manner. Luc. 22. 25. Againe it is vvritten, no man that goeth on vvarfare, intangleth him selfe vvith the affaires of this life. 2. Tim. 2. 4. For if once ecclesiasticall persons, as thei call them, get ciuil offices, thei become that second beast vvhich is antichrist. Reuel 13, 15. For thei get the image off the first beast vvhich is the povver & authoritie off vvicked magistrates, that confirme their authoritie: so thei geue a spirit to the image, that it should speake, that is their church lavves & orders, hauing got ciuil povver, both to deceaue men bi shevve of religion, & to force them vvith threates and penalties, the kingdom of antichrist doeth mightilie vvorck & lift up it selfe. But because thei againe did striue that thei vvere protestantes, & did but as the martyrs had done before them. Thei had sought the Lord sence the time of the martyrs: It vvas ansvuered that so saied the aduersaries of Iudah & beniamin, & added further that thei had sacrificed a long time vnto the true god, Ezr. 4, 2. as these also sai, thei haue the vvord & the sacramēts. So said the scribes & pharises, vvhich builded the tombes of the prophets, & garnished the sepulcheres of the righteous, Mat. 23. 29. as these also haue vvritten & made much of the booke of martyrs, & saie, iff thei hadd bene in the daies of their fathers, thei vvould not haue bene partners with thē in the bloud of the martyrs. But novve sence the Lord hath called vnto thē, & thei refuse to be reformed in so manie & greuous pollutions, & also pursue, imprison & persecute those vvhich call for redresse, euen all the bloud of the righteous shed vpon the earth vntill this daie shall come vpon them. Againe vvhereas thei vnderprop vvickednes by regard off times, of examples, [B 3 verso] of authorities: first for their times, it vvas thus ansvvered, as it is in Hagg. 1, 2. This people saie, the time is not yet come to build the Lordes house: but is it time for you saith the Lord to dvvell in your seiled houses, & this house ly vvast? & againe in Esa. 62. 6. I haue set vvatchmen vpon thi vvalls o Ierusalē vvhich all the day & all the night cōtinuallie shall not cease: yee that are mindfull of the Lord, keep not silence, & geue him no rest, till he repaire, and vntil he set vp Ierusalem the praise of the vvorld. Also for their examples & authorities of men, it Vvas ansvuered as in Exod. 23. 2. thou shalt not follovve a multitude to do euill. But further thei alleged the scripture for themselues: as vvhere it is vvritten of Paul 1. Cor. 3. If a man build haie or stubble, & this his vvorck burne, he shall lose, but he shall be safe himselfe: likevvise thei sai, that thei mai build though imperfectlie, & yet help forvvard the house of God. And againe thei ad that Paul reioised if Christ vvas preached, though it vvere of enuie & strife. Phil. 1. Thus by their shiftinges & excuses, thei hide as in a nest their vntovvardnes & villanie. Thei can vnnestle such packings, & let them flee vvhen thei list, & againe thei can couer them by such deep deuises. For vvhen Paul speaketh of building haie & stubble, he rebuketh their vaine rhetorick & eloquence, and this he saith shall burne vvith the fier, but thei shall be safe, if thei cease to be vaine, & build rightly vpon the foundacion, vvherefore for ansvuere of the enimies, it vvas saied, that if Christ the foundacion vvere vvanting, hovve should ether the builder him selfe be safe, or his vvorck stand & abide? For Christ is the foundacion being dueli preached & duely receaued, & so held 1. Cor. 3. 11. But none can houlde him vvhich openli shevv them selues to be the children of belial. And such are thei vvhich call so manie grosse corruptiōs, to be that haie & stubble laied vpō the foundacion. For thus do thei iustifie their popish kind of parishes vvhich though thei ouerthroe the true planted churches yet forsooth thei are built vpon Christ the foundacion. Behould their vvorthie buildinge: it is made of stravves, the beames be stubble, & the vvalls be hai & vvithered grasse: nai rather those their vile & popish decrees & traditions, are the synevves, & veins of that monster Antichrist: their conclusions & lavves made in popish conuocations likevvise their yearli iniunctiōs made to persecute the forvvardest, be the bloud & marrovv or rather the strength and poinson [sic] of that

---

[1] Possibly bead roll is meant — a catalogue of persons for whose souls' rest one says prayers.

A True and Short Declaration

monster. Their stinted seruice is a popish beadrovv[1] full of vaine repeticions as if seaven paternosters did please the Lord better then syx: & as if the chattering of a pie or a parate vvere much more the better, because it is much more thē enough. Their tossing to & fro of psalms & sentēses, is like tenisse plaie vvhereto God is called a Iudg vvho can do best & be most gallant in his vvorship: as bie organs, solfaing,[1] pricksong, chaūting, bussing & mumling verie roundlie, on diuers handes. Thus thei haue a shevve of religion but indeed thei turne it to gaming, & plaie mockholidaie vvith the vvorship of God. For the minister & people are bridled like horses & euerie thing appointed vnto them like puppies: as to heare, read, ansvuere, knele, sitt, stand, beginn, breake of, & that by number, measure, & course, & onelie after the order of antichrist. Their vvhole seruice is broken, disordered, patched, taken out of the massebook, & a dum & idle ministerie manteined therebie yea a vaine vvorship vvithout knovvelege and feeling.

And vvhat difference is there betvvene praiing on beades, and the mumbling vp of so manye Lordes praiers, so manie bablinges bie the priest, & so manie ansvueres by the clark & people? For no part of the seruice must be left out by the bishops iniunctions. [B 4 recto]. Against such praiers, vvas the companie also strengthned bie the vvord of God. first because thei are redd, and not applied to the vvorde preached: vvhich is against the custome of the church vnder the ould lavve: and also sence the coming of Christ. For When the sacrifices With praier and incense Vvere offered: the Word also Vvas preached. Therefore it is Written in Ecclesiastes. 4. 7. Take heed to thy foote When thou entrest into the house off God, and be more neare to heare, then to geue the sacrifice off ffooles: for thei knovve not that thei do euill. So then to bable ouer praiers, VVhen the people knovve not nether are taught their sinnes, is an abomination. Prouerb. 15, 8 & 21, 27. And to seuer the offices off the pastor, Vvhich God hath ioined, it is iniquitie. For to preach, to praie, and minister the sacraments, are so put together in the scriptures, that iff the pastor did prai or minister the sacramentes, he Vvas also to preach, as it is Written Deut. 33. 10. Likevvise in Malac. 2. 6, 7. Also the Apostles did not publiqueli prai and minister the sacramentes, except the Vvord Vvere preached vvithall. Act. 2. 42. Act. 10. 36. Act. 6. 4. Also because such praiers are off custome and course, thei can not be Vvith true feeling and touch off hart. Therefore in vaine thei Vvorship me, saith the Lord, because thei come neare vnto me Vvith their mouthes, and honour me vvith their lippes, but haue remoued their hart from me. Esa. 29. 13. Novve then iff it be the office off the pastor and preacher, and part off his calling, toe pray, then

---

[1] To sing the notes of a gamut, or scale. The word comes from the names "sol," "fa".

must he be able off himselfe to do it: Whie then should a seruice, or reading off praiers be stinted vnto him? For iff his lippes keep not knovvledge, Malac. 2. 7. iff he can not minister the vvord Vvith praier: Act. 6. 4. he is not meet to be a pastor or vvatchmā ouer the people. But vvhereas the praiers are set dovvne bi number and course, it is alltogether a popish superstition, or rather an heathnish follie. For to Vvhat purpose are such fond repiticions, and vaine bablinges forbidden bie Christ? Mat. 6. 7. And iff all thinges ought to be done in due order 1. Cor. 14. 40. Col. 2. 5. then vvhere is that order in so chiefe a thing as is the vvorship off God? Suerlie such a seruice and vvorship off God is to build vpon the foundacion, as he that buildeth a dunghill vpon the sandes, and vvhen the tempest of vengeance shall come, it shall take him avvaie, Vvith the dongue he hath gathered. But thei obiect that a leiturgie maie be appointed and red, and that most off their seruice is good, and the rest, iff anie be euill maie be left of them that heare, though the minister must nedes read it all. To this it vvas ansvvered, that it is a shame for them to come into such bondage, as ether to suffer the incense of Nadab and Abihu (for such is their seruice and abstractes from the massebook) Leuit, 10. 1. or else to be seruauntes to men to hinder their libertie: vvhich is forbidden 1. Cor. 7, 23. 2 Cor. 11. 20. For bie the capp and the surplisse & the bishops dischargings, vvith other their traditions the VVord is in bondage, & likevvise their Vvorshipping off God bie such stinted seruice, so that thei can nether praie, nor preach as thei should, but as it pleaseth the bishopes.

Nether let them account off the feeling vvhich some saie thei haue vvhen thei heare the seruice red. For euen in vvorshipping Idols, there is a strong feeling, or rather a strong delusion: and though there might be good motions in an euill thing, yet that did not vvarrant the euill, no more then Paules zeale did iustifie his persecuting of the sainctes: nor the teares vvhich come from a troubled hart do iustifie the sinne for the vvhich it is troubled. And Vvhat is it to Vveep before an Idol, or to shed teares in a false & vaine vvorshipp? [B 4 *verso*] And vvhat should thei boast of some good praiers & some good vvordes vvhich are in their commō seruice? For vvitches and coniurers vvill Vse good vvords & good praiers, vvhē thei coniure & charme the deuil. And whi halt thei betvuene good & euil? For iff thei do many things vvell & yet in one thing be open & greuous transgressors, all is made naught. And hovve should anie thing be partli good as thei say, & partli euil? For the euil that is doth make it vvholi euil, as it is vvritten, Iam. 2. 10. 2 Sam. 15, 23. So then such traditions and orders, are so far from building vpon Christ the foundacion, as the Lordes house & temple can not be the synagogue

A True and Short Declaration

of satan, nor his builders the open & knovvē balamits & maisters of iniquitie For Balaam blessed Israel but counseled to make an agremēt & partakeing together of Israel & amalek: So these do blesse the cause, & prai for discipline, but thei tolerat & dispense vvith abominations, to make Christ & belial agree. Yea sai thei, Paul teacheth vs to preach Christ bi all māner of vvaies, Phil. 1. & also reioiseth thereī. So thei vvill preach Christ after the manner of Balaam: & as bi their praiers thei hould stil the mediation & intercession of antichrist, so bi their tolerating & dispensing vvith vvickednes, thei hould still his priesthood, & bi their counsel, decrees & traditiōs, thei hould stil his prophecie. Wherefore, to ansvvere them, it vvas said, that Paul reioised, not that Balamits should be preachers in the church, but that abundance of all sortes of preachers should be, so thei vvere lavuefull. And though thei Vvere hypocrites, & had their enuie & strife, yet that forth-vvith did not make them vnlavueful preachers. For if their brast[1] not forth into open contention, toe make a diuision, nor did vvilfulli tolerate open abuses, nor frovvardli iustifie false doctrine & heresies, Paul Vvould not reiect them. But if it Vvere othervvise, Paul is so far from reioising in them, that he Vvisheth thei vvere euen cut of[f] vvhich disquiet the church. Galat. 5. & againe he saith, that he shall beare his condemnation, vvho so euer he be that troubleth them. And to the Romans 16. 17. he saith, novve I beseech you brethren, marck thē diligētly vvhich cause diuisions & offenses, contrarie to the doctrine vvhich ye haue learned, & auoid them. And if Paul reioised in all manner of preaching, vvhi do not thei reioise in the Pope & in the frears[2] & moncks. For thei vvould preach Christ, & vvithall the lavves & traiditiōs of antichrist: as these also vvill seeme to preach Christ, & yet preach a toleration of the kīgdom of antichrist: as of the povver of lordli bishops, of their sending forth of Warrants, of sitting in ciuil iudgment, off imprisoning & persecuting in shamful manner: likevvise off their spiritual courtes & officers, vvhich ouerrule, threaten, excommunicate and poule the people vvith force & penalties. In deed Vvould Paul reioise in such preachers, vvhich allovve & teach others to allovve, or vvilfulli tolerate that their profane babtisme vvith godfathers & godmothers, Vvith crossing & confirming off children, & other foolish toiinges. off these it vvas said, that thei being superfluous ceremonies, are not onelie the precepts of men, & so make vaine the vvorship of God. Mat. 15. but also are popish superstitions & a miserable yoake laid vpon us by antichrist. For by them, & other such like, is the vvord of God made of none authoritie Mark 7. 13. because his message by his seruantes is stopped, except thei yeeld & subscribe to such trash. Yet the vvord commaūdeth,

[1] Obsolete form of burst.
[2] friars.

that vve should not be seruantes to men. 1. Cor. 7. 23. that is thei must lose no vvhit of their libertie vvhich thei haue in Christ. And this libertie they haue, not to do anie thing after mens traditions, but onelie to do vvhat the Lord commaundeth. Therefore to teach & tolerate the churching of [C 1 *recto*] vveomen vvas shevved to be vnlavvefull: because thei are churched, vvhich ether can be none of the church & people of God, or else vvhich neuer vvere put out of the church: and vvhy then should thei be so solemlie againe receiued to the church ? For the Ievvish vveomen vvere solemlie purified, because of their outvvard vncleanes: but that being then but a ceremonie, can not be novve held vvithout great superstition. And vvhy should there be an open thanckesgeueing for that vvhich is no blessing, but a curse ? For at their trauaile, and vvhile thei are in childbed, it is knovven vvell enough vvhat vanitie is among them. So frō their cursed life at home thei come to the church to haue the priestes blessing, & the vveoman is safely deliuered to liue the more vvickedly. As for the babtisme of the child, iff it be rightly done, & ether of the parentes be godlie, that is a blessing, & in the publik sacrament there should be a publik thanckesgeuing. But the churching of vveomen can be no sacramēt: nether is ther bodelie deliuerance a publique blessing: nai rather it is a curse if thei be vnthanckfull & vvicked. Therefore for their priuat blessing let them priuatlie geue thāckes. But if thei be vnthanckfull, vvhy should the church meet together to be thanckfull for thē or vvhy should thei be honored in that manner & strengthned in their sinne, vvhile thei are so vainlie comforted for their bodelie deliuerance ? For hovve profanelie is that 91 psal. applied to comfort them, as if that priuate & vvorldlie blessing vvere all in all ? or as if for that vvorldlie blessing there should be opē meetings, & none for the spiritual & greater blessings. A[1] for a man to teach his househould, to rebuke sinne in his freind, to acknouledge his fault to his neighbour, Vvith amendment thereoff &c. these are spirituall blessings, & if for these particularlie there can not be publique meetings, because that vvere a troublesōe disorder, vvhy then should there be a disordered meeting for the churching of vveomen ? But as in this point, so in manye such like popish delusions, the pomp, superstition, & vanitie of antichrist vvas shevved: as in their fastinges, feastinges, saincts euens, holie daies, funeralls, manner of marriing, popish attire, vvith other such like. Further it vvas declared hovve vngodlie the bishops do authorise, & the preachers do suffer & tolerate those vvretched blind ministers to minister the sacramēts, & saie seruice, & also dispence vvith the people to heare them, & to receaue the sacraments of thē. Also hovve vvickedlie thei allovve those vvoefull

[1] As text.

A True and Short Declaration

conuocations of bishops in stead of church synodes, & putt their vniversitie degrees, disputations, & common places in stead of church prophecie, & despite & gainsaie the true exercise therof. Likevvise sundrie other wantes in the church & vvoefull defaultes of the preachers vvere shevved, the disproofe vvhereof is novve to long to reherse: as in hovve vile and abominable māner thei are made preachers & ministers. Thei geue their neckes to the yoak of disordered & popish attire, the marckes of antichrist, as the horned capp, the maidenlie surplsse [sic], the graue & florishing tippet, the hoodes, gounes, chimers, rochets, coapes, &c and that according to vaine degrees: as for the lordlie bishops, their attire, & for the doctors, bachelars of diuinitie, ministers & priests, their attier: all vvhich is more vaine & ridiculous then the pharisaical phylacteries & fringes. For the fringes vvere commaūded bie the lavv, but yet of them superstitiously abused. But these their garmentes, & also their offices, are flat against the lavve, & yet of them most proudlie abused. As cheifly vvhen the Beadle & the tipstaffe do go before them to bring them into the pulpitt. Hovve shamefullie doe thei tarie for the magistrates as if thei hindred & letted them to do their full duetie. Hovve like hire-[C 1 verso]-lings do thei leaue the flock vvhen the bishops or the magestrats do vniustlie discharge thē & hang their authoritie & calling on their sleue, but vvil not hould it of the Lord their God? Hovve parcial are thei, could[1], & seruile in suffering greuous corruptiōs to the ouerthrovve off religion & gouernment? What runnings make thei from tovvne to tovvne, to preach for their prais, & leaue their flock destitute a long time for their pleasure, & seek more gaine & honour. Hovve do thei seuer preaching from gouerning, doctrine from discipline, as iff thei could be seuered & vvere partes diuided? Hovve many non residents are there & gredie deuourers off benefices, stipendes & other popish liuings, Which are vtterly vnlavvfull, because thei are bie tythings, vvhich are novve no more to be geven to the ministerie, or bie lavves & customes vvhich hinder the due placing & displacing off ministers, & the right & libertie off the church therein. These & a thousand mo abominations haue thei amongst thē & confesse them selues, that thei can not redresse them. So thei hould one communiō vvith hoggs & dogges, euen open vngodlie persons, & haue no remedie. Behould, do these men preach Christ, vvhich thus do peruert the ghospell of Christ? For this is the sūm of the ghospell, & of Paules preaching, as he him selfe wittnesseth, Act. 20. Repentance tovvardes God, faieth tovvardes our Lord Iesus Christ. This repētance & faith is denied & also Christ & his ghospel is cast vnder foote, vvhere such greuous corruptions doe raigne & nether his gouernment & prophecie can

[1] *I.e.*, cold.

ouersee & trie out such filthines, nor make separation of cleane and vncleane, nor yet by his preisthood anie such vncleannes can be clensed avvaie. Therefor vve say that these men can not preach Christ truelie, but onelie in shevve, nether can build vpon Christ the foundation, for it is not for you saied the lords people, but for vs to build the house vnto our God. for vve our selues together vvill build it vnto the lord god of Israel. Therefor not all builders or preachers are to be receaued or reioyced in, but such as in deed do hould the foundacion & preach Christ aright. For the enuie & strife vvhereof Paul speaketh vvas seacret, or vvhen it appeared, yet it could not and vvas not menifestlye proued, & therefore such preachinge vvas not against the foundacion. But if anie doe vvllfullie [sic] & presumptuouslye stand in anie opē synne, tde [sic] same can not hould the foundacion, for vvhether the sinne be small or great, Mat. 18. if it become open & be duelie brought before the church, & the offeder vvill not heare the church, let him be vnto the[e], saieth Christ, as an heathen man & a publican. & againe it is vvritten, that that man vvhich shall doe presumptuouslie, against the voice of the highe preist.)[1] which figured the voice of Christ Iesus at this daye in his church, that man shall die. dut. 17.[2] And Saul kinge of Israel, though he saied he had sinned, yet betause [sic] he excused it & repented not, Samuel vvould not returne to him, tyll agaīe he had saied I haue sinned vvithout excuse. 1. Sam. 15. So that plainelie it appeareth, that Samuel Iudged Saul not to hould the foundacion, vvhile he openly excused his sinne: for else he vvould not haū [sic] forsaken his fellovvshipp & left him to the shame of the people. But Semuels vvords before doe plainly declare that all open sinne vnrepented & stoud in, is the ouerthrovv of the foundacion. for Rebellion is as the sinne of vvitch craft, & transgressiō is vvickednes & Idolatrie. verse. 23. if then vvitches & Idolaterrs hould not the foundaciō suerli noe more doe thei, vvhich by ane sinne rebell & transgresse against God & vvittinglie excuse it, as did Saule or vvillfullie & presumptuouslie Iustifie it. Novv let it be Iudged, hov ether thei build vpon the foundacion, or hould the foundacion, or preach Christ as thei sai [C 2 recto] thei doe. For this is to lay the foundacion Acts. 8. 12. to preach the thengs that concren [sic] the kingdome of God, & the nāe of Iesus Christ. & this is to ouerthrouve the foūdacion, vvhich vvilfullie thei or vvith persecution & outrage.[3] thei vphould the abominations of a cōtrarie kingdome. This is to lay the foundacion. Mat. 28. to preach & Baptise in the name of the Father teachinge to obserue & doe, vvhat soe euer saieth Christ, I haue commaunded you. &

---

[1] No opening bracket; closing bracket probably in mistake for comma.
[2] Deut. 17. 12.
[3] As text. Perhaps the reading should be: "which vvilfullie they do."

A True and Short Declaration

this is to ouerthrovv the foundacion to teach a toleration & practissing of things, vvhich are cōtrarie to the vvhole gouernment & kingdom of Christ. Novv to hould the foundaciō, is to beleeue, & also receaue that doctrine of Christ in proffession & practise of life. for as soone as thei beleeued thei vvere baptised saieth the text. thei continued in the apotles [sic] doctrine, fellovvship & cōmuniō of praiers & sacramēts. Act. 2. yea thei shevved their vvorkes & their loue, & the singlenes of their harts verse. 46. Act. 19. & vvere seprat frō that frovvard generation. & it is vvritten that if anie man shall breake of the least commanndemēts, & teach men soe, that is shall doe it openlie & geue euil example, & hould & Iustefie it in doctraine and vvords, he shall be called the least in the kingdom of God, Mat. 5. that is he shal be excludede & shut out off his kingdom. And if anie man shall ad or diminish of the vvord of God, either by doctrine or by practisse, & that vvitingli & stubburnlie, he can not hould the foundacion. for God shall add vnto him the plagues that are vvritten. Reuel. 22. Pro. 30. Therefore saie noe more, ye vvicked preachers, that ye hould the foūdacion, or that ye preach. for vvhat is it vvorth to saie vnto Christ, haile King of the Ievves, & bovve the knee before him, vvhē you cast your filthie disorders & popish gouernment as dougne [sic] on his face you haue not yet gathered the people frō the Popish parishes & vvicked fellovvship. nether haue planted the church by layinge the foundacion thereof, for here by is the foundacion laied, vvhen vVe make & hould the couenant vvith the Lord to be vnder his gouernment, vvhen vve haue the povver of the Lord, as it is vvritten Cor.[1] 1. 5. amongst vs, & the septer of Christ Iesus amongst vs. But these doe hould the vvhep & the svvord of Popish excomūicatiou. They are vvithout the Lords couenant, & vvithout his gouernmēt. They haue alltogether corrupted their vvaies, thei haue broken the yoake & Burste the bands in sunder. for euen those vvhich can be none of Christ church, abidinge in such vvickednes, are cheefe in their churches. & so farr are thei from buildinge of gould & tymbere, together vvith hay & stubble, that thei put fier to the better tymber & tūble dovvne the better stones to ouerthrovve the Lords buildinge. Thus haue thei an ansvvere of these places, of the 1. Phil. & 1. Cor. 3. vvhich is this that thir vvickednes & abominacion is more greuous then that can be counted the Infirmitie of speaking toe eloquentlie, or of enuie vvhich is secrett, or of a contentious mynd.

---

[1] As text. The reference is either to I Cor. 2. 5 or I Cor. 5. 4.

THE ORDER AGREED ON FOR THE GIVDING[1] &
establishing of the companie in all Godlines, & such like[.]

This doctrine before being shewed to the companie, & openlie preached a mong them manie did agree thereto. & though much trouble & persecution did follovve, yet some did cleaue fast to the trueth but some fell avvaie. fro [sic] vvhen triall by pursuites, losses, & imprisonment cāe, & further increased then Robert Barker, Nicholas vvoedovves, Tatsel, Bond[2] & sōe others, forsooke vs also & held back, & vvere afraid at the first. There vvas a day appointed, and an order taken, ffor redresse off the former abuses, and for cleauing to the Lord in greater obediēce. so a couenāt vvas made & ther mutual cōsent vvas geuē to hould to gether. [C 2 *verso*] There vvere certaine chief pointes proued vnto them by the scriptures, all vvhich being particularlie rehersed vnto them vvith exhortation, thei agreed vpon them, & pronoūced their agrement to ech thing particularlie, saiing, to this vve geue our consent. First therefore thei gaue their consent, to ioine them selues to the Lord, in one couenant & fellovveshipp together, & to keep & seek agrement vnder his lavves & gouernment: and therefore did vtterlie flee & auoide such like disorders & vvickednes, as vvas mencioned before. Further thei agreed off those vvhich should teach them, and vvatch for the saluation of their soules, vvhom thei allovved & did chose as able & meete ffor that charge. For thei had sufficient triall & testimonie thereoff by that vvhich thei hard & savve by them, & had receaued of others. So thei praied for their vvatchfulnes & diligence, & promised their obedience.

Likevvise an order vvas agreed on ffor their meetinges together, ffor their exercises therin, as for praier, thanckesgiuing, reading of the scriptures, for exhortation & edifiing, ether by all men vvhich had the guift, or by those vvhich had a special charge before others. And for the lavvefulnes off putting forth questions, to learne the trueth, as iff anie thing seemed doubtful & hard, to require some to shevve it more plainlie, or for anie to shevve it him selfe & to cause the rest to vnderstand it. Further for noting out anie speciall matter of edifiing at the meeting, or for talckīg seuerally thereō, vvith some particulars, iff none did require publique audience, or if no vvaightier & more necessarie matter vvere hādled of others. Againe it vvas agreed that anie might protest, appeale, complaine, exhort, dispute, reproue &c. as he had occasion, but yet in due order, vvhich Vvas thē also declared. Also that all should further

[1] *Sic*.
[2] Perhaps the comma was intended after Bond, if so, Tatsel Bond is one person.

A True and Short Declaration

the kingdom off God in them selues, & especiallie in their charge & househould, iff thei had anie, or in their freindes & companions & vvhosoeuer Vvas Vvorthie. Furthermore thei particularlie agreed off the manner, hovve to Vvatch to disorders, & reforme abuses, & for assembling the companie, for teaching priuatlie, and for vvarning & rebukeing both priuatly & openlie, for appointing publick humbling in more rare iudgemētes, & publik thankesgeuing in straunger blessinges, for gathering & testifiing voices in debating matters, & propounding them in the name off the rest that agree, for an order of chosing teachers, guides, & releeuers, vvhen thei vvant, for separating cleane from vncleane, for receauing anie into the fellovveship, for preseting the dailie successe of the church, & the vvantes thereof, for seeking to other churches to haue their help, being better reformed, or to bring them to reformation, for taking an order that none contend openlie, nor persecute, nor trouble disorderedly, nor bring false doctrine, nor euil cause after once or tvvise Vvarning or rebuke.

Thus all thinges vvere handled, set in order, & agreed on to the comfort off all, & soe the matter vvrought & prospered by the good hand of God. But last of all vvas this thing determined. Whether God did call them to leaue their contrie, & to depart out of England.

Some had decreed it to be gone into Scotland, & by vvriting, sending, & riding to and froe, did labour in the matter, & seemed to be Ielouse least their counsell should not take place. But R.B. being then held as prisoner at London, did send dovvne his ansvvere bie vvriting to the contrarie. For he iudged that it vvas against duetie, & so vvrote vnto them, if thei first should agree to go into Scotland, wheas yet thei had not sifted vvhether thei vvere to leaue England. Also he sent vnto them, that thei vvere to do that good in England, vvhich possiblie thei might do before their departure, & that thei ought not to remoue, before thei had [C 3 *recto*] yet further testified the trueth, & the Lord had vvith strong hand deliuered them frō thēse. And rather in deed vvould he haue it to be a deliuerance by the Lord, then a covveardly fleeing off their ovvne deuising. Further he gaue them his reasons, vvhy Scotland could not be meet for them, seing it framed itself in those matters to please England toe much. Wee knevve also that vve could not there be suffered, ether because some corruptiō should come vpon vs from their parishes, vvhich vve ought to auoide, or because vve there should haue great trouble vvrought vs from England, as iff vve kept still in England. So vvhen some vvere better aduised thei chaunged their mindes for going into Scotland. Notvvithstandīg againe thei vvould be gone into Gersey or Garnsey[1] & had the con-

[1] The Channel Islands : Jersey and Guernsey.

sent, as thei saied of diuers others, that thought it meet thei should learne the state off those countries. R.B. saied he vvas not against their going to that purpose[.] But yet he tould them there vvas no such hast to be gone out of England, & that further delay & deliberation should be had in that matter. But at last, vvhen diuers of them vvere againe imprisoned, & the rest in great trouble & bondage out of prison, thei all agreed, & vvere fullie persvvaded that the Lord did call thē out of Englaud.

OF THE BREACH AND DIVISION
vvhich fell amongst the companie.

But vve come to the breach & falling out of these parties. First the lavves vvere broken, vvhereby the church of Christ should be kept in good order. There fel out questions, offenses, & takeing of partes, as vve knovve it hath alvvaies & shall come to passe in the church of God. But for remedie of such thinges the Lordes ordinance vvas reiected and greater presumption further increased, as shall appeare. The mindes in a manner of all vvere estraunged from the pastor, or their consciences vvounded, & thei disquieted by foolish doubtes, accusations, slaunders & quarrels moued & cast abroade bie the chiefest of them. Yet vvas there noething in controuersie vvhich vvas not generallie agreed on by all at the first, & openlie debated vvith mutuall cōsent, though diuers aftervvard fell avvaie, & some also secretlie vvere at variance in their hartes. For the end did declare their hypocrisie & vvhat enuie & grudg laie hidd in their brestes. Notvvithstanding their disposition vvas perceaued of some, & some stirring and disquietnes thei began to make vvas stopped & cut of for the time[.] But vvhen the pastor fell sick & could not be present at the exercises, nor visit them priuatlie in houses, the stirring did freshly beginn againe. Thei made a doe secretly & talcked manie matters among them selues, but neuer told them to the pastor, nor asked counsel for them of the church by admonishmēt, doubt, or question in prophecie, before thei had troubled the vvhole church about them. Hereby the contention grevve so far, that some fell from questions to euill speaches & slaunders, & from slaunders to open defiaunce & railinges.

The matters in controuersie vvere manie, all vvhich, though thei were often times tho-[C 3 *verso*]-rowlie debated, yet therein vvere sooe peruerted them selues, & did also corrupt & hurt others[.] the stirring & busines vvas after this māner. There vvere sundrie

A True and Short Declaration

meetings procured against R.B. By R.H. & his Partkers [sic]. for certaine tales & slanders vvere brought to R.H. vvhich he straight vvay receaued, & delt against R.B. The accusations in the first miettinge Vvere, that R.B. condemned his Sister Allens[1] as a reprobate. alsoe he saied, she had not repented of her abominations in England. also that he saied, except she repented of her abominations that night she should neuer enter into the kingdom of God, to these it vvas āsvvered & vvitnesses taken first that he nether did call nor Iudge his sister for a reprobate, & that he had to[o] hastelie harckned to tales, in that matter, also vvitnes came in that he saied not to his sister, she had not at all repented of these abominations in England, But that nether she nor vve all vvere sufficiently mortified for them[.] for these matters, because R.B. did first priuatlie rebuke R.H. as for that he had beleued & receaued such things vvith out all proufe & vvitnesses: & also for that he saied he knevv more aganst him, but vvould not speake of them he tooke the matter verie hainouslie[.] Straight vvsy [sic, vvay] he vvent forth, & sent others to admonish R.B. for he could not soe suffer the matter to passe. but he cast ot that charge vvhich he had taken vpon him, a litle before, & vvould not medle anie further, except there vvere some remidie procured. Then did he put forth his accusation in vvritinge, vvhich vvas red & receiued of others, but not shevved to the partie vvhom he accused. For this vvriting & handling of matters soe priuilie he vvas blamed. & therefore, vvhen R.B. sent vnto him to see the vvritinge he refused, & kept it backe. then he procured Charles mōemā,[2] Iohn Chāler, Tobie Henson, & others to meet about the matter. at vvhich meeting because diuers things before vvere disorderedlie handled, R.B. did then instantlie call for an order, that thnges [sic] might be rightlie debated. as first that noe accusation might be openlie brought against him vvithout tvvoe or three vvittnesses. for this he saied vvas the vvord of God, 1. Tim. 5. 19. Deut. 19. 15. But R.H. vvhich before had delt vvithoute vvittnesses, did this shift of the matter, that he Needed noe vvittnesses to accuse R.B. Because the mrtters [sic] could not be denied, vvherevvith he charged him, Ansvvere was made that thei had beene denied, & vuere not yet proued & therefore such dealing vvas vtterli vngodlie, Then in tvvoe other things did Robert. B. call vppō thē for ane order amongst them the first vvas that their might be noo fused brablinge But that the accuser and ansvverer hauing both tould their tales, then matters might be iudged by the church, & thei not suffered to make contention, by gainsaing on an other soe offt as thei list.

---

[1] R.B. married (i) [Alice] Allen of Yorkshire. See *Transactions*, C.H.S., ii. 155; Blore, *History and Antiquities of the County of Rutland*, 93.
[2] The name may be Moneman, Moneyman, Munneman, or Munneyman.

ver. 33. & 1 Cor. 11. Soe likevvise did thei in the other point vvhich vvas that R.B. vvould haue one matter first & then an other to be debated & Iudged, & not one accusation, to passe, before the truteth [sic] thereof vvere thorovvli foūd out these things vvere denied him, & could not be grannted, because of the frovvardnes & cōtention of some then did R.B. cōplaine that he had great iniurie dōe him, & vvould depart frō the meetinge if thei proced in that manner: which vvordes vvhen thei hard, they vvere denie & breake order, contrarie to the scripture alleged 1 Cor. 14. But herein also did R.H. Charles Mūnemā, & their partakers both furthr out of order, soe that eihter [sic] tvvise or thrise he vvas forced to rys vp & leaue them then vvas he condemned as an vnlavvfvll Pastor, & it vvas saied vnto him that he vvas not to keep the excreises [sic], also that he vvas to confesse his faults before thei vvould Ioine Vvith hī, the meeting beinge in R.B. chamber, he cāe in agaīe and tould the, that he vvas [C 4 recto] vnvvillinge thī [they] should vees [use] their meetings in his chamber after that manner. Soe aftervvard thei held their meetings in another place: vvhere againe thei condemned R.B. but nor [sic] as before ffor he sent vnto them, that they vvould send him in witinge [sic] the matters vvherevvith thei charged him, & dele in that manner aginst him, But the former slanndres thei had then geuen ouer, & had got vp three nevv matters against him, vvhich then sente him avvaie. one vvas that Robert B. vvith his vvittnesses had falslie accused R.H. of Notable apparēt vvickednes. to this it vvas ansVverd, that he nether had taken Vvittnes nor made accusation in anie matter saue onlie that in defence off him selfe he had called for vvittnes to cleare hī selfe, as that vvhen the aduersarie did accuse him vvithout vvittnes. likevvise he rebukedd Ro. H. off open vvickednes, & vvhen he made that also a public accusation, he vvas faine openli to shevv vvherein he vvas vvicked. namelie in that he openlie brake the order & gouernment of the church in that he had receued false accusations, & report against his brother, & him selfe also did falsly accuse him & trouble the church in that manner: en [sic] other accusation VVas, a bout the pavvning off a siluer spoone, vvherein R.B. vvas cōdēned as an vnlavvfull surmiser. But straight vvay they vvere found by their ovvne vvittnesses, to be vvicked slannderers, & that R.B. had iust cause to admonishe one as beīg cause off offence to her mother in that matter. the third accusation vvas, for Rebuking R.H. off murmuringe, & this vvrs [sic] Iudged a slander. thus vvhen R.B. perceaued hovv that diuers tymes priuilie, & novv also openli they cast him off, he also openli pronounced it, that he had noe charge off them, if they soe continued to vvithdravve them selues. then did R.H. toke [sic] vpon him charge. for his conscience he saied could not suffer him, to let

A True and Short Declaration

them be vvithout teachinge. yet aftervvard, belike their cōsiences did trouble them for casting off Robe. Brov. in such order, Soe in an open meetinge euerie on confessed their ffaultes. RoBe. H. both openlie in the church & particulerlie from man to mā, & From house to house did acknovvledg, that he had delt vnaduisedlie against R.B. in sundrie things. So in all things vvas Robert Brovvne, cleared, & acknovvledged noe ffaulte at all as being innocent in those things vvhere vvith thei had charged him. But yet ffor all this the grudge lay hid in the harts of diuers, & nevv meetings vvere had against R.B, vvhere in agaī accusations vvere had without Vvittnesses, R, Har, againe receaued sundrie tales & slanders & nethr shame vvhich before came on him, nor the Iudgement of God by the death of his children, nor sundrie vvarnings othervvise could cause him to lay doū his malice & troublesome mind. he had diuers partakers that claue fast Vnto him, because he Taught Them that Thei might Lavvfully Returne INTO ENGLAND AND[1] there haue their dwellinge, & Thit [sic, This] DOCTRINE thei liked Because thei VVere VVearied, of the hardnes of that contrie[.] So And So did hould in VVith Robert, H. THEN VVAS Robert BROVVNE the third Tyme condemned, and forsaken off Them.

The faults They Laied Against him VVere, For rebukinge Rob, H, Sister of VVant of Loue AND off abhorring The Pastar: VVhich They Counted A Slander. LIKe VVise FOR Re buking her, oF Ivdgeing VVrong Fullie on The Printer, VVhich VVas also made a slannder. [C 4 verso] But yet againe after this recōcilēmēt vvas made, & the accusers cōfessed their ffaultes: but no ffault as yet Vvas foūd & proued agaīst R.B. Thus agaīe thei all took him for their lavvfull pastor & made a faier shevv, that thei vvould deale no more so ffoolishly against hī. Notvvithstādīg such vvas their enuie, & stomack, & desire to be gōe into Englād, that thei vvere restles til thei had vvholly diuided thēselues. Thē vvas there vvhisperigs, backbitīgs & murmurīgs priuily & amōg thē selues: also opēly greuous threats, taūts, reuilīgs & false accusatiōs vvere rife in their mouthes. The cause vvas for that some had threatned R.B. to accuse & trouble him at the meetīgs, as beffore thei had done verie vvrōgffully: but he charged thē othervvise, & saied thei could not ioine vvith him in publik praier & thāksgiuīg being at opē disagremēt & not first recōciled. This vvas coūted presūptiō intolerable to be spokē of him. And for that he charged some buisie bodies, vvhich vvere also blasphemers, not to come to the meetings, nether to his chāber in that māner, he vvas greuously takē vp & miscalled off diuers. Likevvise for his vvife there vvas

---

[1] It will be observed that as the end of the third sheet approaches the spelling, punctuations, and capitalization become increasingly frantic, and the number of abbreviations increases. A good many letters are upside down.

427

much a doe, & for the povver & authoritie vvhich the Husband hath ouer the Wife. In this latter a doe R.H. vvas sick & came not abroade, but he had tales enovve brought vnto hī, for vvhich he afterward made great stirrīg & busines. But agaīe their ovūe shame cōpelled thē to come to agreemēt, & yet once more vvith one cōsent thei receaued R.B. for their lavvefull pastor. To this agreement, though R.H. had giuen his cōsēt, yet so sone as he had recouered his sicknes he troubled all againe. He vvithdrevve him selffe frō the exercises vpō certaine tales vvhich vvere tould him, & beīg admonished thereoff & for coūseling some to retourne into Englād, he fell out vvith R.B. chargeīg & accusing him in sūdrie things verie vvrōgfully[.] Then vvas he openlie accused & chalēged for an heretick, & cōdemned as vvorse thē the pope & antichrist. The heresies laied against him vvere, becaus he saied, that all the children must not be coūted forthvvith, to be of the church, vvith the parēts beleuing & receaued to the church. Also because he saied, that none can be the people of God, & outvvardly so takē, vvhich ether did not offer & geue vp them selues to God & the church, or vvere not offerd & giuē vp by others. Further he vvas accused off ffalse doctrine, because he saied that England vvas as Ægipt, both ffor the outvvarde bondage & appressiō off the church, by popish fforceings, lavves & penalties, & ffor all kind off wickednes: & becaus he saied thei did sinn vvhich had a ffull purpos to dvvel stil in England, vvhen the Lord did call thē avvay & thei had libertie to depart. Yea though the magistrates giue thē leaue there to dvvel as thei liked, yet the lavves & disorders abidīg stil the same, thei could not there tarie. Likevvise thei cōdemned him as though he had some times saied (vvhich he neuer did) that some might be of the outuvard church of God, vvhile they resorted to that false vvorship & idol seruice then vsed in England, & ioined vvith others therein, but novve blamed them vvhich held such doctrine. Also because he rebuked some for tolerating & excusing abominations at this day, bie the ceremonies of the oulde lavve vvhich in deed vvere tolerable. For thei vvere not simplie euill as be the abuses novve: nether vvere abrogate to the faithfull & vvilling but bie knovveledge off the nevve lavve. With these & such like quarells did thei buisii them selues against R.B. Wherein R.H. C.M. W.H. & I.C. vvere cheiffe.[1] So from this time fforvvard R.H. refused all cōdiciōs & meanes off peace. Likevvise his partakers did vtterlie forsake R.B: & he & thei did most greuouslye despite him. Thei coueted & tooke avvaie his servaūt from him: Thei sould him bookes, & then both stopped the saile & vvould haue burnt thē to his vtter vndoing: debts vvere exacted vvhich

---

[1] Robert Harrison, Charles Munneman, W. H. (William Harrison ?), and John Chandler.

A True and Short Declaration

he neuer did ovve: Some vvere thurst out off their roumes & dvuellings that ioined With him: he himselfe vvas threatned to be thurst out of his chamber &c.

[The narrative comes here to an abrupt end — at the end of the third sheet].

V. AN ANSWERE TO MASTER CARTWRIGHT

His Letter for Ioyning with the English Churches.

The original, in Browne's hand, is Lambeth MSS. cxiii, 203 *recto* — 222 *verso*, where it follows the *Reproofe of certeine schismatical persons*.

It is closely written, with Scripture references in the margin, and with signatures at the foot of the pages. The manuscript is corrected in Browne's hand, and the printed text follows it closely, though the printer introduces his own spelling vagaries. In the text or margin of the manuscript are numbers or signatures indicating the pages of the book; they *may* have been inserted later, but all the indications are that this was the manuscript used by the printer.

Browne was unfortunate in the printing of his books, some of which were set by compositors unequal to their task or unduly handicapped by shortage of type. This applies especially, of course, to the amateur *Trve and Short Declaration*, but also to the present work. The manuscript is in a young man's writing, firm and clear; the style is vigorous and the argument keen; and, for the times, the punctuation is amazingly good. But in the printed form there is the usual lack of uniformity in regard to capitals, the system of italicization of Scriptural quotations often breaks down, and commas are strewn everywhere (it is only the most blatant intrusions that are noted below).

The temptation to print one of Browne's works in attractive form, duly paragraphed and properly punctuated, has had to be sternly resisted. Had those works appeared in a printed dress as attractive in appearance as this manuscript, some of the conjectures which have been made about Browne would scarcely have been given the light of day.

There is no copy of the work in the B.M. The present work follows the copy in Dr. Williams's Library, with the Lambeth MS. (especially serviceable where worms have been busy on the printed copy) open for comparison and checking.

Cartwright's letter is reprinted in *Cartwrightiana*.

[T-p]   An answere to Ma-
STER CARTWRIGHT HIS
LETTER FOR IOYNING
with the English Churches: whereunto the true copie of his
*sayde letter is an-
nexed.*

Ye are deceiued not knowing the Scriptures, nor the power of God Matth. 22. 29.

Search the Scriptures: for in them ye thinke to haue eternall life, and they are they which testifie of me.   Iohn 5. 39.

Let euery one that calleth on the Name of Christ depart from iniquitie. 2 Tim. 2. 19.

And these things that I say vnto you, I say vnto all men: watch. Matke [*sic*, Marke] 13. 37.

Imprinted at London.

T-p. *verso* blank.

[A ii *recto*] To the Christian *Reader, grace and peace* from God the Father, and from the Lord Iesus Christ &c.[1]

Dearely beloued in the truth, you haue in this booke an answere to an answere written vnto Master Harrison at Middleborough by Master Cartwright vpon occasion of controuersie betweene them [concerning the true spouse of Christ or his ordinarie visible Churches in Englande, And it is thought good to put this aunswere before the saide aunswere of Master Cartwright. And although the godlywise, and such as haue onely the glorie of God before their eyes and his pure Religion and seruice together with the saluation of their brethren, will easily perceuie the reasons, and causes: yet least anye might take offence in this offence[2] in this behalfe, it is though[t] meete to shewe some. The first reason therefore is this. Our corrupt nature is more prone and readie to imbrace the errour of man then the trueth of God. Another cause was for that our vntowardenesse is so great, that if an vntruthe be once receiued, it [worketh such a preiudice in the heades and mindes of men, that they will heare neither God his worde, neither reason or argument to the contrary be it neuer so good and effectuall. A thirde cause mooued to place this answere first, for that it shoulde bee an occasion vnto the Reader, to vse more diligent conferring of this aunswere with the other, for the better discerning and finding out of the trueth in this controuersie. It is not necessarie that any man interpose his iudgement at this tyme, but to attende by prayer the good euent which God will giue for the further manifestation of his trueth, and abolishing of the contrary. Nowe these fewe lynes [A ii *verso*] *are thought in this matter sufficient, least it might seeme to foreiudge any truth in either of these answeres, or else by accepting of persons to foster corruption, or a lye in any thing set foorth in the Name of the Lorde. It is expedient therefore that the scriptures be faithfull[y] searched by the godly Reader, to see whether these things be euen so or not. For no man that feareth God is ignorant of the doctrine of our Sauiour christ, that whosoeuer breaketh the least of the commaundements of God, and teacheth men so, is least in the Kingdom of heauen. Neither ye[t] of this generall & uniuersal doctrine of god his word, true repentance, vnfeined faith with amendment of life, to be necessarie vnto saluation.*

But it is said before, these fewe things suffice. There-
fore the faythfull Reader is to be commen-
ded to the grace of God, for his fur-
ther direction in this be-
halfe, farewell deare
brother in the
Lord.

[1] The Preface is missing in the Lambeth MS.
[2] The intrusive phrase as text.

An Answere to Master Cartwright

[1] An Answere to Master Cartwright *His Letter, For* ioyning with the English Churches: *Wherevnto the true Copie of his saide Letter is annexed.*

As there be alwayes both friends and enemies to the Church of God, so some doe giue their handes vnto it as friendes, and some being enemies will giue it their left hande of friendshihpe [*sic*] to turne it cleane out of the way. Howe friendly *Master Cartwright* is to it, let vs examine by this his Letter, and by the grace of God, let vs trie out the trueth betwixt him and vs: his letter is in many mens handes, and was seene[1] abroade vnsealed and open, as if he cared not who shoulde reade it, wherefore I may the more boldly answere it, and the rather because the matter thereof is publike and pertaining to the Church of God. It came but lately to my handes, and was written as they tell me more then fiue or sixe weekes agoe, wherein if he and others that prouoke him, sought not to take vs tardie in the trueth and to worke vs trouble, we would the lesse haue regarded his letter: but seeing he will needes make vs enemies to the common and ordinarie good lawes of the Realme, to the Church of god in the Realme, and to the peace and welfare of the common wealth: Let vs answere his cauilles: and for so much as we haue so small respite of time, let vs shortly gather vp his vntrueths and errours, and hurle them out by manifest & knowen markes, least any man doe beleeue them as trueth.

[2] *Master Cartwright* doeth mooue the first question thus: *That the outwarde profession made by the lawes of the lande, and the assemblyes of the Church helde accordingly, are condēned as vnlawfull*: this is the short (saith he) of M. *Harrisons* lōger discourse, if he vse to make such shorts, he is not meete to deale with short or with long. Let him lappe vp his shortes in his budget, and not sende them abroade in steade of our lengths or larger syse. For at the first brunt he would set against vs all these enemies: 1. *The lawes of the lande.* 2. *The outwarde profession by the lawes.* 3. *The apparant Churches of Christ.* 4. *and the lawfull assemblyes thereof.* First, for the lawes, he knewe well ynough what Lawes we meane: namely, *certaine Popish Cannon lawes*, which though the Magiestrates doe tollerate for a time, yet the common good lawes of the lande are wholy against them. Wherefore let him not deale doubly with vs, as hauing our true meaning in his heart. to fumble out of his mouth or to shuffle vp in his letter a contrary meaning: we know that the lawes doe punish all outward grosse wickednesse, or suffer it to be punished: as namelie, *Idolatrie, forswearing, vsurping of Lordshippe, rebellion, murther, fleshly filthinesse, theft, oppression, raylings, grieuous slanders,*

---

[1] Also in MS.: sometimes "sente" has been conjectured.

drunkennes &c. and if there be any vice not punishable by the lawe, yet the lawes doe suffer either the Church, or euery housholder, or gouernour to correct (so it be not against lawe) such as are vnder their charge. So then the lawes are a wall to the Church rounde about: they stande vp for it as an armed man, that it may shewe it selfe openly without shame or feare. For when they put downe all outwarde grosse wickednesse, and will not suffer it, they doe as it were scatter and driue awaye darkenesse from the Church, that men may see it uisible and cleare as the Sunne. Likewise for the outwarde profession by the lawes, *Master Cartwright* would playe at handie dandie[1] with vs, and yet not giue vs that hand which we doe choose: for there is an outwarde profession after the olde Popish traditions and orders, let him holde this [3] profession in his left hande: and there is a profession more syncerely by some, after some better Lawes and Orders, this he shoulde houlde in his right hand: wherefore then doeth hee reach vs that in his right hande as taking it vnlawfull, which we choose as lawfull. If he saye that wee condemne that ordinarie abused and corrupt profession of the most, I aunswere that the Lawes doe also the same: For the common Lawes are against the cannon Lawes in many hundreth poynts, one giueth checke to the other as two Dames at variance in one house, the cannon is as fire in the house to burne it, the common is as water powring downe to quenche it. The Popishe courtes esteeme all sortes of christians for churches of Christ, much like those harlots, that woulde haue many children though it were by fornication, that they myght rule ouer many, but the Common wealth reiecteth her children, as beyng children of Death, euen for smaller Theftes, Felonyes, Roginges, and Wanderinges, without honest Trades and laboures: as for the right corrections of Adulteryes, those whoorish courtes haue taken so much vpon them, that the Ciuill Magistrates coulde not so well see to it before this time. But nowe euen for this matter they haue giuen a great checke to the cannon Officers. Also for persecuting the brethren and sundry worthye men, their authoritie and cannon power hath receiued a great blowe and wounde. If there be contrary lawes one against another, as through change of tymes, variaunce of people, and other necessities it may fall out, yet through fauour and help of good Magistrates, the lawe shall still be with the Church and not against it: As for the Maiestracie of Byshops there is no lawe to warrant it, but only her Maiesties permission: likewise for the common forme of seruice and prayers, there is exception by the lawe, and it is set downe also in the booke of Common prayer, that the prayers may be changed, intermitted,

---

[1] Handy-dandy — a game in which one person guesses in which closed hand the other person holds some small object.

An Answere to Master Cartwright

and left off by occasions, as when [4] the Minister is to preach or applye him selfe to his studie for preaching. Further whereas the lawe doeth binde vs to come to the church, it doth well, for no man ought to refuse the Church of God, yet if when we come to the church, we finde there an vnlawfull minister, and a wicked confusion of all sortes of people, the fault is not nowe in the law but in the Byshoppes which place such ministers, and in their spirituall courtes which are authours of such confusion: for the Lawe commaundeth that the Minister should be *Doctus* and *Clericus*, which wordes doe require learning sufficient, and godlinesse meete for a cleargie man: otherwise howe shoulde he be *Clericus* that is one of the Lordes inheritance. But the Bishops count him learned if he can but reade onely, and answere to a catechisme as doe children: wherefore good Magistrates will execute the lawe according to the true meaning, and not according to the extremitie of the wordes, and if they see to it, that men shall come to Church, they will first see that the church be better ordered that men may come with comforte, and not with heart burning to their conscience. Also for discipline in gathering the worthie from the vnworthy, the lawe appointeth it and giueth leaue to make exception both in publique iudgement and in churches against vnworthye persons: as against Drunkennesse, fightings, murther, adulteryes, stealth, slaunders, &c. and that before the Constables, Iustices of Peace, Iudges and Iustices of Assises, and yet also doe giue libertie to the Church to vse their owne discipline. But eyther the Popes cannon lawes, and his officers doe quite ouerthrowe it, or the Ministers are so seruile and foolish that they can not, or dare not execute it: It were too long to rehearse what libertie the lawes do yeelde to vs, and what outwarde profession there is by the lawes: but thus we conclude, that seeing very many of the Bishops doings and their officers are vnlawfull, and yet very vsually and ordinarily professed, helde, and practised, we must needes say that such an ordinary profession is vnlawfull.

[5] Nowe followeth the chiefest and greatest matter in controuersie: namely, *Whether the ordinarie assemblies of the professors in Englande be the Churches of Christ.* A part of this question he must make as he doeth the vsuall outward profession. What *Master Harrison* did write in his letter, and vpon what wordes *Master C.* doeth gather this question I can not tell: for I neuer sawe *Master Harrisons* letter: but I hope *Master H.* did not condemne any assemblyes, but abused assemblyes neither any professors, but false professors:[1] wherefore let him take his right meaning, namely, *The ordinarie abused assemblyes of false professors.* But he will admit no such distinction: for belike he will haue no such assemblyes, yet in a time

---
[1] The meaning seems to be this: I hope Master Harrison did not condemn all assemblies indiscrimately, but only the abused assemblies; not all professors, but only false ones.

Ierem. 3. 6. 10 of better reformation then is now in Englande, as in the dayes of King Iosiah, *the Lord witnesseth, that Iudah had not returned vnto him with their whole heart but faynedly.* If they then were false professors, whose hypocrisie was in their hearts, why should not they be false professors, which doe shewe foorth in practise a false profession, and that chiefely in their assemblyes? but whatsoeuer false profession they haue, and howe grosse soeuer their abuses be, *Master Cartwright* will prooue them to bee churches of Christ. But goe to, let vs examine his proofes: those assemblyes haue Christ for their head and foundation, for saith hee, they beleeue in Christ, and haue the spirite of Christ, therefore they are the churches of Christ. Nowe to prooue that they beleeue he bringeth in their profession: so that all *Master Cartwrights* arguments falleth from one to one, till it come to nothing at all, for from the head and foundation of the church, he descendeth to the spirite and to faith, and so at last to the outwarde profession. Nowe the outwarde profession must chiefely be shewed and iustified by the lawfull vsing of publique assemblyes. If they then be so shamefully abused by meanes of the bishoppes, and their officers, then his proofe of the outward profession also falleth to the ground. Thus of necessitie he must iustifie many grosse corruptions both in the assemblyes & in [6] sundry their practises and customes, or else laye by his proofe as vntrue. But what neede hee haue fetched about and made suche adoo, touching faith and the spirite, and the head and the foundation of the Church, and then to haue no other proofe but the question to prooue the question. For the question is, *whether the assemblyes bee lawfull outward Churches, being helde according to so corrupt profession?* or whether *the outwarde profession of the false professours standing as it doeth, the assemblyes that are according, bee lawfull or no?*

Thus he prooueth *idem per idem*: [the same by the same], it is so, because it is so: it shall bee so, because it shall bee so. But marke his turning and shifting to and fro in this matter. For from the outward church and the outwarde profession he leapeth and fleeth to the spirite and faith, which are inwarde: and from the inwarde graces he returneth to the outwarde profession. Thus as one that is hunted with his enemie within, he runneth out, and being in daunger without he runneth

An Answere to Master Cartwright

in: for by faith which is inwarde, and the spirite that is inwarde, hee woulde iustifie an outwarde churche. Againe, by an outwarde, false, and corrupt profession, he will iustifie the inwarde spirite and faith of professours, to bee syncere. Thus with turning and returning to and fro, he woulde establishe his errour, but hee doeth wearie him selfe in vaine. Nowe as his dealing herein is ridiculous, so hee increaseth it vnto a shamelesse and blasphemous doctrine: For he sayeth that there being but one onely true Christian in a church, or congregation, and all the rest wicked, yea and so wicked that they haue but a bare profession in worde onely without any good workes, they shoulde all be counted the church of God, for that one mans cause. I maruaile howe his penne coulde droppe downe such poyson, and he not smell the stinck thereof as he wrote it: For by this doctrine euery faithfull christian shall bee aboue Christ. For *Master Cartwright* doeth giue them power to loose those on earth, which God doeth binde in heauen, and this power Christ neuer [7] had: For if the faith of one or a fewe beleeuers in an assembly be of force to make them all the Church, though the rest be grosse offendours, then neede they to bynde none in earth: And why shoulde Saint Paule alleadge this power of our Lorde Iesus Christ, if all may bee taken for the Church by the faith of some? 1. Cor. 5. 4.

For *Master Cartwright* will giue vs a contrary power, namely, to reckon all for the churche, *But will you steale, murther, commit adulterie, and sweare falsely* &c. sayeth the Lorde, *and come, and stande before me in this house whereupon my Name is called, and say, We are deliuered, though wee haue done all these abominations*? If *Master Cartwright* shoulde answere this question, we shoulde heare those lying wordes (for so the Prophet tearmeth them) namely, *The Temple of the Lord, the Temple of the Lorde, all is the Temple and Church of God*: But a denne of thieues is not the house and Temple of God. And if the faith of fewe will make many wretches to be the church, then the vnfaithfulnes of many shoulde be of force to make them all no Church: But as my wickednesse condemneth no man but my selfe, except they partake with me in my wickednes, so my faith iustifieth no man to be of the church, except they hold with me an outward good profession according to faith. *For shew me thy faith by thy works (saith S. Iam. 2)* as who say, he Ierem. 7. 9. 10.

Iere. 7. 4.

Iames 2.

Rom. 10. 10. would not beleue there were faith, if he saw not the works of faith. And *Paul ioyneth the beleefe of the heart, and confession of the mouth both together, as needeful vnto righteousnes & saluation*: and by the confession of the mouth, he meaneth al outward profession agreeing to faith, because the professiō by mouth is chiefest. He can not turne his words, as if he spake of one truly faithful, and all the rest secret hypocrites, for he speaketh of the outward profession, of the outward works, and of the outward church, & granteth also that there are many outward & grosse abuses: further, he nameth that in wordes only they hold the true faith, as who say, be the deeds neuer so abhominable, yet for that faithful mans sake they are al [8] to be called one church with him. If *Master Cartwright* had sayde cleane contrary, he had spoken more truely: namely, that if among many good liuers, one wicked man were founde, as a murtherer, an idolater, or an adulterer, and the rest become so negligent or wilfull, or are helde in such spirituall bondage, that any one such open and manifest offence is incurable, then the couenant is broken and disanulled with them all, till they repent and redresse such wickednesse. Proofe there is by the 7. *of Ioshua*, the 13. *of Deuteronomie*, the 9. *of Ezra*, the 20. *of Iudges*, the 3. *of Ieremie* and 1. *verse. By the punishment of the whole land for Sauls offence*, 2 *Samuel*. 21 *By the ceremonies of leprosies. Of touching vncleane things. By the leauen (named of Paul) that leaueneth the whole lūpe* 1. *Cor.* 5. & by sundry other places. Wherefore this doctrine of his, as it maketh for the Pope, that a whole wretched multitude may be the Church and depende on one man, & cleane ouerthroweth the discipline of the church: so it is so contrary to God and all godlinesse, that I wonder anye man should haue the face to auouche it. If M.C. say, that hee meaneth not a profession altogether corrupted, but a good profession in other dueties, though that bee nought, which iustifieth such abuses in assemblies, I maruaile howe he dare pronounce it an apparant sanctification, or an holy profession in other dueties, where there is so corrupt and polluted a profession in publique assemblyes. Doth not the Prophet teach vs, *That that man can haue no name of a righteous, iust, and holy man, which offendeth in any one grosse sinne. If he sinne in any one of these thinges* (saith the Prophet) *though he doe not all these things he is a wicked man, all the righteous-*

Iosh. 7. 12.
Ezra. 9.
Deut. 13.
Iudg. 20.
Ierem. 3. 1.
2. Sam. 21.
1. Cor. 5.

Ezech. 18. 10.

An Answere to Master Cartwright

nesse which he had done, shall not be mentioned, but his wickednesse shall be vpon him. And if it be true that Iames saith, Cap. 1. 26. *that not to refraine a mans tongue, is to proue his religion vaine*: then to haue a filthie polluted profession in publique assemblies, is to make all other profession filthy and polluted. And so reasoneth the Prophet Haggi, *That as any holy meate was made vnholy and vncleane, if a polluted person did but touch it, [9] or the skirt of a mans garment did but touch it, so much more vncleane was that people and nation, and all their holy exercises and sacrifices, and all the workes of their handes, because they polluted them selues but in one thing,* namely, *in slacking and fearing to builde the outwarde Temple, which was but a figure of the outwarde Church of god at this day.* Iames. 1. 26. Hag. 2. 13. 14.

But we come to another of Master Cartwrights proofes, which hee giueth thus: They haue the couenaunts of the churches of god, namely *the spirit and the worde of god put in their mouthes, therefore they are the Churches of god.* We doe not denie but that there are sundry churches of god: but the question is of a corrupt profession by Popish Lawes, and of vnlawfull assemblyes made thereby. But whatsoeuer corruption there is, (as he granteth diuers) yet they haue the couenant saith he of the spirite, and the worde of god in their mouthes. So without shame he abuseth that place in *Isaiah* 59. For he leaueth out one part of the couenant, which is, *That the Lorde will come vnto Zion and to those that turne from iniquitie in Iacob, and with them will hee make his couenant*: wherefore the worde is not the couenant to establish a Church except it reigne and rule in the Church, to subdue it in obedience to the Lorde: for the Lorde maketh no couenant, but with those that turne from iniquitie in Iacob. As againe it is written, *Walke before me, and be thou vpright, and I will make my couenant betweene me and thee.* As who say, one condition and part of the couenant is our vpright and good profession. So likewise in *Ieremie* and *Exodus*, the promise of obedience in the people, is set downe as one part of the couenant, *Obey my voyce, and doe according to all these thinges which I commande you, so shall you be my people, and I will be your god: or els cursed be the man that obeyeth not the wordes of this couenant.* For on this condition will the Lorde receiue vs, as *Paul reasoneth, if we come out from among the wicked, and separate our selues: Then will I be a Father vnto you, and ye shall be my sonnes and daughters,* Isa. 59. 20. Gen. 17. 1. 2. Iere. 11. 3, 4. Exod. 19. 2. Cor. 6. 17. 18. Isa. 52. 11. Ierem. 31. 1.[1]

---

1 "31. 2." in MS. wrongly.

saith the Lorde Almightie. Thus shoulde *Master Cartwright* haue conferred[1] [10] place with place, and haue knowen that the worde is no couenant, where the practise thereof is reiected and troden vnder foote: neither can men say they haue the couenant of the spirite, when open and grosse wickednesse so reigneth in them, that there is no power of the spirite to redresse it, but it remaineth incurable. And so Paul reasoneth, *that as many as are led by the spirit of god, they are the sonnes of god,* but he sheweth that they are in the state of condemnation, and not in Christ Iesus, if they walke after the flesh, and not after the spirite. For there is not the couenant of the spirite, where we are not turned from iniquitie as *Isaiah* him selfe witnesseth, and let *Ƶecharie* interprete Isaiah, who sheweth what spirite God will powre vpon his house and people, namely, *The spirit of grace and compassion, vnto repentance and mourning for their sinnes.* Likewise *Ezechiel* doth giue the proofe and tryall of that new spirit and newe heart which God woulde put in his people, namely this, *That they should walke in his statutes, and keepe his iudgements, and execute them, and so doing, they shall be his people, and he woulde be their god.* Wherefore let not *Master Cartwright* account so much of the word in their mouthes, except as it is written in *Deut, it be in their mouthes and in their heartes for to doe it.* Otherwise Christ wil pronounce of them, that in vaine they worship the Lord, and so are they false worshippers: for god is neere in their mouthes, and farre from their reignes: *They drawe neere vnto god with their mouthes and honour him with their lippes, but their heart is far off from him.* Surely such men are not those burning lampes, neither the goldē candlesticks he speaketh of, *but rather as those that will seeke me daily,* saith the lord, *euen as a nation that did righteously, and had not forsaken the statutes of their god: they aske of me ordinances of iustice, they will drawe neere vnto me.* Yet in the next chapter the Lord witnesseth, *that there was a great separation betwene him and them, so that he was to make a newe couenant with them, and they were to turne from their former iniquities, or else they could not be his people and Church.* And therefore when Christ [11] appointeth the Apostles to plant churches throughout the world, he appointeth them not, to talke of and professe the word in their mouthes onely, but he giueth in charge these three things, as being the

Rom. 8. 14

Zech. 12. 10.

Ezec. 11. 19. 20.

Deut. 30. 14.
Mat 15. 8.

Ierem. 12. 2.

Isa. 29. 13.
Isa. 58. 2.
Isa. 59. 2. 20.

Mat. 28 19. 20.

---

[1] That is, compared, collated.

chiefe marks of a planted Church: namely *preaching the word, ministration of the sacramēts, & reformation of life*, which is the chiefest thing of all to set forth his Church & kingdom: for he commādeth to preach and baptize, & because preaching & baptizing is nothing without amendmēt of life, he addeth these words, teaching thē to obserue & do all things, whatsoeuer I haue comanded you. Therfore as appeareth in the acts of the Apostles, was neither the church nor the couenāts of the Church established among any, but where their good & godly profession was shewed, and the contrary refused. I know M.C. will gainsay that there must needes be hypocrites in euery church, & sometimes also open breach of gods commandements. It is true indeede. But yet if any make an open and grosse breach then Paul hath written vnto vs, *that we company not together with such. For if any* (saith he) *that is called a brother, be a fornicator, or couetous, or an idolater, or a railor, or a drunkard, or an extortioner &c. with such a one eate not.* The aduersaries replie to this, that in deede to eat common bread with such, or to partake with them in the feastes of charitie was forbidden, which distinction and shift they alleadge out of Caluin. But who dare say that the godly wife may not eate comon bread with her excomunicated husband? or the godly children with their wicked parents? or seruants with their masters? For otherwise al seruice, ministery & communiō in a common wealth should be ouerthrowen. And so as Paul reasoneth the godly shuld not be able to liue in the world. Who also dare say that when the church held their feasts of charitie they might forbid wicked persons to partake with them in the feastes, and yet suffer them to partake in the Lordes table. Nay they kept their feastes and the Lords Supper together. And hereupon Paul gaue this distinction, that they should suffer none but brcehrē [*sic*, brethrē] to ioyne with them in the holy feastes or in the assemblyes which were [12] *for ministration of the Lordes Supper*: but if we will not eate and drinke with sinners in the worlde we must goe out of the worlde. Wherefore there is an eating with wretches in the worlde, or in worldly meetings and feastings, which is forbidden in the Church meetings. As if a brother being separate and fallen away, should in an Inne or vitailing house sit downe at the table to eate, after we and others were set; it were vnlawfull to

Actes. 2.
Actes. 8.
Actes. 19. 18.

1. Cor. 5 .11.

rise from the table because of him: yea it were both against common charitie and humanitie, and also against the peace & communion of a common wealth. But of this matter it followeth to speake afterwardes.

We haste one to others [sic] proofes.[1] An other proofe is, as though it were graunted him, *that where a preaching minister is, there is a Church*: nay we know that assemblyes of papistes haue preaching ministers, and yet are not the church of God. And though they be Protestants which haue a Preacher ouer them, yet if he for his wickednesse cease to be a brother, and they also for their wickednesse be no brethren, the preaching Minister can not cause them to bee a Church of God. This is manifest before, and shall partly also afterwarde be spoken of: wherefore I let it passe. As for that he saith, of some knowledge receiued by a dumbe ministerie, and of faith receiued by some further Ministerie, it is much like the same tryfling proofe he vsed before, and is answered alreadie. For we said, that the inward faith will not iustifie the outward Church, when there is a wicked profession contrary to the doctrine of faith. Againe a man may beleeue, & be wonne to faith, by meanes of some godly brother, and that before he haue outwardly ioyned him selfe to the Church: so in gods secret election he is of the church: yet because he hath not the outwarde profession, can not be sayde to be the outwarde Church. But here *Master Cartwright* though he dare not iustifie the blind reading Ministers, yet he doeth praise them as doing some good. But of this matter also it followeth afterwarde to intreate, as whether he that doeth so much hurt and mischiefe [13] can be saide to doe any good at all. Likewise it is a trifling to no purpose, that he sayth, *the Church ceaseth not, when a minister faileth or wanteth*: for we knowe that euen two or three agreeing together in the trueth, & separate from wickednesse, if none other will ioyne with them, euen they are an outwarde and visible Church, and haue this power of Christ, *euen to binde men on earth, and to loose them on earth, that they may be bound or loosed in heauen.* For though by persecution they be driuen into corners, yet their good profession is outward and visible in it selfe, and yet hidden from their enemies which are vnworthy to see

Mat. 18. 18

---

[1] Here the MS. is better: "We hast on to other proofes".

it, for the church may increase into thousandes and
decrease also in this worlde, euen to a litle householde, Reuel. 11. 8.
and to foure or fiue persons. For Ierusalem fell away,
and became as Sodome and Egypt, and the Lorde did
blot out the whole name and church of the Iewes, and Isa. 65. 15.
called his people by another name: as it is written Act. 11. 26.
Isay. 65. *Actes* 11. *But in these latter dayes, it is prophecied
that the Church shoulde be small, hidden, and driuen into
corners. So that as in Noas time, eight persons onely escaped,* Reuel. 12. 13, 14
euen so when the sonne of man shall come he shall not finde Mat. 24. 22.¹
*faith on the earth, & those dayes before his comming shall be
so hard, that scarce any flesh shall be saued.* Indeed one
person will not make a church, for the church must
needes be a number, *but where two or three are gathered* Mat. 18. 19, 20.
in the name of Christ, there is he in the middes of them. And Philem. 2.
the housholde of *Philemon* is named a Church. Likewise the Col. 4. 15.
housholde of *Olymphis*,² of *Aquila* & *Priscilla*, and others. Rom. 16. 5.
1 Cor. 5. 4.
For if they haue the power which *Paul* calleth the power
of our Lorde Iesus Christ, and doe meete together fewe
or moe in the Name of Christ, they are surely the
Church of Christ. Therefore this doctryne is still
agaynst *Master Cartwright* for neyther the worde in the
preachers mouth, nor the Sacraments can make an
outwarde Church, except they haue the power of
Christ to separate the vnworthye. For *Master C.*
confesseth that the name of a Church shall remayne,
though the preacher and his preaching doe cease, and
is wanting for a tyme. But without [14] this power of
binding, that is, of declaring mens wickednes, and
forsaking their fellowshippe to leaue them vnto Satan
being open and grieuous offendours, there is no name,
nor shewe of the church of Christ remaining. If he
demande proofe hereof, the scriptures are manifest.
For God hath giuen this power, not onely to the preachers
but to all the saintes of god, as appereth by that Psalme,
namely, *By the worde of god in their mouthes, to binde euen* Psalm 149. 6, 7, 8, 9.
*the Kings and nobles of the earth, and to execute vpon them
his spirituall iudgement,* & the text followeth, *that this
honour shall be to all the Saintes.* Wherefore it is not Isa. 54. 7.
peculiar to some one, or to some fewe alone, but it
belongeth to all: yea this is the heritage of all the
Lordes seruants, as *Isaiah* testifieth. In deede it is

---

¹ An additional Scripture reference in MS., hard to read, part being in the binding: probably " Ezek. 17 ".
² That is, Olympas. See Romans 16 : 15.

true, that we ought ioyntly to execute this power: but if others will not or bee in bondage that they can not ioyne with vs therein, then they are not the Church, but the bondslaues of men. For this power belongeth to euery one seuerally to forsake wicked fellowship, and there is a cōmandement giuen to euery one, *to forsake the vnfruitfull workes of darkenesse, to be no com-* <small>Ephe. 5. 7.</small> *panions with such, to haue no fellowshippe with them, to* <small>2. Thes. 3. 6.</small> *withdraw our selues from euery brother that walketh in ordin-* <small>2. Tim. 3. 5.</small> *ately*: yea, and to turne away from all, which hauing a shew *of godlinesse doe deny the power thereof*: For if we walke in darknes, and say we haue fellowship with god, we lye (sayth S. Iohn) *and doe not truely*: But if we walke in the light, we haue fellowship one with another: otherwise that <small>1. John. 1. 6.</small> *fellowship holdeth not*. And in Hosea commandement is giuen vnto all, *euen to pleade against the mother church, if it fal away, that as god doth forsake it so euery one also should* <small>Hose. 2. 2.</small> *stand against it, if it become abhominable*. And so also all are commanded to saue them selues from a froward generation. <small>Actes 2. 40.</small> But it may be here obiected, howe we answere to the place in *Matth.* 18 *that we must complaine to the Church, and then if the offender heare not the Church, we must take him for a heathen and publican*. I grant that if the offence be priuate, he must be first priuately dealt with. But this proueth not, that either for priuate or open offences, we must waite [15] on them for redresse, which are enemies of the Church, and which haue no power to binde and lose, as hath the church. Wherefore let not *Master Cartwright* accompt so much of the assemblyes he speaketh of: for what is a Church without this power we spake of? yea what are those assemblies which insteade of it, do holde that Antichristian power of the spirituall courtes, or rather are helde in bondage by it? But *Master Cartwright* alloweth not onely those assemblies, but also those vile courtes and officers, and Bishoppes set ouer them to be all the Church of God. For he sayeth afterwarde, namely in the sixt page, that the calling of the dumbe ministers, which is by them, is a calling of the church and sufficient to make them ministers: yea and he seemeth to allowe also their suspendings of preachers, as if it were done by the Church, so that both for complaint and for redresse of defaults, & for establishing and gathering the churches, he alloweth or tollerateth those officers and courtes to haue the power and authoritie of the church. But God

An Answere to Master Cartwright

hath appointed no such kinde of complaintes in the Church, neither such kinde of redresse, nor ordering of matters. First, because they redresse and order matters by money, Brybes, Fees, Ciuill penaltyes &c. wherein the Church discipline ought not to meddle. For the weapons of our warfare sayeth Paul, are not 2. Cor. 10. 4. carnall. He meaneth that the Church maye not deale in matters of reformation, as doeth the common wealth and this present worlde. The Church can deale no further then onely by rebuke, warning and exhortation out of gods worde, and by forsaking & casting of[f] fellowship in grosser sinnes: And therefore rightly may the word and his Spirituall graces be called the weapons of our warfare. Also in the church there can bee no recompence made for sinne by money. For the sinner is the murtherer of his owne soule. And therefore the Num. 35. 31. 3 law of god is, that for murther or killing any, there cā be no recōpence made saue only by the death of the māslayer [16] him selfe, or the high Priest, which figured thus much, that except we see in any transgressour open repentance and faith in the death of Christ, we are to iudge him still dead in his sinne, and that money can not make him to liue, nor redresse his wickednesse. And the officers that take money in such a case, doe euen eate vp the sinne of the people, as it is written *and lift vp their mindes in their iniquitie.* Also because the Iudges Hose 4. 8. and officers of the court doe wrest Gods Lawe, by their Popish cannon Lawe, and respect persons and take rewarde which is forbidden in Deuteronomie (and by Deut. 16. 14. their profession they must needes doe so, or else they can not holde their office,) howe shal any make complaint vnto them for Church matters, which can be counted none of the church. And seeing Christ hath commanded to complaine to the Church against the sinner, howe shall Christs ordinance be broken by complaining vnto such wretches. Furthermore seeing 1. Cor. 5. 12. the Scripture sheweth that the church hath nothing to doe to iudge those which are without, how shal any complaine of such a number of wicked men, as neuer 1. Cor. 6. 1. were worthie to be coūted the church. Againe, seeing no godly man may seeke iudgement vnder the uniust, as Paul sheweth, if he haue a matter against a brother, why shoulde we seeke vnto such for iudgement. Further the rebuke and reforming of a brother ought not to be delayed, till the time of keeping their courtes. *For we* 1. Thes. 5.

knowe perfectly (saith Paul) *that the day of the Lorde shall come as a thiefe in the night*: *and as he that sinneth ought not to delay his repentance, and promise safety to him selfe, least sudden destruction come: so he that seeth his brother sinne, ought to hast his repentance and reformation.* For thou shalt not hate thy brother in thine heart (sayeth the Scripture) but thou shalt plainely rebuke thy neighbour, and not suffer sinne vpon him. And the Corinthians are sharpely rebuked of negligence, because they hasted not to cast out of the Church the incestuous person, and likewise, because they made too long delaye in receiuing him againe being penitent. Againe because those cannon officers are straun-[17]gers, neither knowen to the Churches, nor dwelling among them, no maruaile though Christ say, *that his sheepe will not followe nor seeke to strangers, but will flee from them.* Moreouer, *Because they bring the Churches into bondage* (as it is written) *because they deuoure, because they take their goods, because they exalt them selues, and as it were smite the people on the face, and cast them them [sic] in prison, they do all these things besides the church gouernment, and therefore ought to be reiected, and in no case to be suffered.* Thus it is manifest by the worde of God that such proude prelates, and Antichristian vsurpers, haue no authoritie nor power of the church: neither is [sic] their suspendings to be counted suspensions by the church, nor their calling of Ministers a calling by the Churche. Nay surely the least in the kingdome of God shalbe able by the worde of God in their mouthes, to plucke vp and roote out such plantes if none other will ioyne with them. I meane they shall pronounce them by the worde of god to be abhominable, & haue no felowship with thē in the church: & so to thē they are vtterly plucked out of the Church. For they are kings and priests vnder Christ, to execute the lords gouernement against such: and therefore they ought not to loose their right, which is euen their heritage and glorie, *Isaiah* 54. or rather the glorie or kingdome of god, euen the keyes of the kingdome of heauen to binde and loose, *Mat.* 18. *The power of Christ Iesus to deliuer vp the wicked to Satan,* 1 *Corinth.* 5. The scepter of his worde for rebuke, doctrine, exhortation, promising life, denouncing iudgement. *For this is a right scepter, which subdueth the people vnder vs, and the nations vnder our feete Psalme* 45.

---

[1] May be 1 Cor. 7. 1., which is also relevant.

An Answere to Master Cartwright

He alleadgeth another proofe by peraduenture. For he guesseth, that peraduenture we will say, it were better for an assembly to haue no minister at all, then to haue a blinde reading minister. And then he reasoneth thus, that hauing none at all but yesterday they are the church, or may be the church, then hauing a dumbe minister to day, they are still the Church of god, and can not so suddenly be made the sy-[18]nagogue of Satan. This is a slender proofe, and borowed by imagination: for we make not the minister, whether dũbe, or not dumbe to be the essence, substance, or life of the outward Church, but the keeping of the couenant by the outwarde discipline and gouernement thereof. And the Lorde calleth the keeping of the couenant by this discipline, his staffe of beautie, as appeareth in Zecharie, which being broken, he disanulleth his couenant with the people, and so they become the sheepe of slaughter. For he saith, *I will not feede you: that that dyeth let it dye, and that that perisheth, let it perish, and let the remnant eate euery one the flesh of his neighbour*: Likewise in Iere. & Ezek. as the breaking of the couenant is set downe to be the death, and perishing of the church & people of God: so the keeping thereof by better discipline and gouernement was the life and renuing of the Church. Why then shoulde *Master Cartwright* reason so fondly? as though they that helde the couenant to day, might not breake it to morowe, and as though any grosse wickednesse committed of all, were not the breaking of the couenant by all. Did not the people pleade truely against Reuben and Gad, that if they rebelled to daye against the Lorde, euen to morrowe the Lorde woulde be wroth with all the Congregation of Israel. And they alleadge further, that for Achans sinne, wrath fell on all the congregation of Israel. Howe suddenly and quickly was this sinne committed? and howe soone was the Lorde prouoked, euen to forsake all the congregation, and to be with them no more, except they destroyed the excommunicate from among them: for so are the wordes of the Lorde him selfe. Nowe what was that sinne, which Israel calleth rebellion in Reuben and Gad, both against the Lorde, and against the rest of Israel? And what was the sinne of Achan? Surely they thought that the Reubenites and Gadites had broken that commandement which the Lorde had giuen them, namely, that they should not offer their burnt

Zacha 11. 10.

Iere. 11. 3, 4.
Iere. 31. 32.
Ezek. 16, 60, 61, 62, 63.
Hebr. 8. 8.

Ioshu. 22. 18.
Ioshu. 7. 12.

Deut. 12. 11, 12, 13.

offerings in euery place which they liked, but only in the place which the Lorde had cho-[19]sen to put his name there. Now who knoweth not, but that that place of the name of God, figured the visible Church of god, so that this matter toucheth M.C. very neerely. For if it be true, that as all sacrifices then, so all sacraments now, are rebellion against the Lord, being ministred without the visible Church of God, then that sinne which he calleth a fault, shalbe found to be more then a fault, euen rebellion & falling away from the Lord. And this is a sinne of execration, euen abomniation in the eies of the Lord, to measure the visible church of god, by a compasse of ground, by a nūber of housholdes, by stint of tythes & tenthes as we see in our parishes. For the place maketh not the church, neither is the church or true religiō, to be measured by the place, as Christ him selfe teacheth vs, *for neither in the mountaine where the father worshipped*[1], *neither yet at Ierusalē the citie of god, was God any more to be worshipped, but the true worshippers shall worship the father in spirit & truth.* By which words Christ meaneth thus much, first, that the spirit & trueth being shewed by the outward good profession, declare the outwarde Church of God, and not the places, neither temples, nor cities, nor parishes. For in whome we see the spirit, that is, the graces of the spitit [sic] by their outward good works, and the trueth, that is the lawes and word of Christ which is true, to be kept & obserued, them only we must call the Church of God. And therefore in *Isaiah* it was shewed before, that with those only which turne from iniquitie in Iacob, will the Lord make his couenant, euen his spirite which is vpon them, and his words which he hath put in their mouth. Secondly by those wordes Christ teacheth, that al the Jewish ceremonies shuld be abolished, because the chiefest, euen Ierusalem and the Temple should be no more. For the temple at Ierusalem & circumcision were the chiefest. How great the citie and the Temple were, it appeareth by the prayer of Salomon, 1. Kinges 8. 29. And by sundry other places. *Deuteronom,* 12. 11. *Ierem.* 3. 17. *Ezek.* 43. 7. *&c.*

And of circumcision Paul reasoneth with the Galatians, [20] *That if they be circumcised, they are bounde to keepe the whole ceremoniall lawe*: for it being one of the

Iohn. 4. 23.

Isa. 59. 20.

1. King. 8. 29.
Deut. 12. 11.
Iere. 3. 17.
Ezek. 43. 7.
Gala. 5. 3.

---

[1] As text. The words of the Samaritan woman were: " Our fathers worshipped in this mountain ; and ye say, that in Jerusalem is the place where men ought to worship." John 4 : 20. Browne's quotation combines verses 20, 21, and 23.

chiefest ceremonies, if they still obserued it, they should also obserue all the rest, but if they reiected the chiefest, they should also reiect all the rest. And to that ende Christ reasoneth, that seeing all things are nowe to be verified in spirit and trueth, therefore all ceremoniall and superstitious worship should cease. As also Paul reasoneth, *That if they be led by the spirit, they are not vnder the ceremonies of the lawe.* Gala. 5. 18. So then it appeareth that tithings, because they were ceremonies, belong not to the Church. And because such abomination is committed by them, namely, the due planting and gathering of the church is hindred, and the libertie of the Church for remouing euil ministers stopped, they are euen the execrable things which *Achan* did steale. For if the common wealth (as it ought) had long agoe taken from the ministerie those tenthes, and Popish liuings, then *Iericho* being once destroyed (I meane the Antichristian churches once put downe) had not so soone bene built againe: but nowe such tythings, benefices, and Bishoprickes remaining, they haue builded by them an other *Iericho* in steade of the first, in deede somewhat differing from the first: but as contrary to Gods church and holy citie as was the first: yea and *Master Cartwright* also will iustifie that execrable stealth of *Achan*, and call Iericho, (I meane those woefull assemblies and Parishes) the visible church and citie of God. *But cursed be the man before the Lord* (saith Ioshua) *that riseth vp and buildeth againe this citie Iericho: he shall lay the foundation thereof in his eldest sonne, & in his yongest sonne shall he set vp the gates of it.* Ioshua. 6. 26. Satan is that enuious and malitious man, which hath builded againe this citie, his eldest sonnes were the first beginners of this lamentable state, whome God did afterwarde scourge, and cal to repentance in the time of Queene Marie, and brake their enterprise: and his youngest sonnes are these latter reformers, whome God also will certainely plague except they repēt. But to come againe to *Master Cartwrights* proofe, let him [21] not say that we count any assembly, whether they haue a dumbe minister or haue none to be the outwarde Churches of God, except they keepe the couenant by the outwarde discipline and gouernement of the Church. Further *Master Cartwright* saith that in such assemblyes, the dumbe minister is not chiefe, but Christ, and that wee make nothing of the dumbe minister, and yet will needes haue him to be the head of those Churches.

Indeede we make nothing of him concerning any goodness that is by him, for he helpeth nothing thereto, but concerning the mischiefe and hurt which he doeth, or the sinne that is by him, let him not say wee make nothing of it. *For if they be beastes* (as it is written) *so that by their want of vnderstanding and conscience, the flockes of the pastour be scattered and perish, shall we say it is nothing. If they be those foolish shepheardes whome the Lorde saith by Zecharie, he will raise vp in iudgement, to sell and to slay the sheepe, to eate the flesh of the fat, and to teare them in pieces, which also shall not looke for them that are lost, nor seeke the tender lambes, nor heale that is hurt, nor feede them, but rather feede them selues vpon their flesh, shall we make nothing of such ministers*? But go to: he sayeth that Christ is the head of those assemblyes, and not the dumbe ministers. That Christ is their head or foūdation, he can not prooue, as was shewed before, wherefore for any thing he can prooue, the dumbe ministers in the absence of the Bishops and their officers, are the chiefe and heades ouer them. That they are alwayes chiefe we saide it not, for when the Bishoppes which are greater vsurpers are present, then they are heades, and both the dumbe ministers and hireling preachers, may serue well ynough to bee the tayle. For Satan hath all wayes by such, as by the taile of the dragon, drawing the third part of the starres of heauen, and cast them to the earth. What shall we vnderstande by heauen, but the shewe of the church, as it were set in heauen, & by the starres, but the children of the church, falling to wickednes and loosing their light. Such are the people of those assemblies, whom Satan hath cast vpon the earth as starres with-[22]out light. He bringeth another proofe by *Corah* and his company. For they (saith he) were not cast foorth of the lords host by Moses, therefore should not these assemblyes also which haue a dumbe minister thrust vpon them, be reputed for runnagates[1] from the Lorde, well, let vs see: was not indeede *Corah* with those that claue to him, put apart from the hoste of the Lord ? First, Moses commaunded the congregation (& the Lord so bade him) to depart from the tents of those wicked men, and touch nothing of theirs, lest they perished in their sinnes: was not this a putting apart, or a casting out ? Againe, by the word

Iere. 10. 21.

Zecha. 11. 15,
ibid. 11. 4. 5.
16.
&c.

Reuel. 12. 4.

Num. 16.
verse. 24. 25.
26.

verse. 31.

---

[1] That is, renegades, deserters, apostates.

An Answere to Master Cartwright

of the Lord in the mouth of Moses, the earth opened her mouth, and swallowed thē vp quicke. For assoone as he had ended his words (saith the text) euen the grounde claue asunder that was vnder them: was not this also a putting apart, or a casting out? The next day also fourteene thousand and seuen hundreth dyed by a plague for cleauing still to *Corah* by an aftermurmuring: was not this a putting apart? And these iudgements were both an ensample and a figure of the spirituall iudging at this day, both by excommunication, & by rebuke, and denouncing iudgement. For otherwise to what purpose is it said in the reuelation, *that the witnesses at this day,* meaning euery faithfull preacher, *are as oliue trees, and golden candlesticks standing before the god of the earth: and that fire proceedeth out of their mouthes, and deuoureth their enemies: and that they haue power to shut heauen, and power ouer waters to turne them into bloud, and to smite the earth with all maner plagues, as often as they will.* If he say that *Corah* and his company were not forthwith cast out *(though it be euident that forth-with they did cast out themselues)* he should know that there must be a time to examine their cause, yet in that short time they had of examining being but a day, for the next day they perished. We read that *Dathan* & *Abiram* would not come to be examined, and so of them selues they were put apart. As for *Corah* and his company two hundreth & fiftie, whereas they tooke censers & came before the Lord in the doore of [23] the tabernacle, they did it as vsurpers: and both in the very acte doing were separate by fire to destruction, and before the act, Moses is so farre from ioyning with them, or from allowing or tollerating their act, that he prayeth against it, saying, Lord looke not vnto their offring. Likewise that the people ioyned not with them in their censing, it is euident: for euen while they were burning incense, or before, the cōmandement was giuen, which they obeied, that they should get them away from about the tabernacle of Corah Dothā [sic] & Abiram, and touch nothing of theirs. Now if any will take uantage, that yet their cēsers were holy, as the text saith because they offred them before the Lord: & so will impute some holines to the ministery of dumbe ministers, let vs cōsider what holines this was. First, their action was altogether vnholy, & none might or did ioyne with them therein. And therfore the censers were

Reue. 11. 4.

verse. 12.

verse. 39. 40.

consecrate as a signe & remēbrāce saith the text, that no stranger which is not of the seed of Aaron, come nere to offer incense before the Lord, that he be not like Corah & his cōpanie. Wherfore those censers were holy, because they were made a holy signe of iudgement for warning to all posterities not to do the like: wherefore I would say, there were holines in the dumbe ministery, if all the dumbe ministers were hanged vp in the Churches and publike assemblies, for a warning & terrour to the rest, that are readie to enter such a function. Then indeede they were a holy signe & remēbrance of iudgemēt against such wretches, but other holines haue they none in thē. Yet *M.C.* dare say that their ministration of Sacramēts, & reading of praiers is holy & sanctified, yea so farre sanctified that we may lawfully receiue the Sacraments of them, & ioyne with thē in praiers. Belike because Moses commanded Corah & his cōpany to come with their censers, therfore those also must come with their seruice books. But did Moses cal thē for any other purpose, saue only to destroy thē ? Did he meane as *M.C.* doeth, to ioyne with them, to tollerate their ministerie, to excuse their vsurping, to pronoūce a blessing on their ministery. For indeed it is blessed if it be as he saith, that we may [24] lawfully receiue the Sacraments of them. Did not Moses say plainely, *To morrowe the Lorde will shewe who is his, and who is holy, and who ought to approche neere vnto him* ? meaning that by his terrible iudgement, he woulde shewe that they were none of his, and that there was no holinesse in their action of comming neere to the Lorde. Surely therefore, this holinesse which *M. Cartwright* imputeth to the dumbe ministers and their assemblies, is like the holinesse, whereof *Corah* spake together with his companie, saying, *That all the congregation was holy, euerie one of them, and the Lorde was among them.*

An other proofe Master Cartwright taketh by the seales of the couenant, that is, the Sacraments. They haue the Sacraments (saith he) as seales of the couenant, therfore they are within the couenant, and so are the Churches of god. Here the question falleth out, whether the sacraments are false sacraments, and counterfet seales of the couenant: He saith it is graunted him, that they are true and vncounterfaite sacraments being ministred by sufficient ministers, for (sayeth he) if we condemne the seales set to by dumbe ministers, then we

An Answere to Master Cartwright

must needes iustifie the Sacraments ministred by sufficient ministers: So by his iffs and supposings he will gather against vs what proofes he list. But though they be preaching ministers, yet are they not sufficient ministers, as we shewed before. *For if they goe out of the way, as it is written, and cause many to dash and fall by the lawe, they are not sufficient ministers, but they breake the couenant of Leui, and the Lorde will make them despised and uile before the people, because they keepe not his wayes.* If they be neuer so famous in preaching, yet if they be worldly minded men, *and whose bellies are their gods, and glorie to their shame*, they are not sufficient ministers. But why did *M.C.* so subtlely set contrary to dumbe ministers, sufficient ministers, & not rather preaching ministers. For the question is of false professors, and of a false profession, and therefore also of preachers which hold a false profession, together with their assembles: now [25] such we say are not sufficient, for they are not such as Paul appointeth in his epistle to *Timothie* and *Titus*. So herein we see howe *Master Cartwright* misseth of his proofe, and in missing doeth take a further foyle. for he reasoneth that if the Sacraments doe prooue a Church, then though they haue not the discipline commanded by Christ, yet they are the Church. But howe doeth this followe? belike he thinketh that the Sacraments may be seuered from discipline, yea and the Church also, and yet be an outwarde and visible Church of God. Howe true this is, it followeth afterwarde to be examined. First let vs stande on his proofe, that he taketh by the iudgement of other Churches in Europe, all which (saieth he) giueth the right hande of societie vnto our *English assemblyes*, which proofe he confesseth not to be so strong, yet strong ynough to stay all sudden iudgements, and so long to cause silence til on eyther side the light of the trueth doe breake foorth. I will not heare enter into that question, whether the Churches haue power to sit in mens consciences, and to shut vp mens mouthes from testifying their iudgements and consciences, for in some matters *Master Cartwright* doeth giue them that power, namely *for their verdite and sentence, which be true Churches of God*. What vantage the Pope and Papistes might take hereby for defence of their churches it may be easily iudged: and what a clog to mens consciences it were to iustifie and ioyne with all assemblies, till all the churches by general consent did

Mala. 2. 5, 6, 7, 8.

Phil. 3. 18.

Titus 1. 6, 7, 8, 9.
1. Tim. 3. 2, 3, 4, 5, 6, 7.

condemne them, let euery one iudge. But surely Paul witnesseth, *that the spirit of God in his children searcheth out all things euen the deepe things of God: yea it iudgeth and knoweth all things that are of God.* And againe he saith, *that he which is spirituall discerneth all thinges: yea he himselfe is iudged of no man*: meaning, that indeede worldly men can not rightly iudge of him. wherefore the godly may freely both iudge and giue their iudgement, euen of all assemblies which they knowe, whether they be the true Churches of God. And in another place he cōmandeth *not onely to minde, iudge & think* [26] *on all things that are true, and honest and iust, and pure but also to doe them.* Wherefore as we ought to loue the godly and their assemblyes, so our loue (as Paul teacheth vs) ought to abounde more & more in knowledge and in all iudgement, that wee may discerne thinges that differ, especially that wee may knowe the house of God from a denne of thieues. But herein *Master Cartwright* doeth much abuse vs and allso all the Churches of Europe. For neither we[2] doe cast out the churches of two whole Ilandes as he saith, neither doe they holde them all in. For though the fame of the Martyrs of Englande came to their eares, and also their doctrine & profession at that time, as they thēselues wrote it or testified it by mouth, was knowen vnto them, and then in the time of affliction they tooke them for brethren and churches, yet it followeth not, that nowe in our securitie, they heare of our canon lawes and popish gouernement & of our wofull abuses thereby, or if they doe heare, that notwithstanding they doe hastily iustifie vs. In deede they can not rashly condemne vs, because they knowe not our state: and rather they should take our assemblies to be the churches of God, for the fame they haue sometimes heard of the Martyrs. But that we which throughly knowe them, should not iudge truely and doe accordingly, it is both against reason and duetie. *For as euery plant which the heauenly Father hath not planted shall be rooted vp*: saith Christ: so in the next verse he sheweth the way to roote them vp: namely *that we put away from vs their guiding and gouerning, being blinde guides and leaders of the blinde, and let them alone.* And so with Ieremie *we shall plucke vp and roote out, destroy and throw downe euen kingdomes and nations*: that is as we saide before,

[1] Cor. 1. 10, 11, 12, 13, 14, 15.

Phil. 4. 7, 8, 9.
Phil. 1. 9.

Mat. 15. 13, 14.

Ierem. 1.

---

[1] Should be as MS., 1. Cor. 2. 10-15.
[2] Intrusive comma in text.

wee shall pronounce their wickednesse, and iudgement against them, and forsake their fellowshippe, and so leauing them to the iudgements of God, they shall surely be plucked vp and destroyed, except they repent. Wherefore let not *Master Cartwright* thinke much, if God doe set one man, euen against a whole countrey. For Ierem. 1. 17, 18. Ieremie in as good [27] times as ours are, was set against the whole lande, against the Kinges of Iudah, and against the princes thereof, against the priestes thereof, and against the people of the Lande. And in another place, *he woulde vtterly leaue the people, and goe from them, and dwell alone in the wildernesse.* And so well did he like their assemblyes, *that he calleth them all adulterers and an* Iere. 9. 2. *assemblie of rebels.* And in another place *he is forbidden to haue any fellowshippe with them, whether pleasant or vnpleasant: so that he might neither mourne with them, neither* Ier. 16. 5, 6, 7, *reioyce, neither eate nor drinke with them.* And if it bee said, 8. that *Ieremie* had a speciall commaundement, which we haue not, we knowe that all the commaundements of God, vpon the like occasions, belong vnto vs. And concerning authoritie and power, wee prooued before, that the least in the kingdome of God, hath it equall with Ieremie or any of the Prophetes. Hereby is that also aunswered which *Master Cartwright* inferreth, that if one man bee founde worthie of excommunication, the smaller part of an assembly is not to proceede against him, if the greater part will not. What doctrine is this? and what one worde of God doth he name for profe of this & diuers other such like? For though Kinges & nations & all the world, wuold [*sic*] take any knowen wretched liuer to be a brother, and communicate with him, yet neither the smaller part of an assembly, neyther I alone ought to do it. For there is a flat law set downe by the Lorde: *Thou shalt not followe a multitude to doe* Exod. 23. 2. *euill: neyther agree in a controuersie to decline after many, and ouerthrowe the trueth.* But *Master Cartwright* will saye, that this Lawe was giuen for wittnessing the trueth in publique iudgement, and not that euery one shoulde take vpon him to excommunicate. We knowe that the common wealth of Israell, and their ciuill iudgement did figure out the Lordes Spirituall iudgement in his Church: and therefore it is sayde of Saint Paul that wee are nowe Ephes. 2. 12. no more aliauntes from the common wealth of Israel: which wordes doe shewe that their Common [28] wealth did figure out our spirituall fellowshippe. But whether it did or no, the lawe is generally giuen both for ciuill iudgement, and for all dealings in controuersie, that we ought to giue true iudgement and testimonie, and not to keepe backe iudgement, or peruert the trueth for any mans cause, yet we say not that euery one may excommunicate alone. *For we ought to tell the Church,* (saith Christ), and so we should haue the church to ioyne with vs in that action. And Paul sheweth *that his spirit & theirs being met together, was ioyned as in one for excommunicating the incestuous person.* but what if the rest of the church will not ioyne with vs therein? Surely then, as we prooued before, we must set our selues against them all, we must not be afraid of their faces as the Lorde commandeth, lest he destroy vs before them. For they all, that knowing *Achans* sinne, refuse being warned to cut him off, are guiltie with him in his sinne, or if they touch or come neere the tents of *Corah, Dathan and Abiram,* they shall perish with them: or being in a citie that is fallen away to Idolatrie, if they flee not out of it, or set not them selues against it, they shall be destroyed with it. All which iudgements doe teach the Church at this day, true iudgement: namely, to set it selfe both against small & against great companyes, if they withstande or refuse the true discipline of the church. For Ieremie saith of him selfe, that he was as a contentious man, and a man that did striue with the whole earth: euery one did curse him, his owne familiars watched for his halting, as he saith in another place, he was in derision daily and euery one mocked him: for he called thē al an assembly of rebels, priuate famillar [sic] fellowshippe he brake off with them, as was shewed before, and openly he came not amongst them, but only to proclaime their sinnes, and preach vengeance against them. If it bee then asked, whether *Ieremie* did condemne them al as none of the church and people of God: let *Ieremie* him selfe answere it, for indeede by their vsuall and common profession and trade of life, they shewed not them selues to be the [29] people and Church of god. For as it is written, both the great men and rulers, and also the inferiour and poorer people had all together broken the yoke and burst the bandes. In the streetes of Ierusalem, and in the open places

Matth. 18.

1. Cor. 5.

Ierem. 1. 17.

Iosh. 7.

Nomb. 16.

Deut. 13. 15.

Iere. 15. 10.

Ierem. 20. 7, 8, 9, 10.

Ierem. 5. 1, 2, 3, 4, 5.

Ierem. 9. 23, &c.[1]

---

[1] The correct reference is Jeremiah 9 : 2, 3.

An Answere to Master Cartwright

there could not a man be fonnde [sic], that did execute iudgement and sought the trueth, that the Lord might spare the citie. And he sayeth in another place, *They are all rebellious traytours, they are brasse and yron, they are all destroyers, they shall call them reprobate siluer, because the Lorde hath reiected them. From the least of them, euen to the greatest of them, euery one is giuen vnto couetousnesse, and from the Prophet euen vnto the Priest, they all deale falsely. They are all vnto me* (saith the Lorde againe) *as Sodome, and the inhabitants thereof as the people of Gomorrah.* yet I doe not doubt, but that there was the Church, and children of God amongest them. For Ieremie him selfe and Barucke was with them: for *Isaiah* witnesseth *that when iudgement was turned backwarde, and iustice stoode a farre off, so that all trueth and equitie failed, yet* (I say) *there were some that refrained from euill, and were made a pray to the rest.* In deede openly there was none to reforme the church: of all his children there was none that tooke her by the hande to bring her into the way. For the Lorde sought for a man among them that shoulde make the hedge, and stande in the gappe before him for the land, that he should not destroy it, but he found none. Yet there were those that had a marke on their foreheades, as mourning and crying for all the abominations that were committed. And if it be asked, whether these were a visible church of God, it is answered by Ezekiel in another place, that among the heathen and in the countreyes where the Lorde did scatter them, he was as a litle Sanctuarie, vnto them: whereby is meant, that though they wanted the visible figure signe of the tēple and Sanctuarie at Ierusalem, yet their holy conuersation shoulde shewe the Lord to be among them, and that the Lorde would iudge betweene sheepe and sheepe, betweene the rammes and the goates. It is manifest that the Synago-[30]gues of the Iewes in Antiochia and Ephesus were the churches of God: yet when Christ was preached vnto thē, and they withstoode Paul and Barnabas, did Paul or Barnabas stay for the consent of the most part to cast them off? Did they not foorthwith separate the disciples, and gather the church apart from thē? yea will *M.C.* say: for that they were worthy to be cast off, seeing they refused Christ. Then belike it is true, that one man or a fewe persons may cast off whole churches, for some greater sinnes or offences. How then is it true which *M.C.*

Ierem. 6. 28.

Ierem. 23. 14.

Isa. 59. 14, 15.

Isa. 51. 18.

Ezek. 22. 30.

Ezek. 9. 4.

Ezek. 11. 16.

Ezek. 34. 17.

Act. 13. 46. 51.

Act. 19. 9.

457

saith, that one man being founde & iudged to deserue separation, should not be separate except the most part do consent ? He will say peraduēture, that he excepteth idolaters & apostates frō the Lord. why then did he giue a generall rule, without naming such exceptiōs ? yet Christ for all disobedience in refusing any message of God, doth giue cōmandement, euen to all and euery one of his messengers, to cast off whole cities and churches, as being in a worse case then Sodome and Gomorrha. *For if they receiue you not,* sayeth he, *nor heare your wordes, when ye depart out of that house or that citie, shake off the dust of your feete against them.* He will answere, that their sinne also of not receiuing the messengers of Christ, was the sinne of Apostacie. And is not this a message from Christ, when one or a fewe persons doe iustly rebuke the congregation for ouerthrowing the Lordes discipline and treading his scepter vnder foote ? and is not his scepter cast downe, and his kingdome polluted, when he which is manifestly knowen and prooued to deserue separation, can not be cast out ? But againe he will say, that those cities and churches were not cast off, for refusing the Lordes messengers, but for refusing such a message as they brought: namely that the Christ and Messiah was nowe come in the flesh. Surely til after the death of Christ, they had no such message. For Christ straightly charged his disciples, that they should tell no man, that he was Iesus the Christ: meaning that till his death and rising againe, it is not meete that that doctrine [31] should be blased abroad, but it was sufficient for that time, if they generally beleeued in the Messiah, as the Iewes also did, and refused him not when he shoulde be preached more clearely. yet long before his death was the commandement giuen, concerning those houses or cities, which shoulde refuse his messengers. yet in deede it is true, that they which refuse his discipline and gouernement, do also refuse Christ him selfe: and so it is the sinne of apostacie. For so it is written, *Those mine enemies which woulde not, that I shoulde reigne ouer them, bring hither and slay them before me.* But hereto they will answere, that yet till iudgement was executed by the Lorde him selfe, they were called his Citizens: for so the text sayeth that his Citizens hated him, and sent an ambassage after him, saying, we wil not haue this man to reigne ouer vs. But doe they not

knowe, that they are called his Citizens, because they
should haue bene so, and were not, but became his
enemies. Indeede they were Citizens in name only, but
not in deed. So Ierusalem in name was called the citie Reuel. 11. 8.
of God, yet in deede it became that great Citie, as it is
written, which spiritually is called Sodome and Ægypt,
where our Lorde also was crucified. The Iewes were
planted a noble vine as Ieremie witnesseth: and Isaiah Isa. 5. 7.
sayeth, that the vineyard of the Lorde of Hostes was the
house of Israel, and the men of Iudah (were sometymes)
his pleasant plant, but nowe they are turned vnto me
sayeth the Lorde into the plantes of a strange vine, yea Iere. 2. 21.
that we be not beguiled with the Names of Gods house,
Church, and Citie, he him selfe hath giuen it a name,
as it is written, the name of that city shalbe from that
day. *The Lord is there.* And in this respect also it is Ezek. 48. 35.
called in Ieremie the throne of his glorie. As who say
that amōg whōsoeuer we see not the Lord to reigne by
his gouernement & discipline, as it were in the throne of
his kingdom, them we shuld iudge not to be the city Iere. 14. 21.
& church of God. And though the church do pray, Ezek. 43. 7.
that God would not cast downe the throne of his glory,
nor breake the coue-[32]nant with them: yet Ieremie
bringeth in those wordes as a complaint of the penitent,
and not to proue that the wretched sorte either helde
the couenant, or were the throne of God. Wherefore
to conclude this matter, *The path and way of the Lord
is holy,* as the prophet teacheth, *& no polluted shal passe* Isa. 35. 8.
*by it: there shalbe no lyon, no noysome beast shall ascend by
it, neither shall they be founde there.* Whereby is meant
that open and grosse sinners shall not be suffred in the
Church. For either they shall be separate by excommunication, or els all the godly shall withdraw them
selues from them, and hold them accursed. As it is 1. Cor. 16. 22.
written, If any man loue not the Lorde Iesus, let him
be had in execration, yea excommunicate to death. Luke. 19. 27.
And surely they loue not the Lorde, but are his enemies,
as was shewed before, which refuse his gouernment,
that he can not reigne ouer them. And againe it is
written, *This is the loue of God, that we keepe his commande-* 1. Ioh. 5. 3.
mēts, and he that sayeth I knowe god, or I loue god, and keepe 1. Joh. 2. 4, 5.
not his commaundementes, is a lyar, and the trueth is not in him.
Not that we can keepe his commandements without all
breach or offence, for wee are not Donatistes as the
aduersaries slāder vs: that we should say, we may be

without sinne, or that the church may be without publike offences, or if there fall out some sort of grosser sinnes, that therefore it should cease to be the church of God. We teach no such doctrine, but if in any Church such grosse sinnes bee incurable, and the Church hath not power to redresse them, or rebelliously refuseth to redresse them, then it ceaseth to be the Church of God, and so remaineth till it repent, & take better order.

And here cometh in that question to be decided, whether without the discipline comaunded of Christ, any assembly or church may be called the church of Christ. *M.C.* saith, that for want of this discipline, we giue al the english assemblies, the blacke stone of condemnation. Howe truely he writeth this of vs, his conscience is witnes. for we neuer said that all the English assemblyes doe want discipline. Thogh this matter be sufficiently debated before, yet let vs weigh [33] *Master Cartwrights* answer. H[e] sayeth that faith in Christ is the essence, being, or life of the church: as for discipline it is but accidental, and therefore the Church of God may haue her being and life, and be named the church of God, without discipline. What worde of God doeth he bring for all this? we knowe in deede that Christ is the life and essence of the Church.

Iohn. 15. 6. For except as braunches we abide in him, which is the true vine, we can bring foorth no fruite, we are cast foorth as branches, and are to be consumed with fire. Christ is the resurrection and the life. He is the way,

Iohn. 11. 25.
Iohn. 14. 6. the truth, and the life. So it is true, that Christ is the life of the church, as for faith it is but the hand, whereby we take hold of this life: As it is written, *he that beleeueth in the sonne, hath euerlasting life*, and he addeth vpon it, as a tryall of faith, euen our obedience to the sonne,

Iohn. 3. 36. and saith, *he that obeyeth not the sonne, shall not see life, but the wrath of god abideth on him.* Nowe it was prooued before, that they which are guilty of such horrible abuses, & so grossely offende by their corrupt & false profession, haue not this faith, neither do holde Christ the foundation. But see, how fondly & blasphemously *Master Cartwright* distinguisheth: He will haue a dead Christ, or an Idol christ to be the life of the church. For he will ioyne the church to Christ, without the discipline and gouernement of Christ. He putteth asunder the church and the discipline of Christ, and so must needes sunder Christ from his owne discipline or gouernement. Nowe Paul calleth this discipline, the power of our Lorde Iesus christ. So if wee seuer christ and his power, what is he but a dead christ? Also by his discipline, and gouernement he hath ouer vs, he is our king: as againe it is written, *the scepter of thy kingdome is a scepter of righteousnesse.* So if we seuer christ, and his discipline, rule, and gouernement what is he but an Idol christ? If *Master Cartwright* say, that by the scepter there is meant nothing else but the power of the worde of God, I graunt it: as Paul saith, I will knowe not the speach or wordes of these men, [34] but the power[1]: *For the kingdome of God is not in worde, but in power saith he,* and in the psalme, *The Lorde shall sende the rodde of thy power out of Zion*[.] *And the weapons of our warrefare are mighty through God,* as againe he writeth. So then if the power of the word to bynde & lose, to remit or retaine mens sinnes, to promise lyfe, and to rebuke and giue ouer to execration, be taken from Christ or the church of Christ, what remaineth but an Idol or counterfet christ, an Idol or counterfet church? Thus while *M.C.* wil haue faith in christ to be the life of the church without discipline, he doth leaue christ himselfe without life, & as one that is dead, or turned into an Idol. yet further he proceedeth in his absurdities, & blasphemies, & sayth, *that fayth only is the essence, being, or life of the church, and that besides faith, nothing is necessary to the very essence and being of the church.* Thus belike children which yet through want of discretion, can not haue faith, shall be without the essence & life of the church. How corrupt doctrine this is, I neede not heere stand on it. If he say that by the faith of the parēts they haue life & essēce in the church, the scripture is against him. For by the promise & the couenant made to the righteous & to their seed are their childrē reckoned in the church & not by their faith. Therefore the faythful are called by Paul *the children of promise. For we are* (sayeth he) *after the maner of Isaac children of the promise,* and againe to the Romans, *the children of the promise are counted for the true seede of Abraham.* But that by any mans faith his children or others, should haue life & essence in the church, is the same false doctrine we refuted before. *For the iust shall live by his fayth* saith Habbakk [*sic*]. If then a mā shall liue by his

1. Cor. 5. 4.

Hebr. 1. 8.
Psal. 45. 6. 7.

1. Cor. 4. 18. 19.

Gene. 17. 7.

Gal. 4. 18.
Rom. 9. 8.

Hab. 2. 4.

---

[1] The Scriptural references following are not in the text, but in the margin of the MS. We have some of them : *Ps.* 110. 2., 2 *Cor.* 10. 4.

owne faith, he shall not liue by the faith of another. And by baptising into the fayth and profession of any, we must vnderstande, that we are baptized to holde the same fayth and profession, when wee come to discretion, and not to haue our lyfe and saluation by an other mans fayth, when as yet we haue not the same fayth our selues. And if wee shall liue by faith, then fayth is the meanes to come by [35] lyfe, and is not the life it selfe. Wherefore Christ is the life and essence of the Church, and not faith. Nowe Christ is made as no christ vnto vs, except we holde him, and ioyne with him as our annointed King, priest and Prophet. For so the word (*Christ*) doth signifie. And here I demande of *M.C.* whether the Kingdome, Priesthood, & Prophecie of Christ be of the essence and life of the Church. I am sure he dare not say nay to this: and why then will he haue the Lordes discipline or gouernement, to be but an accident or hangby[1] to the church. *For by Christ as paul sheweth, (that is by the graces of Christes kingdom, priesthood & prophecie) all his body, (that is all his Church) are coupled & knit together by euery ioynt, and so receyueth increase and edifying in God.* So take away the kingdom and gouernement of Christ, and there can be no ioyning, nor coupling together of the church, no offices nor callings in the Church, yea, no face, or shewe, or rather no parte, signe or token of the church. For these graces do we receiue of Christs kingdome or from his imperiall Maiestie. And therefore it is writtē, that *when he ascended vp on hie,* (as our triumphant King and Gouernor) *he led captiuitie captiue, and gaue giftes vnto men,* and againe, he ascended far aboue all heauēs, that he might fill all things. And wherfore is the church and people of God in so many places, called the throne of God and the kingdome of God, but only to shewe that without the discipline and gouernement of Christ therein, it loseth euē her essēce, life & being in christ. And this *M.C.* is forced to cōfesse. For he saith, that the ministery of the word is a part of this discipline, & the obedience of the people is another: & so reasoneth, that, take away all discipline & euery part thereof, & there remaineth no church of christ. Thus the truth hath made him to yeeld in battell, and turned him backwarde, and yet he will resist as it were going backward. For how backewardly doeth he deale in this matter? to say that

Rom. 3. 22.

Eph. 4. 16.

Eph. 4. 8.

Iere. 14. 21.
Ezek. 43.
Mat. 13. 7. &c.

---

[1] hangby — appendage; now obsolete. See *N.E.D.*

discipline is not pertaining to the essence of the church, & now for wāt of discipline, to take away the essence and name of the Church. Againe to say, without discipline, there may be a church, and nowe [36][1] to say that without discipline, there can be no church. So rather then he will be without an enemie, he will fight with a shadowe. For nowe full wisely he doeth cut discipline into partes : namely the ouersight, rule, and gouernement of such as haue charge in the church, and the obedience of the people thereto: which two partes indeede doe conteine[2] all the other partes, and therefore very vainely he speaketh of other partes of discipline as if they might be separate and secluded from these. For he can shewe none in the church, but either gouernours, or vnder gouernement : neither can he shewe any duetie in the church, but onely the dueties of gouernement or of submission and obedience : neither any worke, matter, businesse, or ministerie in the church, but either of charge and ouersight, or vnder charge or ouersight. Wherefore take away both gouernement and ouersight, & also obedience and submission, and there can be no other part of discipline remaining. For the dueties of teaching, exhorting, improouing, rebuking &c. also all dueties of examining and deciding controuersies, of reforming abuses, of relieuing and maintaining the afflicted and poore, of separating the vnworthy &c. are contained vnder that parte of gouerning. Also all dueties of beleefe and learning the trueth, of reuerence, honour, meekenesse and all kinde of seruice and vpright behauiour &c. are contained vnder that part of obedience and submission. Thus it is manifest, that through want of discipline, there is no naturall coniunction of the partes and members of the church together, so that both the head and vitall partes are wanting, and all the other partes are wholy and throughly either displaced and peruerted, or vtterly lost and perished. But why doeth he not shewe what part of discipline may be wanting, yea and of those two partes, which he sayeth can not be wanting, yet what defect there may be. Indeede it[2] is commanded *to forgiue a brother, if he sinne seuen times in a day, and seuen times in a day turne againe to vs, saying, it repenteth me, yea we must forgiue, though it were vnto seuentie times*[2] *seuen tymes.* [37][3] But yet Christ giueth no power

Luke. 17. 4.
Matt. 18. 22.

[1] Wrongly paged (34) in text.
[2] Intrusive comma in text.
[3] Wrongly, " 35 " in text.

to forgiue, if a brother remaine wilfull in his sinne, yea if it be but a priuate sinne, I am to proceede against him, and am not to cease, till either I haue brought him to repentance, or haue broken off all fellowshippe with him, as with a brother. But we must take heed, that they be brethren, and not dogs and scorners whō we rebuke and labour to redresse. *For if thy brother trespasse against thee, saith Christ &c.* then he sheweth howe to deale and complaine for reformation of a brother. But concerning scorners it is written, *Hee that reprooueth a scorner, purchaseth to him selfe shame: and he that rebuketh the wicked, getteth him selfe a blot*: againe, *Rebuke not a scorner least he hate thee, but rebuke a wise man, and he wil loue thee.* But to be short: All the discipline of the church consisteth herein, first that the church be gathered of the worthie: as it is written, *Enquire who is worthie*: and againe, *Giue ye not that which is holy to dogges, neither cast ye your pearles before swine.* And in Ieremie *If thou take away the precious from the vile, then shalt thou be as my mouth: let them returne vnto thee, but returne not thou vnto them.* And in Ezekiel, *They shall teach my people the difference betweene the holy and prophane, and cause them to discerne betweene the vncleane and the cleane.* And in Malachie *the Lorde reiected their offerings, because they offered the scrobled*[1], *and the lame and the sicke and the blinde*, which figureth the reiecting of our sacraments, when dogges and swyne do communicate therein. When Papistes and Atheistes, *drunkardes, Maygamesters, blasphemers, raglers, fighters and such like*, are presented as sweete breade at the table of the Lorde. The seconde point of discipline is, that the couenant, promises, and Gospel of Christ and the sacraments of his kingdome, being established among the worthie, then that they keepe the couenant & sacraments vnpolluted. And for this purpose there are appointed these other partes of discipline: namely *that the Church doe iudge those which are within: for it hath nothing to doe*, saith Paul, *to iudge those that are without.* The discipline of the church poceedeth [*sic*] against the bre-[38]thrē that offend, as was shewed before, & not against scorners, or careles worldlings. For the lord doth now *take vs of the gentiles for priests & leuites*, as it is written, and as wee may not bring into *the lords sanctuary strangers, & vncircumcised in heart, to pollute his house*, that is wicked wretches which haue not the lords couenāt,

Matth. 18. 15.
Prou. 9. 7, 8.

Matth. 10. 11.
Matth. 7. 6.
Iere. 15. 19.

Ezek. 44. 23.

Mala. 1. 13.

Vers. 7

1. Cor. 5. 12.

Isa. 66. 21.
ezek. 44. 7.

---

[1] " torn " in *A.V.* Now obsolete, probably equivalent to modern scrubby, mean, shabby.

An Answere to Master Cartwright

may not be receiued into fellowship of the church: so those that are within being fallen to transgression, *they shal iudge according to my iudgements saith the Lord, and they shall keepe my lawes and my statutes in all my assemblies.* For there is a particular iudging & dealing against any in the church, as by particular rebuke, & pronouncing accursed him that grossely offendeth, & there is a general iudging of any without the church. For it is written, that we shal iudge the angels, And euery nation that shall rise vp in iudgement against the church, shal it condemne. this iudging is no part of the particular iudging we speak of. And here come in, other parts of discipline to be spoken of: namely for priuate rebuke of the brethren that priuately offend, for open rebuke of open sinnes, & for casting off & forsaking felowship & brotherhood with grosse & open offenders. These partes of discipline, although they are prooued & made manifest before, yet because *M.C.* saith that some part of discipline may bee wanting, let vs see which of them may be wanting, and the church notwithstanding haue the essence and name of the church. *First Christ hath gieun [sic] power to euery christian to reteyne the sinnes of euery brother whom he knoweth to trespasse against him, & not to forgiue hym, except he see him repēt.* So that if any person want[1] this power, he is not to be counted a christian. And this power reacheth so far, not only for open but euen for priuate offences, to iudge & take any man for a heathen & a publican, if he wil not be reformed. Now this liberty & power, euery christian must hold, or els he is the seruāt of mē, & not of christ. If then a particular christian cannot want[1] it, how shal the whole church be without it, & yet be named the church of christ? Euery particular christiā [39] is a king & a priest vnto god, a king because he holdeth the scepter of gods word, to iudge the offēders, a priest because in euery place he offreth incense and a pure offring to the name of the Lord *as it is in Malachy.* So thē he is vtterly without the kingdō & priesthod of christ, if that liberty be denied him, I mean of iudging & rebuking the particular offenders, & forsaking their fellowship if they wil not be reformed. Howe much more shall the Church be without this kingdō, & priesthod of christ, & so without christ hymself, if it want this libertie & power. Likewise as we shewed before

verse. 24.

1. Cor. 6.
Isa. 54. 17.

Luke. 17. 4.
Mat. 18.

1. Cor. 7. 23.
Reue. 1. 6.

1. Pet. 2. 5.
exodus 19. 6.
Reue. 2. 26.
Mal. 1. 11

ephe. 5. 7.

---

[1] These are instances where the use of " want " in the sense of " lack " needs to be watched.

2. Thes. 3. 6.	euery christian hath power seuerally to forsake wicked
2. Tim. 3. 5.	fellowship, & not to cōpany together with wicked
1. Iohn. 1. 6, 7.	brethrē. And as by this liberty & power, they vphold
Hose. 2. 2.	their Kingdō in Christ, so without it, both they and
Act. 2. 40.	the whole church do lose their interest in the priesthood
1. Cor. 5. 11.	and kingdom of Christ, and so are none of his church.

For they haue not the keyes of the kingdom of heauē to bind & lose, to reteine or remit mens sinnes, and therefore what right can they haue in the kingdom of christ. If they cannot openly & particularly rebuke,

Iohn. 20. 23.
Mat. 16. 19.

how shall they openly & particularly binde? and if they cañot openly & particularly cast out or excōmunicate the grosser offenders, how shal they binde? For being still reteined as brethrē in the church, how shall they pronounce them to be boūd in heauē? How shall they shut the gates of heauen against those, whom still they keepe in the bosome of the church? If *M.C.* say that a general rebuke, & iudging of the wicked is a binding, let him knowe that the Church hath more liberty & right, particularly to iudge those which are within, then generally to iudge those that are without. And surely, if it haue not power to iudge those which are within, it hath no power of iudging at all. So that it is manifest, that no part of church discipline can be wanting, but the church doth straightway go to ruine thereby. For a cōfused gathering of al together, was proued to be no church of God. Likewise if the couenant of the church, & the sacraments thereof, be broken and disanulled, *Master C.* graunteth that there is no church: and nowe it is shewed that [40][1] without that power of rebuking and iudging those which are within, and of excommunicating those that deserue it, there can be no church of God. As for that his fonde answere, that for some default in preaching, and some default in obedience, the discipline of the church may fayle and yet be the church, let him knowe that though some preacher or other person offende, yet doeth not therefore the discipline of the church fayle or want, except the church be negligent, or wilfully refuse to redresse such offences, or is brought into bondage that it cannot redresse them. And yet also the question is not of some weakenes and failing in discipline but a full want and ouerthrowe either of the whole, or of some parte thereof. Wherefore that proofe they

---

[1] Mistakenly " 37 " in text.

An Answere to Master Cartwright

alleadge by the Corinthians, that they wanted discipline, & yet were the church of God, is false & very vaine. For they wanted it not, but were negligent therein. They were not vnder the bondage of a popish discipline, & power, which denyed and withhelde the Lordes discipline. Nowe negligence was a fault in them, yet not an vtter ouerthrowe and failing of disci- 2. Cor. 7. 11. pline. For being rebuked of Paul, they mended this negligence, in so much that their repentance and sorowe for their negligence wrought a great care in them, yea as the text saith, *a clearing of them selues, an indignation, a feare, a great desire, a zeale, a punishing of themselues.* Likewise for their abuses in the Sacrament 1. Cor. 11. 20. of the Supper, Paul condemneth euen the Supper, and sayeth, *This is not to eate the Lordes Supper.* And for abusing that Sacrament, many of them were plagued of God, and dyed. So that although for a tyme, they turned the Sacrament to be a iudgement against thē, & the discipline of the church did fayle, yet was it not therefore quite ouerthrowē & debarred from thē. Also whereas some beleeued not the resurrection frō 1. Cor. 15. 34 the dead, it was the ignorance of those which had 35. newly imbraced the Christian profession, and not the ouerthrowe of the church discipline. And here is that answered which *M.C.* alledgeth, that Paul calleth the churches of God by the ti-[41]-tle of the faythfull and Sayntes. For though some fall away vnto wickednesse, yet by the discipline of the Church the rest doe remaine as Saintes. And that tytle of Saintes is agaynst *Master Cartwright.* For if they bee Sayntes and holy, howe shall they shewe forth a wicked and vnholy profession, and still be called the Sayntes and Church of God. Though Paul wrote his Epistle to the Church and 1. Cor. 1. 2. Sayntes at Corinth, yet doeth he not thereby call the incestuous person or other grosse sinners, the members or parts of that Church. But in the fifth Chapter *he* 1 Cor. 5. 13. *calleth the incestuous person a wicked man and not a Saynt.* As for his tytle of the faithfull, he can not shewe that Paul vseth it, without addition of other wordes, to shewe the good profession of that fayth: as in that place, (*To* Ephes. 1. *the Sayntes* sayeth Paul *at Ephesus and to the faithfull*). And though the tytle of the faythfull should be vsed alone, yet must we vnderstande their fayth shewed by an outwarde good profession. Here also may that place be aunswered which they alleadge out of Paul,

1. Cor. 11. 28. Rom. 14. 13. Luke 6. 43. Mat. 12. 33. Mat. 7. 16.	*Let a man examine himselfe*: and againe to the Romans, *Let vs not therefore iudge one another any more*, but they abuse these places, as if Paul meant, *that we were not to iudge men by their fruites, or the Church had not power to iudge those that sinne in the Church*: for these things wee haue prooued before, but by iudging in that place, we must vnderstande a rash iudging or condemning of any, for those deedes or workes they doe, whereof they can giue a good and probable reason. Likewise
Mat. 7. 1.	whereas Christ sayeth, *Iudge not that ye be not iudged*, he meaneth that wee must iudge or condemne no brethren as reprobates, or rashly condemne that in them, which is no fault at all, or iudge euery man to be worse then our selues, but rather we must iudge our selues to bee
1. Tim. 1. 15. 1. Tim. 6. 14.	the chiefe sinners of all, *and yet also keepe the Lordes discipline, of iudging and rebuking the wicked, without spot and vnblameable*. Likewise *to examine our selues*, that is our owne heartes and consciences[1] belongeth to our selues: but wee are not thereby forbidden to examine the outwarde abuses and [42] faultes of others. For it is written, *that we are to consider one another. Also to
Heb. 10. 14 Rom. 16. 17. 2. Thes. 3. 14. Phil. 2. 4.	marke others diligently, to note others, that wee looke not euery man on his owne thinges, but euery man also on the things of other men*. Here also is that question answered of the Dutch Churches in hygh Germany, which holde the errour of transubstantiation. For indeede I iudge it to be an error, and not an heresie, except they obstinately pursue it with other grosse absurdities, as doe some heretikes, or with sworde and bloodshed as doe the Papistes, and then without question they are not the Church of Christ, but remaine in the state of condemnation, tyll they repent. As for those of our profession, which are withhelde from the vse of the Lordes Supper, that question followeth afterwarde to be answered, and doeth nothing at all make against vs. Likewyse that matter of neglecting circumcision and the Passeouer the space of fourtie yeeres he shamefully abuseth. For there was no negligence but a necessitie and commandement of omitting. For that seruice of the passeouer was not to be kept after their comming out of Egypt, saue at some speciall charge from the Lord
Exod. 12. 25. Exod. 13. 5. Nom. 9. 13.	as *Nom*. 9. 2. till they came into the land of Canaan: *as appeareth in Exo.* 12. 25 *and other places*. And it figured also their hasting both out of Ægypt and thorowe the

[1] Intrusive comma in text.

An Answere to Master Cartwright

wildernesse: and therefore were they not to keepe it ordinarily euery yeere, till they came to the lande of their rest. And for this cause also was circumcision omited. For being circūcised, they were sore certaine days : by reason whereof, if they had bene circumcised, they could not haue iourneyed after the cloud & tabernacle. So a necessitie was laid vpon thē. *For they were to iourney with the cloud and tabernacle as in Nombers, Whether the cloude vpon the tabernacle was taken vp by day or night. All their iourneying was by the commandement of the Lorde.* Nom. 9. 21.

Now let vs come to other of his profes. A city saith he, may be a citie, though it haue not the walles of a citie. And so he reasoneth that Ierusalem¹ was the Citie of the great King, before *Nehemiah* had builded the walles, whereupon [43] he concludeth that a Church may be the church of God, though it want discipline. Howe greatly here againe doeth *M.C.* deceiue him selfe and others. He knoweth that the Temple did figure out and signifie the church of God, as well as the citie Ierusalem. Nowe as the Temple was noe Temple of God, but a ruinous heape, without the walles of the temple, and the foundation of the walles: so the citie Ierusalem, *was said to lye waste as no citie of God, till the walles were builded and the gates reared vp*: If he require proofe of both these, we shewe him the Scripture. For in the Psalme, in Isaiah, and in Matthewe, *Christ is set downe to be the sanctuarie and head corner stone in the building.* And in the Reuelation, *the twelue Apostles are called the twelue foundations of the wall of the holy citie, and the gates the twelue trybes of Israel*, meaning all the nomber of Gods elect. Nowe therefore let him iudge, that seeing the Apostles, and all the Saintes of God, are builded in the walles of this citie, howe it can bee the citie of God without the walles. Yea he neither doeth, nor can bring any worde of God, that the walles shoulde signifie discipline onely, and not rather the gathering and building of all the saints of god, into one spirituall house & city of god. And therefore is there no mention made of any temple or other houses within the city. yea the text saith, *that there was none such, but the Lord God Almightie and the Lambe are the Temple there of.* And in the 121. psalme that hie cōmendation of the building of Ierusalē, is expounded in the 87. psalme, wherein it consisted, namely in the building of the walles & gates. Neh. 2. 3.

Psal. 118. 22.
Mat. 21. 42.
Isa. 8. 14.
Reu. 21. 14.
vers. 12.

Reue. 21. 22.
Psal. 121. 3.

¹ Intrusive comma in text.

Psal. 87. 1, 2, 3. & therfore he praiseth it, saying, *God laid his foundations*
Psal. 48. 12, 13. *among the moūtaines, the lord loueth the gates of Zion more then all the habitations of Iacob: glorious things are spoken of thee, O citie of God.* And in the fourtie and eyght Psalme, *Compasse about Zion, and goe rounde about it, and tell the towres thereof: marke well the wall thereof, Beholde
Neh. 1. 3 her towers that ye may tell your posteritie.* And in Nehemiah, the people are sayde to bee in great affliction, and in reproch, because the wal of Ierusalem was broken downe [44] and the gates thereof were burnt with fire. Wherefore the city Ierusalem, was a resemblance and figure of the spirituall Ierusalem and Church of God, onely by the walles and gates of the citie & the execution of Iudgement in the gates thereof. For in these 3. things
Psal. 122. 1, 2, 5. is described the ioy of Dauid in that Psalme: namely *That the people should go into the house of the Lorde, that their feete shoulde stande in the gates of Ierusalem, and that there were thrones set for iudgement.* Nay sayeth *Master Cartwright*, the houses & fayre buildings did figure the Church of God, and the walles did figure discipline only. This is his owne dreame, euen an imagination of his owne head. For not the houses of the city did figure the spirituall house of God or his citye, but the Temple. Neyther was the city without the walles any figure, but onely by the walles. And therefore doth
Nehem. 2. 5. Nehemiah say in the seconde Chapter, *That he woulde builde the Citie because hee meant to builde the walles of the Citie.* But let *Master Cartwright* remember himselfe, and shewe any place in the worlde, that is called a city, and yet hath not the walles of a City. Or an orcharde, garden, or close so called, without a hedge, a wall, or some safe inclosing or fensing. Are a clump of fruite trees called an orcharde, yf they stande open in the fielde without any fence? or is a fayre piece of grasse grounde named a close, if it be not enclosed. So by his owne vayne reason he ouerthroweth him selfe. And wheras he sayeth that after their returne from Babylon *the Citie is called the Citie of the great king,* euen before the walles were builded: what proofe bringeth he for that. It is called a city indeede by
Nehem. 2. 3. Nehemiah, *but a destroyed and waste Citie*: hee meaneth that it had bene a Citie, but nowe is destroyed and waste, *and he saith he would builde the citie,* (not that it was nowe a citie, for then it had bene buylded to his
verse 5. hande) but the vse of speach is, that where a citie hath

An Answere to Master Cartwright

bene, to call the place and the ruinous heape of stones by the name of the Citie. And so in Ezra, before their returne from Babylon, *The Heathen King Cyrus calleth the place of Ierusalem by the name* [45] *of Ierusalem*, yet was neither the people of God there, nor the Temple of God. *Yea Zion was plowed like a fielde, and Ierusalem was an heape, and the mountaine of the house, was as the high places of the forest*. And being in that case it figured rather the desolation of the spirituall Ierusalem, which in the *Reuelation is called Sodome and Ægypt*: and howe then could it be the City of God, saue onely in Name, for that it had bene so. Likewyse his descantyng about a vineyarde is against himselfe. For there can be no yarde or court except it haue the walles or fence of a yarde or court, and so where no yarde is, there may be vynes growing, but there can bee no vineyarde. And so where discipline is wanting, there may be some graces of God appearing, as knowledge, and an outwarde subiection to mens lawes and to Magistrates, yea there may be Gods secrete elect children, and an outwarde false shewe of religion and deuotion: and yet no true shewe nor face of an outwarde and visible Church of God.

Ezra. 1. 3.
Micah. 3. 12.
Ierem. 26. 18.
Reuel. 11. 8.

Nowe *Master Cartwright* commeth to that poynt, concerning the dumbe minister: of whome as he, so wee also haue spoken before. But here he prooueth the Sacraments, ministred by such, to be Gods Sacraments, and that men may receiue them lawfully. His proofes are like wynde blowen out of a bladder. he myght rather laugh at them him selfe, then offer them to others to take viewe of his folly. His first proofe is, they are ministers, but no lawful ministers, and they are ministers, though they be Idol mynisters, therefore he concludeth, that though they be Idoles and vnlawfull ministers, yet wee may heare them, and receyue the Sacraments of them. He confesseth them to bee vnlawfull and Idol ministers, and yet their ministration or mynisterie must be good and lawfull. This is as much, as if one should condemne a theefe and iustifie hys theft. For if they be not messengers, nor ministers from Christ, then their message and ministerie is not from Christ, but from the deuill. For these be coniugates, an vnlawfull minister, [46] and his vnlawfull ministerie: a messenger from the deuill, and his message from the deuill: a wicked man to be abhorred and his wickednes to be abhorred. Euen so it must needes followe, that a minister being vnlawfull and of the diuill, his action and deedes of ministration are vnlawfull and of the deuill. And so the Lorde reasoneth, that the people shoulde not heare the prophets that prophecied peace vnto them, for he had not sent, nor commanded them: as who say, because they were vnlawfull messengers, therefore their message also was vnlawfull and to be refused. But *Master Cartwright* sayeth that though they bee vnlawfull messengers and Ministers, & not of God, yet their message and ministerie is of god. For it is not a false or euil message or ministerie as was that of the false prophetes, but good and necessarie for the Churche. For that that is of Christ sayeth he, is good, and by their ministerie they giue us that[1] that is of Christ, hee meaneth the Sacramentes and their reading of Common seruice. And so hee concludeth that they are Ministers of good thinges. Yea and hee addeth[1] a further distinction: that to vs they are ministers of god, but to themselues or in respect of them selues, they are vnlawfull ministers. Surely these are trimme distinctions to carrye him blyndefolde, hee can not tell whether [*sic*]. For whether [*sic*] will hee wander in his vanities? or howe many deuilish doctrines will hee heape vp together? First hee sayeth, they are vnlawfull ministers, and yet ministers of god: then that they are ministers of god, but not lawfull ministers of god: Thirdly that they haue their calling and allowaunce by the Church and yet are thrust vpon the Church: Fourthly that eyther such dumbe ministers, and theyr ministerie is [*sic*] of GOD: or if they bee of the Diuell, yet if the Bishoppe and his officers doe authorize them, then the Churche doeth authorize them, and noe man ought to refuse them: Fiftely that their reading of seruice[1] is to bee heard, as being a good thing from christ: Sixtly that their sacraments [47][2] are to bee receiued as good thinges from Christe: Whereby also it followeth that Christe doeth sende such dumbe, or blynde reading ministers to take charge of the people: also that for a neede, reading ministers may bee in the Churche in steade of preaching ministers: Further that the byshoppes maye thrust vpon the flocke,

Ier. 23.
vers. 16.
vers. 21.

---

[1] Intrusive comma.
[2] Mistakenly "37" in text.

An Answere to Master Cartwright

what Ministers they lyst, and giue them that authoritie and calling which God can not giue them: Also that the people shall bee counted Gods people and Churche, though they bee vnder the deuilles messengers, and subiect to his guyding. Howe vngodly and foolishe doctrine is all this? and yet hee heapeth much more vnto it, before his letter bee ended. It is written that *the Lorde is ryghteous in all his wayes and holy in all his workes.* If then anye Minister bee of God howe shall he bee an vnlawfull minister? or if he bee vnlawfull, howe shall he be of God? If he say a thing may be lawfull before men, which before GOD is not so, and therefore that men maye take it as lawfull before God: Let hym remember him selfe, that hee speaketh of vnlawfull ministers euen before men, yea whome hee himselfe knoweth and calleth vnlawfull. So that beeyng vnlawfull ministers both before men, and before God, how shall they be ministers of god? Wherefore they are of the Deuill, and plantes which the heauenly Father hath not planted, and therefore shall bee rooted vp: and christ sheweth the way to roote them vp: namely, that we let them alone blinde guides, leaders of the blinde, and haue nothing to doe with their guyding and ministerie. For christ did gather his disciples aparte from the Pharisees disciples, so that the Pharisees were to haue no charge, nor ouersight on christs disciples. This appeareth in very many places of the Euangelists. Againe he distinguiseth that he is a minister, and leaueth out his wordes of lawfull and vnlawfull, of god and not of god: So he woulde fray vs with the bare worde (minister). If they bee Satans [48] ministers shoulde we receiue them, because they beare the name of ministers: *There are prophets also, which come to vs in sheepes clothing,* shoulde we receiue them, being false prophets, because they beare the name of prophets? Therefore these are vyle and vngodly mockeries, wherewith *Master Cartwright* woulde delude vs. Further he distinguisheth, that to the dumbe ministers them selues their ministery is a matter of destruction, but to the church, it is, he can not tell what good thing, or gratious benefite from Christ. Wee shewed before, that they doe good to others, *like those foolish shepherdes* named in Zechary, *whom God did raise vp in iudgement to sell and to slay the sheepe. Also like Corah and his companie, by whome so many thousandes perished.*

Psa. 145. 17.

Mat. 15. 13, 14.

Luke. 5. 33.
Mar. 2. 18.
Iohn 3. 25.
Iohn. 9. 27, 28.

Actes. 8. 21
Mat. 7. 15.

Zech. 11. 4, 5.
verse 15, 16.
Nom. 16. 39,
40, 49.

Or like the priestes of Baal, or the shepheardes spoken of in
Ezekiel: *which did eate the fat, and clothe them selues with the wooll, and slewe them that were fedde. but fed not the sheepe: the weake they strengthened not, the sicke they healed not, neither bound vp the broken, nor brought again that which was driuen away, neither sought vp that which was lost: but with crueltie and violence doe they rule them,* as these doe by their cannon power and spirituall courtes. For they, the Byshoppes, and their officers are those *that thrust with side and with shoulder, and push with their hornes all the weake of the flocke, till they vtterly scatter them abroade.* It is a wonder, that any man should speake of any good the blind ministers doe. For through their woeful ministerie, and through that lamentable bondage of popish discipline, we may well say with Ieremie *that wickednesse is gone foorth into all the lande. They strengthen also the handes of the wicked, that none can returne from his wickednesse. They are all vnto me* saith the Lorde *as Sodome, and the inhabitantes thereof as Gomorah.* But let vs see, what are those things[1] of Christ, which he saith the dumbe ministers can giue vs. Forsooth the Sacraments and the reading of common seruice. Indeede *they haue gotten the censers of Corah and his companies* and they are made priestes of such places and churches, as the Lorde as yet doeth not choose to put his name there. Wherefore [49] as we shewed before, both their censings and their offrings, that is their prayers and sacraments are reiected of the Lord as execrable things. They are those strangers named in Ezekiel and in Nombers, which are not of the Leuites nor of the seede of Aaron, but doe pollute the Lordes house, and can not offer the sweete incense and pure offerings, which Malachie speaketh of. Their Sacraments are stollen and counterfet badges, and howe then shoulde we receiue them as markes of the true church of God. They offer the incense of Nadab and Abihu. For their stinted forme of seruice, deuised by the Byshoppes, and translated from the Massebooke, can neuer be prooued to be incense made by fire from the Altar of the Lorde. But yet *Master Cartwright* will iustifie their Sacraments and reading of seruice. Let vs therefore see to his proofes. One proofe is this, the Scribes and Pharises might be heard preaching true doctrine, therefore the dumbe ministers may be heard reading seruice: a goodly proofe. For it was lawfull for

[1] Intrusive comma in text.

the Pharisees to bee preachers of the trueth, and it was a parte of their office and ministerie: but it is not lawfull to be a blinde reading minister, neither is it any parte of the ministerie, to reade ouer such a stinted form of seruice. Wherefore though I may heare and like of that, which is truely preached, yet doeth it not followe, that I shoulde heare, like of, or ioyne with, that which is vngodly, and blasphemously spoken, vttered or done. Againe he abuseth that place in Matthew, *saying, that it was cōmanded by Christ to heare the Scribes.* There is no cōmandement giuen to heare, but to do as they knewe the Pharises taught truely. And though by occasion they might heare them teaching trueth, yet were they separate as was shewed before, from being their disciples: they were not vnder their charge and ministerie, as those are nowe vnder the dumbe ministers charge, whome *Master Cartwright* doeth iustifie in hearing them, and receiuing the Sacraments of them. Hee can not shewe that the Pharises were no Leuites nor Priestes, and yet offered the sacrifices [50] as the Priestes. And yet these doe minister the Sacraments, and will be Priestes ouer the people, beyng neither to bee counted brethren, nor Chrystyans. And though the Pharises or Scribes had so farre vsurped, yet shoulde not the people haue partaken with them the sacrifices, no more ought the people at this day[1] to partake in the Sacraments with such blinde ministers. But why doth not *Master Cartwright* perceiue, that his owne proofe is against him selfe. For if the Scribes and Pharises were to be heard because they preached trueth, then are these dumbe ministers not to bee hearde, because they are no preachers. But this proofe fayling, *Master Cartwright* prepareth another, namely this. The Scribes and Pharisees[1] were as vnfit and as vnlawfull ministers[1] as our reading ministers and yet might be heard, therefore our reading minysters may bee heard. Howe vnfitte ministers the Pharisees were, it is after examined. We saye not, but that the dumbe ministers may be heard. For if standing on the gallouse to be executed, they say they woulde come downe, I knowe we maye heare them. But the question [is] whether we may be vnder their charge and guiding, and so daily and vsually heare them, as our spirituall guides, pastours, watchmen for our soules, and ministers in the church. This *Master Cartwright* can not prooue, and

[1] Intrusive comma.

therefore his proofe serueth for another matter, quite besides the question. Yea if he looke well, this proofe serueth against him. For the disciples of Christ were not to heare the Pharisees, as being their disciples and vnder their charge, therefore may not we be vnder the dumbe ministers charge, to heare them as our teachers, and guides in Christ. Another proofe he giueth thus: The dumbe ministers haue a calling by the Church, as the scribes and Pharisees had: therefore wee may lawfully heare them and receiue them as ministers. In this proofe wee haue these matters to consider whether our dumbe ministers haue as good a calling as the scribes and Pharisees had. Whether the bishops and their officers that [51] call ministers are to be counted the Church: whether if the church shoulde appoint and receiue a dumbe minister, he had thereby any whit more authoritie, or were any whit the rather to be receiued. *It is certaine, that Ezra was a Scribe, and a priest also of the sonnes of Aaron, as wee may reade in the booke of Ezra, and Nehemiah. And in other places other Scribes also were mentiond, which were both writers and preachers of the Lawe and worde of God. And therefore Christ saith, that they sate in Moses seate, That is, as it is in the 8. of Ezra, They were chosen being men of vnderstanding to preache, and minister to the people as their office required. Yea by the Priestes and Elders & consent of the Congregation were they chosen.* But dare *Master Cartwright* say that our dumbe ministers are thus chosen and called? or dare he say that they sit in Moses seate? If then he bring it for a good profe, *That the Scribes & Pharises were to be heard, because they sate in moses seat,* then it is also a good or better proofe, *That these dumbe ministers doe not sit in moses seat, and therefore are not to be heard & receiued as ministers. In the Church and assemblyes of the Iewes, there could be no suche dumbe ministrie suffered, as an ordinarie office and calling.* For herein consisted their ministerie, *To teach Iaacob the iudgements of God and Israel his lawes, to put incense before his face, and the burnt offering vpon the altar.* And so the dumbe minister can haue no office nor calling in the Church, seeing there is no such ministerie, nor parte of ministerie, as to be a reading minister. Furthermore if *Master Cartwright* saye, that the Bishoppes and their officers are the Church, and that therefore the dumbe ministers are called by the Church: First it is to bee shewed, that *Master Cartwright* can not prooue them to bee the

Marginal references: Ezra. 7. 6, 11. Nehem. 8. 1, 2, 4. Luke 11. 46. Ezra. 8. 16. Ierem. 8. 8. Nom. 3. 6. Exod. 29. Mat. 22. 35. Nom. 8. 9. Deut. 33. 10.

An Answere to Master Cartwright

Churche, yea it was prooued before, that they are not the Churche of God.

Then also he is against him selfe herein, for he confessed before, *That the dumbe ministers are thrust vpon the Churche, and howe then can they bee called by the Churche:* Thyrdely, [52] if they were called, and then both the maner of calling bee altogether blasphemous and wicked, and the office whereto they are called[1] is none of the church offices and callings, of what weight or authoritie shall their calling be? Shall wee haue strange officers and ministeries in the Church, which God hath not appointed? or shall wee giue any authoritie or reuerence vnto them, because men account of them? shal the blasphemie and wickednesse of a number, though they be named the Church, make me any whit the more[1] to receiue a dumbe minister, because they doe wickedly and blasphemously call and authorize him. Nay, *I ought not to followe a multitude to doe euill.* Exod. 23. 2. For it is not as *Master Cartwright* would haue it, that the moe which sinne in a matter, the lesse the sinne is: but rather it is the more grieuous, and more to be abhorred. And Paul giueth this libertie to Timothie, *That though other* 1. Tim. 5. 22. *men euen the Elders and people shoulde choose any vnmeete minister, yet hee shoulde not partake with them in their sinne.* And if in the acte of chusing, the authoritie of the church is not to be regarded, when it shamefully abuseth her authoritie, then also in the wickednesse & sinne that is wrought by the choyse, it is lesse to be regarded. For the reading ministerie is abominable wickednesse, and as it first ouerthrewe the Churches of God, and brought 1. Tim. 3. in Antichrist, so is it still the doore and high way to all ignorance, dissolutenesse, and all wicked practises and customes. Wherefore let *Master Cartwright* laye away his fonde distinction that they are ministers, though they be vnlawfull ministers. For if the reading ministerie be no office nor calling appointed by christ, then is it an office of Antichrist: *And why then shoulde he sticke so much on the worde minister, if they be Antichristian and deuilish ministers? And what will he make of the Church?* It is indeede the house of the liuing God, the pillar and grounde of trueth. But *Master Cartwright* will haue it to presume aboue Christ, and so will make it an Antichrist. For if it ordeine strange ministeries and officers in the church, which christ and his Apostles

[1] Intrusive comma.

ne-[53]-uer coulde doe nor woulde do, doeth it not presume aboue Christ? Christ and his Apostles coulde not thrust, no not lawfull ministers vpon any congregation. Neyther coulde he commande any Congregation or Church to receiue vnlawfull ministers, and take them for their guydes. Yet by *Master Cartwrightes* saying, we may receiue such: and if any such be thrust vpon vs, we must account their ministery to be sanctified, for the Churches sake which calleth them. Surely if the Church doe vsurpe and chalenge[1] such a power of ruling, and such a holines in sanctifying, which christ neuer had: it becommeth the church of Antichrist, and quite ouerthroweth the kingdom and priesthood of christ.

Luke 9. 5.
Mat. 10. 13, 14.

But let vs see further what M.C. sayeth. He pleadeth for the dumbe ministers, by comparing them still with the Scribes and Pharises, also with the priestes and teachers in the olde lawe, with the chiefe Priestes at Christes comming, and with vnsufficient and vnable Magistrates. He will haue them to haue as lawfull a calling and ministerie as any of these. The Scribes sayth he, taught vntruely & were deceiued in the chiefe groūds of religion, & yet were to be heard of the people: therfore our dumbe ministers are as lawful ministers as they. Likewise he saith of the priests & of magistrates that some of the priests were dumbedogs, & some false teachers, and some had no lawfull calling, also that some Magistrates are not lawfull & sufficient Magistrates and yet neither the Scribes nor the priestes nor the magistrates were to be reiected as no ministers nor Magistrats. What true or false doctrine there is in all this, we will shew by and by. But graunt it true which he sayth of the scribes, Priestes, and Magistrates: namely that they were so euill, as he sayeth, or taught such false doctrine, yet he him selfe hath giuen the answere before, to condemne him selfe: For he sayde that the Scrybes were not to bee heard, but in that they taught trueth: and that our dumbe ministers were to be heard and receiued so farre, as they can giue vs any thing that is of Christ. Nowe it is shewed that a reading or dumb [54] ministerie is not of Christ, therefore we are not to receiue or heare such a ministerie. Lykewise the Scribes when they preached trueth, were to bee heard and receiued, therefore these being no preachers, are not to be heard nor receiued. The same may be sayde

[1] Intrusive comma.

An Answere to Master Cartwright

of Magistrates, that what duetyes they are able and sufficient to doe, therein we may receiue some good by them, therefore the dumbe ministers hauing no ablenesse nor sufficiencie to that calling, are wholy to be reiected. If he say that the reading of common seruice is some ablenesse and sufficiencie of a minister, hee knoweth well ynough that that is no parte, nor duetie of the ministerie. For though it bee written *That the Leuites reade in the booke of the Lawe, and gave the sense, and cause*[1] *the people to vnderstande the reading.* And againe in the *Actes that Moses was preached being read euery Sabbath*: yet we must not thereby vnderstande a bare reading onely, neither a reading of a stinted forme of seruice. For the order was, as appeareth *in Luke and in the Actes chap.* 13. to reade the Law and word of God, and then to preach vpon it. And therefore as appeareth in Nehemiah *They read in the Booke of the Lawe, and preached the sense and vnderstanding thereof to the people.* And therefore in Timothie, *Reading exhortation, and doctrine are ioyned together.* If *Master Cartwright* doe further alleadge, that the dumbe ministers haue some ablenesse or sufficiencie to minister the Sacramentes, he likewyse knoweth that it is no parte nor duety of the ministerye, to reade a consecration of the Sacramentes, neyther to minister the sacramentes without preaching, and much lesse without the power, and abilitie to preache. This is manifest in the olde Lawe *as in Deuteronomie, Ecclesiastes, and in other places*: *Likewise in the Newe Testament, as in Matthewe, Actes and sundry other places.* By all which places it is euident, *That though preaching may sometymes be without the present Acte of ministring the Sacramentes, yet the Sacraments might neuer be ministred but of preachers and with preaching.* But nowe marke howe fondely hee compareth dumbe Ministers to vnable or vnsuffici-[55]-ent magystrates, which shoulde rather bee compared to Trayterous and vsurping Rebelles. For as anye vsurper were wholy to bee reiected and withstoode, if hee shoulde get from Her *Maiestie* her royall dignity and crowne, or laye clayme thereunto: So also are these minysters to bee reiected, which vsurpe a Kyngdome and gouernement in the Churche: when as they ought not to bee counted brethren, nor members in the Churche. If agayne *Master Cartwright* doe saye, that vsurping Traytours maye geue vs our ryght, and wee are to take it, at

Nehem. 8. 8.
Actes. 15. 21.

Luke 4. 17.
Actes 13. 15.

1. Tim. 4. 13.

Deut. 33. 10.
Eccles. 4. 17.
Mat. 28. 19.
Actes 2. 42.

[1] Rightly "caused" in MS.

theyr handes: Wee aunswere, that this is the questyon, whether the readyng of seruyce in that manner, and theyr mynistring of Sacramentes bee ryght or no. Fyrst wee shewed before, that such Sacramentes so mynistred, and suche a readyng of Seruyce were execrable thynges and also none of our ryght. But if they were our ryght, yet a man is to take his ryght from vsurping Traytoures by force of armes, if hee bee able. Or if hee bee not able, hee shoulde rather loose his righte, then doe suite and homage to a Traytour. In deede the Lordes Sacramentes are our ryghte, and thankes bee to our Lorde GOD, wee may haue them by other meanes, then by the Dumbe Mynisters. And though wee coulde not, yet wee shoulde not take our ryghte on a thyefe to iustyfie his theeuerye. *For these hyrelynges are theeues and robbers comming in by the windowe, as it is written.* So wee shoulde first followe the Lawe on them, to thrust them out of the sheepefolde, and then see if wee can get our right[.] For if all such Ministers were excommunicate from among the brethren, wee shoulde knowe the better, both what were our ryght, and howe to come by it. Againe *Master C.* distinguisheth, that to be able to teache is not of the substance of a minister, but onely of a lawful minister, also that to be able to iudge true iudgemēt is not of the substance of a magistrate, but onely of a lawful Magistrate[.] [56] Such lyke fopperyes as these not worthie the answering, we haue answered before. But here agayne we answere, that the discipline of the Church and of the common wealth are vnlike in this, that vngodly men[1] may bee sometymes lawfull officers and magistrates in a common wealth: and therefore Heathen Kynges, yea Idolatrous kinges and princes are lawfull Magistrates at this daye. Otherwyse wee shoulde condemne our owne Kinges and Queenes, which heretofore haue bene Popish and Idolatrous, as beeing no lawfull Magistrates: But in the Church of God, this holdeth not. For if any be a wretched liuer, or an Idolater, hee can neither be minister nor lawfull minister in the church: yea he is no parte nor member of the Church. Againe we say, that if any be an vnlawfull minister, hee is a Minister quyte out of the Church, as we prooued before, and then what hath the churche to doe with hym? *Master Cartwright* will needes haue hym to bee a minister, and we are content: for he shall

Iohn. 10. 1.

---

[1] Intrusive comma.

An Answere to Master Cartwright

bee a minister, not for rhe [*sic*] Churche, nor to haue any medling in rhe Churche, but for Satan and the children of Satan. Further wee answere accordyng to hys manner of reasoning that to auoyde Idolatrye, or to be no Idolater is not of the substance of a mynister, but of a lawfull mynister: for he may be a minister though he be an Idolatrous minister. But shall wee therefore say that dayly massemongers commyng openly from the masse, to mynister the Sacramentes, in the same order that our dumbe mynisters doe, shall be receyued of the brethren, or that the brethren shall receyue the Sacramentes at theyr handes? And yet agayne wee answere that if a man bee not a lawfull minister, hee hath no essence nor substance of a mynister: except we saye hee hath the substance of a deuelish minister. *For the lawfullnesse of a minister, and of his ministration, is the essence and substance of a minister, and of his ministrating.* Paul saith, *that where no lawe is, there is no transgression. He meaneth that because there is a lawe, therefore the breach of that lawe, is the essence and substance of sinne and transgression.* [57] *The lawe,* saith he, *is it that causeth wrath: For it maketh sinne to be sinne.* Wherefore as that which is vnlawfull or against the lawe of God, hath the being and essence of sinne: so it must needs folow, that the lawfulnes of any thing is the being, the essence & substance of the same. & therfore also that the lawfulnes of ministers is the essence, & substance of ministers. And so we see how vayne his distinction is, that a mā may haue the substāce of a minister, & yet be no lawful minister. I would not so readily vse such schoole tearmes & words, as is essence, substāce, & being, if I were not forced thereto by his vngodly subtleties. And surely except god in iudgement haue blinded his eyes, he may well perceiue thē, not only to be vngodly, but altogether childish & vnlearned. Rom. 4. 15.

Nowe we come to answere other matters, which fall out of the former proofes. As that he saith, the Scribes were altogether deceiued in the Messiah. He might rather saye, they were ignorant, in some mysteries of the Messiah, then all together deceiued. And so Paul saith to them, *That had they knowen, they woulde not haue crucified the Lorde of glorie.* And Peter also saith *That the people did it of ignorance, as also did their gouernours.* Yea the Apostles them selues were a long time ignorant in some mysteries of the Messiah. *And Christ testifieth that* 1. Cor. 2. 8. Act. 3. 17. Mat. 13. 17.

Luke 10. 24.	many *Prophetes and righteous men desired to see and heare*
1. Pet. 1. 12.	*those thinges which the Apostles sawe and heard, but did not*
1. Tim. 3. 16.	*see nor heare them.* Yea *saith Peter, The Angels desire to beholde these thing*[s] *concerning the suffering and glorye of Christ*: And *therefore Paul calleth this a great mysterie, that God should be manifested in the flesh, iustified in the Spirite, seene of Angels, preached vnto the Gentiles, beleeued on in the worlde, and receiued vp in glorie.* The Scribes and Pharises
Mat. 22. 42. Iohn 4. 25.	knewe that the Messiah shoulde come, *that he was the holy one & annointed of God, as appeareth by their answere to Christ. The woman of Samaria knewe that hee shoulde be the annointed Prophet, and tell them all things.* All the
Mat. 2. 6.	Priestes and Scribes knewe *that he was borne King of the Iewes, that he was the gouernour and high Shephearde of Israel that shoulde feede the peo-*[58]*-ple.* They knewe the
Dan. 7. 14 Mich. 4. 7. Isa. 7. 14. &c. Ioh. 6. 14, 15. Ioh. 12. 34.	prophecies that were of him, that are written *in Daniel, in Micah, in Isaiah, in Ieremie, and the rest. Both they and the people coulde readily rehearse such prophecies at their fingers ende, as where he shoulde be borne, whose sonne he was, what was his office, what great workes he shoulde doe, what saluation he shoulde worke to his people, what sufferinges he should endure, and what shoulde be his glorie.* But *Master Cartwright* sayeth, *They knewe not that Iesus was the sonne of God, neither howe the Godhead and manhoode shoulde bee together as in one.* I answere that no more did the Apostles, for a tyme: neyther can any man search this
Iohn 14. 5, 8. Iohn. 16. 17. Iohn 13. 37. Luke 24. 21. Actes 16.	mysterie to the deapth. *For Thomas and Philippe knewe not, as we may reade in Iohn, How* Christ shoulde ascende into heauen to his father, and come againe, that the Father shoulde be in the sonne and the sonne in the Father. Peter also and the rest, were ignorant in such mysteries as appeareth in other places. *Yea they dreamed of a worldly kingdome and a worldly deliuerance, which shoulde be by Christ, as is manifest in the Actes and in Luke.* Wherefore they beleeued not that that Iesus which was then come in the flesh, was the Sonne of God, yet they beleeued and knewe the prophecies. Namely, *that he was to be called Immanuel,* that is *God with vs.* Againe
Isa. 7. 14. Isa. 9. 6.	they knewe another prophecie of Isaiah, *That he shoulde be called by Name, Wonderfull, Counseller, the mightie God &c. that he shoulde sit vpon the throne of Dauid, and vpon his kingdome, and his gouernement shoulde haue none ende.* They knewe of whome that prophecie was giuen in the foure-
Psal. 89. 26. Psal. 2. 7. 12.	score and nynthe Psalme, *Hee shall crye vnto me, thou art my Father, my God, and the rocke of my saluation, also I will*

make him my first borne, higher then the Kinges of the earth. Therefore they coulde not be ignorant, that the Christ was the Sonne of God. They knewe also that they were to trust in the Sonne, as it is written, Thou art my Sonne, this daye haue I begotten thee. Kisse the Sonne least he be angrie, and ye perishe in the way, when his wrath shall suddenly burne. Blessed are all that trust in him. So they well knewe that as hys [59] wrath was destructiō, so to trust in him, was blessing and saluatiō. Therefore it is not truely sayd, that they were altogether deceiued in the Messiah. Rather it is true that they were ignorant but in these two poyntes. First, *howe* Ioh. 6. 51. *that particular man being so poore, despised, and afflicted,* Iohn. 10. 33. *shoulde be the Messiah, and secondly, howe he being man shoulde be God also, and come downe from heauen, to be Manna for the people.* So then, so long as they helde the generall fayth and beleefe, concerning the Messiah, and were ignorant, whether that particular man was the Messias, I say this ignoraunce for the time was no open ouerthrowe of any grounde of Religion. For the Apostles were com- Mat. 16. 20. maunded not to preache Christ particularly to bee the Messiah, till after his resurrection. And the fayth of the holye Fathers before time suffised to saluation, though Heb. 10 [*sic*, 11] particularly they knewe not Christ, neither receiued the 13, 39. promises, as sayeth the text, *But sawe them a farre off, and beleeued them, and receiued them thankefully.* Whereas the wordes are, that they receiued not the promises, and yet receiued them thankefully, it is meant that they receiued not the particular performance of those promises in Christ, but onely the bare promises that were afterwarde to be fulfilled. *In this fayth they dyed* sayeth the text, and verse 39. yet no doubte they were saued. Therefore it was not this particular ignorance that condemned the Pharisees, but their frowarde refusing of a further knowledge. If *Master Cartwright* say that they being so frowarde, yet the faithfull did ioyne with them, it is manifest to the contrary. *For the holy Ghost commaunded them to saue them* Actes 2. 40. *selues from that frowarde generation*: and so they did. *For* Actes 5. 13. *they ioyned with the faithfull onely, and of the other sorte,* sayeth the text, meaning them which beleeued not, durst no man ioyne him selfe to them. *And the man* Iohn. 9. 35. *whome the Pharisees did cast out, or excommunicate, christ tooke him as his disciple.* Whereby it is manifest that Christ both despised and condemned all communion in the Church, with such of them as were persecuters.

[60] Whereas *Master Cartwright* sayeth, that the Scribes and Pharises taught iustification by workes, he hath graunted before, that preaching false doctrine, they were not to bee heard: and therefore the dumbe ministers, being no preachers at all, are not to bee heard. But if they taught that doctrine, yet they taught but a true doctrine, except they taught it as our Papistes doe at this day. For the Scripture sayeth, *That the man that shall doe the workes of the lawe, shall liue in them, or haue life by them.* So then hee that can keepe the Lawe, without breach of the lawe, shall be iustified by the Lawe. But *Master Cartwright* can not prooue, that it was a common doctrine among the Pharisees, that any man coulde keepe the Lawe, without breach thereof. Yea there is proofe to the contrary. *For the chiefe Priest did once euery yeere offer a sinne offering, to make an atonement for him selfe, for his house, and for all the people.* Likewise *were sundry other offeringes and sacrifices obserued, both for the sinnes of the priests, and of the people*: which doeth plainely prooue, that by one common doctrine they acknowledged all to bee sinners, and to haue neede of the grace and mercie of God. What then is to be meant *By those heauie burdens, which they layde on mens shoulders.* Master Cartwright sayeth, *They were the burdens of the morall lawe, that is, the dueties of righteousnesse, which all men perpetually ought to obserue and doe.* Surely this burden, both Christ him selfe, and all the Apostles and prophets doe lay on vs more straightly then euer did the Pharisees. For what strayght commaundements doeth Christ geue, *Against vnaduised anger, reproching, offences, against lust of the heart, wanton lookes,* and all occasions of sinne. Also *against swearing, against reuenge, against hatred, against hypocrisie, against distrustfulnesse,* and a number such like. And he threatneth in the fift of Matthewe, *That for breaking the least commandement, a man shall bee thrust out of the kingdome of God.* And howe often is the burden of the Lorde, the burden of the Lorde, repeated in the Prophetes ? wherefore that burden or yoke is rather meant, which is named [61] in the Actes, *That they tempted God to lay a yoke on the disciples neckes, which neither they, nor their fathers were able to beare.* This burden was the ceremonies of the olde Lawe, which were more intollerable to others, then to the Scribes and Pharises. For they being most of them Priests and Leuites, were not to bring their tythes, first fruites, and offringes to

An Answere to Master Cartwright

Ierusalem, as did others, from all quarters round about. For they dwelt at, or about Ierusalem, especially those whome Christ rebuketh, or else came to Ierusalem to minister in their course. And they tooke tythes and payed none, saue onely the tenth parte of the tythes that were brought them. They did very straightly looke to their tenthes, and to all clensings, purifyings, vowes and offrings &c. for they were their liuing and maintenance. Wherefore it being a great trouble and burden to others, to come from all places of the worlde, to Ierusalem euery yeere, as the Lawe then did bynde them, also to pay their vowes and their tenthes and first fruites, and to obserue their purifyings &c. and no trouble at all to the Scribes which kept at Ierusalem, no maruaile though *Christ say they layed heauie burdens vpon other mēs shoulders, but would not touch them, them selues with the leact [sic] of their fingers.* For there being an hundreth occasions in the yeere, whereby the people might become vncleane, as by touching, tasting, handling, by the death of any that should dye by them, by diseases, by ignorances and escapes &c. they were to bee cleansed by the sprinckling water, and to bring their offeringes to Ierusalem. But *Master Cartwright* might haue alleadged a more likely proofe then these, out of the Romanes: namely *That Israel sought not righteousnesse by faith, but as it were by the workes of the Lawe: for they haue stumbled at the stumbling stone.* For answere hereto, we shewed before, *that the Israelites made a profession of their faith in the Messiah, euen till the tyme, that he plainely shewed him selfe: and then they reiecting him, and yet beleeuing that he was still to come, their faith became as no faith: they beleeued in a Messiah which was to come,* [62] *but they stumbled at him which was come. And so he was vnto them that stumbling stone, and rocke of offence.* And so this worde (*as*) or (*as it were*) is well added of Paul. For hee meaneth, that their doctrine and profession[1] was not openly nor directly to seeke righteousnesse by the bare Lawe, but by their rebellion against the Messiah that was come, they did as much and as they tearme it, indirectly. So as it were they sought righteousnesse by the Lawe, when they kept the ceremonial law, without the Christ that was come, though not simply without the Christ they looked for, yea they beleeued that the ceremonies did still offer and represent

Leuit. 15. 29.

Leuit. 15. 12, 13, 14, &c.
Coloss. 2. 21.
Nom. 19, 11, 12. 13, &c., 16.
Leuit. 5.
Rom. 9. 32.

---
[1] Intrusive comma.

Christ vnto them, & so made profession that to keepe the ceremonial law was to keepe their faith and beleefe in Christ. *But they hauing refused Christ cōe alreadie, and christ hauing abolished that law, they might well be said to seek righteousnes without faith in christ.* Thus it is manifest that the doctrine & sacrifices of the Iewes was to haue righteousnes and atonement by Christ, whome their sacrifices did signifie: but their deeds and practise in refusing Christ[1] was as much[1] as to seeke righteousnesse by the law. *Nowe those which refused christ, and beleeued not in him, were vtterly separate as was shewed before from the communion and fellowshippe of the churche.* And therefore this matter is altogether against him. *As for that place of luke, he abuseth it too much: for the parable of a pharise, which speaketh of matters*[1] *as though they were, when in deede they were not,* he alleadgeth for proofe of all the Pharisees doctrine. First, the fault of one Pharise if he had bene faultie, can not prooue them all faultie: then also the parable of a fault, doeth shewe it to be no fault committed, but imagined or supposed, as if it were committed. Thirdlye Christ in that place, mindeth not to rebuke any doctrine of the Scribes and Pharisees, but as the text sayeth, he spake a parable vnto certaine, which trusted in them selues, that they were iust, and despised others. None are named to teache any such doctrine, but certaine are rebuked for trusting in themselues, wherefore the like proofe to this[1] might [63] I alleadge against him: namely that very many in England both preachers, and others doe trust in their riches, or power, or wisedome or good workes &c. Therefore the preachers in Englande doe teach men to trust in thēselues. But as this proofe is fonde, so the conclusion that followeth is according. For he concludeth that the dumbe ministerie is as lawful and good, as the ministerie of the Scribes: which taught vntruely, saith he, in the chiefe grounds of religion. Although he cannot prooue such vntrue doctrine, yet howe doeth it followe, that their ministerie, which faileth in all poyntes, shoulde bee as good as theirs, which fayleth but in some poyntes. For the dumbe ministers wee prooued, to haue no parte nor worke in the ministerie. And the Scribes hee confessed before to sit in Moses seate, to teache true doctrine, to haue a calling by the Churche. Agayne, they must needes

Actes 5. 13.
Actes. 2. 40.
Luke 18. 9.

† Intrusive comma.

An Answere to Master Cartwright

edifie more, which preache much trueth, then they whiche are no preachers at all. But the Scripture is playne, that if anye preache muche trueth, and yet doe preache heresies withall, they are to be auoided: as it is written, *Reiect him that is an heretike, after once or twise admonition.* And though the Churche is to admonishe such, yet if it will not or can not, then any man particularly hath this libertie to admonishe, except for his scornefulnesse and obstinacie he be vnworthie. And then we are forbidden to receiue them to house, or to bid them God speede. And howe then shall we take them for our guydes and pastours in the Church, or say (Amen) to their prayers? And here followeth that vntrueth to be refuted, which he addeth in these wordes, that the true Prophets are neuer founde to haue forbidden the people to come to the sacrifice of the false prophets, and of the priestes that were dumbe dogges, neither to bring their sacrifices vnto them. First euen that place of blinde watchmen and dumbe dogs, which he quoteth amisse, is against him selfe, For there was a Lawe, that the priestes being vncltane, [*sic*] *they might neither touch nor eat of the holy things: if they* [64] *did, then those thinges were polluted.* Nowe to drinke wine or strong drinke was a pollution both of the Nazarites and Priestes: of the Priestes I say, when they came into the Tabernacle of the congregation to offer sacrifice. Howe then shoulde the people partake in the Sacrifices with Priestes that were common drunkardes. For *the people are commaunded not to touche any vncleane thing*: and therefore those sacrifices being vncleane, howe shoulde the people have any thing to doe with them? Nowe suche drunkards were those dumbe dogges which hee nameth, as is there mencioned: *they were greedie dogges, which sayde, Come, I will bring wine, and we will fill our selues with strong drinke, and to morowe shall be as this day, and much more abundant.* Wherefore being such, howe coulde they put difference, as it is commaunded in Leuiticus, *Betweene the holy and the vnholy, and betweene the cleane and the vncleane.* And howe then shoulde not all their sacrifices be polluted? There be ma-[1] places which shewe, that the priestes polluted them selues, and the holy thinges: as in Ezekiel, *Her priestes defile myne holy thinges, they put no difference betweene the holy and prophane, neither discerne betweene the vncleane and the cleane*, and in

Tit. 3. 10.
Mat. 18.
2. Ioh. 10.
Rom. 16. 17.
Isa. 56. 10.
Hag. 2. 13, 14.
Leuit. 22. 5, 6.
Nom. 6.
Leuit. 10.
Malal. [*sic*] 1. 7.
Isa. 52. 11.
Nom. 19.
Leuit. 22.
verse. 11. 12.
Leuit. 10. 1u.
ezek. 22.
Hag. 2. 15.
Mal. 1.

[1] As text; MS. has "manie".

Haggai, *that which they offer here is vncleane*: and in Malachie, *Ye offer vncteane [sic] bread vpon mine altar &c.* Also in sundry places, as is quoted before, commaundement is giuen not to touch any vncleane thing: Wherefore it is a flat commaundement euen to all the people, not to touche those polluted sacrifices of the Priestes, not to communicate nor partake with them therein. Therefore in his own place quoted out of Isaiah, is that terrible iudgement pronounced both against priestes and against peeople, though onely the sinne of the priestes or watchmen is named. The wordes are these. *All yee beastes of the fielde come to deuorr [sic], euen all ye beastes of the forest.* And then follows these wordes, *their watchemen are all blinde &c.* as who say, that the people, because they did partake with such watchemen, they shoulde also perish with them, If *Master Cart-*[65]*-wright* say, the pollutions we speake of, were by Idolatrie: let him knowe that Malachie spake to those, which were no Idolaters, which also had a generall reformation from Idolatrie: *Likewise Haggai prophecied in a time of reformation, and spake to those which were no Idolaters. And Ezekiel in that Chapter, mentioneth no Idolatrie, but rebuketh other wickednesse, as it were seuering it from Idolatrie.* For in the next Chapter, he toucheth their sinne of Idolatrie more particularly. And to those that accounted so much of the Temple, and of the sacrifices, as *Master Cartwright* doeth of his Churches and Sacraments, *Isaiah saith thus, The heauen is my throne saith the Lord, and the earth is my footestoole.* and so he proceedeth to rebuke their vaine bragge of the Temple, and then commeth to their sacrifices, saying, *He that killeth a bullocke, is as if he slewe a man, he that sacrificeth a sheepe, as if he cut off a dogges necke: he that offereth an oblation, as if he offered swynes blood: he that remembreth incense, as if he blessed an Idol*: by which wordes it is plaine that he rebuketh euen those, that detested Idoles, and swynes blood &c. and telleth them that their sacraments are no sacraments, they are vncleane and polluted, as the most vile filthinesse which they themselues abhorred. If he say, that yet to the godly in those dayes, the sacrifices were lawfull and good, I aunswere that the godly had no medling with such wicked men, nor with their sacrifices. For in the seconde verse after hee speaketh thus to the godly, *Heare the worde of the Lorde, all ye that tremble at his worde, your brethren that hated you,*

An Answere to Master Cartwright

and cast you out for my Names sake, sayde, let the Lorde be glorified: but hee shall appeare to your ioye and they shall bee ashamed. So then there was a great separation betweene the righteous and the wicked in those dayes: in so much that the righteous forsooke all fellowshippe in their sacrifices, and the wicked cast them out from among them. If *Master Cartwright* say that the righteous forsooke not their sacrifices, but were cast out from them, it is answered in another place, *That while they re-frained from euill, they made them selues a pray to the wic-[66]-ked.* So then the cause why they were cast out was, because they woulde not partake with the wicked in their wickednesse. If *Master Cartwright* saye that that was for other wickednesse, but not for their refusing to partake in the sacrifices, *It is said in Samuel That for the wickednesse of the priests, men abhorred the sacrifices.* If he say againe, that they did euill to abhorre thē, he can not prooue it: & it is euident that they were of the better sorte that did so. For in Malache it is written, *that they which feared the Lorde, spake euery one to his neighbour,* cōcerning the abuses and wickednes of those dayes: and the Lord sheweth the badge and marke of all his flocke and people, namely that they should returne & discerne betwene the righteous and the wicked: betweene him that serueth God, and him that serueth him not: As who say, that euery one of the righteous had libertie and were commaunded, to haue no communion with the wicked in the Churche: and howe then shoulde they be ioyned with them in the neerest communion, namely in the Sacramentes. And in the same Chapter it is prophecied, *That the offeringes of Iudah and Ieerusalem shoulde bee acceptable to the Lorde, as in the olde tyme, and in the yeeres afore,* and that was, when the sonnes of Leui (which figured all the righteous)[1] shoulde bring offeringes vnto the Lorde in righteousnesse. For he shewed in the Chapters before, that while open and grosse wickednesse was incurable among them, both the priestes and Leuites broke the couenant, and also the people, & the offerings were no more regarded, neither receiued acceptably at their hands. As for the sacrifices of Elkanah and his wiues, they were offered by the ministerie of *Eli*, as appeareth in that place, and not by his wicked sonnes. Nowe Elie was rather negligent, in correcting his sonnes, then a grosse transgressour, and therefore might Elkanah the rather

Isa. 59. 15.

1. Sam. 2. 17.

Mal. 3. 16, 17, 18.

ibid. 34.

Mal. 1. 10.
Mal. 2. 8, 9, 10
13.

1. Sam. 1.

---

[1] Closing bracket missing in text, present in manuscript.

Psa. 15. 4. partake in the sacrifices with him. But wee reade in the Psalmes, That a vyle person is contemned in the eyes of [the] righteous: howe then shall a ryghteous man[1] receiue the Sacramentes with such, as with brethren in the Churche? [67] *Dauid prayeth that hee might not commit wicked workes, with men that worke iniquitie, and that he myght not eate of their delicates*: and howe then would he eate of their sacrifices, which are the chiefest delicates. If hee saye, that Dauid woulde not eate common bread with such, it is euident that hee daily did so, in the house of Saul. And this matter is before made plaine. And in the Prouerbes it is written,

Psal. 141. 4.

pro. 28. 4. *They that forsake the Lawe prayse the wicked, but they that keepe the Lawe set them selues against them*. Howe shall they set them selues against them, when they ioyne with them as brethren in the Sacramentes. Iudah was sayde to defile the holinesse of the Lorde, because some in Iudah did marrye the daughters of a straunge God: yea and this was counted a synne, transgression, and abomination committed by all Israel and Iudah, and Ierusalem, though some onley had marryed such women. Wherefore were they all guiltie of transgression, but because they did not, or would not redresse such wickednes. For it had bene the duetie of euery one, as appeareth in Ezra and Haggai, to haue offred no oblatiōs, nor to haue partaken with any such in the sacrifices, till such opē wickednes[1] had bene taken away.

Mal. 2. 11.
Ezr. 9. 1.
Nehem. 9.

Hag. 2. 15. Otherwise Haggai woulde not haue saide, that all the workes of their handes, and that whiche they offered there was vncleane: neither would Ezra haue rent his clothes, nor pluckt off the heare[2] of his head, and of his beard, nor haue saide that they all were before the Lord in their trespasse, and therefore could not stand before the Lord because of it. And surely their sin of marrying strange wiues, did but figure out our sinne of mingling and intermedling the Churches: For the daughters of Antichrist, I meane those wicked prelates & popish officers are yet married to our churches: The papists & wicked men are thrust into our churches to receiue the sacraments with vs. Their discipline is the nurture & lady mystres ouer our churches. If *M.C.* aske what proofe we haue, that their marriage, I meane of the

Eph. 5. 32. Iewes, was anye figure or Ceremonie, [68] let him reade

[1] Intrusive comma.
[2] Hair. The reference is to Ezra 9 : 3.

An Answere to Master Cartwright

that of Paul to the Ephesians, where Paul calleth marriage a secrete or mysterie, and sheweth there, that marriage was a signe or figure of the ioyning together of Christ and his Church: also in the song of Salomon this is manifest, and in the Reuelation and sundry other places. Dauid sheweth with whome the godly did partake in the sacrifices, when he saith, I haue not haunted with vaine persons, neither kept companie with the dissemblers, I haue hated the assemblie of the euill, and haue not cōpanied with the wicked, and then followe these wordes, I will wash mine handes in innocence o Lord and compasse thine altar. Which wordes doe teach vs, that when we receiue the sacraments, we can not wash our handes in innocencie, except we receiue them apart from the wicked. For the order of the Jewes was to partake in the sacrifices, familie by familie, as we may reade in sundry places. And therefore they might more easily auoyde the companie of the wicked. And the Iewes contended against Peter, because he went in to men vncircumcised, & had eaten with them, which sheweth howe straite they were, for avoyding all company with the wicked. It is lawfull indeede to eate with Publicanes and sinners as Christ also did, but yet to eate the Lordes supper with opon [sic] vnrepentant & wretched persons is not lawfull. For as I may not offer myne owne oblation, when I remēber that a brother hath ought against me, much lesse may I partake in another mans offring, when I haue ought against him. Yea mercie and pitie in seeking to reforme him is preferred before sacrifice. So that, except he be obstinate and a scorner, I am gentlie to admonishe him, and if he be yet hardened in his sinne, I am as Iude saith, to saue him with feare, pulling him out of the fire. What is this feare which shoulde saue him, but to make him afraide, by sharper rebukes, and refusing to partake with him in the Sacraments. For he will be afraide of nothing, so long as I take him for a brother and ioyne with him in the sacraments. But this is strange that *Master* [69] *Cartwright* sayeth, that the true prophetes did not forbidde the people, to communicate with the false prophetes in the sacrifices. *For commandement is giuen, not onely to communicate with false prophets, but euen to kill them, and our hands to be first against them, yea though they were our brethren, or our owne children, or the wife that lyeth in*

Song. 6. 8.
Reuel. 21. 9.

Psal. 26. 6.

Actes. 10. 28.
Act. 11. 2, 3.

Marke 2. 15.
Mat. 5. 23.
Mat. 9. 13.
Hose. 6. 6.
Mat. 18. 15.

Iude. 23.

Deut. 13. 5, 6
7, 8, 9.
Deut. 17. 2.
Luke. 17. 23.
Zech. 13. 3.

Gal. 1. 8.	*our bosome, or our friende, which is as our owne soule: yet our eyes may not pitie him, nor shew mercie vnto him,* saith the text. If *Master Cartwright* say that this was commaunded for Idolatrous prophets, why then did he not make that exception. But wee haue shewed before,
Deut. 18. 20. Titus 3. 10. 2 Iohn 10. 11. Rom. 16. 17. Nom. 15. 39.	*that for heresie also, the false prophets are not to be bidden God speede, and are vtterly to be auoyded. yea they are to be put to death as well as the other, as againe it is written in Deuteronomie* 18. 20. *And it is testified in Nombers, against the people, that they shoulde make them fringes, that when they looked vpon them, they might remember all the commaundements of the Lorde and doe them, and that they sought not after their owne heart, and after their owne eyes, after the which they went a whoring.* which wordes doe teache vs, *that all heretikes and false prophets doe goe a*
Ierem. 23. 16. Deut. 17. 12. Gal. 1. 8.	*whoring after their owne heartes, and are as euill*[1] *as Idolaters.* And wherefore is it cōmanded, *that the man which hearkeneth not to the voyce of the high Priest,* (which figureth the voyce of Christ in his Churche) *shoulde die*? which wordes doe shewe, *That false prophetes that will not be reformed, are to be held in execration and auoyded of men.* And howe then should the people partake with them in the sacrifices. Yea the Iewes had that custome, as it appeareth from their forefathers, and from the former Prophetes,
Iohn. 9. 22, 34, 35.	*To excommunicate the false Prophetes and those that beleeuede them, and therefore they did wickedly excommunicate the blinde*
Iere. 29. 26.	*man, that beleeued in christ.* And the custome of punishing false prophetes, is alleadged in Ieremie, though wickedly and by a false prophet. And whereas it is commaunded
Zech. 13. 6. Iere. 23. 16. Ierem. 27. 9, 14, 15, 16, 17, 18.	in Ieremie, *That the people shoulde not heare the wordes of the false prophetes, is it not also a commandement, that they should not partake with them in the sacrifices*? For the sacrifices and [70] sacraments are but a seale to the worde that is preached. So the false prophetes hauing a false worde and a false message, if the people shoulde partake with them in the sacraments, they did thereby seale vnto their false message, as if it were true.
Deut. 33. 10. Eccle. 4. 17. Leuit. 1. 4. Chap. 3. 2.	Againe that anye dumbe dogges, which coulde not barke did minister the sacrifices, *Master Cartwright* can not prooue, yea before we haue prooued the contrary. *For the sacrifices were alwayes ministred as it shewed before, by Priestes that coulde preache and did preache. The occasion for which the sacrifice was offered, was shewed before. The sinnes of those that brought the sacrifice, was confessed ouer*

[1] Intrusive comma.

An Answere to Master Cartwright

the head of the Sacrifice &c. All these thinges are manifest in the olde Lawe. Indeede there were dumbe dogges, among the priestes (for there were diuers cities, which belonged to the Priestes onely) *yet none suche being able, nor vsing to minister the sacrifices,* [1](wee speake not here of Idolatrous sacrifices) *I saye it is follye to imagine, that the people did bring their sacrifices to such.* But yet if they did bring, we haue prooued before that they ought not to haue done so. Chap. 4. 4. Mal. 2. 7. 8.

If *Master Cartwright* saye that the Churche indeede might refuse the false prophetes and put them from the sacrifices, but not euery particular man in the Churche: I aunswere that the question is not of forbidding and debarring from the sacrifices, but of withdrawing our selues from wicked companions in the sacrifices. And so it followeth that if the whole Churche ought not to communicate with such in the sacrifices, then no part nor member of the Churche ought to communicate: and if the whole Churche doe sinne and commit wickednesse by communicating with suche: then if any amongest them will refuse to communicate, they shall doe well, and shall not sinne thereby. That the whole Churche ought not to communicate, but to cast out such from amongest them, it is prooued before. But here is that place of Paul to be answered, which the aduersaryes lay against vs: whiche is [71] that some preache Christ of enuie and strife, and some also of good will, and Paul reioyceth that Christ is preached all manner wayes. By which wordes they woulde gather, that we may communicate in the Churche with false teachers, false prophetes, heretikes, and vngodly wretches. Howe shamelessely they gather this, euen Paul in the same Epistle answereth them: For he biddeth them *beware of dogges, beware of euill workes: beware of the concision.* Woulde Paul haue dogges and euill workers to communicate in the Churche? Nay doeth he not call them concision from the Church: meaning that if they preached circumcision, they must needes be cut off from the Church, and others also with them. And so their circumcision, shoulde rather be concision, that is a cutting and renting of the Churche in sunder. Paul is so farre from reioysing in such preachers, that in the eighteenth verse he geueth warning of them, with weeping teares, and calleth Phil. 1. 17, 18. Phil. 3. 2. Verse 18, 19.

---

[1] Opening bracket missing in text, present in MS.

Gal. 5. 12.	them *enemies of the crosse of Christ, belligods, proude and worldly men, and appointed to damnation.* And Paul would not onely not suffer the churche to communicate with such, as is largely prooued before, but wisheth they were euen dead and destroyed which so did disquiet the churche. What is then to be meant by Paules ioy, that Christ was preached all manner wayes? Surely this, that so the church and the discipline thereof were kept vpright, we neede not care for the enemies thereof. yea and if in the churche also, the doctrine of hypocrites doe more good, then their secret faultes can doe hurt, we are therein to reioyce. For Paul speaketh of the enuie and contentious minde of such preachers, and not of anye grosse wickednesse that brake foorth by them. Further if some be deceiued
Phil. 3. 15.	in doctrine, and bee otherwyse mynded then the trueth is, God shall reueile the same vnto them sayeth Paul: he meaneth so long as they are weakelings and not obstinate enemies. For ignorance, so long as it is not a sotted nor wilfull ignorance, [72] nor ioyned with other grosse wickednesse, is to bee borne with. But if
Mat. 5. 19.	any man abuse his ignorance so, that he breaketh but the least commaundement, and teacheth men so, as Christ hath tolde vs, he shall be called the least in the kingdome of heauen: that is, he shall be cleane cast out of the kingdome, or if any man by his ignorance or false doctrine be contentious, we haue no such
1. Cor. 11. 16. Rom. 16. 17.	custome, *saieth Paul*, neither the Churches of God. Yea the custome of the Church is, as it is written againe, *To marke those diligentlye, which cause diuision amongest vs, contrary to the trueth we haue learned, and to auoyde them.* Howe then shoulde Paul reioyce in contentious preaching? Surely as Paul reioyced, so Christ desired to haue contention in the worlde. Contention I say in the
Luke 12. 48, 49, 50, 51. Mat. 10. 34.	worlde, but not in the Church. *For I came not sayeth Christ to giue peace on earth, but rather debate. I am come,* saith he, *to put fire on the earth, and what is my desire if it were alreadie kindled? For from hencefortho there shall be fiue in one house deuided, three against two, and two against three. The father against the sonne, and the sōne against the father &c.* Now there is a lawful ioy in this cōtention, not that mē shuld be so wicked, nether that such contention shoulde be among the true professors, but that the warfare against wickednes is begun, and that the treuth [*sic*] worketh and preuaileth thereby: This was

Pauls ioy, and this should be our ioy, if mē in the world fall out, contend and disagree about the Gospel: for then shall the trueth be sifted and boulted out, and the Church of Christ shalbe builded, and growe the more mightely. But Paul discommendeth contention in the Church, and saith, that when they come together into one place, with such dissention among them, this is not to eate the Lordes Supper. And here also is that place answered, that some men did build hay or stubble in the spirituall buylding, & so their worke cānot abyd the fyer of Gods word, but shall burne, yet they shalbe safe thēselues. Paul thereby rebuketh their vaine elo-[73] quence & other infirmities in preaching, as being but haye and stubble that shall burne, but they them selues being purified from such infirmities as it were by fire, shall be safe. yea and though some be false apostles, yet if they worke so deceitfully, and so cunningly transforme them selues, that none can prooue them to be obstinate false teachers, nor charge them with open grosse wickednes, they are to bee suffered as brethren in the churche. But it is before sufficiently prooued that if any be an obstinate hereticke, or an open wicked wretch, he is not to be suffered.

1. Cor. 11. 20.

1. Cor. 3. 13, 14, 15.

2. Cor. 11. 13.

Againe the aduersaries doe set the practise of the Apostles and brethren against vs, which did communicate, as they say, in the offerings and sacrifices of the wicked Iewes and persecuting priestes. And *Master Cartwright* bringeth in Christ, who commanded the leprous man, purged from his leprosie, to shewe him selfe to the priest, and to offer his oblation. To them both we answere, that neither the Apostles & brethren did communicate with the wicked Iewes and persecuting priestes, neither also was the leprous man commanded to communicate in that manner. For they were of the brethren, as is plaine in the text, with whome Paul did contribute in that matter of purifying. And it is written, that *a great companie of the Priestes, were obedient to the faith*. And therefore no doubt of it, the Apostles made choise of the priestes, as they did of those foure brethren, with whome Paul did contribute & other priestes besides the high priest might accomplish the common seruice of the sacrifices, *Hebrewes* 9. If they say that the sacrifices and oblations were sanctified in the name of the wicked hie priestes, we denie it: For the beleeuers did know that Christ the high Priest

Act. 1. 224 [*sic*, 21. 24].

Mat. 8. 4.

Act. 6. 7.

Heb. 9. 6, 7.

was come alreadie, and therefore in his name they tooke the sacrifices to be sanctified, and not in the name of the other priestes. Moreouer it is manifest, that they did not communicate, neither offer any offering, but rather that they shoulde haue done it, and were letted by the vproare before the dayes of purifying were ended.

Actes. 18. 18.
Actes 20. 22, 23.
Actes 21. 11.

[74] And it seemeth that Paul knewe by the spirite and by the prophecies that went on them, that such an vproare should fall out, and therefore also knewe that the offering shoulde be letted. If here againe they obiect, that the sacrifices them selues¹ were fulfilled in Christ, and also abrogate, and yet for the churches sake were tolerated, I aske them what they would gather hereby, or what vantage they would take against vs? Forsooth they would iustifie thereby a tollerating of our horrible abuses and disorders. But how cā they, by those things which God commandeth, warrant those things which God neuer cōmanded. Againe they are fowly deceiued, as touching the ceremonial law. First because they thinke the accomplishing or fulfilling of the ceremoniall law¹ to be a present and vtter abolishing thereof, without a certaine testimonie and preaching to the people, that it is abolished. Secondly for that they make no difference betweene the law disanulled: and the forbidding thereof, being disanulled, also betweene the acte and manner of abrogating the law, & the law already abrogated. Also because they will haue the new lawe stand in force, before it can be duely proclaimed and receiued in steade of the old. And so to the Hebrewes it is written, *that the old testament being disanulled, is ready to vanish away,* whereby it is ment, that it could not at once be taken away. It was accomplished & fulfilled in Christ, yea it was also abolished in Christ as the head, yet by degrees and measure it was abolished and taken from the body. wherefore it was vanishing, and yet not vtterly vanished. It stoode in some force, because the new testamēt¹ was not yet sufficiently proclaimed and preached to the people. And therefore it is sayde, *Today if ye will heare his voyce.* By these wordes, *To day,* he appointed a certaine time, saith the Apostle, & so he sheweth that time is appointed for receiuing the further & better promises, also a better testamēt & a better professiō, thē was the former. So that we see it was lawful for the Iewes to

Heb. 8. 13.

Heb. 3. 7.
Psal. 95. 7.
Heb. 4. 7.

Heb. 7. 18.

¹ Intrusive comma.

hold stil their ceremonies & sacrifices, till they might surely know the first com-[75]-mādement to be disanulled, because of the weakenes thereof. For what faithful subiect wil forsake the old lawes of his prince, till he be assured that newe lawes are proclaimed which abrogate the olde. Indeede the newe Testament or new Lawe tooke place and was established at the death Heb. 9. 16. of Christ, as the Apostle prooueth, yet by degrees it tooke place in the Churches, as Christ also teacheth, where hee sayeth, *And I, if I were lift vp from the earth,* Iohn 12. 3. *will drawe all men vnto mee,* meaning that at his death hee established a newe Lawe and Testament, by which men should bee drawen vnto him, not that they were drawen at once in a moment, and all together. For the vayle or couering of the olde Testament was first to bee taken away. By this vayle no doubte Paul 2. Cor. 3. 14, 15. meaneth the ignorance of the Iewes, whereby they did cleaue so much to the old law & ceremonies. And therefore the Lord sayeth in another place, that he *will* Isa. 25. 7. *destroye in this mountaine, the couering that couereth all people, and the vayle that is spredde vpon all nations.* For the Temple that stoode on the mountaine, with the ordinances thereof, was as a vayle to blynde the heartes of the Iewes, which dwelt among all nations. And there- Mat. 24. 2. fore Christ did foreshewe the destruction of the Temple, Iohn. 4. 21. which came to passe about fourtie yeeres after. A great parte of which tyme, it was still permitted to the Iewes to holde the olde Ceremonies. If they obiect that the vayle of blindenesse was sinne, and therefore to holde the ceremonies was sinne, I aunswere, that it was no vayle of blindnesse, to those that were willing, ready, and forwarde to receiue the Newe Lawe and Testament when it was offered. If againe they obiect that their willingnesse and forwardnesse appeared not, seeing the Gentiles so quickely reiected the olde lawe, and they in so long time reiected it not: wee aunswere, that all the beleeuing Iewes did straightway reiect it in part, though not wholly: but some of them also reiected it wholy euen in shorte time, [76] yet they were but fewe, and no maruaile. For the Gentiles had neuer receiued the olde lawe, and therefore might the more Actes 21. 20. readily imbrace the newe, but the Iewes were alwaye zealous of the olde Lawe, and therefore coulde not so suddenly be reclaimed from their former zeale. Further that distinction or difference betwixt the acte and maner of doing any thing, and the deede alreadie done, appeareth by that place in the Hebrewes: where it is said, *thou hast put all thinges vnder his feete*: in which wordes the acte done, is put for the doing thereof. For yet we see not, (saieth the Authour) all thinges subdued vnto him. But the worke was in hande, as it were, it was doing and prospered, till all thinges shoulde be subdued. Euen so we may say that the olde lawe was abolished or taken away, at the death of Christ: that is, it was in abolishing, or it was readie to vanish away, and to be vtterly abolished, yea in Christ the head, it was abolished, and in the members also it was readie to be abolished. And therefore Paul giueth this distinction, that some brethren are weake in faith, and are not yet perswaded in their mindes, that the ceremoniall lawe is abolished: others haue knowledge. Now Paul reasoneth, that in such matters concerning the obseruation of such ceremonies, euery mans faith or knowledge must bee his rule. *For to him that iudeth any thing vncleane, to him it is vncleane.* Therefore he that doeth any thing in suche matters, against his knowledge or conscience, he sinneth. For whatsoeuer is not of faith or knowledge is sinne, saieth Paul. So then our answere is true, that the ceremonies of the olde lawe[1] were not vtterly to be remoued, but by faith and knowledge of the full abrogation thereof. Otherwise Paul woulde not haue said, that he which obserueth a day, or he which eateth not vncleane meates, obserueth the day of the Lorde, or eateth not the meate to the Lord. He meaneth, according to his owne interpretation verse 18. vers. 4. that they serue Christ in these thinges, and are acceptable vnto God, and also to be approoued of men. And there-[77]-fore also they that were stronger, and had further knowledge, were to beare with the weaker, and to applie their knowledge and iudgement, that they put no stumbling blocke nor occasion to fall before their brethren. Againe we haue a further answere by these wordes of Paul. That some thinges may be done, vpon iust occasion, as when we are sure that we serue God therein: and some thinges are simply sinne, which may neuer be done vpon any occasion. Such are our vyle abuses and vngodly disorders, which are not as the ceremonies of the Lawe, that by occasion might be obserued or not cbserued : as to make differēce of

[1] Intrusive comma.

An Answere to Master Cartwright

times or of meates: but they are altogether forbidden by the word of God, and therefore not indifferent as they terme them. And though some thinges in them selues, as they are creatures, are rather cleane, good, and lawfull, then (as they terme them) indifferent, yet their vse, or rather abusing in such manner and order, is not lawfull and good, neither indifferent. Rom. 14. 14. 1. Tim. 4. 4.

And here againe is another obiection to be answered, because when King Hezekiah did celebrate the Passeouer, there were many in the congregation[1] that were not cleansed, and yet did eate the Passeouer. And thereby they doe gather, that wicked wretches may partake with vs in the sacraments. That place[1] plainely sheweth, that it was onely a ceremoniall vncleannesse, and no wickednesse in the people. For the people as the wordes doe testifie, prepared their whole heart to seeke the Lorde God. againe the same place answereth it selfe: that they were not cleansed according to the purification of the sanctuary: whereby is ment, as it is written in Numbers, that they were to keepe the Passeouer, notwithstanding such vncleannesse. For it could no way be remedyed before the time of the Passeouer appointed. And againe that ceremonie of vncleannes[1] was cōmanded because of the sanctuarie, which might not be polluted. Nowe therefore they onely eating the Passeouer in their houses or tentes, and not comming to the sanctuarie, [78] their ceremoniall vncleanes was no wickednesse in them. For the Priestes them selues, as the text declareth, were not suffered to come into the Sanctuarie or Temple, being not yet cleansed. And yet also there is a further answere. For that the ceremoniall vncleannesse was no sinne, so long as it was not by their carelessenesse in avoyding it, or if it had bene sinne, yet it was to be counted a smaller escape or an infirmitie, and no grosser wickednesse. And then seeing it was openly rebuked, and openly confessed, and prayed for by the king, and also healed in the people, (*For the Lorde healed the people* saith the text), I say, seeing the matter stoode so, howe shal any man excuse or tollerate thereby, our intollerable disorders, which are also incurable. For if escapes, or open infirmities are not so to bee borne with, but that they must be openly rebuked and mended, before the offenders can communicate in the sacraments. Then much rather are open grosser sinnes to be first

2. Chron. 30. 17, 18, 19.

verse. 19.

Nom. 9. 10.

Nom. 19. 20.

2. Chron. 29. 34.
2. Chron. 30. 16.
Marke 7. 15.

[1] Intrusive comma.

redressed, before the sinners be suffered to partake in the sacraments. But *Master Cartwright* bringeth a place in Ieremie, for defence of suspendings, which the Bishops vse nowe a dayes: or at least for tollerating of them, that the preachers should take and giue ouer their callings, as the Bishops and their officers doe appoint them.

Ierem. 36. 5. Why doeth he so carelessely falsifie the Scriptures. First he saith that Ieremy was suspended from preaching, and then he woulde prooue that Ieremie obeyed that suspension, thirdly he sayeth that Ieremie was at libertie of his bodie, and fourthly that he would not preache in the Temple for making a tumult. All whiche things are vtterly false, and haue no shewe of trueth in thē.

Ierem. 32. 2. *For first it is plaine in the chapter he quoteth, that he was shut vp*: and therefore was not at libertie of his bodye: *and the 32 chapter sheweth that Ieremie was shut vp in the court of the prison.* Then also imprisoning of a man doeth shewe a violent withholding of a man from preaching, and not a suspending. Further that Ieremie would obey no suspendings, it is plaine by the charge and message he

Ier. 1. 10, 18. had from the [79] Lorde. *For he was set ouer the nations and ouer the kingdomes (as is written) and was made an yron pillar, and walles of brasse against the king, the princes and the priestes, and was not to bee afraide of their faces, least the Lorde did destroy him before thē.* Indeede it is true as we haue

Hose. 4. 4. prooued before, *that we are not to preach to the vnworthie, as to scorners, and persecuters. For there is a time when the wise man shall keepe silence, when scarce any is to rebuke, or reprooue another.* But when Ieremie was shut vp, there

Iere. 36. 19. were of the princes that tooke his parte. For by their meanes no doubt, did Ieremie get out of the prison court, and so hid himself with Baruch. There was no such bondage of suspendings, as *Master Cartwright* would tolerate: and though they were, yet Ieremie obeyed them not, but onely gaue place to the tyrannie

Actes 23. 6. of persecuters. As for the tumult he speaketh of, we know that Paul him selfe, though he sought peace, yet he cared more[1] for his safetye, and to witnesse the

Ierem. 26. 9. trueth, then he did for to raise a tumult. And Ieremie also ceased not to preache still, notwithstanding that a tumulte, and much stirring had bene among the people, and priestes, and princes and Prophets, and all for his preaching.

Whereas *Master Cartwright* sayeth, that Christ liued

---

[1] Intrusive comma.

An Answere to Master Cartwright

in the corruptest times of the Churche, and when things
were most confused, and fewest steppes of any lawfull
calling to be seene, he is therein fowly ouerseene. For   Zech. 12. 10.
those were the dayes, wherein the Lord did powre[1]   Zech. 13. 2.
vpon the house of Dauid & vpon the inhabitants of
Ierusalem, the spirit of grace & of compassion, wherein
also he did cut off the names of the Idoles from amongst   Luke 1. 8, 9.
his people, as againe it is prophecied: So that they   luke 2. 21.
were no more remēbred, and he did cause the false   Mar. 1. 40.
prophets, & the vncleane spirits to depart from amongst   Act. 10. 28.
thē. They had the true worship of God, the true   Iohn 4. 9.
sacrifice, the order of the priestes and Leuites, & their
callings according to the Law of Moses. *The church was
separated frō the wicked, frō the sect of the Saduces, frō the
idolatrous Samaritans: There were uery many good men &
women, as Zacharie the* [80] *Father of Iohn Baptist and
his wife, Simeon and Anna, and Nathaniel and many*   Mat. 3.
other. all which I neede not to recken vp. *For there*   Luke 3.
*were great multitudes that heard Iohn Baptistes doctrine, and
were baptised of him, yea among the Pharisees, there were
those that touching the righteousnesse which is in the lawe were*   Phil. 3. 6.
*vnrebukeable. They were as it appeareth, most of them Leuites,
openly called and authorised to preach by the Elders and people
in the Synagognes* [sic]. And surely that is but a vaine
exception, which *Master Cartwright* maketh of the high   Nom. 20. 28.
Priest, *That he was made a yeerely officer, and came in by
Simonie into his office. For Eleazar was made high priest,*   1. King. 2. 35.
while Aaron the high Priest yet liued. And Zadok was made   1. King. 1. 42.
high Priest, and Abiathar and his sonnes put from the priest-   1. Sam. 2. 30.
*hoode, when as yet the couenant of the priesthoode pertained by the
lawe vnto Abiathar and his house.* But necessities and iust
occasions did oftentimes make change of the ceremoniall
lawes, and yet no corruption nor abuse came thereby.
Wherefore for aunswere I say, that the priesthoode was
not made a yeerely office, but that by course euery yeere
two priestes did execute the office. And this seemed to
be tollerable by the Lawe, seeing that if one priest should
be sicke, or letted by some greater occasions, the other
might be in his steade. *As wee shewed before, that Eeleazar*   Iohn. 18. 13.
*was chosen high Priest, while Aaron yet liued, and Zadok in
Abiathars steade, and yet were there not two high Priestes in
the office at once, but onely one at once to execute the office. Also
there seemed to be much doubt and controuersie, to which of the
pniestes* [sic], *the priesthoode did belong* (as also we may

---

[1] Intrusive comma in text.

reade in Iosephus.) *And therefore two chiefely standing for it, there were two chosen to it. And because the lawe of God did not suffer two at once to bee in the office, they did succeede one another in the execution of the office.* Againe seeing they were of the sonnes of Aaron, and called after the order of Aaron, no doubt their calling was lawfull and good. Otherwise if any at that time[1] had bene lawfull high Priestes, and yet not lawfully called as was Aaron, then the Apostle woulde not haue set downe this for a generall [81] trueth, *That no man taketh this honour vnto him selfe, but he that is called of God, as was Aaron.* Neither let him here shift off our answere, by his fonde distinction of the essence of a priest, and of a lawfull priest, which before is refuted. As for Symonie wherewith he chargeth the high Priestes, hee can not prooue it against them. For if the Romanes ouerruling them, did grieuously exact their tributes and paiments both of Christ himselfe, as we may reade in Matth. and of the high priestes: it was no more Symonie in the priestes, then it was in Christ to pay them their exactions. For the priesthoode was their right, seeing it pertained vnto them, being the sonnes of Aaron. yet can not *Master Cartwright* prooue that they payed any monie when they tooke their right, or if they did, that they thereby bought their right, and not rather payed an exaction, which the Romanes demanded when they tooke their right. But suppose that secretly they gaue bribes to the Romanes, & delt by Symonie, yet that being hidden and not manifest to the people, they were to be taken of men as lawfully called to that office. For if the Lawe and common tribute exacted monie of them, they might pay it as well as Christ. If the officers did exact any besides lawe, they did it secretely, lest they them selues should be condemned by lawe: and so it is manifest that no symonie could be laid to their charge.

And therefore no maruaile though Christ bad the man shewe him selfe to the high Priest. For before the high priestes became open persecuters, there was a lawfull communion to be had with them. But this communion was afterward broken, and made vnlawfull through their open wickednesse. Also it is false, which Master Cartwright saith, that Christ did reuerence the high Priest, and gaue him accountes of his doctrine. For he gaue

Heb. 5. 4.

Mat. 17. 25.

Iohn. 18. 23.[2]

---

[1] Intrusive comma in text.
[2] MS. has 18. 20. Both would serve.

An Answere to Master Cartwright

him no accountes, and answered him so roundly, that one of the officers whiche stoode by, smote him with a rodde. Also his aunswere is false cōcerning that place in Hoshea, that the Lord would refuse the priestes, for being any more his priestes: seeing [82] they were without knowledge, of which wordes he sayeth, that the prophet rather giueth a rule to be followed in their election or deposition, then howe farre they may be vsed. Nay the Prophet there speaketh nothing of electing them, or deposing them by men, but rather of the plague or destruction that shoulde come vpon them. yee hee sheweth that through the ignorance of the priestes all wickednesse and idolatrie reigned, and therefore he saith that there shal be like people like Priest, meaning that they shall haue a like destruction. Now *Master Cartwright* dare not say, that all abominable wickendnes and Idolatrie reigning, and the priests them selues being wicked idolaters, I say, he dare not affirme, that they helde the couenant, or were the people, or church of God. For before he hath said the contrary. And howe then dare he say, that such priestes[1] were yet priestes vnto God, and were not deposed from their priesthoode, when as their owne wickednes and idolatrie did depose them. For that whole chapter of Hoshea is altogether against their wickednesse and idolatrie. And let *M.C.* knowe that our open grosse sinnes & abuses, being not curable by the discipline of the Church, are as euill as Idolatrie: as Samuel the Prophet doeth witnes, saying, that *rebellion is as the sinne of witchcraft, and transgression* (he meaneth trāsgression which is stoode in, and wil not be mended) *is wickednes & idolatry*. But this matter is made manifest before. Hose. 4. 6.

Verse 9.

1. Sam. 15. 23.

Now followeth the last part of his letter, & the last matter in controuersie, as whether by communicating with or reading minister, we do communicate with their impietie, & establish their ministerie. *M.C.* herein doth more shamefully erre, then if he should, with the bishops, altogether iustifie such reading ministers. For he might better say, they were lawfull ministers, and that their ministerie were lawfull, then that he should confesse them to be vnlawfull ministers, & yet iustifie that we may receiue them, as hauing the essence[1] and substance of ministers, and partake in their wicked ministerie, without impietie or establishing their ministerie.

[1] Intrusive comma.

[83] But he may playnly see (except his eies of vnderstanding be vtterly darkened) that if any do vsurpe, as traitors, against her maiesty, then they also that come vnder their vsurped rule and gouernment, being once free from it, are also trayters together with them: So likewise those men vsurping a ministery[1] which Christ neuer gaue them, neyther sanctified to be in his Church, both they doe wickedly, and they also, that wil come vnder theyr ministery, do establish theyr wicked ministery, and partake with them in theyr impiety. *If a man of the winde,* (sayeth the prophet) *and false fellowe doe lie saying, I will prophecie vnto you of wine and of strong drinke*; *he shall euen be the prophet of his people.* Yea why not, sayth *Master Cartwright*, if the Church doe call such a one, is it his sinne onely, sayth he, and not theyrs that receaue him. And the prophets, sayth he, doe not lay it to the peoples charge, though they communicate with such. Doe they not indeede? doth not this prophet Micha laye it to theyr charge? doth not also Zecharie shewe how vnlawfull it was to communicate with false prophets, where be sayeth, *that when any false prophet shall yet prophecie, his father and his mother that begate him*[1] *shall saye vnto him, Thou shalt not liue: For thou hast spoken lyes in the name of the Lorde: and his father and his mother that begate him*[1] *shall thrust him through, when hee prophecieth.* But the trueth of this matter, I haue prooued before. Let vs further examine his wise reasons. He confesseth that if by communicating with him, we doe make him minister, then we are guilty of his wickednes. But we make him not minister sayeth he, though we communicate with him. But I demaunde, should we haue such ministers, if no parishioner, nor other did communicate with them? Woulde there be any magistrates, if there were no subiectes to bee vnder theyr guiding, or any master, if there were no seruants? So then as the hauing of seruants and subiects, to cōmunicate in the same houshold or kingdom, doth make [84] masters and magistrates, so to haue parishioners to communicate with such ministers, doth make them such ministers, and also establish their ministerie. If *Master Cartwright* were not voide of common reason in this matter, he would neuer affirme such absurdities. But before he graunted as much in effect, that the church which receiueth and calleth a minister doeth especially

Micah. 2. 11.

Zech. 13. 3.

---

[1] Intrusive comma.

make him minister: and therefore herein he is contrary to him selfe. And therefore it is written, that the congregation of the people[1] made Salomō king, and Zadok high priest. Indeede if the false prophets, or reading ministers doe runne of them selues onely, and were not called nor receiued of any, neither had any office nor ministerie in the Church, then the deuill onely[2] might be said to make them ministers, but the parishioners receiuing them for their ministers, and taking them to be called to that office by the Church, as *Master Cartwright* teacheth vs, and yeelding them selues to be their flocke and charge[2]. I say, those parishioners together with the diuel and his officers do make them ministers. As for partaking with the impietie of the minister, we haue prooued before, that if anye wickednes be open, and the church will not redresse it, it is guiltie of the wickednes committed, neither ought it to alleadge, that it can not redresse it. For it hath the power of Christ, to iudge those that are within, & those strong weapons of the spirituall warrefare, which can cut off all wicked disorders in the church. Otherwise as we haue shewed, it is not the church of God. Paul sheweth that except we purge out the olde leauen we can not be a newe lumpe to the Lord, neither keepe the Lordes feastes. he sheweth his meaning in that place, that they suffering such a grosse offender amongest them, were guiltie of his wickednesse, and coulde not partake in the sacraments, but it must needes be done with the leauen of wickednesse, and not with the vnleauened bread of sinceritie and trueth. And therefore in the next epistle it is shewed, that they all repented and sorrowed, as being guiltie of his sinne, whom they had no soo-[85]-ner excommunicate.

1. Chron. 29. 22
Ierem. 23. 21.

1. Cor. 5.
2. Cor. 10.

Mal. 1. 13.
2. Cor. 7. 11.

And why was king Hezekiah afraide, and all the people. For the ceremoniall vncleannes of some, but onely that they feared, least they all were polluted thereby, and the Passeouer not accepted. And therefore that vncleannesse, which the Lawe also did suffer, and which was without sinne, as we haue shewed, was openly confessed, and healed by prayer: least the keeping of that feast should be wholly vncleane. Howe much more then shal open grosse wickednesse, when it breaketh forth in the Church, make them all polluted and

2. Chron. 30.
17, 18, 19.

---

[1] Intrusive comma.
[2] MS., better, has comma.

guiltie thereof, if they refuse and will not redresse it.

Finally his similitude of receiuing goods or landes of a mans father being a murtherer, is vaine. For the sacraments which the reading ministers doe geue vs, are neyther his sacraments, neyther the Lords, as we prooued before, but are polluted pledges of a wicked communion. Againe wee may not receiue golde of a thiefe, to iustifie his thieuerie. And wee haue shewed that such ministers are theeues and robbers, and can not as fathers giue vs the Lordes holye thinges. Likewise is that answered of communicating with adulterers whome we can not (as he saith) auoide. For if their sinne be open and prooued, then both all the Church and euery one of the Church, ought and may auoyde them, I meane their fellowship in the sacraments. If their sinne is secret and not prooued by witnesses, then the question is not of them.

FINIS.

VI. SUBMISSION AND COMMENTARY

Browne's Submission to the Archbishop of Canterbury, 7 Oct., 1585, and his later commentary on it.

This is known only through Bredwell's *Rasing of the Foundations of Brownisme* (1588).

I. I do humbly submit my self to be at my Lord of Cant. commandemēt, whose authority vnder her Ma. I wil neuer resist nor depraue, by the grace of God.

Rasing, 127.

Commentary:
The bishops ciuill authoritie Browne did acknowledge lawfull in his subscription, and their magistracie to be obeyed. hee doeth by those wordes, neither iustifie those for brethren which doe persecute, nor allow an idle and Lordly ministerie in the Church as a part of the brotherhoode.

Rasing, 141.

II. [I acknowledge that] where the word of God is duly preached, and the sacraments accordingly ministred, there is the Church of God.

Rasing, 134.

III. [I acknowledge] the Church of England to be the church of Christ, or the church of God and promise to cōmunicate with the same in praiers, sacramēts, & hearing of the word and to frequent [the] Churches according to law.

Rasing, 134.

IV. [I promise] quietly to behaue myselfe, and to keepe the peace of this church: and not to preach nor exercise the ministerie, vnlesse lawfully called thereunto.

Rasing, 137.

V. I refuse not to communicate in the Sacraments. For I haue one childe that is alreadie baptized, according to the order and lawe, and by this time in mine absence, if God haue giuen my wife a safe deliuerance, and the childe doe liue, I suppose it is also baptized in like maner. Further, my seruants being three, doe orderly come to their owne Parish Church, according to the lawe and communicate also according to the Lawe.

Rasing, 140.

Commentary:

his childe was baptized according to order of lawe, But yet it was done without his consent, and contrary to an order he had taken and appointed; for it was baptised in England he being beyonde the sea . . .

he was not to force his seruants agaynst their conscience and custome, being newly come to him. he neuer came to the same Church with them, the parson beeing a common drunkard, and infamous by sundrie faults . . . there was no lawe to force him to take such a parson for his lawfull minister, neither to ioyne with him in the prayers and sacraments,

Rasing, 142 - 3.

VII. FRAGMENTS

From Browne's controversy with Stephen Bredwell it is possible to gather extracts from some of his writings, though not to reconstruct those writings to any extent.

Bredwell's works are two in number. In 1586 there appeared his *Detection of Ed. Glouers hereticall confection . . . . togither with an admonition to the followers of Glouer and Browne*[1]. In this work " Steph. Bredwell, Student in Phisicke ", scarcely mentions Browne, who seems to be dragged in merely that he might be smeared with Glover's heretical opinions. The only sentence of Browne's definitely quoted (p. 124) is from his

(a) Conference "with M.F. and M.E[dmundes]"; "there may be a true church of God without the presbyterie".

The second is *The Rasing of the Fovndations of Brownisme* (1588), to which reference has already been made. This work contains :

T-p.
T-p *verso* (¶ 1 *verso*) The chiefe conclusions in *this Booke*,
¶ 2 *recto* — 3 *verso* Epistle Dedicatorie [to Thomas Hussey]
¶ 1 *recto* — A 3 *verso* To the Christian Reader.
1—2 The doubts and obiections of a *certaine disciple of Robert Brownes*, wherein, being vrged to come to Church, the said partie desired first to be resolued.
3—10 An Answere resolutorie to *the doubtes and obiections* aforesaid; running title, " The first Answere for Communicating ".
11—60 A seconde Answere or Reioynder to *Brownes replie for the doubts* and obiections of his Disciple; running title, " The second Answere for Communicating ".
61—145 A Defence of the Admonition *to the followers of Browne*: made in reply to a raging Libell of Brownes, *sent abroade, in sundrie written copies*, against the same.

From the two works of Browne here mentioned, the " Replie to the First Answere for Communicating ", and the " Raging

[1] No copy in B.M. Copy in Cambridge University Library, 8. 58. 10.

Libell ", Bredwell quotes *ad lib*. It seems clear that Browne is often drawing on his previous writings; sometimes sentences are identical, at others slightly altered.

(b) " Replie for the doubts and obiections of his Disciple " [about communicating with the Church of England].

12. First hee sayth, *I make an Eldership, a part of your seconde point, leauing out discipline.*
13. Secondly hee sayth, *by Elders we meane Aldermen, as that we seeke no other but by ciuill power and authoritie to force the vnruly.*
13. Againe, . . *that the forward of euery Parish put forth themselues by visiting, counsailing, withdrawing, comforting.*
13. Hee supposeth, *considering the times, that an agreement were better than a choise.*
13. Hee giueth another reason: *that rather God may haue the praise in prouoking and calling them* [Elders] *then men in choosing them.*
14. *As for the names of Elders and other ceremonies in ordeyning, seeing they are made mockeries and matters of persecution, I iudge it superstition to make them vnchangeable.*
    hee addeth, *that it is to make in force the Popish sacrament of orders.*
15. he telleth you in plaine words: *That the obedience of the worthy vnto them, is a calling by man, and the agreement of the wisest is a choosing.*
15. My answere to your question hee sayth is *darke, doubtfull, shifting, vntrue, and cauelling.*
21. But he saith (Pag. 7) *If the Church bee established and refuse to debarre him, whome they confesse to bee so wicked and vnreformed, all are made wicked by our complaining.*
22. yet still he vrgeth, *that I warrant him to be a companion or brother in Christ, by communicating with him.*
22. But he cryeth, *that in this wise I admitte a diuision in the Communion.*
23. (p. 5) *if there be any open breach of the couenant by any one knowne to the rest, the sacrament is of no force* . . . (P. 4.) *The communion is not a diuision that is halfe good to the one part, and halfe bad to the other part, but eyther wholly good, or wholly bad.*
24. [Paul proueth the sacrament no sacrament to the Corinthians because] *the forme and institution of the Supper was violated by them all* [and] *so was the end and vse.*
31. *An Apostle is but one member, and yet might any one Apostle or messenger of Christ forsake or cast off whole Cities or Churches, that refused or withstood their message.*

Fragments

32. [Asks whether] *we be schismatiques for departing from* [the Popish Church].
32. *To deny Christes discipline and gouernment, is to denie Christ.*
32. [pp. 10. 15] Asks *Whether if the Church will ioyne in the Sacrament with an vnlawfull Minister, a Wolfe, a hireling, a theefe, those amongst them that knowe and can proue him such a one, may withdraw themselues?*
34. *particular members may depart from the bodie of the Congregation for default of separating the vnworthie.*
42. (p. 13). *The Sacrament of the Lordes Supper is a Sacrament of order, or orderly communion: . . order or orderly communion is the very fourme, matter, manner or essence, and nature thereof.*
43. *What places enforce an outwarde vniting in the Sacrament with the members of Christs body only, the same inforce a deuyding or refraining in the Sacraments, from those that outwardly are manifest to bee no members of his body: But all these places enforce such an outward vniting with members onely: Therefore they inforce a refrayning and diuiding in the Sacrament from open wretches, which are knowne to bee no members.*
44. *as euery particular mēber of a body, may shake of[f] the rotten, and yet not forsake the bodie: so may euerie particular member of a*
45. *Church . . . . As the members of a natural bodie, refuse to vse the seruice of the rotten ones: so ought the members of a spirituall bodie, refuse to communicate in the sacraments with such.*
45. [Asks] *What if the Church, or the rest of the bodie, will not withdrawe themselues from that dead and rotten member, neither will cast it off, what shall one member doe?*
    [Answers] *That if one member doe cast it off, the rest will not be angrie . . . it is a token, the rest of the members are not so liuely.*
46. (P. 16) *one Congregation is not the whole Church of Christ.*
50. *But then he woulde haue vs* crie out by nameagainst *those that restraine vs, yea though it cost vs our liues.*
53. *as sweete water intermingled with poyson, is poysoned and turned into the nature of poyson:* so the *notorious wicked openly mingled in one outward Church with the righteous, or the righteous with them, they become one wicked crewe together, euen all of them poysoned and infected together.*
57. (Pag. 15) he sayth *The wicked man remayned not among them*
58. (the Corinthian Church) . . . *They communicated not with him in the Sacraments being knowne . . . . they wanted not Christes power and discipline to seuer him[,] being in bondage to popish*
59. *discipline . . . They refused not to seuer him, but onely neglected it.*

132. *Thus your writing condemneth you of iniquity, that speake not one word in the pulpit[1], against the restraint by popish discipline, that ye cannot separate. How sore do you labour, and how much do you suffer, that dare not speake a word by name against those officers and courts, neither name nor protest openly against those wicked, against whom you would haue vs protest particularly by name.* [And by and by after] *But why labour you not also to charge them openly, though it cost you your life and liuing?*

(c) The " Raging Libell " — " sent abroade " (*i.e.*, broadcast, dispersed, with no suggestion of beyond seas) in sundry copies. Known only through *Rasing.* Apparently it contained 120 points. Five of these are quoted, apparently in full, possibly also a sixth (34, below) :

P. 134. No. 3. *Glouers popery or popish heresies, being long ago by many diuines refuted, needed not Bredwells childish refutation, whereas the cause wherin Bro[wne] hath stood as yet is refuted by none.*
P. 132 - 3. No. 20. *Thou hast written it heretofore, that there is no Aegipt in England, and hast thou now found vs out to be in Aegipt. Doest thou not perceiue, that thou and thy partakers, abusing your knowledge to persecute those which are come out of Aegipt, are worse then Aegipt, yea princes of Sodome, and people of Gomorrha? looke thou to it, that thou remain not in Aegipt. Thou hast confessed that we were once come out of Aegipt, thou canst not say so of thy selfe, if still thou iustifie thy Aegiptian doctrine & pollutiōs, as is to be seen by thy pamphlet.*
P. 133. No. 28. *We haue gained, by fleeing from persecuting wolues, not wealth, nor bellycheere, nor fauour in the world, but losse, imprisonment, all maner euil speaches, and death it selfe.*
P. 136. No. 105. *While they raile & resist the truth we may heare them as enemies, but ioyne with thē as brethren we dare not.*
Pp. 143 - 4. No. 108. *No part of Church Discipline can bee wanting, but the Church doeth straight way goe to ruine thereby.* .... *there may be a true Church of GOD without the Presbiterie,* [meaning] *that a Church remayneth still, though all the officers of discipline should die at once, because yet still the office and right of gouernemente shoulde remaine.*

To others reference is made as follows (page references are to *Rasing.* There is no reply to Nos. 1 — 29.

---

[1] Marginal note: " He supposed he had spoken it to our minister."

Fragments

P. 64. 30. In 30 Browne said he condemned truth as well as falsehood, because he [Bredwell] *could not distinguish betwixt the regenerate part of a man, (which though the man sinne, yet that parte sinneth not) and the vnregenerate part, which (though the man be iustified in Christ)*[1] *yet it is condemned.*

P. 114. 34. *The hypocrisie of rayling F. and Bredwell with their partners, is hidden in rich mens houses, sometimes in deceytful fastings, as though we should haue present reformation, and somtimes in delicate feastings, in bribes, gifts, shew of almes to the poore, when all goeth into their owne bellies or purses.*

Three examples of what Bredwell calls Browne's "reuiling phrases" are:

P. 114. 53. *O blind Pharisee: or rather O froward heretike.*
P. 114. 54. *Thou blind Pharise.*
P. 114. 60. *O false tongued man, shall not God plucke thee out of the land of the liuing?*

Pp. 77 - 8. 72[2]. *They that holde the power, authoritie, and gouernement of Christ not to bee of the essence of a Church, doe faine a counterfaite Christ, and a counterfaite Church: But they that say, discipline is not of the essence of a Church, hold the power authoritie, and gouernement of Christ, not to be of the essence.*

Therefore they that say discipline is not of the essence of a Church, feigne a counterfaite Christ, and a counterfaite Church.

Pp. 114 - 5. 75. *If all were such persecuting wretches as Bredwell is, they were not onely infidels, denying the fayth, but also worse than infidels because they yet suffered the beleeuers to dwell in the same house with them: but Bredwell and his partners would not suffer them to dwell in the same Citie with them, no not in the same Countrey, no not vpon the face of the earth.*

P. 115. 77. *Nay false hypocrite, this word onely is thine owne addition, &c. It is thy maner and thy partners, to force, to threaten, to make stirrings and hurlie burlies, and to driue man and wife asunder. Thine and their outrage cannot be satisfied with bloud. Thine and their raylings, slaunders and false accusations, haue brought diuerse of vs to death, some by the Gibbet, some by long imprisonment, some by flight and pursuit, some by extreame care, death*[3], *and sicknesse: some by seas, some by necessitie and want, some by chaunging aire, dwelling and place. The bloud of all these shall bee vpon thine and thy partners heades.*

[P. 134 gives from 77: *None of you all can show any fault, false doctrine or wickednes in vs.*

---

[1] Text mistakenly has closing bracket at the end of the sentence.
[2] Margin says from No. 72 and from the Answer to Cartwright (see above, p. 460).
[3] On p. 133, where the words are again quoted, "thought" is in the text.

513

114. Quoted by Bredwell as examples of Browne's " reuiling phrases " :

 78. *Nay thine and thy partners hypocrisie, ioyned with enuie, outrage, and crueltie, shall be better knowne. Thou teachest F. thy fogging Phisike, and hee teacheth thee his lying diuinitie.*
 79. *The wretch careth not what he forgeth against vs* . . . *O caitife, thou wouldest fayne heare of it, that wee were all hanged.*
 103. *Thou vnpitifull and gracelesse wrester*[1] *and falsifier, &c.*

---

1 Corrected from " writer " in some copies.

VIII. "A TREATISE AGAINST ONE BAROWE". 1588.

This is a reply to Henry Barrow's *Four Causes of Separation*, for which see *Trans. Cong. Hist. Soc.*, II. 149-50, [292-]301, T. G. Crippen's *Relics of the Puritan Martyrs*, 1593 (1906), 7-16, and the forthcoming edition of Barrow's work. The treatise is known only through a fragment quoted by Bancroft in his sermon at Paul's Cross, 9 Feb., 1588/9 :

Whereas you charge us in denieng Christ in his offices, and consequently not to be come in the flesh: it shall appeere by your presbyterie or eldermen, that indeed you are and will be the aldermen even to pull the most ancient of all, Christ Iesus himselfe by the beard: yea and seeke not onely to shake him by the lockes of his haire out of his offices, but also all his ancients under him, I meane the lawful magistrates and ministers, which haue lawfull authoritie from him.

Wherefore not we but you rather seeke the glistering blase of great name: and if once you might get up the names of Elders and Presbyters, what mischiefe, crueltie, and pride would not streame from that name, even as fire from a blasing star to set on fire the whole world ? For every busie foole, the more busie he were in discrediting others, and seeking mastership among the people, the better elder he should be judged. Yea and this new name of an elder given him, were even as a sacrament of grace, and would seale up all his knaverie: that whatsoeuer filthines dropped from him, yet the skirte of his ancients gowne should cover it.

---

[1] Richard Bancroft, *A Sermon Preached at Paules Crosse the 9. of Februarie, being the first Sunday in the Parleament, Anno* 1588 [1588/9] (London, 1588) [1588/9], pp. 76-77.

IX. AN AUNSWER TO Mr. FLOWERS LETTER 1588/9.

Dated "this last of December, 1588", the letter was edited by Mr. Champlin Burrage for the Congregational Historical Society in 1904, under the title *A " New Years Guift "*.

The identity of Mr. Flower, to whom Browne refers as "Louing Vnckle", "My good Vncle" and "Your Worships humble to command" remains a secret. If "uncle" is a literal uncle it implies that an aunt of Browne's married one named Flower, or that Browne's wife had an uncle so named. Students of Norfolk history have failed to discover any contemporary "Worshipful" Flower. A John Flower signed a Puritan "Supplication of Norwich men to the Queens Matie" in 1580[1]. In 1590 John Procter, the publisher of C.S.'s *A Briefe resolution of a right Religion. Touching the Controuersies, that are now in England*[2] wrote a Dedicatory Epistle to "The Right Worshipful Mr. Francis Flowar, Esquire : Iustice of Peace & Quoram" in which he spoke of Flowar's " bountie to some, & good will to all ", and his " daily furtherance to such as spend their time in matter of consequence " and urged that no " newe sects or erronious errours " can spring vp where there is right religion.[3]

The letter is in the British Museum (Add. MS. 29546, ff. 66 - 72), being purchased with a bundle of other papers for 6/- in 1874. It had some time previously formed part of the Harbin Collection, having apparently been owned by the Rev. George Harbin, Non-Juror, Chaplain to the Bishop of Ely (1684 - 91), and Librarian at Longleat.

It is written in Browne's clear and well-formed hand, and lacks some pages — perhaps a sheet of four. Instead it has

---

[1] See Peel, *The Seconde Parte of a Register*, I. 159 and the same writer's *The Brownists in Norwich and Norfolk about 1580*, p. 8.
[2] The book itself is entirely concerned with the Roman Church and the Pope.
[3] Mr. Flower may have been an uncle of Browne's wife, Alice Allen. There is a Tristram Flower, who married the niece of Browne, but since she was born in 1593, her husband cannot be the one intended. Conceivably, Tristram Flower is a son of the " Louing Vncle," Mr. Flower.

An Aunswere to Mr. Flowers letter

inserted an entirely irrelevant passage on the book of the *Reuelation*, perhaps part of the work on that book to which Browne referred in the Preface to *A Booke which sheweth* (above, p. 225).

The manuscript is thus endorsed by Richard Bancroft on 72 *verso* :

" Mr Brownes aunswer to Mr Flowers letter: for his iudgement in diuerse particuler pointes in this letter yo^u may not accompte of it: for he hath reformed them & hym selfe likewise. The wordes to be looked vppe I haue rase [underlined] wth my pen."[1]

It was this endorsement, *plus* the recognition of the writing as Browne's, which enabled Mr. Burrage to identify the letter as the one which Bancroft quoted in his famous sermon at Paul's Cross, 9 Feb., 1588/9, for the words underlined are those quoted in the sermon. Dexter had assumed that Bancroft was citing a lost printed work of Browne's, but clearly he was using this letter, which no doubt had been intercepted by the remarkably efficient detective agency he controlled.

[67 *recto*] My good Vncle, I would I myselfe were resolued as I should be, in such waightie matters/.* We both must confesse this true, which is written. 2. Thess. 2. 7. that the mysterie of iniquitie hath wrought, sence S^{ct} Paules tyme hethertoe. How hard it is to sound the depth thereof, & how far it hath spred it selfe, all the world hath felt, and in wofull manner tried it, and none I suppose can denie, but that Antichrist is come allredie and hath bene declininge theis manie years: I except onely those whose eyes the God of this world (as Paul saieth) hath blinded. Herein therefore hath bene and shall be much labor, to disclose those mysteries of Antichrist, & to auoied the pollution of them/: yea and the combrance and trouble, about names, offices, gouernment and right or order[2] of rules & succession hath bene & shalbe so great, and that both in ciuil & ecclesiastical state, that all mens witts shall faile them (as Christ saieth) for feare & for looking after those things, that shall come vpon the earth. Euen in this matter

---

[1] The same hand endorses the " Notes owt of ¶Harrysons ſbooke " in the same volume of MSS. (f. 116 *verso*) and also, I think, the endorsement " The copie of my lbe to Mr. Cartwright " on Bancroft's letter in Add. MSS. 32092. 124 *verso*. The inscription on the title page of Harrison's *Three Formes of Catechismes* (see above, p. 124) is in a more formal hand, perhaps Bancroft's, perhaps a scribe's.
* The oblique lines are in the original text and serve as marks of punctuation.
[2] order. Paper damaged, may have been " orders ".

you write of, concerning names & titles, aucthoritie & gouernment there is a mysterie. Christ gaue warning thereof, when he saied, call no man Rabbi, nor Doctor, nor father vpon earth, and prophecied of his first & latter coming to Judgement / forewarning that deceiuers should come, vnder colour of titles, & should pretend gouernment, chieftie & prærogatiues to vsurp ouer others/. Yea euen those lawfull titles of Pastor, Doctor, presbyter, Deacon/ etc, may become antichristian. For what difference is there betwene Father & Elder, & the name of (Doctor) which Christ forbiddeth, & the same name which other scriptures do iustifie. Who so euer therefore will be so a Pastor or doctor, or presbyter or Deacon, as that without those names, he condemneth the offices, or accounteth them voied, the same man is branded with a marcke of this mysterie. Thus did Antichrist clime vp first, when ministers called first for names & titles of offices of those first Christiā Emperors. They were ashamed to call for ciuil dignities & promotions: but chalenging their spiritual titles by prærogatiue of lawe, & so vsurping by them, they made those names essential, as they terme it to their ministerie: so it came to passe, that who so euer had the name geuen them by law, being neuer so vnmeet for the office, yet men must needs call them & take them for their pastors, or doctors or presbyters/: Wherefore the meaning of Christs words is this, that we should not so be bound, to the titles of Doctor or pastor or father or anie other name, as that for the names sake, or for their vnlawful authorising or consecrating by such titles or names, we should anie whit more receiue them for our pastors or doctors/. Wherefore he saieth, Mat. 23. be not ye called doctors, that is intrude or inforce not your selues vpon anie by lawe or by custome to be counted & called doctors: but if you haue the guift of teaching, teach & discharge your calling to them that willīgly will be vnder your chardge/. If anie refuse, though the Magistrate may force a kind of hearinge, yet may no man be forced to take anie man for his pastor or doctor against his conscience, / nether should the Doctor vrge his name and charge so far, as to præsume against anie by anie such title or vsurped preheminence/. Againe call no man your doctor or Father vpon earth, that is receiue no man by those names for anie law or custome, or dignitie & honor sake except in deed you fynd them to be teachers & fathers called & sent of God which you shal perceiue by their doctrine & fruites/, which being good, they may also be called of men/.

[67 verso] This therefore is my Judgement, good Vnckle, that though the names of pastors, doctors, & presbyters be lawful, being found in the scriptures, yet that a pope or proud popelinge may ly hyd vnder the names/. yea and further I Iudge, that if the Parliament should establish such names, and those the officers according

An Aunswere to Mr. Flowers letter

to those names, which seeke their own discipline / that then in stead of one Pope we should haue a thousand / & of some Lord byshops in name, a thousand Lordly Tyrants in deed, which now do disdaine the names/. This haue I found by experience to be trewe, both in forreine contries and in myne owne Contrie. I can testifie by trial of Scotland which haue traueled it ouer in their best reformed places, as in Donde [Dundee], S^{ct} Andrewes, Edenborowe & sundrie other Townes / And haue knowne the king in great daunger & feare of his lyfe by their Lordlie Discipline/, the nobles & people at great discord & much distracted, & yet all men made slaues to the preachers & their fellowe elders/. So that myne owne ears haue hard the king by name to be verie spitefully abused by their preachers in pulpitt, his doings & commaundements called in, reuoked, or repealed, or els established & performed as he durst or could do for feare or daunger of them. Also in euerie Towne I found the chiefe Magistrates in awe of them, much murmuring grudging & whispering conspiracies to be made on all hands, some tymes them on the kings syde to be put out of office, & their aduersaries put in / & some tymes them on the preachers syd put downe, & others sett vp. Further I haue sene all manner of wickednes to abound much more in their best places in Scotland, then in our worser places here in England. And to conclude when I came away, all the whole land was in a manner wholie diuided into parts, much people in armes, & redie to ioine battel, some with the king, & some against him, & all about the preachers discipline. In England also I haue found much more wronge done me by the preachers of discipline, then by anie the Byshops / & more Lordly vsurping by them, then by the other, so that as in Scotland, the preachers hauing no names of byshops did imprison me more wrongfully then anie Bishop would haue done, so theis having nether the name, nor the power, haue yet vsurped more then the Byshops which haue power. For before my first voiag beyond sea, & sence my last retourne, I have bene in more then twentie prisons / And for once imprisonment by the byshops, I haue bene more then thrise imprisoned by the preachers or their procuringe/.

This I haue written for the names of Elders, pastors, doctors, deacons./

Now for the offices I will write a few lines as you will me, & then lastly wyll come to our Byshops/.

Wherefore for the offices of Pastors & elders etc. I say that euerie Church of Christ hath them in effect, though not in name, & that no church of Christ can be or is without them. Yet againe I say that such offices of Pastorship, eldership & doctorship etc / as they seeke for, is in no church of Christ nor can be/. For then doeth the Church degenerate from Christ, when such vsurping Elders or aldermen, shal ambitiously, furiously, & as Lordlie Tyrants bring in subiection vnto them the Magistrats & people, & make mens consciences slauishly to yeild vnto the Bondage they shall lay vpon them / Iude. 8. Reuel. 13. 11. 2 Thes. 2. 7.

That the Church of Christ can not be without a pastorship or eldership it is euident, because the Church it self is that most graue & ancient elder whereof Christ is the Elder & pastor being called the ancient of Daies & the cheif shepherd & pastor of the flocke. The testimonies of scriptures you know for this, I need not rite them/

Yea the Church is elder then Christ concerning his manhood, because he was borne of the promised seede & so is often called in the scripture the sonne of man. [68 *recto*] By which title of being the sonne of man is ment that he is a sonne & child of the church which was his elder, because he had so manie fathers his ance[s]ters before him/. yet concerning his Godhead he was without beginning of daies or end of tyme / & is the first fruits & eldest by the resurrectiō frō the dead

Againe we know that a church must needs be, before anie particular elder can be chosen / . for one partie can not make a church, nether beget bodelie children to be of the Church but by an helper, And therefore no elder did breed or beget a Church, except there were first a church whereof he was/.

And though Paul be saied to beget a church in Corinth & therefore in tyme to be elder & father to that one particular church, yet he speaking of eldership by dignitie & aucthoritie & not in tyme, doeth confesse that though by comparison with particular persons in Corinth he was inferior to none, yet in respect of all the Church, he saieth that he was the seruant of the Church, & that Paul & Cephas was theirs, & they Christs, & Christs Gods/: Noting that euerie one member sauing Christ is inferior to anie whole bodie of the Church, & that the whole bodie is yet inferior to Christ, & Christ touching his Manhood is inferior to God. 1. Cor. 3. 2. // 2. Cor. 4. 5.

Also where it is saied, tel it to the Church, Mat. 18/. And if he heare not the Church, let him be vnto the[e] as a publican / where they all take (Church) to signifie an eldership/.

Yea they them selues confesse, that though Paul could or might plant some particular churches as being an extraordinarie elder, yet that the ordinarie elders whereof they speake, must needs be called by the church allredie planted so that the church is in deed by consequence vpon their owne words an eldership.

Further seing an elder is nothing els in the scripture but anie person of special wisdome & honestie, lawfully allowed & called

An Aunswere to Mr. Flowers letter

in the church to counsel, teach & geiue aduise without anie forcing, it is [*sic*] must needs follow that there are manie such elders in our churches / or at least wise may be without anie such titles or popish vsurping as they seek for/.

Wherefore if in anie Church neighbours can wisely & godlie take vp matters end controuersies & redresse disorders without anie iniurie to other officers, & if some haue special direction by authoritie to deale in such manner, they are no doubt lawfull elders before God & Man / & yet haue no name of presbiters & elders/.

And as for them that make imposition of hands, & a solem̄n fast to be of the essence of presbyters also the name & tytle it selfe, they stil establish that popish sacrament of orders / & so againe with their ellders, doctors & deacons do bring in Papisme/.

If then it be demaunded who shal call & consecrat Ministers, excommunicat, depose & put downe false teachers & bad fellowes, & iudg in a number of ecclesiastical causes, let the word of God answere, which appointeth the cheifest & most difficult matters to be iudged by them of cheifest authoritie & guifts. & other matters of inferior gouernours Exod. 18. 22. 1. Cor. 6. 5. Rom/. 12. 3. If it be asked who be of cheifest guifts or ought to haue cheifest authoritie, I answere that the ciuil Magistrates haue their right in al causes to iudge & sett order, & it is intolerable præsumption for particular persons to skan of euerie Magistrats guifts or authoritie or to denie them the power of iudging ecclesisiastical causes. For murthers, felonies, Adulteries, rebellions, blasphemies, vsurpings / Idolatries, oppressi[ons] & all other causes should be & are ecclesiastical, from which if we debar the magistrat, we vtterlie make voied his office, & leaue him nothinge of a Magistrate but the bare name.

[68 *verso*] Now for chosing & deposing ministers, let Christs ordinance be kept, that no man be called or taken for a doctor, pastor, preist or presbyter, for anie name title, custome or consecration by men, except they bring good proofe & assurance not onelie in general but euen to those that do or may make doubt or exception against their callinge/.

If againe it be saied, that while men might take & refuse their ministers as they list, all factions & heresies might grow / I answere that the ciuil Magistrat must restraine that licentiousnes. But the way to restraine it is præscribed of God/. First that a number of vnlawful ministers being now descried & made manifest to the world, that the Magistrats if they can not remoue them, do yet quietly suffer the people to fall away from them, which if they do not suffer, there will be in tyme, ten fould more factions & diuisions then otherwise there should be, especially because God hath prophecied that he wil disclose euen this mysterie of iniquitie also concerning hirelings & ignorant caitiffes/.

Secondlie if anie will forsake a preacher being his minister, & that preacher be found vnmeet for that office for some notorious wickednes or other vnsufficiencie, if the preacher can not wel be remoued, & the partie not able to stand in lawe with him & to driue him out/, that yet without charges of lawe, he may haue the matter tried by neighbours & freinds. But yet not so far as to displace the preacher nether simplie to refuse the hearing of his doctrine vpon good occasions, but onelye to refuse him for his pastor or minister, tyll further tryal, if he be found so vnmeet, or if not, that then the recusant which is in suspence for receiuing the communion of his minister, do so remaine suspended but yet without bitter, sharpe or chargeable dealing against him, till he be iustly condemned as willful in his fault/.

Thirdly that for auoiding of heresies & strange opininions [sic], none be admitted or suffered to refuse or withdrawe them selues which hould not the doctrine of christianitie after some exacter forme of catechisme, & be also able to geiue a good reason of their religion & profession in all such matters/. And that therefore if they haue conference, readings or expositions, in priuate houses, the officers appointed for that purpose do serch & trie their opinions & doctrine & see their orders / & if nothing be erroneously & disorderedlie attempted, that they be suffered, yea though some smaller fault or error be committed or escaped, yet if a greater fault happen, that they be punnishable accordingely.

Lastly that none be suffered to haue their voice or right in chosing church offices & officers but onely such as are tried[1] to be sufficiently grounded & tried & to be able to geiue a reason of their faieth & religion / And that the ciuil Magistrats may if they will, be both present & directers of the choise, yet permitting anie man to make iust exceptions against them which are to be chosen Further that they which are to ordeine, consecrate or pronounce them authorised, do it not in their owne name, but by voice & testimonie of the most of those wyser sort, whose consent & voices for the most part he hath gathered & doth shew. Also it skilleth not who do pronounc[e] & consecrate them whether bishop or other, so that it be according to the forme aboue mencioned & the partie be a wise & good man/, & the officers chosen be not by number, as that there must needs be but one preacher & no moe suffered in such a parish/ also two, three, or syx other helpers, arbitrators or presbyters if they will haue them so called, but that for teaching, who so hath bene priuat[e]ly tried verie often, & then is both willing & called openly to vse his guift may so continew, yea & be further also authorised if no dislike be iustly shewed

---

[1] " are tried " may be crossed out.

An Aunswere to Mr. Flowers letter

Likewise that sundrie wiser parties not able to preach, may yet by consent, when solemne agreement is needles or can not be had, may deale for matters of aduise

[Here page 68 *verso* ends, and evidently the following pages are missing. Page 68 seems to be part of the treatise of *Revelation* mentioned in the Preface to *A Booke which Sheweth* (above, p. 225). This subject occupies 69 *recto* and the first two lines of 69 *verso*.]

[69 *recto*] Then followeth the sixt degree, namelie the raising vp of his fellow Antichrists, that is the Turcks, saracens, persians, barbarians, Aegyptians etc / which are those foure angels appointed to ouerruñ the greatest part of the world / which allredie is come to passe/, sence the cheif Antichrist that man of Rome was exalted/. Then is the seauenth degree fullfilled in the worcking of all this mysterie of iniquitie euē tyll the end of [the] world specified in the 11. chapter/. and againe it is repeated in the 12. 13. 14. & 15 chapters, But in the sixteenth is shewed the seauen degrees of the falling of Antichrist/.

The first as is shewed before. The second by disclosing the woful state of the people / signified by the vial poured into the sea / & the rotten bloud killing the creatures in the sea/.

The third by displaiing false doctrine & heresies/

The fourth by notifiing all grosse ignorance, whereby much rage, blasphemies & factions followed/.

Yet all theis were the pulldowne of Antichrist / So that by & by followeth his fyft fall euen the shaking of his throne & seat so that his kingdome waxed darck, & they blasphemed & gnew[1] their tongues for anger/.

This is that plague of Antichrist which at this day is to be fulfilled namelie in speaking & preaching against their Lordships, great liuings, & all their vsurpings : For this is that vial powred out vpon his throne / which now is in pouringe, For the former are all poured out allredie, saue that the fourth also is not yet fullie finished/

This I write good Vnckle, that we may take heed how we iustifie & vphould that seat that must needs fall, I meane that pompe, glorie, riches, power etc/ of the clergie least we be taken in the sixt plague, Namelie that the three euill spirits bewitch vs to stand in that last battel of Gog & Magog, to defend this totteringe state to our euerlasting confusion/.

Rather this we must do, euen ioine with those kings of the east, & endeuour with them to drie vp the water of that great riuer Euphrates, that is to spoile & take away the merchandice

[1] Obsolete preterite of gnaw.

of Antichrist by sea & land / & thē shal the way be prepared, euē to burne Rome it selfe/, for that also must be burnt as is prophecied/. Reuel. 17. 16. Reuel. 18. 9. 22. 23. & this is the sixt fall of Antichrist.

And that it is Rome which shal be thus serued, it is euident, first because it is called the great cietie which reigned ouer the kings of the earth, stāding on 7. hils for Rome is called septemcollis/

But specially because the Number of the name of that man of Rome is six hundreth sixtie six/. let him that hath witt saieth the text. Reuel. 13. 18. count the Number of the beast, for it is the nūber of a man / for in deed the number of 666. doeth in hebrew letters, by which John being a Jew vsed to number, as the manner of the Jewes was, doeth I say make the name R O M A N U S. By which is signified that the Romanists & the abuse of the romane tongue should hinder & falsifie all religion / & learnīge And therefore [the] word (latinus) counting it by the greek letters doeth amount to the same number/.

Now the kings of the east are the Protestants which are all eastward in respect of Spaine & Rome & all their enimies the Papists are westward vnto them / And though some take them for the Turcks & barbarous people yet I haue proued in a seueral treatisse in latine,[1] touching the herring fishes hauing a writing of letters vpon them, taken in the east seas, that they signifie the princes of the protestants, & that they shal prosper in all their warrs against the Papists, euen tyll Rome it self be burned, & then shall Gog that is Antichrist of Rome & Magog that is Antichrist of the barbarians be ioined in league & come vp in battel aray euē into the plaine of the earth, & when they shall haue compassed in the poore church on all sids redie to deuoure it, Reuel. 20. 8. 9. thē shal Christ come with fier to Iudge [69 *verso*] all the wicked & so shall be the end / or that full, last or euerlasting plague of Antichrist which is the seuenth plague/.

Thus you see my whole Iudgement concerning this state of the Church saue that I haue conceiled some matters, offensiue to be delt in, & haue not as yet also shewed that commō mistaking of Discipline / as it followeth in the articles vnderneath sett downe/.

Concerning ecclesiastical discipline some are deceiued, & do mistake it for it is not that ciuil discipline, nor bodelie puñishing, nor outward forceing of good & bad / Nether is it a violence, outward power, Maiestie, dignitie or honour of the world, as some proud ministers would haue it/. This is proued by sundrie scriptures alledged before/.

---

[1] This Latin treatise seemingly has disappeared.

An Aunswere to Mr. Flowers letter

But it is the power of Christ by his word/I meane a spiritual power in ruling his Church/
   1. Cor. 4. 20.
   1 Cor. 5. 4.
   Mat. 16. 19.
   Rom. 1. 16.
   Luk. 19. 17.
   Rom. 14. 17.
   1. Cor. 1. 18.
   2. Cor. 10. 4. 5. 6.
   Ezek. 48. 35.
   Psal. 45. 6. 7.
   Heb. 1. 8.
   Reuel. 1. 6.
   Micah 4. 2. 3.
   Exod. 19. 6.
   Luk. 17. 20. 21.

Now that I condemne or at anie tyme haue condemned all England or all Churches of England for wanting or as wanting discipline, it is vntrue.

for I say and alwaise haue saied, that who so hath the word of God, & doeth liue according to it, he hath the discipline, gouernment or kingdome of Christ/.
   1. Cor. 4. 20.
   Rom. 14. 17.
   Luk. 17. 21.
   Mat. 13. 19.
   Mat. 4. 23.

Further I say that this discipline consisteth in sundrie points or dueties, of the least of which there can be no full ouerthrowe, denial or spiritual bondage, but the church doeth go to ruine thereby/.
   Mat. 5. 19. 20.
   Iames. 2. 11.
   Ezek. 18. 11.
   Hebr. 12. 16.
   Reuel. 3. 15.
   1. Sam. 15. 23.

I meane not, that for some default, negligence, or ignorance of the Church in some part of discipline, or in some doctrine & trueth it should be no church/. But for an vtter bondage, refusal, denial or ouerthrow of anie of theis followinge/.
   1. Cor. 10. 13.
   1. Cor. 5. 2.
   Gala. 6. 1. 2.
   1. Cor. 15. 34.

Namely without the word of God, or when it is denied, debarred or brought into miserable bondage of mens dispensations or traditions against the word/.
   2. Chro. 15. 3.
   1. Tim. 3. 15.
   Gala. 1. 8.
   Deut. 12. 8.
   Daniel. 7. 25.
   Isa. 59. 20. 21.

They I say that are guiltie herein & are depriued of the libertie, ether to confesse & testifie the true religion or to practisse the same, are vnder the thraldome of Antichrist, & not partakers of the kingdome of Christ/.
   Rom. 10. 10.
   14. 15. /.
   Micah. 4. 2. 3.
   Amos. 8. 11.
   2. Thess. 2. 10. 11.
   Reuel. 22. 18. 19.
   Zecha. 11. 10.
   1. Sam. 15. 23.
   Rom. 1. 16.

Also if no man haue libertie to commaund or instruct by this word, among such the church of God is not established/.
   2. Tim. 4 : 3 :
   Isa. 29. 10. 11.
   12. 13. 14. 15.
   Hose. 4. 4.
   Mat. 15. 8.
   Mat. 23. 13.

[70 recto] Nether are those the Church, which are in such spiritual bondage that they will not dare not or may not, counsel, exhort, admonish & edifie one an other/.
   Hose. 4. 4.
   Amos. 5. 13.
   Hebr. 10. 25.
   Isa. 59. 21.
   Deu . 30. 14.
   2. Tim. 4. 3.
   Mat. 23. 13.

Mat. 18. 18.
1. Cor. 5. 4.
1. Cor. 6. 12.
Mat. 23. 13.
1. Cor. 4. 19. 20.
2. Cor. 10. 4.
1. Cor. 7. 23.

Nether they which haue not the power or keyes of bynding & losing among them/. of releising or pronouncing remitted the sinns of the penitent, & of deteining or pronouncing deteined the wickednes of the vnrepentant/, and that particularlie by particular appliing, as occasion serueth/.

Heb. 10. 24.
Leuit. 24. 11.
Phil. 2. 4.
Deut. 13. 14.
Hebr. 12. 15.
16.
Joshua 7. 24.
Ezra. 9. 2.
Ezra. 4. 2. 3.
Act. 2. 40.
Reuel. 18. 4.
Reue. 14. 19.
Ezra. 6. 21.
Ephes. 5. 7. 11.
Joh. 10. 5.
2. Thes. 3. 14.
Rom. 16. 17.
Gala. 1. 8. 9.

Nether they wch haue no libertie, to inquire or make trial of abuses among them, nether to put difference betwixt good & bad, but are in bondage to ioine in one communion of the Church, with those whose profession indeed is most abominable, & are open atheists, vowed, & geuen ouer vnto prophanes of life.

Act. 5. 13.
Zecha. 8. 21.
Hebr. 10. 25.
Dan. 11. 34.
Psal. 133. 1. 2. 3.
Act. 2. 42.
Ezra. 4. 2. 3.

Nether they which thinck it vnlawful & for feare of man dare not or will not keep companie with the breethren for mutual edifiinge & so ether loseth his libertie herein, or doeth vtterlie condemne such meetings.

Joh. 5. 43.
Joh. 10. 5.
Ezra. 4. 2. 3.
2. Tim. 4. 3.
Zechar. 11. 16.
1. Joh. 4. 1.
2. Cor. 11. 20.
Rom. 16. 17.
2. Thes. 3. 6. 14.

Nether they which haue vnlawful ministers thurst vpon them in mans name, by dispensation against Gods word, & nether will refuse them, nether thinck it lawful because of mans Inhibition onely/.

1. Cor. 6. 2. 3. 4.
Rom. 10. 10.
Leuit. 24. 11.
Phil. 2. 4.
Reuel. 1 6. 1.
1. Pet. 2. 5.
Heb. 10. 24.
1. Cor. 2. 10. 15.
Ezra. 9. 1. 2.
Phil. 1. 9. 10.
Deut. 13. 14.
Hose. 2. 2.
Nom. 14. 6. 7. 8. 9

Nether they which geue ouer & lose their libertie of testimonie, accusation, or making exception, or right of their voices & speaking, also of Judging the trueth & true religion, of standing for, defending & laboring for the same, so that greuous abuses are incurable thereby/.

1. Cor. 11. 16.
Mat. 12. 25.
Luk. 16. 13.
Reuel. 13. 4.
Hose. 5. 11.
Reuel. 14. 9. 10.

Nether they which so far disagree of the orders & common dueties of worshipping & seruing God & ruling the Church, that seeming to striue for the Lords ordinance, the deeper they are plunged in the contrarie ordinances/.

An Aunswere to Mr. Flowers letter

Nether they whose dealing & whole endeuour in the ministerie for reformation is alltogether by extremitie, crueltie, violence, force & ciuil penalties, & neuer by lenitie, gentlenes, patience, mercie, kindnes & charitie /. Further all theis & such like are those greuous [ ]¹, for which the offenders therein, are breakers of the couenant, ouerthrowers, of discipline / & so are no mēbers of the church of God/.

Isa. 66. 5.
1. Pet 5. 3.
2. Cor. 11. 20.
Isa. 59. 15.
Ezek. 34. 4.
Zecha. 11. 16.
2. Chro. 15. 3.
Mala. 2. 8.
Ezek. 18. 11.
Jere. 11. 3. 4.
8.
Psal. 50. 16. 17.
Mat. 5. 19.
James. 1. 26.
Isa. 59. 20. 21.
Gene. 17. 1. 2.
Zech. 11. 10.

[70 verso] Namlie prophanes & Atheisme / of professors.² Hebr. 12. 16. 2. Tim. 3. 5. Reuel. 3. 15. falling to infidelitie & paganisme / 2. Cor. 6. 15. Ezek. 18. 6. 11. 2. Chro. 15. 3. Ezra 6. 21 from the true religion/-
Obstinacie in refusing to heare, iudg & learne anie special duetie of religion /. Act. 13. 46. 51. Act. 19. 9. Luk. 19. 17. 1. Cor. 11. 16. Isa. 30. 10.
Obstinat rebellion against the law & word of God in knowne dueties. Mat. 5. 19. Mat. 18. 17. 1. Tim. 5. 8. Rom. 16. 17.
Falling to Idolatrie from the true religion / 2. Cor. 6. 16. 17. 1. Cor. 10. 2. Exod. 34. 14. 15. 16. 2. Chro. 15. 3.
Contempt, disdaine, or condemning the sacraments. Nom. 19. 13. Mark. 16. 16. Gene. 17. 14. Act. 2. 42.
Blasphemie, cursing, heresie, against the true religiō & the name of God Leuit. 24. 14. 15. 16. Nomb. 15. 35. Deut. 18. 20.
Schisme & forsaking of the church of God. Hebr. 10. 25. Dani. 11. 34. Joh. 6. 66. Hebr. 12. 15. Hebr. 10. 38. 39.
Witch[c]raft, coniuring, sorcerie/. Reuel. 22. 15. Gala. 5. 20. Leuit. 19. 31. Deut. 18. 19. 20.
Blasphemous swearing & foreswearinge. 1. King. 2. 42. 43. Zecha. 5. 4. 1. Tim. 1. 11. Jam. 5. 12. Mat. 6. 13.
Reuolting & deniing the true religion for feare or worldlie welfare. Luk. 12. 9. Mat. 10. 33. Hebr. 12. 16.
Wilful præsumption to dispense against the word of God & to break his commaundements/. Deut. 18. 20. Gala. 1. 8. Rom. 16. 17. Mat. 5. 19.
The confounding & intermingling of the Church / Ezra. 9. 1. 2. 1. Cor. 10. [ ]³ Ezra. 6. 21. Exod. 34. 14. 15. Heb. 12. 15. 16. 1. Cor. 5. 11.
Vsurping & confounding the offices of the Church/. 2. Sam. 6. 6. 7. Act. 19. 13. 16. 1. Cor. 12. 29. 30. Hebr. 5. 4. Ezra. 2. 62. 63.

---

¹ Obviously some such word as "abuses" missing.
² From this point the Scripture references are part of the text, and not in the margin.
³ Verse omitted; perhaps 26.

Seeking to new mediators & intercessors for vs, as to Pope or Saincts / Isa. 8. 19. 1. Joh. 2. 1. 2. Reuel. 22. 8. Leuit. 19. 31.
Seking saluation or iustification by merit of worcks/ Rom. 11. 6. Rom. 4. 2. 14. Gala. 2. 11.
Contumacie & hardning the hart being called by extraordinarie Judgments & by our superiors in Gods name to mortificatō & humbling of our selues/. Isa. 1. 4. 5. 6. Leuit. 26. 21. Deut. 29. 19. 20. Mat. 3. 10.
Presumptuous breach or contempt of the sabbath & holie exercises/.
Presumptuous contempt & rebellion against superiors as by cursing, resistīg treasons etc.
Spiritual bondage to Antichrist or to other vsurpers in the church, whereby abuses do grow incurable/. Willfullie or for feare of man to geiue ouer their calling, to denie or refuse the testifiing or preaching of Gods trueth or of hearing & obeiing the same.
Also willfully to denie or refuse the vse of the keies / or to seeke to or execute Antichristian absolutions & pardons / or cursings & excommunications./ To geue false Judgement or sentence of malice or parcialitie/. Extremitie & crueltie in seeking the bodelie or spiritual distructiō of anie.
Railings, fightings, obstinat contentions, murthers/ etc.
Betraiing, forsaking or persecuting the breethren/. Knauerie by dispightfull & malicious touches/. Obstinat & malicious refusal to help releiue or succour the distressed breethrē.
Adulterie, fornication, Ribaudrie etc. Drunckennes, rioting, excessiue vanitie & pride. Commō Idlenes by geuing ouer or ceasing their calling.
Vnthriftines by shamelesse [71 *recto*] mispendings. Shameles couetousnes, briberie, extortion, Symonie etc.
Shameles couenant breaking, oppression, vsurie, robberie, Theuerie, cousinage, etc. Shameles & common lying, discrediting, slaundering, backbyting, false accusinge etc or Shameles excusing, iustifiing, conceiling or partaking with others therein etc

Theis are those open greuous or notorious offences, And to denie the trueth herein if it be with obstinacie is heresie/.

These I thought good to note downe, because none is to deale in discipline, except they lay some such platforme before them as this[1] to which those heresies also which are against the mysterie of the Godhead & of our creation, & likewise of our redemption in Christ must be added/. I did omitt them heare, because they are commonly knowne / & auoided/.

And if euerie weeke there might be inquirie in euerie congregacion of these things & redresse takē accordingly, it would sone be perceuied what the vse of true discipline is/.

---
[1] Edge of paper, word beginning "1".

An Aunswere to Mr. Flowers letter

Thus Louing Vnckle I haue spent some howers, to shewe my duetifulnes towards you, & to gratulate you with a peice of scribled paper this new yeares euen/. I would it were such, as that you might take it for a new years guift: which if you like not, it is no more worth, then your fancie thereto, doeth afford it. Yet I beseech you, how so euer you dislike it, let it rather ly in the bench hole safe, then be consumed with fier, because I haue no copie thereof/, & if it appere in the light at anie time, that in no case it be anie præiudice or daunger to me, seing I wrote it by your demaund. For I am pore enough & broken to to much with former troubles, & therefore had no need of further affliction.

      Your Worships humble
      to commaūd Robert Browne/
      writtē this last of December: 1588.

After I had finished this writing I red ouer your letter againe & found that I had forgotten to write of the word πρεσβύτερος which I am suer no learned writer will denie to signifie an elder. Now you take it onely to signifie a preist or minister / But if you will haue our word preist to come of πρεσβύτερος then must you interpret them both according to their natural sence, which is a senior or elder or one of more age/. For otherwise preist is a word of no sence, except it haue the interpretation by the first original. Yet in deed the scriptures wittnes, that the word presbyter is attributed to the Apostles: for so S$^{ct.}$ Peter nameth him selfe an elder. 1. Pet. 5. 1. allso to other ministers of the word, & to those that are rulers with them but are not able to preach publiquely. And therefore Paul saith, that the presbyters or elders, which rule wel, are worthie duble honor, specially they that labor in the word & doctrine. 1. Tim. 5. 17.

But what I iudge of the vse of theis names & offices I haue before writtē / this onely I add, that the former elders in age & tyme in the cæremonial lawe, were figures of the elders or first & former[1] in guifts & graces sence the abolishing of ceremonies, & therefore the names are not so much to be stuck vpon, nether the eldership by birth or continuance, but the vse of the guiftes & graces are specially to be regarded/.

---

[1] Perhaps "foremost" intended.

X. LETTER TO LORD BURGHLEY, 15 April, 1590.

From Lansdowne MSS. lxiv. 34, f. 89, endorsed :

"M^r. Rhobt Browne to my L. Offers a treatise to my L., made by hym self, wherein is discouered, the error of all arts. and how the same may be confuted out of gods woord, and learned in a very short tyme. And now thynks, that therby ye old verse is verefyed, made of Oxford and Stamford ".

Printed, not quite in full and not quite correctly, in Strype, *Whitgift*, III, 229 - 30.

>To the right honorable Lord Burghley
>Lord High Treasurer of England

With especiall reuerence and dutifull submission I exhibite this treatise to your Honour. The latine tables and definitions thereof I haue before tyme written to your Lordship, which as I understand, haue bene shewed to some learned & reuerend Fathers the Bishops, but are ether neglected or through greater busines forgotten. Neuerthelesse I assure my selfe, & dare offer the chalendge that here in this treatisse, I haue iustly altered the arts & the rules & termes of Art, by euidence of the word, & haue corrected manie errors of all our professors, yea manie falsified points of learning bothe in the methode & trueth of the arts & also of religion. Allso I am able to Justifie this treatise and the exact methode & truethe thereof against the multitude of philosophers, doctors & writers heretofore. Further I offer to proue that the Word of God doth expressely sett downe, all necessarie & general rules of the arts & all learning: as may appeare by this book: but should more appeare if examples were added, and the contrairie errors more largely discouered. O that our universities were herein yet better aduised & reformed, I dare say no more: But I Judge that, that prophesie was of God touching Oxford & Stameford, & that some good menn long ago striuing against Antichrist, did foresee & foretell of the returne of good studies & profession[1] of learning to Stameford, & that to the shame of Oxford, which then withstood & preuailed against Stameford, suppressing it & the trueth therewith. O right Ho. & prudent, I speak noe toie but euē in this poore treatisse of me a Stamford man do see it

---

[1] Corrected. The word "profession" instead of "professors" seems to be the better reading.

Letter to Lord Burghley

partly verefied, yea I dare by Gods helv & your Lordships fauour vndertake this plea or cause, that in one yeare schollers may well learne together those arts, which scarcely in ten yeares they vntowardly learne in the vniuersities. And that by diuine wisdome, & prudence they shal confute their Logick, by right speach and languag disproue their Grammar, By right vse of prouerbs & prouerbial speaches or bywords disproue their Rhetorick. Allso their Arithmetick, by the right rules of nūbering, their geometrie by better measuring. Their musick by better melodie, Their metaphysicks by the lawes of creatiō, coueñant, and sanctificatiō. Their Ethicks, Aeconomicks, politicks, by true Religion & righteousnes. Yet I condem̄ none of the arts, but onely the falsifiing of them: And if it were not that I am become odious to manie for the trueths sake, I would not doubt by Gods grace, to bring manie thousands of my mind & iudgmēt, & in verie short tyme profit them in the former studies, as is aboue specified. I meane if I were authorised to read publique lectures & make profession according. For as Plato, Aristotle, Sokrates & Pythagoras made manie thousands scollers, & that without anie publique mantenance & charge, & in verie few yeares, so much rather in the arts & pointes of religiō more truelie handled, & vtterly differing from them all, I would hope by your Lordships good countenance onely, to performe much rather the like, & that in all quietnes also, not medling to condemne or controule anie learned man or anie kind of profession.

Thus being longer herein than I would, I cease[,] praiing for your Honours health & eternal blisse.

Your Ho. poore Orator
Robert Browne.

APPENDIX A
NOTES OWT OF HARRYSONS BOOKE

The following notes evidently were extracted from Harrison's writings as a preliminary step to the issuance of the royal proclamation of 1583 against the works of Harrison and Browne. The probable date of compilation would be the winter or spring of 1583. There are two copies of these notes, the original set, in my judgment, being in the British Museum, Additional Manuscripts 29,546, folios 113-116. The other set of notes is in the Public Record Office, State Papers, Domestic, Elizabeth, Volume 146, No. 20 [S.P. 12].

It is interesting to note the selection of items from Harrison's writings. Since these extracts constitute a part of the *raison d'etre* for the proclamation of 1583, they provide an insight into the attitudes of the officials of state and church just prior to Whitgift's appointment as Archbishop of Canterbury.

[f. 113 *recto*] A treatyse styrringe vp vnto carefull desyringe an[d]¹ dutiful laboringe for true churche gouer[n]ment./

To all Xp̄ian Brethren in England wch wayte for the kingdome of Christe./ [p. 70]

1. fol: 3   The fyrye sworde did hange over vs in Qucene Maryes tyme wherof the Lord delivered vs. [p.74]

2. fol: 4   But o^r clergye wch should haue labored about
faults in   the lordes worke first before they were installed in
the clergy   there roomthes, [rooms, places] they contrarywise layd hould vppō these liveinges. [p. 75]

3. fo.: 5   But those thynges they receaued of the cananytyshe Romane [womane?] wch ought to haue bene execrable. [p. 76]

The Lord gaue vs victorye, w[i]thout battayle &c. meaninge by the deathe of Queene Marye, And the lorde also gaue vs the earnest of assured victorye in thes bat[t]ayles¹ that weare to insue, in the behalfe of his son[s]¹ kingdome against Antechriste. [p. 76]

4. fo: 6. 7.   But wee refused to goe to battayle against him, we hau[e]¹ more made covenāt wth Antechristes burdes [burdēs, birdes?] knowing [borrowinge]² many of there ceremonyes, entertayninge theire fo[rm]¹ of

¹ The manuscript is torn along the right-hand margin.
² This is the reading of the Public Record Office manuscript. Henceforth, all such variations are indicated by the letter ¶.

532

Notes owt of Harrysons booke

	service for the most parte makinge our selues willing slaves to there Ecclesyasticall sworde and byca[use][1] this practise could soonest be attchyved [achieved] and this vngratio[us][1] worke could soonest be mumbled [iummbled?]¶ vp, then was it accompted pollycye to wyppe mens noses & to geue them a necke [neecke], [mocke]¶ youe should not haue admitted any tolleraton of vanityes wth a smoothe and feigned p[ro]mise to haue taken them away in tyme. [pp. 76, 77]
5. fol. 8.	Thos y^t haue beene cheefe m^r [master] workmen at the firste in reformatōn of religion, cannot espye that they haue framed ther tymber some to[o] longe, some to[o] shorte and ready to reele: yt waythe [wayteth]¶ but for a blast from the lorde to cause it to fall, and slaye all thos [thes?] that commytted them selues to suche a false buildinge./ [p. 78]
6. fo. 9. 10. many thinges amisse.	Many do confesse that thinges be amisse in the church. maye the churche [the Lordes Worke]¶ aboue other thinges, suffer delaye [or][1] [and]¶ wayte vppō o^r good leasure. [p. 79].
7. f. 10: 11	[f. 113 verso] But they saye we must beare nowe for the tyme is past: Indeede there was a tyme carelesly slypped [skypped?] at the begininge when the Iron was hott but the workmen weare laysye and neglected to frame there worke before the Iron was coulde. [pp. 79, 80]
8 [f.] 11. gods royall throne wantes	As we haue harde there wanted not some gracyouse offer concerninge thes [those]¶ thinges but they [the Lorde]¶ laye not to o^r chardge the thinges paste [past, passed]. [p. 81]
9.	He affirmethe in effecte that gods Royall throne wch is churche gouerment wantethe amonge vs and p[er]swadethe to erecte a tabernacle to the lord. [p. 81]
10. [f.] 12. people	Howe the people hauinge some knowledge and zeale haue agreeed [sic] wth there guydes in there negligence for they haueinge gotten seruice into englysshe thoughte them selues excused. [p. 81]
11.[ff.] 12: 13	The people haue been as a strange [stronge]¶ asse cowcheinge [towcheinge?] downe betweene diu[er]se burdens of sperytuall bondage and haue beene subiecte vnto the yocke wch is contrarye vnto

[1] The manuscript is torn along the right-hand margin.

12. [ff.] 15. 16. [reli]gion¹ evill reformed	that lybertye where in Christ hathe sette vs free./ [p. 82] What reprochefull and myserable men are wee wch see not our reproche &c. But boast in o^r shame and saye, we haue religiō reformed better then others where o^r wante is more than one thousand cytye walles and all the cytyes in the worlde be not worthe one lyuelye churche./ [pp. 84, 85]
13. f. 16	He exhorteth the people to mourne vntill they see this brought to passe and them selues lyvelye stones of this lyevlye [sic] buildinges [sic] and p[ro]ceedethe wth exhortacōns to that end and saythe that Christ hathe left [liste]¶ vs.// [p. 85]
14. fo. 17. Bondage and cawses	That Christ is not withe vs because the sworde of his enymies exalted, and his sword troden vnder foote and that wee are in greater bondage then the Iewes were in Babylon[.] [p. 85]
15. fo. 17	He appoyntethe for one cause, that the guyderes of our soules, are appoynted w[i]thout o^r counsaylle or aduise.// [p. 86]
16. fo. 18.	Further yt [that]¶ wee haue noe power to complayne in o^r [owne]¶ congregacōn but other lordes besydes Christ doe rule ouer vs and ouer the whole churche.// [p. 86]
17. [stin]ted¹ service	Moreouer we cannot serue god publiquelye in speryte as we ought for we are tyed to the deade letter, and stinted [folio 114 *recto*] out o^r measure yt [that]¶ we must giue god this daye &c. [and so]¶ other dayes &c. w[i]th many lewed [lowde?]¶ wordes agaynst godes servyce, appoy[n]ted by the lawe./ [p. 87]
18. fo. 19:	And yt [that]¶ we are forced to make [mocke?]¶ the lorde, in brin[g]ing [torning?] to him suche worshipe as he spuethe out of his mouthe. [p. 87]
19. electio de minister [*sic*]	Yf halfe a score chuse a man fytt to guide them can they bringe him in: or maye they goe to another place, noe by lawe they must come to their p[ar]yshe. [p. 87]
20. f. 20 vt sup. bondage	He seemethe to moue the people rather to dye, therto [then to]¶ suffer theise bondages w[hi]ch sayth he be more greuous and more daungerous then the Babylonyan bondage of ye churche [Jewes].¶ [p. 88]
21. fol. 20, 21. inf[ra] [?]	After p[er]suasyons to them that there is cause to lament[,] concludethe, that albeit at the begininge

¹ The manuscript is torn.

Notes owt of Harrysons booke

exhortations to all people
wee haue not done faythefullye yet let vs sweare and vowe t[o] seeke his face &c. and not to rest tyll we haue p[erfor]med o[u]r vowes. [p. 89]

22. fol. 22
Many that haue bene zealous to remoue ceremon[ies] and stinted seruice and hoped longe for redresse by p[ar]lymt and disapoynted they houlde them selues excused, but that is not enoughe for that they must not cease to seeke the kingdome of god. [p. 91]

23. prayer and practice
Nor yt is not enought [sic] to praye for a mendemt [amendment] for prayers w[i]th out practyse are but poore prayers, and the harte w[hi]ch settethe not by the hand and [on]¶ work dothe not burne w[i]th much heate. [p. 92]

24. fo. 25. government ecclesiasticall
We haue labored to o[u]r power in the behalfe of true ecclesiasticall gouerm̄t and haue returned emptye. [p. 92]

He perswadethe to seeke reformacōn and to girde vp our loynes yt we maye w[i]th more swiftnes and courage wake [walke]¶ therin. [p. 92]

25. fo. 30 no worldly iurisdiction
It is the callinge of euery Christian to remoue himselfe from the comm[un]yon w[hi]ch worshippe god vaynely &c. and to ioyne only where the lords worshipe [is]¶ [114 verso] free and not bound or w[i]th holden w[i]th bandes [bondes]¶ of wordlye [worldly] Iurisdictiō nor wayte vppon there leasure for a commandem[en]t thervnto. [p. 97]

26. fo. 31 : 32.
Lawfull callinge of mynisters &c. and the meanes of our saluacōn must be kepte awaye vntyll a cyuill lawe send them vnto vs albeyt there be neuer so longe delaye. [p. 97]

27. fo. 37.
No mynister now is lawfully called. [p. 99]

fo. 38.
The chefe of the clergye and the chefe w[hi]ch haue the [reanes — reins¶] roomthes, [places, positions] of cyuill regym[en]t are against thestablishm̄et of churche gouerment. [p. 103]

28. faythe and thervpon procurement of rebellion
He asketh wheare is the [that]¶ faythe where by o[u]r fathers subdued kingdomes and of weake weare made stronge. [p. 103]

[29.] ff. 38, 39
The children of Israell weare ready to haue entred into there rest but throughe vnbeleef of thinkges [sic] brought by espyes, they shutt vp there dores the thinges brought weare that the walles were hyght [high] and the people stronge. [p. 103]

[30.] fo. 39,
Even so we wold enter into a trewe reformed

40. [A lyon]¶ [31.]	churche but some bodye is agaynst it[.] I knowe wherof you mean a Lyon is in the waye. [p. 104] He contynuethe a p[er]suasion that thos [thes?] thinges and the hyghe walles by faythe shall fall downe. [p. 104]
32. fo. 41.	Nehemyahe [Nehemiah] doubted not the fewnes or pouertye of the Iewes nether the mallyce of enymies but stepped to the worke in the middest of theire [theise]¶ vnlyklyhoodes so when the hartes of gods people by faythe be encoraged and theire handes strengthened and put to the busynes god will reforme for he will teache o[u]r handes to warre and o[u]r fingers to feight[.] [p. 105]
33. fo. 46: stinted service	In the churche yt we are ioined vnto we submitte o[u]r selues vnto the ordyn[a]nces [ordynūces?] of Antechrist[,] for prayers and thankes gevinge must be measured out and appoyncted after the Popes fashion. [p. 110]
34. fo. 47: abusinge of estates	[115 recto] One of the greatest lettes [hindrances] in finishinge the lordes worke is for that yt cannot be done w[i]thout abusinge [abasinge]¶ of the loftynes of many wch are exalted w[i]thout the lord./ [p. 111]
35. fo. 52. the Church of Englande	There be wittnesses in England yt knowe how that exceedinge many mouthes of the teachers, and of thos that speake as the[y] are taught have confessed concerninge theire churche and say it is naked and yet a church [&c.]¶ [pp. 114, 115]
36.	Some saye it is a man that wantethe a legge and yet a churche &c. But all this while they espye not wherin the great deformitye lyethe, namely in that it hathe a lytle prety bodye and a great sorte of monstrouse greate heades, and sayth that other lordes besydes Christ hathe [haue]¶ ruled. [p. 115]
27 [37.] f. 53.	Concerninge the churche of England as the[y] entyle it [, it] is a notable dishonor to Ihesus to make all the p[a]rishes in England his churche, he denyethe as it semeth yt euer god knoweth the booke of common prayer to be his. [p. 115]
38. f. 56. who ought to begin reformation	He saythe yt there is a questyō expounded [pponed, proponed]¶ and flyinge abroade w[hi]ch is whether the Prynce or the people ought to begy[n] reformacōn in the churche where vnto he answereth that kinges ought to reforme as far as to them appertaynethe./ [p. 118]
39.	And that the people ought to reforme w[i]th out

Notes owt of Harrysons booke

kinges office	tarrying as far as the bondes [bandes]¶ of there callinges reache also and settethe forthe what ap[er]teineth to the prynce that is./ [p. 118]
40. ff. 57, 58	[115 *verso*] To breake downe Idolatrous altars[,] to burne theire Images w[i]th fyer[,] staye [slay]¶ those that haue revolted from Christianity vnto Idolatry[,] to take away Bishoprickes[,] Deanryes[,] [pr[e]bendes[,] cathedralles theyr chauntryes [chaunters]¶[,] musicke[,] Bishopes Chauncelores, archdeacons[,] Com̄issaryes[,] proctores[,] officialles[,] Som̄oners and Questners [questmen] w[hi]ch robbe the Church or her authoritye. [p. 119]
40 [41]. stinted service	Theyr Courtes[,] Cannon lawes[,] frehold p[ar]sonages[,] vicarages[,] w[hi]ch hinder the election of the minister[.] [p. 119]
42.	Blinde and dumme ministery [mynisters]¶ & stinted service to be read[.] [p. 119]
43. ff. 58: 59: no law	The duty of gods people is to remoue them selves from this & all other abhominacōns [,] not to ioyne handes w[i]th open wickednes [,] not to goe vnder the yoke of spirituall bondage, but to stand fast in the libertye wherin he hath made vs free./ [p. 120]
44.	And after he asketh what vngodly tounge [being?] [tonge]¶ dare be so bold as to say that we ought to tary one howre, but yf we tary for a newe grawnt from men to doe our dutyes in the true worship of god when we haue sufficient grawnt frō heaven we shall dye in our sinne. [p. 121]
[45]¶	If this be [the]¶ true Church government why doe the ministeres sue to the p[ar]layment or to the prince even for a law to compell to yt [that]¶w[hi]ch the Lord hath com̄aunded them to doe./ [p. 121] And so end [endeth]¶ w[i]th [a]¶ prayer./

APPENDIX B

BY THE QUEENE

A Proclamation against certaine seditious and scismatical Bookes and Libelles, &c.[1]

THE Queenes most excellent Maiestie being giuen to vnderstande that there are sent frō the partes beyond the seas, sundry seditious, scismaticall, and erronious printed Bookes and libelles, tending to the deprauing of the Ecclesiastical gouernment established within this Realme, set foorth by ROBERT BROWNE and RICHARD [ROBERT] HARRISON, fled out of of the Realme as seditious persons, fearing due punishment for their sundry offences, and remaining presently in Zealande: which seuerall bookes, doe manifestly conteine in them very false, seditious, and scismatical doctrine and matter, and haue notwithstanding bene secretly solde, published, and dispersed in sundry places within this Realme, to the end to breede some scisme among her Maiesties subiectes, being persons vnlearned, and vnable to discerne the errors therein conteined: Her highnesse therefore perceiuing the wickednesse of these euil spirits, and the malicious disposition of lewd and euill disposed persons to be readie to violate and breake the peace of the Church, the Realme, and the quietnesse of her people, and knowing it also to be most requisite and conuenient for her highnesse to vse those meanes which God hath appointed for preuenting thereof, doeth will, and also straightly charge and commaunde that all manner of persons what so euer, who haue any of the sayde Bookes or any of like nature in his or their Custodie, that they and euery of them doe foorthwith vpon the publishing hereof, bring in and deliuer vp the same vnto the Ordinarie of the Diocese, or of the place where they inhabite, to the intent they may bee burned, or vtterly defaced by the sayde Ordinary. And that from henceforth no person or persons whatsoeuer, be so hardy as to put in print or writing, sell, set foorth, receiue, giue out or distribute any more of the same or such like sedicious bookes or libels, as they tender her Maiesties good fauour, and wil answere for the contrary at their vttermost perils, and vpon such further paynes as the Lawe shall inflict vpon the offendours

[1] *A Booke Containing All Svch Proclamations, As Were Pvblished Dvring the Raigne of the late Queene Elizabeth. Collected Together By the industry of* Humfrey Dyson, of the City of London Publique Notary. London, 1618. Folio 225. (British Museum, Press Mark G 6463). This is probably a unique volume, collected by Mr. Dyson, Clerk of the Parliament. He caused a printed page to be placed at the beginning of this volume, but there are no other copies. Similar collections, however. are in the Bodleian Library, and in Queen's College, Oxford.

By the Queen

in that behalfe, as persons maintayning such seditious actions, which her Maiestie myndeth to haue seuerely executed. Giuen at her Maiesties Mannor of Greenewich the last day of June, in the fiue and twentieth yeere of her highnesse Reign [June 30, 1583].

God saue the Queene.

Imprinted at London by Christopher *Barker, Printer to the Queenes most excellent Maiestie.*

APPENDIX C

THE WILL OF ROBERT BROWNE

Robert Browne died on or about October 1, 1633. His widow and second wife, Elizabeth Warrener Browne, secured letters of administration on October 19, 1633, from the Prerogative Court of Canterbury, on the grounds that her husband had left no written will. The following is the earliest document relating to a commission issued to Mrs. Brown.[1]

Decimo nono die [October 19, 1633] emanavit Com[missio] Elizabethe Browne rel[i]c[t]e Rob[er]ti Browne cl[er]ice nuper r[e]ctoris ecclesie parochialis de Achurch in Com[itatu] North[amp]ton def[uncti] h[ab]entis etc.[2] ad ad[mini]strand[a] bona iura et Cred[ita] d[i]c[t]i def[uncti] de bene etc.[3] coram Will[el]mo Allen Cl[er]ico[4] vigore Com[missionis] etc. iurat[a].[5]

Petriburg
Blassii
In^m ext 1°
p[er] Andree
1634

Evidently Mrs. Browne was dissatisfied with the arrangements of 1633, for the following year she produced a nuncupative will, which was proved April 21, 1634.[6]

MEMORDANUM that vpon or about the ffirst daie of October in the yeare of our Lord God one Thousand sixe hundred thirtie and three Robert Browne late of the Parish of Thorpe Atchurch [Achurch] in the Countie of North[amp]ton Clerke deceased haveinge an intent to declare by his will nuncupative whoe should have and enioy those temporall goodes which God in mercie had blest him withall exprest his will therein in manner and forme followeinge vidlt [videlicet, namely]

I doe giue and bequeath all my goodes chattles and estate whatsoeuer vnto my Deare and Loveing wiefe Elizabeth

---

[1] This document is in Somerset House, Administration Act Book, Prerogative Court of Canterbury, 1631-1633, folio 198 *verso*.
[2] Having an intent to declare and appoint his wife administratrix, or some similar expression.
[3] De bene et fideliter administrando eadem.
[4] The manuscript reading is clici, but an ablative case seems necessary.
[5] A marginal note reads : "Introduct sunt he lre et adco cu testo nunc comiss Apr anno dni 1634." (Introductae sunt hae litterae et adiuncto cum testamento nuncupativo commissae Aprile anno domini 1634).
[6] Somerset House, Prerogative Court of Canterbury, 32 Seager.

540

The Will of Robert Browne

Browne who hath euer bine a most faithfull and a good wiefe vnto me. And I will and my mind is that none of my Children shall haue or enioy any parte of my said estate and to that end I haue securitie to shewe from some of them[.] But if anye person or persons shall thinke or saie that I haue not delt like a ffather with them I doe hereby lett such knowe that I haue heretofore my selfe advanced preferred and giuen vnto each of them more then their due & proportionable part of and out of all my said estate.

These wordes or the verye like in effecte were spoken by the said Robert Browne beinge in perfecte mind and memorie in the p[rese]nce of vs whose names are herevnder written[1]

Signum Willimi Browne
John Coles.//

Vicesimo primo die mensis Aprilis Anno Domini 1634 emanavit commissio Elizabethe Browne relicte dicti defuncti ad administrand[a] bona iura et credita eiusdem defuncti iuxta tenorem et effectum testamenti nuncupativi dicti defuncti eo quod Idem defunctus nullu[m] in eodem nominavit Executorem[.] De bene et fideliter administrand[o] eadem ad sancta Dei Evangelia in debita Juris forma Iurat[a] Willimo Browne et Iohanne Coles testibus tempore condic[i]o[n]is et declarationis Testamenti nuncupativi predicti personaliter presentibus De et super eiusd[em] etiam Jurat[is?]

Mrs. Browne may have considered herself a "Deare and Loueing wiefe," but her step-son, John Browne, contested successfully the will in 1637, as revealed in the following summary:

Sentence was pronounced by Henry Marten knight LLD, Master of the Prerogative Court of Canterbury, Saturday 20 May 1637, in the Cathedral Church of St. Paul's London, at the petition of George Gaell notary-public procurator of John Browne and in the presence of Thomas Webb notary public, procurator of Elizabeth Browne, in a cause touching the exhibition of an inventory and rendering account of the goods of Robert Browne,

[1] A marginal note reads : Testum̃ ac lre adnis huḿod pronuntiũr pro nullis p Sniam (Sm̃am?) diff. lat 2do Ascen 1637. (Testamentum ac litterae administrationis huius modi pronuntiantur pro nullis per Sententiam definitivam latam 2do Ascensionis). In 1637 Easter fell on April 9 and Ascension Day on May 18. Hence the second of Ascension would be Friday, May 19, but the second day after Ascension (*post festum Ascensionis*) would be Saturday, May 20, which is the correct date. See James T. Law, *Forms of Ecclesiastical Law* (2nd edition; London, 1814), pp. 1-12, and Thomas Oughton, *Ordo Judiciorum; Sive Methodus et Litibus in Foro Ecclesiastico-Civili Britannico et Hibernico* (2 volumes; London, 1728, 1738), I, p. 2.

late of Achurch, county Northants, clerk, deceased, which was promoted before the said Master by John Browne son of the deceased against Elizabeth Browne widow and administratrix.

Whereas the court has found insufficient the case [*partem*] of the said Elizabeth as set out in an allegation & account and in an allegation & will on her behalf, therefore it is found that the said Robert died intestate, & after his death letters of administration were granted to the said Elizabeth; & thereafter *pendente lite* she obtained surreptitiously & by guile letters of administration with a will nuncupative: therefore the said letters of administration with will are revoked & annulled; She is charged with £240 of the goods of the said Robert remaining in her custody; she is to pay the costs of both parties.[1]

S[ente]n[t]ia condemnatoria et p[ro] revocac[i]one ad[ministratio]nis bonor[um] Roberti Browne.

In Dei nomine Amen, auditis visis et intellectis ac plenarie et mature discussis p[er] nos Henricum Marten militem et legum D[o]c[t]orem Curie Prerogative Cantuar[iensis] m[agist]rum Custodem sive Com[m]issariu[m] l[egi]time constitutum meritis et circumstantiis cuiusdam negotii exhibic[i]onis Inventarii et reddic[i]o[n]is Computi bonoru[m] iuriu[m] et credit[orum] Roberti Browne nup[er] de Atchurch in Com[itatu] North[amp]ton Cl[er]ici def[uncti] quod coram nobis in Iudicio inter Johannem Browne filiu[m] n[atu]ralem et l[egi]timu[m] d[i]c[t]i def[uncti] partem h[uius]mo[d]i nego[tiu]m promoven[tem] ex una et Elizabetham Browne relic[t]am et Admi[ni]stratricem bonor[um] iuriu[m] et Creditor[um] eiusdem defunct[i] partem con[tra] q[ua]m h[uius]mo[d]i nego[tiu]m p[ro]movetur partibus ex altera vertitur et pendet indecis[um] rite et l[egi]time proceden[tibus] partibus p[re]d[i]c[t]is p[er] ear[um] procur[ato]res coram nobis in iudicio l[egi]time comparen[tibus] Parteq[ue] p[re]fati Johannis Browne S[ente]n[t]iam ferri et Justitiam fieri pro parte sua Parte vero memorate Elizabethe Browne Justitiam etiam pro parte sua instanter respe[ctive] postulan[tibus] et peten[tibus] Rimatoq[ue] [Priuatoq[ue]?] primitus p[er] nos toto et integro processu in h[uius]mo[d]i causa coram nobis habito et facto ac diligenter recensito Servatisq[ue] p[er] nos de iure in hac parte servandis ad n[ost]re Se[n]tentie diffinitive sive n[ost]ri finalis

---

[1] Somerset House, Prerogative Court of Canterbury, 64 Soare. I have used the original Latin document, but have also relied upon the excellent summary given by A. Matthews in *Transactions of the Congregational Historical Society*, X, no. 1 (April, 1927), pp. 8-10.

The Will of Robert Browne

Decreti prolac[i]onem in h[uius]mo[d]i nego[ti]o ferend[e] sic duximus p[ro]cedend[um] fore et procedimus in hunc qui sequitur modum. Quia p[er] acta inactitata Deducta all[ega]ta ex[hibi]ta p[ro]posita probata pariter et Confessata in h[uius]mo[d]i nego- [ti]o comperimus luculent[er] et invenimus partem p[re]fate Elizabethe Browne intenc[i]o[n]em suam tam in quibusdam all[egatio]ne et computo quam in quibusdam allegac[i]one et testamento p[ro]v[i]s[ori]o ex parte sua in hac causa dat[is] exhibit[is] et admiss[is] deductam minus sufficienter quoad inferius pronunciand[um] fundasse et probasse sed in probac[i]o[n]e all- [egatio]nis ac comp[ut]i et testamenti p[re]d[i]c[ti] quoad inferius pronunciand[um] deficisse et deficere.

Idcirco nos Henricus Marten miles et legum D[o]c[t]or Iudex an[te]d[i]c[t]us Christi no[m]i[n]e primitus invocato ac ip[su]m solum deu[m] oculis n[ost]ris preponen[tes] et haben[tes] De q[ue] et cum consilio Jurisperitor[um] cum quibus in hac parte co[mmuni]- cavimus Preno[m]i[n]atum Robertum Browne Def[unctum] ab intestat[o] nullo p[er] eu[m] condito testamento (quat[en]us nobis constare possit) decessisse et citra mortem eiusdem defunct[i] l[itte]ras ad[ministratio]nis bonor[um] iuriu[m] et creditor[um] d[i]c[t]i defuncti tanquam ab intestato Deceden[tis] fuisse et esse p[re]fate Elizabethe Browne au[ctori]tate huius Curie l[egi]t[im]e concess[e] p[ro]nunciamus et declaramus. Et citra p[ro]miss[e] et penden[te] hac lite p[re]fat[am] Elizabetham Browne l[itte]ras p[ro]v[i]s[orias] ad[ministratio]nis bonor[um] iuriu[m] et Creditor- [um] p[re]fati Roberti Browne def[uncti] cum testamento p[ro]- v[i]s[ori]o nuncupativo eiusdem def[uncti] eisdem annex[ato, o] surreptitie et dolo malo sibi com[m]itti obtinuisse etiam pronun- [cia]mus et declaramus.

Ideoq[ue] easdem p[ro]v[i]s[ori]as l[itte]ras admi[ni]strac[i]- o[n]is cum testamento nuncupative[o] p[re]d[icto] eisdem annex- [ato, o] ad o[mn]em iuris eff[e]c[t]um revocamus cassamus et annullamus proq[u]e nullis et invalidis ad o[mn]em iuris eff[e]c- [t]um p[ro]nunciamus et declaramus Nec non sum[m]am decentar[um] [ducentarum?] et quadraginta librar[um] leg[a]lis monete anglie ex bonis iuribus et creditis d[i]c[t]i Rob[er]ti Browne def[uncti]computatis computandis et allocatis de iure in hac parte allocandis in manibus custodia et possessione p[re]fate Elizabethe Browne ad[ministra]tricis p[re]dict[e] quat[en]us nobis constat remanere et existere seu p[er] eam stare quominus sic remaneat Eandemq[ue] Elizabetham Browne cum d[i]c[t]a sum[m]a onerari debere ad o[mn]em iuris effectum pronunciamus decerimus et declaramus D[i]c[t]amq[ue] Elizabetham Browne in expensis l[egi]timis ex parte et p[er] partem prefati Johannis Browne in h[uius]mo[d]i Causa factis et faciend[is] eidemq[ue] seu parti sue solvend[is] condemnamus p[er] hanc n[ost]ram S[ente]n[t]iam diffinitivam sive hoc n[ost]r[u]m finale Decretum quam sive q[uo]d ferimus et promulgamus in hiis scriptis Taxac[i]o[n]em vero sive moderac[i]o[n]em ear[um]dem expensar[um] nobis aut alii Iudici in hac parte competen[ti] cuicunq[ue] reservando reservamus.

Lecta lata et promulgata fuit S[ente]n[t]ia diffi[niti]va p[er] D[i]c[tu]m Henricum Marten mi[li]tem legum D[o]c[t]orem Curie Prerogative Cant[uariensis] m[agist]r[u]m Custodem sive Com[missiar]iu[m] l[egi]time constitutum s[e]c[un]do die Juridico post festum sive diem Ascentionis D[omi]ni n[ost]ri die Sabb[at]i vicesimo vizt [videlicet] die mensis Maii Anno D[omi]ni mill[es]imo sexcentesimo tricesimo septimo in loco Cons[istoriali] [Cons[tituto]?] infra Eccl[es]iam Cathe[dral]em Divi Pauli London iudiciali et pro tribunali seden[tis] ad petic[i]o[n]em Georgii Gaell no[ta]rii pub[li]ci procur[ator]is d[i]c[t]i Johannis Browne ac in p[rese]ntia Thorne Webb no[ta]rii pub[li]ci procur[ator]is D[i]c[t]e Elizabethe Browne Sup[er] cuius S[ente]n[ti]e p[ro]lac[i]o[n]e d[i]c[t]us Gaell requisivit me Robertum Erswell no[ta]riu[m] pub[li]cum tunc p[re]sentem ad conficiend[um] sibi vnu[m] vel plura instrumenta pub[li]ca ac testes &c p[rese]ntibus tunc et ib[ide]m Mag[ist]ris Basilio Wood Will[el]mo Clarke Will[el]mo Merricke et Josepho Marten legum D[o]c[t]oribus Henrico Iremonger Georgio Cole Jacobo Hulet et Johanne Fish no[ta]riis pub[li]cis d[i]c[t]e Curie procur[ator]ibus testibus &c.[1]

[1] Somerset House, Prerogative Court of Canterbury, 64 Soare. I wish to express my thanks to my friends, R. B. Pugh, Professor Otto Skutsch, and Dr. Hartmut Erbse, for advice in editing this document.

A SELECT BIBLIOGRAPHY

MANUSCRIPTS

Additional Manuscripts   British Museum
29,546, ff. 67-72, 113-116
117-118, 32,092, ff. 123-133
Burghley Manuscripts   Marquess of Salisbury
                                     Hatfield House, Hatfield
                                                 Hertfordshire
Congregational Manuscripts   Congregational Library
I. e. 14   Memorial Hall, London
Egerton Manuscripts   British Museum
1693, ff. 87, 100, 105
Harleian Manuscripts   British Museum
7581, ff. 50-56
Lambeth Manuscripts   Lambeth Palace Library
113, ff. 187-202 (No. 11)
ff. 203-242 (No. 12)
Lansdowne Manuscripts   British Museum
33, f. 26 (No. 13); f. 40 (No. 20)
38, ff. 162, 163 (No. 64)
64, f. 89 (No. 34)
103, f. 176 (No. 60); f. 206 (No. 71)
982, ff. 100, 111-113, 130, 139, 143
165, 169, 170
1029, f. 43
Morrice Manuscripts   Dr. Williams's Library
                                                 London
State Papers, Domestic, Elizabeth   Public Record Office
146, No. 20
161, No. 33

BIBLIOGRAPHICAL AND REFERENCE WORKS

AMES, JOSEPH. *Typographical Antiquities.* Augmented by William Herbert. 3 volumes. London, 1785-1790

ARBER EDWARD. *A Transcript of the Registers of the Company of Stationers of London, 1554-1660.* 5 volumes. London, 1875-1894

BATESON, F. W. (ed.). *The Cambridge Bibliography of English Literature.* Volume I, 600-1660. Cambridge: University Press, 1940

Bibliotheca Norfolciensis. A Catalogue of the Writings of Norfolk Men and of Works Relating to the County of Norfolk, in the Library of Mr. J. J. Colman, at Carrow Abbey, Norwich. Norwich, 1896

COOPER, C. H., and COOPER, THOMPSON. *Athenae Cantabrigienses.* 3 volumes. Cambridge, 1858, 1861, 1913.

CRIPPEN, T. G. " Bibliography of Congregational Church History," *Transactions of the Congregational Historical Society,* Volume II, nos. 2, 5 (May, 1905; May, 1906).

[CRIPPEN, T. G. ?.] *A Catalogue of the Congregational Library, Memorial Hall, Farringdon Street, London, E.C.* 1895.

CRIPPEN, T. G. " Early Nonconformist Bibliography," *Transactions of the Congregational Historical Society,* Volume I, nos. 1, 2, 3, 4, 6; II, nos. 1, 3, 6 (April, 1901 — October, 1906).

DARLOW, T. H., and MOULE, H. F. *Historical Catalogue of the Printed Editions of Holy Scripture in the Library of the British and Foreign Bible Society.* 2 volumes. London, 1903-1911.

DEXTER, HENRY MARTYN. *The Congregationalism of the Last Three Hundred Years, As Seen in Its Literature.* New York: Harper & Bros., 1880. There is a bibliographical appendix of 286 pages, with 7250 items and a brief guide to manuscript collections.

GANDY, HENRY. *Bibliotheca Scriptorum Ecclesiae Anglicanae.* London, 1709.

GIBSON, EDMUND. *Codex Juris Ecclesiastici Anglicani*: *or, the Statutes Constitutions, Canons, Rubricks and Articles, of the Church of England, Methodically Digested under Their Proper Heads.* Second edition. 2 volumes. Oxford: Clarendon Press, 1761.

GILLETT, C. R. *Catalogue of the McAlpin Collection of British History and Theology in the Union Theological Seminary Library.* 5 volumes. New York, 1927-1930.

GODWIN, FRANCIS. *De Praesulibus Angliae Commentarius* . . . . . Cambridge, 1743.

HENNESSY, GEORGE. *Novum Repertorium Ecclesiasticum Parochiale Londinense or London Diocesan Clergy Succession from the Earliest Time to the Year* 1898. London, 1898.

LE NEVE, JOHN. *Fasti Ecclesiae Anglicanae.* 3 volumes. Edited by T. Duffus Hardy. Oxford, 1854.

NEWCOURT, RICHARD. *Repertorium Ecclesiasticum Parochiale Londinense.* 2 volumes. London, 1708, 1710.

POLLARD, A. W., and REDGRAVE, G. R. *A Short-Title Catalogue of Books Printed in England, Scotland, and Ireland And of English Books Printed Abroad* 1475-1640. London, 1926.

READ, CONYERS. *Bibliography of British History, Tudor Period,* 1485-1603. Oxford: Clarendon Press, 1933.

SAYLE, CHARLES EDWARD. *Early English Printed Books in the University Library, Cambridge* (1475 to 1640). 5 volumes. Cambridge: University Press, 1900-1907.

A Select Bibliography

SMITH, J. C. CHALLENOR. *Some Additions to Newcourt's Repertorium* — Vol. II. Reprinted from *Transactions of the Essex Archaeological Society*, Volume VII (1898-1899).
SOUTHERN, ALFRED C. *Elizabethan Recusant Prose, 1559-1582. A Historical and Critical Account of the Books of the Catholic Refugees Printed and Published Abroad and at Secret Presses in England together with an Annotated Bibliography*. London, 1950.
SURMAN, CHARLES E. *A Bibliography of Congregational Church History, Including Numerous Cognate Presbyterian-Unitarian Records and a Few Baptist*. [Birmingham], 1947. A typescript in the British Museum (4999. k. 18); contains many valuable and less-known items not found in standard lists. Especially useful for local church history.
TODD, HENRY J. *A Catalogue of the Archiepiscopal Manuscripts in the Library at Lambeth Palace*. London, 1812.
WILKINS, DAVID. *Concilia Magnae Britanniae et Hiberniae, ab Anno MDXLVI ad Annum MDCCXVII*. Volume IV. London, 1737.

BOOKS

[AINSWORTH, HENRY].
An apologie or defence of such true christians as are commonly (but vniustly) called Brownists: against such imputations as are layd vpon them by the heads and doctors of the university of Oxford, in their answer to the humble petition of the ministers of the Church of England, desiring reformation of certayne ceremonies and abuses of the Church. [Amsterdam?], 1604.
[AINSWORTH, HENRY?].
A Trve Confession of the Faith, and Hvmble Acknowledgment of the Alegeance, which wee hir Maiesties Subjects, falsely called Brownists, doo hould towards God, and yeild to hir Maiestie and all other that are ouer vs in the Lord. [Amsterdam?], 1596.
ALLEN, WILLIAM CARDINAL. *The Letters and Memorials of William Cardinal Allen.* [1532-1594]. Edited by the Fathers of the Congregation of the London Oratory. With an historical introduction by Thomas Francis Knox. London, 1882.
ARBER, EDWARD. *An Introductory Sketch to the Martin Marprelate Controversy. 1588-1590*. Westminster, 1895.
BACON, FRANCIS. "Certain Observations Made upon a Libel Published This Present Year, 1592," in James Spedding, *The Letters and the Life of Francis Bacon*, I (London, 1861), pp. 146-208.
BAILLIE, ROBERT. *Anabaptisme, the True Fountaine of Independency, Brownisme, Antinomy, Familisme, and Most of the other errours which for the time doe trouble the Church of England, unsealed.* London, 1647.

BAILLIE, ROBERT. *A Dissuasive from the Errours of the Time.* London, 1645.

BANCROFT, RICHARD. *Davngerovs Positions and Proceedings, published and practised within this Iland of Brytaine, vnder pretence of Reformation, and for the Presbiteriall Discipline.* London, 1593.

BANCROFT, RICHARD. *A Sermon Preached at Paules Crosse the 9. of Februarie,* being the first Sunday in the *Parleament, Anno* 1588 [1588/9]. London, 1588 [1589].

BANCROFT, RICHARD. *A Svrvay of the Pretended Holy Discipline.* London, 1593.

BARCLAY, ROBERT. *The Inner Life of the Religious Societies of the Commonwealth.* 3rd edition. London, 1879.

BILSON, THOMAS. *The Perpetual Gouernement of Christes Church.* London, 1593.

BLOMEFIELD, FRANCIS. *An Essay towards a Topographical History of the County of Norfolk.* 5 volumes. Norwich, 1739-1775.

BLORE, THOMAS. *The History and Antiquities of the County of Rutland.* Stanford, [1811].

A Booke of the Forme of Common Prayers, Administration of the Sacraments: &c. agreeable to Gods Worde, and the Use of the Reformed Churches. London: Printed by Robert Walde-grave, [1584-5]. There are editions in 1586, 1587, and 1602, the first probably, and the others certainly, printed at Middelburg by Richard Schilders.

BREDWELL, STEPHEN. *Detection of Ed. [Edward] Glouers hereticall confection, lately contriued and proffered to the Church of England, vnder the name of* A Present Preseruatiue. *Wherein with the laying open of his impudent slander against our whole Ministrie, the Reader shal find a new built nest of old hatcht heresies discouered, (and by the grace of God) ouerthrowne: togither with an admonition to the followers of Glouer and Browne.* London, [1586].

BREDWELL, STEPHEN. *The Rasing of the Fovndations of Brownisme.* London, 1588.

BRIDGES, JOHN. *A defence of the government established in the Church of England for ecclesiastical matters.* London, 1587.

BROOK, BENJAMIN. *The Lives of the Puritans.* 3 volumes. London, 1813.

BROOK, BENJAMIN. *Memoir of the Life and Writings of Thomas Cartwright, B. D., the distinguished Puritan reformer; including the principal ecclesiastical movements in the reign of Queen Elizabeth.* London, 1845.

BROWNE, JOHN. *History of Congregationalism, and Memorials of the Churches in Norfolk and Suffolk.* London, 1877.

BURGESS, WALTER H. *John Robinson Pastor of the Pilgrim Fathers. A Study of His Life and Times.* London, 1920.

A Select Bibliography

BURRAGE, CHAMPLIN. *The Church Covenant Idea. Its Origin and Its Development.* Philadelphia, 1904.

BURRAGE, CHAMPLIN. *The Early English Dissenters in the Light of Recent Research* (1550-1641). 2 volumes. Cambridge, 1912.

BURRAGE, CHAMPLIN. *A New Years Guift.* London, 1904.

BURRAGE, CHAMPLIN. *The 'Retractation' of Robert Browne, Father of Congregationalism, Being ' A Reproofe of Certeine Schismatical Persons [i.e.,* Henry Barrowe, John Greenwood, and their Congregation] *and their Doctrine Touching the Hearing and Preaching of the Word of God.*' Oxford and London, 1907. R. Browne or T. Cartwright is the author. Printed in Albert Peel and Leland H. Carlson, *Cartwrightiana,* 201-261.

BURRAGE, CHAMPLIN. *The True Story of Robert Browne* — 1550 ?- 1633 — *Father of Congregationalism* . . . . London, 1906.

CARLSON, LELAND H., and PEEL, ALBERT. *Cartwrightiana.* "Elizabethan Nonconformist Texts," volume I. London, 1951.

CLAPHAM, HENOCH. *Antidoton: or a soveraigne remedie against schisme and heresie.* [London ?], 1600.

CLARK, HENRY W. *History of English Nonconformity from Wiclif to the Close of the Nineteenth Century.* 2 volumes. London: Chapman and Hall, Ltd., 1911, 1913.

CURTEIS, GEORGE H. *Dissent, in Its Relation to the Church of England.* London: Macmillan and Co., 1872. Bampton lectures, 1871.

DALE, R. W. *History of English Congregationalism.* Completed and edited by A. W. W. Dale. London: Hodder and Stoughton, 1907.

DAVIDS, T. W. *Annals of Evangelical Nonconformity in the County of Essex, from the Time of Wycliffe to the Restoration.* London, 1863.

D'EWES, SIMONDS. *The Journals of All the Parliaments during the Reign of Queen Elizabeth, both of the House of Lords and House of Commons.* London, 1682.

DEXTER, HENRY M. *The Congregationalism of the Last Three Hundred Years, as Seen in Its Literature.* New York, 1880.

DEXTER, HENRY M., and DEXTER, MORTON. *The England and Holland of the Pilgrims.* Boston: Houghton, Mifflin Co., 1905.

DORE, JOHN R. *Old Bibles: An Account of the Early Versions of the English Bible.* Second edition. London: Eyre and Spottiswoode, 1888.

FAIRLAMBE, PETER. *The Recantation of a Brownist, or, a Reformed Puritan.* London, 1606.

FENNER, DUDLEY. *A defence of the godlie ministers against the slaunders of D. Bridges,* . . . . London, 1587. Also in *A parte of a register.* [Edinburgh; 1593 ?].

FLETCHER, JOSEPH. *The History of the Revival and Progress of Independency in England.* 4 volumes. London: John Snow and Co., 1847-49.

FOSTER, C. W. *State of the Church in the Reigns of Elizabeth and James I as Illustrated by Documents Relating to the Diocese of Lincoln.* " Publication of the Lincoln Record Society," volume 23. Horncastle, 1926.

FRERE, WALTER H. *The English Church in the Reigns of Elizabeth and James I.* (1558-1625). London, 1904.

FRERE, WALTER H., and DOUGLAS, C. E. *Puritan Manifestoes.* London, 1907.

FULLER, THOMAS. *The Church History of Britain.* 6 volumes. Edited by J. S. Brewer. Oxford: University Press, 1845.

FULLER, THOMAS. *History of the Worthies of England.* 2 volumes. Edited by J. Nichols. London, 1811.

GREENHAM, RICHARD. *The Workes of the Reverend and Faithfvll Servant of Iesvs Christ, M. Richard Greenham.* 5th edition. Edited by Henry Holland and Robert Hill. London, 1611-1612.

HALL, PETER. *Reliquiae Liturgicae. Documents Connected with the Liturgy of the Church of England.* 5 volumes in 2. Bath, 1847. Volume I, entitled *The Middleburgh Prayer-Book*, contains a reprint of *A Booke of the Forme of Common Prayers.*

HALLER, WILLIAM. *The Rise of Puritanism or the Way to the New Jerusalem as Set Forth in Pulpit and Press from Thomas Cartwright to John Lilburne and John Milton, 1570-1643.* New York: Columbia University Press, 1938.

HANBURY, BENJAMIN. *Historical Memorials Relating to the Independents, or Congregationalists: from Their Rise to the Restoration of the Monarchy, A.D. 1660.* 3 volumes. London, 1839, 1842, 1845.

The Harleian Miscellany. 8 volumes. London, 1744-1746. Another edition, 10 volumes. London, 1808-1813.

HARRIS, JAMES R., and JONES, STEPHEN K. *The Pilgrim Press. A Bibliographical & Historical Memorial of the Books Printed at Leyden by the Pilgrim Fathers.* Cambridge, 1922.

HARRISON, G. B. *The Elizabethan Journals. Being a Record of Those Things Most Talked of during the Years 1591-1603.* London: George Routledge and Sons, 1938.

HERREY, ROBART [or ROBERT] F. *Two right profitable and fruitfull Concordances, or large and ample Tables Alphabeticall.* In the 1580 and subsequent editions of the Geneva version of the Bible. Fitz Herrey is regarded by some as a pseudonym for Harrison.

HOPKINS, SAMUEL. *The Puritans: or, the Church, Court, and Parliament of England, during the Reigns of Edward VI and Queen Elizabeth.* 3 volumes. Boston, 1859-1861.

JESSOPP, AUGUSTUS. *One Generation of a Norfolk House, A Contribution to Elizabethan History.* 3rd edition. London, 1913.

A Select Bibliography

JOHNSON, FRANCIS. *A short Treatise concerning the Exposition of those Words of Christ, Tell the Church, etc.* Mat. 18, 17. [Amsterdam?], 1611.

JORDAN, WILBUR K. *The Development of Religious Toleration in England from the Beginning of the English Reformation to the Death of Queen Elizabeth.* London: George Allen & Unwin, Ltd., 1932.

KNAPPEN, MARSHALL M. *Tudor Puritanism: A Chapter in the History of Idealism.* Chicago: University of Chicago Press, 1939.

KNAPPEN, MARSHALL M. [ed.]. *Two Elizabethan Diaries by Richard Rogers and Samuel Ward.* "Studies in Church History," volume II. Chicago, 1933.

LAVATER, LUDWIG. *Of Ghostes and Spirites Walking by Nyght.* Edited by J. D. Wilson and May Yardley. London, 1929.

LAWNE, CHRISTOPHER, et al. *The Prophane Schisme of the Brownists or Separatists.* [London?, 1612].

LE LOYER, PIERRE. *Discours et histoires des spectres.* Angers and Paris, 1586.

MACKENNAL, ALEXANDER. *Sketches in the Evolution of English Congregationalism.* Carew Lecture for 1900-01. Delivered in Hartford Theological Seminary, Connecticut. London, 1901.

MACKENNAL, ALEXANDER. *The Story of the English Separatists; Written to Commemorate the Tercentenary of the Martyrdom of Greenwood, Barrowe, and Penry in 1593.* London: Congregational Union of England and Wales, 1893.

MARSDEN, J. B. *History of the Early Puritans from the Reformation to 1642.* 2nd edition. London, 1853.

McGINN, DONALD JOSEPH. *The Admonition Controversy.* New Brunswick, New Jersey: Rutgers University Press, 1949.

MITCHELL, W. F. *English Pulpit Oratory from Andrewes to Tillotson. A Study of Its Literary Aspects.* London: S.P.C.K., 1932. Has a bibliography.

MULLINGER, J. B. *The University of Cambridge from the Royal Injunctions of 1535 to the Accession of Charles the First.* Cambridge: University Press, 1884.

NEAL, DANIEL. *The History of the Puritans.* 5 volumes. London, 1822.

NEALE, J. E. *Queen Elizabeth.* London, 1934.

PAGITT, EPHRAIM. *Heresiography, or, A Description of the Sectaries of These Latter Times.* 6th edition. London, 1661.

A parte of a register, contayninge sundrie memorable matters, written by diuers godly and learned in our time, which stande for, and desire the reformation of our Church, in Discipline and Ceremonies, accordinge to the pure worde of God, and the Lawe of our Lande. [Edinburgh, 1593].

PEARSON, A. F. SCOTT. *Church and State: Political Aspects of Sixteenth Century Puritanism.* Cambridge: University Press, 1928.
PEARSON, A. F. SCOTT. *Thomas Cartwright and Elizabethan Puritanism, 1553-1603.* Cambridge: University Press, 1925.
PEEL, ALBERT. *A Brief History of English Congregationalism.* London, [1931].
PEEL, ALBERT. *The Brownists in Norwich and Norfolk about 1580. Some New Facts, together with " A treatise of the Church and the Kingdome of Christ,"* by R.H. [Robert Harrison?], *now printed for the first time from the manuscript in Dr. Williams's Library, London.* Cambridge: University Press, 1920.
PEEL, ALBERT. *The Congregational Two Hundred, 1530-1948.* London: Independent Press, 1948.
PEEL, ALBERT. *The First Congregational Churches. New Light on Separatist Congregations in London, 1567-81.* Cambridge, 1920.
PEEL, ALBERT. " From the Elizabethan Settlement to the Emergence of Separatism," *Essays Congregational and Catholic Issued in Commemoration of the Centenary of the Congregational Union of England and Wales.* Edited by Albert Peel. London: Independent Press, [1931].
PEEL, ALBERT. *The Noble Army of Congregational Martyrs.* London: Independent Press Ltd., 1948.
PEEL, ALBERT [ed.]. *The Seconde Parte of a Register. Being a Calendar of Manuscripts under that title intended for publication by the Puritans about 1593, and now in Dr. Williams's Library, London.* 2 volumes. Cambridge, 1915.
PEEL, ALBERT, and CARLSON, LELAND H. *Cartwrightiana.* " Elizabethan Nonconformist Texts," volume I. London, 1951.
POWICKE, FREDERICK J. " English Congregationalism in Its Greatness and Decline (1592-1770), *Essays Congregational and Catholic Issued in Commemoration of the Centenary of the Congregational Union of England and Wales.* Edited by Albert Peel. London: Independent Press, [1931].
POWICKE, FREDERICK J. *Robert Browne, Pioneer of Modern Congregationalism.* London, [1910].
RAINOLDS, JOHN. *The svmme of the conference betwene Iohn Rainoldes and Iohn Hart: touching the head and the faith of the Church ....* London, 1584.
SAVILE, JOHN. *Les Reports de Sir John Savile Chevalier,* Nadgairis *Baron de l'Exchequer, de Divers Special Cases cybien en le Court de Common Bank, Come l'Exchequer en le Temps de Royne Elizabeth.* Edited by John Richardson. London, 1675. See Browne's case, CIV, pp. 49-50.
SCHEFFER, J. G. DE HOOP. *History of the Free Churchmen Called the Brownists, Pilgrim Fathers and Baptists in the Dutch Republic, 1581-1701.* Ithaca, New York, [1922].

A Select Bibliography

SCOT, REGINALD. *The Discouerie of Witchcraft.* London, 1584. Other editions in 1651, 1665, 1886, and 1930.
SELBIE, W. B. *Congregationalism.* London, 1927.
SELBIE, W. B. *Nonconformity, Its Origin and Progress.* London, n.d.
SERJEANTSON, R. M. *A History of the Church of St. Giles, Northampton.* Northampton, 1911.
SHAKESPEARE, J. H. *Baptist and Congregational Pioneers.* London, 1906.
SOAMES, HENRY. *Elizabethan Religious History.* London, 1839.
SPALDING, THOMAS A. *Elizabethan Demonology.* London, 1880.
STOW, JOHN. *The Annales of England.* London, 1605.
STOW, JOHN. *A Survey of London.* Edited by C. L. Kingsford. 3 volumes. Oxford: Clarendon Press, 1908.
STRYPE, JOHN. *Annals of the Reformation.* 4 volumes in 7. Oxford: Clarendon Press, 1824.
STRYPE, JOHN. *Historical Collections of the Life and Acts of the Right Reverend Father in God, John Aylmer, Lord Bp. of London in the Reign of Queen Elizabeth.* Oxford: Clarendon Press, 1821.
STRYPE, JOHN. *The History of the Life and Acts of the Most Reverend Father in God, Edmund Grindal....* Oxford, 1821.
STRYPE, JOHN. *The Life and Acts of John Whitgift, D.D.* Oxford: Clarendon Press, 1822.
SUTCLIFFE, MATTHEW. *A Treatise of Ecclesiasticall Discipline.* London, 1590.
TAILLEPIED, NOEL. *Psichologie ou traite de l'apparition des espirits.* Paris, 1588; Rouen, 1600, 1602.
TAILLEPIED, NOEL. *A Treatise of Ghosts.* Edited by Montague Summers. London, [1933].
TENISON, E. M. *Elizabethan England.* 10 volumes. Royal Leamington Spa, Warwick, 1933-1950.
TRAVERS, WALTER. *A Defence of the Ecclesiastical Discipline Ordayned of God to Be Vsed in His Church.* [London?], 1588.
USHER, ROLAND G. *The Presbyterian Movement in the Reign of Queen Elizabeth as Illustrated by the Minute Book of the Dedham Classis 1582-1589.* "Royal Historical Society," 3rd series, volume VIII. London, 1905.
USHER, R. G. *The Rise and Fall of the High Commission.* Oxford: Clarendon Press, 1913.
VAUGHAN, ROBERT. *English Nonconformity.* London, 1862.
WADDINGTON, JOHN. *Congregational Church History, from the Reformation to 1662.* London, 1863.
WADDINGTON, JOHN. *Congregational History, 1200-1567.* 5 volumes. London, 1869-1880. Volume I, for 1200-1567, and Volume II, for 1567-1700, are most pertinent.
WADDINGTON, JOHN. *1559-1620. Track of the Hidden Church; or, the Springs of the Pilgrim Movement.* Boston, 1863.

WADDINGTON, JOHN. *Historical Papers (First Series). Congregational Martyrs.* London, 1861.
WAKEMAN, HENRY O. *The Church and the Puritans,* 1570-1660. London, 1887.
WALKER, WILLISTON. *The Creeds and Platforms of Congregationalism.* New York: C. Scribner's Sons, 1893.
WHITE, FRANCIS O. *Lives of the Elizabethan Bishops of the Anglican Church.* London, 1898.
WILSON, THOMAS. *The Arte of Rhetorike, for the use of all sutche as are studious of Eloquence, sette foorthe in Englishe, by Thomas Wilson,* 1553. *And now newly set foorthe again, with a Prologue to the Reader,* 1567. 6th edition. London, 1580.
WILSON, THOMAS. *The Rule of reason, contayning the Arte of Logike.* London, 1567.
WILSON, WALTER. *The History and Antiquities of Dissenting Churches and Meeting Houses, in London, Westminster and Southwark* . . . 4 volumes. London, 1808-1814.
WRIGHT, THOMAS. *Queen Elizabeth and Her Times.* 2 volumes. London, 1838.
YOUNG, ALEXANDER. *Chronicles of the Pilgrim Fathers of the Colony of Plymouth, from* 1602 *to* 1625. Boston, 1841.

ARTICLES

" The Bampton Lecturer on Dissent." *Congregationalist,* I (1872), 502-509, 553-562, 618-631.
" The Brownists Faith and Beliefe Opened." *Trans. C. H. S., IV,* No. 6 (September, 1910), pp. 343-346.
" The Brownists' Paternoster." *Trans. C. H. S., V,* No. 1 (February, 1911), pp. 34-39. A lampoon.
CATER, F. IVES. " The Excommunication of Robert Browne and His Will." *Trans. C. H. S., V,* No. 4 (January, 1912), pp. 199-204.
CATER, F. IVES. " The Later Years of Robert Browne." *Trans. C. H. S., III,* No. 5 (May, 1908), pp. 303-316.
CATER, F. IVES. " New Facts Relating to Robert Browne." *Trans. C. H. S., II,* No. 4 (January, 1906), pp. 235-246.
CATER, F. IVES. " Robert Browne and the Achurch Parish Register." *Trans. C. H. S., III,* No. 2 (May, 1907), pp. 126-136. This article has two full-page illustrations of the parish register.
CATER, F. IVES. " Robert Browne's Ancestors and Descendants." *Trans. C. H. S., II,* No. 3 (September, 1905), pp. 151-159.
CLEAL, EDWARD E. " The Church of the Pilgrim Fathers." *Trans. C. H. S., II,* No. 3 (September, 1905), pp. 201-205.

A Select Bibliography

COWELL, HENRY J. "Valerand Poullain. A Precursor of Congregationalism." *Trans. C. H. S.*, XII (1933-1936), pp. 112-119.

[CRIPPEN, T. G.?]. "Anti-Brownist Pamphlets, 1641-42." *Trans. C. H. S.*, V, No. 2 (May, 1911), pp. 83-91.

CRIPPEN, T. G. "The Brownists in Amsterdam." *Trans. C. H. S.*, II, No. 3 (September, 1905), pp. 160-172.

[CRIPPEN, T. G.]. "The Morrice Manuscripts in Williams's Library." *Trans. C. H. S.*, IV, No. 5 (May, 1910), pp. 294-298.

[DALE, R. W.?]. "Dr. Dexter on Congregationalism." *Congregationalist*, IX (1880), pp. 928-936.

[DALE, R. W.?]. "Robert Browne." *Congregationalist*, XI (1882), pp. 867-872, 946-952, 1044-1048.

[DALE, R. W.?]. "Robert Browne and Brownism." *Congregationalist*, XI (1882), pp. 225-236.

DEXTER, HENRY M. "Dr. Waddington's Congregational History." *Congregational Quarterly*, July, 1874.

DEXTER, HENRY M. "Elder Brewster's Library." *Proceedings of the Massachusetts Historical Society*, second series, V (1888-89), pp. 37-85.

DIXON, H. N. "The 'Free Churches' of Norwich in Elizabethan and Early Stuart Times." *Trans. C. H. S.*, XI, No. 1 (April, 1930), pp. 28-37.

"The 'Gathered Church': Robert Browne and the Tradition of Congregationalism." *The Times*, May 9, 1950. Reprinted by the Independent Press, London.

GRIEVE, A. J. "Extracts from Robert Browne's *Booke which sheweth, etc.*" *Trans. C. H. S.*, XII, No. 1 (April, 1933), pp. 11-18.

HERIOT, DUNCAN B. "Anabaptism in England during the 16th and 17th Centuries." *Trans. C. H. S.*, XII (1933-1936), pp. 256-271, and pp. 312-320.

"The Humble Petition of the Brownists." *Trans. C. H. S.*, V., No. 1 (February, 1911), pp. 59-63.

MATTHEWS, A. G. "Robert Browne's Will." *Trans. C. H. S.*, X, No. 1 (April, 1927), pp. 8-10.

NEALE, J. E. "The Elizabethan Political Scene." *Proceedings of the British Academy*, XXXIV (1948).

NIPPOLD, FRIEDRICH. "Heinrich Niclaes und das Haus der Liebe." *Zeitschrift fur die historische Theologie* (Gotha, 1862), pp. 323-394.

NUTTALL, GEOFFREY F. "The Early Congregational Conception of the Church." *Trans. C. H. S.*, XIV (1940-1944), pp. 197-204.

OAKLEY, H. H. " Why Sir Andrew Aguecheek ' had as lief be a Brownist as a Politician '." *Trans. C. H. S.*, X, No. 2 (September, 1927), pp. 66-72.
PEEL, ALBERT. " A Conscientious Objector of 1575." *Transactions of the Baptist Historical Society*, VII (1920).
PEEL, ALBERT. " Robert Browne's Wife — A Correction." *Trans. C. H. S.*, VIII, No. 2 (August, 1920), pp. 82-83.
PEEL, ALBERT. " William White: An Elizabethan Puritan." *Trans. C. H. S.*, VI (February, 1913), pp. 4-19.
POWICKE, FREDERICK J. " Lists of the Early Separatists." *Trans. C. H. S.*, I, No. 3 (July, 1902), pp. 141-158.
SCHEFFER, J. G. DE HOOP. " The Brownists in Amsterdam," edited by T. G. Crippen. *Trans. C. H. S.*, II (September, 1905), pp. 160-172.
SHAW, WILLIAM A. " Elizabethan Presbyterianism." *English Historical Review*, III (1888), pp. 655-667.
SLAUGHTER, STEPHEN S. " The Dutch Church in Norwich." *Trans. C. H. S.*, XII (1933-1936), pp. 31-48 and pp. 81-96.
SMITH, DWIGHT C. " Robert Browne, Independent." *Church History*, VI (December, 1937). A summary of his Ph.D. thesis.
WILSON, J. DOVER. " Richard Schilders and the English Puritans." *Transactions of the Bibliographical Society*, XI (October, 1909, to March, 1911), pp. 65-134.
YORKE, A. C. " Kinsfold of Robert Browne in Cambridgeshire." *Trans. C. H. S.*, VI, No. 4 (August, 1914), pp. 248-260.

PERIODICALS

The Biblical Review and Congregational Magazine. 6 volumes. London, 1846-1850.
The Congregational Magazine. New Series. 12 volumes. London, 1825-1836. New Series. 9 volumes. London, 1837-1845.
Congregational Quarterly. 20 volumes. January, 1859 — October, 1878. Boston, Massachusetts. Congregational Library Association.
The Congregational Review in Which Are Incorporated The Congregationalist *and* British Quarterly Review. 4 volumes. 1887-1891.
The Congregationalist, volumes I - XV. London, 1872-1886.
The London Christian Instructor, or Congregational Magazine. 7 volumes. London, 1818-1824. Useful for brief articles on dissent and dissenters, and for book reviews. Continued as *The Congregational Magazine*.
Transactions of the Congregational Historical Society. London, 1901-1952.

INDEX

Achurch, 7
Allen, ——— (Browne's sister-in-law ?), 425
Allen, Alice, see Browne, Alice
Anabaptists, 65
Anderson, Sir Edmund, Lord Chief Justice of the Court of Common Pleas, 124
Arras, 80
Authority, civil, see Magistrates
Aylsham, 2, 29, 60
Aylsham Grammar School, 2

Bacon, Francis, 18
Bancroft, Richard, 20, 124, 405, 515, 517
Baptism, 256-261, 507, 508
Barclay, Robert, 65
Barker, Robert, 20, 397, 422
Barrow, Henry, *viii*, 4, 7, 30, 515
Bastwick, John, 20
Benneyman, Henry, 26
Bernard, Richard, 42
Beza, Theodore, 175
Bishops, 218, 220, 246, 272, 398, 399, 401-405, 436, 472, 474, 476, 503, 519
Blore, Thomas, *History and Antiquities of the County of Rutland*, 425
Bond, 422
Bonner, Edmund, Bishop of London, 218
Booton, 29
Boyce, Gray C., *viii*
Bredwell, Stephen, 6, 7, 509, 513, 514; *Rasing of the Foundations of Brownisme*, 1, 5, 24, 149, 396, 507, 509, 512

Brewster Press, 70
Brewster, William, 70
British Museum, 26, 70, 430, 516
Browne, Alice (Mrs. Robert Browne), 6, 7, 425
Browne, Elizabeth (Mrs. Robert Browne, second wife), 7
Browne, Philip, 20, 397
Browne, Robert, *vii*, *viii*, 1, 2, 4, 6-8, 13, 16, 17, 19-22, 25, 30, 38, 93, 149, 383, 396, 397-429, 430, 509
Browne, Robert, Writings of :
An Answere to Master Cartwright, 3, 21, 430-506
An Aunswere to Mr. Flowers Letter, 24, 516-529
A Booke which sheweth, 6, 19, 150, 209, 221-395
Fragments, 509-515
Letter to Lord Burghley, 25, 530-531
A New Years Guift, see *An Aunswere to Mr. Flowers Letter*, 516-529
Submission and Commentary, 23, 507-508
A Treatise of reformation, 6, 15, 30, 38, 149, 150, 151-170
A Treatise vpon the 23. of Matthewe, 6, 17-19, 29, 149, 150, 171-220, 225, 396
A True and Short Declaration, 7, 8, 19, 71, 396-429, 430
Undiscovered works, 5, 6, 24, 225, 383, 509, 510, 512
Brownists, 15, 29
Burghley, William Cecil, Lord, 6, 7, 25, 124, 530

557

Burrage, Champlin, 4, 5, 42, 65, 517
Burton, Henry, 20
Bury St. Edmunds, 2, 6, 7, 124

Calling, see Ordination
Cambridge, 1, 2, 6, 17, 20, 172, 173, 208, 397, 398, 404, 407
Carlson, Leland H., 25
Cartwright, Thomas, *vii*, 3, 5, 21, 22, 31, 430-506, 517
Cartwrightiana, *vii*, 3, 5, 124, 430
Catechisms, 3, 124-148, 220, 522
Cater, F. Ives, 4
Ceremonies, 40, 59, 91, 93, 286-295, 417
Chanler, or Chandler, John, 425, 428
Channel Islands, 20, 423
Christ, Jesus, 243-249, 263-269, 515
Church, gathering of, 252-255, 262
Church government, 119
Church of England, 115, 507, 525
Church officers, 32, 36, 119, 157, 214, 518
Clapham, Henoch, 42
Congregational Historical Society, *Transactions*, 30, 40, 151, 221, 425, 515
Congregational Library Manuscripts, 30, 31-37, 39, 40
Congregationalist, The, 396
Congregationalists, 20, 21
Coppin, or Copping, John, 2, 4, 7
Corpus Christi College, 1, 6
Covenant, 255-257, 422, 439, 461, 510
Cranmer, Thomas, Archbishop of Canterbury, 218
Creede, Thomas, 26
Crippen, T. G., 4, 151, 515

Darlow, T. H., 15
Deering, or Dering, Edward, 408
Dertford, 5
Dexter, Henry M., 1, 4, 70, 517

Discipline, 460, 461-467, 510, 512 515, 524, 526, 528; see Ecclesiastical authority
Dr. Williams's Library, 29, 430
Dry Drayton, 6, 398

Ecclesiastical authority, 32, 41, 48, 59, 62, 91, 120, 155, 214, 269, 272-275, 329-337, 407, 463, 515, 521, 524, 526
Edmondes, 5, 509
Elders, 117, 270, 271, 275, 510, 515, 518-521
Elizabeth, Queen, 8, 14-16, 23, 66, 152, 173, 202, 412
Erastianism, 8
Excommunication, 120, 444, 466, 521

Family of Love, 65
Far. and Har., 5
Fenner, Dudley, 3
Fenton, Edward, 10, 12, 29, 42-45, 51-53, 55-67
Fenton, John, 10, 12, 29, 42 - 45, 51 - 53, 55 - 67
Field, John, 68
Flower, Mr., 5, 7, 24, 516
Freake, Edmund, Bishop of Norwich, 6, 404

Galileo, Galilei, 18
Glover, Edward, 509
God, attributes of, 226-243, 249-251; reverence of, 302-325
Greenham, Richard, 6, 20, 398, 406
Greenwood, John, *viii*, 4, 7, 30
Guernsey, see Channel Islands
Gunns, W., *ix*

H., R. (Robert Harvey), 4
Hall, Peter, 3
Harbin, George, 516
Harrison, Robert, *vii*, *viii*, 1-4, 7, 8, 15, 21, 26, 30, 93, 149, 396, 397, 406-429, 430, 431, 517

Index

Harrison, Robert, Writings of :
    Letter on Robert Browne, 149
    A Little Treatise, 2, 12, 13, 15, 29, 37, 70-123
    Of ghostes, preface to, 9, 26-28
    Three Formes of Catechismes, 2, 124-148
    A Treatise of the Church, 2, 9-12, 13, 31-69, 71
Harrison, William, 20, 397, 428
Heaton, Herbert, *viii*
Henson, Tobie, 425
Herrey, Robert F., 14, 15
Hooper, John, Bishop of Gloucester 218
Howland, Richard, Bishop of Peterborough, 7
Huxley, Thomas, 18

Jersey, see Channel Islands

Knappen, Marshall M., *viii*

Lambeth Palace Library, 124, 150, 396, 430
Latimer, Hugh, Bishop of Worcester, 218
Laud, William, 20
Lavater, Ludwig, 2, 26, 27
    Of ghostes and spirites walking by nyght, 2, 9, 26
Leland, Simeon E., *viii*
Le Loyer, Pierre, 9
Little Casterton, 7
Logic, use in preaching, 173, 181, 191-193, 194, 196, 197, 203, 210, 223
London, 6, 7, 423

Magistrates, civil, 38, 39, 56, 57, 61, 118, 119, 131, 152-154, 156, 158-167, 201, 434, 471, 478, 480, 504, 515, 519, 521
Marprelate, Martin, 20
Marriage, 380-385
Martyrs, 218, 454

Mary, Queen, 74, 219
Middelburg, 1, 3, 6, 7, 20, 29, 150, 396, 432
More, John, 408, 412
Moule, H. F., 15
Munneman, Charles, 425, 426, 428

Neale, J. E., *viii*
Niclaes, Heinrich, 65
Nippold, F., 65
Nonconformity, 2, 3, 7
Norfolk, 6, 29
Norwich, 6, 30, 406, 407
Norwich, Bishop of (Edmund Freake), 6, 404
Norwich Congregation of, 5, 6, 7

Of ghostes and spirites walking by nyght, 2, 9, 26
Old Men's Hospital, Norwich, 2, 407
Ordination, 98, 100, 216, 219
Oundle, 6
Oxford, 530

Painter, Richard, see Schilders
Parishes, 115, 199, 205
Parliament, 121, 153, 157, 213, 217, 518
Parte of a register, 4, 408
Peel, Albert, *vii, viii, ix*, 29, 68, 124
Peel, Albert, Writings of :
    Brownists in Norwich and Norfolk about 1580, 2, 33, 61, 516
    Opinions and Dealings of the Precisians, 124, 405
    Seconde Parte of a Register, 29, 68, 406, 516
Peel, Mrs. Albert, *viii*
Peel, Miss Margaret, *viii*
Penry, John, *viii*
Peterborough, Bishop of (Richard Howland), 7
Philpot, John, Archdeacon of Winchester, 219

Pope, 152, 518
Powicke, F. J., 4
Preaching, 59, 64, 65, 67, 172, 173, 199, 200, 202, 410, 419-421, 475, 478
Presbyterians, 7, 21, 24
Presbyters, 117, 512, 515, 518, 519, 522, 529
Prynne, William, 20

Relics of the Puritan Martyrs, 1593, 515
Rhetoric, 180, 182-189, 195, 210
Ridley, Nicholas, Bishop of London, 218
Roberts, Thomas, 406, 408, 412

Sabbath, 328, 329, 528
Sacraments, 39, 59, 61, 139, 140, 212-214, 256-261, 278-285, 401, 441, 452, 466, 467, 471, 475, 506, 507, 511
Saint Giles', Northampton, 8
Saint John's College, 1, 124
Saint Olave's School, 6, 7
Saint Paul, 10, 17, 54, 63, 67, 154, 160, 169, 174, 189, 404, 414
Schilders, Richard, 3, 221, 222, 396
Scotland, 3, 7, 20, 423
Seconde Parte of a Register, 29, 68, 406
Smith, Dwight C., 4
Smithfield, 219
Smyth, John, *Paralles*, 42
Snape, Edmund, 3
Spirits, 27
Stamford, 6, 530

Sterling Memorial Library (Yale), 70
Stiffkey Papers, 43
Strype, John, 530
Summers, Montague, 9
Surman, Charles E., *v, ix*
Swainsthorp, 29

Taillepied, Noel, 9
Tatsel, 422
Tebbutt, Arthur R., *viii*
Thacker, Elias, 2, 4, 7
Thorpe Waterville, 7
Transubstantiation, 468
Travers, Walter, 3

W., T., 30, 42, 43, 45, 48, 53, 62, 63, 66-68
Waldegrave, Robert, 3
Walker, Williston, 221
Warrener, Elizabeth, see Browne, Elizabeth
Watkyns, Richard, 26
White, Thomas, 42
Whitgift, John, 23, 507
Wiggenton, Giles, 30
Williams's Library, Dr., 29, 430
Wilson, J. Dover, 26, 150
Woedowes, Nicholas, 422
Wray, Sir Christopher, Lord Chief Justice of the Queen's Bench, 124
Wymondham, 60
Wyndham, Sir Francis, 43

Yardley, May, 26

For Product Safety Concerns and Information please contact our EU representative GPSR@taylorandfrancis.com
Taylor & Francis Verlag GmbH, Kaufingerstraße 24, 80331 München, Germany

www.ingramcontent.com/pod-product-compliance
Lightning Source LLC
Chambersburg PA
CBHW070748020526
44115CB00032B/1397